UNDERSTANDING
AMERICAN
GOVERNMENT

About the Author

Robert Weissberg is Professor of Political Science at the University of Illinois at Urbana-Champaign. He is the author of numerous books on public opinion and methods of analysis in political science, and he has had articles published in the *American Political Science Review* and other scholarly journals. Born in New York City, Professor Weissberg received his Ph.D in political science from the University of Wisconsin. He is married and has two children.

Reviewers

William Fetsko
Social Studies Supervisor
Liverpool Central School District
Liverpool, New York

Corinne Wright
Social Studies Teacher
Hunter's Lane High School
Nashville, Tennessee

UNDERSTANDING AMERICAN GOVERNMENT

First Edition

ROBERT WEISSBERG
*University of Illinois
at Urbana-Champaign*

 RANDOM HOUSE SCHOOL DIVISION • NEW YORK

First Edition
987654321

Project Editor: Charles Roebuck
Manufacturing Supervisor: Lenore Zani
Cover Design Concept: Thomas Vroman Associates, Inc.
Cover Photo: © Wes Thompson, The Stock Market
Photo Research: Frost Publishing Group, Ltd.

Editorial Development, Text Design, and
   Production by Helena Frost Associates, Ltd.
New York, New York

Library of Congress Cataloging-in-Publication Data

Weissberg, Robert.
   Understanding American government.

   Includes index.
   1. United States—Politics and government.
I. Title.
JK274.W38   1988   320.473   87-16649

International Standard Book Number: 0-676-35579-X

Manufactured in the United States of America

your understanding of important concepts and issues.

● Extending Your Understanding. This set of activities encourages you to look beyond the classroom and the textbook to examine various aspects of government and politics. Many of these activities are designed to help you discover how government relates to your own life and to your community.

● Making Decisions. This final activity in the end-of-chapter material enables you to participate in the kinds of decision making that occur at different levels of government.

Special Features

Four different kinds of special features appear at intervals throughout the text. The Biography features, one in each chapter except Chapter 1, focus on individuals who have had a significant impact on a particular aspect of government or politics. Points of View, Issues, and Commentary provide enlightening information or discussions of important topics and concerns.

Preface

The primary goal of *Understanding American Government* is not only to provide you with all the basic information about our system of government but also to help you understand how the political process works. To accomplish this, it provides opportunities for you to analyze the significance of important political issues and events. *Understanding American Government* will do more than inform you; it will challenge you to examine, analyze, and evaluate our complex system of government, in which many groups and individuals interact.

Learning to look beyond the basic information in order to examine issues and events is not a simple task, and *Understanding American Government* has several important features to assist you. Chapter 1, for example, provides several questions that can serve as guidelines for helping you organize what may seem like unrelated events into meaningful patterns. For instance, by asking yourself who is on which side of a political controversy and why, or by examining which tactics are used by each side in a dispute, you can clarify and analyze the issues.

The remaining chapters of the book are organized around broad questions related to government and politics. These questions help to set the context for analysis; each chapter then goes on to explore these questions comprehensively. For instance, rather than examining the Constitution article by article, Chapter 2 asks, "Does the Constitution promote government by the people?" Exploring answers to this question requires that you think analytically and should make the Constitution more meaningful to you.

Each chapter of *Understanding American Government* has been arranged to make the subject as accessible to you as possible. Thus each chapter, except the first, includes a Preview. This is a fairly detailed summary of the chapter, and it provides a description of the most important topics covered in the chapter. There are also frequent summaries, both in the body of the chapter and at the end. In addition, the book includes many features, described below, that will help you in your study of American government and politics.

Learning Activities

One of the primary concerns of *Understanding American Government* is to stimulate thought and discussion, as well as to make the material clear and understandable. The following elements appear in each chapter to help you review what you have read, examine important issues, and apply your understanding of government and politics to situations you may encounter in the real world.

- Check Your Understanding. These questions appear at the end of each section and will help you review what you have read.

- Important Terms. This list of key vocabulary words, which appears at the end of each chapter, contains several terms that may be new to you. Key words and terms are boldface in the text and are defined in the glossary at the end of the book.

- Thinking Critically. This series of questions appears after the list of important terms. The questions challenge you to explore in depth

Contents

UNIT 3 Institutions 261

Unit 1

THE BASIC FRAMEWORK

Chapter 1: **Introduction**

Chapter 2: **The Constitution**

Chapter 3: **Federalism**

Because the United States is a democracy, citizens have both the right and opportunity to participate in politics. Effective participation is not always easy in a complex society of some 240 million citizens. An important first step is to gain some understanding of the nature of politics in the United States. Chapter 1 offers some guidelines to unraveling the complexities of political disputes, the limits of political action, and the relationship between politics and social and economic factors. Chapters 2 and 3 then explain the basic principles of how power is organized and distributed in the American political system. Although the separation of legislative and executive power and the coexistence of a national government with fifty separate state governments are rarely discussed as being part of "politics," they exert a powerful influence on day-to-day politics.

Chapter 1
Introduction

Every year government officials at the national, state, and local levels make tens of thousands of decisions. These decisions may affect what we earn, our physical well-being, which books we read, which food we eat, which cars we drive, and virtually every other aspect of our lives. Even if we wanted to have nothing to do with politics, we could not escape it. If we moved to a remote mountaintop and lived in isolation, we could not avoid breathing air whose pollution level is determined by government regulation. If the mountaintop is public land, the campsite would have to conform to Department of Interior rules or we would face eviction and a fine. Numerous government restrictions—for example, state building codes—would apply if we were to buy property on the mountain. For better or worse, what goes on in government has an inescapable and important impact on our lives.

THE CITIZEN AND POLITICS

In the United States, politics is not a one-way process by which government is free to shape the lives of its citizens. Our political system is a democratic one. Each person can play a role in deciding such questions as which part of our income will go to taxes or which drugs will be illegal. A mountaintop hermit who cannot breathe the air or drink the water can do something about it. However, the mere existence of a democracy does not mean that citizens will participate effectively. We may intensely want to change a particular government policy, but unless we understand how politics works, we will have difficulty in getting our view across. Success in politics requires considerable knowledge in addition to the opportunity to participate.

Becoming knowledgeable about politics is not easy. There are over eighty thousand governments in the United States and tens of thousands of laws. Even professional politicians do not know all the ins and outs of politics. Nor are there any obvious, simple rules that guarantee success in politics. Some people believe that having a great deal of money is all that matters, but if we gave an uninformed person a million dollars with the instructions "influence politics," he or she would likely wind up poor, in jail, and without much to show for the effort. Obviously, money is useful, but we have to know how to use it.

Fortunately, however, the situation is not hopeless. This book will help provide the understanding necessary for making wise choices about policies and how you might influence government. Since contemporary politics is exceedingly complex, acquiring sophistication means learning about many different aspects of politics. Let us begin by examining the term *democracy* and what it means for citizens in the real world of politics.

Democracy and Politics

What does it mean for citizens that the United States has a democratic political system? To answer this question we must define *democracy*. This is not easy, since experts offer dozens of different definitions. Moreover, many nations usually described as dictatorships call themselves democracies. Rather than try to determine the "proper" definition of *democracy*, it is more useful to think of different types of democracy, each with its own set of attributes.

One common conception of democracy is simply "rule by the people." This was the classic definition offered by the Greek philosopher Aristotle some 2,300 years ago. In current politics this view is known as **direct democracy** and means that people themselves decide important issues. Government exists to carry out the will of the majority. The New England town meeting, in which citizens periodically met to decide local issues, is a famous example of direct democracy. The practice in many states and cities of allowing citizens to propose and pass laws through *initiative*—citizen-sponsored measures accepted or rejected in an election—is consistent with direct democracy. An even greater emphasis on an active citizenry is found in **participatory democracy.** In this, people decide their own fate in all institutions of soci-

Town meetings in the 1800s were often marked by vigorous exchanges of views. Gatherings of citizens participating in direct democracy still take place in some New England towns.

ety—government, the workplace, fraternal organizations, sports teams, and so on.

At the opposite end of the scale in terms of citizens' activity are what may be called **output theories of democracy.** There are actually several types of such theories, but the common element is that government decisions are to be made on behalf of citizens. Citizens do not participate in these choices. Communist governments characterize themselves as democratic in this sense because they claim to rule in the interests of all citizens. Capitalist systems such as the United States, they assert, are not true democracies because government is run only for those who own property, rather than for all citizens.

The type of democracy that applies to the United States is called **representative democracy.** Representative democracy balances citizen participation with the existence of a large nation facing a multitude of complex problems. The term **representation** indicates that citizens choose leaders who represent them, rather than govern themselves directly. The essential features of representative democracy are the following:

1. Political leaders are selected through regular, fair, and contested elections, and virtually all adults can seek office and vote.
2. Candidates winning a majority are elected.
3. Citizens, individually or in groups, are permitted to try to influence their government once it has been elected.
4. The right to express views and attempt to persuade others is strongly protected.

Obviously, this list is not absolutely precise. People may disagree, for example, over how strongly the right to express one's views needs to be protected. How do you handle groups that advocate violence or use obscenities? Some supporters of representative democracy would limit the participation of such groups. Also, some divergence between this ideal and the real world is inevitable. It is unlikely, for instance, that all elections will be judged completely fair by all participants. In recent years many people have expressed fears that a candidate can use huge sums to overwhelm the opposition. Nevertheless, these are the traits that on the whole apply to the U.S. political process:

In an Iowa town during the 1984 presidential campaign, voters express their preference for candidates. Both parties hold caucuses around the state to help choose delegates to the national conventions.

elections occur regularly, many people run for office, groups are free to influence government, and our right to criticize leaders or suggest new policies is protected. Abuses happen, but they are the exception, and action can usually be taken to correct them.

For citizens, the fact that we live in a representative democracy implies both opportunities and restrictions. We have opportunities to influence the political process by voting, organizing election campaigns, writing letters, contributing time and money to groups, or convincing others of our cause. Each of us therefore must answer such questions as "Should we get involved?" "What is the best way to be involved?" and "How can a viewpoint best be defended?" If we were citizens in a political system that did not encourage citizen participation, such questions would be far less relevant. In a representative democracy, they are important even if we are apathetic.

But there are also restrictions on how we may influence the political process. The existence of a representative democracy means that interference with the fairness and openness of elections is not permitted. We cannot, for example, intimidate potential candidates or voters. Nor is it permissible to obstruct people's efforts to influence government or express their views. Tactics such as assassination, bombing, and blackmail are off-limits. In other words, the answer to the question "How should I be involved?" cannot be something like "Forbid people who disagree with you from voting."

Check Your Understanding

1. Which type of democracy applies in the United States?

2. List five opportunities citizens in our system of democracy have to influence the political process.

3. What are two restrictions on how people in our system can influence the political process?

Throughout American history, outdoor rallies have provided communities with a forum for expressing opinions. In the early days of the Republic, when literacy was not widespread, public oratory played a vital role in educating the citizenry.

ANALYZING POLITICAL ISSUES

In a representative democracy more is required than deciding whether or not to participate and by what means. A citizen must also be able to analyze political situations. Without analysis, participation may come to nothing or, even worse, it may be harmful to our interests. Consider the following situation.

A group in your state supports charging tuition for public high schools. The group says that parents of high school students should pay $1,000 a year for each child in a public high school. This group plans to wage a vigorous campaign to convince the state legislature that this is a good idea. What is your position on this issue? Does this proposal have any chance of success? How would it affect you and your family? Questions such as these can rarely be answered quickly and easily. To analyze an issue such as charging tuition at public high schools, it is necessary to ask a few additional questions. Answers to these questions may not provide a precise formula for action, but they will increase the probability of intelligent action.

How does the issue relate to your own goals? Each of us has our own set of goals. Some people, for example, may have personal wealth and power as their primary objectives. Others value world peace and equality as most important. In varying degrees, political issues relate to these goals. Tuition of $1,000 for public high school students not only affects your finances but it may determine the type of education you receive and the people you meet at school. Moreover, it may have an impact on the educational opportunities available to poor people.

The first question to ask, therefore, is "How does a $1,000 tuition relate to my own goals?" Such a tuition would likely mean lower taxes for those with no children in high school and an increased school dropout rate, especially among families making modest incomes. There may also be changes in the size of school staffs as well as less competition for admission to college. Suppose that you come from a wealthy family, you prefer a smaller, less crowded high school, and you are worried about your chances of getting into a good college. A $1,000 tuition is probably in your best interests. If, on the other hand, you believed that all citizens should have the same opportunity for a high school education, you would oppose charging tuition.

Who is on which side of the issue? Politics involves the conflict among groups and interests to achieve their values. Parallels between politics and sports are often drawn and, as in analyzing sports, much can be gained simply by asking who is on which side. You would not, for example, want to place a large even-money bet on your local high school football team in a contest with the Dallas Cowboys. In many situations, simply asking who is on which side of a conflict helps clarify your course of action.

Let us again consider the issue of charging $1,000 tuition for public high school. Suppose the following people oppose the idea: the governor, most state legislators, teachers' unions, and leaders of parent-teacher associations. Opinion polls also show most citizens opposed, as well. On the other side are private schools, who charge tuition, and several groups working to reduce taxes. Since enactment of tuition would require state government action, and most government officials oppose such action, the group favoring tuition faces serious obstacles. For the time being, at least, those fearing a high school tuition have little to worry about.

What tactics are being used in the conflict? The conflicts that characterize the political process are not abstract, philosophical debates. Participants can use a variety of methods to advance their cause. Often what may initially appear to be inefficiency or incompetence can be a well-disguised political maneuver. On occasion, simply asking "What is the other side doing?" can simplify a bewildering situation.

Suppose that, through their tireless efforts, the groups favoring tuition have created enough publicity to force officials at least to consider it. Moreover, the group believes that it has the necessary votes in the state legislature. At this point, the governor, who opposes tuition, announces that a special commission composed of leading educators and distinguished citizens will be appointed to study the matter and prepare a comprehensive report. Moreover, the head of the group favoring tuition will be asked to serve on this commission. If all goes as the governor hopes, most commission appointees will be opposed to tuition, it will take two years before a report is ready (by then, enthusiasm for tuition may have faded), and the public will be convinced that the governor handled the issue fairly and squarely—even though the process was intended to delay consideration of the proposal by the legislature. An alternative tactic might be for the governor's supporters to introduce a bill in the legislature that calls for high school tuition and also abolishes all high school athletic programs. This would allow the governor to support a bill favoring tuition while knowing that the measure had no chance of success.

What are the consequences of the conflict? Political decisions usually have consequences far beyond the particular issues at hand. These spillover, or ripple, effects must, if possible, be considered when the choice is first made. While you may favor a particular policy, it may have so many negative side effects that, on the whole, you might lose more than you would gain. Since many of these consequences are hard to predict, such calculations are not always easy. Nevertheless, numerous mistakes can be avoided by simply working through some of the likely effects of a political choice.

What might happen if tuition were charged at public high schools? One consequence could be a higher dropout rate, especially among students from poor families. This, in turn, could increase the number of young people looking for jobs. Many of these job seekers may not be able to find employment. Eventually, this group of dropouts may become a financial burden on society, and this burden could exceed $1,000 a year. The high school tuition may also make private schools more attractive. The higher dropout rate plus transfers to private schools could significantly reduce the size of the public school system. The people who would benefit most from a tuition charge would be property owners with no children in high school, since most communities finance education from the property tax. Students who had completed high school would also benefit, because there would be less competition for jobs or admission to college.

How do the rules affect the conflict? All political conflict is governed by rules. For example, we choose a President every four years by holding an

Citizens working for changes in policy at the local level often seek assistance from state legislators and the governor. In Nashville, Tennessee, legislators discuss an issue.

election on the first Tuesday following the first Monday in November. Such rules generally favor one interest over another, regardless of how fairly they are enforced. Holding elections on a weekday, for instance, means that most people in hourly wage jobs either have to leave work to vote or vote after work when polling places are crowded. Thus, hourly wage earners may be more easily discouraged from voting than lawyers, business people, professors, and others whose work hours are more flexible. By examining the rules surrounding a conflict, we can frequently see that one side or one strategy has a built-in advantage over the other.

Let's suppose that the group favoring tuition is planning to spend its money to elect a few state legislators. What rules determine whether this strategy is a good one? A good question to begin with is "Who makes these decisions?" You *may* discover that such decisions are *not* made by the state legislature or if they *are* made by the legislature, the vote may be taken in a committee whose membership is decided by party leadership. If this is the case, it may be wiser to give support to established party leaders rather than fund new legislators who will possess little influence upon election. To ignore the rules of politics is like playing baseball without knowing that you only get three strikes.

What are the alternatives to pursuing a particular policy? There are usually many different ways a goal can be achieved. Unfortunately, it is sometimes easy to be so engrossed in one specific solution that we don't consider all the alternatives. Some of these alternatives may be far easier to accomplish and more effective. For example, if safe cars are our goal, we might find it cheaper and quicker to use the courts to sue manufacturers for selling unsafe cars than to get Congress to pass tough car safety laws (judges are not influenced by large campaign contributions from auto makers). It might even be more effective to avoid politics altogether—to convince the insurance companies to raise premiums for unsafe cars, thereby discouraging their purchase.

Consider some of the alternatives to a plan of a $1,000 a year tuition. One possibility is to charge

tuition but also to provide an extensive loan and scholarship program for children of low-income parents. Another possibility is to create programs within the high schools to find work for students so they can more easily afford to pay the tuition (such work experience may even be considered as part of the educational process).

How are words and slogans used in the conflict? Words are an important resource in political conflict. By choosing words carefully, supporters can emphasize the most positive aspects of a program and minimize the less-desirable aspects. For instance, political leaders who know that the public is not eager for higher taxes may label a tax increase "revenue enhancement." Cleverly worded

Demonstrators publicize their cause with handlettered signs. Citizens' goals may not always be easy to achieve, but displaying simple, eyecatching slogans and images can help capture the public's attention.

slogans can make it easier for the public to understand and remember what may actually be a complex issue.

In the conflict over charging tuition for high school, supporters might claim that this plan "makes everyone pay a fair share" and "lightens the taxpayers' burden." On the other hand, those favoring no tuition might claim that a free high school education is a fundamental right of all citizens and tuition would deprive the poor of an equal opportunity to achieve the American dream. Each side is merely stating its position in the best possible light. This is typical of political conflict. We must see beyond such language, however, if we are to make intelligent choices.

In sum, because the United States is a representative democracy, citizens have an opportunity to influence politics. But the effective use of this opportunity requires an ability to analyze political conflict. Without an intelligent analysis, the opportunity is wasted. Often, asking a few simple questions will help clarify both the conflict and your own course of action. These questions include: How does the issue relate to your own goals? Who is on which side of an issue? What tactics are being used in the conflict? Answers to these and other questions will not necessarily provide a complete and perfect course of action, but they are a way of making a highly complex process more comprehensible.

Check Your Understanding

1. Why are goals important in analyzing a political conflict?

2. Why is it important to determine who favors and who opposes a proposed program?

3. Why is it important to examine alternatives to a proposed policy?

4. What role does language play in a political conflict?

THE LIMITS OF POLITICS

We have described the importance of politics in contemporary society and offered some guidelines for making wise political choices. At this point, politics may appear to be an all-inclusive process regulating every aspect of your life. While it is true that decisions made in government have wide consequences, it is not true that government decides everything. This situation—politics affects almost everything yet government cannot decide everything—seems like a contradiction. To understand how this can occur, let us examine three additional topics: (1) the idea of limited government, (2) politics and economics, and (3) politics and social relations.

The Idea of Limited Government

When the present system was created in 1787, government existed to provide those services that citizens acting on their own could not provide, such as national defense, rules of commerce, and officials to enforce the laws. Government could do only what it was specifically permitted to do. Over time, especially since the 1930s, the permissible role of government has greatly expanded. Today, for example, the national government is responsible for eliminating racial discrimination in restaurants and monitoring the purity of our food. These were once off-limits to government.

Nevertheless, despite the steady growth in government activity, governments at the national, state, and local levels remain **limited governments.** That is, many areas of our lives are beyond the direct reach of government, even though our actions in these areas may be influenced by government. Consider, for example, the role of government in family matters. Government agencies may provide a minimum level of shelter, food, and health care to the family and ensure that children are protected from physical abuse. However, the government will generally not interfere with the moral and religious training of children or their discipline, or make rules about how the husband and wife should take care of the family's

Commentary: Political Language, Washington Style

The importance of words for the images they convey is well understood by experienced public officials. A skilled wordsmith can often disguise a disaster or make inaction appear to be a bold dramatic move. Here are some illustrations of how words can transform the meaning of an event or situation.

When caught in an outright lie, a politician will gladly admit that he or she had "misspoken" or had given a "misstatement."

A government employee who can serve employers of various ideological views with equal enthusiasm is called a "pro."

A political appointee with little knowledge of the facts becomes a "person of vision."

When the State Department speaks of serious rights violations in other nations, "unlawful or arbitrary deprivation of life" is substituted for "killing."

The CIA calls its Latin American mercenaries "unilaterally controlled Latino assets."

A Defense Department official advocating the overthrow of the Nicaraguan government spoke of "unconsolidating" it.

When asked whether U.S. troops were withdrawing from Lebanon, Secretary of Defense Caspar Weinberger said, "We are not leaving Lebanon. The marines are being deployed two or three miles to the west." That is, they were being put aboard ships in the Mediterranean Sea.

Source: Leslie H. Gelb, "I Can't Hear You, I Have a Career in My Ear," *New York Times*, March 7, 1985; and "1984 Doublespeak Award," compiled by William Latz, Camden, N.J.

---

finances. Government-provided assistance may play a role in such family matters, and such things as domestic violence may require direct government involvement, but the government has no right to regulate all aspects of family life.

The idea of limited government stands in contrast to **totalitarian government.** Here, as in the Soviet Union and China, the government claims the right to control all aspects of a person's life. Authority is total, even though in practice certain areas may be left alone. This means that, if it so desired, the government could decide which languages the parents teach their children, whether religious ceremonies will be permitted, and which values a child will be taught. If Congress or the state governments were to pass similar laws, most Americans would be outraged at this unwarranted intrusion into private life.

Politics and Economics

The idea of limited government is especially relevant for understanding the complex relationship between the political and the economic systems. Nations differ in their economic systems. In **Communist** systems the state controls all the major elements of the economy—industry, transportation, banks, housing, medical care, education, and so on—though some personal property is allowed (for example, clothing, furniture). Moreover, economic decision making is done through central planning rather than in the marketplace. Government planners decide how much of something is to be produced, what its price will be, and how it will be distributed. Some European nations such as Sweden have an economic system often described as **democratic socialism.** Here, some but not all key economic elements are state-owned and non-state-owned enterprises are heavily regulated, but there is no overall management of the whole economy. The extreme opposite of communism is **laissez-faire capitalism.** Under this system the economic role of government is minimal—enforcing laws, providing defense, and administering various "housekeeping" functions. All economic power is privately held, and economic decisions result from the competition of people in the marketplace.

The United States possesses what has been called a **mixed economy.** From democratic socialism it borrows the idea of government control of some key economic elements and the regulation of non-state-owned economic activities. The federal government, for example, owns the mail delivery system, many power-generating installations, numerous medical facilities, and so on. It also regulates banks, transportation, health care, commerce, and almost every other significant economic endeavor. Nevertheless, the bulk of industry and commerce in the United States is in private hands. And even when government owns an industry, there if often a private business in competition with it (for example, United Parcel Service competes with the Postal Service). Equally important, the government in our mixed economy does not engage in comprehensive, long-term economic planning. Through its various economic powers it can influence the overall growth rate and the well-being of many industries, but the government does not set rates of production, prices, employment levels, and so on. It might, for example, try to encourage the housing industry, but the government traditionally leaves the actual decisions up to private builders, realtors, and home buyers.

To appreciate what a mixed economy is, consider the example of two friends, Maria and Carl, who wanted to go into business by selling pizza. Although they are free to undertake this enterprise, there are several government restrictions they must follow. They must first legally establish themselves, and the particular form they choose (for example, a limited partnership versus a public corporation) will have an impact on their financial arrangements, on the way they raise capital for the business, and on the kinds of business activities that will be allowed. Once properly created in the eyes of the law, the business must obtain licenses to open a retail store and sell food. The store must also meet local building and fire regulations. A bookkeeper may have to be hired to keep track of employee payroll contributions to Social Security, unemployment insurance, and various taxes.

Once the business is in operation, Maria and Carl must obey antipollution laws that prevent businesses from conveniently dumping trash into the nearby river. Numerous antidiscrimination laws also apply to their customers and employees. If their employees want to unionize, the right to do so is legally protected. Meanwhile, the restaurant

An artisan in China applies glaze to an intricate piece of pottery. Although some craft manufacturing is privately run, the centralized government owns all the nation's factories and regulates industrial productivity.

"*I personally see nothing wrong with giving a sucker an even break. However, federal regulations strictly prohibit it.*"

(Drawing by Levin; © 1985 The New Yorker Magazine, Inc.)

may be periodically inspected to ensure that restrooms are clean and that the food is prepared under sanitary conditions. The restaurant's advertising could not violate the law by making false claims. If Maria and Carl fail to pay their taxes, the business will be sold at auction.

Though all these government requirements may seem restrictive, they should not obscure the freedom we enjoy. No government official decided that Maria and Carl should, or should not, go into the pizza business, and they can always leave it. They also have considerable leeway in what they will serve, whom they will hire, what prices they charge, how they market the product, and issues like expansion and diversification. There is no Ministry of Food where all the choices are centrally made or that assigns business managers or owners to a restaurant. Maria and Carl can replace the pizza with fried chicken, remodel,

change locations, spend more on advertising, hold sales, put in entertainment, or sell out to the competition and retire to Florida.

The significance of economic activity as a mixture of government control and individual freedom is that the political process cannot be used to deal with *every* economic issue. In recent years, for example, the national government, in response to public pressure, has vigorously intervened in the auto industry, setting standards on safety, pollution, and gas mileage. at the request of American manufacturers, Washington has taken steps to protect the auto industry from foreign competition. The government has not yet, however, gone so far as to set wages for auto workers and management, design the cars, approve advertising, and make production-related decisions. At least for now, these remain private economic decisions, not choices to be made by the political process. If

These chickens may eventually end up for sale in a privately owned grocery store or supermarket, but they are being inspected for wholesomeness by the U.S. Department of Agriculture. Much private enterprise in the United States is subject to at least some government regulation.

you believe that automobiles should be safer, you can advance your cause through the political process. But if you object to the styling of American cars, there is little you can do politically.

Politics and Social Relations

Coexisting with the economic system are numerous social groups, including family relationships, educational institutions, professional societies, religious organizations, and recreational clubs. Here, as in economic matters, the government has a limited role. On some issues the government will determine just what you can and cannot do. In other areas the government may have some influence, but considerable freedom exists.

Perhaps the most complex role of government in what many consider to be private matters occurs in the area of religion. Though the First Amendment to the Constitution provides for the separation of church and state, religion is not beyond government regulation. Even perfectly ordinary religious organizations must obey numerous complex laws dealing with taxes, fire and safety requirements, and the certification of clergy. If the church operates a school, there are laws regulating teacher qualification, pupil attendance, and educational content of secular subjects.

Nevertheless, as is true of the economic sector, there are major limits to government activity in social relations. Social and religious groups are not created and administered by government officials, and nobody can be forced to attend religious services. This is not true in many totalitarian societies—everything from professional societies to local sports clubs is created by government and administered to suit the political objectives of the regime.

Here again we find limits to the political process. As a citizen in a representative democracy, you can make use of the political process to deal with some, but not all, social relationships. It is permissible, for example, to pass laws preventing a local organization from selling food prepared in an unsanitary kitchen. An effort to pass a law requiring members of that organization to spend their time reading literary classics would, however, be judged a totally inappropriate exercise of political power. If this were your goal, it would have to be pursued through nonpolitical means.

The Changing Meaning of Limited Government

We have seen that many areas of economic and social life are off-limits to government. It would be a mistake, however, to conclude that the boundaries of government are perfectly clear or forever fixed. These boundaries are fluid, people disagree over where they are, and controversies occur over where they should be.

The changing meaning of limited government is apparent when we compare the activities of government today with government in the nineteenth century. Today many people agree that Washington should establish a minimum wage for nearly all workers, act to prevent numerous types of discrimination, and regulate workplace safety. Such activities would have been considered beyond the reach of politics 100 years ago. No doubt, such changes will continue—100 years from now it may be politically acceptable for Congress to enact a law requiring citizens to eat well-balanced meals.

Disagreement always exists over just where the appropriate role of government begins and ends. In the area of economic activity, this controversy frequently involves regulation of buyer-seller relationships. Today very few people believe that buyers and sellers should negotiate without any government restrictions. Almost everyone accepts the idea that certain deceptive practices should be prohibited. Differences are common, however, in what level of government involvement is thought proper. For example, a used-car dealer is prohibited from charging excessive interest rates, but should the dealer be required to list every defect in a car? Should the dealer also be required to guarantee each car in writing? Similar disputes occur in the regulation of social relationships. Many once completely private activities have partially come under government scrutiny. For instance, sexual harassment on the job was once considered a purely personal matter. Today, however, in some situations a person who was harassed on the job may be able to receive assistance from a government agency that deals with problems in the workplace. Should this type of protection also be extended to derogatory racial or ethnic remarks?

The significance of these changes and uncertainties is that the political process can alter the boundaries of limited government. In other words,

Especially since the 1930s, the government has substantially increased its role in the area of disease prevention. Here, in a program sponsored by the federal government, local residents line up for inoculations.

not only can you try to influence government policy, but the boundaries of government policy making can also be decided politically. If you are concerned about the quality of family life, you may work for greater government financial aid to poor families (a traditional area of government involvement) as well as advocating government regulation of child-rearing practices (an area now off-limits). The government's role may also be restricted. Some women's groups have, for example, successfully argued that it is not the role of government to tell a woman whether she should or should not have an abortion. Many of these same people have also worked to get the government *into* new policy areas, such as enacting legal protections against sexual discrimination in employment, credit, and life insurance.

Check Your Understanding

1. In what way has the scope of government activity changed since the 1930s?

2. How does a mixed economy differ from a Communist system, laissez-faire capitalism, and democratic socialism?

3. In what way can government regulate the activities of religious groups?

4. Why are there shifts in the boundaries of limited government?

CHAPTER SUMMARY

Politics in the United States affects almost every aspect of our lives. Because we live in a democracy, there are many ways we can influence the political process. The effective use of the vote and other means of influence, however, requires our understanding of how politics works. Analyzing politics is a complex process, but a good place to begin is to ask a few simple questions, such as "How does an issue relate to my own goals?" to enable you to participate more intelligently and efficiently. There are, however, constraints on the use of politics. Because we have a limited government, in many areas of life the government cannot directly intervene. But the limits of government are not always clear or permanent.

IMPORTANT TERMS

Explain the following terms.

direct democracy
participatory democracy
output theory of democracy
representative democracy
limited government
totalitarian government
mixed economy

THINKING CRITICALLY

1. Is it possible to have direct democracy in a modern, complex society? Discuss your answer.
2. Should citizens who are eligible be required to vote? Why or why not? What effect would such a requirement have on our political system?
3. Are some policy areas permanently beyond the reach of government? Should such restrictions be decided by leaders or by the people themselves? Discuss your answer.
4. In recent years there has been much talk about reducing the scope of government intervention in the economy. How might our daily lives be different if we lived under a system of laissez-faire capitalism?
5. In what ways are economic systems and political systems (types of government) linked?
6. Should there be restrictions on allowing citizens to pursue political goals that will bring them personal gain? Should they be allowed to work only on goals for which there is no personal conflict of interest? Discuss your answer.

EXTENDING YOUR UNDERSTANDING

1. Make a list of at least five different ways government policy affects your own life. Compare

your list with your classmates'. Explain how these policies have influenced your life.

2. Contact an organization, like the League of Women Voters, that provides information on voting activities. What kinds of activities is the organization involved in? What does the organization hope to achieve through its activities? Present your findings in a report.

3. Find out how democratic socialism works in a nation like Sweden. How would life in the United States be different if we adopted such a political-economic system? Would you favor such a change? Prepare an argument either for or against adopting a system of democratic socialism.

MAKING DECISIONS

Most of the funding for public schools comes from property taxes. All property owners help pay for public education even if they have no children or if they send their children to private schools. You are a member of a commission set up to study alternatives to this system of funding. Your goal is to decide on a system of funding that is fair to all citizens. Present your recommendations to the class.

THE PLAN OF THIS BOOK

The chapters that follow describe important aspects of American government and politics. These chapters have two general goals. First, each presents some of the facts, events, and debates that are an important part of American politics. Such information constitutes the building blocks of political understanding. Second, each chapter includes discussions of important questions, such as "Does the Constitution promote government by the people? and "Is federalism still politically relevant?" The questions are asked at the beginning of each chapter, and the material is then organized to provide answers. By raising, and then examining, important issues, we illustrate the analysis of the political process. Many of the questions we have already described as useful in clarifying the role of government will be found in these chapters; the answers will help you make intelligent choices about your own political involvement.

Chapter 2
The Constitution

The study of American government must begin with an examination of the basic framework that regulates the political process. Ignoring this framework would be like trying to understand a baseball game without knowing that a batter is allowed three strikes or that each team is allowed three outs in an inning. By examining the Constitution and the philosophy of divided, limited government that underlies it, we can better understand contemporary politics. It is the Constitution that defines our basic political institutions—the presidency, Congress, the court system. The Constitution also describes key power relationships—for example, it authorizes the President's right to veto legislation passed by Congress. Moreover, the Constitution is the supreme law of the land, and if other laws conflict with it, as determined by the Supreme Court, they may be declared invalid. Numerous laws dealing with such topics as religion in public schools and the size of election districts have been overturned by the Supreme Court because they conflicted with the Constitution. In many instances Congress has refused to take certain actions that might be at odds with the Constitution. In order to understand the significance and contemporary role of the Constitution, we shall seek answers to four important questions:

- What are the origins of the American Constitution?
- Does the Constitution promote government by the people?
- How should we interpret the Constitution?
- Has the Constitution become politically outdated?

1787   We the People 200   1987

PREVIEW

What are the origins of the American Constitution? The Constitution was an attempt to resolve problems created by the Articles of Confederation, the first written rules that governed the United States. The Articles, ratified in 1781, created a weak government that did not rule the people directly and lacked the power to resolve the financial and commercial problems of the day. Attempts to revise the Articles failed until delegates from eleven (later twelve) states assembled in Philadelphia in 1787. Originally charged with revising the Articles, the Constitutional Convention instead created a brand-new government.

There has been a great deal of debate over whether the Constitution was designed to protect wealthy interests or to safeguard the rights of all citizens. Those who see the Constitution as drafted and promoted by wealthy interests point to the elite backgrounds of the Framers of the Constitution, the provisions in the Constitution that benefited commercial interests, and the undemocratic nature of the ratification process. Those who dispute this interpretation note that delegates to the Constitutional Convention supported the rights of the common people and that they were not a unified economic group. In addition, these defenders argue, many small farmers and tradespeople supported ratification.

Does the Constitution promote government by the people? The Preamble, or introduction, to the Constitution declares that the document draws its authority from the people of the United States. Yet the Constitution does not easily allow for policy making by ordinary citizens. The Framers feared that people could be misled or that well-estab-

lished groups would tyrannize less-powerful groups. Thus, only the House of Representatives was to be directly elected by the people. In addition, several key constitutional provisions prevented a popular majority, or large group, from acting quickly. Separation of powers and checks and balances set up barriers to the control of government by one group. It is difficult for one individual or group to gain control of all three branches of government, and each branch can limit the actions of the others. *Federalism*—the division of power between the national and state governments—also helps prevent rule by popular majorities. Finally, majorities sometimes are thwarted by constitutionally required "supermajorities" of two-thirds or three-quarters. For example, amending the Constitution requires ratification by three-quarters of the states.

How should we interpret the Constitution? Because the Constitution plays such a vital role today and because it is often sketchy on details, it must be interpreted if it is to be applied. There are three main approaches to interpretation. One approach emphasizes the meaning of the words in the Constitution. Although this approach is straightforward, constitutional language is frequently vague, and the document omits many topics altogether. A second approach, in which scholars, judges, and others try to determine what the Framers intended, is also limited. Records of intent are incomplete and, of course, nonexistent in such areas as electronic media. A third approach, which stresses contemporary political realities, has the advantage of being flexible but can also be hard to pin down.

Has the Constitution become politically outdated? The social, economic, and political changes that have occurred in American society since 1789 raise important questions concerning the contemporary relevance of the Constitution. Critics of the constitutional system argue that it is biased toward inaction, promotes unnecessary conflict among public officials, and gives disproportionate power to the interests of small groups. Its defenders claim that the Constitution is flexible and adaptable because it gives leaders leeway through such provisions as the "necessary and proper" clause and the granting of executive power to the President. They point out that the Constitution is also a unifying symbol for all citizens. Their strongest argument is that the document has facilitated the emergence of a strong, nontyrannical government.

WHAT ARE THE ORIGINS OF THE AMERICAN CONSTITUTION?

The Constitution did not come into existence until eleven years after America declared its independence from Great Britain. Between July 4, 1776, and May 28, 1787, when the drafting of the Constitution officially began, numerous events greatly affected the content of the document. The Constitution was not written as an abstract, ideal form of government. Rather, it represented a practical attempt to resolve several crucial problems of American society following the Revolutionary War. To understand some of the important features of the Constitution, we need first to consider the failure of previous attempts to create a national government.

Government Under the Articles of Confederation

During the eleven years after they declared their independence, the thirteen states were largely self-governing. The first "national" government was the **Continental Congress,** which existed from 1774 to 1781. The Continental Congress existed primarily to fight the war and thus mainly concerned itself with raising an army and conducting necessary diplomatic business. Because its orders were not binding on either the state governments or on citizens, it cannot be considered a true national government. The Continental Congress was more like a committee created to coordinate the actions of sovereign, or independent, nations than a central government.

On March 1, 1781, the Continental Congress was replaced by a government created under the **Articles of Confederation.** Despite the change in name, the new central government continued the tradition of the largely ineffectual Continental Congress. Under the Articles almost all power was vested in a single legislative chamber—the **Confederation Congress**—with no formal distinction between legislative and executive authority. Executive functions, such as negotiations with foreign governments, were performed by temporarily appointed committees or special officials. Provisions for a national judicial branch were very limited.

The central government under the Articles was subordinate to the separate states. It possessed no direct power over the American people. It could only request—not order—that state legislatures take certain actions. Delegates to the national Congress were selected and paid by the state legislatures. No matter how many delegates it sent, each state had one vote. Although the central government had some power to regulate international commerce, agreements with foreign governments could be (and were) overridden by individual states. The crucial area of interstate commerce was off limits to central control. Attempts by the Congress to increase its powers over the states were unlikely to succeed because major rule changes required approval by two-thirds of all state delegations—that is, by nine states. Amendments to the Articles of Confederation required unanimous approval. The national government was especially limited in its power to raise money. Congress could not tax directly but had to make "requisitions" to state legislatures for funds. During its first two years the Confederation Congress requested $10 million from the states but received only $1.5 million.

The government under the Articles of Confederation was almost powerless to resolve the many problems that occurred in the post-Revolutionary period. Commercial competition among states frequently resulted in discriminatory taxation that interfered with commerce. Public finance was frequently mismanaged and chaotic. Payments on the public debt were not regularly met, and some states printed more and more money to pay their bills. Inflation was widespread. What was most disturbing to business interests and large landowners was that economic problems were contributing

Commentary: The Real First President of the United States

The government under the Articles of Confederation has sunk into obscurity. Perhaps the greatest loser as a result of this neglect has been John Hanson.

The Articles of Confederation came into existence on March 1, 1781, and John Hanson was subsequently elected president of the

Peyton Randolph.

pointed to that state's delegation to the Continental Congress. On September 5, 1774, he was elected the first President of the Continental Congress but resigned seven weeks later to attend the Virginia state legislature. In 1775, he was again elected President of the Continental Congress, served for two weeks, and then resigned for health reasons.

John Hanson.

Congress of the Confederacy. This would make John Hanson—not George Washington—the nation's first President. Hanson, who served a one-year term and retired from public life, should not feel alone, however. An even more obscure first President of the United States was Peyton Randolph. Randolph was a prominent, highly respected Virginian who was ap-

George Washington.

to the growing strength of radical forces in the several states. Faced with large debts and an uncertain future, many small farmers and tradespeople spoke out against the banks and laws that facilitated the collection of debts. The most extreme example of this attack on wealthy interests was **Shays' Rebellion** in Massachusetts. This protest of farmers, led by Daniel Shays, sought relief from debt and mortgage foreclosures. Armed and angry debtors broke up court sessions hearing debt cases and gained control of a number of towns. Although Shays and his followers were ultimately defeated, this outbreak of violence showed a need for a stronger central government that could deal with growing economic problems.

The Movement to Reform the Articles

Although many people believed that the central government under the Articles of Confederation had to be strengthened, several proposals to accomplish this goal came to nothing. The first step toward change in the form and power of government began in 1785, when representatives from Maryland and Virginia met at George Washington's home, Mount Vernon, to discuss navigation problems on the Potomac River and Chesapeake Bay. This meeting resulted in agreements between the two states concerning currency, import duties, and commerce. When the Virginia legislature later ratified the agreements, it also proposed a gen-

Daniel Shays and his troops do battle with the Massachusetts state militia in Springfield. Shays' men were defeated, but their rebellion sent shock waves through the other states. Many people feared similar uprisings by the nation's debtors.

eral meeting of all states in Annapolis, Maryland, to discuss their problems further. In September 1786, delegations from only five states met in Annapolis, but they issued a call for another meeting to resolve common problems, to take place in Philadelphia in May 1787. The purpose of this meeting was to propose amendments to the Articles of Confederation. Under the leadership of James Madison and Alexander Hamilton, this attempt at revision was to produce a complete change in the form of government.

The Constitutional Convention of 1787

The first session of the convention took place on May 28, 1787. Seventy-four delegates were selected by the states, but only fifty-five attended. Delegates from New Hampshire arrived two months after the convention began, and Rhode Island never participated.

The delegates quickly chose George Washington as their presiding officer. They agreed that all deliberations were to be secret, and this secrecy was maintained for thirty years afterward. Compared to the general population, delegates were better educated (half were college graduates) and came from such professions as law, medicine, and business. Many of the people closely associated with the Revolution—Patrick Henry, for example—were absent. In fact, of the fifty-six signers of the Declaration of Independence, only eight were present at Philadelphia. Two other prominent citizens—John Adams and Thomas Jefferson—were overseas on diplomatic missions.

The actual drafting of the Constitution was a slow process marked by numerous compromises. Even though the Constitution has come to be revered almost as a divinely inspired document, a much more apt description would be "a bundle of compromises." Almost every word, phrase, power, and prohibition was the result of negotiation among competing interests. Many of these compromises did not come easily, and at times it looked as if the Convention might collapse for lack of an acceptable middle ground. Frequently a serious conflict was resolved by omitting the issue from the Constitution.

Consider the selection of the President. In the first draft the President was to be elected by Congress for a single seven-year term. Delegates differed, however, over how Congress would select the President. Should each state have just one vote? Should the voting be based on state populations? The suggestion that citizens elect the President directly was rejected decisively. The final decision—that the number of presidential electors (the *electoral college*) selected by each state would equal the number of that state's senators and representatives—was settled upon as a compromise because it offended the fewest delegates.

Slavery was another complex issue resolved through numerous compromises. Because the economy of Southern states depended on slavery, any effort to outlaw the practice would be the end of the Constitution. Slavery involved several issues—how much power Congress had in regulat-

ing foreign trade, who was to be counted in determining how many representatives each state would have in the House, how taxes were to be calculated—as well as the morality of slavery itself. Some Northern delegates feared that the counting of slaves as citizens would give the South undue influence in choosing the House of Representatives and the President. A bargain was struck in which slaves (called "other persons" in the Constitution) were to be counted only as three-fifths of a person for purposes of representation and taxation. And delegates agreed that, although slavery was permitted, Congress could ban the importation of slaves after 1808. By setting the maximum duty, or tax, on imported slaves at $10, however, delegates made sure that Congress could not tax the institution out of existence before 1808. They also provided for the return of runaway slaves and forbade Congress to tax exports (slave-produced cotton was a vital Southern export). On the whole, the protection of slavery was the price paid for making the Constitution acceptable to the South and thus preserving the Union.

Perhaps the most important compromise concerned representation in Congress. This issue involved two questions. First, *who* was to be repre-

George Washington presides at the Constitutional Convention, 1787. The painting gives no hint of the deep divisions and political deals that on several occasions nearly destroyed the attempt to create a new central government.

sented in Congress—citizens or states? If citizens were to be represented, a member of Congress would be accountable directly to the people. On the other hand, if states were to be represented, a national legislator would merely be the agent of the state government. This had been the arrangement under the Articles of Confederation, and national lawmakers acted more as ambassadors from states than as representatives of the people. The second question was *how* representation should be apportioned. One possibility was to continue the practice under the Articles—equal representation for each state regardless of population. An alternative would be to base representation strictly on population.

These choices had major political implications. One of the major weaknesses of the government under the Articles was that national government officials acted to protect their individual states' interests at the expense of the nation as a whole. Allowing national legislators to represent the people directly would weaken state power and strengthen the central government. The assignment of legislative seats was also important, because the thirteen states differed considerably in population. Pennsylvania, for example, had a population of about 430,000, whereas Georgia, Rhode Island, and Delaware each had less than 100,000. If only size of population were used, the national government could be dominated by three or four of the thirteen states.

One set of proposals to settle these issues was offered by the state of Virginia. The **Virginia Plan** was basically a call for a strong central government in which national legislators represented citizens, not state governments. This sharp departure from the Articles called for a two-house Congress. One house would be elected by the people for a three-year term. Representatives' salaries would be paid by the national treasury and not by the states, as under the Articles. Members of the second legislative house would be nominated by the states, but the final selection would be made by the lower house, elected by the people. Both houses would then choose a chief executive for a single seven-year term, as well as judges for a national court. This new national legislature would have the pow-

er to overrule the actions of the individual states. The chief executive would administer the laws, but Congress would be the dominant branch of government.

The Virginia Plan drew strong opposition from two sources. Many delegates to the Convention were still reluctant to create a national government that could impose its will on the state governments. Opposition also came from many smaller-state delegates, who objected to having representation in Congress based solely on population. These two groups of opponents did not always overlap. Some delegates from New York, for example, objected to the Virginia Plan because of the powers given to the national government, even though New York would benefit from the principle of population-based representation.

Shortly after its introduction, the Virginia Plan was countered by an alternative offered by William Paterson, a New Jersey delegate. The **New Jersey Plan** was more a modification of the existing Articles than a new form of government. Under this plan the national government would be given greater powers, especially in its ability to raise revenue and regulate commerce. The national government would have some power to overrule state governments, national law would be the supreme law of the land, and the chief executive could use force to compel obedience. A national judiciary also was to be created. However, as under the Articles of Confederation, the one-house national legislature was to be chosen by the states and not be based on population. This plan favored the smaller states and appealed to those who feared a strong central government. Nevertheless, it was rejected by seven states, with only three states in favor.

The rejection of the New Jersey Plan did not, however, clear the path for acceptance of the Virginia Plan. Still unresolved were the questions of whether states or individual citizens were to be represented and of how legislative seats were to be apportioned. For a time it seemed as if the problems were insolvable. Finally, after much bargaining, the deadlock was broken. The solution offered by Roger Sherman and Oliver Ellsworth of Connecticut called for seats in the House of Representatives to be based on population. In order to bal-

A *lithograph shows Independence Hall—the site of the Constitutional Convention—nearly one hundred years after the drafting of the document. In this idealized depiction of Philadelphia in 1876, men, women, and children ride or stroll past the historical structure in the background.*

ance the victory for the populous states, the Senate was to consist of two members from each state elected by the state legislature. The **Connecticut Compromise** thus gave something to both sides and calmed fears that the new government would be used by one group of states against the other. So crucial was this accommodation that it is often called the "Great Compromise."

On September 17, 1787, the delegates to the Constitutional Convention assembled for the last time. One final revision was proposed—changing the ratio of seats in the House from 1 per 40,000 citizens to 1 per 30,000 citizens. George Washington made his one speech at the Convention favoring this amendment, and it was passed unanimously. The Constitution was then approved by all except three delegates. After the new government had been created, at least on paper, the delegates adjourned to the City Tavern on Second near Walnut to dine and, in the words of Washington, take "cordial leave of each other." Instead of reworking the Articles, the Convention had created a new form of government. A weak single-house legislature was replaced by a two-house leg-

islature, and a separate executive was established. The groundwork was laid for a national judiciary. Most important, this new government was given significant powers in taxation, regulation of commerce, and military matters.

Ratification

The drafting of the Constitution did not bring the new central government into existence automatically. Considerable debate had occurred over the ratification, or approval, process. Some delegates to the Convention argued that the unanimous consent of all state legislatures was required for adopting the Constitution (the legal method under the still-existing Articles of Confederation). Other delegates rejected this position as too difficult. Several state legislatures were heavily influenced by groups of citizens, such as farmers and shopkeepers, who were heavily in debt. These groups were likely to oppose the Constitution because it prohibited states from printing money and altering contracts. Eventually delegates agreed that the decision would be left to special conventions in each state. Citizens would choose delegates to these conventions, but citizens themselves would not decide on ratification. Approval by nine of the thirteen states would put the Constitution into operation.

The ratification process frequently involved hard-fought, close battles. Those favoring the Constitution were known as **Federalists;** their opponents came to be known as **anti-Federalists.** Especially in the large, politically important states, such as Virginia, New York, and Massachusetts, the debate revolved around two issues: the power of the central government under the proposed Constitution and the need for a bill of rights to protect citizens from government interference. The anti-Federalists claimed that the Constitution gave far too much power to the central government and put too many limits on state government. Although many anti-Federalists agreed that some state legislatures had abused their power to print money, they feared that the national government, with its considerable power to tax and its control of the military, would soon resemble a monarchy. They also expressed fears regarding the ability of the new government to govern a nation as large and as varied as the United States. Much was made of the fact that the Convention was conducted in secret, that the Convention had no legal authority to draft a new Constitution, and that the whole idea behind the Constitution was too novel.

The pro-Constitution forces strongly denied the charge that too much power was being concentrated in the central government. Alexander Hamilton, John Jay, and James Madison, in a series of articles called *The Federalist*, asserted that the power of the proposed central government was in fact greatly limited by provisions of the Constitution. They argued that presidential power would be limited by the legislature, that important powers were divided among several branches of government, that the people would retain some power through elections, and that the states did not relinquish significant independent power (these points will be considered later in this chapter and in other chapters). Such arguments were generally persuasive, especially because antiratification forces commonly did little more than conjure up possibilities of disaster if the Constitution were adopted.

The call for a bill of rights by opponents of the Constitution was a more difficult issue to resolve. In several states antiratification forces pointed to this omission as a shortcoming of the Constitution and as proof that the Framers were intent on restricting the liberty of citizens. Several state ratification conventions issued calls for specific guarantees of individual rights. Protection of free speech, freedom of religion, the right to a jury trial, and limitation on government searches were among the more common guarantees demanded. Defenders of the Constitution argued that the organization of government power—rather than written guarantees—best protected citizen rights. This reasoning was not very persuasive, however, and in order to help assure ratification, the Federalists promised that once the Constitution was ratified, a bill of rights would be added.

The actual ratification process took only about seven months (see Table 2.1). Delaware ratified first, and it was soon followed by Pennsylvania, where a Federalist-inspired mob dragged opponents of the Constitution to the legislature to ensure a quorum (the required minimum number of participants at the meeting). Three more states—New Jersey, Georgia, and Connecticut—followed with overwhelming proratification votes. In Massachusetts the contest was very close and often revolved around economic issues. Only after promises were made regarding amendments did Massachusetts become the sixth state to ratify. Meanwhile, the New Hampshire proratification forces *lost* 70 to 30, but the voting was adjourned. Rhode Island soon followed with a second "no" vote. Maryland and South Carolina became the seventh and eighth states to ratify. On June 21, 1788, the Federalists overcame their earlier defeat and New Hampshire reversed itself. With the nine "yes" votes, the Constitution was now officially ratified.

Despite these nine "yeses," however, the key states of Virginia and New York had yet to vote. Because of their size and importance, both were essential if the Constitution was to survive. In Vir-

Chronology of Important Dates and Activities in the Creation of the Constitution, 1787–90

Date	Event
May 25–28, 1787	Convention formally convenes and organizes itself.
May 29	Virginia Plan on representation is proposed.
June 15	New Jersey Plan is proposed.
July 16	Connecticut Compromise is adopted.
August 8–10	Agreement reached on qualifications of voters, representatives, and regulation of elections.
August 15–23	Powers of Congress are debated.
August 24–25	Powers of the President are debated.
August 29	The conflict over the slavery issue is resolved.
September 6	Means for electing the President is decided.
September 10	Amendment procedures are adopted.
September 17	Constitution is signed.
December 7	Delaware ratifies, 30–0.
December 12	Pennsylvania ratifies, 46–23.
December 18	New Jersey ratifies, 39–0.
January 2, 1788	Georgia ratifies, 26–0.
January 9	Connecticut ratifies, 128–40.
February 16	Massachusetts ratifies, 186–168.
April 26	Maryland ratifies, 63–11.
May 23	South Carolina ratifies, 149–73.
June 21	New Hampshire ratifies, 57–47. Constitution now officially adopted.
June 25	Virginia ratifies, 89–79.
July 26	New York ratifies, 30–27.
November 21, 1789	North Carolina ratifies, after ratification was rejected on August 4, 1788.
May 29, 1790	Rhode Island ratifies, 34–32.

TABLE 2.1

ginia the anti-Federalists were ably led by several distinguished citizens (including Patrick Henry), but ratification carried by an 89 to 79 vote. The situation in New York originally appeared bleak—only 19 of the 65 delegates to the ratification convention openly supported the Constitution. However, mostly because of the politicking of Alexander Hamilton and threats by New York City to secede from New York State to join the Union on its own, New York State ratified 30 to 27, but with reservations. North Carolina and Rhode Island, having little choice now because the new national government already was functioning, both eventually ratified despite strong anti-Constitution sentiment.

When Congress first assembled in 1789, one of the issues on the agenda was the promise to enact a bill of rights. As noted, such a promise had played a major role in securing ratification of the Constitution in several states. Nevertheless, many—perhaps most—legislators seemed more concerned with the financial problems facing the country than with guarantees of liberties. The fight for the amendments was led by James Madison, who had been elected from Virginia on a pledge of securing a list of protections for citizens. Madison was worried that failure to fulfill commitments might enrage public feeling. Equally important, many anti-Federalists still had not given up their opposition to the Constitution and were hoping to use congressional delay as a means of undermining the new government. Specifically, they wanted to use the commitment to enact amendments as a justification for a second Constitutional Convention. Madison believed that such a convention could be used to weaken the new government.

Relying on suggestions originally made at the Virginia ratification convention, Madison proposed twelve amendments. After considerable delay and numerous objections, they were approved by Congress on September 25, 1791, and sent to the states. The states failed to approve two proposed amendments—one dealing with the apportionment of seats in the House, the other forbidding members of Congress from raising their salaries until after a later election. On December 15, 1791, Virginia became the eleventh state to ratify

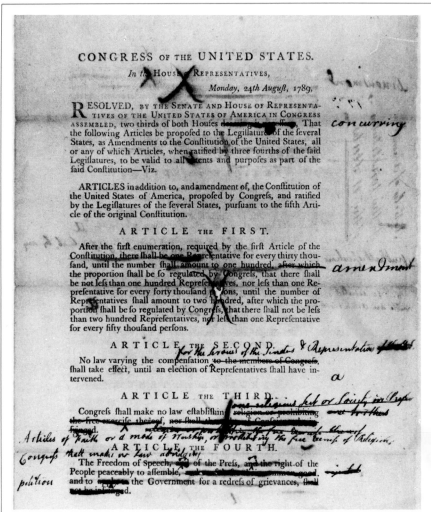

In an early draft of the Bill of Rights, part of what is now the First Amendment, protecting free speech, was in "Article the Fourth." The original first two amendments were rejected and the third and fourth were combined.

the ten amendments, and they became part of the Constitution. Only many years afterward did these guarantees of individual liberty become known as the **Bill of Rights.**

The Controversy over the Constitution's Origin

Although most Americans revere the Constitution and those who created it, one school of thought asserts that the whole adoption process was an antidemocratic seizure of power on the part of the privileged classes. Those who hold this view argue that the Constitution was created to protect the economic interests of the wealthy and then was imposed on an unwilling population. This position was stated first by Charles Beard, who in 1913 published the widely acclaimed *An Economic Interpretation of the Constitution of the United States.*

The Beard Thesis

The economic interpretation of the Constitution rests on three major arguments.

1. *The business and professional interests of the delegates.* Convention delegates represented the economic establishment: large propertyholders, merchants, plantation owners, and successful lawyers. Small farmers and tradespeople were totally absent from the Convention. The drafters of the

According to the Beard thesis, the Constitution was written to protect the economic interests of plantation owners and other substantial propertyholders. In preindustrial America, acreage and livestock represented a primary source of wealth.

Constitution were likely to gain financially from a strong central government that could protect their property from the radical-minded, debtor-influenced state legislatures. Moreover, most delegates owned public securities, such as bonds, issued by the government, which were practically worthless so long as the national and state governments could not pay their debts. Clearly, says Beard, most delegates stood to advance their own welfare by abolishing the ineffectual Articles of Confederation.

2. *The procommercial provisions of the Constitution.* Beard points out that men of property incorporated directly into the Constitution provisions highly beneficial to their interests. For example, Article VI, Section 1 guarantees that all public securities issued before adoption of the Constitution would be redeemed by the new government. This was a boon to several drafters of the Constitution who owned securities issued by the old government. Article I, Section 10 prohibits states from making "any Thing but gold and silver Coin a Tender in Payment of Debts." This provision eliminated a favorite tactic of debtors, which was to have states print so much money that their

debts could be easily discharged. Section 10 of Article I also prohibited states from "impairing the obligations of contracts"—that is, states could not abolish debts or any other contractual commitment.

3. *The undemocratic nature of the ratification process.* According to Beard, the established economic interests won ratification of the Constitution despite widespread opposition from most ordinary citizens, who were aware that the Constitution favored the wealthy. In some states poor citizens could not vote for electors to the ratification conventions because of restrictive property qualifications. In other states—for example, New Jersey, Georgia, and Connecticut—the ratification process moved so swiftly that the opposition had almost no time to organize. In all, not more than a fifth to a quarter of all adult white males participated in the ratification process. Furthermore, the indirect system of ratification—citizens selected convention delegates and these delegates then voted on ratification—allowed popular antiratification majorities to be ignored. In New York, Massachusetts, and New Hampshire many delegates violated voters' antiratification instructions and

approved the Constitution. In South Carolina pro-Constitution forces never won a clear majority of the popular vote.

Arguments Against the Economic Interpretation

Opponents of the Beard argument assert that a careful reading of the debates during the Constitutional Convention shows that there was considerable concern for the interests of ordinary citizens. The Convention was not a conspiracy against the people. Numerous proposals were rejected on the grounds that ordinary citizens would not tolerate them. Moreover, several delegates expressed great confidence in the political good sense of workers. And although many delegates were concerned primarily with the protection of property, others were devoted to the protection of the rights of all citizens. James Madison, who probably had more of an impact on drafting the Constitution than any other delegate, stated that if human rights and property rights were in conflict, human rights—such as the right to vote—had priority.

Opponents of the economic interpretation point out that delegates to the Constitutional Convention were not a unified "economic establishment." They were a varied group, and their own economic interests were often in conflict. Slave-owning Southern planters did not always agree with merchants from New England. Moreover, many of the delegates supported policies that were against the narrow interests of the economic elite. For example, some wealthy convention delegates favored allowing states to issue paper money, a favorite tactic of debtors. A quarter of the delegates had participated in state legislatures that were sympathetic to the poor and had voted for laws protecting debtors. Perhaps the most telling piece of evidence against the Beard thesis is the fact that several wealthy delegates—including the holder of the largest block of public securities—opposed ratification of the new Constitution.

Finally, those who disagree with Beard's interpretation assert that the ratification process was not simply a contest between the rich and the poor. In most states the majority of delegates to the ratification convention were small farmers. In Delaware, the first state to ratify, not a single manufacturer, banker, or security speculator was at the convention. In several states numerous large landholders and merchants opposed ratification. Nor was the vote very close in these ratifying conventions. Among the first nine in favor of ratification, the proConstitution forces received 66.75 percent of the total vote.

Resolving Conflicting Interpretations

Which of these two positions is closer to the truth? Because both arguments rest on incomplete information and subjective interpretations, the conflict cannot be resolved completely. There are many gaps in the historical record. Nevertheless, both sides would agree that several facts are reasonably clear. First, the Constitution did not result from widespread popular demands for a new form of government. Whether the proratification forces were largely the rich (as Beard argues) or a more varied group does not change the fact that the movement for a new form of government came from a minority of citizens. Second, the overall thrust of the new Constitution was to limit the antirich policies of several state legislatures. Some historians interpret this as a self-serving, conservative counterrevolution organized by the wealthy, but others see the same events as merely a reasonable corrective to a widely acknowledged problem. Finally, the proportion of citizens voting for the Constitution was tiny. Only a small portion of the population could vote—women, blacks, and those without property were excluded. Many who could vote did not, and the election was indirect—citizens selected convention delegates and these delegates voted for or against. By today's standard, this mandate for ratification might seem undemocratic. However, in the context of the late eighteenth century, this might be considered a resounding popular endorsement. In sum, both perspectives have merit. Supporters of the Beard argument are correct when they point out economic motives in the drafting and ratification process. However, such motives and the absence of overwhelming majority endorsement do not automatically mean that the Constitution was a conspiracy of the rich against the poor.

Biography: James Madison

There were a lot of things James Madison did not have: a robust physique, a powerful speaking voice, the quality called charisma that advances political careers in today's world of mass media. The qualities he did possess, however, included great learning, intelligence, and understanding, and these he devoted tirelessly to his

country's welfare. From the time of his birth in 1751 until his death eighty-five years later, Madison served the United States in a host of roles. But nothing else he did equaled the accomplishment for which he is most famous—shaping our Constitution and thus helping in a very real sense to create a new nation.

Madison was born into a Virginia family of comfortable means. The family plantation was worked by slaves, although Madison himself hated the institution of slavery. He encouraged the government to help slaves resettle in Liberia, Africa. Educated at the College of New Jersey (now Princeton University), he developed a strong interest in history and government. Like many other young men of his time, he also studied Latin, Greek, and Hebrew.

During the Revolutionary War, Madison served in the Virginia legislature, in 1776–78, and in the Continental Congress in 1780. (It was at this time that he began his close friendship with Thomas Jefferson, which was to endure for the rest of his life.) After the war, Madison returned to the Virginia legislature. There, in opposition to such conservatives as Patrick Henry, he worked successfully against religious teaching in the public schools.

Like many of his peers, Madison regarded the national government set up by the Articles of Confederation as inadequate. If the Articles were not amended, he felt, the new United States would split into several small and ineffectual nations. With this concern in mind, Madison worked to organize the convention at Philadelphia, and represented Virginia there.

Madison was a firm believer in republican government. At the same time, he feared that, without adequate safeguards, popular rule might result in tyranny by the majority. Madison's great contribution at the Philadelphia convention was the development of practical ways to achieve the former and avoid the latter. His approach was embodied in the Virginia Plan, in the idea of federalism, and, indeed, in the whole concept of checks and balances so central to the American system of government.

Madison's contributions to the Constitution did not end with the drafting of the document itself. He kept the most complete records of the Constitutional Convention. His many essays in *The Federalist* eloquently defended the kind of government the Constitution would establish, and helped pave the way for ratification. Moreover, when delegates to state ratifying conventions demanded a bill of rights in return for their support of the Constitution, Madison was instrumental in drawing up the nation's first guarantee of civil liberties.

Madison went on to serve Jefferson well as Secretary of State, but he himself did not excel as President. His administration (1809–17) was preoccupied with the conflict with Britain that culminated in the War of 1812. Madison lacked the temperament to be a good wartime President. He retired to Virginia, where visitors sought advice and encouragement from one of the Founders of the Republic.

DOES THE CONSTITUTION PROMOTE GOVERNMENT BY THE PEOPLE?

We have seen that the Constitution was not the result of widespread public desire, nor was it approved by the majority of citizens. Many delegates to the Constitutional Convention also had doubts about the ordinary citizen's ability to choose policies wisely. After all, the delegates did not allow the people to ratify or to reject it. These historical facts stand in sharp contrast to a view that sees the Constitution as the basis for citizen control of government. Does the Constitution promote popular rule despite the philosophy of those who wrote it? Or are many people misinformed about the true nature of the Constitution? To answer these questions, we must explore two interrelated aspects of the Constitution: its source of authority and the provisions that affect citizen control over government.

The Principles Behind the Constitution

All governments must somehow justify their authority. In the early seventeenth century King James I of England asserted that his power came from God and therefore that he ruled by **divine right**. According to this view, ordinary citizens could not replace a monarch because they did not create the monarchy. Governments have also claimed that their authority rests on the innate superiority of leaders over subjects. For example, in the nineteenth century British and French colonial regimes in Africa and Asia justified their rule on the basis of alleged white superiority. Here, too, it would be wrong and contrary to so-called natural laws—as *they* defined them—for the ruled to overthrow the government.

The political philosophy that dominated American thought during the eighteenth century held that the people, not God or natural superiority, were the ultimate source of government authority. The writings of the English philosopher John Locke (1632–1704) were especially important in

John Locke's belief that government's authority rests on the consent of the citizens was an important influence on the drafters of the Declaration of Independence and of the Constitution.

promoting the view that people create governments to serve their interests and that the people can withdraw this authority. This notion, which was the basis of the Declaration of Independence, was accepted by the delegates to the Constitutional Convention. The principle of the people's authority is expressed directly in the Preamble to the Constitution:

> We the People of the United States, in Order to form a more perfect Union, establish Justice, insure domestic Tranquility, provide for the common defence, promote the general Welfare, and secure the Blessings of Liberty to ourselves and our Posterity, do ordain and establish this Constitution for the United States of America.

Basing the new government on the consent of the governed was more than just a symbolic gesture. It was a practical step intended to ensure the new government's survival. A persistent theme throughout the constitutional debates was that no system of government would last without popular support. After all, the delegates had seen the British colonial governments overthrown and thus knew that the divine right of kings was little protection against dissatisfied citizens. Many delegates also believed that the new government would be more effective if its authority came directly from the people. (Recall that one of the weaknesses of the Articles of Confederation was that the document drew its authority from the state legislatures, not from the people themselves.)

It is important to understand, however, that basing the authority of the government on the people is *not* the same thing as letting citizens decide government policy. The Framers intended that the people were to be the source of authority, not the executors of policy. Their reluctance to encourage popular control of government stemmed both from the political conditions of the day and from the political philosophy of such leaders as James Madison and Alexander Hamilton, who helped draft the Constitution. In the late eighteenth century, public debates and elections were seldom orderly, dignified affairs. Most citizens were not well educated, and their sources of information were limited and often highly biased. Appeals to ignorance and prejudice were common. Candidates often competed with each other by offering the voters free food and whiskey. Madison and other Founders believed that to allow ordinary people to decide government policies under these conditions would be a risky business.

This distrust of direct popular rule resulted from the Founders' beliefs about the nature of humankind, the organization of society, and the purpose of government. Madison and other leaders did not have a very charitable view of human nature. They believed that people were not angels and that those with power would attempt to tyrannize those who lacked power. Society consisted of numerous antagonistic groups—which Madison called *factions*—the most important of which were the wealthy and the poor. Given the tyrannical nature of humanity and the existence of factions, what was to prevent one faction from achieving a dominant position and depriving others of their rights and liberties? The answer was to create a government strong enough to control what Madison called the "mischiefs of faction." It was particularly important that this government be able to prevent the majority from tyrannizing the few. To ensure a government that would be strong but in which the interests of the less powerful would be protected, several Constitutional mechanisms were employed.

Selection of Public Officials. Even though the Constitution permits citizen involvement in the selection of government officials, it minimizes the risk that a single group of citizens could capture all government power through the election process. First, only members of the House of Representatives were to be elected directly by the people. Senators were to be chosen by state legislatures, and the President was to be chosen by **presidential electors,** who were selected in a manner decided by state legislatures. Hence, the same group of citizens could not elect both Congress and the President (some of these provisions have changed, as we will see a little later in the chapter). In addition, judges at the national level are appointed and serve for life. Finally, terms of office are not identical. Senators' six-year terms are *staggered*, with

Points of View: Bill of Rights: U.S. Versus Soviet

The Constitution guarantees Americans many important rights. Putting these guarantees in a document does not, however, necessarily mean that they will exist. The U.S. Constitution has been characterized as a "living constitution" because it has a real impact on contemporary politics. Some constitutions, however, are more statements of ideals than enforced principles. The fact that putting something in a constitution does not automatically bring it into existence is illustrated by a comparison of the U.S. and Soviet constitutional protections of free speech.

U.S. BILL OF RIGHTS

I. Congress shall make no law respecting an establishment of religion, or prohibiting the free exercise thereof; or abridging the freedom of speech, or of the press; or the right of the people peaceably to assemble, and to petition the Government for a redress of grievances.

SOVIET CONSTITUTION

(ADOPTED OCTOBER 7, 1977) Article 52—Citizens of the USSR are guaranteed freedom of con-science, that is, the right to profess or not to profess any religion and to conduct religious worship or atheistic propaganda.

Article 50—Citizens of the USSR are guaranteed freedom of speech, of the press, and assembly, meetings, street processions and demonstrations. Article 49—Every citizen of the USSR has the right to submit proposals to state bodies and public organizations for improving their activity, and to criticize shortcomings in their work.

---

about one-third of the Senate up for election every two years. The President's term is four years, while House members serve for two years. These provisions ensure that only a portion of the government can be replaced at any one time. Thus for one faction to seize control it would have to win a series of elections. If, for example, a strong antitax sentiment swept the nation in 1992, tax opponents could, theoretically, elect the House and the President but only one-third of the Senate.

Separation of Powers. Besides limiting citizen influence through the electoral process, the Constitution is designed to minimize the consequences if a particular group of citizens gained control of one part of government. One way this is accomplished is through the **separation of powers**—the separation (but not the complete independence) of legislative, executive, and judicial functions. If, for example, angry taxpayers successfully gained control of the House, the impact would be limited, because the House does not by itself usually have enough power to cut taxes. The House might pass antitax legislation, but the Senate could reject such legislation. House-Senate disagreements are encouraged by the differences in what these legislatures represent: the House is intended to represent citizens, while the Senate is intended primarily to represent the states. Even if the two houses of Congress were to pass an antitax measure, the President has the power to veto it. Power is also shared with the judicial branch of government— judges interpret laws and enjoy considerable independence from the other two branches. Similarly, Presidents may not impose their will on the legislative branch. If all powers were concentrated in one branch, controlling government would be much easier—a simple majority could make the laws, enforce them, and decide the resulting court cases.

Checks and Balances. A principle related to separation of powers is the doctrine of **checks and balances.** Whereas separation of powers divides authority among different branches of government, checks and balances give each branch the opportunity to "check," or control, the actions of the other branches. For example, Article II, Section 2 gives the President the power to make treaties and to appoint ambassadors and Supreme Court justices, but these appointments require Senate approval. Likewise, the President is commander-in-chief of the armed forces, but only Congress may declare war and authorize the money to wage it. The President is also given the power to **veto,** or reject, legislation. Presidents who overstep their powers or commit other crimes may be *impeached* (indicted) by the House and tried by the Senate. Checks and balances also apply to the courts. It is the President—with the consent of the Senate—who appoints all federal judges, but Congress creates new court systems. Both the separation of powers and checks and balances are designed to encourage conflict within government, in order to prevent groups or factions from imposing their will.

Federalism. A fourth feature of the Constitution that can thwart citizen control of the national government is *federalism*—the division of power between the national government and state governments. This principle is explicity stated in the Tenth Amendment: "The powers not delegated to the United States by the Consititution, nor prohibited by it to the States, are reserved to the States respectively, or to the people." This means that a majority cannot force the national government to take action in an area that falls in the domain of state power. Even if the American public demanded that Congress do something about the chaotic pattern of local traffic regulations, for instance, Congress could not act because this area is off limits to the national government. At best Congress might provide some economic incentives to change the laws, as it did when it told states that they would lose federal highway funds if they did not enact certain speed limits. But it could not impose these rules directly. Thus, for a group to use government to impose its will, it would have to control both the national and the state governments, a situation not easily achieved.

Supermajorities. A fifth brake on popular control of government is the provision in the Constitution for what we might call "**supermajorities.**" a *simple majority* is 50 percent plus 1; a supermajority is a majority larger than a simple majority. The Constitution frequently requires that to accomplish something, a two-thirds or three-quarters vote is necessary. Treaties with foreign governments, for example, must be approved by a two-thirds vote in the Senate. A simple majority in the House is needed for impeachment, but conviction by the Senate requires a two-thirds vote. The two-thirds requirement applies also to proposals for amending the Constitution, but ratification of a proposed amendment requires a three-quarters majority of either state legislatures or special state conventions (see Figure 2.1). The existence of supermajority requirements means that a minority of officials can effectively block highly popular proposals.

Policies Off Limits to Government. Finally, the Constitution explicitly prohibits government from enacting certain types of measures, so that if the people want the national government to act in these areas, they must adopt a constitutional amendment. For example, Congress is prohibited in Article I, Section 9 from passing an **ex post facto law** (a law that makes an action illegal after it has been committed). Nor can Congress permanently suspend the right to a **writ of habeas corpus** (a court order directing an official holding an individual in custody to explain why the person is being detained). The importance of such constitutional restrictions was made clear when the government first tried to pass a national income tax in 1894. The Supreme Court struck down the tax as a violation of Article I, Section 9, paragraph 4, prohibiting taxes on grounds other than state population. The Sixteenth Amendment had to be adopted (1913) in order for a national income tax to be constitutional.

A Perspective on the Constitution

How you regard these constitutional checks on a majority depends on your political values. For the Founders, preventing tyranny was more important than creating a government that would closely follow public opinion. Given the events of this historical period, this priority was understandable. The Founders personally had experienced the un-

FOUR DIFFERENT WAYS THE CONSTITUTION CAN BE AMENDED

Amendment is proposed by

1. **2.** **3.** **4.**

 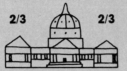

2/3 2/3 2/3 2/3

| Two-thirds vote in both House and Senate | Two-thirds vote in both House and Senate | A national convention called for by Congress at the request of legislatures of two-thirds of states | A national convention called for by Congress at request of legislatures of two-thirds of states |

Amendment must be ratified by

| Legislatures of three-quarters of states (currently 38 states) | Specially convened conventions in three-quarters of the states | Legislatures of three-quarters of states | Specially convened conventions in three-quarters of states |

When used

| For all amendments except Twenty-first (repeal of Prohibition) | For Twenty-first Amendment | Never used | Never used |

FIGURE 2.1

reasonable and unjust power of George III and of various colonial governors, as well as the more recent excesses of some state legislatures. Without this fear, the various checks on government action appear less justified. Indeed, if one has no fear that large groups, or majorities, might deprive smaller, less powerful groups of their rights, the constitutional structures seem old-fashioned and undemocratic. If, however, one agrees with the Founders that preventing tyranny is the most important value, these constitutional provisions still are appropriate.

The Constitution and Contemporary Politics

Clearly, then, the Constitution was designed to limit popular control over government despite the fact that the government draws its political authority from the people. The question now is whether these safeguards are still relevant.

The Constitution has been changed somewhat—but not drastically—to provide greater citizen control of government. The most significant changes have occurred in the method of selecting public officials. In 1913 the Seventeenth Amendment was adopted, providing for direct election of senators. Also, voters, not the states, select presidential electors, and these electors automatically follow voter majorities in their states (although exceptions can and do occur). Constitutional amendments have extended voting rights to blacks (Fifteenth Amendment) and women (Nineteenth Amendment). The Twenty-fourth Amendment, adopted in 1964, forbids the use of the *poll tax* (a fee charged for voting) in federal elections; and the Twenty-sixth Amendment, ratified in 1971, extends the vote to citizens eighteen years of age or older.

Despite these changes, most of the constitutional features designed to limit popular control of government remain intact. House, Senate, and presidential terms of office still overlap, so that a complete change in government requires more than one election. Judges and many other officials are still appointed, not elected. The principle of separation of powers remains in effect despite periodic pleas by members of Congress and the President for less bickering and more cooperation. Presidential complaints about "do-nothing" or "obstructionist" Congresses and congressional irritation at presidential stubbornness have been regular features of twentieth-century politics (see Chapter 10). And both of these branches are frequently frustrated by judicial decisions. The principle of checks and balances is also very much alive. No President, regardless of electoral success, has received total legislative cooperation on budgets, laws, and appointments.

The federalism principle, too, remains relevant despite considerable blurring of purely national and state responsibilities. A national majority cannot always impose its will in each state. As we shall see in Chapter 3, state governments still dominate in such key policy areas as education, crime, and housing. A national majority might, for example, try to persuade Congress and the President to take strong action against drunk drivers by making twenty-one a national minimum drinking age, but it would still be largely up to the states to enact such laws.

The supermajorities required by the Constitution remain very much in force. The three-quarters rule for ratification of constitutional amendments proved a major impediment to the adoption of the proposed Twenty-seventh amendment, or **Equal Rights Amendment (ERA)**. This amendment, which would have forbidden the abridgment, or reduction, of rights on the basis of sex, was first presented by Congress to the states for ratification in 1972. Between March 1972 and November 1978, when the allotted period for ratification expired, only thirty-five states ratified the amendment—three states short of a three-quarters majority.

Finally, while the Constitution has displayed considerable adaptability to changing situations, it remains effective in keeping certain actions beyond the reach of citizens. For example, abolishing the electoral college and replacing it with the direct election of the President would take a huge effort, merely because the procedure is spelled out in the Constitution. A similar difficulty would be encountered if we wanted Supreme Court justices to be elected rather than appointed or if we wanted to increase the terms of members of the House of Representatives from two to four years. All of these proposals have been considered and have some public support. They have come to nothing, though, in part because the constitutional obstacles are so difficult to overcome.

Check Your Understanding

1. The government created by the Constitution draws its authority from what source?

2. According to those who drafted the Constitution, what might happen if one interest controlled government?

3. What was the basic purpose of incorporating into the Constitution the principles of separation of powers and checks and balances?

4. List three types of votes for which the Constitution requires a "supermajority."

5. To what extent are the rules embodied in the Constitution still relevant to contemporary politics?

HOW SHOULD WE INTERPRET THE CONSTITUTION?

The Constitution is far more than an abstract set of rules handsomely written on parchment. What the Constitution says plays a vital role in every aspect of life today. Imagine, for example, that a President refused to leave office after an electoral defeat. Such complete disregard of a constitutional provision would arouse widespread outrage. Ours has often been called a "living Constitution" because of its continuing influence. This is not true everywhere. In some nations the written constitution is conveniently ignored as a historical relic.

Our Constitution is also a relatively short document that gives key powers only brief mention. The language is often vague, and there are numerous omissions. The Framers who drafted the document did not want to bind future leaders with a great many detailed regulations. Making such a document relevant means that it must be constantly interpreted. All public officials—from the President to the local police—must deal with its often imprecise grants of authority, restrictions on power, and guarantees of rights. For instance, federal judges hold office "during good Behavior," but what precisely is "good Behavior"?

The process of interpretation can have serious political consequences. Consider, for example, the question of whether abortion should be permitted. Until the early 1970s, all states had laws prohibiting abortions except under specific conditions—for instance, if the woman's life is endangered by the pregnancy. The Constitution is completely silent on abortion. Until 1973, state abortion laws were considered constitutional, because states historically were given considerable freedom in regulating health matters. However, in the case of *Roe v. Wade* (1973), the Supreme Court invalidated a Texas law greatly restricting abortions. The Court's decision was based partly on an interpretation of the Fourteenth Amendment's guarantee of due process and partly on the Ninth Amendment's provision that the Constitution's enumeration of certain rights "shall not be construed to deny or disparage others retained by the people."

Many public officials and ordinary citizens attacked the *Roe* decision as a rewriting of the Constitution through interpretation. They asserted that neither amendment had anything to do with abortion. Other observers acknowledged the document's silence on abortion but held that the Court's reasoning was proper if the Constitution was to be applied to modern society. Without such "reading into," the Constitution would become an irrelevant historical relic.

This type of controversy occurs often. In recent years, for example, Presidents have had to interpret their constitutional grants of power in questions involving U.S. military commitments. How is this interpretation to be made? How much leeway do public officials have in interpreting the Constitution? Let us consider several different ways the Constitution can be interpreted.

The Meaning of the Words

This is the simplest and most straightforward approach: we merely ask what the words mean. For example, when Article I, Section 10 says that no state may coin money, this means just what it says: no state may coin money. A more sophisticated version of this approach is to ask what the words meant when that portion of the Constitution was drafted. This acknowledges the fact that words can change over time. Thus, the Eighth Amendment's ban on "cruel and unusual punishments" would be interpreted by examining what this phrase meant in the late 1700s. We might consider hanging a cruel form of punishment today, but it was not considered cruel in 1791, when the amendment was ratified.

The emphasis on what words mean has had widespread appeal. As Chief Justice Charles Evans Hughes wrote in *Wright v. United States*, in 1938:

"The first principle of constitutional construction [is to honor the] deliberate choice of words and their natural meaning." Writing in 1827, in *Ogden v. Sanders*, Chief Justice John Marshall stated: "The intention of the instrument must prevail; this intention must be collected from its words; and the words are to be understood in that sense in which they are generally used by those for whom the instrument was intended."

Many constitutional experts and public officials endorse this approach. They argue that unless we pay close attention to just what the words mean, the Constitution will be rendered almost meaningless by endless and varying "interpretation." The strength of the Constitution, they believe, is its ability to provide enduring, clear rules. Moreover, these rules must be plain and visible to everyone. Sticking to the words and their obvious meaning preserves the Constitution as a "real" document.

Despite its simplicity, this approach presents problems. First, many key words and phrases resist precise definition. The First Amendment prohibits Congress from interfering with the "free exercise" of religion, but what exactly is a "religion"? The Eighth Amendment bans excessive bail and

In the Eighth Amendment, Americans sought protection against unreasonable punishment. Notions of what constitutes "cruel and unusual punishments" have evolved over time. Compared to some types of torture practiced in Europe in the eighteenth century, tarring-and-feathering, shown here, was a relatively less severe form of punishment.

fines, but what makes a bail or fine "excessive"? The English language is filled with ambiguity, and it is unrealistic to expect universal agreement on words, especially when these words are part of a political controversy.

A second problem occurs when the literal meaning of words and phrases leads to obviously undesirable consequences. The Constitution, for example, prohibits states from issuing bills of credit. Taken at face value, this prohibition means that states may not borrow money, a rule that would greatly impair the operation of state government. In the case of *Craig v. Missouri* (1830), however, Chief Justice Marshall—clearly a believer in sticking to the words—interpreted this clause as meaning a ban on paper money that is widely circulated. It would seem that a degree of linguistic leeway might be needed in order to avoid calamities.

Perhaps the most serious criticism of the literalist approach is that it creates a rigid and unadaptable Constitution. It makes the present and future prisoners of the past. What was reasonable and worthwhile in the late eighteenth century might make little sense in modern society. Consider, for example, the Second Amendment: "A well regulated Militia, being necessary to the security of a free State, the right of the people to keep and bear Arms, shall not be infringed." Taken literally, this language would block any national regulation of firearms. Many have argued, however, that such a provision is unwise in a modern, largely urban society that is protected by professional police force and military.

Intention of the Framers

This approach goes beyond the literal meaning of words and asks what was intended by those who wrote the Constitution and its amendments. This intention can be discovered in several ways. In the case of the Constitution itself, there are votes from the Philadelphia Convention, records from state ratifying conventions, and writings, such as *The Federalist*, that describe the purposes of various provisions. For later amendments, there are the records of congressional and state ratification debates. The circumstances of the times also can be considered as evidence of what was intended. For example, if we wanted to determine what was meant by the Eighth Amendment's ban on excessive bail, we might do research to find out what was deemed excessive bail in the late eighteenth century.

The intention-of-the-framers approach has long been popular. When the Supreme Court in the 1890s debated the constitutionality of a national income tax, attention was often focused on discussions at Philadelphia and in several state ratifying conventions as to what was meant by a "direct tax." In 1945 the Supreme Court turned to the original convention's proceedings for guidelines on how "treason" (Article III, Section 3) was to be interpreted. Many of the Court's controversial decisions in such areas as the death penalty and the rights of criminals have made use of historical research on the drafters' intent.

Conservatives are especially fond of this style of constitutional interpretation. They often view the Founders as sources of great political wisdom whose writings remain worth following. Such guidelines, moreover, are a necessary protection against the maneuverings of politicians who would undermine the Constitution for short-term gain. If the Constitution is silent or unclear on a matter, it is far better to ask, "What did the original drafters mean?" than to proceed as if there were no constitutional guidance.

And yet the intention of those writing the Constitution is not always a practical guide. For one thing, there is often significant diversity among those who created the document. Even when the record does not reveal controversy, it may well be that the delegates differed among themselves on certain provisions but remained silent for fear of presenting obstacles to the creation of a new system of government. Certainly many provisions exist not because they were desired but because they were the least objectionable or the best compromise. Another difficulty is the absence of a clear historical record of intent. Records of conventions or legislative debates were often not kept or were imcomplete. Even when statements of intent do exist, they might mask true opinions.

Convention speeches, such writings as *The Federalist*, and the like might reflect political expediency. Opponents of the Constitution regularly accused people like Madison and Hamilton of using misrepresentation in order to sway state ratification conventions.

As especially convincing argument against this perspective is that original intent is frequently no help in modern situations. How are we to consult the intentions of those who drafted the First Amendment (ratified in 1791) in dealing with electronic mass media? What could the Framers have to say about the legitimacy of such presidential actions as sending U.S. troops to Korea and South Vietnam without a congressional declaration of war? This critique of the writers' intentions was well stated in 1816 by Thomas Jefferson:

> Some men look at constitutions with sanctimonious reverence, and deem them like an ark of the covenant, too secret to be touched. They ascribe to the men of the preceding age a wisdom more than

human, and suppose what they did to be beyond amendment. I knew that age well; and belonged to it, and labored with it. It deserved well of its country. . . . Laws and institutions must go hand in hand with the progress of the human mind. As that becomes more developed, more enlightened, as new discoveries are made, new truths disclosed, and manners and opinions change with the change of circumstances, institutions must advance also, and keep pace with the times.

The Political-Reality Approach

Although the two previous approaches to interpretation differ, they share a view that the Constitution should be impervious to the ebb and flow of political conflict: the meaning of a word or phrase is permanent. The political-reality approach, however, sees the Constitution more as a set of broad principles and ideals than as a detailed, unchanging guide for governing society. The Constitution must be interpreted in light of current political conditions, taking into account the real consequences of interpretations. The key point is not the literal meaning of a word or the Framers' original intent, but whether the interpretation is consistent with the values of American society.

To see what this approach means, consider the issue of racial segregation in education. The Constitution itself makes no mention of education. Only the Fifteenth Amendment explicitly mentions race, but this amendment deals with voting. The Fourteenth Amendment's guarantee of equal protection of the laws can be interpreted to ban racial discrimination in public schools, but the intentions of the amendment's drafters on this matter are unclear. An interpretation of the Constitution based on the meaning of the words or on the drafters' intent would thus seem to offer little to opponents of racial segregation in public schools.

In the late 1930s, however, the federal courts began attacking the legal basis of segregated education, which was widespread in both the South and the North. This attack continues into the present, and although it relies on particular provi-

On the White House grounds, TV camera crews await the President's appearance. Electronic journalism raises constitutional questions the Framers could not have anticipated.

The landmark Supreme Court case Brown v. Board of Education *(1954) was the first in a series of rulings, by the federal judiciary, invalidating the concept of "separate but equal" education for blacks and whites. Pressure from concerned groups and the need, in an industrialized society, for the best education available have also played a significant role in bringing about school integration.*

sions of the Constitution (especially the Fourteenth Amendment), it much more closely reflects new political circumstances: access to a decent education has become an essential part of life; racial integration is accepted as a major social value; and government action to eliminate segregation is widely regarded as desirable. To use the words of the Constitution or the Framers' intent to maintain eighteenth-century views on education and race relations would create social and political problems. Thus the Constitution provides guidance, but not rigid rules, on how leaders must deal with a changing society.

The advantage of this approach—the fact that it permits the Constitution to be readily adapted—is also, according to its critics, its greatest defect.

Critics assert that such "adaptability" merely allows political leaders to use the Constitution any way they choose. The Constitution's basic purpose of providing rules and principles beyond the reach of everyday politics would be defeated. Thus the flexibility that makes the approach useful can also become a drawback.

Choosing Among Different Approaches

Obviously, no agreement exists on which is the best way to interpret the Constitution. Advocates of each approach can count on the support of scholars and distinguished judges. (There are numerous additional approaches we have not described.)

It is probably useful to think of these alternative approaches as being more, or less, relevant under different conditions. The meaning-of-the-words approach makes sense when dealing with specific sections of the Constitution (for example, the language describing what kinds of cases the Supreme Court will rule on). When words and phrases are not self-evident, the intent of the Framers can prove helpful. A good example of this was the Supreme Court's use of historical research in 1972, when it said that the death penalty was accepted by those who drafted the ban on "cruel and unusual punishments."

The political-reality approach may be most appropriate when leaders are confronted with strong political pressures. A rigid emphasis on words or history might preserve the traditional meaning of the document, but at enormous cost. Imagine what might have occurred if the Constitution had been used in the 1950s and 1960s to maintain racial segregation or how modern government might function if the President were bound by a late eighteenth-century view of the office? Clearly, survival might often require new ways of reading the Constitution.

We should realize that each of these approaches could benefit various groups very differently. Advocating one approach over the other can be a way of achieving political victory while appearing to be neutral. For example, an advocate of unlimited free speech might say: "The First Amendment clearly states that 'Congress shall make no law . . . abridging freedom of speech.' " An opponent of this view would answer, "Surely the historical record shows that the Founders were willing to accept numerous limits on free expression." Put bluntly, the method of interpretation can be part of the political process.

Check Your Understanding

1. What is the "meaning-of-the-words" approach to interpreting the Constitution? What are some of the strengths and weaknesses of this approach?

2. What are two major problems in using the Framers' intent as a guide to interpreting the Constitution?

3. What is the "political-reality" approach to interpreting the Constitution? What is the major advantage? the major disadvantage?

HAS THE CONSTITUTION BECOME POLITICALLY OUTDATED?

The Constitution became effective on June 21, 1788. Two years later, the first census reported a population of 3.93 million people living in 888,881 square miles. Much has changed since 1790. The U.S. population in 1985 was over 237 million, the thirteen states have increased to fifty, and the United States has an area of 3.615 million square miles. More important, the world has become much more complex. Problems that are common today—the nuclear threat, pollution, poverty, racial and sexual discrimination—were not major issues leading to calls for government solutions two hundred years ago. The transformation of society has understandably raised serious questions about the current political relevance of the Constitution. It is reasonable to ask whether the Constitution provides an adequate framework for dealing with the problems facing our nation today. To examine this issue, we will summarize arguments posed by both critics and defenders of the document.

Criticisms of the Constitution

Perhaps the most important criticism of the Constitution concerns whether the original design—which emphasizes the division of political authority, checks and balances, and limits on government action—lends itself to solving contemporary problems. In 1788 government played a relatively limited role; it was concerned with securing peace, constructing roads and canals, and performing other "housekeeping" functions. This view was widely accepted. (Recall that a major argument of the anti-Federalists was that the central government under the Constitution had too much power.) Defenders of the Constitution accepted the underlying premise of this argument—that a strong government was bad—but argued that the Constitution did not create too strong a government. The Framers believed that extensive power could result only in harm, because most of the rightful duties of government—for example, creating a uniform money system—did not require vast authority.

Today, however, the basic assumption that government ought to be limited is open to question. In such areas as managing the economy, providing for our health and welfare, and eliminating racial and sexual discrimination, it is necessary for a government to be strong and energetic. In 1788, people were concerned that the national government could become a tyranny. Today the fear is that the national government will be unable to cope with complex, deep-seated problems. It is inappropriate, some observers say, to impose an eighteenth-century Constitution rooted in a fear of strong government on a twentieth-century society concerned with problems whose solutions require a less limited government.

It can also be argued that the Constitution's built-in encouragement of conflict and delay leads to poor policy making. When the Constitution was drafted, policy making was far simpler. Fewer people were involved and decisions could be made on a year-to-year basis. Today, however, it is often necessary to coordinate the actions of numerous officials, and systematic long-term planning is essential. Such coordination and comprehensive planning are difficult under the principles of separation of powers and checks and balances. Typically, the President proposes one solution to a problem and the House and Senate each offer their own versions. Often the result is a stalemate or an uncoordinated series of compromises. Two years later, after another congressional election, the policy may be changed. Meanwhile, the possibility always exists that the actions of both Congress and the President will be overruled by the Supreme Court. Delays, constant bickering, and a piecemeal approach might have been acceptable in planning a canal; when the problem is to reform the Social Security system, the result could be one crisis after the other.

Another contemporary criticism of the Constitution focuses on the power it gives to small but powerful groups. A few officials in strategic positions can effectively block a majority. Recall that supermajorities—two-thirds and three-quarters—are common in the Constitution. On numerous occasions simple majorities (50 percent plus 1) have been thwarted in their attempt to amend the Constitution, ratify treaties, or override presidential vetoes. Having two senators per state—regardless of population—also permits rule by a minority rather than a majority. For example, if a number of senators from the less-populous states are joined by a few senators from the large states, they could make up a majority—fifty-one senators—that actually represents only about 20 percent of the total American population. That group could block legislation that the other senators wanted. Some of these provisions were a necessary price for getting the Constitution ratified. Others were rooted in a fear that a simple majority might act too hastily on important issues. Today both of these justifications are less compelling. It is especially difficult to justify the practice of allowing a small group to frustrate the will of an elected majority.

Defenses of the Constitution

The Constitution Is Flexible

Even though the Constitution was drafted two hundred years ago and reflects an eighteenth-century view of government, its relevance can be defended on several grounds. One important defense is that the Constitution allows for flexibility and change. Since its adoption, the document has been amended twenty-six times; the amendments have concerned such fundamental issues as prohibiting congressional interference with speech and abolishing slavery. Nor has the Constitution prevented the national government from creating new organizations to meet new needs. The Constitution makes no mention of a Department of Commerce, a Federal Aviation Administration, a Federal Reserve Bank, or any other Cabinet office or federal agency, yet all of these necessary organizations were created under constitutional authority (for instance, the power to regulate commerce). Important nongovernment organizations, such as political parties and interest groups, also have developed apart from the Constitution. Thus it cannot be claimed that the Constitution locks us into a late-eighteenth-century government.

Flexibility is provided by certain clauses in the Constitution itself. The delegates in Philadelphia realized that no document could ever anticipate in detail all future circumstances and emergencies, and leeway had to be granted to public officials. A well-known example is Article I, Section 8, paragraph 18, which gives Congress the power "to make all Laws which shall be necessary and proper for carrying into Execution the foregoing Powers, and all other Powers vested by this Constitution in the Government of the United States, or in any Department or Officer thereof." This provision, sometimes called the *necessary and proper clause* (or the *elastic clause*), follows a long section spelling out specific powers given to Congress and provides Congress with the general authority to make whatever laws are necessary to carry out these explicit powers. Over the years this clause has enabled Congress to deal with new and important issues.

Flexibility is provided also by the constitutional responsibilities given to the President. In particu-

lar, two key phrases in Article II have laid the groundwork for a wide variety of presidential actions not explicitly authorized in the Constitution. The first sentence of Article II states, "The executive Power shall be vested in a President of the United States of America." **Executive power** has usually been interpreted by all three branches of government to give the President considerable authority even in areas not included in a specific provision of Article II. It has been the basis for presidential declarations of neutrality, removal of executive branch officials from office without congressional consent, the signing of executive agreements with foreign nations (which are legally equivalent to treaties), and various measures taken during emergencies. None of these actions are explicitly mentioned in the Constitution, but each has been allowed as an exercise of executive power.

The second key clause that provides considerable presidential flexibility is in Article II, Section 3, which states that the President "shall take Care that the Laws be faithfully executed." Here again the vagueness of the language allows considerable leeway. The importance of this general grant of authority was illustrated several times in the conflict over the civil rights of Southern blacks in the 1950s and 1960s. For example, when Governor Orval Faubus of Arkansas refused to allow court-ordered integration of Central High School in Little Rock, President Dwight Eisenhower ordered U.S. troops to Little Rock to ensure compliance. President John F. Kennedy also dispatched troops to overcome Southern resistance to court-ordered integration of public schools in 1962 and 1963. In all three cases it was up to the President to decide how the laws would be enforced. A variety of legal options were available, but the President's final decision depended on complex circumstances that could not have been anticipated by the drafters of the Constitution.

Finally, the Constitution's provisions for the judicial system encourage adaptability. Basically, the Constitution creates the Supreme Court, authorizes the future creation of other courts, and deals with the kinds of cases the national courts may rule on. It does not require federal judges to

*For most U.S. citizens the
Declaration of Independence
and the Constitution symbolize
the nation's commitment to the
ideals of equality and rule
under law. An examination of
the original copies of the
documents evokes a sense of
historical continuity.*

interpret narrowly the letter of the law. Such leeway is not found in the judicial systems of many
other nations. The significance of this leeway is
that judges can adapt constitutional requirements
to changing situations and modern problems. For
example, when the Constitution was drafted, there
was no such thing as electronic surveillance of private conversations. Nevertheless, when cases involving "bugging" came to the courts beginning in
the 1920s, judges were able to use the Fourth
Amendment's protection against unreasonable
searches and seizures as a guide. In fact, the
Supreme Court generally has held that the
amendment, written nearly two hundred years
ago, is applicable to modern technology.

The Constitution Is a Unifying Symbol

The Constitution can be defended as a valuable
symbol that helps unite Americans of varying po-

litical perspectives. It has been argued that any
nation, if it is to remain united, must have common, highly regarded symbols. Most Americans,
whether Democrats or Republicans, liberals or
conservatives, share positive feelings about the
Constitution. The Constitution is the written em-
bodiment of our freedoms, our rights, and the rule
of law. Politically, the Constitution and other
symbols, such as the flag, help to create a sense of
national identity and thus help reduce sharp disagreements.

The symbolic value of the Constitution can be
seen when groups of citizens with very different
views on an issue both cite the Constitution in
support of their position. For example, many citizens opposed to federal efforts to integrate the public schools believe that their stance is perfectly
consistent with the Constitution. Civil rights
groups, favoring government-sponsored integra-

tion, claim that the Constitution supports their position. Thus both sides share an admiration for the document that creates and defines our basic political structures. Conflict occurs over the meaning of specific phrases in the Constitution or the relative importance of various provisions. The political system itself, embodied in the Constitution, is not directly challenged.

The Constitution Has Worked

A third defense of the Constitution is the most fundamental: it has worked. Especially when compared to many other nations, government under the Constitution has survived despite numerous obstacles. The major goal of the Constitution was to create a nontyrannical central government. Although there have been occasional acts of political repression—for example, the mass deportation of suspected radicals in the early 1920s—the United States has escaped the dictatorships that have befallen Italy, Germany, Japan, and many countries in Africa, South America, and Asia. Two hundred years without a dictatorship is no small accomplishment. Of course, nobody would argue that the Constitution all by itself prevented such tyranny, but it is likely that such principles as separation of powers and checks and balances have played a significant role.

The Constitution has also created effective government. This is demonstrated by the emergence of the United States as a world power. A major criticism of the government under the Articles of Confederation was that it left the United States open to foreign domination. Under the Articles there were no unified commercial policies, and the central government lacked the resources to pursue American overseas interests vigorously. The government created by the Constitution clearly overcame these weaknesses. The national government now spoke with one voice in dealing with foreign nations, and it could defend itself. Moreover, in times of war and international crisis, the government—despite separation of powers, checks and balances, and other impediments to action—has moved quickly and decisively. In foreign affairs at least, a constitutionally limited gov-

ernment has not proved to be a weak, disorganized government.

Finally, the soundness of the basic constitutional design is demonstrated by the later modifications of this design through amendments. Several amendments have had a profound impact in extending the rights of certain groups. But the basic structure has been changed only slightly. For example, the Twelfth and Twentieth amendments settled some details concerning presidential elections and when the President would take office, but they did not touch on the basic powers and responsibilities of the President. The Fifteenth, Nineteenth, Twenty-third, Twenty-fourth, and Twenty-sixth amendments opened up the electoral process to blacks, women, residents of Washington, D.C., and eighteen-to-twenty-year-olds and prohibited poll taxes (fees for voting), but they left the electoral system otherwise untouched. The Seventeenth Amendment gave the people the right to elect senators directly, but the Senate itself was left unchanged. If the basic design of separated powers, checks and balances, and so on, were defective, we would expect much greater changes. After all, if citizens could call a convention to overhaul the Articles of Confederation, they could do the same for the Constitution—and such a convention is explicitly provided for in Article V.

Check Your Understanding

1. What are three major criticisms of our Constitution?

2. In what way is flexibility built into the Constitution?

3. In what way is the Constitution a symbol of unity?

4. What evidence supports the claim that the Constitution has worked?

Commentary: Amendments That Never Survived

The bias of the Constitution against fundamental political change becomes apparent when we examine attempts to amend the document. Since the first ten amendments were ratified, in 1791, only sixteen amendments have been adopted (and one of these—the Twenty-first—merely canceled out the Eighteenth). Five more proposed amendments have received the necessary two-thirds vote in both houses, and four of the five have been ratified by a majority of the states. But since a simple majority is not sufficient for adoption, these four proposed amendments are not yet part of the Constitution.

Over the years several thousand attempts to change the Constitution have failed. One compilation of these failed efforts found, for example, that between 1889 and 1928, fifty-three amendments were proposed dealing with presidential elections. Despite several clear problems with the existing method—an individual can win, for example, with a minority of the popular vote—no change was made. Between 1790 and 1928, 210 amendments were introduced regarding the length of the President's term. One such proposal—the Twenty-second Amendment, which limits a President to two terms—finally made it in 1951.

Before 1928, seventy amendments were proposed to give the President power to veto part of a bill (commonly called an item veto). None has yet succeeded. Between 1900 and 1928, there were thirty-nine proposals to limit the terms of federal judges, but these, too, failed.

For an interesting description of failed amendments, see *Proposed Amendments to the Constitution*, prepared by M. A. Musmanno, 70th Cong., 2nd sess. (Washington, D.C.: Government Printing Office, 1929).

THE CONSTITUTION AND CONTEMPORARY POLITICS

One of the most remarkable features of the Constitution is its appeal to so many different groups. Almost every political group finds something of value in this document. Even citizens who, if called upon, could not recite a single constitutional provision probably believe that their freedom to do what they think is right is guaranteed explicitly in the Constitution. And Americans who are more familiar with the document have no trouble in finding support for their views. Citizens devoted to popular control of government can look to the Preamble (which proclaims the people as the ultimate source of power) and to the provisions for elections. Those fearful of popular influence are reassured by the provisions that prevent a momentary majority from seizing control of government. Groups concerned about preserving individual freedom have the Bill of Rights and numerous other restrictions on government action—for example, the prohibition against suspending the writ of habeas corpus except in emergencies. On the other hand, those who favor a strong, vigorous government can take comfort in the vast powers given the President.

No doubt, this capacity to mean so many things to so many people helps explain the survival of the Constitution despite enormous political changes since its creation. Nevertheless, it would be a serious mistake to view the Constitution as a document that treats all interests equally. As in the supermarket, we can all find something we like, but some tastes are better satisfied than others. No system of political rules is perfectly neutral, and the system of rules embodied in the Constitution is no exception.

Basically, when the provisions of the Constitution are considered as a group, it is clear that the document generally favors the status quo—that is, things as they are. In this sense it is a conservative political force. For example, for a bill to become law, it must receive majorities in the two legislative houses and be signed by the President; and if the law eventually becomes the subject of a court action, it must be favorably interpreted by the judiciary. Defeat at *any one* of these four stages usually means complete defeat. To make a real impact, a new political group must exert electoral influence in numerous states and in several separate elections. Even if a new group did win majorities in Congress and won the presidency, it would still not possess a free hand to do whatever it pleased. Resistance in the form of court actions, supermajority votes, and the checks and balances system would have to be overcome.

The tendency of the Constitution to support the status quo does not, however, automatically mean that advocates of conservative policies always have an advantage. The Constitution is conservative in the sense that it makes change difficult, not in the sense that it favors policies advocated by conservative groups. The conservative tendency of the Constitution can even be advantageous to liberal groups. Getting new policies adopted may be difficult under our constitutional system, but once in place, those policies are protected by the same inertia that was so hard to overcome.

A good example of how liberal policies can benefit from the status quo tendencies of the Constitution occurred when Ronald Reagan was elected President in 1980. During the campaign, Reagan promised to undo many of the liberal programs that had been enacted since the 1930s. In particular, Reagan called for deep cuts in social welfare spending, relaxation of environmental protection laws, return of many powers to the states, and abolition of several government agencies. The President and his conservative appointees had some successes, but by no means was there a wholesale change. Many of the more drastic proposals were resisted by the more liberal House. Even the Republican-controlled Senate did not always follow the President. In addition, many states were reluctant to assume the responsibilities offered by the President. Overall, despite his promises, the President was largely unsuccessful in dismantling the liberal policies established under Presidents John F. Kennedy and Lyndon B. Johnson. President Reagan and his supporters might bemoan the liberal tendencies of the House of Representatives. Other than to work for the election of more conservative members of Congress, however, there was little they could do. Even the Supreme Court, widely viewed as generally in tune with the President's philosophy, resisted the President in several decisions.

From a purely practical perspective, the Constitution is most useful after a group has been successful. When its policies have become law, a group can then talk about the dangers of popular majorities, the importance of checking the accumulation of political power, and the need for new proposals to pass through the traditional obstacle course of Congress, the presidency, and the courts. On the other hand, on the outside looking in, these arguments have little appeal. "Outgroups" are likely to emphasize the need for quick action, the popularity of their cause, and the obstructionist tactics of those in power. Neither side is being deceptive; rather, the virtues of the Constitution often depend on whether one's cause is helped or hurt by the Constitution's provisions.

CHAPTER SUMMARY

What are the origins of the American Constitution? The Constitution was created to remedy faults of the Articles of Confederation. The central government under the Articles was weak and ineffective. Economic problems were common, and in some states debtor groups threatened established financial interests. The specific provisions of the Constitution were a series of compromises intended to satisfy many different groups. Ratification involved a number of closely fought battles. Only a small number of Americans actually participated in the ratification process. Disagreement continues over whether the Constitution was a necessary remedy for problems of the day or a means to protect the holdings of the wealthy.

Does the Constitution promote government by the people? The Preamble states that the document was established by the people. The Constitution itself provides for citizen influence in choosing leaders. Nevertheless, it is designed to thwart majority control of government policy. The Founders had a pessimistic view of human nature and believed that an unchecked majority surely would deprive the minority of their rights. Such provisions as separation of powers, checks and balances, federalism, and supermajorities are intended to make it difficult for a popular majority to act quickly and decisively.

How should we interpret the Constitution? If our Constitution is to play an important role in contemporary politics, it must be interpreted repeatedly. Among the approaches to interpretation are the one that stresses the meaning of the words, the one that emphasizes the Framers' intent, and the one that takes into account changing political realities. Each approach has its advantages and limitations. How useful each one is depends, usually, on the circumstances.

Has the Constitution become politically outdated? Because the constitutional system is designed to restrain government, it could be argued that this system is obsolete in a world in which a rapid response frequently is necessary. The Constitution has been criticized because it encourages bickering and thwarts systematic planning. However, defenders of the Constitution assert that the document has adapted to modern circumstances. Many provisions allow officials considerable flexibility in carrying out their responsibilities. Perhaps most important, the system has worked for the past two centuries. The United States has not become a dictatorship, and the national government has proved to be an effective political authority.

IMPORTANT TERMS

Explain the following terms.

Articles of Confederation
Shays' Rebellion
Connecticut Compromise
The Federalist
divine right
separation of powers
checks and balances
supermajority

THINKING CRITICALLY

1. Why didn't the ratification process for the Constitution simply require the approval of a majority of citizens in each state, rather than a majority of delegates to state conventions? Can this indirect method of ratification be justified? Why or why not?

2. Is the use of supermajorities basically undemocratic? Why or why not?

3. The Constitution was written in such a way that it has been open to interpretation and reinterpretation throughout our nation's history. Should key sections of the document be rewritten and made more precise so that interpretation is unnecessary? Why or why not?

4. Nobody alive today has voted to ratify the Constitution. Since it is the basic law of our land, should citizens have the opportunity to vote to accept or reject the rules and political institutions established in the Constitution? Explain your answer.

5. Is it accurate to say that the Constitution provides fundamental guidelines when Congress, the President, and the courts frequently offer different—and often conflicting—interpretations of the Constitution? Give reasons for your answer.

6. Should the process of amending the Constitution be revised so that major changes can be made more easily? Why or why not?

EXTENDING YOUR UNDERSTANDING

1. Research what proposals were made at the Constitutional Convention. Select one proposal that was defeated. Describe how you think our government might have been different if the proposal had been accepted.

2. If you had been a delegate to the Constitutional Convention, what provisions that were included in the final document would you have wanted to change? What provisions would you want to include that are not found in the present Constitution? Present your proposals to the class.

3. Select several of the powers that Article I, Section 8 gives to Congress. Explain how our government might have been different if the Constitution had given these powers to the President instead.

4. Research the Magna Charta and the Declaration of the Rights of Man and Citizen (French Revolution). Compare the major provisions found in these documents with the provisions in our Constitution. What main principles do the three documents have in common? Make a chart that expresses your findings.

MAKING DECISIONS

As a delegate to a local constitutional convention, you are given the responsibility of drafting a constitution for your town or city. Using the U.S. Constitution as a model, develop a constitution based on local needs, problems, and issues. Present your constitution to the class.

Chapter 3
Federalism

When people think of the government, they often picture the national government in Washington, D.C. Though this is an understandable association, the President, Congress, and the Supreme Court are not the only important political authorities in the United States. The national government may be the single most powerful one, but it does not monopolize political authority. In addition to the national government and fifty state governments, a 1982 survey reported a total of 82,341 other governments in the United States. The relationship among these governments, especially that between the national and state governments, is important and raises complex issues in American politics. Many important current controversies—for example, the shipping and storing of toxic wastes—involve the powers and responsibilities of Washington and the fifty state governments. Our analysis of federalism addresses three key questions concerning the division of power between the national and state governments.

- What are the basic principles of American federalism?
- How does contemporary federalism operate?
- Is federalism still politically relevant?

PREVIEW

What are the basic principles of American federalism? Federalism exists when two or more levels of government have authority over the same citizenry, with each level having at least one area in which it sets policy independently of the other. An important issue in American federalism has been whether the national government or the states have final authority. In *McCulloch v. Maryland* (1819) Chief Justice John Marshall said that on the basis of the supremacy clause and the "necessary and proper" clause of the Constitution, the national government was supreme in most areas. Although the doctrine of national supremacy has often been challenged, current interpretations give supremacy to the national government in conflicts with the states. A second important issue concerns the actual division of political responsibility between national and state levels. The Constitution indicates some areas in which one level has authority; custom has defined other cases. In matters such as the regulation of commerce, the line separating national from state authority is not clearly defined. The question of which has final authority often generates intense political conflict.

How does contemporary federalism operate? Over the years federalism has evolved from a doctrine emphasizing the division of power between governments to a process by which the national government cooperates with states and cities to solve problems. Especially since the mid-1960s, federal aid to local governments, given through a variety of methods, has grown enormously. Numerous conflicts, however, continue to exist over the administration of cooperative federalism. One such conflict is over the distribution of federal aid—whether it should be in the form of categorical grants, block grants, or general revenue sharing. The formulas for aid have also caused disputes, since different formulas favor different interests. Moreover, contemporary federalism has made the traditional national–state–local relationship much more complex. Recent Presidents have adopted different approaches to resolving these controversies.

Is federalism still politically relevant? The transformation of federalism has raised important questions regarding its relevance. In recent years the Supreme Court has almost always ruled in favor of the national government in disputes between Washington and the states. Nevertheless, the states enjoy considerable independence—an independence that has resulted in a lack of uniformity in state court decisions, a complex legal system, and charges of excessive bureaucracy. Federalism has been defended, though, on the grounds that such diversity is necessary and useful.

WHAT ARE THE BASIC PRINCIPLES OF AMERICAN FEDERALISM?

Federalism exists when (1) two or more levels of government have authority over the same citizenry, and (2) each level of government has at least one area in which it sets policy independently of the other. The United States is a federal system because the national and state governments both have direct authority over citizens, and both governments have complete responsibility in certain policy areas. A federal system is usually contrasted with a unitary government and with a confederation (see Figure 3.1). In a **unitary government** all political power ultimately resides in a central government. Some powers may be delegated to regional or local officials, but these can be modified or withdrawn at the discretion of the central government. Great Britain, France, and Italy are unitary governments. A **confederation** is a system in which the central government is created by other governments. It has no direct authority over citizens and remains subordinate to the powers that established it. Under the Articles of Confederation, the Confederation Congress was ultimately subordinate to the authority of the member states and could not govern citizens directly (see Chapter 2).

While defining federalism may be simple, applying the principle is complex. In a unitary system it is clear who has which powers and who makes the final decision: The central government decides everything, though for convenience it may delegate some authority to local units. The principle of federalism, however, says nothing about the

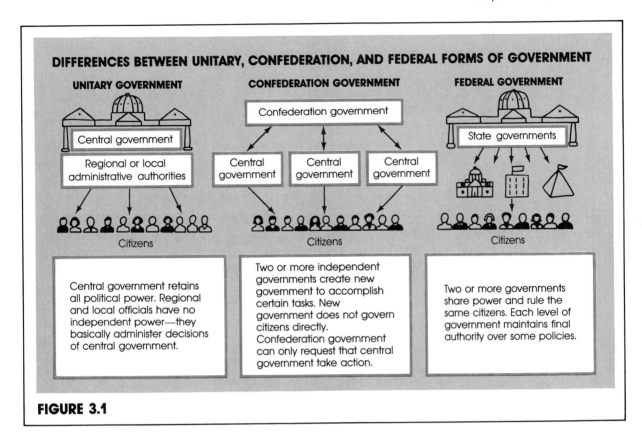

DIFFERENCES BETWEEN UNITARY, CONFEDERATION, AND FEDERAL FORMS OF GOVERNMENT

UNITARY GOVERNMENT

Central government

Regional or local administrative authorities

Citizens

Central government retains all political power. Regional and local officials have no independent power—they basically administer decisions of central government.

CONFEDERATION GOVERNMENT

Confederation government

Central government | Central government | Central government

Citizens

Two or more independent governments create new government to accomplish certain tasks. New government does not govern citizens directly. Confederation government can only request that central government take action.

FEDERAL GOVERNMENT

State governments

Citizens

Two or more governments share power and rule the same citizens. Each level of government maintains final authority over some policies.

FIGURE 3.1

way specific powers are to be divided or the way conflicts between two levels of government are to be resolved. Federalism merely means some (unspecified) division of political labor. Let us consider two key aspects of federalism in American politics: What level of government—the national or the state—retains ultimate political power? How is political responsibility divided between the national and the state governments?

The Question of Supremacy

The system of federalism created by the Constitution was at first greeted with skepticism. When the Constitution was drafted, there were many examples of unitary and confederation governments. The idea of a central government sharing final authority with thirteen state governments was new, though. Many people doubted whether two governments could be coequal. As a practical compromise to enlist state cooperation in ratifying the new Constitution, federalism—with its promise of sovereignty to both levels of government—

was an attractive plan. Yet two centuries after ratification, the possible contradiction of the federalism principle is still with us: If both levels have sovereignty, which has the ultimate power in a conflict?

Early Attempts to Resolve the Supremacy Question

The question of which level of government has ultimate power has been answered in many different ways over the years. Both the nationalist position (that the central government has final authority) and the state sovereignty view have been vigorously advocated. One of the most important nationalist arguments was set forth by the Supreme Court under Chief Justice John Marshall in the landmark case of *McCulloch v. Maryland* (1819). The case arose when the federal government established a national bank located in Maryland. The state of Maryland believed that the national government had no right to do so, since the Constitution makes no mention of the power to establish a bank. Maryland put a tax on the

Biography: John Marshall

The third Chief Justice of the United States, John Marshall was one of the most influential jurists ever to serve on the Supreme Court. Almost singlehandedly, he established the power of the judicial branch of the national government. He also did much to establish the supremacy of the national government in its relations with the states.

Marshall was born in 1755 in the wilderness of western Virginia. The oldest of fifteen children, he exhibited many of the traits we think of as typical of the frontier: a love of the outdoors, a directness of manner, and a certain casualness in dress. But this famous jurist was influenced, as well, by later experiences that modified the individualism we associate with frontier life.

Marshall came of age during the American Revolution and fought with the Continental Army. After the war, the young Virginian served in the state legislature and was appalled by its subservience to the interests of debtor-farmers. His goal became a strong national government—one that would, for instance, enforce contracts to protect people of property from fiscally irresponsible state legislatures. His beliefs were those of the Federalists, a party with whom he identified throughout his life.

After studying at the University of Virginia, Marshall became a lawyer and was elected a delegate to the Virginia convention that ratified the Constitution.

During the administration of President John Adams, he served briefly as Secretary of State. In 1801, Adams appointed Marshall to be Chief Justice—a position he held until his death in 1835. The appointment angered the political opposition, the Jeffersonian Republicans, who dominated the federal government at the time. To them, the strong national government advocated by the Federalists represented a threat to the sovereignty of the individual states.

Marshall's strong will, intelligence, and ability to organize arguments made him a dominant figure in the Court and in the government as well. His judicial decisions were based on his firm conviction that, in a federal system like the United States, the central government must have greater authority than the states; that the Constitution was sacred; and that the Supreme Court be recognized as the ultimate judge in interpreting the document.

The first important Marshall decision, in *Marbury v. Madison*, established the principle of judicial review (see Chapter 12). Other cases dealt more directly with the relationship between the national and the state governments. *Fletcher v. Peck* in 1810, was the first Supreme Court case to strike down a state law on the grounds that it was in conflict with the Constitution: the Court ruled that a Georgia law invalidating contracts violated Article I, Section 10 of the Constitution. Nine years later Marshall's decision in *Mc-*

Culloch v. Maryland further promoted the supremacy of the national government. In 1821, in *Cohens v. Virginia*, the state of Virginia challenged the concept of judicial review. In a brilliant opinion, Marshall argued that the states had given up part of their sovereignty in ratifying the Constitution and that state courts had to submit to federal jurisdiction; if they did not, he warned, the national government would become simply the servant of the states. In *Gibbons v. Ogden*, Marshall further underscored the supremacy of the federal government.

By the time of Marshall's death, in 1835, the United States had overcome some of its youthful weakness. There was little doubt that the country owed much of its strength to the vision, purpose, and dedication of Chief Justice Marshall.

bank, hoping to shut down its operation. The bank cashier (McCulloch) refused to pay the tax. This conflict eventually went all the way to the Supreme Court. For Marshall the issue was basically a question of who should prevail when the national government and a state government disagree.

The Supreme Court ruled that the national government did not have to pay Maryland's tax. Marshall held that paying the tax would open the door to state domination of national government. A state that objected to a national program could, theoretically, tax the program out of existence. The Supreme Court's decision in *McCulloch* came down strongly on the side of national government supremacy. This decision rested on two important provisions of the Constitution: the supremacy clause and the necessary and proper clause (this clause is also discussed in Chapter 2). Article VI, paragraph 2, usually called the supremacy clause, reads:

> This Constitution, and the Laws of the United States which shall be made in Pursuance thereof; and all Treaties made, or which shall be made, under the Authority of the United States, shall be the supreme Law of the Land. . . .

The supremacy clause means that if the laws of the national government made in accordance with the Constitution conflict with state legislation, national law prevails. But the power to establish a bank is not an **enumerated power,** because the Constitution does not specifically allow the national government to set up such an institution. Can national law be supreme even if it does not rest on power explicitly mentioned in the Constitution? Marshall argued that the power to create a bank is implicit in the constitutional grant of powers to the national government. It is an **implied power,** according to Marshall—that is, a power *based* on a specifically listed duty and backed up by the "necessary and proper" clause (Article I, Section 8, paragraph 18). Creating a bank may be necessary for collecting taxes and paying debts (both of which are enumerated powers). Marshall's position essentially means that the authority of the national government is final when Congress acts in accordance with enumerated *or* implied constitutional power.

Advocates of state supremacy, however, have looked at the Constitution and reached different conclusions. One argument in favor of state sovereignty focuses on the nature of the original agreement between the states and the national government. Since the states created the national government for particular purposes—for example, to regulate commerce—the states are not bound by actions of the national government that go beyond the original purposes of the unifying agreement. The Constitution, like a contract, specifies obligations; it can enforce only obligations that are spelled out.

The argument favoring state supremacy first appeared when Congress passed the unpopular Alien and Sedition Acts in 1798. These laws, which made it a crime to criticize the government or its officials, outraged many citizens. The Kentucky legislature even passed a resolution (drafted by Thomas Jefferson) declaring that national laws not specifically authorized by the Constitution have no force and that each state can judge for itself which laws are valid. James Madison—who helped draft the Constitution—concurred with this judgment in a similar resolution passed by the Virginia legislature. He argued that a state could block the enforcement of unauthorized laws by **"interposing"** or placing itself between its citizens and the national government. This conflict was eventually resolved by the election of Jefferson to the presidency in 1800 and the expiration of the Alien and Sedition laws.

In 1832, the issue of state versus national supremacy surfaced again when South Carolina declared federal tariff acts null and void (that is, having no effect) and refused to allow federal agents to collect tariffs in the state. President Andrew Jackson responded to the **nullification,** or cancellation, of national law by sending gunboats into Charleston harbor to collect the tariff. Eventually the issue was resolved by a compromise on tariff rates.

The strongest claims for state sovereignty were made in the context of the debate over slavery. Southern leaders such as John C. Calhoun and Jefferson Davis argued that in the case of repressive action by the national government, the states

John C. Calhoun, who served as Vice President under John Quincy Adams and Andrew Jackson, provided much of the intellectual support for the rights of states to secede from the Union.

could reassume even powers explicitly given to the national government by the Constitution. **Secession,** or breaking away, from the Union was permissible, it was argued, because the states had not surrendered their sovereignty for eternity. It was the Civil War, of course, that settled once and for all the issue of whether a state, like a sovereign nation, could withdraw from the original compact.

Dual Federalism

Perhaps the most important and influential doctrine challenging the supremacy of the national government has been **dual federalism.** This doctrine emerged when Roger B. Taney was Chief Justice of the Supreme Court (1836–64), but its influence was felt until the 1930s. The guiding principle of dual federalism was the Tenth Amendment—"The powers not delegated to the United States by the Constitution, nor prohibited by it to the States, are reserved to the States respectively, or to the people." This amendment was interpreted to mean that unless a power was expressly given to the national government, it belonged to the states. The national government and the states were coequal in sovereignty. In areas such as public health, where the national government is granted no explicit constitutional authority, the states' authority, in the words of Taney, was "complete, unqualified, and exclusive."

If pushed to its limits, the doctrine of dual federalism can greatly limit the national government. The national government would be the supreme authority only when it acted in accordance with specific constitutional authority. No longer could Congress use the "necessary and proper" clause to legislate in areas related to its explicit grants of power. This view was most forcefully argued in the case of *Hammer v. Dagenhart* (1918). In a 5–4 vote the Court invalidated the Federal Child Labor Act of 1916, which restricted the interstate shipment of goods produced by child labor. The Court said that the powers not expressly delegated to the national government are reserved to the states and the people. Since the Federal Child Labor Act concerned manufacturing, and since the power to regulate manufacturing was not specifically granted to Congress by the Constitution, Congress had overstepped its authority. An interesting aspect of this decision was that in order to reach this view of national power, the Tenth Amendment was misquoted. Justice William Rufus Day, writing for the majority, quoted the amendment as "the powers not expressly delegated to the National Government. . . ." The original does not have the word *expressly*. Its inclusion was debated when the amendment was first drafted, but the term was rejected as too restricting.

The Decline of Dual Federalism

The notion of two separate levels of government, each with its own political authority, came under increasing attack in the 1930s. Today dual federalism has been almost entirely rejected, and most judges and legislators have returned to the interpretation first offered by Marshall in *McCulloch v. Maryland*. The national government is supreme whether its power is *expressly enumerated* (for example, the power to coin money) or *implied* (for example, the power to create a national bank).

National laws made under both types of powers prevail when they conflict with state laws. Moreover, the Tenth Amendment—contrary to claims made by supporters of dual federalism—does *not* say that powers not expressly given to the national government belong exclusively to the states. Rather, the contemporary interpretation of the Tenth Amendment is that the states retain the ultimate power only where *no* authority—explicit or implicit—is given to the national government. For example, because the Constitution makes no mention of the Social Security program, this does not mean that the states have ultimate power in this area (this program may be justified under Congress' implied power).

Does the reemergence of national supremacy suggest that the federal system has really become a unitary system in all but name? Are state officials little more than agents of the Washington government? As we shall see, the powers of the national government still do not cover everything, and in many issues the states have a major voice.

Current Interpretations of Federalism

In our previous discussion we saw that, according to current thinking, when the national government acts on the basis of its expressed or implied constitutional powers, it has final say. Yet this doctrine does not mean that the national government can dictate to the states on any and all issues. The "necessary and proper" clause may grant broad power, but it does not cover everything. Even today, there remains a division between the national and state levels.

In contemporary politics the division of power between the national government and the states rests on the Constitution, court decisions, and numerous customs. Some duties of the national government are **exclusive powers.** They are spelled out in the Constitution and may not be taken over by other levels of government. The Constitution, for example, permits only the national government to print money, declare war, establish rules for citizenship, admit new states, and engage in several other activities. The national government also possesses certain **inherent powers**—duties that belong exclusively to the national government by virtue of its rule over a sovereign nation. Making treaties with foreign countries and acquiring territory are examples of inherent power. Such powers are defined by custom.

At the other end of the scale are exclusive state powers. Although the Constitution does not specify such powers, they exist by custom and implicitly through the Tenth Amendment. They include the authority to enact laws to protect public morality, regulate land use, provide fire protection, maintain internal order, make laws regarding marriage and divorce, and license professions such as law.

Many powers are **concurrent,** or shared, **powers.** Here both the national government and the state governments can legislate in the same general area. For example, the Constitution grants the national government the power to tax, create courts, and build roads. The states may also engage in these activities. Of course, if state and national activities conflict, the supremacy clause of the Constitution allows the national government to override state activity.

This division of authority is not forever fixed. In many important areas changes can and do occur. In the early nineteenth century, for example, providing police protection was in fact an exclusive state power. Today, with the FBI and Treasury agents, providing police protection is a concurrent power. A similar change has occurred in education: a power once exercised solely by the states has become a concurrent power. These shifts in who makes policy are frequently complex. The federal government may have no constitutional authority in an area, but it may use financial incentives to gain state cooperation (the 55-mph speed limit is such an example). To understand this changing division of political power, let us consider the power to regulate commerce.

Regulating Commerce and Federalism

Article I, Section 8, paragraph 3 of the Constitution gives the national government the power "to regulate Commerce with foreign nations, and among the several States, and with the Indian

Tribes." This grant of power, known as the "commerce clause," has been the subject of great controversy. Every change in its interpretation has resulted in a shift in the nature of American federalism. The first and third areas—foreign commerce and commerce with Indians—have generally been interpreted as an exclusive national power. It is commerce among the "several States" that has produced the most disagreements.

To begin with, what is meant by *commerce?* If you are the proprietor of a pizzeria, are you engaging in commerce? Does it make a difference constitutionally whether you not only manufacture but also deliver pizza? Might it also make a difference whether your pizzas are delivered in more than one state? Suppose someone buys a pizza and carries it across a state line (but you yourself do not ship across the state line)? Moreover, what does *regulation* imply? Would a national law setting the diameter of small, medium, and large pizzas be consistent with the constitutional power to regu-

The concept of interstate commerce has been expanded over the last century. Today, most small stores are subject to regulations established by the federal government.

late commerce? What about a regulation stating that you cannot discriminate among customers in your business? Obviously, if the commerce clause allowed the national government to specify every detail of your pizza business, the nature of federalism would be quite different than if the national government had a say in only the most limited aspects of your business.

The first of many answers to these questions was given in the landmark case of *Gibbons v. Ogden* (1824). The case came about when New York State granted Robert Fulton and Robert R. Livingston a monopoly to navigate the waters of New York. They, in turn, granted Ogden a license to operate in New York waters. Meanwhile, Gibbons had been granted a license by the national government to operate steamboats between New York and New Jersey. Ogden—who had authority from New York—brought suit to stop Gibbons, who had been licensed by the national government. The basic issue was whether national authority in commerce was superior to state authority. The first question to be decided was how the commerce clause would apply to this conflict. Writing for a unanimous Court, Chief Justice John Marshall interpreted the term *commerce* broadly to refer to all commercial transactions. Second, Marshall asserted that commerce "among the several States" (the language of the Constitution) may involve transactions wholly within the borders of a single state. At this point it appears that Marshall's view was that Congress can regulate just about anything by virtue of the commerce clause. Marshall drew back from this conclusion, however, and observed that such regulation would be "inconvenient" and "unnecessary"—but not unconstitutional. The Court ruled in favor of Gibbons and thus in favor of national authority over state authority in regulating commerce.

Marshall never distinguished *inter*state commerce from *intra*state commerce. Regulating commerce within a state, according to Marshall, was inconvenient but not unconstitutional. But the ultimate impact of *Gibbons v. Ogden* was to exclude almost all intervention by the national government in commerce that took place wholly *within* a state. The federal government could intervene only when the crossing of a state line was involved. Especially in the late 1800s, *interstate commerce* was construed very narrowly. When Congress under the **Sherman Antitrust Act** (1890) sought to break up a monopoly of the sugar industry, its actions were overruled by the courts on the grounds that sugar manufacturing was not part of interstate commerce. Only the transportation of sugar was interstate commerce; therefore as long as shipping sugar was not monopolized, the national government could not touch the manufacturing monopoly (*United States v. E. C. Knight Co.* [1895]).

Current interpretation of the commerce clause allows national regulation of almost every aspect of commerce (broadly defined), even when commerce occurs solely within a state. This change in interpretation has its roots in a revised definition of *interstate commerce*. The broadening of the commerce power first occurred in the early twentieth century. The Supreme Court acknowledged that when *intra*state and *inter*state are inseparable commercial transactions, the entire process becomes part of *inter*state commerce. For example,

in *Swift and Co. v. United States* (1905) the Supreme Court ruled that if you buy cattle in Chicago that have been shipped from Texas (and the processed meat may be sold in many states), your purchase is part of *inter*state commerce even though it takes place completely in Chicago. Moreover, even if the cattle were raised in Illinois and are to be sold in Illinois, the transaction can be regulated by the national government if these intrastate transactions will have a substantial effect on interstate commerce.

In the late 1930s and early 1940s, a series of Supreme Court decisions further reduced the limits on the use of the commerce power by the national government. In the key case of *National Labor Relations Board v. Jones & Laughlin Steel Corp.* (1937), the Court ruled that the national government can regulate labor practices within manufacturing plants because working conditions clearly affect the nation's commerce. In *United States v. Darby Lumber Co.* (1941) the Court ruled that Congress could prevent all goods produced in violation of nationally set wage laws from being shipped in interstate commerce. The princi-

Points of View: Conflicts Between the States

An ongoing problem of American federalism is disputes between the states. Since 1789, more than 120 disputes have wound up in the courts, and in at least four there was a show of armed force. Several court cases have involved claims of Arizona, California, and Colorado on the water from the Colorado River. Other cases have involved pollution as sewage from one state enters the water of another state. Despite the supposedly fixed nature of state boundaries, conflicts over the exact location of state lines continue to occur (in

1970, Arkansas and Tennessee had such a dispute).

The Constitution specifies that cases involving disputes between states are to be resolved by the Supreme Court. The Constitution or other national laws, however, are frequently of little help in resolving questions of water rights, air pollution, or border disputes. The response of the Court to these issues has been to rely on certain principles of international law (modified when necessary) plus its own precedents.

The continuing difficulty as-

sociated with interstate conflicts is illustrated by the lengthy battle between Iowa and Kansas over birds and flowers. In 1970, the Iowa legislature proposed a bill to declare the sunflower—the state flower of Kansas—a "noxious weed." Kansas struck back by trying to declare the goldfinch—the state bird of Iowa—a public nuisance. In 1977, the Iowa legislature again proposed legislation to label the sunflower a noxious weed. The battle simply could go on forever.

ple set forth in the *Hammer v. Dagenhart* case of 1918 was now reversed. The national government could now regulate employment in nearly all industries in the United States, even in small, largely local businesses. Perhaps the most extensive use of the commerce power has been in the area of civil rights. On the basis of the commerce clause, Congress banned racial discrimination in hotels, inns, restaurants, theaters, and employment.

The evolution of the meaning of the commerce clause tells us something very important about the federalism principle: the division of political labor between the national government and the states is neither sharply defined on all matters nor forever fixed. On some issues—for example, prohibition of the printing of money by states—there is a clear division of labor, but on crucial questions such as regulating commerce, no such clarity exists. Federalism is thus what political leaders, especially Supreme Court justices, say it is.

Conclusions

We can return now to the general question posed at the beginning of our analysis: What are the basic principles of American federalism? These principles may be summarized as follows:

1. The United States has a federal system because there are two levels of government, each with its primary areas of responsibility, and citizens are governed by both levels.
2. Where the Constitution, expressly or implicitly (through the "necessary and proper" clause), grants the national government authority, this authority is supreme if there are conflicts with state laws.
3. The national government cannot, however, act as a unitary government. There are many powers in the domain of state government.
4. This division of political labor is far from fixed. In 1800, an attempt by the national government to decide wages and working conditions in local businesses would have been considered a violation of federalism. Today such national power is widely viewed as consistent with the principles of federalism.

Check Your Understanding

1. On what two clauses of the Constitution did John Marshall base his decision in the *McCulloch* case?

2. What was the chief effect of dual federalism?

3. When does a commercial transaction become interstate commerce?

HOW DOES CONTEMPORARY FEDERALISM OPERATE?

In the nineteenth century and the first half of the twentieth century, the key issue in federalism was which—the national or state government—was supreme. Though still relevant, this is no longer the central issue in federalism. Today, the key question concerns how governments at all levels can cooperate to solve common problems. The emphasis has shifted from conflict to cooperation. Discussions today involve such issues as how money from Washington will be given to the states rather than whether states can nullify national laws.

The Change in the Meaning of Federalism

The roots of contemporary cooperative federalism go back to the pre-Constitution period. In 1785 the Confederation Congress authorized money to enable states to establish schools in the Northwest Territory (today's upper Midwest). Eighty years later the Morrill Act (1862) gave the states public land to be sold to finance colleges offering training in agriculture and mechanical arts. The Morrill Act was followed by national aid programs in agricultural assistance, highway construction, vocational training, child care, and the treatment of venereal disease. Though many of these programs were important, such national-state cooperative efforts were infrequent. Moreover, national involvement in their administration was limited. The federal government gave the states considerable freedom in how the money was to be spent.

The election of Franklin D. Roosevelt in 1932 and the Great Depression gave a boost to national-state cooperation. Some of the New Deal programs were short-lived emergency measures, but others helped set the style for policy for the next half century. The Social Security Act of 1935, for example, provided federal money to the states for public welfare, child health care, and unemployment insurance. This assistance was provided, moreover, with national standards as to who could receive benefits, how funds were to be apportioned, and how Washington would monitor state programs. The Housing Act of 1937 gave cities

access to federal money to construct public housing, although state approval was still necessary.

The 1940s and 1950s saw the creation of new programs and increased federal aid to states and cities, but the scale of activities remained modest. In the mid-1960s, under the presidency of Lyndon Johnson, the pace changed dramatically. Between 1965 and 1966, 130 programs involving state and national cooperation were created. In the late 1960s and early 1970s many innovative ways of channeling aid were developed, and states and cities were strongly encouraged to participate in the programs (in some instances, programs did not even require state and local contributions). To encourage participation in aid programs, advisory groups were established to help state and local officials with administrative complexities. As Table 3.1 shows, between 1955 and 1987 the dollar amount of Washington **grants-in-aid,** or funds given to the states, rose from $3.2 billion to $100.4 billion. Also note that national funds now play a

The response by all levels of government to the human tragedy of the Great Depression created, even after the immediate crisis, a sense of cooperation among local, state, and federal authorities.

National Grants-in-Aid to States and Localities, Selected Years	Fiscal Year	Amount (billions)	As Percentage of State and Local Revenue	As Percentage of National Government Expenditures
	1955	$3.2	11.8%	4.7%
	1960	7.0	16.8	7.6
	1965	10.9	17.7	9.2
	1970	24.0	22.9	12.3
	1975	49.8	29.1	15.0
	1980	91.5	31.7	15.5
	1982	88.2	25.6	11.8
	1983	92.5	24.7	11.4
	1984	97.6	23.7	11.5
	1985 (est.)	106.0	23.7	11.2
	1986 (est.)	102.6	21.4	10.7
	1987 (est.)	100.4	19.5	10.1

Source: Advisory Commission of Intergovernmental Relations, *Significant Features of Fiscal Federalism*, 1985–86 (Washington, D.C.: ACIR), p. 19.

TABLE 3.1

much larger role in state and local finances—in 1955, 11.8 percent of state and local revenues originated at the national level; in 1987 the figure was 19.5 percent. These transfers are now a major federal government budget item (about one in eight of all dollars spent).

This dramatic change in intergovernment relationships has many sources. Since the 1930s a shift in expectations regarding the appropriate role of government has occurred. In the past, the role of government, especially the national government, was limited to such activities as providing roads and military protection. Today, Washington tries to deal with almost every social and economic problem, from funding local sewage treatment plants to providing health care to the elderly. This broadening of responsibilities has been reinforced by the increased complexity of problems facing governments at all levels. In transportation, health care, environmental protection, public welfare, and education, problems are no longer local or statewide in character. As a result, involvement by Washington has become essential to coordinate

planning and ensure common standards. Imagine the outcome if, for example, the fifty states independently attempted to plan and construct an interstate highway system or to set air pollution standards.

Financial factors have also contributed to the growth of federal aid programs. The national government has a much greater capacity for raising revenue than do the cities and states. Federal individual and corporate income taxes are more easily adjusted than local property or state sales taxes. While state and local officials are reluctant to raise taxes for fear of losing industry to other cities or states, this concern is of less importance for members of Congress or the President. Because of the high cost of dealing with many contemporary problems, then, the financially well-off national government takes the lead.

The need to ensure their reelection has also encouraged government officials to devise programs to channel federal money back to states and localities. Especially in recent years, members of Congress have discovered that directing federally

Senior citizens have been among the many groups of Americans benefiting from increased social services as more federal money became available to states and localities.

sponsored programs into their districts can impress voters at election time. By helping local groups obtain funds, working in behalf of district interests, or simply claiming credit for some aid package, a legislator shows concern for the people back home. Finally, the emergence in Washington of organizations that represent state and local governments has encouraged cooperative federalism. Groups such as the National League of Cities and the U.S. Conference of Mayors can usually be counted on to make a forceful case on why the national government should enact a new program to help the cities or states.

Administering Federalism—The Types of Grants

The operation of hundreds of aid programs involving thousands of separate governments and tens of billions of dollars is exceptionally complex. A multitude of decisions must be made on how funds will be distributed, who will receive assistance, and how program results will be monitored.

Many of these decisions are not simply administrative details—*how* money is dispensed can influence *who* receives benefits. Let us first examine how federal aid can be distributed.

Basically, the grant-in-aid program can operate through three kinds of mechanisms: *categorical grants, block grants,* and *general revenue sharing.* A **categorical grant** is money given by the national government for some specific purpose, to be spent according to specific rules. An example would be funds to build low-income housing in New York City—money that could be used only for housing and in accordance with federal rules regarding construction, discrimination in employment, access to completed facilities, and so on. Usually the local authorities are required to contribute funds to the project as well. Categorical grants are sometimes classified as either *formula grants* or *project grants.* In a **formula grant,** funds are given as a matter of right to all eligible recipients according to some government-defined formula. A grant given to state agencies to establish programs to help the blind is an example. A **project grant,** in contrast, is awarded only to those government units or agencies that apply for it, rather than to all who are in principle eligible. Funds for a community eye disease center in a particular city would be given through a project grant. Categorical grants are the most common type of aid and allow either Congress or the administrating agency considerable influence over state and local officials in the program.

Block grants, the second-most-common form of federal aid, are funds given to state and local agencies for some broad general purpose. Block grants were first established by Congress in 1966 and were intended to achieve efficiency and save money by giving state and local officials greater discretion. Instead of applying for several grants, each with its own complex rules, officials could instead apply for a block grant covering such broad areas as crime prevention, community development, or retraining for the unemployed. However, on occasion Congress has required that money authorized under a block grant be spent for more specific purposes, so in practice block and categorical grants may be similar.

Issue: A Grant by Any Other Name May Not Be Worth as Much

"Categorical grant," "block grant"—terms like these tend to become abstractions unless we have some idea of how the money is distributed and how it is spent. In order to make meaningful comparisons between the types of grants, it is helpful to look at a specific area that has received federal funds administered in two different ways. Education provides a good example.

Starting in 1965, the federal government offered schools categorical grants through the Elementary and Secondary Education ACT (ESEA). At first, the funds were given, in about equal proportions, to two main groups: (1) the general school population, and (2) disadvantaged groups. The money was allocated according to complex formulas. For instance, one ESEA program provided specifically for aid to school districts that were undergoing desegregation.

By 1980, schools in disadvantaged communities were receiving about three times as much money as other schools under the ESEA. The newly elected Reagan admin-istration wanted to redress what it saw as an imbalance, as well as cut overall funding for education. In 1981 Congress, following Reagan's initiative, repealed ESEA and provided that its (now reduced) funds should be awarded in block grants. These became known as Chapter 2 grants, because they were outlined in that section of the bill. Chapter 2 money, given through state education departments, was to be allotted to local districts strictly on the basis of student enrollment. The primary goal was no longer to lend a helping hand to those most in need. Instead, equality in education would now mean that the available money would be distributed more or less equally throughout the population. Moreover, local schools were allowed to spend the money pretty much as they pleased.

Did the shift from categorical to block grants help education? The answer depends on which aspect of the educational picture you focus on. In general, administrators favor block grants because they offer flexibility and reduce paperwork. But block grants have benefited surburban and rural schools at the expense of inner-city schools, mainly because funds are no longer targeted toward the disadvantaged.

According to one expert, the main drawback of block grants to education is the use to which they have been put. School districts receive money no matter what they do. Although some schools have used these funds to develop innovative ideas—for instance, a Michigan program to welcome new immigrant families—many have used the money for routine purchases. If a school district is large enough, it may buy new computers. If a school's small enrollment translates into a tiny grant, on the other hand, the money may end up simply as a supplement to petty cash.

There's often more difference than a name change between one grant and another. Types of grants can reflect political and social goals as well as just administrative approaches.

The third aid mechanism is **general revenue sharing,** first enacted in 1972. It is the automatic return of money collected by the national government to states and localities according to a complex formula based on income levels in a community, urbanization, and levels of taxation. Under the present general revenue-sharing law, funds to the states can be withheld, and they were in fiscal 1981. The money received from general revenue sharing can be spent with very few restrictions. The principal restrictions concern the length of time a government has to spend the money (twenty-four months), some public participation in allocating funds, and provisions regarding record keeping and compliance with antidiscrimination laws. In 1982, over $4.5 billion was distributed through general revenue sharing to nearly 40,000 units of government.

In fiscal 1986, about $4 billion was sent to some 39,000 towns and cities (after 1983, states no longer received general revenue sharing funds). However, in 1985, in the face of mounting federal budget deficits, President Reagan called for an end to this program. In 1986, despite intense lobbying by local governments, Congress refused to renew the program for 1987. Thus, unless it can be reenacted in the future, this program, which dispensed an estimated $83 billion to states and cities between 1972 and 1986, will become history.

The Politics of Federal Grants
Disagreements over the Efficiency of the Types of Grants

Considering all the money involved in these programs and their complexity, it is not surprising that political disputes are common. One ongoing conflict concerns the relative role of categorical grants, block grants, and general revenue sharing in the aid process. Each method has its advocates and detractors. Many members of Congress and top federal administrators favor categorical grants because they believe that this type of aid ensures that the money will be spent properly. If Congress wants to help disadvantaged inner-city children, channeling funds through a categorical grant virtually guarantees that this money will not be spent for some other purpose. The narrow nature of these grants also allows the aid to be targeted to specific problems. Many state and local officials, however, oppose categorical grants. They assert that all the complex rules attached to these grants make them difficult to administer. In addition, uncertainty often exists over how long the funds will be available, since money is given out only for a specific period. They also claim that if an agency undertakes a project such as building a park, it must apply for numerous separate categorical grants—a wasteful, time-consuming, and discouraging process. The city of Boston, for instance, once had to make seventy-two applications to nine federal agencies in order to improve four acres of its downtown area.

Advocates of block grants claim that this type of aid balances the right of the national government to decide how the money will be spent with the need for communities to adjust to local condi-

tions. In addition, by consolidating grants, administrative costs are reduced, planning is simplified, and there is less duplication. Block grants have not escaped criticism, however. Studies show that because of the lack of specific spending guidelines, funds were sometimes spent in ways quite different from Congress' original intent. For example, the Comprehensive Employment and Training Act (CETA), passed in 1972, was a collection of block grants to train the hard-core unemployed. Often, however, funds were used to hire people who already had a high potential for employment. Regular civil service positions were also supported by CETA funds, and the program was occasionally used by officials to advance their own political goals.[1]

General revenue sharing has received its strongest endorsement from elected state and local officials, who believe that the program sharply reduces paperwork, curbs Washington's meddling in local affairs, encourages flexibility, and eliminates the need for frequent applications for aid. Its defenders feel that it is particularly valuable to older cities with numerous problems and a declining tax base. Revenue sharing is also supposed to prevent "creeping centralism," whereby all important decisions are made in Washington, not locally.

Critics of general revenue sharing, especially those who want government to address problems of poverty and inequality, feel differently. They argue that communities that do not need money receive funds anyway, because even the wealthiest localities are given money. At the same time, the critics say, communities with severe revenue shortages don't receive as much as they need. Moreover, many localities are ill-equipped to handle the large quarterly checks from Washington. Funds are sometimes spent on projects of limited value, such as lavish swimming pools, or to replace local taxes to pay for regular services such as police and fire protection. Finally, some observers fear that despite antidiscrimination provisions in revenue sharing, the poor and members of minority groups are unlikely to be given a fair shake when funds are divided by local and state governments.

Controversies over Allocation Formulas

Running parallel to the disagreements over the best means of distributing federal assistance is the controversy over the formulas for allocating benefits within each program. The importance of the particular formula can be seen if we examine a program to improve state highways. In determining how much each state should receive, Congress could consider such factors as population, miles of roads, highway use, conditions of the roads, highway upkeep costs, and so on. Just which elements are taken into account and how much weight is given to each element will determine a state's share of the funds. A formula that stressed highway mileage would yield more money to large Western states than a plan emphasizing use of highways, which would favor small but populous states in the Northeast.

Funds allocated through categorical grants, block grants, and general revenue sharing are usually dependent on complex formulas set by the federal government. No single type of formula exists that can be applied generally. Formulas are usually defined by Congress on a program-by-program basis, and the bargaining is lengthy and intense. A good example of the consequence of different formulas is provided by the mass transit plan offered by President Nixon in 1974. Originally the plan distributed money solely on the basis of population. When members of Congress from New York City protested the plan, Congress revised the formula to include the number of passengers carried and the miles traveled. This change increased New York City's share by $80 million.

Political factors influence the construction of formulas in several ways. Especially in large programs, elected leaders and administrators try to use formulas that ensure that almost every state and numerous localities get something. This promotes extensive political support for the program. Wide distribution of benefits appeals to those who favor a "fair share" for everybody. An aid formula sometimes reflects power in Congress. In 1978, for example, eighty-nine urban development grants were announced; 73 percent of the money went to cities represented by legislators on the House and Senate committees that monitored the activities of the granting agency. Moreover, formulas can occasionally be revised as economic and political conditions change. For example, a 1974 community development block grant calculated allocations on the basis of population, poverty levels, and overcrowded housing. In 1977, to aid the economically hard-hit Northeast and Midwest states (which had a lot of older housing), an alternative formula was permitted that included housing built before 1940.

Contemporary Federalism and State and Local Government

The replacement of conflictual federalism with cooperative federalism has changed the relationship between the national, state, and local governments. Until fairly recently the relationship between these three levels of government was marked by three rules. First, towns and cities within states exercised no independent legal authority. The form of government, types of municipal programs, methods and rates of taxation, and everything else had to follow state requirements. Second, the relationship between localities and the national government was supervised by the state government. City or county officials could not bypass state government in dealing with Washington. Third, political power was clearly in the hands of elected public officials—governors, state legislators, mayors, and so on. In other words, if a city needed a new bridge, the mayor might visit the state capital to plead with the governor for state funds.

This relatively simple set of relations has changed significantly under cooperative federalism. First, the grant-in-aid program has allowed cities, towns, and counties to get funds directly from Washington and thus avoid state political control. This has been especially important in states like Illinois and New York, where large urban areas have traditionally pleaded their cases to rural-dominated legislatures. In the past, for example, if Chicago needed money for a new sewer system, the final decision was made in Springfield, the capital. Today, the mayor of Chicago can go directly to Washington for funds. In 1982, the national government spent nearly $21 billion in direct aid to local governments. Though some form of state approval is sometimes needed for this funding, such aid nevertheless weakens the traditional state domination of local government.

A second change resulting from cooperative federalism has been the creation of numerous types of government and semipublic organizations to administer assistance programs. Traditionally, the mayor and the city council were the most important political power in a city. Now, because of provisions in some grants, some of this power may be shared with **special district governments**—that is, local or regional units created to oversee such responsibilities as recreation, waste disposal, soil conservation, and various education programs. Other groups that have been set up include community development boards, citizens' advisory councils, and private groups that owe their existence to federal grants requiring community involvement in local decisions.

A third, closely related change brought about by cooperative federalism has been the rise of the professional administrator as a political force. Obtaining categorical and block grants is a complex and time-consuming task. Correctly administering these programs, with all their rules and regulations, is highly demanding. Elected public officials rarely have the time or training to become involved. The responsibility is therefore given to the technically expert bureaucrat or outside consultant familiar with **"grantsmanship"**—an informal name for the complex process of obtaining aid. These technicians, who often are not elected and not accountable to the public, form a parallel government. Thus, the local recreation program may be worked out by city, state, and national administrators rather than by the mayor and other elected officials.

A fourth important consequence of the emergence of cooperative federalism has sometimes been described as the nationalization of state and local government. As each new federal aid program came into existence, more requirements were added on to what states could and could not do (so-called creeping conditionalism). Such regulations concerned discriminatory practices, environmental protection, proper administrative procedure, and more. For example, the Environmental Protection Agency has held up federal highway funds to California, Colorado, Pennsylvania, Kentucky, and Tennessee in order to force these states to create auto emission control programs. When Illinois, in the early 1980s, dragged its feet on establishing a program in Chicago, the EPA threatened to cut $100 million in federal aid. The collective impact of all the made-in-Washington rules was to bring many diverse state and local administrative practices into line with national government standards. Administrators in Sacramento or Albany are no longer completely free to do things the California or New York way; if the money comes from Washington, it is administered the Washington way.

Finally, the continuously changing nature of federal aid programs has encouraged a great deal of political maneuvering among subnational governments. Several large, older, and financially strapped cities now have lobbyists in Washington looking for grant money, suggesting new programs, and working on behalf of favorable aid formulas. Such efforts are often resisted by representatives of rural or suburban governments, who see the large cities as competition. The state governments have been active too; in 1982 some twenty-five states maintained lobbying offices in Washington. One study found a definite relationship between having a lobbyist and obtaining economic benefits from the national government.[2]

This competition for funds is especially evident in the conflict between the Northeast and upper Midwest—a region called the **Frostbelt**—and the South and Southwest—known as the **Sunbelt**. The clash pits an area characterized by slow population growth, older heavy industry, numerous decaying large cities, and a declining tax base against a region that is growing in population and in wealth but has other problems (for example, water shortages). Many of the choices faced by Congress in grants-in-aid generate sectional rivalry. For example, a program to help poor people would be more useful to Northern states if the aid

In the Frostbelt, top, an old mill now houses a few small businesses, as residents of a northern state seek to revive a faltering local economy. The gleaming cities of the Sunbelt, bottom, may mask other social problems: overburdened municipal services as citizens from other areas relocate in search of employment, vulnerability to changes in the price of oil, and inadequate water supplies.

formula included the recipients' utility bills and clothing costs, since these items are higher in cold climates. On the other hand, a formula stressing wages would benefit the Sunbelt, since salaries there tend to be lower. Conflicts also frequently occur over where federal money is to be spent. As Table 3.2 shows, sizable discrepancies exist in the amounts of aid received by states. Citizens of Alaska, for example, receive nearly four times as much grant-in-aid assistance as do citizens of Florida. In general, Frostbelt states send more money to Washington than they receive back in the form of aid and spending programs. According to one study, in fiscal 1983 the eighteen Northeast and Midwest states received only 89 cents for every $1.00 in federal taxes paid, compared to $1.07 for all other states.[3] Frostbelt states like Illinois and Michigan argue that such inequality further contributes to already severe financial problems. Officials of poorer Sunbelt states counter that without

such federal assistance they would be unable to provide adequate levels of service.

Both regions are well organized in Congress. The 1982 House, for example, had a 200-member Northeast–Midwest Congressional Coalition as well as a Sunbelt Caucus. Mayors and governors from these regions have also formed coalitions to advance sectional interests. These regional disputes often cut across party and ideological lines— liberals and conservatives, Democrats and Republicans will sometimes join forces to protect their sectional interests. These conflicts are often bitter and resemble the regional rivalry of an earlier period in American history.

Contemporary federalism has made the once simple state-local relationship highly complex. Power has become more dispersed across different governmental levels, many more elected and non-elected officials now have a say in policy making, and competition for resources is now intense.

State Differences in Grants-in-Aid Received from National Government, Fiscal Year 1984	*Five States Receiving the Most Aid, per Capita*	*Per Capita Grants to State and Local Governments*
	Alaska	$986
	Wyoming	919
	New York	617
	Vermont	574
	North Dakota	548
	Five States Receiving the Least Aid, per Capita	
	Florida	$268
	Texas	275
	Arizona	281
	West Virginia	294
	Indiana	323

Source: Advisory Commission on Intergovernmental Relations, *Significant Features of Fiscal Federalism*, 1985–86 (Washington, D.C.: ACIR), p. 63.

TABLE 3.2

Attempts to Reshape Cooperative Federalism

Given the huge costs of the federal grant-in-aid programs, it is not surprising that the administration of cooperative federalism has been widely debated since its emergence in the mid-1960s. As we have seen, questions involving how grants should be distributed and the precise formulas for allocating funds are politically important. A decision to allow Congress greater power over grants is likely to draw support from groups with influence in Congress, while opposition will probably come from governors and local officials. Administrative decisions often affect policy decisions on who is to get funds and for what purpose. Nearly all Presidents since Lyndon Johnson have made the reshaping of national-state-local relationships one of the major issues on their agenda.

Issue: When the Strings Are Too Tight

Accepting federal money almost always entails observing federal regulations. Compliance with federal guidelines—the strings attached to most authorizations—may seem especially burdensome when the federal government makes an offer the states can't refuse. A case in point involves federal highway funds and the 55-mph speed limit.

Late in 1973, the United States was in the midst of an oil shortage that drove gasoline prices up and caused widespread concern about future petroleum supplies. As a temporary measure, Congress passed and President Nixon signed a bill requiring states to mandate a 55-mph limit on interstate highways within their borders or lose all their federal highway funds. Slower speeds would not only conserve gas, it was argued, but would save lives as well. The result, as intended, was enactment of the limit by all fifty states.

Temporary measures have a way of lingering on well past the end of the emergency they were designed to combat. So it was with what came to be called the "double nickel" limit. The longer it was on the books, the more opposition it aroused.

Opponents of the 55-mph limit were especially vociferous in the western states, where distances are great and the terrain flat. Many of these states found ways of making life easier for their lead-footed drivers. They charged minimal fines—as low as $5 in Montana and Nevada—for speeding violations. And they termed the offense "wasting motor fuel" so that it did not count as a violation on drivers' licenses.

Exceeding the speed limit, however, was still a violation as far as the federal government was concerned. Its regulations provided that in any state where over half the cars exceeded the 55-mph limit, up to 10 percent of federal highway funds might be forfeited. Thus a state like Maryland, which received some $215 million in highway funds in 1984, could, theoretically, lose $21 million. The Department of Transportation, monitoring compliance by means of electronic devices, threatened to withhold funds from several states. But it also allowed states to do some creative tinkering with their statistics in order to keep the funds flowing. For instance, it permitted downward adjustments to compensate for presumed inaccuracies in speedometers. Even with the tinkering, however, several states were not in compliance with the law. Arizona was fined $5.1 million and Vermont $1.9—penalties that were subject to negotiation.

According to most polls, a majority of the American public favored the limit. But tests of monitored roads indicated that over 70 percent of vehicles routinely exceeded it. In 1987, Congress finally passed a bill allowing states to set a 65-mph limit on rural interstates. President Ronald Reagan vetoed the legislation. According to Reagan, the nearly $90 billion price tag for highway and mass transit improvement that was part of the bill was too costly. Both houses of Congress overrode the veto, however, and the measure became law in April 1987.

Johnson's "creative federalism." As noted, it was under President Johnson that modern federalism made its dramatic break with the past. Johnson's approach involved not only sharp increases in Washington's assistance but new, creative ways of dispensing aid. Creative federalism, as he put it, meant "the cooperation of the state and the city, and of business and labor, and of private institutions and private enterprise." Its purpose was to improve dramatically the quality of life through extensive federal government aid. In practice this meant that even private companies, or religious groups could receive federal funds. Moreover, Washington became active in many policy areas once left almost entirely to state and local governments—improving neighborhood parks, training police, providing jobs to teenagers, and the like. It was also a federalism of much paperwork and nationally administered guidelines.

Nixon's "new federalism." Almost as soon as Richard M. Nixon assumed the presidency in 1969, he began advocating a "new federalism" that would shift decisions from Washington to state and local governments. This approach reflected the traditional Republican view that state and local officials were closer to citizens' problems and thus better qualified to solve them. The national government would continue to supply the funds, but with fewer restrictions on spending. Decentralization would be accomplished through several mechanisms. Block grants, with their emphasis on greater local discretion, would replace categorical grants. Where possible, funds in such areas as housing and health care would be given directly to individual recipients rather than to government agencies. Finally, money would be turned back to states and localities through general revenue sharing. The Nixon program had a major impact. Many categorical grants were consolidated into block grants, and general revenue sharing was enacted. Nevertheless, Congress, with its Democratic majorities, still managed to keep control over most grant-in-aid programs in Washington during Nixon's two administrations.

Carter's "partnership federalism." Unlike Nixon, who was frequently in conflict with the Democrat-ic-controlled Congress, the Democrat Carter did not emphasize a reduction in Washington's role. Carter's stand was also consistent with his view that control by Washington was necessary to ensure compliance with antidiscrimination regulations. Instead of shifting administrative responsibility, he called for the greater cooperation of officials at all levels of government to make existing programs more effective. This was to be accomplished by creating a special task force on problems of federalism, placing officials with state and local experience on the staff of a key White House advisor, and setting up close consultation between the President and mayors and governors. The approach made few changes in the overall grant-in-aid program.

Reagan's "new federalism." Compared to the changes offered by Nixon and Carter, the "new federalism" of President Reagan has been very ambitious and might have far-reaching consequences if completely enacted. The Reagan program basically requires a sharp reduction in Washington's role in defining and curing the nation's problems. President Reagan in his first term proposed major cuts in many categorical grant programs, the complete elimination of others, and consolidation of more than ninety categorical programs into block grants. This was to be coupled with a major high-level attempt to reduce the paperwork burden put on state and local governments by Washington. Ultimately, Reagan would give the states primary financial and administrative power over major programs now controlled by the national government (for example, the food stamp program). Other programs administered in part by the states would be turned over entirely to Washington.

In 1986 President Reagan's Cabinet-level Domestic Policy Council released a report, called "The Status of Federalism in America," that called for greater state sovereignty. The report criticized the national government's interference in state policy in such areas as minimum wage, legislative apportionment, and abortion law. It also called for tough guidelines or even a constitutional amendment to give states more independence. In

Commentary: But Just Wait Until You See the Comfort Station That Goes with the Recreational Center

One consequence of the large grant-in-aid program is a blizzard of paperwork and the need to satisfy numerous layers of bureaucracy. A city wanting assistance to build a recreational facility might have to make separate requests to get money for the land, build a swimming pool, plant trees, operate a senior citizens' center, and purchase sports equipment. Sometimes funds for an identical project can come from different agencies, depending on the size of the city.

One of the frustrating features of the grant system is that requisitions must pass through several different hands before they are approved. A small town might apply for money for a new jail, but several state and national officials could change the request as it

moves (slowly) toward final approval. Naturally, with so many people involved, a breakdown in communication between the origi-

nal need and the actual grant can readily occur. The following story about a proposed recreation facility illustrates this problem:

Stages of a Grant-in-Aid Project As It Advances Through the Approval Process

As proposed by the person completing the grant application

As modified by the State Department of Recreation

As modified by the Department of Health, Education, and Welfare, Washington, D.C.

As finally approved in Washington

Actual construction of project

What town originally wanted

---

addition, it supported a limitation on the scope of grant-in-aid regulations.

The Reagan program has existed largely on paper. Part of the reason for this slow movement is the administrative headache of transferring dozens of complex programs. Even more important has been the reluctance of most states to assume the burdens of costly programs now handled by the national government. Though states have traditionally complained about excessive Washington paperwork and meddling, they are unwilling to take on the financial responsibility that would eliminate this aid. The Reagan program calls for financial assistance to the states, but there is no guarantee that such funding will be adequate or permanent. Congress has also played a role in modifying dramatic departures from existing pro-

grams. Finally, the whole emphasis on restructuring the grant-in-aid programs has taken a back seat to more pressing economic and foreign policy problems.

Moreover, the President's call for greater state independence has been weakened by the administration's inconsistent policies. At times it says, "Leave the states alone" but at other times it says, "Let Washington decide." For example, on several occasions Reagan appointees in the Justice Department have attempted to replace state business law with more probusiness national law. In 1986 the administration tried to block an Indianapolis plan to recruit more women and minorities for city jobs. The administration also attempted to interfere with state laws dealing with parents' right to decide whether or not to use life support systems for fatally impaired infants. Such actions reduce the administration's credibility when it calls for reforming federalism.

The consequences of different approaches. These different approaches will affect who wins and who loses in the competition for money and influence. Where a decision is made and under what rules can determine whose policy objectives are followed. Consider the way different approaches to cooperative federalism can have an effect on a poor black citizen. Since civil rights groups often have their greatest influence in Washington, a policy of federal government control over aid programs will probably be most beneficial to blacks. Such programs may contain strict antidiscrimination provisions. On the other hand, if key choices are made entirely at the local level, it is less likely that poor blacks could be as influential. Civil rights groups are strong only in some of the localities where poor people and blacks live. This biasing of programs is not necessarily due to local prejudice. Rather, in most localities there is far more pressure to reduce taxes and support traditional municipal services than to develop social welfare programs to eliminate the effects of discrimination. In short, support for "partnership federalism" or "new federalism" is also support for one set of interests over another. Calls for making the system more "efficient" are often calls for changing the distribution of funds and influence.

Check Your Understanding

1. What are the three basic types of grant-in-aid programs?

2. Why do political leaders like to include as many localities as possible in a program?

3. Describe briefly the conflict between the Frostbelt and the Sunbelt.

4. Describe the approaches to federalism that have been taken by Presidents Johnson, Nixon, Carter, and Reagan.

IS FEDERALISM STILL POLITICALLY RELEVANT?

Throughout most of our history there was no debate over the relevance of federalism. Numerous court decisions and doctrines such as dual federalism provided a strong legal basis to separate national and state spheres of power. This was reinforced by customs regarding the limits of national involvement in state affairs. National regulation of matters such as police protection and sanitation was considered both unconstitutional and inappropriate. Even the most ardent supporters of national supremacy did not believe that the United States was, or should be, a unitary political system. Today, however, some critics argue that federalism is becoming little more than a historical relic, since the national government has so much influence over the states.

The Legal Standing of Contemporary Federalism

Since the 1930s the Supreme Court has approved the steady expansion of national power at the expense of state power. When Congress moved to regulate areas traditionally within state jurisdiction, the Supreme Court has usually ruled in its favor. In some instances the Supreme Court interpreted the Constitution very broadly to achieve this pronational position. For example, in *Heart of Atlanta Motel, Inc. v. United States* (1964) the Court ruled that Congress could use the commerce clause to prohibit racial discrimination in motels, restaurants, and theaters. In 1968 the Court in *Maryland v. Wirtz* ruled that states must pay their nonprofessional and nonadministrative employees the national minimum wage set by Congress.

Many state and local officials feared that the Supreme Court would eliminate all obstacles to national domination. These officials were delighted, therefore, when the Supreme Court in *National League of Cities v. Usery* (1976) for the first time in several decades ruled in favor of state power over national power (but see the *Garcia* case below). The case concerned a 1974 federal law dealing with wages and overtime that applied to state employees. The Court ruled that Congress had gone too far in taking over state authority. The justices held that the Tenth Amendment puts certain state policies clearly out of Washington's reach. Justice William Rehnquist wrote, "There are attributes of sovereignty attaching to every state government which may not be impaired by Congress, not because Congress may lack an affirmative grant of legislative authority to reach the matter but because the Constitution prohibits it from exercising the authority in that manner."

The *National League of Cities* decision did not, however, indicate a return to reinvigorated state sovereignty. In several cases involving the right of public employees to strike, and the regulation of mining and of public utilities, the Court returned to a policy of favoring national sovereignty. In 1981 the Supreme Court, faced with several earlier decisions that conflicted with each other, tried to establish a set of conditions under which a federal law would be invalid if it went against state policy. Each of three conditions would have to be satisfied: (1) the national law regulates "states as states" (deals with state actions rather than just the citizens of the state); (2) the law concerns indisputable aspects of state sovereignty; and (3) the law directly interferes with traditional state functions. If all three conditions were met, the national law would be unconstitutional.

While this set of conditions allows state sovereignty in principle, in practice it is hard to imagine that the Court would rule on behalf of a state in conflict with Washington. This point was made clear in the 1985 case of *Garcia v. San Antonio Metropolitan Transit Authority et al.* In this case the San Antonio Metropolitan Transit Authority (SAMTA), a public mass-transit agency, was held to be in violation of the minimum wage and overtime requirements of the national Fair Labor Standards Act. SAMTA defended its wage policy on the principles established in the *National League of Cities v. Usery* (1976) case—Congress cannot override state authority in areas of traditional state functions. The Court ruled against SAMTA's wage policy. It also said that the very

idea that Washington cannot interfere with traditional state responsibilities is unworkable and inconsistent with the established principles of federalism. *National League of Cities v. Usery* was thus overruled. The majority opinion did assert, however, that the decision was in no way an attack on state sovereignty. In short, while the Court views the states as sovereign, there seems to be little that states can do if a conflict arises with the national government.

State and Local Government Policy Independence

Although the national government now plays a more vigorous role in areas once limited to the states, state and local governments continue to exercise considerable independence in many policy areas. The legal preeminence of Washington has not turned subnational governments into numerous carbon copies of the federal government. We are still a long way from a unitary system, in which state governors would be mere administrators charged with mechanically implementing policy made in Washington.

One indicator of state independence is the diversity in the organization and powers of state government. Even though all fifty states generally follow the national model of an elected chief executive, a two-house legislature (except in Nebraska), and a separate judiciary, there are numerous variations. Many states, for example, limit the term of governor, while in others the governor may serve an unlimited number of terms. Likewise, differences occur in whether top state officials are elected or appointed and how these officials are removed from office. Also, thirty-nine of the governors, unlike the President, possess an *item veto* that allows them to reject only a portion of a bill drafted by the legislature (in North Carolina, the governor lacks any kind of veto). State legislatures vary in size, length of session, committee structure, pay, and available support services. A major difference between the national government and state governments occurs in the selection of judges. Almost all federal judges are appointed for life, but judges in most of the states

State capitols symbolize the independence and diversity of the federal system. States vary tremendously, for instance, in the ways they allocate financial resources and in the services they provide to their citizens. Because state governments can sometimes respond more readily to community needs, state and local officials may initiate programs that are later adopted by other states or by Washington.

are elected and must run regularly for reelection. Finally, there are frequent differences in the forms of local government and in the authority possessed by cities and counties. For example, not all states have counties and some states allow local government considerable independent authority.

The independence of state governments is also evident in their spending and taxing policies. By custom and tradition all states spend heavily on education, highways, and public welfare. Yet vari-

ation exists in how much states spend and where funds are allocated. For example, Table 3.3 indicates that in 1983 the state of California spent $1,449 for every man, woman, and child in that state; the comparable figure for Florida was $856. California spent nearly seven times as much on education as it did on highways and was generous in public welfare spending. In Florida, however, relatively little was spent on health and hospitals but highway construction was well supported.

Comparison of California and Florida in Expenditures, Fiscal Year 1983	Per Capita Expenditures				
	State	*Education*	*Highways*	*Public Welfare*	*Health and Hospitals*	*Total*
	California	$13,921	$1,836	$10,000	$2,274	$1,449
	Florida	4,077	956	1,142	895	856

Source: *Statistical Abstract of the United States, 1986*, p. 279.

TABLE 3.3

Differences also exist in how money is generated to pay for these services. States have different ways of collecting money—user fees, income tax, sales tax, property tax, or corporate income tax—and each state has a particular combination of taxes and tax rates. The total tax burden that states impose on their citizens also varies. As Table 3.4 shows, a citizen of Arkansas in 1984 on average had to pay only about one-third as much tax as a citizen of Wyoming. Almost 16 percent of the income of New Yorkers went for state taxes, compared to less than 10 percent for Arkansas residents. While in 1983 a resident of Illinois had to pay at most 3 percent of his or her income in state income taxes, a New Yorker might pay as much as 14 percent.

The independence of states is significant in the lives of their citizens. Some states have made strong financial commitments to education, health care, public assistance, and other services. A resident of New York State, for example, has the benefit of an extensive system of public education from kindergarten to college. Other states have chosen to keep taxes low by providing only limited publicly supported facilities. Someone who moves from high-tax Massachusetts to neighboring low-tax New Hampshire will pay lower taxes but may have fewer public services.

Problems of Contemporary Federalism
Legal Diversity
One source of problems that have regularly existed under our federal system concerns how states treat the legal actions of other states. Article IV, Section 1, of the Constitution requires that "Full Faith and Credit shall be given in each State to the public Acts, Records, and judicial Proceedings of every other State." This means that states are obligated to respect the civil (but not criminal) court decisions of all other states. A California court decision in a civil suit—a court case involving disputes among individuals—will be recognized as valid in all other states, but a California law making certain acts criminal violations does not automatically apply in other states.

The "full faith and credit" clause has contributed to the confusion that occurs when each of the fifty states has its own distinct set of laws. The classic illustration has occurred over divorce laws. Until 1906, if a husband and wife lived in separate states and one got a divorce (even if the other spouse was not involved in the legal action), the divorce was valid in every state. In *Haddock v. Haddock* (1906), however, the Supreme Court ruled that each state could decide for itself whether to honor the divorce actions of another state. In this particular case, when both husband and wife were in New York State, they were considered married; when both were in Connecticut they were considered divorced; when he was in Connecticut and she was in New York, he was legally single while she was legally married! Not until 1942 did the Court rule that states must respect each other's divorce decisions. Even today there are unresolved issues regarding whether divorce settlements reached in one state are binding on

Variations on State and Local Taxation, Fiscal 1984	*Five States with Highest Tax Rates*	*Per Capita Tax Collection*	*As Percent of Personal Income*
	Alaska	$4,704	28.6%
	Wyoming	2,504	20.9
	New York	2,103	16.5
	Minnesota	1,706	14.4
	Connecticut	1,655	11.2
	Five States with Lowest Tax Rates		
	Arkansas	$866	9.7%
	Mississippi	871	10.8
	Tennessee	878	9.3
	Alabama	916	10.0
	Idaho	953	10.1

Source: Advisory Commission in Intergovernmental Relations, *Significant Features of Fiscal Federalism*, 1985–86 (Washington, D.C.: ACIR), p. 182.

TABLE 3.4

ex-spouses living in another state. For example, if a husband leaves his wife in New York and gets a divorce under California law, do California laws about dividing up family property apply to the ex-wife, who never set foot in California? This diversity of state laws has resulted in people "shopping around" to find states that have the most favorable laws for their purposes. Citizens who believe that they were libeled in the press, for example, might bring suit in the state with the laws most favorable to their case.

Federalism also creates confusion regarding what is or is not a crime and how a crime will be treated. Despite efforts to create national uniformity in criminal law, state-to-state variations still exist. Take, for example, the bewildering array of state and city laws regarding marijuana. In one state a person may be subject to a relatively small fine for possessing marijuana; in another state the fine might be ten times as large.

Such legal variations can hinder enforcement of state and local laws. For example, minimum drinking ages might vary from state to state. Young people living in a state where the legal drinking age is twenty-one could drive to a neighboring state where the drinking age is lower and purchase drinks without penalty. This, of course, undermines the intent of the law in their home state and also increases the chances of car accidents. A similar problem exists with gun control laws—a restrictive state law may become ineffective if residents can drive to a nearby state where firearms can be easily purchased.

Economic Costs

The existence of fifty separate states, each with its own laws and economic interests, contributes to economic waste and inefficiency. As explained in Chapter 2, economic conflict among the states was one of the major reasons for calling the Constitutional Convention. Before the adoption of the Constitution, states would often place tariffs on imports from other states or otherwise give an advantage to in-state commercial interests. The results were artificially high prices that slowed down national economic development. To prevent this situation, the Constitution in Article I, Section 10, expressly prohibits states from placing duties on exports or imports (except if necessary for inspection laws). Such actions are also made subject to congressional review and control.

Nevertheless, despite constitutional intentions, economic discrimination still occurs. It has been estimated that artificial interstate trade barriers add billions of dollars a year to the cost of goods and services. States can "protect their own" in numerous ways. Through its power to license professions such as medicine, real estate, and teaching, a state can maintain shortages of professionals to the economic gain of state residents. For example, Florida can discourage non-Floridian veterinarians from moving to Florida by imposing strict examination requirements for graduates of out-of-state schools. If fewer out-of-state veterinarians can come to Florida, those already there will face less competition. A second tactic is to give home industries a built-in advantage in bidding for government contracts. States and localities may specify that nonresident firms must underbid local firms by more than 5 percent.

States also enact scores of complex "administrative" regulations to discourage out-of-state competition. For example, since 1967 you cannot sell a grapefruit in Texas unless it tests at nine parts sugar to one part acid. This "consumer protection" law is really designed to ban Florida grapefruit, since these are usually seven parts sugar to one part acid. Similarly, several states discourage the sale of out-of-state wine by imposing difficult-to-meet requirements on storage and marketing (and in some cases, state taxes are higher on non-state-produced wine). According to one study, the eleven Western states impose some 1,500 restrictions on interstate agricultural trade.[4] Many states also impose higher financial standards on out-of-state banks and insurance companies.

Many of the actions the states take run contrary to the intent of the Constitution. But the Supreme Court and Congress have acted only where abuses are blatant. For example, the Court has invalidated a Louisiana tax on oil-drilling equipment manufactured out of state and a North Carolina tax on soft drinks bottled out of state. For the most part, however, Congress and the Court have tolerated such discrimination as either lawful administrative

regulations or constitutionally permitted inspection requirements.

Administrative Conflicts

Finally, critics of federalism say that multiple levels of government have increased bureaucracy, delay, and administrative confusion. The involvement of state agencies, which have their own political perspective, in national programs frequently results in unnecessary competition for control over programs, conflicts over administrative procedures, and inaction due to a lack of communication. In some cases, having nationally created programs administered by fifty different state governments results in redirection (or misdirection) of goals. For example, because of the need to get the cooperation of innumerable state and local officials, national antipoverty programs in the 1960s did not always reach the people most in need of help. In cities like New York and Chicago, aid was used by local leaders to reward their followers. The differing administrative abilities of the states also make it difficult to set up national programs in some localities. For example, some national programs require that projects such as hospitals be licensed by state authorities, but a state may not have an appropriate licensing agency.

Strengths of the Federal System

Can the federal system of government be defended against the charge that it promotes confusion and administrative inefficiency? Basically, three arguments can be used to defend the present system. First, variations in state policies are necessary because of the enormous diversity of the American people. It might be that divorce laws, education laws, and traffic laws that work well in South Dakota would be a disaster in California. In sparsely populated farm states, driver's licenses at age fourteen allow young people to operate tractors. In a big city, it would be dangerous to allow fourteen-year-olds to drive. A certain degree of inconsistency is the price we pay for the right of citizens to create laws that best fit local and not national needs.

Second, there is no logical reason to believe that the centralization of policy making in Washington would necessarily result in better, more efficient programs. State independence is a problem only if you are convinced that Washington is always in the right. Take, for example, the efforts of the national government to help cities clean up their water. Between 1972 and 1978, the national government spent $9.4 billion in grants-in-aid to help clean up sewage. The national government insisted that some of this money be used to construct complex advanced water treatment plants (AWT), which cost $2.2 billion in federal funds and over $700 million in state and local money. The problem is that the AWT plants do not always work, and they cost a great deal to maintain. Such experiences with made-in-Washington policy are not isolated exceptions. Many nationally conceived and funded programs have had a fate similar to that of the advanced—but frequently non-operating—sewage treatment facility.

Third, the ability of the states to act independently has occasionally allowed them to develop new and successful policies that were then adopted nationwide. States are thus laboratories of experimentation where new ideas are tested. Important national policies such as unemployment compensation, civil service, conservation laws, the income tax, and regulatory commissions were first set up at the state level. When the interstate highway system was in its early stages, officials in Washington drew on the experiences of New York and Pennsylvania. Policies such as no-fault automobile insurance, decriminalization of marijuana, and liberalized abortions were tested in a few states before being adopted more widely. The growing concern for the quality of public education has resulted in experimentation by many states, with different solutions. Such innovations would probably be more difficult if all important decisions were made in Washington.

In answer to the question of whether federalism is still politically relevant, what can we now say? Our answer is a clear yes if by "relevant" we mean that federalism still exists. As we have seen, the United States is far from a unitary government. The Supreme Court has, though to a very limited extent, reaffirmed the idea of state sovereignty, and states continue to exercise a significant degree of independence. But if by "relevant" we mean necessary or useful, then the answer is less clear. A reasonable case can be made that the principle of federalism is left over from the eighteenth century. Its existence complicates Amerian politics. Of course, it is not always easy to determine if the costs outweigh the benefits. For example, are variations in divorce laws good because they allow citizens a choice, or are these variations bad because they create confusion? What might be an innovative state policy to one observer may be a dangerous manifestation of local prejudice to another. We can say for sure, however, that because abolishing federalism would require rewriting the Constitution, and rewriting the Constitution would require overwhelming state approval, federalism is likely to exist well into the future.

Although the federal government provides much of the funding for pollution cleanup, localities may prefer to tackle the problem with solutions of their own devising.

THE POLITICS OF FEDERALISM

American federalism has undergone enormous changes. It has been transformed from a doctrine emphasizing sharp divisions of political authority into a system of intergovernmental cooperation to accomplish a wide variety of goals. Those who drafted the Constitution would probably not recognize contemporary national-state relationships as being consistent with their idea of federalism.

This change in American federalism is more than just a shift in procedure. The present system of multibillion-dollar grant-in-aid programs, national guidelines, and other features of cooperative federalism is not just the old system supplied with more money to accomplish more goals. Contemporary federalism has resulted in major shifts in political influence. Groups that once were weak have gained new strength, and many traditionally powerful interests now have less influence.

Under the old system of federalism, powerful groups in one state could not necessarily influence policies in other states. A group might secure antipollution legislation in New York, but this success would have no bearing on policy in New Jersey. As a result, New Yorkers would suffer the pollution created by industry in New Jersey. Appeals to Washington would be pointless because the national government had little concern with pollution. For better or worse, old-style federalism limited the national impact of strong state and local interests.

Today, because so many key decisions are made at the national level, a relatively small number of citizens in a few states can have considerable influence. For example, suppose a group opposes putting billboards alongside highways. In the past, when highway construction was handled by hundreds of semi-independent governments, attaining the goal would be pretty hopeless. Thousands of officials would have to be swayed. Under contemporary federalism, however, the group might accomplish its goal if it could persuade a comparatively small number of national officials. Congress could require that no state could receive a national grant-in-aid for highway construction unless it prohibited billboards within 100 feet of a highway.

Of course, not every group has suddenly found its influence multiplied a thousandfold because it can now act through one central government rather than fifty separate ones. Many groups that were especially strong in a few states have lost influence to groups better able to persuade Congress or Washington-based bureaucracies. Consider how present-day federalism has affected blacks in the South. Until the early 1960s, Southern blacks were virtually at the mercy of hostile state officials. The Supreme Court could order integration of schools and other facilities, but resistance was difficult to overcome. Battles had to be fought one at a time in several states and in thousands of school districts. This required enormous resources and commitments. Successes were rare. The national grant-in-aid program provided a powerful weapon for civil rights groups, who persuaded Congress to include antidiscrimination laws in grants-in-aid. Thus, if a state hospital practiced discrimination in its admissions policy and it wished to receive financial aid from Washington, it was forced to stop this discrimination. Most of the time, the threat of a cutoff in federal funds encouraged compliance. In short, civil rights groups with their allies in Congress and in government agencies now had the advantage over once-powerful state officials.

The lesson we draw from this shift in power is clear. Federalism is not a fixed, well-defined principle; it is an evolving concept, and changes in the relationship between Washington and the states help determine who wins and who loses in political conflict.

CHAPTER SUMMARY

What are the basic principles of American federalism? The American system is based on a division of authority between the national and state governments. Both Washington and the states exercise authority over citizens. The actual division of authority has changed considerably over time. Once the states were viewed as the final authority in disputes; today the national government is supreme. The authority of the national government derives from the Constitution—especially the "necessary and proper" clause and the supremacy clause—and custom. It is the political process that in practice decides who has what authority in a policy area.

How does contemporary federalism operate? Especially since the mid-1960s, federalism has emphasized intergovernmental cooperation instead of conflict and sharply drawn lines of authority. Because of its extensive financial contributions, the national government plays a major role in state and local affairs. Grants have also altered traditional national-state-local relationships. Aid is given in several ways—from specific grants for particular projects to unrestricted funds that can be used for almost any purpose. Aid programs have generated strong political battles, however. Controversy has centered in particular on who controls the funds and on the allocation formulas.

Is federalism still politically relevant? Despite much centralization of power in the national government, important elements of traditional federalism survive. States and localities often differ in government structure, and they follow different policies in such areas as welfare, education, and taxes. State independence has often been criticized as encouraging legal confusion and administrative complexity. Federalism has been defended on the grounds that it is necessary in a large, diverse society, that it encourages experimentation, and that the national government cannot always deal effectively with local problems.

IMPORTANT TERMS

Explain the following terms.

confederation
supremacy clause
necessary and proper clause
enumerated power
implied power
nullification
dual federalism
exclusive power
inherent power
concurrent power

THINKING CRITICALLY

1. How would our government have been different under a unitary system rather than under our federal system?
2. Could a Constitution be written that would spell out precisely the division of political power between the national government and the states? Why or why not?
3. The 1930s saw a great increase in the number of government programs. Did these programs serve the purpose they were intended to serve? Why or why not? What events might happen in our own day that would require an expansion in the role of government?
4. Should the present, complex system of federal grants be abolished and replaced by lower federal taxes? Give reasons for your answer.
5. Should the federal government require states to follow federally established minimum standards regarding important services such as education and health care? Defend your answer.

6. How important a role should states have in the development of national policies? Should primary responsibility lie with states or with the federal government? Explain your answer.

EXTENDING YOUR UNDERSTANDING

1. The U.S. government under the Articles of Confederation and the structure of the United Nations are both examples of confederations. Compare the problems faced by the United Nations with those faced by the United States under the Articles of Confederation.
2. The Constitution does not give the national government any authority over education. Yet the national government plays a vital role in education. How has this change come about? What educational issues are of major concern to the national government? Discuss these issues in class.
3. Why did the national government under President Lyndon Johnson greatly expand federal grants-in-aid? What were some of the major programs established? Write a report of your findings.
4. Contact an agency within your local government. Find out whether this agency must follow any rules and regulations from the national government. Determine who benefits from the regulations. In what ways do these rules help or hinder the operation of the agency? Present your findings to the class.

MAKING DECISIONS

Your community is eligible to receive federal aid. You are a member of a task force responsible for developing proposals to get this money. Identify five major local problems that could benefit from federal aid. Decide what types of programs could be set up to help solve these problems. Present your proposals to the class.

Unit 2
CITIZENS AND POLITICS

The opinions and behaviors of citizens are of central importance in American politics. In many ways, what occurs in Washington or state capitals is dependent on the views and votes of ordinary people. The way this process works is highly complex. We begin in Chapter 4 with public opinion—what views Americans hold, how we ascertain these views, and the sources of opinion. Chapters 5 and 6 focus on the voting process, including both the institutional mechanisms of elections and the forces that shape individual voting choices. Chapter 7 analyzes an important mechanism that helps to organize the electoral process—political parties. Citizens can, however, do more than just vote. In Chapter 8 we shall see how a multitude of diversely organized groups convey citizen opinion to officials in all three branches of government.

Chapter 4
Public Opinion and Political Socialization

Like atmospheric pressure, public opinion seems to be a powerful but not easily observable force. Many activities in American politics are said to be influenced by public opinion. Newspapers sometimes speak of Presidents taking actions to boost their standing in opinion polls. Corporations and political groups often spend large sums on creating a more favorable public image. Disagreements regularly occur on what public opinion is, however. Many experts believe that describing public opinion is as much an art as it is a science. Nor can we always agree on how public opinion works. Why do some unpopular laws survive while others are abandoned because public opinion is against them? Why do some leaders pledge themselves to serve the people and then make decisions opposed by the vast majority of citizens? Public opinion in politics is far more complex and subtle than the results of any opinion poll suggest. This chapter explores four crucial aspects of public opinion:

- How do we measure public opinion?
- How are political opinions acquired?
- Is the American public today basically liberal or conservative?
- Do political leaders follow public opinion?

PREVIEW

How do we measure public opinion? The opinions of citizens are not self-evident; if they are to be recorded and measured, we must first find out what they are. Many different methods of determining public opinion exist. The written record and personal conversations are two such methods. Today polls are the most common and accurate. Polling involves preparing questions, selecting a sample, asking the questions, and tabulating the results. Polls do not necessarily provide a clear picture of public thinking. People do not always answer truthfully, the surveys may be poorly designed, and the results can be misinterpreted. All polls distort public opinion to a degree.

How are political opinions acquired? The process by which children form their opinions is called political socialization. The family is an important source of political attitudes and beliefs, especially basic loyalties and identities. The family's influence is less strong on more specific issues. Schools teach obedience to authority, national loyalty, and a variety of other political skills. Education has had less success in shaping attitudes on political participation. The mass media also help determine political beliefs and values, particularly knowledge about and interest in politics.

Because of early political socialization, we do not arrive at our positions on issues simply on the basis of intellectual choice. Some issues will never be seriously debated because they have come to be widely and deeply accepted as the truth. Finally, the diversity of sources of learning and the degree of choice people have make it difficult to manipulate people.

Is the American public today basically liberal or conservative? The terms "liberal" and "conservative" can be defined in many different ways. Most definitions focus on the role of government in society, attitudes toward change, willingness to spend public funds, and approaches to morality. If liberalism and conservatism are measured by self-identification, most people take a middle-of-the-road position. However, people differ in how they define these terms. On many specific issues associated with liberalism and conservatism, the pattern of responses is complex and inconsistent.

Do political leaders follow public opinion? Debate occurs over whether leaders should follow public opinion, even in a democracy. Arguments against the idea are that polls do not provide clear guides to policy making and that citizens are uninformed on many issues. But it could be said that citizens can offer guidelines to leaders through polls.

The relationship between opinion and policy is mixed. On issues of basic political and economic arrangements, considerable agreement exists. As we move to day-to-day concerns, differences frequently occur. Public officials sometimes ignore public opinion because the opinions of some people are more important than those of others, poll results are viewed skeptically, the policy desired by the public is not practical, or leaders are simply unaware of public opinion.

HOW DO WE MEASURE PUBLIC OPINION?

Discussions of the Constitution or federalism deal with concrete documents, court decisions, laws, actions, and policies. Public opinion, however, is far less obvious than a section of the Constitution or a federal grant-in-aid program. Public opinion is not like the weather—you cannot look into a crowd of people and know what policies or candidates they prefer. There are millions of people, and each one holds numerous and frequently complex ideas about a wide range of issues and personalities. Correctly measuring public thinking can be a difficult and often controversial task.

Though measuring public thinking involves many considerations—for example, who might be included in a poll—far more is involved than technical details. The type of measurement used can have important political consequences. For example, in the 1960s public opinion on U.S. involvement in Vietnam was frequently inferred from the numerous vocal antiwar demonstrations, rallies, and disruptions. On the basis of such highly visible behavior, many people concluded that the war was having a profound impact on people's lives and that opposition was intense. Opinion polls, however, painted a somewhat different picture. This approach to determining public sentiment showed less intensity of feeling and considerable support for U.S. military involvement. The specifics of polls also had political implications. Sometimes questions were worded in order to suggest support or opposition to the war effort (for example, supporters could call U.S. involvement the "fight against world Communism," while opponents could characterize the war as "fighting other people's battles"). Since public support for the war was a major political issue, deciding how to measure public opinion was often a political choice.

Let us briefly consider some of the different ways we can measure public opinion.

The Written Record

Historians have traditionally relied on the written record to learn about the opinions of people. By using newspaper stories, personal letters, novels, and documents, scholars and popular writers have tried to piece together what people thought during a particular period. From surviving documents it is possible to get some idea of the political issues and conflicts of ancient Athens or Rome. This approach can also be used today. Scholars analyze popular books, magazines, and even graffiti to see how they reflect people's ideas and values. Unfortunately, the written record, though frequently the only evidence available, may not present an accurate picture of public sentiment. Until fairly recently illiteracy was widespread, so the written record expressed the concerns of only a small number of citizens. There is also the problem of whether a popular book or magazine reflects the opinion of those who read it. A person can read an article without accepting the ideas in the article.

Public Contact

A second popular method of learning about public opinion has been to travel and talk with ordinary people. This technique is popular with journalists who crisscross the country chatting with homemakers, students, workers, business persons, taxi drivers, and just about everyone else to get a feel for the "national mood." Many political officeholders rely heavily on this approach. Some spend a great deal of time visiting shopping centers, factories, or neighborhood groups to get a sense of what constituents want. Here again, however, we face the problem of overall accuracy. Even the most energetic correspondent or officeholder can interview only a fairly small number of people. Some people may also be reluctant to express their views. Moreover, the interviews can fill thousands of pages or miles of tape, and selecting "typical" passages can be a real problem. Intentional or unintentional bias can easily distort the results. Despite its personal touch, measuring public opinion by traveling and talking to ordinary citizens is of limited use, especially when we are interested in the opinions of large numbers of people.

Opinion Polls

A third method of taking the public's pulse is the opinion poll. Here a large number of people are asked one or more questions. Opinion polling is common today, but it has roots in earlier times. Several newspapers and magazines in the nineteenth century conducted what were called **straw polls**—before an election the newspapers would print a ballot so the public could register its preferences. Readers themselves decided to participate. Straw polls frequently drew many responses. Since there was no way to prevent people from voting in the poll several times or to prevent people who were not eligible to vote in the election from taking part in the poll, inaccuracy was a problem. Often the straw poll was a way for a newspaper to generate publicity and increase circulation, not to assess public opinion. Today some TV stations use a modern version of the straw poll by having viewers phone in to register a yes or no response to a question.

In the 1930s a more scientific approach to opinion polling emerged. The emphasis shifted from the number of people responding to the quality of the response. In part, this shift was a reaction to a 1936 straw poll conducted by the respected *Literary Digest*, which predicted a landslide for Alf

Not all opinion polls are conducted by professional poll takers. Students interested in raising an issue in the community, for instance, may take a poll to determine how other students feel about the issue. As they ask questions, they are also publicizing their cause and perhaps enlisting supporters.

Landon over Franklin Roosevelt (of course, the results were exactly the opposite). In particular, greater care was taken to ensure that people who answered the questions (they are called *respondents*) were representative of the general population. Attention was also given to how questions were worded and how results were analyzed. Though accuracy was far from perfect—in 1948, for example, a Gallup poll predicted the election of Dewey, not Truman—there was a clear improvement over straw polls.

Today, especially since the development of computers, polling has become big business. Many television networks, newspapers, and magazines conduct their own polls (for example, the *New York Times*/CBS poll). Almost all candidates for high office hire a polling organization to run

surveys on their image, campaign impact, and public issue preference. There is even a magazine—*Public Opinion*—that regularly prints poll results and articles analyzing poll data. Several universities have polling organizations associated with them as well as departments—sociology, political science, marketing, among others—that deal with polling. In a few cases—the late George Gallup or Louis Harris, for example—the people who run polling organizations have become well-known public figures who are asked to testify before congressional committees or otherwise comment on the public mood.

Though there are hundreds—perhaps thousands—of organizations conducting polls and numerous variations on how polls can be conducted, all surveys basically involve four steps.

Biography: George Gallup

When George Gallup died, in 1984, one newspaper headline referred to him as the "man who made polling what it is." Certainly this good-natured Midwesterner did not invent the public opinion poll, but he did turn it into a powerful force in American society. Using scientific techniques,

he broadened polling to include vast ranges of topics; for example, he was the first to conduct presidential popularity polls. He even did a poll on polls, revealing in 1975 that one in seven Americans nineteen years old or older had

been interviewed in at least one survey. Many of Gallup's findings appeared in weekly reports in several hundred newspapers.

Born in 1901 in a small Iowa town, Gallup earned advanced degrees in psychology and journalism at the State University of Iowa. After teaching journalism in the Midwest, he moved to New York City to become director of research for the advertising agency, Young and Rubicam. In his fifteen years there, Gallup researched, among other things, audiences' reactions to radio programs and readers' opinions of various advertising campaigns.

While still at Young and Rubicam, Gallup founded the American Institute of Public Opinion (later renamed the Gallup Organization), with headquarters in Princeton, New Jersey. The new firm made a name for itself by correctly predicting Franklin D. Roosevelt's victory over Alf Landon in the 1936 presidential election. This success contrasted with the failure of the best-known poll of the day, sponsored by the *Literary Digest* magazine, which predicted a Landon victory. While Gallup used scientific sampling, the *Digest*'s straw poll drew names chiefly from the telephone book; this technique resulted in an unrepresentative response, since many poorer people (most of them FDR voters) didn't have phones. In later presidential elections, Gallup miscalled only the 1948 contest between Truman and Dewey.

Although Gallup continued to conduct consumer polls for advertisers and the mass media, his work in the area of politics was probably the most noteworthy and the most controversial. As polling became more widespread, critics asserted that political leaders, in making policy choices, were paying too much attention to poll results. Gallup's response was simple: "To the extent that a political leader does take public opinion into account in making his decisions, he should have an accurate and objective measure of that opinion."

And what about his own politics? Gallup claimed to have stopped voting—in presidential elections, at least—after 1928, when he cast his ballot for the loser, Al Smith. If he were to reveal his choice, Gallup remarked, he might be accused of trying to influence the outcome. But if he refused to reveal the information, he said, "How could I ask anyone else such a question?"

Largely as a result of Gallup's innovations, polling has become a highly visible aspect of national life. On most important issues the public's reaction is closely examined and the findings well publicized by the media. Political leaders may seek guidance from polls; they may use them to justify their actions. However it is used, there seems little question that poll taking is here to stay.

Prepare Questions

Questions may range from very specific ones requiring a simple yes or no response to **open-ended questions** such as "What should we do about energy problems?" that allow respondents to provide their own answers. Careful researchers will test questions several times to eliminate unclear terms or misleading implications. To weed out answers based on lack of information, **filter questions** are sometimes used. They inquire whether the person has thought about an issue or is familiar with a problem. If the answer is no, the person's opinion is not asked for.

Select a Sample

Pollsters have discovered that it is unnecessary to ask everyone's opinion to get an accurate measurement of overall opinion. A **random sample** of 1,500 people can give a good picture of how the entire population would answer a question. In a random sample, each person in a population has an equal chance of being included in the sample. The goal is to produce a perfect cross section of the population—that is, a sample that includes all the variations of opinion on an issue. In practice this never happens, though the results are frequently close.

There are several different types of samples. A common variation of random sampling is **cluster sampling.** Groups of people (states, schools, etc.) near each other are selected, subdivisions within the units are selected (counties, classrooms), and finally people within the subunits are chosen. A second variation is **stratified sampling** in which the population is divided into groups—whites, blacks, men, women, and so forth—and random samples are drawn from each strata. In **quota samples,** people are selected to create a sample that accurately reflects the makeup of the population. For example, if the population is 11 percent black and the desired sample size is 1,500, 165 blacks will be found and interviewed. Quota samples can lead to bias if interviewers are given too much leeway in filling quotas. For example, an interviewer who "needs" fifty women may interview only employees from a local hospital in order to fill the quota. Their views may not reflect those of women

This opinion poll was "sponsored by leading Republican, Democratic and independent newspapers." What effect might such sponsorship have on the poll?

in general. Though using a sample instead of asking everyone will produce some errors, the amount of error can be estimated and the cost vastly reduced.

Ask Questions

Organizations like Gallup or Roper usually ask questions in face-to-face interviews to allow the interviewer to probe responses and get a good sense of whether respondents understand the issues. Telephone interviews and mailed questionnaires are also popular. Face-to-face interviews are usually preferred but are expensive and time-consuming. When a quick response to a current issue is needed, polling is usually conducted over the telephone.

Tabulate the Results

Hundreds of separate responses must be condensed, or the results will be bewildering. When questions are of the yes/no variety, the process is straightforward. However, when responses are open-ended, judgments must be made concerning how to present the information—for instance, should "don't-know" responses be included in the tallies? Should similar answers be combined? For example, if 2 percent of a group favor a policy, 3 percent oppose it, and 95 percent don't care, do you conclude that 60 percent oppose the policy? (This is based on the fact that of the 5 percent who expressed an opinion, 3 percent—or 60 percent of the small group—opposed the policy.)

Problems with Opinion Polls

There is no single way to conduct an opinion poll. Experts often disagree on how to word questions or provide the most accurate sampling techniques. The quality of opinion surveys can differ significantly, especially since cost factors can lead to cutting corners. The result is that it is often difficult to evaluate the truthfulness of poll results. Here we touch on the most basic issue on polling: Do opinion polls present a truthful picture of public sentiment? The answer is that to a greater or lesser extent *all* polls contain a certain amount of distortion. Discrepancies between true public opinion and poll results come from three main sources: (1) people give inaccurate answers, (2) polls may be poorly designed, and (3) results may be interpreted inaccurately.

Inaccurate Answers

When citizens are asked their opinion on an issue such as unemployment or energy, their answers do not always correspond to what they really think. This discrepancy can stem from several factors. One factor is the pressure people feel to give socially acceptable answers. If you ask about sensitive issues such as racial prejudice, support for unpopular political causes, or odd personal behavior, respondents may answer on the basis of how people *ought* to act or think, not their own feelings. This pressure to conform probably also explains why people's responses to questions on whether they have voted do not always match official records. Some people prefer to say that they have registered and voted when in fact they have not. According to one study, in the 1976 presidential election about 14 percent of the respondents misrepresented themselves when asked if they had vot-

ed. Also, many of those who voted for the loser claimed that they had supported the winner.[1]

Fear of how the information could be used can also encourage misrepresentation. People holding unpopular views might fear that they would suffer if their views were known. In addition, some campaign and commercial organizations have used polls as a way of "selling" their candidates or products. For example, a campaign might conduct a poll by asking: "Do you believe that our present mayor's plan to reduce taxes and improve education has done the most to help our community?" Obviously this is a disguised sales pitch, not a poll. Sophisticated citizens have learned to spot these pseudo-polls and sometimes give fake information in response. Legitimate survey organizations may also receive answers that are not accurate.

VIETOR'S FUNNY BUSINESS

"Thank you for seeing me. Would you mind answering a few loaded questions?"

(Copyright, 1983 USA TODAY. Reprinted with permission)

Finally, people may not offer their real opinions because they do not understand the question or important terms. Consider a question like "Should the government guarantee loans for private companies?" Since this question could easily be misperceived as pertaining to government loans, not simply guarantees of these loans, a "no" answer does not really indicate opposition to loan guarantees. Problems of this type are especially likely when complex, highly controversial terms are used (for example, "affirmative action," "military intervention").

Poorly Designed Polls

Measuring public opinion, like measuring temperature, requires an accurate instrument. Inaccuracies can occur at every stage of the measurement process. An accurate poll should be based on a sample that closely mirrors the group whose opinions are to be measured. Obtaining a good, representative sample is expensive and time-consuming. Sometimes there are groups—isolated rural dwellers, people who travel a lot, and so on—who are difficult to contact and are thus underrepresented in state or national samples. Problems can also occur if interviewers avoid high-crime neighborhoods or people who look unfriendly and uncommunicative. If a poll is done by telephone, there is a good chance that poor people will be underrepresented, since many poor people do not have a phone.

The question itself may be faulty. Besides including unfamiliar terms, a question may use emotion-laden words that influence the way respondents answer. In a 1978 poll, people were asked, "If a situation like Vietnam were to develop in another part of the world, do you think that the United States should or should not send troops?" About 18 percent said "send troops." When the phrase "to stop a Communist takeover" was added, the proportion favoring sending troops doubled.[2] Questions may also offer people no alternative responses that match their own opinions. For example, a 1974 Harris poll asked citizens if they "favored," "opposed," or were "not sure about" expanding U.S.–Soviet trade.[3] How would a person respond who favored expanding agricultural

trade but opposed trade involving technology? When alternative responses are not offered, the poll gives an incomplete view of public opinion.

An opinion poll can also yield distorted results if interviewers are poorly trained, biased, or likely to generate misleading answers by mistake. Respectable survey organizations train their interviewers not to encourage one response over another by offering cues such as a smile, a change in tone of voice, or a bored look. Nevertheless, such influence does occur.

Inaccurate Interpretation of Results

Even after the information has been collected and tabulated and every possible precaution has been taken to ensure accuracy, a misreading of public opinion can occur. The "message" of a poll can depend on the interpretation given to it, and this interpretation can be faulty. For example, between 1964 and the early 1970s, the public was repeatedly asked whether the United States had made a mistake in getting involved in Vietnam. Some poll takers and leaders interpreted this question as offering a choice between staying in Vietnam or withdrawing (they assumed that those saying "mistake" wanted the United States out of Vietnam). A more careful analysis of this information, however, found that many of those saying "mistake" also desired continued U.S. military involvement.

Problems can also occur when sophisticated preferences are read into fairly simple questions. For example, in his 1981 testimony before the House Subcommittee on Health and the Environment, polling expert Louis Harris testified that 51 percent of the public wanted to keep the Clean Air Act without change. This act is a highly complex piece of legislation dealing with many situations, standards, and technologies. Shortly after Harris' testimony, a national survey found that 65 percent of the public had heard "nothing" or "little" about this act.[4] Even those who had some general idea of the legislation probably had no familiarity with its specific provisions. Obviously, the 51 percent spoken of by Harris were not basing their response on a complete understanding of the Clean Air Act. More likely, they were simply indicating support for the general idea of antipollution legislation, not a particular law.

Measuring just how close opinion polls come to being perfectly accurate is very difficult. To do so would require a 100 percent accurate standard against which a particular poll result could be compared; the difference between the two would reveal the degree of poll inaccuracy. Perhaps the closest thing to such a test occurs when polls try to predict the outcome of an election. What the poll shows can be compared to what really happens.

In the 1984 presidential election, nine major polling organizations made final predictions of the outcome. The actual result was that Ronald Reagan received 59 percent of the vote, Walter Mondale 41 percent. One pollster—Gallup—called the outcome exactly. While the others predicted a Reagan victory, the size of the projected win varied significantly from poll to poll. For example, the USA *Today* poll gave Reagan a 25-point margin, while the Roper poll saw a 10 percent difference (the final difference was 18 percent). These differences among polls result from such factors as how their samples were drawn, how the questions were asked, and how last-minute "undecided" voters were assigned to the two candidates.

It is quite likely that on issues other than elections, even larger differences between polls and the "true" distribution would occur. For one thing, since results of an issues poll will not be checked against a voter tally, poll takers may not conduct as careful (and therefore expensive) a poll as they should. Second, compared to a "how will you vote?" poll, the choices on an issue poll are far more complex—decisions regarding language, number of alternatives, and so on can shape responses. Finally, citizens are more likely to have a clearer view of candidates than of issues. A well-formed preference for a particular candidate is much easier to measure than a vague idea about a complicated public matter.

A Perspective on Polling

Our analysis of how public opinion is measured has focused on the problems of accurately gauging public thinking. We are not suggesting, however, that opinion polling is hopeless. Reasonably accurate polls are possible and improvements are being made in polling techniques and methods of analysis. What we must realize is that "public opinion" is not self-evident; it must be measured, and measurement will always involve some distortions.

Check Your Understanding

1. What are the four steps in conducting an opinion poll?

2. What are four types of samples used in public opinion polls?

3. List three reasons why poll results may be inaccurate.

HOW ARE POLITICAL OPINIONS ACQUIRED?

People are not born with opinions on political issues. Nor are these opinions suddenly acquired when an individual reaches adulthood. Political opinions are learned, and learning begins at an early age. The process by which people acquire their political identity and preferences on issues is called **political socialization.** Political socialization in the United States is a complex and individualistic process. Citizens get their values and beliefs from many sources—family, school, mass media, friends, and so on. Moreover, people are not passive recipients of messages. They can accept or reject information and help shape their own identities. Political learning is a continuous process that occurs over a lifetime. Our analysis will focus on the sources of this learning and on some of the consequences of early political socialization.

Sources of Political Learning
The Family
The family is probably the most important source of political learning. Especially before their chil-

dren reach adolescence, parents typically have the most influence. Obviously, few parents have total control of their children, but most parents shape the general values of their offspring. Most of the time, for example, a child raised in a family whose values are similar to those in the community will retain those values. Even when this child grows up, the family can exert influence. Feelings of "what would my mother and father think?" may encourage the young adult to hold on to the values even when pressured to change.

The family shapes the political socialization process in several ways. The most direct way is by teaching political values. A father who strongly favors one political party over the other may consciously convey this feeling to his children. The teaching process may also be less deliberate, more informal—children may become interested in government if their mother is active in a local political group. Families also play a major role in exposing their children to socializing forces outside the home. Parents usually decide such matters as whether a child will have religious training, exposure to television, books in the house, whether a child will attend public or private school, and so on. Even though learning may occur from, say, television, it is often the parents who decide whether the child can watch a particular program. The general atmosphere and exercise of authority in a family may also have political consequences. It has been argued, for example, that families that are very strict and believe in firm discipline are unlikely to raise their children to accept democratic ideals.

The role of parents is probably most pronounced in molding basic loyalties and identities. A person who thinks of himself or herself as a loyal American, a Methodist, and a supporter of labor unions probably owes much of this self-perception to family influence. Identities like these tend to be gotten early in life, are persistent, and can greatly influence subsequent opinions. A black child with a strong sense of black identity may grow up to feel that a black should run for President, whereas a black child without a sense of racial identity may, as an adult, be indifferent to black political issues. Family learning regarding the relationship among

Memorial Day parades are a typical event all across the nation. The splash of color of waving flags and the excited cheers of citizens help instill a sense of national pride and loyalty.

identities and loyalties is especially important. In the United States children are usually taught to place national loyalty ahead of religious loyalty. This is not true in many Middle Eastern and African nations, where religious, not national, loyalty comes first.

On more specific issues, the family continues to play a role, but the influence appears to be less obvious. One particular political orientation that has received special attention from researchers is **partisan affiliation,** or feelings of loyalty to and identification with a political party. The importance of affiliation comes from the fact that it is usually a good indicator of how a person votes (that is, Democratic identifiers usually vote Democratic). One major national study of young adults (aged twenty-five and twenty-six) and their parents (aged forty-eight to sixty-two) found that most parents and children had similar party loyalties. For example, about two-thirds of the young Democrats had Democratic parents, while only about a fifth of young Democrats had Republican parents.[5]

On such issues as prayers in public school, racial integration of schools, the legalization of marijuana, and evaluations of various people and groups, parent-child agreement is usually weaker. For example, in 1973, among parents who felt that the government in Washington should ensure racial integration in schools, 59 percent had children who shared this view. The issues of prayer in public school, the divine nature of the Bible, and the right of people to make antireligious speeches showed relatively high parent-offspring agreement. Significant disagreement occurred over issues of equality between men and women, ratings of radical students, and support for consumer advocate Ralph Nader.

There are several reasons why parents do not turn out carbon copies of themselves in their children. First, few if any parents want their children to be precisely like themselves on every political issue. A mother and father may not care very much which political party their children belong to if party loyalty is not important to their household. This is reinforced by the fact that politics does not have a high priority in most American families. Second, the transmission of political identity from parent to child can sometimes be disrupted. Parents can disagree among themselves, children can become emotionally distant from their families, and offspring can misperceive where their parents stand on issues. All of these conditions have been shown to reduce parent-child political agreement. Finally, parents and children may lead very different lives, and even people with similar basic political orientations can differ if their circumstances differ. This was dramatically illustrated during the war in Vietnam, when many draft-age males disagreed with their parents over U.S. military intervention. The two generations may have shared the same overall values, but specific circumstances led to different issue positions.

The School

The school is probably the second most important source of political learning. Due to compulsory education laws, young people spend at least ten years in school. Besides conveying information and imparting skills, schools often shape friendship groups and can introduce students to people from diverse ethnic and economic backgrounds. Extracurricular activities—from the French Club to football—can also affect one's political orientations.

Assessing the role of schools in highly complex, and there are many controversies over the schools' role in political education. We know the number of years spent in school bears a relationship to particular political attitudes and behavior. For example, those who are well educated are usually more knowledgeable politically, more attuned to political events, more likely to vote, more likely to hold opinions and discuss politics, and more likely to tolerate those with unpopular views. Whether these traits are a result of schooling or have their roots in family or personal factors remains an unanswered question. It may be that people who pursue an education also tend to be more politically active, and therefore that schooling is not the major influence.

One type of political learning in which education does have an impact is in instilling obedience to authority. Willingness to accept political authority, whether in a law of Congress or a police officer's traffic command, is an important attitude. Unless such obedience is widespread, bribery or force would be the basis of society. The typical school, with its elaborate rules and penalties for violations, reinforces the family in this type of socialization.

The school also plays a major role in creating people's sense of national identity and respect for traditional political values. This is accomplished by such mechanisms as American history courses that emphasize the colonists' struggle for freedom, the celebration of events like Thanksgiving, the special honor given the flag, pictures of famous

These youngsters watching a movie in their classroom are not simply being entertained. When the film is over, they will explore, with their teacher, whether the movie changed their attitudes on topics the film brought up.

patriots, and the like. Such activity is so widely accepted that we may forget that it is political teaching.

One area in which American schools seem to have only a limited impact is in courses that deal explicitly with political subjects. One major study concludes that high school civics courses do little to change students' political knowledge, interest in politics, feelings of political influence, disposition toward political activism, and so on. Even civics courses rated highly by students did not seem to influence their political views.[6]

One reason why schools have limited impact on their students' political views is that there is often disagreement within a community on certain controversial issues. Parents, teachers, community leaders, and others may have differing opinions on issues like abortion, U.S. military intervention, environmental protection, and so on. Textbook publishers too may want to avoid covering controversial subjects in their books. As a result, classroom discussions on political issues often stick to topics that most people agree on. The discussions may not be very inspiring, but at least

nobody is offended. According to one study, in those few cases in which teachers did discuss controversial issues and students were encouraged to participate, the courses had a sizable impact on political learning.[7]

The Mass Media

Only in the last few years has the mass media's role in political socialization received widespread attention. It is now clear that before adulthood a person may spend as much time watching television, listening to the radio, reading magazines, and so on as he or she spends in school or with the family. Moreover, technological progress gives the mass media powerful means to shape opinions. A message about war can be dramatically underlined by a television picture direct from the battlefield.

Various studies have examined the consumption, by both children and adolescents, of politically relevant material in the mass media. In general, only about a third of grade school children follow the news presented by television, radio, or newspapers. Among adolescents, about half pay some attention to the news, but the figures may increase during political campaigns.[8] Explicit messages are, however, only part of the political role of the mass media. Political socialization may also occur as children and teenagers watch programs on war, crime, space adventure, and cowboy-and-Indian Westerns. If we consider all types of political messages, it is clear that by age eighteen, young people have been exposed to a considerable amount of politically relevant material in the mass media.

What is the impact? A number of studies show that exposure to television news programs and newspaper stories increases political interest and knowledge.[9] Moreover, when asked where they acquired their political information, young people gave the greatest weight to the media, especially television.[10] Other studies show that watching presidential campaign advertisements or news stories about a person increases the attractiveness of the candidate or the person. However, among adolescents, news watching appears to be negatively related to views of the national, state, and local government. One analysis of high school seniors found that media exposure encourages discussing politics and engaging in campaign activities. Political discussions with family and friends were also shown to result from greater exposure to the mass media.[11]

The impact of "nonpolitical" messages on political opinions has also been examined. One study, for example, found that watching crime shows encouraged beliefs about police effectiveness, but feelings toward the police themselves did not change. Another study found that the images young people had of lawyers and judges were similar to the stereotype media images of these groups. Moreover, frequent viewers of detective programs overestimated the crime level in society and police violence. The type of television program watched also seems to be related to feelings toward government. *M*A*S*H* watchers were less positive than those who watched *Happy Days* or *Wonder Woman*. The viewing of sports programs was associated with greater national loyalty, conservatism, and respect for authority. It should be emphasized, however, that it is difficult to say what causes what

Using a QUBE, TV audiences can express their opinions, which are tabulated at a central location.

in these findings. It may be, for instance, that people prefer shows on which the characters have attitudes similar to their own. It's not a matter of influence so much as shared views.

The Importance of Political Socialization

Our analysis has highlighted some of the many studies of how people acquire their political opinions. What do these research findings tell us about public opinion in the United States? Though numerous unanswered questions remain, we can draw three general conclusions.

People Do Not Freely Choose Opinions

Though people may like to think they freely choose their views based on objective information, research suggests that strong predispositions exist on many issues. As they grow up, people may retain some political values they learned in childhood and discard others. Yet experiences at home and in school may influence people longer than they realize. Consider, for example, the evidence on how families influence their children's party affiliation. As an adult, deciding to be a Democrat Republican, or independent is, in principle, an uncomplicated choice. There is no application, membership fee, loyalty oath, or any other requirement. Nevertheless, relatively few people completely abandon their early party leanings. Their initial socialization inhibits a purely objective review of the pros and cons of each position.

The pull of this learning is sometimes less obvious. One major study has shown that early in their lives Americans develop a powerful attachment to the electoral process.[12] This infatuation with voting may derive from the school curriculum, the numerous school elections, and mass media coverage of campaigns. For adults, the existence of American-style elections seems to be an important criterion in judging foreign governments. That a particular government was *voted* into office is considered far more important than, say, the persistence of economic inequality, the use of repression by the government, or inept administration. Not surprisingly, U.S. public officials have frequently insisted that nations without a tradition of elections at least go through the motions of selecting candidates, holding campaigns, and the like. The possible inappropriateness of elections may not be seriously considered—our desire to see elections is almost instinctive.

The pull of early learning may also lead some citizens to choose issue positions that run contrary to their own self-interest. For example, after the Civil War white Southerners became loyal Democrats, and this attachment was passed down from generation to generation. The appeals of Republicans usually fell on deaf ears. Many white Southerners have persisted in this long-standing attachment despite their differences with the Democratic party on many issues, especially race. As a result, Southern whites have helped elect Democratic Presidents who pursued policies they personally opposed. Only recently have many white Southerners begun abandoning their historic attachment to the Democratic party.

The Public Agenda Is Limited

Because many political beliefs and attachments are deeply rooted and characterized by a high decree of consensus, they cause little political controversy. This is especially true on matters relating to national loyalty, the structures of the government, the selection of public officials, and the abstract rights of citizens. If citizens were asked, "Do you favor keeping the present Constitution?" virtually everyone would answer yes; these results would occur poll after poll. Because most people's answers are predictable and the overall pattern hardly changes, such questions are not even asked by polling organizations.

These strongly held views limit public debate. Those few people who insist on raising such issues and offering alternatives are either ignored or treated as political outsiders. In the 1960s, for example, a few people proposed the elimination of all economic inequalities, the democratization of workplace relationships, the legalization of certain drugs, and the transformation of traditional family relationships. These proposals were so contrary to deeply rooted beliefs that they failed to become part of the agenda of issues before government. If one examines the issues that are part of the continuing public debate, it will be clear that some issues are never seriously discussed. There is no point in debating what everybody believes to be true.

Political Persuasion Is Limited

Research has suggested that there is great diversity in the way people acquire their attitudes and beliefs. No one source—family, the school, the mass media—dominates this learning process. In addition, people can select the kinds of political information and ideas they read, see, and hear. A young adult deeply committed to conservative political values can seek out books, movies, friends, and school programs that reinforce conservatism. Such choice is not universal. A teenager in the People's Republic of China would have a difficult time surrounding himself or herself with anti-Communist books, activities, and friends.

This diversity of sources and individual choice over political exposure means that it is difficult—perhaps impossible—for one group to control early political learning. Let us imagine that a group wanting drastic limitation of the power of government decided that its only real chance of success lay in reshaping people's thinking about the role of government. To accomplish this goal, the group decided to convey their messages to children via television shows, free comic books, discussion materials provided free of charge to schools, seminars for parents, and other means. At best, even a campaign lasting years would significantly influence only a limited number of children. Such anti–big government messages could easily be avoided and, even where exposure occurs, the messages would have to compete with a great deal of contrary information. If this anti–big government group persisted in trying to saturate schools, families, and the media with their ideas despite public resistance, steps could be taken to restrict such propaganda. School administrators could simply ban the material from classrooms.

These limitations on controlling the socialization process also apply when the objectives are more positive. Campaigns to reduce prejudice, increase support for democratic values, promote greater political awareness, and teach political participation run into many of the same problems as do campaigns to indoctrinate a particular point of view. To be effective, a program has to reach millions of parents, tens of thousands of classrooms, and television and newspapers throughout the country. The potential recipients of these messages must also be willing to heed and absorb them. The most brilliant program to encourage political activity among young people will come to nothing if teachers are not committed to it, if parents give contrary messages at home, and if youngsters daydream in civics courses.

Conclusions

Political opinions do not suddenly emerge at adulthood. Many of our opinions are acquired

Learning can take place in all kinds of settings. At a demonstration by the deaf in support of legislation to provide needed emergency services, participants intently observe the events.

from parents, the schools, the mass media, and other sources. People are not, however, the passive recipients of messages—even young children can choose among competing messages and reach their own conclusions. No one centrally controlled source dominates political learning. As a consequence of this socialization, people can hold opinions that do not derive from a careful analysis of their situations, many types of issues are excluded from public debate, and it is very difficult to systematically control the formation of public opinion.

Check Your Understanding

1. What is "political socialization"?

2. Young people learn political attitudes from what three major sources?

3. On what two types of issues is public discussion likely to be limited?

IS THE AMERICAN PUBLIC TODAY BASICALLY LIBERAL OR CONSERVATIVE?

As we saw at the beginning of the chapter, measuring public opinion is a complex process. There is no one way to measure public opinion, and reasonable people can differ in how they interpret the evidence. To illustrate this complexity, let us consider an often-debated question that deals with the overall pattern of public thinking: Is the contemporary public basically liberal or conservative?

Defining "Liberal" and "Conservative"

The first step in answering this question is to decide what we mean by these terms. Both concepts have been in existence for many years, have been written about extensively, and are part of an ongoing political discussion. We have all heard statements like "The campaign for mayor in that city is a contest between a liberal and a conservative." Although the terms are used frequently, they are not simple to define. In fact, the opposite seems true—the words have been used so often in so many different ways that a multitude of definitions exist. This situation is not unusual when we seek to measure public opinion. A number of terms in common use—"racial integration," "free trade," "environmental protection," for example—are subject to widely differing interpretations.

One approach to a definition of "liberal" and "conservative" focuses on the role of government in regulating the economy. This approach has been common in the United States in the twentieth century, especially since the 1930s. Basically, a liberal is one who views government as a potential means for improving the economic well-being of the population. Liberal programs would include regulation to improve working conditions, enactment of minimum wage laws, legal protection of the right to join unions, protection against unfair business practices, government-financed health care and retirement, and so forth. A conservative, on the other hand, emphasizes individual initiative and minimal government regulation. Government exists to provide essential services—defense, highways, a currency, and so on. To regulate such elements of the economy as wages or working conditions is to create inefficiency. For a liberal, a large government with numerous programs, especially those that help the poor and the middle class, is a force for good; to conservatives, big government means higher taxes, manipulation of the marketplace, and interference in people's lives.

A second approach to defining "liberalism" and "conservatism" stresses attitude toward change. Basically, a liberal favors change in the belief that it is essential to improvement. In contrast, a conservative is suspicious of change, preferring to stick with what is known to work. Given a new proposal, a liberal would typically say, "If it looks as if it will make things better, let's try it." A conservative might say, "Let's not abandon the present approach for something that is untested." Both, however, reject either too-rapid change or rigid adherence to the way things are.

A third definition, which contains some elements of the two previous ones, focuses on money. Here a liberal is someone willing to spend public money generously to accomplish his or her goals. People-oriented objectives such as education and a clean environment are placed ahead of financial goals such as low taxes. A conservative, on the other hand, does not reject these goals but feels, rather, that they are often secondary to financial considerations. Faced with a decision on a program, a liberal might ask "Will it help all people?" To a conservative, the question is "Can we afford yet another government program?"

The fourth and final definition we shall consider revolves around certain moral and social issues. This definition is the most difficult to spell out since it is more a collection of issue positions than a single philosophical principle. From this perspective a liberal is one who supports policies that encourage individual choice rather than obedience to tradition. It is the individual, not the state, who decides which books should be read or whether a speech is worth hearing. Government intervention in morality is to be minimized. In foreign affairs, the goal is world peace, to be pursued as much as possible through nonmilitary means. Conservatives, on the other hand, say that the government must ensure the survival of what they call traditional moral values—respect for authority, strong family structure, patriotism, sexual restraint, and religious devotion. Conservatives therefore oppose abortion and pornography as threatening to traditional society and favor greater promotion of religious values. Patriotism is often viewed as opposition to the atheistic regime of the Soviet Union and the spread of world communism. This goal requires a strong military and a willingness to use it.

All four of these definitions are widely accepted. What makes matters complex is that they are sometimes combined in different ways. The existence of several differing packages of positions under the "liberal" and "conservative" labels has resulted in the invention of terms such as "neoconservative," "neo-liberal," and "libertarian conservative," among others. Some people consider themselves "true" liberals and yet endorse a strong military, less government economic regulation, and antipornography legislation, all positions usually associated with conservatism. Some conservatives argue that government restrictions on abortion or prayers in public schools are inconsistent with "real" conservatism. Some people classify themselves as, say, a liberal on domestic policy and a conservative on foreign policy (or the reverse). In other words, neither in principle nor in practice are the terms "liberal" and "conservative" precise guides to what people believe.

The imprecision and complexity surrounding these terms has important implications for determining whether the public is liberal or conservative. An opinion pollster might, for example, simply ask people to classify themselves. Because the terms are so hard to pin down, people who hold different political positions might choose the same label to describe themselves. And people who hold similar views might select different labels to characterize their positions. Or the poll taker might present a few issue areas, label some positions "liberal" and some "conservative," and then measure people's opinions. A person who considered himself or herself a liberal might be classified by the poll taker as a conservative. Such discrepancy occurs because the poll taker and the respondent differ on the common meaning of "liberal" and "conservative."

Measuring Liberal and Conservative Opinion

Thus far we have somewhat abstractly considered the question of whether Americans are liberal or conservative. Let us now turn to some specific data that deal directly with this question. In 1980, a nationwide survey of 1,614 people was conducted by the Center for Political Studies at the University of Michigan. One of the questions was as follows: "We hear a lot of talk these days about liberals and conservatives. Here is a seven-point scale on which the political views people might hold are arranged from extremely liberal to extremely conservative. Where would you place yourself on this scale, or haven't you thought much about this?" In other words, people were asked to label themselves using terms supplied by the interviewers.

Table 4.1 shows that of all the people responding to this question, about 67 percent were willing to place themselves on this seven-point scale. Perhaps the most striking thing about these data was that most people gravitated toward the "moderate, middle of the road" position or the adjacent position. In fact, 65 percent of the sample occupy the three middle positions. Barely 6 percent used the label "extreme" in defining their overall political viewpoint. The information collected in 1980 is

Self-Identification by the Words *Liberal* and *Conservative*, 1980	Label	Percentage	Number of Respondents
	Extremely liberal	2.5% *	25
	Liberal	9.3	93
	Slightly liberal	13.5	136
	Moderate, middle of the road	30.6	307
	Slightly conservative	21.0	211
	Conservative	19.2	199
	Extremely conservative	3.3	33
	Haven't thought much about it	33.4	504

* These are percentages of those who offered a response.

Source: Center for Political Studies, University of Michigan, American National Election Study of 1980.

TABLE 4.1

similar to the results of the same questionnaire in 1972, 1974, and 1976. In sum, we can say that of those people willing to use the terms "liberal" and "conservative," most are either slightly liberal or conservative, or middle of the road.

These data provide, however, only part of an answer. As we noted, these two labels are complex and can mean different things to different people. In the same 1980 survey, respondents were also asked, "People have different things in mind when they say that someone's views are liberal or conservative. . . . What sorts of things do you have in mind when you say that someone's views are liberal (conservative)?" Up to three different definitions of "liberal" and "conservative" were recorded. Table 4.2 and Table 4.3 display some of the most common meanings given to these terms.

These two tables (and information not shown) tell us several things about what the terms "liberal" and "conservative" mean to people. First, even among those people willing to use these terms to describe themselves, there were some people—86 for "liberal," 68 for "conservative"—who could not supply a definition. In other words, some people might say that they were "slightly liberal" but could not define "liberal." Table 4.1 shows that about a third of the respondents could not even

label themselves. Thus, while a political analyst might talk of the public in terms of these labels, more than a third of the people questioned did not use the terms to describe themselves or, if they did, could not define them.

Second, the large number of possible definitions we described earlier is reflected in public thinking. For both "liberal" and "conservative" several themes are more popular than others, but no one concept has a majority. The most common definition of "liberal" includes willingness to change, to use government to solve social problems, and to spend public money. Many people, however, offer definitions that do not fit well with more accepted definitions. They use terms such as "irresponsible" or focus on specific issues or political figures. A similar pattern exists in how the public defines "conservative." Some themes—resistance to change, support for free enterprise, less government spending—are more frequent than others, but no sharp agreement emerges. As was true for liberalism, many definitions focus on specific issues or personality.

In short, if we approach the question of whether the public is liberal or conservative by allowing people to describe themselves, we find a preference for middle positions. What these preferences

Common Meanings Given to the Term ***Liberal***	*Meaning*	*First Mention*	*Second Mention*	*Third Mention*
	Accepts change, flexible, innovative	18% *	3%	1%
	Responds quickly to problems, not cautious	4	3	1
	Irresponsible	3	1	**
	Independent in thought	4	3	**
	Favors equality	2	**	1
	Extreme, radical	2	1	**
	Compassionate, helps others	2	1	**
	Sensitive to social problems	3	2	1
	Favors government intervention in social problems	8	7	1
	Depends too much on Washington	3	3	1
	Opposes catering to special interests	2	2	2
	For "little people"	2	2	3
	Favors government spending: spends too much	17	8	5
	Favors social welfare, giveaways	8	7	3
	Favors abortion	2	2	**
	Favors women's rights	2	2	1
	Other definitions	18	33	48
	No second or third definition	—	34	66

* Each entry is the proportion of all respondents offering at least one definition who offered this particular definition.
** Less than .5 percent.

Source: Center for Political Studies, University of Michigan, American National Election Study of 1980.

TABLE 4.2

mean, however, is not completely clear. People disagree about what these terms stand for. Two people adopting the same label might have quite different things in mind. For one liberal, liberalism may mean a tolerance for change. A second liberal might call himself or herself a liberal because of a commitment to programs to help the poor.

Liberalism and Conservatism on Specific Issues

As we mentioned earlier, liberalism and conservatism can be approached on an issue-by-issue basis.

Instead of asking, "Are Americans liberal or conservative?" we find out how people feel on more specific issues associated with liberalism (for example, should the government spend more money on social welfare?). Here we are labeling some views as liberal or conservative rather than depending on people themselves to use and understand these terms.

Figures 4.1 through 4.6 present the results of the Center for Political Studies (CPS) 1980 survey for six questions that touch on issues relating to liberalism and conservatism. In general, the patterns of responses suggest that Americans are neither distinctly liberal nor conservative on these

Common Meanings Given to the Term *Conservative*	Meaning	First Mention*	Second Mention	Third Mention
	Patriotic	2%	1	**
	Has definite moral standards	2	1	**
	Resistant to change	17	5	1
	Has cautious approach to problems	7	3	**
	Thoughtful	4	3	**
	Does not think independently	3	1	**
	Moderate; not extreme	2	**	**
	Favors free enterprise; opposes socialism	8	5	1
	For states' rights	4	3	1
	Favors individual responsibility	1	1	**
	Favors less government spending	21	9	4
	Opposes social welfare	3	3	2
	For strong national defense	2	3	3
	Other definitions	25	42	44
	No second or third definitions	—	33	70

* Each entry is the proportion of all respondents offering at least one definition who offered this particular definition.
** Less than 5 percent.

Source: Center for Political Studies, University of Michigan, American National Election Study of 1980.

TABLE 4.3

issues. For example, on the questions of whether government should provide more services (Figure 4.1) and whether the government should guarantee jobs for workers (Figure 4.5), responses are scattered across all seven positions. On the issue of how to get along with the Soviet Union (Figure 4.3), only the middle category draws an appreciably larger response, but again there is no agreement on a specific position. Figure 4.6 indicates that a bare majority of respondents favor keeping environmental regulation even if this means limiting sources of energy (the liberal position). Many citizens (47 percent), however, would accept more relaxation of standards. On the question of equality for women (Figure 4.4), 35 percent accept complete equality, and most people are at the "equal-role" end of the seven-point scale. Yet it is also possible to say that a majority endorses some degree of inequality (positions 2–6).

The complexity of opinions is further demonstrated when we compare responses to several different questions. Figure 4.2 shows that a large majority favors at least some cut in taxes, though there are disagreements over just how much. Note, however, that there is less enthusiasm for the idea of government cutting services (Figure 4.1). Specifically, 78 percent favor a tax cut, but only a third would slash government services (categories 1–3 in Figure 4.1). Such contradictory patterns are not all that unusual when we examine several separate opinion polls. Many citizens have little difficulty in wanting policies that may conflict—for example, clean air and their own freedom to burn garbage or use polluting leaded gasoline.

One final point that deserves attention is the relationship between how people define themselves in terms of liberalism and conservatism and

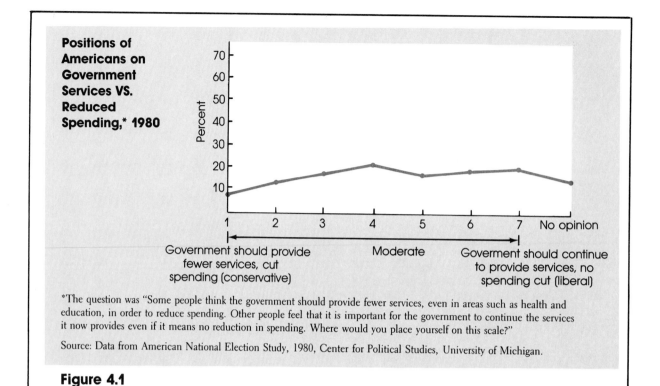

Positions of Americans on Government Services VS. Reduced Spending,* 1980

*The question was "Some people think the government should provide fewer services, even in areas such as health and education, in order to reduce spending. Other people feel that it is important for the government to continue the services it now provides even if it means no reduction in spending. Where would you place yourself on this scale?"

Source: Data from American National Election Study, 1980, Center for Political Studies, University of Michigan.

Figure 4.1

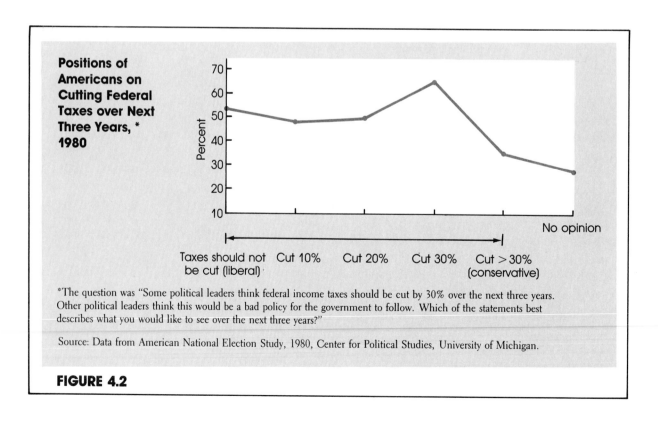

Positions of Americans on Cutting Federal Taxes over Next Three Years, * 1980

*The question was "Some political leaders think federal income taxes should be cut by 30% over the next three years. Other political leaders think this would be a bad policy for the government to follow. Which of the statements best describes what you would like to see over the next three years?"

Source: Data from American National Election Study, 1980, Center for Political Studies, University of Michigan.

FIGURE 4.2

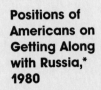

Positions of Americans on Getting Along with Russia,* 1980

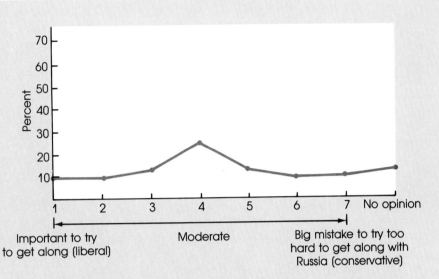

*The question was "Some people feel it is important for us to try very hard to get along with Russia. Others feel it is a big mistake to try too hard to get along with Russia. Where would you place yourself on this scale?"

Source: Data from American National Election Study, 1980, Center for Political Studies, University of Michigan.

FIGURE 4.3

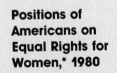

Positions of Americans on Equal Rights for Women,* 1980

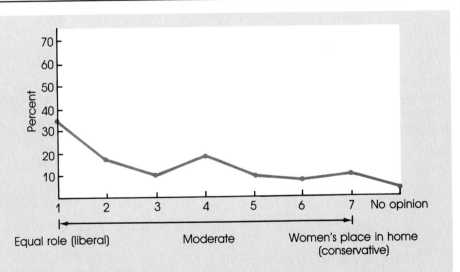

*The question was "Recently there has been a lot of talk about women's rights. Some people feel that women ought to have an equal role with men in running business, industry and government. Others feel that women's place is in the home. Where would you place yourself on this scale?"

Source: Data from American National Election Study, 1980, Center for Political Studies, University of Michigan.

FIGURE 4.4

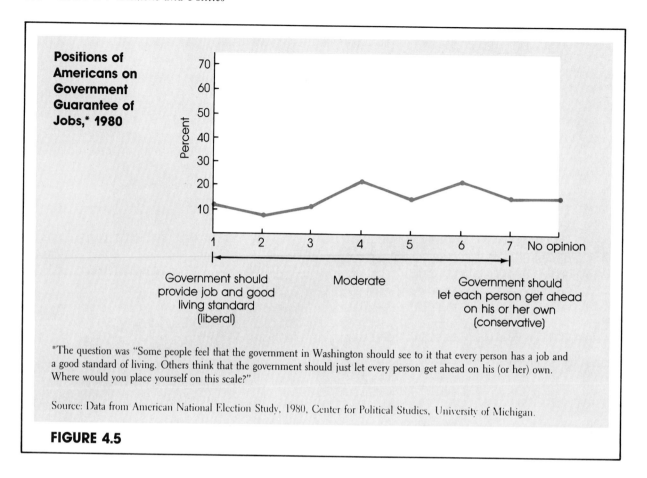

Positions of Americans on Government Guarantee of Jobs,* 1980

*The question was "Some people feel that the government in Washington should see to it that every person has a job and a good standard of living. Others think that the government should just let every person get ahead on his (or her) own. Where would you place yourself on this scale?"

Source: Data from American National Election Study, 1980, Center for Political Studies, University of Michigan.

FIGURE 4.5

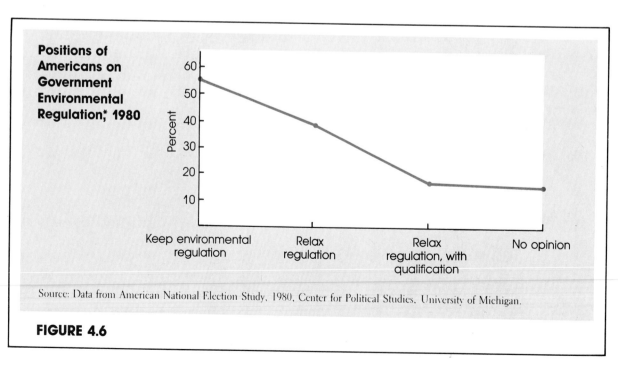

Positions of Americans on Government Environmental Regulation,* 1980

Source: Data from American National Election Study, 1980, Center for Political Studies, University of Michigan.

FIGURE 4.6

their stands on specific issues. Many public officials assume that, for example, a person calling himself or herself a conservative favors those stands traditionally associated with conservatism. The fact of the matter is that this is only partially correct. General labels and specific preferences can be inconsistent. For example, in the 1980 CPS study, of those calling themselves liberals, only 65 percent also agreed with the liberal position that the government should continue to provide extensive services. Thirty percent of the self-described conservatives took the liberal side on this specific issue. A similar pattern occurs on other specific questions. Many liberals hold positions associated with conservatism on the issues of cutting taxes, dealing with the Soviet Union, government guarantees of jobs, and environmental protection. Overall, there is usually a relationship between what people call themselves and specific issue positions, but there are many exceptions.

Conclusions

Our examination of the question "Is the public today basically liberal or conservative?" has shown us two important things. First, there are many choices to be made in measuring public opinion, and these choices have consequences for what we find. Earlier we noted that polls are not the only measure of public thinking; had we examined written materials, speeches, or people's behavior, we probably would have reached different conclusions. When we used polls, we saw that choices existed on how terms are to be defined and results interpreted. For example, should you ask people to label themselves or do you ask them about specific issues? Do you give people a choice of "liberal" or "conservative" or do you include other options such as "middle-of-the-road" or "radical"? Should you include in the analysis people who have given little thought to the whole issue of liberalism and conservatism? How these choices are made will affect our determination of public opinion.

Second, the complexity of measurement is often paralleled by the complexity of the substance of public opinion. It is simplistic to describe Americans as basically liberal, conservative, or somewhere in-between. Further investigation shows that much diversity exists in how "liberal" and "conservative" are defined. Thus, two people who describe themselves as "middle-of-the-road" may hold different opinions. The picture alters when we examine opinions on specific issues. Here there are a wide range of responses—on some issues, opinion leans toward the liberal direction, on others toward the conservative direction. Finally, not all people hold opinions that are consistent with how they describe themselves generally. In short, the answer to our question is that it depends on how the question is approached and the particular policy issues are examined.

Check Your Understanding

1. What are four approaches to defining "liberal" and "conservative"?

2. What might be the difference between a liberal and a conservative in their attitude toward change?

3. Why might a poll taker label a respondent a liberal, while the respondent thinks of himself or herself as a conservative?

DO POLITICAL LEADERS FOLLOW PUBLIC OPINION?

The issue of government by public opinion has been a persistent and controversial one throughout American history. As we saw in Chapter 2, the Founders were suspicious of popular influence in government. Their fears that misguided citizens would enact dangerous policy is reflected in the Constitution's many checks against direct popular rule (for example, the indirect election of the President, appointed judges). Even nineteenth-century reformers who advocated giving the vote to those without property, blacks, and women did not propose direct policy making by ordinary citizens. The people were to be given a say in government by choosing leaders in occasional elections, but governing was to be left to officials.

Beginning in the early twentieth century, however, the idea of more direct citizen control gained a degree of support. A number of people, often called Progressives, argued that by allowing citizens to pass or reject laws, the quality of government would be improved. Laws would be better, corruption would be reduced, and the public would be better informed. The emergence of public opinion polling in the 1930s further encouraged the idea of more direct popular rule. In 1944, George Gallup argued that democracy would be greatly advanced by the modern opinion poll. No longer would the voice of the people have to wait for an election, and the popularity of leaders could be separated from the popularity of specific policies. Polling would also thwart narrow, unrepresentative interest groups. Today, with the advent of communications technology, some people have advocated a form of "electronic direct democracy." Through mechanisms such as two-way cable television (the "QUBE" system, now installed in several cities) or a national satellite hookup, citizens could sit at home and vote on the questions before government.

Let us begin our analysis of the questions of whether leaders *do* follow public opinion by first examining the question of whether leaders *should* follow public opinion.

Should Leaders Follow Public Opinion?

Perhaps the strongest argument in favor of having leaders follow public opinion rests on the belief that this is central to the idea of democracy. From this perspective the ancient city-state of Athens and the New England town meetings are the ideal, because citizens themselves made the laws. Elected leaders were more like caretakers. This view gained a degree of support in the 1960s, when some citizens, especially college students, favored greater use of participatory democracy. Basically,

advocates of participatory democracy felt that people ought to control their own lives and that this goal could be accomplished politically by decentralizing power and encouraging widespread citizen participation.

Opposed to this view of direct citizen policy making are a number of differing positions. One argument distinguishes between the interests of citizens—what is advantageous—and their preferences. These critics of direct rule by public opinion believe that leaders should act in the best interests of the majority. These interests are not necessarily the same as the preferences people express on opinion polls. To illustrate the difference between an interest and a preference, consider how most people would answer a question on the tax rate. If asked, "Do you want higher or lower taxes?" most people would probably choose lower taxes. Should the government then lower taxes? Some leaders might say no, because lower taxes would increase inflation and reduce essential services, and this would be against the interests of the majority. Put another way, citizens do not always know what is good for them.

Other critics argue that democratic leaders must interpret, not follow, public opinion. Even the best polls rarely show crystal-clear results. Without interpretation there would be no need for leaders. Government would consist of technicians who would mechanically follow the results of opinion surveys. Because public opinion is subject to interpretation by political leaders, however, there will always be a gap between what the public says and what it gets. For example, a leader might interpret a poll showing that 90 percent of the public wants pollution eliminated to mean "eliminate as much pollution as possible without causing economic disruption." This reasonable interpretationd could create a difference between opinion poll results and government action on pollution.

Opposition to government by public opinion also rests on the inadequacy of polls as a means of providing guidance. A poll result may be of little value to leaders because of its vagueness. Opinion polls focus on general preferences, but leaders must make specific decisions. For example, over the years opinion polls have asked whether defense spending ought to be increased, decreased, or kept the same. Even if a large majority say "increase," the message is still not clear. Increase by how much? What should the money be spent on?

Asking more specific questions on polls does not solve the problem. Many people simply lack specific opinions on complex policy matters. Giving them more concrete choices would probably produce blank stares. Even if they did have opinions, there are so many possibilities for disagreement on details that a consensus would probably be impossible. Suppose this question were asked: "What exactly should the President do to reduce unemployment? Be as detailed as possible." So many different answers would be offered that few respondents would agree on a particular policy. How can the President be held responsible for following what the majority wants if there is no majority?

Of all the arguments against government by public opinion, perhaps the strongest is that the average citizen is too uninformed to offer wise judgments on complex issues. The day-to-day business of government is beyond the grasp of most citizens. In a nutshell, while citizens may offer their opinions, they frequently have little or no information to base their opinions on. For government to follow such uninformed opinion may be to act irresponsibly.

Advocates of this position can offer considerable evidence to support their case. A study conducted in 1968 reported that most citizens were relatively ill-informed about how much money the federal government spends on national defense, social welfare, and foreign aid. Nevertheless, many of these people would probably offer their opinions on what the government should do in these areas. Several studies report that many people give opinions on nonexistent bills. For example, one-third of a sample of Cincinnati residents had an opinion on the fictitious "1975 Public Affairs Act."[13] Would any sensible leader follow the polls if he or she suspected that a large proportion of the responses were based on ignorance?

Of course, defenders of government by public opinion oppose the view that the public cannot offer informed opinions. They claim that while citizens may be ignorant on some questions, they are knowledgeable in other areas. Particularly on close-to-home issues, such as tax rates or racial integration of neighborhoods, people are sufficiently knowledgeable to provide valid opinions. These opinions *are* politically relevant, according to this view. More important, however, is the belief that even if people are ignorant on details, their opinions on issues are still worth following. A poll result that indicates opposition to gasoline rationing is a genuine message to political leaders even if most citizens know nothing of the complex economics of supply and demand. After all, one does not have to go to cooking school to give a worthwhile evaluation of a meal.

In sum, the question of whether leaders should follow public opinion or not is difficult to answer. Advocates of government by public opinion claim that in a democracy the people must play a role in shaping policy and that citizens are capable of offering opinion-poll responses that are worth following. Opponents say that the public interest, and not mere opinion, should be the guide. They view the results of opinion surveys as imprecise, frequently contradictory, and often based on ignorance. We shall have more to say about this perplexing issue in our concluding session.

Public Opinion and Public Policy

Are the actions taken by legislators, executives, judges, and administrators consistent with public opinion? Because government makes thousands of important decisions each year, the answer to our question must be yes *and* no. In some cases leaders do follow public opinion, and in other instances their decisions are contrary to the preferences of most citizens. The main questions, therefore, are: Which decisions are consistent with public opinion? Which policies run contrary to public opinion?

Policy and Opinion Agreement on Broad Issues

We find the greatest agreement between public opinion and government policy in overall political goals—those that both citizens and leaders take for granted. National defense is such an issue. While many political leaders as well as private citizens may disagree on the specifics—for example, exactly how much money to spend—it is fair to say that most people favor maintaining American military strength. Similarly, leaders and citizens agree that our present form of government—with a President, a two-house national legislature, and a Supreme Court—should be preserved. There is also general agreement on the role of government in society. Here again, there are differences on specifics, but the consensus is that government has major responsibilities for promoting the general welfare. Much of this agreement is the result of the common socialization of leaders and citizens. Leaders and citizens have been exposed to the same messages from families, schools, and the mass media about our nation and its political institutions.

Citizens' and leaders' preferences are also in agreement on several general economic questions. The most obvious is a shared commitment to economic prosperity and growth, though disagreements exist over the means of achieving these goals. A second point of agreement involves the maintenance of our system of free enterprise. In the United States, unlike many other countries, the government does not own the banks, utilities, transportation and communications systems, and large industries. A leader advocating such ownership policies would have a very short career. At the same time, however, most government officials as well as most citizens believe that some degree of government economic control is needed in these areas. Neither citizens nor leaders want a system in which private economic interests are completely free to do whatever they wish.

Policy and Opinion Agreement on Specific Issues

What about more specific policy questions? Do leaders follow public opinion on the more concrete types of issues debated in legislatures or discussed in the mass media? The answer to this question is sometimes yes, sometimes no. People who have examined this question report a varying

amount of agreement between public opinion and government policy. The extent of agreement depends on the time period, the specific issues analyzed, and how the research was conducted. One study that examined the relationship between opinion and policy on 357 issues between 1935 and 1979 reported that government responded to changes in public opinion most of the time. This was especially true when opinion changes were large and the shifts persisted over time.[14] A different study examined about 250 issues between 1960 and 1974 and found that government action was consistent with the majority about 64 percent of the time.[15]

However, a more intensive study of eleven major issues over long time periods found that disagreements between public opinion and policy were fairly common.[16] On only one question— whether the United Nations should admit the People's Republic of China—was there clear agreement between what the public wanted and government policy. On a second issue—U.S. involvement in Vietnam—the evidence was extremely complex, but public opinion and government action usually went hand in hand. On the other nine issues, however, there were numerous contradictions between opinion and policy.

One good illustration of the contradictions that exist between popular desires and the government policy concerns government assistance for medical expenses. Between the mid-1930s and the early 1960s, clear majorities of the public wanted such assistance, yet the government did almost nothing. Only during the 1960s and 1970s, when the government enacted the Medicare program and made major expenditures on medical research, did opinion and policy begin to show agreement. Overall, for about forty years, citizens and leaders were in agreement on this issue about a quarter of the time.

Another clear-cut issue on which public opinion and government policy disagree is gun control. Numerous surveys taken between 1959 and 1974 showed overwhelming public support for a law requiring a police permit to buy a gun. Despite such sentiment, however, leaders have not taken decisive action on gun registration. At both the

Points of View: Charting Changes in Attitude

A favorite technique of public opinion poll takers is to ask the same questions at intervals over time in order to learn whether and how attitudes have changed. With the revived feminist movement that began in the late 1960s, one area of ongoing investigation has been the role of women in American society. Topics of special concern have included changing attitudes toward jobs and careers, marriage, and children.

Statistics tell part of the story, of course. For example, in 1960 less than a third of married women were in the work force. By the mid-1980s, this total has risen to over half. But polls can shed light on the human feelings behind the figures. In 1974 and 1985, the Roper Organization asked this question:

Question: Considering the possibilities for combining or not combining marriage, children, and a career, and assuming you had a choice, which *one* of these possibilities do you think would offer *you* the most satisfying and interesting life? (Card shown respondent)

	Women 1974	Women 1985
Combining marriage, career, and children	52%	63%
Marrying, having children, but not having career	38	26
Having career and marrying, but not having children	4	4
Having career, but not marrying or having children	2	3
Marrying, but not having children or career	1	1
Don't know	3	2

Source: The Virginia Slims American Women's Opinion Poll by The Roper Organization.

Clearly, in spite of the difficulties that choosing to "have it all" may entail, an increasing number of women want to try this option.

As women have joined the work force in greater numbers, they have also made successful efforts to break down discriminatory barriers. For instance, women are far more numerous than they used to be in such professions as medicine, politics, and the law. Do such shifts translate into changes in public attitudes? Apparently so. Asked whether women are more respected today than they were ten years ago, 60 percent of women and 61 percent of men answered in the affirmative. When asked the same question in 1970, only 38 percent of women and 40 percent of men gave a "yes" answer.

The table below indicates that overall efforts to improve women's status have gained increasing approval.

Question: Do you favor or oppose of the efforts to strengthen and change women's status in society today?

It is interesting to note not only the great changes between 1970 and 1985 but also the fact that—except in 1974—the viewpoints of men and women have been remarkably similar.

	Women Favor	Women Oppose	Men Favor	Men Oppose
1970	40%	42%	44%	39%
1972	48	36	49	36
1974	57	25	63	19
1980	64	24	64	23
1985	73	17	69	17

Source: The Virginia Slims American Women's Opinion Poll by The Roper Organization.

In an abandoned inner-city neighborhood, signs plastered on the crumbling walls of buildings send a poignant message to political leaders. Whether the public officials will respond to their constituents' needs depends, of course, on a variety of political factors.

national and state levels, attempts to regulate the sale of handguns have met opposition from a well-organized minority. As a result, the preference of the national majority is not being followed.

In general, such evidence indicates that as we move away from broad issues into specific policy areas, public opinion and government action may diverge. While few leaders would propose broad policies inconsistent with public opinion, they might ignore the results of opinion polls when considering more specific programs. For example, a President who supports the general principles of economic growth and prosperity might neverthe-less call for such unpopular economic policies as higher taxes. In short, the extent to which leaders follow public opinion depends on the level of gen-erality at which we are talking. On broad issues leaders almost always do follow public opinion. However, on more specific day-to-day questions we find differences between public opinion and leadership behavior.

When Leaders Ignore Public Opinion

Why would an elected official faced with clear public support for such measures as tougher gun control or prayers in public schools choose to ignore these demands? Don't politicians who dis-regard public preferences risk being defeated for reelection? Further analysis of this question shows that there are good explanations for why leaders ignore opinion poll results. Let us briefly consider four reasons why a leader might act against majority opinion.

Not All Opinions Are Equally Relevant Politically

Suppose that a public opinion poll in a congressional district showed that 65 percent of the people favored a particular bill. Would it be wise for the representative to follow the majority? Not necessarily. It is possible that among those voting for the member of Congress (or those likely to vote for him or her the next time), only a minority favors this bill. Support for the bill might therefore alienate the very people who put the representative in office. More generally, a public official's career may depend on keeping certain people satisfied, and these certain people may not be among the majority in an opinion poll.

A related argument concerns what are called **issue publics**—groups that are especially concerned about one particular issue. For example, grain farmers are keenly aware of policies that affect their livelihood. Many American Jews pay special attention to U.S.–Israeli relations. Often such groups are united in their opinions and are willing to vote for and give money to candidates who agree with them. The huge majority who are not members of an issue public often have a limited concern for the issue and will do little if their wishes are not followed. For grain farmers, a government subsidy program can generate intense feelings; for the 98 percent who are not directly affected, legislative votes or presidential orders on this topic are probably not very important. By dealing with a constituency as a large set of issue publics rather than as a single group, an elected official may pursue policies that the overall majority opposes. The will of a multitude of groups is followed, not the public will.

Another factor that can explain why leaders do not always follow public opinion concerns intensities of opinion. What should leaders do if the 65 percent who favor a bill are only mildly in favor of it, while the minority opposes the bill very strongly? Can you equate a weak and an intense opinion? Because those holding intense opinions are more likely to act on the basis of their opinions, an intense minority will sometimes outweigh a weak majority in a leader's thinking. The classic instance occurs with citizens opposing handgun registration. Though a small minority, these people are often so committed to their cause that numerous members of Congress are careful not to offend them. Leaders may reason that voting for something favored by an apathetic majority has few benefits; but if they oppose an intense minority, they can cause themselves problems.

Opinion Poll Results Are Viewed Skeptically

We have already seen that when the public speaks, it does not always make precise, informed, and useful suggestions. Leaders are aware of the problems in conducting accurate polls and are thus reasonably cautious in following the results. A frequent claim leaders make about poll results is that citizens would offer different opinions if they were fully aware of the situation. Perhaps for this reason many leaders, if confronted with poll results contrary to their own position, will not change their position but rather insist that the public needs to be educated. In some cases, especially on complicated issues, leaders may be justified in thinking that the public does not understand an issue and therefore poll results are not useful.

This process was illustrated by President Carter's stand on the Panama Canal treaties. During much of 1977, President Carter defended the new treaties, which would eventually turn the canal over to Panama. From the beginning, public opinion was very much opposed to Carter's position. Why didn't the President follow public sentiment? On several occasions he stated that he would *not* follow the majority because it did not understand the treaties. In particular, he felt that many citizens mistakenly believed that the United States would lose control over the canal and that the treaties were a surrender. If the public were "educated," according to President Carter, it would favor the treaties. In effect, the President was saying, "I will follow informed opinion, and informed opinion will support me." He was right. In October 1977, a Gallup poll showed that citizens who were not familiar with the issue opposed President Carter's position by a 2-to-1 margin.

Issues: Figuring Out Public Opinion

The problems facing a leader trying to make sense out of public opinion were especially well illustrated in 1979 and 1980 when the second Strategic Arms Limitation Treaty (SALT II) was being debated. This was a complex treaty between the United States and the Soviet Union dealing with limits on missiles, missile warheads, and the development of new missile technology. The treaty was highly controversial, and leadership opinion was divided. A senator who looked to the public for guidance in voting for or against ratification faced many problems.

First, because of the complexity of the treaty, was this something on which the public could offer an informed opinion? Even experts diverged on how significant the treaty was, whether it could be enforced, and who would benefit from it. Could the public reach an intelligent decision?

Second, did the public really care what the government did on SALT II? It was plausible that many citizens held no informed opinion but were quite willing to defer to the more knowledgeable opinion of elected officials. Thus, officials might follow popular sentiment, but they had no strong obligation to do so.

Finally, if we assume that the public wished its "true" opinion to be followed, what was that opinion? Consider the following poll messages, all conveyed approximately during the same period:

1. NBC/AP poll of February 1979:
   "Do you favor or oppose agreements between the United States and Russia which limit nuclear weapons?"
   Favor agreements: 81%
   Oppose: 14%   Not sure: 5%

2. CBS/*New York Times* poll of December 1978:
   "Do you think the United States should or should not negotiate a treaty with the Russians to limit strategic weapons?"
   Should have treaty: 63%
   Should not: 24% No opinion: 13%

3. Roper poll of January 1979:
   "The U.S. and Russian negotiators have about reached agreement on a SALT treaty. The treaty, which would last until 1985, limits each country to a maximum of 2,250 long-range nuclear missiles and bombers. As you know, there's a good deal of controversy about this proposed treaty. Do you think the U.S. Senate should vote for the SALT treaty or against it?"
   For: 40%   Against: 21%
   Mixed feelings: 19%
   Don't know: 20%

4. Fine poll of February/March 1979:
   "The United States is now negotiating a strategic arms agreement with the Soviet Union in what is known as "SALT II." Which ONE of the following statements is closest to your opinion on these negotiations?"

   I strongly support SALT II
                               8.3%

   SALT II is somewhat disappointing, but on balance I would have to support it 11.3%

   I would like to see more protection for the United States before I would be ready to support SALT II   41.7%

   I strongly oppose the SALT II arms agreement with the Russians   8.6%

   I don't know enough about the SALT II treaty to have an opinion yet   29.6%

   Which of these four polls reflects true public opinion? The first two suggest strong support for SALT, but it could be argued that both questions are too vague to be of value. In particular, each asks support for agreements to limit nuclear weapons. Opposing such efforts would be like opposing motherhood. Questions 3 and 4 are more detailed, and both show less than majority support for SALT. Do these polls indicate that when people are given specifics or allowed to state reservations, public support declines? Choosing one interpretation over the other is not easy, and these conflicting data sparked an exchange among experts over just what the public was saying.

In a time-honored tradition that dates back to the American Revolution, citizens protest against what they consider unjust policies of government. Here, demonstrators march in front of the White House to demand an end to military aid to the contras in Nicaragua.

However, among those acquainted with key details of the treaties, 51 percent favored the treaties and 46 percent opposed them.

Leaders may also be unsure of which opinion poll to believe. It is not unusual for different polls to report different results on the same issue. For example, a May 1979 NBC News/Associated Press poll reported that only 26 percent of the public favored the Strategic Arms Limitation Treaty (SALT II), 7 percent opposed it, and the remainder said they were not sufficiently informed to give an opinion. Three days later, an ABC News poll found that 72 percent favored SALT II, 18 percent opposed it, and only 10 percent offered "don't know." Leaders who monitor polls may also conclude that opinion is too unstable to be a guide to decisions with long-term consequences. When the Roper organization asked people whether a Soviet invasion of Western Europe would justify using U.S. troops, 43 percent said yes in July of

1978, 60 percent in February of 1980, and 51 percent in February of 1981.

Leaders have other indicators of public opinion besides the opinion poll. Public opinion can be gauged by reading newspapers, talking to ordinary citizens, reading the mail, observing events, and contacting friends. Because some of these techniques are more trusted than national opinion polls, leaders may place greater reliance on them. If the messages conveyed by these sources differ from those from national opinion polls, it may appear that a leader is violating public opinion. Actually, the leader may be heeding a different version of public opinion and is following public sentiment *as he or she perceives it.*

Messages Conveyed by Polls Are Not Practical

All political leaders—from a small-town mayor to the President of the United States—operate under limitations. American public officials are not dictators. Their actions are limited by laws and regulations, the power of other officeholders, budgetary considerations, and numerous other factors. Citizens answering poll questions, however, do not operate under such limitations. Hence, it is not unusual to find a majority of citizens demanding policies that would be difficult—if not impossible—to enact.

Consider the issue of allowing prayers in public schools, a matter on which the public has for many years favored a policy that the government refuses to follow. In view of court decisions stating that school religious observances are unconstitutional, the only way leaders could satisfy public demands for school prayers would be to enact a constitutional amendment. In fact, hundreds of congressional bills and resolutions have been offered to allow prayers in public schools. But to change the Constitution requires far more than a simple majority. Supporters of a constitutional amendment also disagree among themselves over the precise content of an amendment—yet another obstacle to following the will of the public.

A related problem occurs when polls provide contradictory messages to political leaders. Polls conducted in the early 1980s found majorities agreeing that in general the national government had become too large and that the best government was one that governs least. At the same time, however, majorities favored strong government involvement in such specific areas as providing health care, promoting economic development, caring for the poor, helping people to achieve minimum living standards, and regulating industry for the common good. How can these contradictory demands be satisfied? It is inevitable that some public demands will go unmet.

Leaders Are Unaware of Public Opinion

Every year thousands of polls are conducted on a variety of issues. Yet despite all these efforts, surveys of public thinking do not exist on many contemporary issues. There are just too many issues, and polls are too expensive for public opinion to be measured on every question. This is especially true of the details of public policy—precisely the points on which leaders must make decisions. On many topics leaders must therefore function with only a rough knowledge of public opinion, and misjudgments can easily occur.

This lack of knowledge about public opinion becomes even more severe at the state and local levels. Results from national studies of public opinion cannot be generalized for separate states and localities. That 75 percent of a national sam-

In 1948, a victorious Harry Truman displays a headline, based on an incomplete vote count, incorrectly declaring Thomas Dewey the next President. Although Truman had been a popular campaigner, the press had insisted that he could not win.

ple favors a particular policy does *not* necessarily mean that 75 percent of the citizens of each state favor that policy. Consequently, for all elected officials except the President, a national poll says little about how an official's own constituents feel on an issue. State or local surveys would be required to answer these questions, but such surveys are rarely available on more than a few issues. Members of Congress, governors, and mayors must therefore make educated guesses about public opinion instead of using poll results.

Conclusions

Much debate takes place over whether leaders *should* follow public opinion. On many important issues, especially those dealing with institutions and general goals, leaders do follow public opinion. Such consistency often goes unnoticed and is taken for granted. On more specific issues the pattern is mixed—in some instances opinion and policy agree; in others, sharp discrepancies occur. Many factors help explain why leaders do not always heed the majority as expressed in an opinion poll: not all opinions are equally important politically, polls may not be trusted, the messages conveyed by polls may not be practical, and leaders cannot always know what the public thinks on each and every issue.

Check Your Understanding

1. List five reasons why some people feel that leaders should not follow public opinion in making policy.

2. When might the opinions of a small number of constituents outweigh the opinions of a large majority of constituents in influencing an elected official?

3. Why is it difficult for state and local leaders in particular to know about public opinion?

THE POLITICS OF PUBLIC OPINION

In recent years there has been much talk about making government more responsive to citizens. More than one candidate has run on a platform of "giving the government back to the people" or "making the people's voice heard in Washington." Government by public opinion may be an attractive idea, but do we really want it? On deeper analysis many people would probably reject such a system.

First, to have government act solely on the opinion of the majority, as expressed in opinion polls, would require drastic constitutional changes. As noted in Chapter 2, many key features of the Constitution (for example, checks and balances) are designed to prevent majorities from deciding policy. Why should we have a Supreme Court if major policy decisions are made by asking citizens? Clearly, government by pubic opinion would mean changing the institutions of government, not merely adapting the existing system. Ironically, many people who want government by public opinion also want to keep the present consitutional system, which works against government by public opinion.

Second, many people have conflicting feelings about leaders following public opinion. Along with our interest in public opinion, we admire leaders who make "tough" decisions that run contrary to popular views. A President who conducted a poll before each action and then always followed the majority position would probably not earn the respect of voters. This contradiction on the part of the public was well illustrated in answers to a 1960 poll conducted in Detroit. People were asked if a President should commit U.S. troops overseas *even if a majority of the public opposed such action*. Three-quarters of the public approved of the President's defying public opinion.[17]

Finally, though the public may be revered as a source of great wisdon, there is no guarantee that government by public opinion would be enlightened. Policies chosen by 100 million citizens can be just as oppressive as policies enacted by a few irresponsible officials hidden in a massive Washington bureaucracy. Indeed, over the years numerous polls have indicated the willingness of a majority of the public to infringe upon the rights of unpopular political and religious groups. If political freedom were decided solely by asking every citizen what he or she thought, the United States might well have less freedom than a system in which leaders can ignore public opinion. There is also the possibility that citizens would refuse to take necessary actions that, at least in the short run, would harm their self-interests. How many citizens, for example, would approve a tax increase or restrictions on energy use?

Who would gain by having government run in accordance with public opinion? Such a change would bring enormous power to those (nonelected) people who control the mass media. Top television and newspaper executives would become the new political elite because of their direct access to the public. Advertising and public relations people, who can package and market new public policies, might also gain in political power. The politician who currently survives by his or her ability to provide benefits to comparatively small groups of citizens would probably be the loser in government by public opinion. In short, following the opinion of citizens on issues would be most advantageous to those able to shape public opinion.

CHAPTER SUMMARY

How do we measure public opinion? Several methods exist—including the written record and personal observations—but the opinion poll is today the most common and accurate instrument. It is not, however, perfect—people can misrepresent their opinions, polls can be poorly executed, and the results may be misinterpreted.

How are political opinions acquired? The family, schools, and the mass media help shape our political attitudes and beliefs. No one source of learning dominates the process, however, and there is a degree of individual control over the socialization process. This learning has important consequences for the choices we make as adults, the issues that are widely debated, and the extent to which opinion in the United States can be influenced.

Is the American public today basically liberal or conservative? There are many different definitions of these terms. One approach to this question is to ask people to describe themselves. Most people say they are near the middle of the two extremes, but not everyone defines "liberal" and "conservative" in the same way. If we examine opinions on more specific issues, the picture is more complex. There is no clear liberal or conservative agreement on issues, and discrepancies occur between a general label like "liberal" and particular issue stands.

Do political leaders follow public opinion? The prior question of whether leaders *should* heed public opinion remains unsettled. Even supporters of democratic government do not say that leaders should follow public opinion. On basic issues, leaders and citizens almost always agree. On more detailed, day-to-day issues, disagreements can occur. There are, however, several understandable and valid reasons why leaders cannot always do what the people want.

IMPORTANT TERMS

Explain the following terms.

opinion poll	partisan affiliation
straw poll	liberalism
political socialization	conservatism

THINKING CRITICALLY

1. Public opinion polls may be important elements in the public debate on issues and may influence what policies are established. Should the government regulate opinion polling? Why or why not?

2. Should the government subsidize private polling firms to guarantee high-quality, accurate poll results? Why or why not?

3. Some critics contend that violence on television has a negative influence on children. Should television programs that contain violence be restricted? Defend your answer.

4. What might the writers of the Constitution have said about efforts to give public opinion a greater role in foreign policy making?

5. The school is an important source of political socialization. Who should determine the political context of this socialization process—parents? teachers? the local community? the federal government? Explain your answer.

6. In what way can forms of entertainment, such as movies, influence public opinion? What movies have you seen that have had a political message? What was the political message of each of these movies?

EXTENDING YOUR UNDERSTANDING

1. Contact a local newspaper or TV station that conducts its own polls. Find out how questions are selected, how the sample is drawn, and how results are reported. Are there any factors that would limit the accuracy of the results? Present your findings to the class.

2. Examine several different national news magazines such as *Time, Newsweek, New Republic, National Review,* and so on. Examine these magazines for messages about the U.S. political system. What is the basic political message of each magazine? Present your conclusions in a report.

3. Interview your parents, teachers, classmates, and others. Ask them to define the terms "liberal" and "conservative." Compare how these various people defined these terms. How would you define these terms?

4. Ask a local public official in what ways he or she follows public opinion. Also ask how the official is able to learn about the public's attitude on important issues. From what the official has told you, do you think he or she follows public opinion? Does his or her perception of public opinion seem accurate to you? Why or why not?

MAKING DECISIONS

Prepare a questionnaire on an issue of importance in your school or community. Consider your questions carefully so that you will be more likely to get accurate and clear responses. Ask your classmates or other students to answer the questions. Tabulate the results. Based on the results, what would your recommendations be on this issue?

Chapter 5
The Electoral System

In the United States, elections are perhaps the most dramatic form of political activity. Moreover, Americans seem to like the idea of holding elections. Every two years we elect 435 members of Congress, at least 33 senators, dozens of governors, and thousands of state and local officials. Quite understandably, most of the attention given to the electoral process is focused on the behavior of candidates, campaign issues, and explanations of victory or defeat. This is the perspective of the mass media, and it appeals to people who view politics as they do sporting events. However, many important questions about the nature of elections are ignored during the heat of battle: Why are some officials elected and others appointed? How should elections be conducted? How should votes be added up? These crucial questions are far more important politically than merely asking who won the election. In this chapter we shall consider three fundamental aspects of elections:

- Why have elections?
- How are American elections organized?
- Does the electoral system promote political equality?

PREVIEW

Why have elections? Elections allow citizens to replace objectionable leaders; they allow citizens to help shape government policy; they legitimize the transfer of political power; they help channel political dissatisfaction into politically "safe" participation; and they enhance feelings of political solidarity. The electoral system has persisted in the United States because most citizens are deeply attached to it. Elections have been challenged on the grounds that they provide only the illusion—not the substance—of citizen political power and that they discourage highly qualified individuals from seeking public office.

There are several methods besides elections for selecting leaders: (1) hereditary aristocracy, (2) performance on examinations, and (3) appointment. States vary concerning which offices are to be elective, which are to be appointive, and which are to be filled on the basis of examinations.

How are American elections organized? The organization of elections can have a major political impact. Because in our system elections are staggered—not all leaders are elected at the same time—it can take years to replace all the officeholders. American elections are determined by the calendar, so we must wait until the fixed election date to vote on issues and candidates. Electoral representation is determined on the basis of geography. Widely diversified districts can make it difficult for leaders to learn about their constituents' opinions. Our electoral system also operates on the winner-take-all principle. Therefore, if more than two candidates are running, a candidate could win with less than 50 percent of the vote. At the national level, citizens can vote only on candidates, not on issues. Finally, the electoral college creates inequalities in the value of votes. It is thus possible that Presidents can be elected with only a minority of the votes cast.

Does the electoral system promote political equality? Although it was not true in the past, today almost all citizens eighteen and over have access to the ballot. The administration of the electoral system—registration and residency requirements in particular—can, however, discourage voters. Such rules may be necessary to prevent fraud. The drawing of district lines can be used to great political advantage. Supreme Court rulings now require districts of equal population. Political inequalities nevertheless continue to exist; some of them might be necessary and have been allowed by the courts.

WHY HAVE ELECTIONS?

Elections might be as American as apple pie, but as everyone knows, there *are* alternatives to apple pie. If it seems unnecessary to justify having elections, remember that historically elections have been a rarely used method of choosing leaders. Even today there are probably some Americans who view the electoral process as a poor way to choose leaders. For thousands of years people have been ruled by hereditary monarchs or by dictators who came to power by force. It is fair to ask, then, why we should have elections.

To Replace Unpopular Leaders

One of the most important benefits of elections is that they provide an opportunity to replace objectionable leaders. Thanks to regular elections, we do not have to be stuck forever with a corrupt, incompetent official. This does not mean that elections ensure the selection of good leaders. After all, voters might replace a corrupt incompetent with an unscrupulous psychopath. Moreover, more than once voters have returned to office people convicted of crimes, leaders guilty of personal misconduct, and even public officials who have served time in jail. In 1984, for example, Tennessee voters reelected Tommy Burnett to the state legislature even though he was serving an eighteen-month federal prison sentence. Voters also have knowingly elected dead people. The frequent opportunity to throw undesirable officials out of office is a benefit of major political significance. This opportunity is not available in absolute monarchies and dictatorships. Just think of what might have happened in 1776 had the colonists been able to vote King George III out of office.

To Influence Government Policy

The existence of elections also gives citizens a degree of influence in directing government policy. This occurs in a number of ways. First, citizens can elect those candidates who offer programs they prefer. For example, if most citizens are unhappy with high taxes, they can elect antitax candidates. Especially since the emergence of polling, many candidates actively search for appealing campaign issues. Second, the prospect of having to be reelected can motivate an officeholder to pay attention to public desires. A member of Congress elected on a promise to reduce taxes might believe that failure to deliver will result in electoral defeat. Finally, regular election campaigns can operate as a learning experience for both constituents and candidates. Campaigns give all citizens a good opportunity to learn what government is doing, how successful these policies are, and where office seekers stand on issues. Candidates also learn from campaigns, through polls, personal conversations, reactions to speeches, and so on. Such mutual learning can help to keep both citizens and government in tune with each other. It is important to realize, however, that elections provide influence, not complete citizen control of policy. A candidate might promise to lower taxes if elected, and citizens might threaten not to reelect an official who votes for a tax increase, but elections cannot dictate an officeholder's behavior during the term of office.

To Legitimize the Transfer of Power

A third advantage of elections is that they are an efficient means of legitimizing, or making acceptable, the transfer of political power. When one political leader replaces another after an election, virtually all citizens—even supporters of the ousted leader—accept the change. To most of us, accustomed to the process in which new leaders replace old ones without much fuss, this legitimizing benefit might not seem important. Yet if one looks at history or at many other nations, the value of having regular elections becomes clearer. In countries without an established electoral tradi-

tion, new leaders have had to continue fighting their opponents, and chaos frequently prevails. All governments must have some means to ensure the smooth transfer of political power—even in dictatorships, when the dictator dies. Of all the mechanisms that have been devised to deal with this problem, elections are perhaps the most efficient.

To Channel Disruptive Behavior into "Safe" Participation

Elections also can channel political dissatisfaction into politically "safe" and routine behaviors. Because election campaigns frequently appear disorderly, this claim might at first appear false. Yet consider what might happen if we did *not* have regular, free elections. Suppose that the only way you could capture political power was to be of royal blood. What could you do if you were extremely dissatisfied with a government policy? When citizens cannot easily and regularly take part in the electoral process, they must improvise outside existing channels. Such behavior could range from petty violations of the law to organized terrorism.

On the other hand, because it is easy to "vote the rascals out," organize election campaigns for sympathetic candidates, or even run for office one-self, politically disruptive hostility is channeled into safe, in-the-system activities. The process of channeling has been particularly well illustrated in the civil rights movement from the late 1950s to the present. Initially, especially in the South, blacks were largely excluded from the electoral process. They could not vote, run for office, or play much of a role in campaigns. As a result, dissatisfied blacks turned to such actions as boycotts, marches, and demonstrations. Some of these ended in violence, and threats of violence from both sides were common.

By the 1960s, there was a possibility that the civil rights movement would become radical and highly violent. Militant organizations, such as the Black Panthers, attracted many followers, and several large cities experienced large-scale rioting. However, beginning in the late 1960s, blacks began making modest electoral gains—the election of a city council member here, of a state legislator

Since the 1950s, black political participation has evolved from front-line struggle to electoral gains. Clockwise from upper left: U.S. marshals enforce court-ordered school desegregation (1950s); a National Guardsman stands by a school bus that was the scene of racial violence (1970); marchers call for integration (1975); John Lewis, left, former civil rights activist, is elected to Congress from Georgia (1986).

there, and so on. Several former civil rights activists were elected to office. Black activists began focusing their energies on electoral politics rather than on confrontations with whites. The Black Panthers even ran a candidate for mayor in Oakland, California. Today, blacks are scoring electoral victories in such cities as Los Angeles, Chicago, and Philadelphia as well as in Congress. In 1984 Jesse Jackson ran an impressive campaign for the Democratic presidential nomination. Between 1970 and 1985, the total number of black elected officials increased from 1,472 to 5,654. The rhetoric of violence and separatism has almost vanished.

This is *not* to suggest that elections are a good way to stifling dissent. Rather, elections provide a way to bring political dissatisfaction safely into the system. Voting replaces violence. Political dissidents benefit as much by electoral activity as do those who worry about a revolution in the United States.

To Enhance Political Solidarity

Periodic conflict centering on elections draws people together and reinforces attachments to the political system. At first this might appear to be a contradictory argument, because many elections are hard-fought battles in which both sides engage in name-calling. The focus on the divisive effect of elections overshadows the possibly unifying effect of conflict. Sociologists have observed that as long as conflict is held within certain boundaries, the combatants can feel better toward one another after the conflict. Obviously, it is an exaggeration to say that all conflict leads to better feelings afterward. However, limited conflict can increase the sense of unity and heighten feelings of community.

Does this apply to American elections? Elections promote political solidarity in at least two important ways.

First, elections can clear the air of a lingering, troublesome issue. Differences are ever-present in society and must be tolerated, but if too many differences accumulate, the antagonisms can be destructive. By giving proponents of an issue a chance to be heard, elections can help end certain conflicts. In the 1972 election, advocates of immediate withdrawal from Vietnam secured the Democratic party nomination for George McGovern, who campaigned on a platform of immediate withdrawal from Vietnam. McGovern's decisive defeat by Richard Nixon, who favored a more cautious approach, helped eliminate the immediate withdrawal option from heated debate. By acting as a safety valve for sharp differences of opinion, elections can contribute to the long-term moderation of conflict and help keep society united.

Second, election campaigns provide regular, shared experiences that help reaffirm people's common political values. This role is similar to that of high school pep rallies to enhance school spirit. Electoral participation in the United States is akin to a civic religion in which all participants

come away with a heightened awareness and appreciation of our system of government. Feelings of togetherness are also enhanced by the rituals following most elections. Despite the animosity of the campaign, losers customarily congratulate winners and offer whatever help is necessary to make government work. It is almost unthinkable in American politics for losers to attack winners publicly or to encourage their supporters to reject the electorate's verdict as final. The upshot of all the conflict, then, is that the basic agreements and shared purposes of citizens are reaffirmed.

The unifying role of elections is demonstrated by comparing people's votes and opinions before and after an election. Table 5.1 shows that despite accusations, mudslinging, and bad feelings during presidential campaigns, newly elected Presidents received considerable public support. And—what is perhaps most significant—much of this support came from people who probably voted against the winner. The proportion giving high ratings to a newly elected President is always much larger than the winner's proportion of the popular vote.

Explaining the Survival of the Electoral System in the United States

One of the most remarkable features of American political history is the survival of the electoral system over such a long time. This might not appear notable until we consider the number of countries that have been unable to maintain a tradition of genuine elections. In many African, Asian, and Latin American nations, elected officials are often overthrown by the military and new elections postponed indefinitely. Many historical factors help to account for the persistence of elections in the United States. These include the emigration of British Royalists following the Revolutionary War, the success of early elections in attracting the support of powerful interests, and the incorporation of newly arrived ethnic groups into electoral politics.

An important though less obvious explanation is that the idea of voting is deeply ingrained in American citizens. Little can compete in popularity with elections as a means of resolving political disputes. The strength of citizen commitment to

Popular Support for the President Before and After the Election		Percentage of popular vote received by President	Percentage of citizens "approving" of the way the President is handling job (first poll following inauguration)
President (election year)			
Harry S Truman (1948)		49.6	87
Dwight D. Eisenhower (1952)		55.1	68
Dwight D. Eisenhower (1956)		57.4	79
John F. Kennedy (1960)		49.7	72
Lyndon B. Johnson (1964)		61.1	79
Richard M. Nixon (1968)		43.4	59
Richard M. Nixon (1972)		60.7	68
Jimmy Carter (1976)		50.6	66
Ronald Reagan (1980)		50.7	73
Ronald Reagan (1984)		59.2	62

Sources: Election data are from *The U.S. Fact Book: The American Almanac for 1977* (New York: Grosset and Dunlap, 1977), p. 452. Gallup data are reported in *The Gallup Poll: Public Opinion 1935–1971* (New York: Random House, 1971), p. 2234, and Gallup poll, release of February 6, 1977. Poll data on Reagan in 1980 are from ABC News/*Washington Post* poll reported in *National Journal*, October 19, 1983, p. 2282. 1984 Reagan poll data are from a Gallup poll conducted January 11–14, 1985.

TABLE 5.1

the voting process becomes clear when we examine what young children learn about elections. Even in the early grades children are knowledgeable about voting and talk about the day when they will be able to vote. One study, for example, found that most grade-schoolers talked to their parents and friends about the presidential candidates, read about the candidates, and wore campaign buttons. Young children also view the right to vote as one of the most valuable characteristics of the American political system. Indeed, the idea of free elections seems to be basic to everyone's concept of democracy.

Major Arguments Against Elections

No doubt most of us believe that elections are the best method of choosing leadership. Nevertheless, reasonable criticisms of elections exist. We shall consider only two of the most important: (1) elections provide merely the illusion of citizen control

of government, and (2) elections discourage qualified people from seeking public office.

Elections Are Illusions of Popular Control

According to this argument, elections and campaign activity are more like tribal rain dances or pagan religious rites than a method of citizen political control. The candidates' appeal for voter support and the rhetoric stressing the power of the voters give the appearance, but do not contribute to the substance, of popular control. Such rituals can reassure citizens that they have control, make the ordinary person feel important, and fit well with common-sense notions of democracy. But according to this view, the ultimate purpose of elections is to hide the fact that the ordinary citizen has almost no control over government. This argument is not an attack on the idea of elections; rather, it focuses on the conduct of modern, mass-media-oriented elections.

Advocates of this position note that many citi-

Commentary: We Like Elections, But We Don't Like to Vote

Perhaps the best evidence of our attachment to elections is the fact that we have so many of them. Rather than have a single, all-purpose election every few years, most states and localities offer citizens at least one election each year. One result is that turnout goes down when there is no top office to be decided. To see how the process works, consider the elections that voters in Champaign County, Illinois, faced in the period from the 1980 presidential election to the 1984 presidential race. There were eleven separate elections in the four-year span.

Date	Election	Turnout
November 4, 1980	General election for President, Congress	73%
February 4, 1981	Primary for city and town races	7
April 7, 1981	General election for city and town races	27
November 3, 1981	Nonpartisan school board election	18
March 16, 1982	Primary for governor, state, and local races	19
November 2, 1982	General election for governor and Congress	64
February 22, 1983	Primary for city and town races	27
April 12, 1983	General election for city and town races	24
November 8, 1983	Nonpartisan school board election	29
March 20, 1984	Presidential primary	40
November 6, 1984	General election for President, Congress	78

Only in three instances—when the President or the governor ran—did turnout exceed 50 percent.

Source: Champaign County Clerk (Illinois).

zens know little about what candidates stand for or about their qualifications and backgrounds. Moreover, this lack of awareness is encouraged by mass media campaigns that frequently stress physical appearance, personal style, ethnicity, and other characteristics irrelevant to important political questions. According to this view, political contests are decided by poorly informed citizens who have been heavily influenced by the media. Such campaigns, these critics say, provide no clear-cut policy direction.

It is also claimed that even if citizens were to provide clear instuctions to their leaders, elected officials do not possess the power necessary to implement public demands (even if elected officials wanted to follow popular desires). Vast quantities of political power, the argument continues, lie in the hands of nonelected public officials, such as bureaucrats or judges, or in private hands, such as executives of large corporations or lobbying groups.

Hence, because the public responds much more readily to symbols than to substance, and because considerable political power is held by nonelected officials, elections, it is argued, merely provide a relatively cheap way to keep the people happy. Citizens will think they have control, and leaders will reinforce this satisfying belief. The truth, so these critics say, is otherwise. Elections are facades that hide the real exercise of political power.

These arguments are difficult to evaluate. Obviously, they have some validity. Campaigns often do avoid key issues in favor of superficial ones, voters frequently are ill-informed, and much political power lies in the hands of nonelected officials and private individuals. But it is also true that choices made by voters can convey clear messages and be of real consequence. In 1980, for example, despite all the superficialities, the presidential election was widely viewed as a contest between two philosophies of government. When voters decisively elected Ronald Reagan over Jimmy Carter, they were choosing lower taxes, increased military spending, and a greater commitment to certain programs. Once elected, Reagan followed through on his commitments and did significantly redirect government policy. Obviously, then, elections can be mechanisms of popular influence. Not every election, of course, is of great consequence, and illusions, citizen ignorance, and deception are probably part of every election.

Elections Discourage "Good" People from Seeking Office

The second important argument against elections is that they do not encourage the emergence of the best leadership. This belief is fairly widespread, and it is a difficult assertion to argue against precisely. The most perplexing aspect concerns what constitutes the "best" people for the job of President, member of Congress, mayor, or justice of the peace. Nevertheless, the argument is sufficiently important to deserve our attention.

Those who believe that elections provide only second-rate leaders usually make the following points. First, the process of getting elected requires wheeling and dealing and even deception. American electoral politics demands that leaders gain the support of varied groups and interests. A candidate must therefore learn how to avoid being pinned down on controversial issues and how to make contradictory statements without offending either side. Integrity, high principles, and frankness, the argument goes, simply have no place in electoral politics—at least not for winners. Even a good person can be corrupted by the electoral experience.

In addition, running for office is burdensome. It is time-consuming and expensive; family life is disrupted; and candidates must put up with all kinds of personal abuse. Given the opportunities and absence of hassles in private life for intelligent, talented individuals, why should such people go into electoral politics? In 1972, for instance,

Walter Mondale dropped out of the Democratic presidential primaries, saying he didn't want to spend the rest of his life in motels (obviously he had a change of heart by 1984). As a result of the strains on decent citizens, the argument goes, only second-raters, lacking better opportunities in private life, venture into electoral competition.

Finally, it can be claimed that seeking elective office is such a demanding, exhausting activity that only power-oriented individuals succeed. Thus, according to this view, electoral politics produces government by overambitious, self-serving individuals, rather than government by idealistic leaders concerned with the public interest.

Do elections discourage high-quality leadership? Probably we all can agree that American political leaders as a group are neither prime candidates for sainthood nor members of the world's intellectual elite. Nevertheless, much evidence shows that the more extreme charges against elections are untrue. Although successful candidates might be gluttons for punishment it does not seem that elected officials as a group suffer from personal difficulties that interfere significantly with their jobs. Nor does it appear that public officials are second-raters who could not otherwise succeed in society. To be sure, political leaders do not always have skills that would make them successful outside politics. Several studies have demonstrated, however, that officeholders as a group are several cuts above ordinary citizens in education and possess a wide variety of experiences and accomplishments outside politics.

More important, however, many of the supposed defects in character that elections are said to bring out might not be defects at all. Consider, for example, the ability to satisfy conflicting groups. Perhaps we want leaders skilled at seeking compromise and reducing conflict. Politics, it is often said, is the art of the possible. To insist on one's principles regardless of political realities might make for martyrdom, but in American society it is bad politics. The "failure" of electoral politics to recruit high-level intellectual leadership might not be a failure at all. Citizens probably want leaders who are more like ordinary people, not geniuses. It might be that elections discourage "the very best" from entering public life, but it is also likely that Americans do not want such individuals in public office.

Alternatives to Elections

Elections play a key role in American politics, but it would be a mistake to conclude that they are the only way to choose political leaders. Elections are but one of several ways of selecting leaders.

Hereditary Aristocracy

One alternative is to follow the example of medieval Europe or contemporary Saudi Arabia and have a hereditary **aristocracy** (in an aristocracy, leaders hold power as a result of birth, wealth, or other attribute). Such a system would have the advantage of continuity because leaders serve for life, the transfer of power is usually clear-cut, it would probably be cheaper than periodic elections, and it would perhaps please fans of pomp and ceremony. As a realistic political alternative, however, it is not feasible.

Selection of Officials by Examinations or Appointment

A much more realistic alternative would be to select leaders on the basis of special skills determined through examinations. Instead of electing a member of Congress, we could fill the position much as a corporation hires an executive trainee. Applicants would take a written exam and be interviewed, and the top candidate would become a congressional representative. Before you dismiss this possibility as absurd, you should realize that many powerful public officials in the United States *are* chosen on the basis of written examinations and expertise in a particular area. Indeed, although we might glorify elections as the method of choosing leaders in a democracy, we probably have more nonelected than elected positions of power in the United States.

One important group of nonelected public officials are **civil servants**, who get their jobs through competitive examinations. In government agencies such as the Internal Revenue Service, the Environmental Protection Agency, and the Feder-

al Bureau of Investigation, nonelected officials make decisions of enormous importance. Some people have complained that these civil servants, who may serve for many years, sometimes dominate elected leaders, who often serve for only a few years. Another group of nonelected public officials are federal judges, who serve for life and can be removed only with great difficulty. Thus appointed judges generally are unaffected by the electoral process. The consequences of this are illustrated by the fact that the Supreme Court has supported numerous policies that the public widely opposes (for example, the ban on prayers in public schools). Finally, many cities have replaced popularly elected mayors with professionally trained, appointed **city managers** who are supposed to replace "politics" with businesslike decision making.

The important point is that despite the popularity of elections in the United States, their use is not preordained. Most political systems have *not* employed elections, and even in American politics many powerful positions are not filled by elections. An important question, one usually obscured by all the campaign hoopla, is why some officials are chosen by election while others are appointed or selected by written examination. In certain states, for example, such positions as attorney general are elected; in others they are appointed. Unlike federal judges, many state judges must run regularly for election. In short, there *are* alternatives to elections, and at least two alternatives have their merits and advocates.

Check Your Understanding

1. What are five purposes that elections serve?

2. What are two major arguments against elections?

3. What are some of the alternatives to elections? Which of these methods are appropriate for our political system?

HOW ARE AMERICAN ELECTIONS ORGANIZED?

A crucial aspect of any electoral system is the way the system is organized. Organization refers to such factors as the timing of elections, the qualifications for voting, and the procedures for counting votes. All of these regulations are important, even though they are frequently overshadowed by day-to-day events. To take one simple example, consider the fact that national elections are held on Tuesdays. Sounds inconsequential, doesn't it? Who could possibly lose or gain from this technical requirement? One group of potential losers are people who work Monday through Friday for hourly wages. Unless the polls are open early in the morning or late at night, this rule puts many of these citizens at a disadvantage. Business executives or college professors, however, can more easily vote during the middle of a Tuesday. Holding elections on Sundays—as in many European nations—would probably increase turnout among working-class citizens and thus make the less wealthy more influential in politics.

Let us examine six important features of the American electoral system: (1) staggered elections, (2) calendar-determined elections, (3) geographically defined election districts, (4) the winner-take-all system, (5) choice of candidates rather than issues, and (6) the electoral college.

Staggered Elections

At all levels of government—national, state, and local—elections are **staggered**: only portions of the government are elected at any one time. At the national level, for example, only one-third of the Senate is up for reelection every two years; presidential elections occur every four years; and House of Representatives elections take place every two years. Many states have even more fragmented elections: federal elections occur in November of even years, and local elections in April of odd years (it is even more confusing when primaries and school board elections are considered).

The net results of the staggering of elections are twofold. First, citizens must frequently wait comparatively long periods to change political leadership completely. For example, if citizens wanted to throw every public official out of office, the process would take six years at the national level. Second, because not all officials are elected at the same time, government could be composed of individuals who owe their success to different issues, issues that were popular during their particular electoral campaigns. Clearly, political life would be much more straightforward if all officials faced reelection at the same time.

The spreading out of elections over several years also influences voter motivation and participation. Generally speaking, participation levels are higher when an important, visible office is being contested. People get more excited about a presidential contest than about a race for Congress. For example, in the presidential race of 1980, the overall turnout in congressional races was 47.4 percent. In 1982, without a presidential contest, turnout dropped to 38.1 percent. In 1984, it rose again to 47.9 percent. If all officials were chosen at one time, voters who came out to elect a President would, in most cases, press the lever for other offices on the ballot as well—from senator to the local park commission. If, on the other hand, the most important office to be decided attracted relatively little attention (for example, county supervisor), fewer people would participate—why bother to undergo the inconvenience of voting if the stakes are small? Hence, having several separate elections rather than one grand election reduces turnout.

Low voter turnout can be of political advantage to one political interest or another. For example, the Democratic party of Chicago conducts its **primary**—the election to choose party nominees—in February of odd-numbered years, a period of no other election and frequent bad weather. This choice of time discourages all but the most highly motivated from participating. In this instance, the most actively involved voters are city employees. Their disproportionate participation allows party officials with influence over job appointments to exert considerable influence over the primary. In many cases the decision to separate state from national elections was based on a desire to prevent poorer, less-informed citizens from having a voice in the selection of state officials. It was believed that these citizens would vote in state races only if they could also vote for President; they would not make a special trip just to choose state officials. In some cases this separation of elections worked to the advantage of Republican candidates, who had their greatest support among better-educated, more politically interested citizens.

Calendar-Determined Elections

Suppose citizens wanted immediate government action on some major issue that suddenly dominated the political scene, but leaders ignored the clamor. What could be done? Very little until the next election. For better or worse, we are constitutionally bound by rigid, **calendar-determined elections,** no matter how pressing the issue. This is not true in such nations as Great Britain, where elections can be called when crucial political issues emerge (for example, Britain's entry into the Common Market). In fact, it has been argued that if we want issue-oriented campaigns, we should schedule elections when important issues arise. This would be more effective than hoping that the important questions will surface in the autumn of predetermined election years.

The disadvantage of calendar elections is well illustrated by the Watergate crisis in 1973 and 1974. Evidence began to come out regarding the illegal break-in, by members of President Nixon's reelection committee, at the Democratic national headquarters. Congress and President Nixon became preoccupied with the possibility of impeachment (removal from office), the lack of public confidence in government, and the President's ability to govern effectively. In European nations, where election dates are not permanently fixed, the question of whether a leader should be replaced is solved by calling for a new election. If the United States had had such a system, President Nixon could have taken his case directly to the people in 1973 or 1974, received a quick answer, and Watergate would have been resolved. Instead, the cri-

sis lingered on until enormous pressure, including the beginning of impeachment proceedings, brought about President Nixon's resignation. Unfortunately, the constitutional requirement of fixed terms means that a popular majority might not be able to take action against discredited officeholders until their terms expire. In some states and cities voters have the legal option of instituting a petition to **recall** elected officials (that is, to force them to face reelection before the end of their term). This process rarely is successful, however.

Geographically Defined Electoral Districts

Suppose we want a political system in which citizens choose leaders to represent them. Which citizens should elect which leaders? The specific way in which the people who are eligible to vote for particular candidates are chosen is crucial. Several reasonable alternative methods are possible. One is to have all citizens elect all officials (**at-large elections**). This occurs, for instance, when all voters choose all members of a city council. A second alternative, one popular in university elections, is to divide citizens into groups on the basis of some common characteristic. For example, university legislative bodies include representatives of such groups as undergraduates, graduate students, faculty, and nonacademic staff. A third alternative is to divide citizens into geographically defined electoral districts. Elections in the United States are based on such geographical divisions, with public officials representing a state, county, ward, or other territorial unit.

The importance of how districts are created is illustrated in Figure 5.1. It shows three different ways of organizing election districts. In the first case—geographically based representation—a minority interest receives half of all legislative seats, and two interests receive no legislative seats at all despite their substantial numbers. By way of contrast, the other two systems are likely to give all interests a share of legislative power in closer proportion to their numbers in the population. Clearly, grouping people together solely on the basis of geographical closeness has an impact on which candidates are likely to be elected.

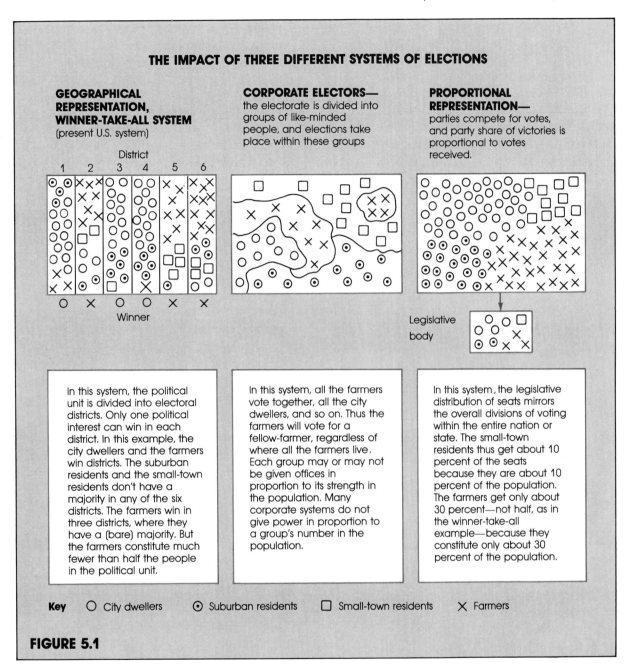

THE IMPACT OF THREE DIFFERENT SYSTEMS OF ELECTIONS

GEOGRAPHICAL REPRESENTATION, WINNER-TAKE-ALL SYSTEM (present U.S. system)

CORPORATE ELECTORS— the electorate is divided into groups of like-minded people, and elections take place within these groups

PROPORTIONAL REPRESENTATION— parties compete for votes, and party share of victories is proportional to votes received.

District
1 2 3 4 5 6

Winner   O X O O X X

Legislative body

In this system, the political unit is divided into electoral districts. Only one political interest can win in each district. In this example, the city dwellers and the farmers win districts. The suburban residents and the small-town residents don't have a majority in any of the six districts. The farmers win in three districts, where they have a (bare) majority. But the farmers constitute much fewer than half the people in the political unit.

In this system, all the farmers vote together, all the city dwellers, and so on. Thus the farmers will vote for a fellow-farmer, regardless of where all the farmers live. Each group may or may not be given offices in proportion to its strength in the population. Many corporate systems do not give power in proportion to a group's number in the population.

In this system, the legislative distribution of seats mirrors the overall divisions of voting within the entire nation or state. The small-town residents thus get about 10 percent of the seats because they are about 10 percent of the population. The farmers get only about 30 percent—not half, as in the winner-take-all example—because they constitute only about 30 percent of the population.

Key   O City dwellers   ⊙ Suburban residents   ☐ Small-town residents   X Farmers

FIGURE 5.1

Such geographically based elections generally make it more difficult for leaders to respond to— or even to know—citizen preferences. Geographically defined electorates are often more diverse politically than those determined according to a common social or economic characteristic. Many congressional districts contain such a variety of groups that it is impossible for any elected official to satisfy everyone. Representation might be much easier if officials were elected by citizens who shared certain political preferences. Instead of having leaders who represented northwest Chicago, for example, we might have a leader elected by middle-class homeowners of European descent.

Basing electoral districts on geography does not, however, discriminate equally against all citizens. Specifically, citizens sharing common interests who happen to be clustered geographically are likely to fare better than citizens with the same interests who are geographically separated. To see how this works, compare the congressional representation of farmers, a group with strong geo-graphical concentrations, with that of manual workers, a group much more dispersed. Despite their small numbers, farmers frequently receive effective representation in Congress. This is due in large part to farmer domination of many electoral districts. The more geographically separated man-

Some congressional districts contain citizens from a variety of economic and social backgrounds. Their representative in Washington may pay greater attention to the views of voters likely to support his or her reelection.

ual workers, in contrast, do not have this political clout because they make up majorities in few congressional districts.

Winner-Take-All Systems

Elections in the United States, unlike those in many European democracies, operate on the principle of **winner take all.** The candidate with the most votes (even if only a **plurality,** or less than 50 percent) wins everything. Those who place second, third, or fourth get absolutely nothing. Three important points need to be made regarding this system. First, although the winner-take-all system is widely accepted, a workable alternative exists—namely, the system of **proportional representation.** The essential feature of this system is that political parties offer lists of candidates, and voters choose lists, not individual candidates. Offices—for example, legislative seats—are then assigned on the basis of the proportion of the vote won by each party. Suppose we have two parties—the Conservative party and the Liberal party. In an election the Conservatives win 61 percent of the vote; they therefore get (as closely as possible) 61 percent of the offices up for election. The Liberals get 39 percent. Under the winner-take-all system, in contrast, the losing party has no guarantee of winning anything. Theoretically, it is possible for the losing party to get 49.9 percent of the vote in every legislative district and yet win no seats! Proportional representation, on the other hand, ensures that losers get a share of the power that corresponds to their electoral strength. Supporters of proportional representation have argued that the winner-take-all system is undemocratic because many people—those voting for the loser—receive no representation.

A second feature of the winner-take-all system is that it allows the election of leaders who receive less than 50 percent of the vote. This happens when three or more strong candidates split the vote so that one candidate is victorious with only a plurality, not a majority. In primaries, where getting on the ballot is comparatively simple, it is not unusual for the winner to receive 30 percent or less of the vote. Even in general elections many office-

holders win with less than a majority. In his 1982 race for Congress, for example, Ronald Packard of California won election with 37 percent of the total vote. Presidential candidates can win a state with less than a majority if there is a strong third-party candidate. On occasion this system results in the election of a comparatively unpopular candidate. For example, in the 1980 New York Senate race a very conservative candidate (Alfonse D'Amato) won with 45 percent of the vote when his two opponents—Elizabeth Holtzman and Jacob Javits—split the liberal vote. A similar situation occurred in 1970—a Conservative (James Buckley) won with 39 percent of the vote when two opponents divided the liberal and moderate vote. Plurality victories could be avoided by having **run-off elections.** In this procedure the two candidates with the highest votes face each other in a second election. This is not required in our system (some states do provide for it, however). Even a run-off election might not guarantee that the majority will prevail. In the 1977 New York City Democratic primary for mayor, six candidates each received between 10 and 20 percent of the vote. The run-off election pitted a candidate who previously received 19.8 percent of the vote against one who got 18.6 percent.

A third important point about the winner-take-all system is that it distorts the translation of votes into political power. Generally, it exaggerates the impact of certain majorities and lessens the representation of those in the minority. Consider the situation of black voters trying to elect a black U.S. senator. If blacks constitute 40 percent of a state's electorate and both blacks and whites vote along racial lines, what proportion of the state's two senators do blacks win? Zero percent. The winner-take-all system is not antiblack, it discriminates against all groups that are less than a majority. Not only are minorities at a disadvantage at the polls; they also are probably discouraged from political action. After all, what is the point of working hard to increase one's vote from 20 percent to 40 percent if the effect is the same? Hence, groups with a small following in a geographical area are disadvantaged in obtaining power. Of course, in a close election the votes of a minority can be crucial

Issues: Proportional Representation as an Alternative

The United States is one of the few democracies that use the simple plurality system of voting (the one candidate with the most votes is elected). Over the years the practice has been criticized as being inconsistent with democracy. In particular, besides allowing victory to a candidate lacking a majority, it does not provide representation to citizens who are not part of the plurality or the majority. In other words, if the winning candidate receives 55 percent of the vote, citizens who cast the remaining 45 percent of votes receive no representation at all. For an electoral system to provide representation to all citizens, it is argued, both the majority and the minority must be given a voice in government in proportion to their strength.

Numerous alternatives have been suggested and adopted in the hope of eliminating the alleged lack of representation. For many years Illinois employed a cumulative-vote, multimember district system for electing its lower house. The state was divided into districts, with each district electing three legislators. Voters were given three votes, which could be used cumulatively—one, two, or three votes could be cast for a single candidate. This allowed those who were in the minority in a district to cast all their votes for one of the three candidates. For example, instead of a Democratic district automatically electing three Democratic legislators, Republicans, by concentrating all three votes on

one candidate, might get at least some representation.

The most common alternative to ensure minority representation is *proportional representation (PR)*. The basic idea of PR is simple—seats are awarded to parties in proportion to their share of the vote—but in practice there are a multitude of variations. In some nations—Israel and the Netherlands—the whole country is one election district; in others—Belgium, Greece—the nation is subdivided into election districts. In some countries the list of candidates cannot be changed; in others, citizens can cast votes to move a candidate higher up on a party's list. Variations also occur in the mathematical formula employed to add votes and distribute seats. In West Germany a party receives no legislative seats unless it wins a minimum of 5 percent of the popular vote.

Despite its claim to be more democratic in allocating legislative seats and its widespread use in European democracies, PR has its

critics. One major criticism is that it encourages political fragmentation. PR can result in many small parties, each appealing to narrow interests. Often, no one party can by itself win a legislative majority, so it must form coalitions with smaller parties. The price paid for such backing can be far out of proportion to the parties' electoral support. Moreover, PR can encourage extremism—a group such as the Ku Klux Klan is completely shut out of the present system, but under PR it could win a few seats and exercise some influence. PR has also been accused of promoting political instability. Governments tend to become weaker when no one party is able to win a clear majority on its own. Disputes among coalition partners can mean the breakup of the ruling majority in the legislature.

Proportional representation has been tried in the United States. In 1937, for example, New York City employed the system for elections to its City Council. Any group that could muster even a small percentage of the total vote got a city council seat (rather than needing more than 50 percent in one electoral district). When several Communists were elected, the system was discontinued. Obviously, proportional representation would greatly help small minorities in getting at least some members elected (if the House of Representatives were elected by PR, only about 0.223 percent of the total vote would be needed to get one member elected.

and thus highly valued. The fact remains that the winner-take-all system usually works against groups that lack the power to win a majority.

To show how this distortion works on a national level, compare the proportion of votes won by Republican congressional candidates between 1960 and 1984 with the number of seats the Republicans actually won. Table 5.2 shows that if House seats were exactly proportional to votes received, the Republicans would have done much better in each election. In 1982, for example, the Republicans' 44.7 percent of the vote translated into only 38.2 percent of the seats, a discrepancy of twenty-nine seats. The major culprit in this distortion was the winner-take-all system.

Experts who have examined the distortion of votes into electoral victories have noted a pattern, which has been stated mathematically in the **cube law.** If votes are divided in the ratio of A:B, legislative seats will be divided in the ratio of $A^3:B^3$. For example, let us say that party A wins 40 votes

and party B gets 30 votes. Party A has won 57.1 percent of the popular vote. According to the cube law, however, the division of seats will be $40^3:30^3$: the winner will get 75.9 percent of the seats. As the margin of victory increases, distortions become even greater. It should be noted, however, that the cube law is a general tendency rather than a rigid scientific principle. In 1982, for example, the cube law would have predicted that the Democrats would gain 70.0 percent of all House seats based on their 55.3 share of the vote. In fact, they won only 61.8 percent of the 435 seats.

Choice of Candidates, Not Issues

At the national level voters choose only among candidates for office. These candidates typically make promises regarding what they will do if elected, but there is no guarantee that they will make good on their promises. Ronald Reagan, for example, promised to appoint a woman to the

Votes Received Versus Congressional Seats Won, 1960–84 Year	Proportion of Votes for House Candidates Given to Republicans (percents)	Proportion of Seats Won by Republican Candidates (percents)	Number of House Seats "Lost" by Republicans Because of Distortion
1960	45.0%	39.8%	23
1962	47.4	40.7	29
1964	42.5	32.2	45
1966	48.7	43.1	24
1968	49.1	44.1	22
1970	45.8	41.5	19
1972	47.3	44.6	12
1974	41.4	33.3	35
1976	43.8	32.9	47
1978	45.6	36.2	41
1980	48.7	44.1	20
1982	44.7	38.2	29
1984	48.3	41.9	28

Sources: Statistical Abstract of the United States, 1960, 1964, 1968, 1974, 1977, 1978, 1982–83, 1984. The proportion of the total House vote received by Republicans in 1984 comes from David W. Brady and Patricia A. Hurley, "The Prospects for Contemporary Party Realignment," *PS* 18 (Winter 1985), p. 65.

TABLE 5.2

Supreme Court; he did make such an appointment, but he was under no particular legal obligation to do so.

Not all election systems limit the choices of voters to candidates. Other nations have occasionally used **plebiscites,** in which citizens may vote "yes" or "no" on an important issue, such as a change in the form of government. At the state and local level there are two electoral mechanisms—the initiative and the referendum—that enable citizens to make policy choices. The **initiative** allows citizens to propose and adopt laws by putting them on the ballot (typically, a petition containing the signatures of a certain number of registered voters must be filed before an issue can get on the ballot). The **referendum** is a measure placed on the ballot at the request of the legislature or city council. Many states legally require certain actions, such as the issuing of bonds or a change in

the size of the legislature, to be approved by voters. State constitutional amendments also require voter approval by referendum. Not all initiatives and referendums are binding on public officials, and even when they are binding, they can be overruled by the courts.

These mechanisms, which permit citizens to express their opinions through the vote, are used frequently. For example, in the November 1982 elections, forty-two states and the District of Columbia presented their citizens with about 200 propositions. Many of these involved a freeze on nuclear weapons, the regulation of public utilities, and proposals to limit taxes. Some of these actions have had clear consequences for peoples' daily lives. In 1983, San Francisco voters, by a narrow margin, required the creation of nonsmoking areas in workplaces. On November 6, 1984, voters in forty-four states had some 230 issues on the ballot.

In 1978, California voters passed Proposition 13, an initiative placed on the ballot by groups of citizens seeking lower property taxes. Because some municipal services had to be cut back as a result of reduced revenues, however, the state government eventually raised taxes to help finance those services.

Voters in California, for example, had to make decisions about a lottery, tax reductions, and cutbacks in welfare benefits. In Oregon, citizens voted to restore the death penalty. Nevertheless, despite the demonstrated workability of initiatives and referendums at the state and local level, voters in federal elections must rely on candidates to keep their promises. The system denies citizens the means to force government to take a particular action.

Another point to be noted about the existing system is that voters cannot express degrees of support. They can cast only a simple "for" or "against" vote (although if a large number of citizens don't vote, that, too, carries a message). This rigidity of alternatives can lead to distortion of the public's preferences. Consider the following situation. There is a liberal candidate (L), a conservative candidate (C), and a moderate candidate (M). The liberal and conservative candidates each have the full support of 35 percent of the electorate. Each also generates widespread opposition. The moderate candidate, by contrast, is the first choice of only 30 percent but is acceptable to 80 percent of all voters. Under the present system, this widespread acceptability counts for nothing. In all likelihood, either L or C will be elected by a plurality, and a majority of the electorate will be dissatisfied with the outcome.

In recent years a political scientist named Steven Brams has suggested a plan to overcome this problem—**approval voting.**[1] Basically, in approval voting each voter may vote for as many candidates as he or she chooses (but may cast only one vote per candidate). The candidate with the most total votes wins. In the illustration above, among one hundred voters candidate L might get fifty votes, candidate C sixty votes, and candidate M seventy-five votes. The moderate candidate thereby wins, and most people have an acceptable outcome. According to Brams, approval voting would help ensure the election of the strongest candidate, increase voter turnout, and encourage the supporters of candidates with less than an absolute majority; and it could be implemented with little change. Although this idea has generated some interest, it has yet to be seriously debated within government.

The Electoral College

Delegates to the 1787 Constitutional Convention were sharply divided on how the President should be selected. As a compromise, they adopted a system in which each state would be assigned a number of **electors** equal to the state's number of U.S. senators and representatives. The states were to decide how these presidential electors were selected. In principle, these electors choose the President; if there is no majority among the electors, the House of Representatives makes the choice, with each state casting one vote. The group of 535 electors that chooses a President is called the **electoral college.**

Over time, the actual operation of the electoral college has changed. Electors are now selected by the popular vote in each state; in all states except Maine the **unit vote system** is used—the candidate winning the most votes in a state receives all of the state's electoral vote. (In Maine a candidate who carries a congressional district receives an electoral vote even if he or she does not win the entire state.)

One consequence of the unit vote system is that large states, such as California, New York, and Texas, are given more attention by presidential candidates than states with smaller populations. In these large states a 1- or 2-percent shift in the vote can result in the gain or loss of thirty to forty electoral votes, whereas the same shift in a less populous state would mean a mere three or four electoral votes. For example, a California resident's ballot for President helps to select forty-seven electors; a South Dakota resident's ballot helps to select only three. It is not surprising then that presidential candidates have come disproportionately from large states and that their campaigns tend to focus on groups and issues that are important in the larger states.

A second important consequence of the electoral college is the possibility of the election of a President with less than a majority vote. This can happen in several different ways. If one candidate barely wins in numerous populous states and is defeated overwhelmingly in smaller states, he or she can lose the popular vote but still receive an electoral college majority. This happened in 1888, when Grover Cleveland won the popular vote by 23,737 votes but lost in the electoral college to Benjamin Harrison. A popular majority can also be frustrated if there is no majority in the electoral college, the decision is made in the House, and the House selects a candidate who did not win the popular vote. This occurred in 1824, when the House chose John Quincy Adams over Andrew Jackson despite many more popular votes for Jackson. If more than two candidates are in the race, the other candidates might receive enough votes to deprive the electoral college winner of the popular majority. The elections of 1860, 1912, 1948, 1960, and 1968 saw presidents elected without a popular majority. That is, the combined votes of the losing candidates were more than 50 percent of the total votes cast. Finally, and most unlikely, electors pledged to the victorious candidate can refuse to honor their pledges. Although there have been several cases of "faithless electors" in recent years, no election outcome has been affected by this action.

These and other features of the electoral college have been severely criticized. At least four major changes have been suggested. The smallest departure from the present system would legally require electors to follow their instructions. Proponents of the **automatic plan,** as it is sometimes called, would also change House voting procedures in the case of a tie so as to make House voting proportional to state population (that is, larger states would have more votes than smaller states). A second proposal, the **district plan,** would divide each state into districts of one electoral vote each; the winner in each district would receive the vote. A variation is the **proportional plan**—a state's electoral vote would simply be divided according to the vote received by each candidate. Finally, the least complex reform is the **direct election plan,** in which the candidate with the most votes nationally would become President. Although each of these reforms has its merits and has received serious attention, none has come very close to adoption.

Despite what may appear to be major flaws, the electoral college does have its defenders. One defense focuses on the disasters that could occur in the system (for example, the House selecting the popular-vote loser). Such disasters, though possible, are highly unlikely and are not problems requiring immediate attention. More important, all electoral systems can, under special circumstances, produce disasters. For example, in a three-candidate race, the direct election plan would not guarantee that the eventual winner will be approved by a majority of citizens. A second defense of the electoral college challenges the idea that some citizens—citizens of large states or small states, for example—are over- or underrepresented. Such arguments are neither mathematically inevitable nor supported by evidence. Finally, the present arrangement has its advantages. In particular it discourages voter fraud by reducing the incentive to cheat, since it makes no difference whether a state is won by 5,000 or 50,000 votes. By contrast, in a straight popular election, there would be an incentive to cheat in every state. Also, the unit rule system helps to preserve a moderate, two-party system. Only the Democrats and Republicans are capable of mobilizing majorities in numerous states. If the electoral college were abolished, there might be a far greater incentive for groups appealing to small minorities to run presidential candidates in the hope of holding a balance of power in a deadlocked election.

Conclusions

It should be clear that the electoral system of the United States is not set up to achieve the easy translation of the public will into electoral outcomes. Such practices as staggered elections and calendar-determined elections prevent the public from acting comprehensively and when it wants to. Geographical representation and the winner-take-all system can produce distortions in the outcome. Allowing citizens only a single vote for or against a candidate also limits what the public can say in elections. Finally, it has been charged that the electoral college can allow minority rule and gives some well-placed groups an unfair advantage. Whether or not these are serious problems in need of correction is an issue we shall consider at the end of the chapter.

Check Your Understanding

1. What impact do staggered elections have on the political process?

2. What are the two features of the winner-take-all system?

3. What electoral mechanisms at the state and local levels permit voters to make choices directly on issues?

4. How does the electoral college work? What are two important consequences of the electoral college?

DOES THE ELECTORAL SYSTEM PROMOTE POLITICAL EQUALITY?

Elections are an important means of citizens' political influence. However, the mere existence of elections does not mean that all citizens have the same power over government. Depending on numerous election rules, some citizens and groups can have far greater influence than others. After all, elections have existed in the United States since its beginning, yet not every group has shared equally in political power. To determine whether all citizens are equal in the power of their vote, we shall examine (1) access to the ballot, (2) the administration of elections, and (3) the drawing of district lines.

Access to the Ballot
Historical Development
The right of all adults to vote has emerged slowly. In the colonial period the **suffrage,** or right to vote, was greatly restricted. Only white males owning property, usually land, could vote. Although land ownership was fairly common in most states, many white males still could not vote. Some states

added religious and moral restrictions as well. The Constitution did not alter things. The states, not the federal government, set voting qualifications (Article I, Section 2, defines the federal voting requirement as identical to the qualifications for voters in a state's most numerous legislative house). Only gradually did the suffrage expand, as personal property or payment of taxes was substituted for land or dropped altogether. Access to the ballot was most open in the newly admitted Western states.

The period following the Civil War saw a mixture of forward and backward steps in opening up the electoral process. The Fifteenth Amendment, adopted in 1870, gave black males twenty-one or older the right to vote. After a brief period of electoral participation by blacks in the South, this guarantee was rendered meaningless by the courts and state legislatures. In particular, three obstacles reduced voting by blacks: the **poll tax,** or fee paid for the right to vote; the **literacy test,** to see whether the prospective voters could read (sometimes they were required to interpret a law as well); and physical threats. A prospective black voter might have to use a large portion of his monthly income to pay off past poll taxes, interpret a law to the satisfaction of a hostile official, and worry about losing his job because of a desire to vote.

The flood of immigration that began in the 1840s drew a mixed response. In some areas immigrants were welcomed as a source of easily influenced votes; they were enrolled as voters soon after disembarking. In other areas, immigrants faced barriers such as the literacy test, lengthy residency requirements, and few polling places in their neighborhoods. Women were given the right to vote by Wyoming when it became a state in 1890. Several other states followed Wyoming's lead and finally, in 1920, the Nineteenth Amendment was adopted, giving women the right to vote in all elections.

Modern Developments
Since 1960, the access-to-the-ballot issue has focused mainly on two groups—those between eighteen and twenty-one years of age and blacks, especially Southern blacks. The age issue has been the

Biography: Susan B. Anthony

Susan B. Anthony did not live to see her life's work—the achievement of women's right to vote—become a reality. Without her, however, the cause would have lacked one of its most single-minded advocates. During Anthony's lifetime, the idea that women should be able to vote evolved in the eyes of the public from an outlandish notion to a worthy objective whose time would surely come. Abuse that had once been hurled at her gave way to admiration and affection.

Anthony was born in 1820 into a Quaker family. She received enough education as a young girl to qualify her for teaching, the only professional job then open to women. The inequities between women and men seemed unjust to her, and she soon turned her attention to reform: not only women's rights but also temperance and the abolition of slavery. She was one of several women to wear the trouser-and-tunic costume advocated by Amelia Bloomer in order to free women from the cumbersome skirts of the time. Like the others, she found herself the target of so many cruel jokes that she returned to more conventional clothing after a year. "The attention of my audience was fixed upon my clothes instead of my words," she later wrote. It was difficult enough trying to persuade hostile audiences of the rightness of her cause; if her attire were to provoke ridicule, the task would be that much harder.

When she was thirty, Anthony met Elizabeth Cady Stanton, a suffragist who had organized the first women's rights convention in the United States, in 1848. The two women formed a close working relationship that was to last the rest of their lives. Stanton, often tied down by the demands of a large family, was the better thinker and writer; Anthony, single and thus free to travel, was the better organizer.

In 1868, Anthony and Stanton founded the National Woman Suffrage Association. A year later other women formed a rival organization, the American Woman Suffrage Association (AWSA). Among doctrinal differences between the two groups was the interest of Anthony and Stanton in issues such as divorce and working conditions—an interest that AWSA leaders believed distracted the public's attention from the suffrage crusade. In 1890 the two groups finally merged, with Stanton and then Anthony at the helm.

Supporters of women's suffrage relied on many methods—which included petitions, pamphlets, periodicals, and lectures—in an effort to persuade both Congress and the state legislatures to give women the right to vote. Suffragists turned to the courts, too. In the 1872 presidential election, Anthony took advantage of startled election officials by casting a ballot before they realized what she was doing. She was arrested and brought to trial. The federal judge ordered a guilty verdict, which the jury delivered. Anthony, fined $100, vowed never to pay, and held to her vow. Unfortunately, because no efforts were made to collect the fine, she could not take the case to the Supreme Court.

The first successes of the suffragists were in the West; a landmark was the adoption of women's suffrage by the Wyoming Territory in 1870. Eight years later a constitutional amendment was introduced in Congress; in language similar to that of the Fifteenth Amendment, the new proposal went a long way in extending the right to vote to all adult Americans. The measure was reintroduced in every session thereafter until the Nineteenth Amendment was finally ratified, in 1920. Anthony had died fourteen years earlier, after delivering a final message to her followers: "Failure is impossible."

simpler in its formation and resolution. Only occasionally did the twenty-one-year minimum become a serious political issue (some states, however, allowed eighteen-year-olds to vote). In 1970 Congress, perhaps in response to arguments that eighteen-year-olds were being sent to Vietnam but not allowed to vote, set eighteen as the age for all federal and state elections. However, the Supreme Court in *Oregon v. Mitchell* restricted the law to federal elections. The Twenty-sixth Amendment, adopted in 1971, overcame this distinction and set the minimum voting age at eighteen for all national and state elections.

Gaining access to the vote has been much more difficult for blacks. Numerous obstacles stood in their way: economic dependency in many areas, histories of intimidation, white fears of black rule, openly hostile election officials, and numerous legal barriers. The first major attempt to remove these obstacles was the Voting Rights Act of 1965. It forbids the use of restrictions—such as literacy tests, educational achievement, moral character, or testimony of qualification by other registered voters—to deny the right to vote on the basis of race or color. The act was enforced in states or portions of a state where less than 50 percent of the population had registered or voted in the 1964 presidential election. An important provision was the appointment of federal examiners to inspect voting records and procedures. Also, the U.S. attorney general was given powers to intervene on behalf of a person denied the right to vote, and anyone preventing citizens from voting was subject to federal criminal charges. In 1970, 1975, and 1982 the Voting Rights Act was extended and enforcement provisions were strengthened. Among other things, the literacy test was suspended in all states, and other groups, such as Hispanics and Indians, were now covered by the act.

The act has had a dramatic impact. Within the first three years of its passage, some 150,000 blacks (and 7,000 whites) were enrolled by federal examiners to vote in five Southern states. In Mississippi, the proportion of blacks registered to vote jumped from 6.7 percent in 1965 to 59.8 percent in 1967. Overall, in the ten states of the South, black registration jumped from 35.5 to 57.2 percent follow-

Women in Boston exercise their newly won right to vote. Constitutional amendments and a variety of federal laws have enabled blacks, women, residents of Washington, D.C., and eighteen-year-olds to vote.

ing this law. Perhaps in response to this change, the proportion of whites also increased, though not as dramatically.

Some citizens, however, remain legally barred from voting. In forty-seven states, prison inmates, people convicted of a felony, and former prisoners cannot vote. One or more states also exclude paupers, those with dishonorable military discharges, the legally insane, and people who violate election law, among others. On the whole, though, it is probably fair to conclude that almost all U.S. citizens over eighteen today have access to the ballot.

The Administration of Elections

Elections do not happen on their own. Arranging an election involves several important administrative tasks. Facilities for voting must be established

Before the passage of the landmark Voting Rights Act of 1965, blacks, especially in the South, were often barred from registering and voting. Methods used to block their political participation included literacy tests and threats of harassment. In 1966, blacks in rural Alabama voted in large numbers for the first time in history. The polling place shown here is a local store. At left, a young man takes part in an outdoor voter registration drive.

and staffed, rules must be made regarding who can get on the ballot, and steps have to be taken to minimize vote fraud.

One important administrative requirement is that voters must register before they can vote. The **registration,** or enrollment, rule developed out of widespread fraudulent practices in the nineteenth century. Votes were cast on behalf of dead people

or by people with false names or with no fixed address. To eliminate such abuses, prospective voters must enroll in advance so that their address and qualifications can be checked; people cannot suddenly appear at the polling place on election day and expect to be allowed to vote.

The precise operation of registration can vary considerably. The time period between registration and the election, whether voters must register before each election, the effort spent to register voters, and the ease of actually registering can be important details. In 1984 five states—Maine, Minnesota, North Dakota, Oregon, and Wisconsin—allowed registration on election day (November 6). At the other extreme, such states as Alabama, Arizona, and New Mexico required registration at least six weeks before the 1984 presidential election. Some states make registration optional at the county or local level.

The administrative details associated with registration can have a significant impact on voter turnout. A 1972 study reported that the existence of registration reduced people's likelihood of voting by between 3.3 percent and 8.7 percent, depending on how motivated they were to vote.[2] The length of the period between the end of registration and the election also had a sizable impact on a person's likelihood of voting, the study found. Other practices lowering turnout included irregular hours for registering, closing registration offices on evenings and Saturdays, and not allowing any form of absentee registration (see under "absentee ballot" below). This study concluded that if in all states registration had been allowed up until the election, registration offices had had longer hours and had been open evenings and Saturdays, and

Commentary: Government Employees as Second-Class Citizens

The most recent battles over the right to participate politically have focused on women, minorities, and those between eighteen and twenty-one. Legal barriers against these groups no longer exist. There is, however, one group of people who still have legal limits on their political activity—federal employees. The Hatch Act, passed in 1939, prohibits federal employees from participating in partisan elections. The act's original purpose was to prevent government workers from being forced into "voluntary" campaign work. The law covers almost all executive branch employees (including postal workers) and employees of the District of Columbia, as well as state and local government employees in programs receiving federal funds. Exceptions are employees paid by the office of the President, department heads and assistant department heads, and presidential appointees.

The Hatch Act prohibits covered employees from (1) running for national or state office, (2) running for local office under a party label, (3) campaigning for or against a political party and candidate, and (4) being involved in party affairs—organizing groups, making financial or time contributions, addressing meetings, and so on. Penalty for violations is suspension or removal from government employment.

In actual practice the Hatch Act has produced complex problems. For instance, what happens when federal employees constitute a large portion of a community (as in Washington, D.C., and several surrounding cities)? Rigid enforcement of the act could interfere with the political process in such areas. The Office of Personnel Management can exempt individual employees from some restrictions. One federal employee asked for permission to write a letter to a newspaper editor on a partisan issue. Permission was granted, but the letter could not be part of a concerted effort (in other words, the limit was one letter to one newspaper). Another case involved a pig roast. When a federal employee in the Southwest asked if he could roast a pig for a political fundraiser, he was told no because he had not established this activity as a regular part-time business. Problems also occur when government workers associate with political groups that endorse party candidates. Does such involvement constitute "partisan involvement"?

Numerous attempts—thirty-three since 1975—have been made to amend the Hatch Act. Obviously, federal employees are second-class citizens politically, even though the original purpose of the act was to protect them.

At a food stamp distribution center, left, members of a volunteer organization help visitors register to vote. By providing an opportunity to register at a convenient time and place, the group hopes to encourage participation in political activity among citizens who may be poorly informed about voting procedures. At right, citizens turn out at their local voter registration office.

absentee registration had been permitted, turnout in 1972 would have increased approximately 9.1 percent. Increases would have been largest among Southerners, blacks, the poorly educated, the poor, and the young.

Another important aspect of election administration is the residency requirement, a rule intended to prevent people from switching election districts at the last moment in order to influence the outcome. Its defenders also argue that voters should be familiar with local conditions. Until recently many states had lengthy residency requirements—in some states during the 1960s, in order to vote in a state election, a person had to have lived there one year; in a county, six months; and in a locality, thirty days. Given the mobility of the American population, this requirement no doubt prevented many from voting.

A major change occured when the Voting Rights Act of 1970 made thirty days the maximum state residency for presidential elections. In 1972, in the case of *Dunn v. Blumstein*, the Supreme Court ruled that lengthy state and local residency requirements violated the constitutionally protected rights to vote and to travel. Subsequent court decisions established a fifty-day residency requirement as the acceptable maximum.

Although the residency requirement generally is no longer a factor in access to the ballot, it still can be important sometimes. For many people— college students, military personnel, migrant workers, and the institutionalized—there is a difference between "home" and where they happen to be on election day. The decision on what constitutes a person's legal residence can make a difference in localities where there are tens of thousands of college students or a large military base.

Another administrative issue that deserves mention is the handling of **absentee ballots**—ballots cast by individuals who will be unable to come to the polling place on election day. Typically, an individual requests an absentee ballot; thirty days (sometimes less) before the election the ballot is mailed out; and for the vote to count, the returned ballot must be received on or before election day. (Registration can also be done by mail for those unable to register in person.) The issue of the absentee ballot is not a trivial one. Many individuals travel frequently on their jobs; others might be on vacation at election time; and some might be in jail awaiting trial. In addition, there are between four and five million eligible citizens living abroad who must vote by absentee ballot. Finally, absentee ballots allow the ill or physically disabled to vote. Absentee ballots can sometimes make a difference in who wins. In the 1982 race for the governorship of California, for example, when the regularly cast votes were totaled, Democrat Tom Bradley won, but when the absentee ballots were added, Republican George Deukmejian was the victor.

In general, state election laws do not encourage absentee voting. Most states give absentee voters only a month or less to receive and return their ballots. This can pose obstacles to voting when foreign mail services are involved or military personnel are stationed in remote areas or on ships. State and federal notarization requirements are another serious obstacle. A special form must be notarized, or signed by an official, before one registers or votes. For an American living abroad this could mean as many as four separate trips to the U.S. embassy or consulate to get a form notarized. It is no wonder, then, that turnout among citizens abroad tends to be much lower than among Americans in the United States.

Another legal detail that can be important is whether prospective voters are permitted time off from work in order to vote. Because U.S. elections are held on a working day rather than on a weekend and polls are rarely open after about 9 P.M., many citizens have to schedule their voting around their work time (especially factory and office workers on an hourly wage). In 1984, only thirty states legally allowed workers time off to vote. In twenty of these, the employer may not withhold wages for time taken to vote. Thus, for many prospective voters the decision to cast a ballot can mean loss of wages and even can jeopardize job security.

Finally, even the apparently simple decision on how to arrange candidates' names on the ballot can have consequences. According to one study of election returns in Michigan, where ballot order is systematically varied, the name that appears first always receives extra votes. When the voter sees a long list of candidates, the first few and the last name seem to receive "bonus votes."[3]

Thus the rules on registration, residency, absentee ballots, time off to vote, and the like are not simply administrative details. Rarely are they the subject of great political controversy, and yet they are important in view of the role elections play in a democracy. For many years in the South, manipulation of administrative rules was a major way blacks and some poor whites could be shut out of the electoral process. No matter how fairly it was administered, a system that had few election officials, that limited hours of registering, and that had highly complex absentee ballot requirements

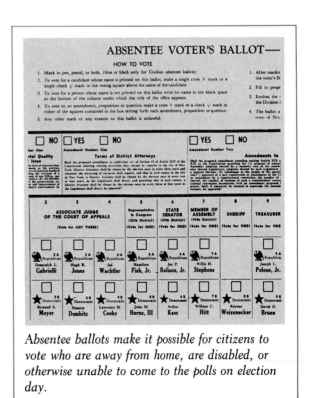

Absentee ballots make it possible for citizens to vote who are away from home, are disabled, or otherwise unable to come to the polls on election day.

was biased against those with modest motivation and little if any experience in dealing with bureaucracy. In the 1980s many leaders intent on registering black voters have discovered the importance of administrative details (for example, whether registration can be done by mail rather than in person, whether registration officials can be self-appointed volunteers, what types of identification are required, and so on). These rules can determine whether tens of thousands of citizens will be able to vote.

The Drawing of District Lines

As noted earlier, elections are organized around geographically defined districts. The precise way in which these district lines are drawn can have a major impact on political power. Consider the hypothetical situation shown in Figure 5.2. In all three plans we have a central city surrounded by rural areas. In plan A the sparsely populated rural areas are divided into eight districts, with one legislator per district, and the central city, which has one quarter of the state's population, gets one legislator. In plan B the state is divided into four districts of equal population, but the urban population is divided up among the four rural-dominated districts. In plan C, the city gets its own legislator, the three rural areas get three (one each), and the districts are of equal population.

Because of the importance of the way district lines are drawn, districting decisions have generated intense controversy. Until the 1960s, states had almost complete freedom in setting up districts for national, state, and local elections. This frequently resulted in gross inequalities. Most commonly, rural areas were overrepresented in state legislatures at the expense of large cities (as in plan A in Figure 5.2). Another common situation, labeled **gerrymandering,** involves the drawing of district lines to give one political interest an advantage over another. For example, if Democrats wanted to dilute the power of Republicans, they might create district lines that excluded certain neighborhoods or zigzagged around neighborhood streets; the district might even be composed of disconnected islands of people. District boundaries were often manipulated to ensure safe seats for many officeholders.

The freedom to draw election districts began to be limited in 1962. The Supreme Court, in *Baker v. Carr*, ruled that inequalities in the size of voting districts could be addressed by the federal courts. A number of important decisions soon followed. In *Gray v. Sanders* (1963), the Court held that a Georgia system of considering counties of unequal population as equal voting units was unconstitutional. (Under the county unit system, Atlanta and a much smaller rural county each "cast" a single vote—regardless of the vote tallies in each—in the

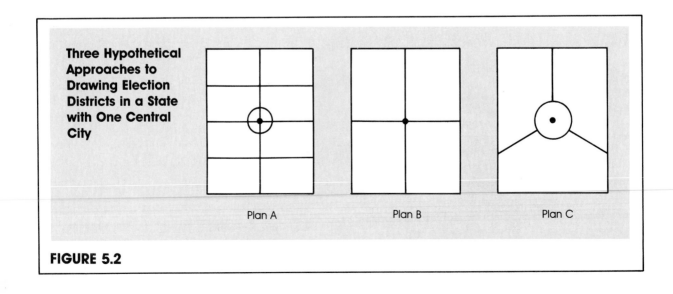

Three Hypothetical Approaches to Drawing Election Districts in a State with One Central City

Plan A   Plan B   Plan C

FIGURE 5.2

primary for state-level offices. Thus, two small rural counties could outvote much-more-populous Atlanta.) In *Reynolds v. Sims* (1964) the Court established the rule of "one person, one vote" and ordered that lawmakers in both houses of all state legislatures must represent districts of equal population. The same principle was applied to congressional districts in *Wesberry v. Sanders* (1964).

These cases proclaiming the rule of "one person, one vote" do not, however, ensure political equality of all citizens. Several problems remain. One such problem is the meaning of "equal." Must two congressional districts in a state be exactly equal in population? The Supreme Court has imposed strict standards on congressional district size but has accepted significant differences in state legislative districts (as much as 16.4 percent in the case of a Virginia legislative district, on the grounds that such variation was necessary to maintain traditional boundaries).

Another set of problems concerns the creation of districts to provide adequate representation for different political interests. This issue has emerged frequently in the context of Democratic and Republican representation in state legislatures and Congress. If, for example, citizens of a state are evenly divided along party lines, should districts be drawn to ensure that representation in the state legislature will reflect this proportion? It is entirely possible that modest changes in district lines, without violating the one person, one vote rule, can have a major impact on a party's success. Consider an example in Michigan. Suppose a district is drawn that would guarantee overwhelming Democratic victories in Detroit (a heavily Democratic area). At the same time, many other districts would contain strong but not overwhelming Republican majorities. This set-up would greatly benefit the Republicans. Under the circumstances, the Republicans could win a strong majority in the state legislature while winning only a bare majority of the overall popular vote. The Supreme Court has said that sometimes the need to represent certain interests fairly may require a small departure from "one person, one vote" (*Gaffney v. Cummings*, 1973).

An even more complex set of district boundary issues is associated with the representation of black interests. The 1965 Voting Rights Act, as amended, requires several states, and areas within other states, to receive Department of Justice approval before election districts (and other election laws) can be changed. This rule was to prevent white-dominated legislatures from weakening the power of black voters by gerrymandering districts. Recently, however, the thrust of the Justice Department's concern has gone from preventing white manipulation to promoting the election of blacks. In particular, the Justice Department has encouraged the creaton of districts that are about 65 percent black, in the hope that such districts would elect blacks. The Supreme Court has even permitted some black districts to be significantly smaller than largely white districts in the state (*United Jewish Organization of Williamsburg v. Carey*, 1977). According to one study of this practice in the South, the creation of heavily black districts has helped black candidates, although this provides no guarantee that a black will be elected.[4]

A related point is whether an election system is at-large or district-based. As described earlier, in an at-large election an entire city, county, or state selects a number of representatives. Voters choose several candidates, and a certain number of top vote-getters are elected. In a district system, in contrast, only a single candidate is elected. Several studies suggest that the use of an at-large system hinders blacks from gaining political office.[5] This seems especially true when the black population is greater than 10 percent but less than 50 percent of the population. A corollary of this electoral underrepresentation in an at-large system is an absence of programs to assist blacks and the poor in general.

To see how this can occur, imagine a city of 100,000 voters with a black voting population of 20,000 clustered in one neighborhood. Voters are allowed to cast five votes, and the top five finishers are elected to the city council. If voting is strictly according to race, the black candidates will receive 20,000 votes. Because the top five white candidates will likely receive more than 20,000 votes each, no black will be elected. If, however, the city were divided into five districts, it is very likely that blacks will dominate at least one district and a black will be elected.

Thus, use of at-large elections to dilute the power of blacks and other minority voters is illegal under the 1965 Voting Rights Act, as amended. But it is not easy to determine whether the mere existence of an at-large system is the clear culprit when blacks are underrepresented. After all, other factors—divisions among blacks, weak leadership, and so on—can produce the same result. In the case of *City of Mobile v. Bolden* (1980), the Supreme Court attempted to address this issue. The case involved the city of Mobile, Alabama; in its at-large system, blacks were unable to translate their votes into electoral victories for black candidates. The Court invalidated the system as a violation of the Voting Rights Act. It also said that for other, similar systems to be invalid, there must be evidence of discriminatory intent. In other words, unequal electoral outcome in and of itself did not invalidate an at-large system. However, the 1982 extension of the Voting Rights Act outlawed district plans and election laws whose consequences are discriminatory, even if there is no intent to discriminate. Thus far, in a case involving congressional district lines in Mississippi, the Court has accepted the principle that discrimination can be shown by results as well as by intent.

There is one final aspect of the one person, one vote principle. The existence of states as the election districts for Congress creates major violations of this principle. The Constitution guarantees each state two senators regardless of population. This means that California, with a 1980 population of 23,667,902 had one senator per 11.8 million citizens. Alaska, with a population of 401,850, had one senator per 200,000 citizens. It is mathematically possible for senators representing only a minority of citizens to defeat the will of senators representing a majority.

A similar, though less severe, violation of the one person, one vote principle occurs in House districts. It sometimes happens that whereas districts within a state are of equal population, significant variations exist in district size from state to state. For example, Nevada had a 1980 population of 800,493; thus each of its two members of Congress represented about 400,000 people. In contrast, representatives from New York State typically have districts of about 515,000 people. In California, congressional districts run around 525,000.

Conclusions

We return to our original question of whether the present electoral system promotes political equality. Compared to what existed one hundred or even fifty years ago, the system is accessible and inequalities produced by gerrymandering are relatively minor. Government-imposed barriers to the ballot—the outright exclusion of women and blacks, the poll tax, the literacy test, and lengthy residency requirements—no longer exist. Registration might continue to discourage some potential voters, but this barrier is hardly in the same league with, say, a literacy test. The one person, one vote principle has eliminated some of the most blatant exclusions from power of minorities and other groups.

It remains clear, however, that we have not achieved perfect equality. Some people (for example, well-motivated citizens who are not easily put off by bureaucratic delays) and some interests still have an advantage. Inequities exist in the requirement that each state have two senators and in the differences among states in the population size of congressional districts. It is clear that perfect equality in electoral politics might not be desirable. Allowing people with severe mental handicaps to vote probably serves no useful purpose. Laws, such as registration requirements, are necessary to prevent fraud, but such laws may also discourage prospective voters with little motivation. Finally, the principle of one person, one vote might be an abstract ideal, but the need to give some interests adequate representation might require some gerrymandering and unequal district size. In short, perfect access and districts with identical numbers of voters can conflict with other, perhaps equally important values.

THE POLITICS OF THE ELECTORAL SYSTEM

The description given here of how elections are organized in the United States might disturb some readers. Particularly for those who think that elections should be a neutral mechanism for translating citizens' desires into public policy, such features as staggered elections, unrepresented minorities, and unequal weighting of votes are serious flaws. Indeed, many sophisticated analysts who share this opinion have proposed ways to remedy these supposed defects.

The question now becomes this: Is the system of elections—regardless of the outcome of specific contests—so seriously flawed that it requires a drastic overhaul? Rather than discuss each possible defect separately, let us offer two general defenses of the existing system. The first concerns citizen satisfaction with the existing electoral procedures, and the second emphasizes the purpose of elections.

The first defense of the electoral system is that most citizens are basically content with the present arrangements, or at least they can think of no better alternative. Certainly, few people strongly believe that the system is perfect. If we review both the changes that have been made and the proposals for reform that have been put forward, it is clear that there is no widespread support for fundamental revision. Electoral reform efforts rarely are aimed at changing the basic structures. Successful reforms have focused on such issues as broadening the suffrage to include blacks and women and restructuring campaign financing, not on the timing of national elections or the underrepresentation of geographically divided minorities. Perhaps the last great successful reform that altered the structure of the electoral system was the establishment of direct election of senators in 1913. Advocates of more extreme proposals—for example, proportional representation—have had a hard time finding a friendly audience. In short, our system may not be perfect, but it is generally what most of us want.

A second, and much more sophisticated, defense of the electoral system begins with a question: "What is an electoral system supposed to accomplish?" If the answer is, "To produce a government *that accurately mirrors public sentiment*," then indeed the existing system is highly flawed. This answer would not, however, be given by those who designed the system. The drafters of the Constitution were not interested in increasing popular influence in government. Essentially, the electoral system was originally designed to accomplish two goals:

1. Allow citizens to choose public officials.
2. Prevent the emergence of a tyrannical faction, whether a majority or a minority.

The first goal is comparatively simple to accomplish: you merely hold elections. The second goal requires considerable ingenuity to meet. As James Madison makes clear in *Federalist No. 10* (see Chapter 2), the possibility that a majority faction would take power, bringing with it tyranny, is a problem when leaders are directly elected. If the American electoral system is viewed as a solution to this problem—to prevent a single faction from dominating government—many of its "faults" become virtues. Staggered elections, fixed terms of office, and highly varied election districts become obstacles to potential tyrants, *not* impediments to citizen rule. American elections are constitutionally *designed* so that public opinion is not immediately and automatically converted into electoral votes.

Thus our evaluation of the electoral system depends on what we think the electoral system is intended to accomplish. Should it act as a direct channel for citizen preferences? Or should it enable citizens to participate in leadership selection but not allow a single faction to gain control? If we want extensive political change and are convinced that the people are behind us, the existing electoral system is clearly a hindrance. If, however, we are satisfied with the status quo and fear sudden and drastic shifts, the present system is to be preferred. It is not a question of what type of electoral system is inherently "good," but of what political values we wish to pursue.

CHAPTER SUMMARY

Why have elections? Elections are not the only way of choosing leaders, but in the United States they serve several important functions—to allow citizens to remove objectionable leaders, help shape the direction of government policy, help legitimize the transfer of political power, channel political participation into "safe" activities, and promote political solidarity. Elections have been criticized for providing only the illusion of citizen power and for discouraging qualified people from seeking public office. There are also many alternatives to elections. Nations have used the principle of hereditary transfer of power; in the United States we choose some leaders on the basis of examinations or by appointment. Among states there are variations as to which offices are elective and which are filled by appointment.

How are American elections organized? Basically, elections are organized in ways that determine how votes are translated into outcomes. Staggered elections and calendar-determined elections frequently make it difficult for citizens to change leaders immediately. The winner-take-all principle and the geographical basis for determining election districts are important features of the electoral system. On the national level, citizens must choose leaders rather than policies. Voters are also limited to an "accept" or "reject" alternative. Finally, the electoral college makes some votes more important than others and has allowed Presidents to be elected without a popular majority.

Does the electoral system promote political equality? Historically, the right to vote has been greatly restricted. With few exceptions, citizens today are free to vote, although such requirements as registration and residency might discourage some. The courts have vigorously implemented the one person, one vote rule, but exceptions can and do occur. Some of the exceptions are built in (for example, two Senate seats per state) and others are deliberate (for example, government encouragement of the election of blacks).

IMPORTANT TERMS

Explain the following terms.

staggered election	runoff election
at-large election	referendum
winner take all	electoral college
plurality	suffrage
proportional representation	

THINKING CRITICALLY

1. Should candidates be held legally accountable for promises they make during election campaigns? Why or why not?
2. Many top officials in the national government are appointed rather than elected. Would it be wise to elect people who occupy these key positions, such as the Attorney General or the Chief Justice of the Supreme Court? Explain your answer.

3. How would our government system be different if we did not have staggered elections?
4. What would be the advantages and disadvantages of having elections when the majority decides they are needed, rather than on a constitutionally determined date?
5. Because the winner-take-all system permits candidates to win with less than a majority of votes, is this system of election inconsistent with majority rule? Explain your answer.
6. What might be the effect of having initiatives and referendums on the national level?
7. Should voter registration be banned on the grounds that it discriminates against poor, less educated citizens? Defend your answer.
8. What might happen if no exceptions were permitted to the court-implemented "one person, one vote" principle?

EXTENDING YOUR UNDERSTANDING

1. Make a list of what you consider to be the key political issues in your community. Find out what your congressional representative's attitude is on these issues. Compare your views with the position your representative has taken on the issues.
2. There is a long history of attempts to reform the electoral college. Research these reform movements and describe (a) what the reform was; (b) who supported it; and (c) why it failed. Prepare a statement outlining your own plan for reform.
3. The Voting Rights Act of 1965 has had a significant impact on black voting. Research this act and prepare a report that considers the following: (a) What are the major points of the act? (b) What pressures brought about this legislation? (c) Has the act worked as intended? Discuss your answers in a report.
4. Locate a map of your city or community that shows the election district boundaries. Do there seem to be any irregularities in the way these districts are divided? What might account for these irregularities? Contact the local election board to try to find out why election districts are divided as they are.

MAKING DECISIONS

Use back issues of newspapers and magazines to examine a recent state or local election as to how the candidates differed on key political issues. Based on the candidates' stands on these issues, for whom would you vote? What are the reasons for your choice?

Chapter 6

Voters, Campaigns, and the Mass Media

Elections are among the most publicized and well-studied subjects in American politics. Libraries are full of books on successful campaigns and manuals on running for office. A multitude of consultants stand ready to provide expert advice. Nevertheless, elections have an element of mystery. Events during a campaign are frequently understood only after all the votes have been counted. Although the election returns may have been carefully analyzed, considerable debate can still occur over why one candidate defeated another. The meaning of particular elections and the election process in general is also widely discussed. Some people think of elections as circuslike rituals that decide little. Others view elections as a great revelation of the people's will. Finally, election procedures have undergone many changes over the years. Numerous campaign reform laws have recently been enacted, and suggestions for additional changes are frequently made. This chapter examines four questions dealing with these issues:

- Who participates in elections?
- What determines how people vote?
- Are campaigns conducted fairly?
- Do the mass media exercise too much power?

PREVIEW

Who participates in elections? Many citizens do not regularly vote or otherwise take part in elections. Whites, the well-off, the middle-aged, and the employed tend to vote more regularly than other citizens. Legal factors, especially registration, deter some people. Other citizens choose not to vote for social and psychological reasons. The nature of our political system also encourages apathy. To some, apathy represents a threat to democracy; others see nonvoters as an untapped resource for the Democratic party. Neither, however, may be correct.

What determines how people vote? Voting is a complex act, and no one explanation holds for all people under all conditions. One possible factor is party identification. Early in life, citizens acquire loyalty to a party; this loyalty shapes perceptions; and these perceptions are translated into votes. The concept of issue voting, on the other hand, stresses that people choose candidates who come closest to their own issue positions. Citizens often do not know where candidates stand on a particular issue, however, or may misinterpret a candidate's political philosophy. Some issue voting occurs, especially what is called "retrospective" voting. Issue voting can also play a role when traits such as leadership and integrity are looked at. The group explanation accounts for voting in terms of group identities. All three explanations have their advantages and drawbacks.

Are campaigns conducted fairly? Two issues relating to fairness in contemporary campaigns are money and the packaging of candidates. Today's campaigns are expensive in large part because of the emergence of a "new politics" that makes use of the mass media and paid advisors rather than political parties. Incumbents—officials running for reelection—raise and spend more than challengers, but money itself is no guarantee of success. Although reforms have eliminated some abuses, money remains important—money is generally given to candidates whom people agree with, and access to officeholders is more important than outright favors. The merchandising of candidates is common. There are, however, major limits on what such techniques can accomplish.

Do the mass media exercise too much power? The mass media are a widespread and well-regarded force in society and politics. For many citizens, it is the mass media that interpret complex events. These events are often presented from a particular point of view. Overall, the mass media cannot sway huge numbers of voters. Nevertheless, the media can help reinforce preferences and mobilize supporters to vote. There are also major limits on the mass media: they are diverse, many people have access to them, and citizens have minds of their own. The media are powerful, but they do not dominate politics.

WHO PARTICIPATES IN ELECTIONS?

As we saw in Chapter 5, the right to vote has not come easily for many groups. Today, however, almost all U.S. citizens 18 years and over have this right. Nevertheless, despite all the efforts to guarantee this right, many Americans choose not to use it. Figure 6.1 shows the turnout in congressional and presidential elections for the last several years. Presidential elections usually draw the largest turnout. Even then, over 40 percent of those eligible in 1976, 1980, and 1984 chose not to participate. At the congressional level, turnout is usually below 50 percent. (Turnout for state-level offices is also often less than 50 percent.) These figures stand in sharp contrast to participation levels in many other Western democracies. In Italy, Sweden, and the Netherlands, for example, over 85 percent of the population regularly votes in national elections.

When we move beyond voting and examine other types of election-related activities, widespread apathy is even more common. After the 1980 presidential election, the Center for Political Studies at the University of Michigan asked citizens about their campaign activity. Only 36 percent said that they had tried to convince someone else how to vote. A mere 7.5 percent had attended a political meeting, fundraiser, rally, or other such event. And no more than 6.7 percent of the sample had even worn a campaign button or put a bumper sticker on a car.

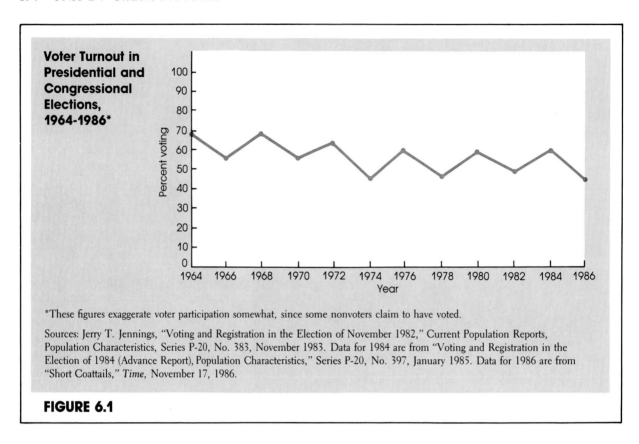

Voter Turnout in Presidential and Congressional Elections, 1964-1986*

*These figures exaggerate voter participation somewhat, since some nonvoters claim to have voted.

Sources: Jerry T. Jennings, "Voting and Registration in the Election of November 1982," Current Population Reports, Population Characteristics, Series P-20, No. 383, November 1983. Data for 1984 are from "Voting and Registration in the Election of 1984 (Advance Report), Population Characteristics," Series P-20, No. 397, January 1985. Data for 1986 are from "Short Coattails," *Time*, November 17, 1986.

FIGURE 6.1

Differences in Participation Rates

It is important to understand that nonvoters are not evenly distributed among the population. Those who drafted the Constitution feared that the less well-off would flock to politics in order to redress inequalities. In fact, just the opposite occurs. In general, the more social and economic advantages a person has, the more likely he or she is to vote. In 1980, for example, whites had a 10 percent higher turnout rate than blacks. The voting rate of whites was double that of Hispanics (60.9 percent versus 29.9 percent). White-collar and professional workers were also much more likely to vote than blue-collar workers. Surprisingly, in view of the attention given to the unemployment issue in 1980, working people were much more likely to vote than those without a job—61.8 percent versus 41.2 percent. This pattern pretty much persisted in the 1984 presidential election, despite highly publicized efforts to register more blacks and Hispanics. Again, blacks and

Hispanics trailed whites in voting. The turnout for whites was 61.4 percent, for blacks 55.8 percent, and 32.6 percent for those of Hispanic origin.

Two characteristics that are closely tied to voter participation are age and education. Despite the image created in the 1960s and 1970s of politically active young people, the under-twenties are the most apathetic age group in the population. Only a little more than a third of this group voted in 1980 (35.7 percent), compared to nearly 70 percent of those between forty-five and sixty-four. In 1984, 40.8 percent of those between eighteen and twenty-four voted. Education also makes a large difference. Turnout among college graduates in 1980 was nearly double that of people who had completed eight years or less of schooling (79.9 percent versus 42.6 percent). Factors that were once important but no longer seem to make a difference are sex and population density. Men and women vote at just about the same levels, as do people in cities, towns, and rural areas.

Rather than using a well-known curtained voting booth, a number of states are trying new types of voting machines that record votes more quickly and, generally, reduce the chance of error or breakdown.

Reasons for Apathy

The relatively low levels of voter turnout, especially in contrast to voting rates in other Western democracies, has been the object of great concern. There is no one explanation of why tens of millions of Americans choose not to vote despite the importance of elections and the publicity given to campaigns. Let us examine three reasons for much of this apathy: legal restrictions, social and psychological factors, and political considerations.

Legal Restrictions

As we noted in Chapter 5, nearly all states, counties, and cities have some administrative barriers to voting. The most important of these are registration requirements. Typically, a prospective voter must go to the local registration office at least thirty days before the election and show proof of residency or other voting requirement. The burden of registering is on the prospective voter, although organizations such as unions and civil rights groups often conduct registration drives. In Great Britain and Canada, by contrast, the government actively seeks to register citizens with house-to-house visiting (enumeration). As a result, participation rates are higher in those nations. U.S. citizens usually remain registered unless they move or fail to vote over a period of several years (the time period varies from state to state).

According to a Gallup poll conducted just after the 1984 election, 31 percent of those who did not vote gave "not registered" as the reason. Compared to the poll tax and the literacy test, registration is a modest barrier to voting. For people with only a slight interest in the election or who dislike

Until the 1960s, blacks in the rural South were often prevented from voting. Their political powerlessness, in turn, contributed to the cycle of poverty and lack of education.

any contact with government bureaucracy, however, even registration is a high hurdle to overcome. In some localities the hurdle is made even greater because registration facilities are closed on evenings and Saturdays, and registration ends a month or more before the election. In those states where citizens can register on the day of the election—Minnesota, Wisconsin, Maine, and Oregon—voting levels are higher than in the rest of the nation. Registration is also made more difficult if it must be done in person rather than by mail. The elderly, those with disabilities, and those who travel a lot may find the bother of going to register and then waiting in line too much of an effort. In general, a reduction in registration requirements would provide a modest boost in voting among those groups that presently vote the least—blacks, the poor, young people, and those with little education.

The importance of registration is made clear if we examine voting rates among people who have registered. Overall, in 1984, 87.7 percent of those who were registered actually voted. Voting is generally low among young people and those with little education. However, if young people and the poorly educated are registered, almost all of them will go to the polls on election day. According to one study of voting in 1980, 86 percent of *registered* eighteen- to twenty-four-year olds voted (in 1984 this figure was 79.4 percent), 79 percent of those with less than eight years of schooling voted *if they were registered*. In other words, the problem of nonvoting is really a problem of nonregistration.[1]

Social and Psychological Factors

Studies of who does and who does not vote suggest that people who are interested in and concerned about politics are more likely to vote. A sense of civic obligation—"I should vote because it is part of being a good citizen"—also serves as a motivation. Those with a strong party attachment are also more likely to vote, as are people with a preference for a particular candidate.

One of the most important psychological factors in electoral participation is a person's **sense of political efficacy**—the feeling that one can influence political events. People with a low sense of political efficacy see politics as beyond their control; they consider themselves to be the objects of political events and processes. Feelings of political control or of powerlessness often are related to early family experiences and socioeconomic status. People with a strong sense of political efficacy are more active in both campaigning and in voting.

Apathy is another response to one's social and personal environment. Sometimes too strong an interest in politics can disrupt families, friendships, and on-the-job relationships. A conservative who is surrounded at home and at work by liberals may choose political indifference as a way of reducing conflict. A business person who became politically active might alienate customers.

Other people simply find political activity uninteresting or socially unrewarding.

Political Factors

The way elections are organized, the types of candidates who run, the consequences of elections, and other political factors all may have a bearing on participation levels. Consider how the present operation of the electoral college can discourage voting for President (see Chapter 5). Under the winner-take-all system, the losing candidate in a state receives no electoral votes. Thus, if it is almost certain who the winner in a state will be, it makes little sense for the loser's supporters to vote. Voter discouragement is a general feature of our winner-take-all electoral system. This is especially true in elections for state and local legislative seats. For example, a Democrat in an overwhelmingly Republican district has little reason to vote, since his or her vote will not affect the outcome. If we had a system of *proportional representation*, in which each vote counted for something even if it did not contribute to a majority, voting levels would probably be higher. (See Chapter 5 for a more complete analysis of proportional representation.)

It is also true that our political system generally limits the consequences of elections. Several features of our system of government make it difficult to bring about instant, major changes through elections. Among the most important reasons are the separation-of-powers principle in the Constitution, and staggered elections and calendar-determined elections. Thus, for instance, a victorious presidential candidate must still overcome potential opposition in Congress and in the courts. This built-in resistance to change lowers the stakes of each election. Even a conservative victory over a liberal (or vice versa) is unlikely to produce large, systematic changes. These lowered stakes, in turn, reduce the incentive to vote. Why bother to vote if the outcome will have a limited impact?

The importance of an election's impact on participation can be seen if we examine the voting behavior of government workers. For many government employees, a clear relationship exists between who wins and whether they will keep their jobs. In some states and localities, a government employee's job is on the line at election time. At the national level, where most jobs are protected by civil service regulations, employees cannot generally be fired for political reasons. However, electoral outcomes can affect pay increases, the creation of new programs, and other personnel matters. In 1980, 77 percent of those working for governments at all levels voted, compared to 59.2 percent of the population in general. Moreover, a concern for their livelihood seems to be the greatest among government workers with the least education. Local government employees in particular are more likely to vote than similar people in private industry. Here again we see that if people have a good reason to vote, they will.

Consequences of Apathy

Low voter turnout is not a new problem in the United States. Recently, though, concern has increased as participation rates have declined. Between 1964 and 1980, for example, turnout in presidential elections went down by 10 percent (from 69.3 to 59.2 percent). In 1984, turnout increased, but only slightly—about three tenths of a percent. What is the significance of the fact that 40 percent or more of eligible citizens choose not to vote?

Some people feel that widespread apathy represents a crisis in American democracy. They see nonvoting as an expression of no confidence in the electoral system, the particular choices it offers, and the results it produces. Eventually, it is argued, nonvoters may seek to replace electoral politics with a more authoritarian way of choosing leaders. Apathy may also indicate feelings of political powerlessness. Nonvoting, then, is a problem that requires serious attention.

This view has some validity, but there is little evidence that the rate of apathy points to a political crisis. It is true that, as we saw, people with a low sense of political efficacy are less likely to vote. And it is also true that some of the decline in voting since the 1960s stems from a sense that government is unresponsive. On the other hand, nonvoters are not necessarily more dissatisfied with the government than are voters. According to a 1976 national survey conducted by the Center for Political Studies at the University of Michigan, voters and nonvoters offered pretty much the same responses to questions dealing with the wasting of taxpayers' money, the domination of government by special interests (such as big business, some trade associations and some labor unions, and so on), and dishonesty in government. Nor was there much difference in voters' trust of Jimmy Carter and Gerald Ford. Another study of nonvoting over a twenty-year period concluded that much nonvoting has its roots in satisfaction—not dissatisfaction—with the political system.[2] Finally, even if a sizable number of nonvoters are distrustful of the government, this does not mean that such people will use violent, unconventional means to replace the entire system. Hostility may be directed at particular officeholders, not at the system. Their apathy in voting may well apply to other forms of participation. That is, many people who do not vote are content with both the candidates and the political system.

A second possible consequence of apathy is its supposed impact on the future of the Democratic party, especially the more liberal wing. This argument goes as follows: Nonvoters disproportionately come from the disadvantaged, less well-off groups—blacks, blue-collar workers, the poorly educated—that in general support Democratic candidates. Often, the margin between Republican victory and Democratic defeat is much smaller than the size of the pool of disadvantaged nonvoters. In 1980, for example, Carter would have won easily if blacks had turned out in much larger numbers (assuming, of course, that they had followed the Democratic lead of black voters). Therefore, this argument goes, widespread apathy gives the advantage to the Republicans. More specifically, since well-educated, well-off people almost always vote, the conservative policy preferences of this group play a major role in who wins the elections.

The evidence is mixed on whether low participation hurts the Democratic party. There certainly are elections (for example, the Johnson–Goldwater contest of 1964) in which some of the Democratic party's success is traceable to a high turnout. It is also true that the Democratic party has benefited from the surge, beginning in the 1960s, of blacks into the electoral process.

Nevertheless, there is no one-to-one relationship between turnout and Democratic success at the presidential level. Democratic candidates won in 1932, 1948, and 1976, when turnout was low, but lost in 1952 and 1968, when turnout was relatively high. Second, evidence suggests that nonvoters may be fickle in their preferences. Rather than follow the traditional party loyalties of voters of similar backgrounds to their own, they tend to follow the crowd, even if the crowd is going off in a conservative Republican direction. One analysis

The United States has had experience with democratic procedures longer than other Western countries, and yet voter turnout in America is lower than in many European nations.

of white nonvoters found that, in 1960, many of these people were Nixon supporters; in 1968 they tended to favor George Wallace, who ran as an independent, and not Hubert Humphrey, the Democrat.[3] Finally, issue differences between voters and nonvoters are not all that large. One analysis of the 1980 election found no differences between voters and nonvoter on issues such as government guarantees of jobs, cuts in government services, or government aid to minority groups. In terms of their overall liberalism/conservatism, nonvoters were on average midway between Carter and Reagan voters.[4] It is certainly not true that most nonvoters take liberal positions on issues.

In sum, though much has been said about apathy in American politics, the significance of non-participation is unclear. It is not likely to result in a crisis or otherwise undermine our political system. Furthermore, if habitual nonvoters were brought to the polls, the outcome would probably not be a Democratic landslide, as some observers have predicted.

Check Your Understanding

1. What are the characteristics of people most likely to vote? Of people least likely to vote?

2. What are three major reasons for low voter turnout in the U.S.?

3. What are some consequences of voter apathy?

4. Why do government workers generally have a higher voting participation rate?

WHAT DETERMINES HOW PEOPLE VOTE?

Voting is a complex process. No two elections are alike, numerous offices are filled in each election, and each person probably has his or her own way of deciding. Analysts have tried to disentangle how people make their choices. Dozens of books have been written on the subject, and consultants and officials all have their own views. Unfortunately, there are no simple, generally accepted answers. Our approach to the question of what lies behind the voters' choices will be to examine three general answers that have frequently been offered: party identification, issues, and group voting.

Party Identification

The party-identification explanation consists of three elements. First, most Americans—between 60 and 75 percent—early in life acquire a feeling of loyalty to either the Democratic or the Republican party. Party identification, as we explained in Chapter 4, is usually acquired from parents. Party loyalty often remains over a lifetime, though it may ebb and flow in strength. Typically, it is weakest in early adulthood but strengthens as people grow older.

Second, party affiliation acts as a powerful filter in the perception of political events. For example, Democratic identifiers are likely to exaggerate the virtues of Democratic candidates and their policies while playing down the positive attributes of Republicans. The same is true for Republicans.

Third, perceptual biases encourage voting for the candidates of one's party. As might be expected, Democrats choose Democrats, while Republicans support Republicans—especially when, as voters, they have little information about candidates and issues. If, for example, a person had to choose between unknown candidates for the state legislature, the party label would probably be the decisive factor.

Evidence exists for the party-identification explanation of voting. At the presidential level, most identifiers have supported the candidates of their party. This is particularly true of people who say that they "strongly" identify with their party. In 1980, for example, nearly 90 percent of the "strong" Democrats who voted chose Carter, while over 95 percent of the "strong" Republicans voted for Ronald Reagan. During the 1982 congressional elections, over 80 percent of the voters remained loyal to their party's candidate. In the 1984 landslide for Reagan, a Gallup poll revealed that 79 percent of Democrats remained loyal to their party (and 96 percent of Republicans voted for President Reagan). A 1986 NBC exit poll of voters found that 85 percent of Republicans voted for the Republican House candidate. In contrast, a mere 8 percent of Democrats supported a Republican candidate. Many voters almost automatically support their party, election after election, regardless of who runs under the party label.

Despite the supporting evidence, though, some people criticize the idea that party identification is generally the result of early learning experiences and often leads voters to select candidates automatically on the basis of party. These critics believe that people become attracted to a political party because they favor that party's issues and candidates. People can, and do, change their party loyalties. Someone who was raised as a Democrat but opposes the candidates and issue stands of the party may become a Republican. When such a person regularly supports Republicans, his or her choices are mainly issue-motivated.

Still other critics see the party identification explanation as an incomplete description of voting behavior. They argue that party loyalty is weakening. In 1984, according to a study conducted by the Center for Political Studies at the University of Michigan, when asked for their party affiliation, some 35.6 percent said "independent" or "no preference." Party loyalty cannot explain the voting behavior of this group. Furthermore, even among party loyalists, an increasing number temporarily abandon their party. Ronald Reagan's 1980 and 1984 victories, for example, drew heavily on support from many traditional Democrats (one in five Democrats voted for Reagan in 1984). **Split ticket voting**—supporting candidates of both parties—has also grown in recent years. In general, for many voters and in many situations party loyalty is no longer the overwhelming consideration. It remains important, but other factors are involved, as we shall see.

Issue Voting

According to the issue-voting explanation of voting behavior, citizens select candidates who come closest to their own policy preferences. In other words, if you believe that the government should enact vigorous antipollution regulations, and one candidate is closer to your position than another, you would select the candidate who agrees with your position.

The issue-voting explanation has considerable popularity. Candidates are aware of its importance when they take positions on a wide variety of topics. In his 1984 campaign, for example, Walter Mondale presented voters with a host of issue positions on such topics as the rights of homosexuals, economic equality for women, reductions in nuclear arms, and so on. Analysts often use candidates' issue stands to interpret election outcomes. A common theme following the 1980 election, for example, was that the inflation issue greatly hurt President Carter. Reagan, on the other hand, benefited from his promise to reduce taxes.

Determining whether a person votes on the basis of the issues is often complex. A person may choose a candidate whose physical appearance he or she finds attractive and then justify the choice in terms of issues. Also, elections often involve several issues, and a voter may prefer candidate A on some issues and candidate B on other issues. Thus, no matter which candidate is finally chosen, the voter will both agree and disagree with his or her candidate's issue positions. People can also misperceive where a candidate stands. A liberal may choose a conservative on the basis of wrong information. Does the mistake still constitute issue voting? Experts differ, as well, on just how issue voting is to be measured.

Specific Issues and the Vote

One careful analysis of issue voting in the 1980 presidential election is offered by Abramson, Aldrich, and Rohde. These authors came up with three conditions that would have to be met before issue voting could be said to occur. First, a person must have an opinion on a current political issue; second, he or she must have an accurate view of where both candidates stand on that issue; third, the voter must see differences between the candidates.[5] For instance, a person could be an issue voter if he or she favored lowered taxes and viewed

Reagan and Carter as differing on this issue, with Reagan being more in favor of tax cuts than Carter.

In 1980, most people met the first requirement—having an opinion. On nine issue questions covering topics such as government spending, income tax cuts, and women's rights, between 61 and 96 percent of the public offered an opinion. However, many of the respondents could not identify either Carter's or Reagan's position on these issues. Finally, less than half of the people in the survey could correctly state which of the two candidates held the more liberal or conservative position on each issue. For example, 83 percent of those interviewed had an opinion on the issue of cutting government spending; 65 percent could make a guess about Carter's and Reagan's positions; but only 48 percent knew that Reagan, and not Carter, favored spending cuts.

Did citizens who knew the candidates' views select the candidate whose views were closest to their own? On some issues—for example, government aid to minorities and government spending—there was a fairly close relationship between a person's vote and the perceived issue position of the candidate he or she supported. On other issues—for example, how to deal with the Russians—the relationship was weaker. Finally, on the issues of women's rights and abortion, there was no relationship between a person's issue stand and his or her choice for President. On the basis of these results, the authors conclude that, at least in 1980, issues did play an important role, but they were far from the most important factor. A major reason why they did not play a larger role is that people did not always agree with one candidate on all issues—for example, a voter might agree with Reagan on cutting taxes but disagree with him on the abortion issue.

Retrospective Voting

The previous discussion focused on the relationship between several specific issue positions and the vote. There is, however, another approach to

"*I'm voting my pocketbook again this year. How about you, Winstead?*"

(Drawing by C. Barsotti; © 1976 The New Yorker Magazine)

assessing the role of issues. Rather than rate a candidate on specific policies, a voter can make an overall judgment on the performance of the incumbent—the officeholder running for reelection. The voter can then decide whether the opponent, or challenger, would do a better job. In other words, in 1984 a voter could simply have asked, "Has Reagan done a good job in office?" If the answer was "No," and Mondale seemed to offer a better choice, the voter would have rejected Reagan in favor of Mondale. Making a choice based on past performance—not on current stands on issues—is called **retrospective voting.** The key factor is results, not the policies a candidate favors—in short, actions speak louder than promises.

The 1980 and 1984 presidential elections both show considerable evidence of retrospective voting. In 1980, voters in general believed that President Carter had done a poor job, particularly in economic matters. Eighty-four percent of the respondents in the University of Michigan election survey believed that the economy had gotten worse in the year before the election. The number of people who felt that their own financial situation had worsened outnumbered those who believed that it had improved. The negative views were strongly translated into anti-Carter votes. For example, of those voters who disapproved of the government's performance on inflation and unemployment, a mere 23 percent supported Carter (among those who approved of the government's economic performance, 88 percent supported him). In 1984, 41 percent of the voters said that their own financial status had improved; these voters supported Reagan by a 4-to-1 margin. However, respondents who said that their economic situation had declined preferred Mondale by about a 3-to-1 margin.[6]

Evidence from the 1984 presidential election also suggests that voters select future leaders on the basis of past performance. When a Gallup poll asked Reagan voters why they had voted for the President, 24 percent said that they liked his economic policies. Another 11 percent favored his other policies. Many Reagan voters saw their vote as an endorsement of his accomplishments.

Candidate Personality and the Vote

An important variation of the issue-voting explanation focuses on what might be described as a candidate's "character"—traits such as leadership, integrity, judgment, decisiveness, and vision. A voter might say, "I do not necessarily agree with candidate X on all the issues, but I believe that he (or she) is more capable of leading the country than candidate Y." The major issue, then, is the candidates' abilities, honesty, and other personal qualities.

The "character issue" is usually a major theme in campaigns. In the 1980 Carter–Reagan presidential contest, for example, Carter's ability to provide decisive leadership was frequently questioned. Moreover, while few questioned Carter's personal honesty, doubts were often raised about the integrity of some of his advisors. On the other hand, while Ronald Reagan held out the vision of strong leadership, many people were worried about his judgment, especially in international crises. A similar situation occurred in 1984. Many citizens again expressed the feeling that Reagan would provide strong leadership—make tough decisions, stand up to the Russians, and not yield to special interests. Mondale, on the other hand, was often looked upon as paying too much attention to groups such as organized labor and women's groups and lacking the backbone to deal with Communist challenges.

There is evidence that such character ratings do affect voting. In 1980, for example, 97 percent of those who had a more favorable image of Reagan than of Carter supported Reagan. Among those who had a more favorable view of Carter, 97 percent voted for him. Positive personality assessments may even make up for disagreement on specific issues. In 1980, voters often disagreed with Reagan on a number of policies, but evaluated Reagan more positively on leadership qualities, self-confidence, effectiveness, and clarity of position. A common justification given for supporting Reagan in 1980 was that he was a strong leader. In 1984 Reagan also benefited from people's beliefs about his leadership. Compared to Mondale, Reagan was judged more capable of handling such important matters as the economy, inflation, and

In the 1984 presidential campaign, Jesse Jackson, right, sought to attract liberal whites as well as blacks; Geraldine Ferraro became the first woman to run for Vice President on a major party ticket.

dealing with the Russians. "Strong leadership" and "experience" were often mentioned as reasons for choosing Reagan over Mondale.

Overall, citizens' conclusions about a candidate's abilities and character are significant. It may be impossible, however, to say just how significant. Beliefs about a candidate's honesty may simply reflect party affiliation or preference for the candidate's stand on specific issues. It is difficult to separate the impact of any one attitude in voting.

Group Voting

The third explanation of voting says that a person chooses candidates on the basis of group identity. Like issue voting, this is a fairly common explanation among politicians, campaign managers, and journalists. In 1984, Jesse Jackson originally built his presidential campaign on a group approach. His goal was to create a "Rainbow Coalition"—an alliance of blacks, Hispanics, women, and others. Basically, this explanation sees people as belonging to various groups—business executives, Poles,

Irish, Catholics, farmers, and so on. Group membership in turn affects voting. People vote for candidates who either share their characteristics (for example, Jews vote for Jews) or who advocate policies favorable to the group (Jews support pro-Israel candidates). Candidates are successful when they are able to put together a winning coalition of groups.

The explanation receives a certain amount of support when we examine voting patterns over a long period. For example, since the 1930s and the elections of Franklin D. Roosevelt, blacks, Jews, union members, and city dwellers have tended to support the Democratic party. In turn, the Democrats have frequently run candidates who make strong appeals to these groups. Likewise, Republican candidates have campaigned successfully among voters who are well-off, better-educated, and so on. According to the group-voting explanation, the vote is a medium of exchange—it is given by people in return for some group-related benefit.

Despite the existence of group differences in voting behavior, the explanation has several weaknesses. In the first place, many groups show considerable variation in their voting, from election to election. For example, while Jews supported Carter by a nearly 2-to-1 margin in 1976, in 1980 they supported him by only a 45-percent to 39-percent margin over Reagan. In some elections Catholics have voted as a group but have sharply divided in others. Perhaps the only group that has regularly voted as a bloc, or group, in recent years has been blacks.

A second problem with the group-voting explanation concerns the determination of which group trait is most important in a given election. Most people belong to a number of social, ethnic, and religious groups. Are well-off Catholics supposed to vote Republican because they are well-off, or do they vote Democratic because they are Catholic? People also may not automatically identify with a group just because they might qualify to belong. A Protestant may not think of himself or herself as a Protestant, despite being classified as one. Also, some groups—young people, old people, city dwellers—are extremely diverse in their membership. Here again, the group explanation encounters problems.

An interesting situation occurred in 1984 when Walter Mondale selected Geraldine Ferraro, a woman and a Catholic of Italian ancestry, as his running mate. Democrats hoped that she would appeal to voters sharing these traits. The strategy was unsuccessful. Women supported Reagan by a 56-to-44 margin; Catholics gave the President 58 percent of their vote; and Italian-Americans went 57 to 42 for Reagan. In other words, the voting patterns of these three groups resembled those of the population in general.

The group-voting explanation makes the most sense in elections in which the issues directly touch group interests. If a black is running against an antiblack candidate, or one candidate favors government aid to parochial schools and the other does not, group characteristics can help explain voting behavior. Jesse Jackson received high levels of black support in the 1984 Democratic presidential primaries, for example, because he was a black who vigorously advocated the cause of minorities. In 1960 John F. Kennedy, a Catholic, did relatively well among Catholics. However, most elections are far too complex to be interpreted solely in terms of the group traits of voters. Group voting plays a role, but by itself cannot explain how people vote.

Conclusions

It should be clear that there is no single explanation for voting behavior. Each approach has its good points and bad points. It is also important to understand that the three approaches we have described are not separate categories. A person may be a Democrat (party affiliation) because he or she agrees with the Democratic party on issues (issue voting). One of these issues may be strongly related to his or her group identity (group voting). A second point is that all three explanations may be valid, but at different times. In some elections issues may be most important; in others, the contest is primarily between opposing group interests. In still other elections people vote their party loyalty. In 1984 a black might have chosen Walter Mondale over Ronald Reagan on the basis of party loyalty and issues; in the Democratic primary, he or she might have chosen Jesse Jackson over Mondale on the basis of group values.

Check Your Understanding

1. What are some of the weaknesses of the party-identification explanation of voting?

2. How do evaluations of candidates' personality and character help determine the way people vote?

3. What is the group-voting explanation of voting behavior?

4. What are some of the weaknesses of the group-voting explanation?

ARE CAMPAIGNS CONDUCTED FAIRLY?

In principle, the purpose of a campaign is to allow voters to decide which candidate to support. Its role is educational. The use of physical threats, bribery, and vote fraud obviously undermines the purpose of a campaign. Moreover, it is important that some balance be maintained among candidates. An election campaign in a democracy is hardly fair if a candidate is not allowed to appear in public or otherwise appeal for votes.

Over the years, open and honest campaigns have not always been the rule. In the nineteenth century, abuses were common. Citizens would sometimes cast more than one vote, and campaign violence sometimes occurred. Voting returns might disappear or be misreported. Gradually, however, most of these abuses were corrected. For example, the **Australian ballot** was introduced. This type of ballot was printed and administered by the government (national, state, or local). This system helped to reduce the fraud that occurred when parties provided the ballots. Today, problems of fairness remain, but these are more subtle and complex. Two problems in particular deserve our attention: the enormous importance of money and the "packaging" of candidates.

Money and Campaigns

The role of money in elections raises two important issues. The first is the "buying" of elections. We would hardly consider an election fair if one candidate spent huge sums of money to overwhelm the less well financed opposition. The second issue concerns the motivation of campaign contributors. It is one thing to contribute $25 to a candidate because you support his or her policies. It is quite another to give $25,000 in the expectation of direct personal benefits as a result of your contribution. In short, money itself does not subvert the electoral process. The expenditure of large sums to manipulate voters and the sale of favors for contributions can undermine the democratic purpose of elections.

Fraud was once a major problem in U.S. elections. A nineteenth-century illustration shows fraudulent voters crowded into a jail cell. Today, irregularities at the polling place sometimes occur, but the vast sums of money spent on campaigns may pose a greater threat to democracy.

The Rising Cost of Campaigns

Campaigns in the United States are expensive, and they are getting even more so. In 1977–78, the total amount of money spent on House elections was $109.6 million. In 1983–84, the cost of House elections was $165 million. The sixty-five candidates running for the Senate in 1984 spent a total of $136.9 million; the average cost of running for the Senate was $2.1 million. In populous states like New York and California, running a campaign is extremely expensive. The Pete Wilson–Jerry Brown California State campaign of 1982, for example, cost $12.3 million. Phil Gramm spent $9.4 million to be elected a Republican senator from Texas in 1984. In 1984, Jay Rockefeller spent more than $12 million to be elected senator from West Virginia; some $23 million was spent in the Jesse Helms–James Hunt Senate race in North Carolina the same year.

Spending in presidential contests has shown a more complex pattern. Table 6.1 shows that between 1960 and 1972, expenditures skyrocketed, especially on the Republican side. In 1976, federal financing of presidential campaigns began, and government subsidies, or payments to candidates, were limited. As a result, expenditures dropped sharply. But because federal outlays provided for a cost-of-living increase, campaign expenses again started moving upward. In 1984, each presidential candidate was allowed to spend $40.4 million. In addition, a candidate could spend up to $20.2 million in primary elections.

There are many reasons why campaigns are expensive, including, in most campaigns, the size of the electorate—that is, the number of people voting. Though our population has grown, since 1910 the number of national elected officials has remained constant (with the small exception of new senators from Hawaii and Alaska). Representatives and senators must now reach more people than before. House districts average nearly 500,000 citizens, frequently a diverse mixture of people. Even a modest, "folksy" campaign emphasizing personal contact does not come cheap under these conditions. The popularity of primaries has also increased the expense, as many congressional candidates must now conduct two separate election campaigns. Even where there is no primary challenge, candidates sometimes wage vigorous, costly campaigns to discourage future primary opponents.

Perhaps the major reason for the big jump in

Cost of Presidential Races, 1960–1984

Year	Democrat	Total Expenditures	TV Expenditures	Republican	Total Expenditures	TV Expenditures
1960	Kennedy*	$ 9,797,000	$ 1,142,000	Nixon	$10,128,000	$18,645,000
1964	Johnson*	8,757,000	4,674,000	Goldwater	16,026,000	6,370,000
1968	Humphrey	11,594,000	6,143,000	Nixon*	25,402,000	12,598,000
1972	McGovern	30,000,000	6,200,000	Nixon*	61,400,000	4,300,000
1976	Carter*	21,800,000	9,081,321	Ford	21,800,000	7,875,000
1980	Carter	29,352,767	18,400,000	Reagan*	29,188,188	12,324,000
1984**	Mondale	46,000,000	—	Reagan*	50,000,000	—

*Winner

**Approximate amounts. Figures on TV expenditures not available.

Source: Herbert E. Alexander, *Financing Politics: Money, Elections and Political Reform* (Washington, D.C.: CQ Press, 1984), pp. 7, 13.

TABLE 6.1

campaign costs is the rise of what has been called the **"new politics."** In the "old politics," candidates relied heavily on political parties. Parties, through their control of government jobs and related benefits, provided many campaign services: registering potential supporters, distributing campaign material, gathering information, getting voters to the polls, and so on. The direct cost of these services was modest. Services were typically given free by people whose jobs or city contracts depended on the outcome of an election. If the

dollar value of these "free" services were calculated, the races would be fairly expensive, but relatively little money actually changed hands. In addition, the emphasis was on the overall ticket—not on a particular candidate—so the total cost was distributed over a number of candidates.

In the "new politics," campaigns are much more candidate-centered. Rather than rely on a state or county party organization, each candidate builds a personal organization run by paid professionals. The style and strategy of the "new politics"

In a flag-decorated convention hall, Republicans choose presidential and vice presidential nominees, 1880, top. As Democrats select their national standard-bearers at the 1984 presidential nominating convention, flags are prominently displayed.

also differs from the "old politics." Whereas the "old politics" stressed personal contact and strong, well-managed organizations, the "new politics" emphasizes the mass media (newspapers, TV, and so on), polling, and the personal qualities of the candidate. Political parties are still relevant—they continue to perform several valuable services—but they are no longer *the* campaign organization.

"New politics" campaigns are expensive. Essential activities such as opinion polling, advertising, and consulting (providing special advice) cannot be performed by government workers "volunteering" their services. Though many campaigns make use of volunteer labor, professional campaign personnel are the rule, and they are well paid. With the "old politics" a candidate would ask a campaign worker to gauge public opinion in his or her area. Today, a polling service costing thousands of dollars might be used.

Reliance on the mass media is perhaps the greatest difference between the old and the new politics. The cost of creating and presenting material through television, radio, and print can consume half of the entire campaign budget. For candidates who run in large cities, even the simplest media campaign is very expensive. For example, in 1982 a single thirty-second television commercial in the Minneapolis area during a Minnesota Vikings football game cost $3,650 just to air. On prime time over network television, thirty seconds can cost $100,000. These figures do not include the costs of producing commercials, which can run several times the cost of broadcasting them. The need for such large sums generated yet another expense—fundraising. Here again, this service has become dominated by paid professionals who provide computerized mailings, telephone calls, and other expensive fundraising activities.

The Pattern of Campaign Expenditures

Though it takes a good deal of money to run a campaign, differences exist in who spends how much. One important factor is incumbency. At least in congressional elections, an **incumbent,** or officeholder, almost always outspends the challenger. For example, in the 1984 House election, incumbents averaged about $326,000 for their

campaigns, while challengers spent $129,000 on average. In Senate races in 1984, incumbents on average outspent their challengers by nearly $1.3 million. These figures do not tell the whole story, though. Officeholders have access to free services that challengers must pay for: office staff, free postage for contacting constituents, and a travel allowance. An incumbent can sometimes get thousands of dollars' worth of television exposure simply by calling a press conference to announce the passage of a bill to help an industry in his or her district. Thus congressional challengers must spend tens of thousands of dollars more just to keep even.

Incumbents spend more because they find it much easier to raise funds. As Figure 6.2 shows, House incumbents in 1986 raised six times as much money from political action committees (PACs) as did challengers. In 1986 the average House incumbent raised $381,218; his or her challenger on average raised $128,024. (PACs will be discussed in the next section.) Giving money to an established officeholder who has proved that he or she can win—even if the candidate does not completely support your view—is a much better investment than supporting an opponent with no track record. It pays to be on the good side of a person with whom you may partially disagree rather than antagonize someone in power. An incumbent already occupies a position of influence. That is why, for instance, a member of the House Ways and Means Committee, which deals with health care legislation, is likely to receive contributions from groups like the American Medical Association (a physicians' organization). A challenger can make no claim that he or she will be on that committee. It is not surprising, then, that even incumbents who face no challengers frequently get substantial contributions.

A very important question concerns the relationship between campaign spending and electoral success. Can candidates spend their way to victory? The answer seems to be that while winners generally outspend losers, no one-to-one relationship exists between spending and victory. Figure 6.3 shows the difference between winners and losers in the 1986 congressional races. One reason for the connection between spending and electoral

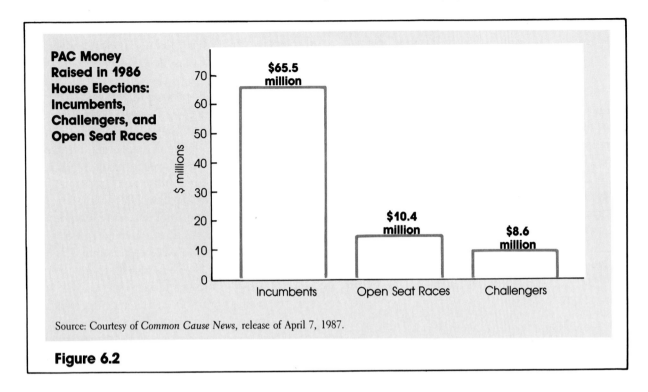

PAC Money Raised in 1986 House Elections: Incumbents, Challengers, and Open Seat Races

Source: Courtesy of *Common Cause News*, release of April 7, 1987.

Figure 6.2

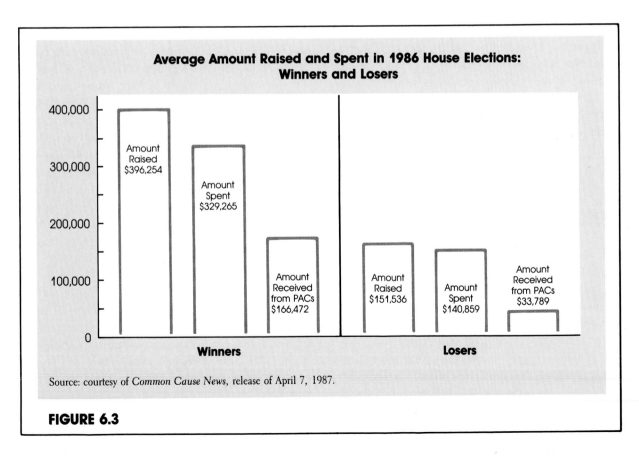

Average Amount Raised and Spent in 1986 House Elections: Winners and Losers

Source: courtesy of *Common Cause News*, release of April 7, 1987.

FIGURE 6.3

success is that many incumbents who are sure of reelection receive generous contributions. On the other hand, there are numerous instances in which candidates greatly outspent their opponents only to lose. In the 1982 Senate contest in Minnesota, for example, David Durenberger was outspent by nearly $3 million, and yet he won. William Proxmire spent nothing on his 1982 campaign, but was nevertheless returned to Washington by Wisconsin voters (we must remember, of course, that figures such as these do not include millions of dollars' worth of free publicity in press conferences, government-paid-for newsletters, and the like). In general, having access to large campaign funds is a necessary condition for victory, but vast expenditures are no guarantee of success.

The Pattern of Campaign Contributions

For most of our history few restrictions were placed on campaign contributions. Laws passed in 1907, 1939, and 1945 forbid banks, corporations, and labor unions from contributing to federal campaigns. However, these and other regulations contained numerous loopholes, or ways of legally avoiding the restrictions. A corporation, for example, could give its executives "bonuses," which they then gave to candidates. For better or worse, secret contributions were fairly common. Large contributors, known as "fat cats," frequently played a significant role in campaigns at all levels of government.

In the 1970s, in response to the role of large campaign contributors, Congress passed legislation, including the Federal Election Campaign Act, that has greatly changed the pattern of campaign giving. First, limits were placed on individual contributions in both presidential and congressional races. A person could give no more than $1,000 to each candidate per election (primaries count as separate elections); $5,000 could be given per year to a political action committee (see below), and up to $20,000 to a political party. The total of all donations from an individual could not exceed $25,000 per year. However, in the case of *Buckley v. Valeo* (1976), the Supreme Court ruled that no financial limits could be imposed on

expenditures on behalf of a candidate as long as the expenditures were not under the candidate's control. The Court reasoned that by forbidding a person from spending freely on behalf of a candidate, the person's exercise of free speech—a constitutionally protected right—had been violated. The Court also ruled that the Federal Election Commission, the Federal Election Campaign Act's enforcement agency, had been improperly constituted, since members were appointed by both Congress and the President, violating the separation-of-powers principle. Contributions of $100 or more and candidate expenditures of $100 or more had to be reported to the Federal Election Commission.

Originally, limits had been placed on both congressional and presidential campaign expenditures. However, the *Buckley v. Valeo* decision invalidated limits on congressional campaign outlays. Thus, limits currently apply only to presidential races. Since 1976, candidates for the presidency have been able, if they choose, to receive government subsidies to cover both primary and general election expenses. Funds are raised through a check-off systems on federal income tax forms. Taxpayers can request that one dollar of their taxes be set aside for the campaign fund (the dollar is not refunded if the option is not checked). In presidential primaries these subsidies are given on a matching basis—each individual contribution of $250 or less is matched up to a limit set every four years, provided that a candidate independently raises $5,000 or more in at least twenty states. The general election campaign of the nominees of the two major parties is completely government-financed. Expenditures vary from election to election, depending on changes in the cost of living. In 1984 each candidate was permitted to spend $40.4 million. Raising additional private funds is generally forbidden (though each candidate's administrative costs can be privately financed). Provisions are also included for dispensing funds to minor parties. (Political action committees are permitted to spend without limit on behalf of a presidential candidate, provided that the candidate does not control these funds.) Though government subsidies—and the total campaign expenditure limits—are voluntary, all presidential candidates so far have accepted them.

The purpose of the reforms was to limit the role of large contributors, especially in presidential campaigns. A multitude of small contributions, plus government subsidies, supposedly would make officeholders less beholden to well-off donors. There was also a desire to hold down the rising cost of campaigns. On the whole, these reforms have changed the character of campaign contributions but have not reduced the importance or amounts of money in campaigns. First, the big-time individual contributor has been replaced by the **political action committee (PAC)**. PACs are organizations sponsored by corporations, unions, trade associations, and issue-oriented groups that raise and distribute campaign funds. PACs are permitted to give $5,000 per candidate per election. In 1983–84, PACs contributed $86.1 million to congressional campaigns. Among the largest PAC contributors were the National Conservative Political Action Committee, the Fund for a Conservative Majority, the Realtors Political Action Committee, and the American Medical Association.

Moreover, the reforms have several loopholes. One tactic is to delay the official declaration of one's candidacy—contribution limits do not apply to "noncandidates." Also, a wealthy person can spend freely on behalf of a candidate so long as the expenditures are not under the candidate's control. Candidates in congressional elections can use their own funds in unlimited amounts (presidential candidates who accept public funding are limited to $50,000). An increasingly popular loophole is to channel money through state party organizations to avoid federal regulation and restrictions. Finally, there are no limits on the donations of services. Candidates have discovered that a free concert given on their behalf by a famous rock group can generate tens of thousands of dollars, but this contribution of valuable services is not covered by contribution limits.

The Consequences of Campaign Money

The link between large campaign contributions and government action is very complex and con-

troversial. There certainly exists a long history of campaign contributions directly linked to favorable treatment by federal officials. For example, in 1971, after President Nixon rejected increased government support for the milk industry, he changed his mind when milk producers agreed to contribute $2 million to his campaign. In 1982 all the members of Congress who received $3,000 or more from contractors involved with the Clinch River Breeder Reactor voted for additional federal funding of the project; among those not receiving contributions, only 29 percent voted for funding. Several Presidents have appointed heavy contributors to diplomatic posts. At one time it was even alleged that ambassadorships carried specific campaign donation price tags—a million-dollar contribution might get you the ambassadorship to France. In 1982 some people said that heavy campaign contributions by used-car dealers led Congress to defeat a proposed rule that would have required the dealers to reveal used-car defects to prospective buyers. The American Medical Association has been accused of using its ample funds to convince legislators to leave medical matters in the hands of doctors.

Nevertheless, despite such charges of corruption and vote-buying, many people play down the impact of campaign money. In the first place, most donors give money not in order to change minds, but to support candidates who basically agree with their positions. Trade union PACs, for example, support prolabor candidates; corporation PACs contribute to probusiness legislators. Electing a sympathetic legislator is a far better strategy than trying to convince an unsympathetic one with a contribution. When a person or group is dealing with an unsympathetic official, a contribution may buy access—that is, a chance to be seen and heard—but rarely much more. Such access may be important, but it is not vote-buying. In general, a group making a $5,000 donation to a legislator must compete with other, perhaps opposing groups, as well as pressure from constituents, party leaders, and the President. Powerful groups such as medical and insurance organizations often work against each other.

A less obvious impact of campaign money concerns the way candidates conduct their campaigns.

Basically, the need for large sums means that nominees must devote considerable efforts to fundraising—giving speeches, hiring extra staff, sending out special appeals, and the like. Not only is this time- and energy-consuming, but it can influence the issue positions that candidates take. In the prereform days, a candidate for Congress might receive the bulk of his or her campaign funds from a small number of interests. Today, however, no one group is permitted to contribute more than a drop in the bucket (a PAC could give $5,000, but the total campaign expenditure will almost certainly exceed $100,000, probably $250,000 or more). This means that numerous sources must be tapped—candidates may now have asked for support from every imaginable group to run a decent campaign. On occasion, a candidate will seek support from groups outside their districts or even from groups that seemingly have no stake in the district.

In sum, campaign contributions are important, but except on rare occasions, large benefactors cannot buy public officials. Being able to raise and spend millions in campaign contributions pro-

Points of View: Do PACs Endanger the Democratic Political Process?

LASTPAC is one of the most unusual of all the special interest groups in politics today: its goal is to eliminate political action committees altogether. Leaving aside the question of whether the aim is realistic, is it worthwhile? Do PACs undermine the American democratic system?

Observers agree on some basic facts. One is that the number of PACs is growing. In the mid-1970s, there were about 600 political action committees: in 1986, there were more than 4,000 (see Figure 8.1). Another trend is the ever increasing amounts of money PACs spend on political campaigns. In 1981–82, PACs paid out a total of some $87 million to candidates in federal election campaigns. In 1986, they contributed almost this much to House candidates alone (see Figure 6.2)—and another $44 million to Senate candidates. In percentage terms, PAC contributions in 1986 accounted for over a third of all the money raised by candidates for the House and about a fourth of that raised by Senate candidates. These amounts do not tell the whole story, for PACs also give money to candidates in state elections.

Not all candidates—even all winning candidates—are equally dependent on PAC funds. In 1986, Congressman Augustus Hawkins of California represented one extreme; he received 92 percent of his campaign money from PACs. Hawkins felt that he had no alternative because his district was so poor. "I cannot possibly get a lot of individual contributions in a high unemployment poverty district," he said. At the lower end of the scale was the winning senatorial candidate in New Hampshire, Warren Rudman. Less than 1 percent of his campaign money came from PACs. One unsuccessful Senate candidate, Mark Green of New York, refused to accept any PAC money whatsoever.

There is no limit on the total PAC money a candidate may receive, nor on the total contributions a single political action committee may make. The law does restrict each PAC to one $5,000 contribution per federal candidate per election. But there is no ceiling on so-called independent expenditures—money spent on behalf of a candidate that is not coordinated with the candidate's campaign. For example, a PAC may disburse unlimited funds on television commercials extolling a candidate (or attacking his or her opponent) as long as it does so without consulting the candidate's campaign staff. Independent expenditures are increasing rapidly. For example, the National Association of Realtors—whose PAC is one of the biggest spenders of all—gave out $355,000 in independent expenditures in 1984 and $2 million in 1986.

Are PACs good or bad for the American political system? One criticism is that they buy votes. In

vides political influence, not total control. Contributions are also important in the way they shape candidate behavior, but here too, it is rare for one or two contributors to dominate.

The "Packaging" of a Candidate

The dependence of officials on campaign contributions is but one worrisome issue in a democratic election process. Another frequently expressed fear focuses on the way in which some candidates are being professionally marketed. This fear involves several elements. First, by clever media

use, speechwriting, and staged events, a candidate's character and ability can be misrepresented. An indecisive incompetent may appear firm and intelligent. Second, merchandised candidates will avoid difficult, complex issues at the expense of superficialities. A candidate's "position" on unemployment, for instance will be a thirty-second television spot showing him or her shaking hands with the out-of-work. In addition, such tactics give an unfair advantage to candidates who do well on television. Finally, the packaging of candidates give undue influence to the behind-the-scenes

other words, accepting money from an interest group—an organization devoted to achieving certain goals—obligates a politician to vote in its favor on any legislation that may affect the group. Politicians counter that they frequently receive PAC funds from groups whose interests conflict (such as pro- and anti-gun lobbies), so that the pressures cancel each other out.

Another criticism is that PAC money gives undue weight to big corporate and business interests, which support more PACs and spend more money than do groups concerned about labor, consumers, or the environment. One prominent Republican senator, commenting that "poor people don't make campaign contributions," added that "you might get a different result if there were a Poor-PAC" in Washington. Defenders of PACs reply that corporate giving amounts to only about 10 percent of total campaign spending—not significant enough to sway votes.

A third criticism of PACs is

that they contribute to the decline of political parties. PAC money given directly (or indirectly) to candidates enables them to campaign independently of party and, once elected, to vote without concern for the compromises and coalitions that are necessary to carry out a coherent political agenda. PAC supporters claim that American political parties have always been weak in relation to interest groups and that PACs alone are certainly not responsible for this situation.

Finally, PACs are criticized because their support goes overwhelmingly to incumbents rather than to challengers. In the 1986 congressional election, for example, PAC contributions to House candidates favored incumbents by a margin of six to one. This imbalance, say critics, strikes at the very heart of the democratic process by making real competition impossible. PAC defenders admit that special interest money favors incumbents, but no more so than does the entire political system. All the PAC contributions to-

gether cannot begin to equal the financial advantages incumbents have. Newsletters sent out at government expense, and a staff paid for by the taxpayers, are not supposed to be used for campaigning. Yet these resources enable incumbents to keep in touch with constituents, and such publicity can be highly beneficial when voters make their choices.

While LASTPAC wants to do away with PACs altogether, other suggested remedies are less extreme. They include reducing the $5,000 maximum to a lower figure, limiting the total amount or percentage of funding a candidate can receive from PACs, and funneling all PAC contributions through party committees. PAC critics feel that such measures would do little to correct abuses; for one thing, they fail to control independent expenditures. And those who favor PACs want fewer, not more, restrictions. The fewer limits, the more PACs; and the more PACs, the less danger of undue influence by any one PAC or group of special interests.

professionals. The candidate's consultants, not the candidate, may decide how and when an issue should be raised.

There is considerable evidence to suggest that this fear of "packaged" candidates is well-founded. Since the 1950s the political campaign industry has grown enormously. Today there are probably more than a thousand consulting organizations dealing with the election of Presidents, members of Congress, and judges, as well as referendums and bond issues. Some of these organizations offer limited specialized advice—for example, how best to reach certain ethnic groups. Others provide almost every possible election service, from running a voter registration drive to researching the issues. While some firms are fairly selective about whom they will work for, others will support anyone who can afford them.

By necessity, these professional advisors place enormous stress on winning. To gain a reputation as a winner means financial rewards and prestige. It is not surprising, then, that deceptive and unethical practices are sometimes employed. In some instances this may be fairly innocent. For example, one consultant made a senator who was fairly short appear taller by filming him in a specially constructed chamber whose seats were designed for smaller, nineteenth-century legislators. Other practices raise more serious questions. In one case careful film editing made a U.S. Senate candidate appear to be healthy despite partial paralysis due to brain surgery (the candidate died, however, prior to the election). During the 1984 presidential campaign Reagan advisors invented an entire ethnic festival in Milwaukee. A "Family Oktoberfest" complete with 13,500 participants, including polka dancers in colorful German costumes, was staged before television cameras to boost the President's standing among ethnic voters. Many examples also exist of using quotations out of context, misrepresenting endorsements, and portraying an ad as a genuine news broadcast.

There are also numerous stories of how political unknowns with many liabilities were transformed into successes thanks to well-organized, expensive public relations efforts. A well-known example is Ronald Reagan's first venture into pol-

Despite support from actor Warren Beatty, left, Mark Green lost his 1986 race for the Senate from New York.

itics. In his 1966 try for the California governorship, Reagan had two major handicaps. Though well known as an actor, he lacked political experience. He was also widely perceived as being a conservative in a largely liberal state. To overcome these disadvantages, he hired a public relations firm. The candidate's political inexperience was changed from a handicap to an asset. Reagan presented himself as an "ordinary citizen" who could bring some commonsense thinking to all the problems created by "professional politicians." His image was carefully nurtured to show him as youthful, vigorous, moderate, responsible, and decent. The candidate's appearance at events was always carefully planned. A team of consultants conducted in-depth interviews on Reagan's image as an "extremist" and advised him to stress taxes, government spending, and morality. He won decisively and launched a successful political career.

Campaign consultants have developed an impressive and varied bag of tricks. A candidate who wants to reach the "youth vote" can be filmed against the backdrop of a surfers' beach or playing in a football game. If necessary, voice coaches and special diets can be arranged. One candidate for the Democratic party's presidential nomination in 1976 even had corrective cosmetic surgery to help project a better image. In 1976 the television ads for Malcolm Wallop, who was running for the Senate from Wyoming, stressed his cowboy image and resembled cigarette commercials. The messages were convincing despite the fact that Wallop was born in New York, graduated from Yale University, and was a cousin of Queen Elizabeth II.

The Limits of Political Merchandising

The activities of modern campaigning managers raise serious questions about the integrity of the electoral process. An election in which the public can pick only from among second-raters cleverly presented as wise lawmakers hardly provides a meaningful choice. Fortunately, however, there are limits on deceptive political marketing.

One important limiting factor is the integrity of political managers themselves. Though some managers will do almost anything to win, most realize that acquiring a reputation for unscrupulousness is harmful in the long run. A consultant might advise a liberal in a conservative area to avoid certain issues, but not many would recommend lying. Reinforcing professional ethics are a multitude of state and national laws dealing with campaign finance, as well as the fear of exposure by the media or the opposition. Playing "dirty politics" is rarely successful over the long haul, and most consultants realize this.

A second factor is that not all candidates are willing to be packaged and marketed as if they were a soap. For those who enter politics through a commitment to a cause, a consultant's advice to stress family rather than issues will probably fall on deaf ears. Nor can most politicians be persuaded to support policies they oppose. It would be hard to imagine, for example, Ronald Reagan supporting the nuclear freeze movement on the basis of advice from a paid political consultant. Moreover, there are limits on what can be done even with a candidate willing to do anything to get elected. As noted political consultant Bob Goodman put it:

You can't put a candidate completely in a new package. You can take his polyester off and put him in a decent-looking suit. You can have him blow-dry his hair. You can teach him how to keep his eyes on the camera. You can try to inspire certain attributes. But you don't have the complete freedom that you do when you're dealing with a bar of soap.

There is also the uncontrollability of the campaign and political events. A candidate can be carefully prepared by his or her advisors, yet mistakes can and do occur. In 1976, for example, during the televised presidential debates, President Ford stated that Poland was not under Soviet domination. Given the intense scrutiny of candidates for major offices and the opportunities for blunders, it is unlikely that their personality and position will remain disguised forever.

Perhaps the best evidence of the limits on political merchandising are the failures of well-financed, professionally managed campaigns. In 1976 Gerald Rafshoon, a highly successful Atlanta advertising agency owner, was praised for his handling of the Carter campaign. In 1980, Carter lost despite Rafshoon's efforts.

Conclusions

To return to our original concern over whether money and merchandising undermine the democratic role of elections, we see that both pose problems. Money has, on occasion, been used to overwhelm the opposition, campaign contributions have bought favors, and second-rate candidates have successfully been sold as first-rate. Such defects, however, are not fatal flaws. In the first place, no one group or interest can monopolize financial contributions and political merchandising techniques. We do not have a situation in which, say, only conservative candidates can raise lots of money or hire clever consultants. In the second place, many correcting mechanisms are built into the system. The constitutional design helps to minimize the damage that any one corrupt, incompetent official can do. A bad President can be resisted successfully by Congress. Voters are usually given many opportunities to make a judgment. Voters who chose Carter in 1976 had a chance to change their minds in 1980. Money and skilled merchandising can help, but they probably cannot by themselves sustain the career of a disastrous politician.

Check Your Understanding

1. Why have political campaigns become so expensive?

2. Why is incumbency an important factor in raising campaign funds?

3. List the major elements in the post-1971 federal campaign finance regulations.

4. How is a candidate "packaged"?

DO THE MASS MEDIA EXERCISE TOO MUCH POWER?

In the nineteenth century, powerful leaders of political parties were described as "kingmakers." Today many people believe that the mass media— radio, magazines, newspapers, and especially television—have become the political kingmakers. The idea of media influence has greatly disturbed many people. Perhaps their greatest fear is that the media, and those who can use them, will dominate politics: the media, not the public, will decide which candidate deserves to be elected, which issues should receive attention, and what constitutes appropriate government policy. Such power, it is claimed, is unaccountable to the public and constitutes a threat to the very idea of free and open elections. Our analysis of the mass media's power will examine the pervasiveness, or wide range, of the media, how they affect citizens, and possible limits on their influence.

Mass Media Pervasiveness

For better or worse, the United States is saturated by the mass media. In 1982 over sixty-two million newspapers were sold each day. The print media cater to almost every possible taste, from the latest Hollywood gossip to complex analyses of foreign policy issues. The electronic media in particular have influenced the lives of most Americans. In 1984, for example, some 98 percent of all homes had at least one television set, and viewers watched television an average of seven hours a day. Whereas news of a major event would once take days to reach most of the population, now, thanks to radio and television, one hundred million people can, within hours, witness an event thousands of miles away.

The political use of the mass media has grown considerably. As we mentioned, the "new politics" relies heavily on the mass media. Candidates now use television commercials and radio spots to do what party workers once did. In big states such as California or New York, the campaign has become largely a mass media event, with candidates spending at least half of their funds on television. Media consultants often play a central role in campaign planning.

Citizens get a great deal of political information from the mass media, particularly television. In the 1984 election, for example, some 83 percent of a national sample conducted by the Center for Political Studies said that they had watched between some and a large number of programs about the campaign on television; two-thirds said that they had watched the national network news at least three or four times a week. By way of comparison, only about 30 percent said that they had discussed politics with their friends or family more than three or four times a week. In other words, there was more exposure to politics on television than through personal experience.

Statistics on the number of TV viewers or newspaper readers do not provide a complete picture of the impact of the media, however. Even those people who avoid reading newspapers or listening to the radio can be influenced by them. Through what has been called the **two-step flow of**

Biography: Edward R. Murrow

Perhaps more than any other single person, Edward R. Murrow helped make radio and television respected media in American society. The accuracy and objectivity of his early radio reporting gave him the prestige that later enabled him to pursue a remarkably independent course as a television news reporter. His knowledge of national and world affairs became so admired that many people urged him to run for the U.S. Senate. He declined, however, commenting that he "had never had a horizon of more than 90 days."

Born in North Carolina in 1908, Murrow grew up in the state of Washington, where he received a bachelor of arts degree in speech from Washington State, the first university in the nation to offer a course in radio broadcasting. After working briefly for the National Student Federation and the Institute of International Education, Murrow was hired by the Columbia Broadcasting System in 1935 and was soon sent to Europe to arrange for broadcasts of interviews and cultural events.

When Hitler's aggressive actions in Europe threatened war, Murrow was on the spot to report the events. His broadcasts from Vienna when German troops marched into the city in the spring of 1938 were highly successful and helped propel the young American to the position of European news chief for CBS. Among the reporters he hired to help cover the war—men who later became famous in their own

right—were William L. Shirer, Eric Sevareid, and Howard K. Smith.

During World War II, Murrow, based in London, attracted a radio audience of millions with his low-key but dramatic news reports. Listeners could often hear bombs in the background as he described the German blitz, or air raids. He flew on twenty-five combat missions to report on the air war over Germany, and was the first Allied war correspondent to witness the horrors of the Buchenwald concentration camp—one of the few experiences to upset his usually calm manner.

Back in the United States after the war, Murrow launched a weekly radio program, "Hear It Now." With the advent of the new medium, the program became a television staple, "See It Now," in 1951; Murrow was the only major broadcaster to switch media successfully.

Murrow became noted not only for his informative, probing style but also for innovations that were to shape television journalism for decades. One of the most

important of these was what Murrow and his co-producer Fred Friendly called "giving the little picture." Instead of presenting the news in abstract generalities, they focused on the small, telling detail. A memorable story on the Korean War, for example, followed the activities of a single platoon and the men's daily round of eating, sleeping, complaining, and fighting.

Murrow's brand of journalism had a powerful impact. His most famous telecast, in March 1954, presented a devastating picture of Senator Joseph R. McCarthy, who was then causing furor with his accusations of communism in high places. By showing the Wisconsin Republican as a bully and a boor, Murrow did much to diminish the fear McCarthy inspired—a factor in the Senate's subsequent censure of him.

"See It Now" was taken off the air in 1958, prompting Murrow to accuse the networks of "decadence, escapism, and insulation from the realities of the world in which we live." Murrow himself left CBS shortly afterward and directed the U.S. Information Agency for three years. Though he died in 1965, his legacy goes on. Television came of age in the 1950s, and it was Murrow's calm, informative manner that helped make millions of Americans comfortable with the new medium. During this period of rapidly changing international events, Murrow influenced the way Americans viewed the world they lived in.

communication, people who acquire information from the mass media pass it on to others. Thus someone who follows the nightly news may tell non-news-watchers what happened. The two-step flow helps explain the importance of the so-called **prestige press**—the *New York Times*, the *Washington Post*, and a few magazines. Though these news sources have small audiences compared to, say, the *CBS Evening News*, the people who follow the prestige press are often community opinion leaders (for example, prominent business people, lawyers, other journalists), who pass the messages on to many others.

It is also important to realize how much Americans trust the media. Though accusations of bias and misrepresentation are commonplace, in fact people are relatively trusting of the media, especially television. This was demonstrated in a 1980 survey, in which citizens were asked to rate the performance of various political institutions. Some 53 percent of the respondents gave national television news a rating of "good" or "very good"; less than 10 percent gave it a poor rating. In contrast, only about 11 percent gave Congress high ratings, and nearly 29 percent gave it poor ratings.[7] Several television commentators—Dan Rather, Roger Mudd—are highly regarded, as are such programs as *60 Minutes*, *20/20*, and *Meet the Press*. Thus, the mass media can be both widespread and authoritative sources of information.

The Political Impact of the Mass Media

Creating Political Reality

Most people have only a limited firsthand knowledge of politics. Whether it is the inner workings of Congress or Soviet agricultural problems, much—if not most—of what we know comes from the mass media. In the late 1960s and early 1970s, for example, television in particular showed college students and various "counterculture" types as the major opponents of U.S. military involvement in Vietnam. For many people this was reality: antiwar people were mostly defiant college students. In fact, antiwar sentiment was just as widespread—if not more so—among blue-collar workers. Because this aspect of reality was

not as newsworthy as a draft-card burning, however, it was rarely shown to the public.

The reality presented by the mass media favors certain kinds of approaches. W. Lance Bennett, in his analysis of news programs, notes that the media usually stress personalities rather than political processes, power relations, and economic forces. Journalists believe that in terms of commerical success it is better to devote five minutes to a single hungry, sick child than to give an in-depth treatment to such complex subjects as the administration of nutrition programs. A topic like tax reform becomes a battle among political personalities—the President, members of Congress, and so on—rather than a conflict over political philosophies and goals. Corruption in government becomes a corrupt person, not the system that encourages corruption. In 1987, the publicity the mass media gave to Gary Hart's personal affairs was decisive in forcing Hart to pull out of the presidential campaign for the Democratic nomination in 1988. This type of emphasis, according to Bennett, provides little understanding of the causes and effects of political events.

The mass media's version of reality also emphasizes dramatic events at the expense of routine happenings. For example, the existence of widespread unemployment and alcoholism in a city is a nonevent until, perhaps, an unemployed alcoholic commits a serious crime. This is "news" because it is out of the ordinary. In addition, interviews with the police and neighbors, pictures of the accused being taken to jail, and the unfolding of the trial are more likely to boost television ratings or newspaper circulation than thoughtful stories on drinking among the jobless. Emphasis on the dramatic is probably most evident in the coverage of foreign affairs. No doubt many people see life in Africa or India as an endless series of riots, assassinations, famines, and revolutions. Here again, the media encourage a superficial understanding of politics.

The importance of drama is especially evident in the way the mass media cover campaigns. Campaigns for high office are important events, yet their day-to-day operations have only limited news value. A newspaper that ran stories such as "Can-

The media may treat news conferences as staged events to attract large audiences. Presidents, for their part, may use the prime-time television coverage as an opportunity to present their policy goals to the public. Here, President Jimmy Carter calls on a reporter during a televised press conference.

didate Meets with Top Advisors" or "Candidate to Study Economic Proposals" would probably bore readers. To stimulate interest, the mass media often engage in what has been described as **race-horse journalism,** the practice of emphasizing who's ahead at the moment and the tactics of each candidate rather than the issues of the campaign. For example, shortly after Geraldine Ferraro became the Democratic vice presidential nominee in 1984, numerous stories appeared on how she would boost the Democrats' chances of victory. Stories also appeared on how the Republicans would respond. Polls asking the question, "If the election were held today, who would you vote for?" became important news stories. In a nutshell, the focus is on campaign "action," not policy issues.

Finally, the image of the world shown in the mass media is highly fragmented, or disconnected. Stories are presented as if the average television viewer or newspaper reader has an extremely limited attention span. The typical newscast or front page is a collection of numerous brief stories with little or no overall context. A three-minute film clip on a member of Congress expressing fears over a mounting budget deficit may be followed by a story on a liver transplant, which in turn is followed by a report on a record Florida cold wave. Such fragmentation makes it very difficult to show the relationship between various happenings.

It is hard to fix blame for the way the media present reality. Most media people argue that they are merely giving people what they want. If newspapers, radio, and television offered lengthy treatments of complex issues, they would lose their audiences. Being entertaining is more important than being thoughtful. In addition, the mass media in the United States are privately owned and therefore must earn a profit to survive. Moreover, media defenders claim that there are limits on what the average person can grasp. A live report on a single hungry child conveys the problem of hunger better than tables and charts on caloric intake.

Defining Political Situations

The mass media tell us what is going on out there in the world; they can also interpret those events for us. When the media devote time and energy to a story, the public is being told that "this is important." This is sometimes called the *agenda-setting role* of the mass media. What is not discussed becomes "not important." The capacity to make some issues important is illustrated in the mass media's handling of crime. Since the early 1960s, with few exceptions, crimes of all sorts have increased. Each day there are thousands of crimes, ranging from the petty to the most gruesome. By suddenly giving even a small proportion of these stories front-page attention, a newspaper can create the image of a "crime wave." By singling out a dozen of the most brutal crimes, the media can give the impression that civilization is on the verge of collapse. With enough attention, "fear of crime" and "crime in the streets" can become major political issues.

The meaning of a political event is shaped by the language used to describe it. This is illustrated by the treatment the media have accorded the Social Security program in recent years. The central fact is that the program is paying out more than it receives, and this gap will probably increase in the near future. The media have repeatedly called this situation a "crisis" leading to possible "bankruptcy." The image suggested is that millions of elderly and disabled citizens could, at any moment, be deprived of their life-supporting benefits. Rarely is it mentioned that the government's obligation is not dependent on the program's bank balance and that Social Security recipients will not lose their assistance unless Congress changes the law.

The mass media also provide ready-made interpretations of complex events. This regularly occurs in deciding who "really" won in a presidential primary. A media-defined victory depends on two things: the proportion of the vote received and prior expectations. Thus, if the media predict that the frontrunner—the candidate who is *expected* to win—will get 75 percent of the vote, but he or she receives "only" 55 percent, the media call the result a "defeat." Perhaps the clearest example occurred in the 1968 New Hampshire presidential primary. Senator Eugene McCarthy, running as an antiwar candidate, lost to President Lyndon Johnson by nearly 8 percent of the vote. Nevertheless, the primary was declared a tremendous loss for the President and a clear rejection of his pro–Vietnam war policy (later but not highly publicized poll data showed many McCarthy voters to be prowar). The mass media turned reality around again in 1972—Edmund Muskie defeated George McGovern in New Hampshire, but McGovern was called the "big winner," since the victory margin was far less than "expected." In 1976, Jimmy Carter received only 30 percent of the New Hampshire Democratic vote, yet was described by one network as "the man to beat" and appeared on the covers of both *Time* and *Newsweek*.

One noteworthy aspect of the media's instant interpretations is their frequent similarity. That is, most television and radio stations and newspapers report an event from the same perspective. Such uniformity has been called the result of **pack journalism.** Pack journalism is perhaps easiest to see in presidential campaigns. Each candidate travels with a group of reporters, all of whom receive the same information. These reporters also spend a great deal of time with each other and may come to develop a common view of events. In addition, a reporter who writes from a different perspective from dozens of other reporters can worry an editor or television news director. Imagine if all three networks, the *New York Times*, and the *Washington Post* declare that the President's economic proposal will cut taxes and one reporter tells his editor that it will raise taxes. The editor will probably follow the pack. Sometimes one well-respected journalist can even set the overall theme of a particular campaign news story or event.

Influencing the Voters

Thus far we have considered how the mass media shape the political environment. For candidates and campaign managers the most important point, however, is whether the media can sway votes. In one sense the answer is obvious. Candidates spend lots of money on media advertising. Therefore, they must believe they are getting something in return. On the other hand, studies of the media's impact on elections are inconclusive. It is difficult to disentangle all the effects of all the media on millions of citizens. Each voter reads, watches, or hears a unique combination of news and paid advertisements, and people differ in how they interpret this information. Moreover, the mass media can influence people without their being aware of it.

Evidence suggests that the media do play a role in informing citizens about the candidates and issues. One study of the 1976 election reported that public awareness of Ford and Carter increased in the course of the campaign.[8] Several other studies report that people learn from television commercials, newspaper stories, broadcast candidate debates, and various campaign events.[9] After Gary Hart did unexpectedly well in the 1984 New Hampshire Democratic primary, for instance, the media focused a great deal of attention on him.

The media's educational role does not, however, operate equally for all candidates and for all segments of the population. In 1976, for example, public awareness of a number of contenders for the Democratic presidential nomination did *not* increase despite expensive campaigns. A similar situation occurred in 1984—candidates such as Reuben Askew remained virtual unknowns despite all the attention given the Democratic presidential primaries. Studies also suggest that the media may have their largest educational impact on those who begin with minimal information.[10] If you have never heard of any of the candidates, watching the news will make a big difference.

Research on the ability of television commercials to change votes suggests that the media's power may be exaggerated. For example, during the 1972 presidential election the research team of Patterson and McClure followed the television watching patterns and political views of a group of citizens in Syracuse, New York. Both before and after the campaign, these citizens were asked to rate McGovern and Nixon on various personality and leadership traits (for example, experience, trustworthiness). During the course of the campaign these images changed. However, the researchers concluded that these changing images were unrelated to the viewing of television commercials. People who liked a particular candidate used the ads to bolster their favorable image; if they disliked a candidate, the ads provided "evidence" for the dislike.[11] Negative views rarely became positive, or the other way around.

To measure the impact of advertising on actual voting decisions, Patterson and McClure focused on the small group (20 percent) within their sample that switched their voting intentions sometime during the campaign. These people were asked to explain their change of heart. The largest group of switchers (42 percent) offered some major event as a cause. Most important, only 23 percent of these switches seemed to be a consequence of the mass media, and many of these were only loosely related to specific advertising themes. In sum, the belief that televised political advertising can influence a large number of voters is not true.

Studies of the role of newspapers and magazines suggest that coverage of events and editorial endorsements can have a limited though still significant impact on voters. This seems to be especially true in races for lower offices—mayors, state senators—when local newspapers may devote attention to contests ignored by television and the national print media. In such contests a local newspaper may be the most important source of information. For example, one study of ten elections in Texas towns found that nine of the ten candidates endorsed by local newspapers won.[12] Newspaper endorsements also seem to play a role in presidential contests. A study by John Robinson, for example, reports that in 1968 a newspaper endorsement could increase a presidential candidate's share of the vote by about 6 percent.[13]

There is one highly controversial area of possible media impact on voting. It concerns the election day predictions made by the three television networks. Since the 1960s, the networks have competed with each other to "call" elections before complete returns are in. Such calls are usually made on the basis of sample precincts in the eastern portion of the nation. If, for example, a traditionally Democratic area has gone Republican, this is evidence for a national Republican victory. More recently, the networks have used **exit polls**—surveys of voters as they leave the polling booths—to make predictions. Because of time differences, this has resulted in the networks' announcing their choice of the "winner" for the presidency long before the West Coast voting booths have closed. The fear is that with the election "over," many people do not vote, while others may change their decisions (for example, not to support the "loser"), so that the outcome itself may be influenced. National legislation has even been proposed that would prohibit early projections and declarations.

The evidence of the ability of the mass media to alter West Coast voting by declaring one candidate the winner is mixed. Let us first consider the media's impact on turnout levels. In a number of studies, analysts interviewed West Coast residents the day before the election and on election day. Several respondents who had said they intended to vote failed to do so. Only a few of these nonvoters gave television coverage on election night as the reason they did not vote.[14] In the 1980 election the evidence is conflicting. One study found no decline in West Coast voting, but another using a different approach showed an impact.[15]

The evidence is also contradictory on the question of whether television projection results in switched votes. One 1964 study in California reported that only 3 respondents out of a total of 1,212 changed their vote because the outcome had already been announced on television. A group of undecided voters who heard the news of the Lyndon Johnson landslide voted pretty much the same way as those who had not heard the news. A similar pattern was found in the much closer 1968 election. Most citizens did not hear election night projections, but even among those who did, very few (0.7 percent) changed their voting behavior.[16] The major contrary evidence to this view is an analysis of the 1980 election conducted by John E. Jackson. He examined the way

citizens had planned to vote, their exposure to events such as Carter's concession speech or television projections, and their actual vote. Overall, he found that supporters of the winner (Reagan) were more likely to stay home because the election was a foregone conclusion.[17] However, given the size of the Reagan victory, this particular response had no political consequences at the presidential level—though it may have influenced state and congressional contests.

Part of the reason for the contradictory findings probably lies in the different character of each presidential election. Some elections—1964 and 1972—were not expected to be close. Others—1968 and 1976—turned out closer than expected. In 1980, the election was expected to be closer than the final outcome. West Coast voters may respond differently depending on circumstances. For example, where there was little contest to begin with, election evening projections may have a minor impact. In contrast, the impact of television can be greater in a "surprise" such as 1980 (that is, many citizens, in anticipation of a close contest, had expected to vote, but when the race turned out not to be a cliffhanger, some stayed home).

These and several other studies should not be taken as evidence that the mass media play only a minor role despite all the money spent on them. Even without producing actual change in voters' behavior, the media can play an important role. In the first place, television news shows, commercials, and newspaper stories may push people toward a particular candidate, but since voters receive pushes in different directions, the net shift may be small. If only one candidate makes use of the media, however, the media may contribute to a landslide. In other words, part of the media's impact may be simply to lessen the impact of the opposition.

Second, a major purpose of mass media campaigns is not to persuade the opposition but to motivate likely supporters. American elections tend to have relatively low turnouts—even presidential races rarely exceed 60 percent. Sometimes merely getting one's supporters registered and to the polling place on election day can ensure vic-

In Idaho a citizen fills out a paper ballot. Choices on election day are influenced by a number of sources, including the media.

tory. A television advertising campaign could thus have a dramatic impact without ever changing a vote. Also, mass media exposure is necessary for raising funds and attracting campaign workers. Here again, success does not depend on conversions.

Third, the mass media can be used to make the opponent's supporters less sure of their commitment. Advertising won't necessarily persuade them to switch their votes, but they may decide not to vote for either candidate. Given the high regard Americans have for voting, this tactic is not often openly discussed, but it exists.

Finally, even if only a few citizens switch their votes, that fact can be decisive in a close election. This is especially true in the race for the presidency because of the winner-take-all rule (except in Maine) and the electoral college. A few thousand votes in a few states out of several million

total votes can sometimes shift enough electoral votes to change the outcome. In 1976, for example, a few more votes for Gerald Ford in Ohio and Hawaii would have sent Ford rather than Carter to the White House.

Limits on the Power of the Mass Media

Most people agree that the mass media have considerable power over politics in general and over elections in particular. Such power has generated fears that citizens and government will be manipulated by television and newspaper coverage of events. No doubt, there are many specific situations in which a political event and its impact were entirely the creation of the media. Nevertheless, it is an exaggeration to argue that the mass media have great political control in the United States.

One important check on media power is their diversity. Even in television, where programming tends to be similar throughout the country, there is no single point of view. Besides the three major networks, there is the Public Broadcasting System, "superstations" such as TBS, and a growing number of specialty cable stations. In 1980 there were 725 stations operating. No one station, even if it dominates the ratings, reaches most citizens at any one time, and many points of view can be heard. Radio is even more varied. In 1980, there were 6,603 radio stations, ranging from big-city rock 'n' roll outlets to FM stations serving small ethnic communities. The print media are the most diverse of all—there were nearly 20,000 newspaper and magazines published in 1982. These publications probably gave voice to every possible political viewpoint.

The mass media in the United States are also privately owned. There are no state-owned radio and television stations, as there are in many European nations (for instance, the BBC in Great Britain). Moreover, media ownership is not concentrated among just a few companies. While some corporations own several television stations and newspapers, no one company comes close to having a monopoly. There is even a government policy of preventing a communications monopoly. Companies are not permitted to own more

Commentary: Television and the Negative Campaign

Mudslinging has a long history in American politics. As far back as 1840, presidential incumbent Martin Van Buren was accused of being an aloof aristocrat who lolled about the White House drinking champagne and eating off gold plates. He lost to William Henry Harrison, who was portrayed—with equal disregard for the truth—as a simple man of the people who lived in a log cabin. The 1840 election was essentially an issueless contest, the type of race especially likely to result in negative campaigning. When there is little of substance to differentiate candidates, they tend to fall back on smears and whispering campaigns.

There is no question that, since the 1960s, television has played an increasingly important role in political campaigns. Its effects on negative campaigning, however, are unclear. While this popular mass medium has probably not raised the overall level of negative campaigning, it may have added a dimension of subtlety to the way accusations are publicized. An example is afforded by one of the most famous, and most controversial, television ads of all time.

In 1964 Barry Goldwater, the Republican candidate for President, was running against the Democratic incumbent, Lyndon Johnson. In his comments on the conflict in Vietnam (which was just beginning to be a major political issue), Goldwater implied that the war might be won sooner if military commanders in the field were not restrained by the President in their use of nuclear weapons.

The Democrats' response was a commercial showing a little girl plucking petals from a daisy and counting. When she reached ten, a voice-over began an ominous countdown to zero, followed by an atomic explosion. Finally, Johnson's voice boomed out pleading for a peaceful world. The ad mentioned neither Goldwater nor the Republican party, but clearly conveyed the message that the Republican candidate was a trigger-happy danger to society. Outraged protests from Republicans forced the Democrats to take the commercial off the air. This incident illustrates another point about negative campaigning: it often backfires when maligned candidates gain sympathy from the public.

Probably the best defense against negative campaigning— whether on television or anywhere else—is candor coupled with humor, especially if these qualities can be called into play before smear tactics have a chance to gather momentum. In the 1984 presidential election, Ronald Reagan's staff worried about the age factor, for the President was seventy-three—not only a senior citizen but twenty years older than his opponent, Walter Mondale. Reagan used the occasion of a televised debate with Mondale to face the issue squarely: "I want you to know," he said to millions of television viewers, "that I will not make age an issue of this campaign. I am not going to exploit for political purposes my opponent's youth and inexperience."

In evaluating negative campaign tactics, voters have become more sophisticated. They may wonder why politicians have to resort to smears against their opponents. The result is often that candidates who take the low road in a campaign end up on the losing side on election day.

than a certain number of television stations or dominate the flow of information. Even locally owned affiliates of the three networks have some independence in their programming.

Thus it is very difficult for the media to impose one view or interpretation on the public. Imagine if the head of one network decided that a particular candidate was an incompetent fool who should

not be elected. Stories would be run on national news programs that made the candidate look bad, and reporters would be encouraged to dig into the person's past for damaging material. If the other media did not share this opinion, the network's treatment would be so obvious that people would begin to examine why it stressed only negative stories. Locally owned affiliates might threaten to drop the national news. Sooner or later it would come out that somebody was "out to get" the candidate, and this would greatly harm the reputation of the network. Such a scenario would not be possible if all the mass media were centrally controlled or owned.

Reinforcing this diversity is accessibility. Candidates or political groups that feel themselves discriminated against by television networks, for example, can usually find some way of expressing their views. One way is simply to buy television and radio time or newspaper space to convey their message. Also, according to the Federal Communication Commission's rules, all candidates must be given equal access to free or paid-for airtime on television or radio (however, this has been modified by Congress on occasion to allow televised debates among just the Democratic and Republican candidates for the presidency). The mass media's enormous appetite for news and entertainment also means that someone with something interesting to say can frequently get some attention. Indeed, the media have sometimes been criticized for giving too much attention to groups and individuals who resort to dramatics for the sake of media attention (for example, covering candidates who walk across their state as a publicity gimmick).

Perhaps the biggest obstacle to media domination of politics is the built-in resistance of citizens, who do not begin each election campaign with blank minds that are then "filled in" by television, radio, and newspaper stories. There are some politically significant events—economic depressions, inflation, unsuccessful war efforts, for example—that are not easily "managed" by the media. The dramatic gasoline price increases of the late 1970s could not be made acceptable through a well-orchestrated public relations campaign. Many people also start each campaign with strong beliefs about political parties and candidates. According to the Center for Political Studies, in the 1980 elections about 55 percent of voters had made their choices by the time the conventions were over. A Gallup poll of voters in 1984 found that 84 percent never wavered in their choice for President during the campaign.

Televised nominating conventions focus on the hoopla rather than on serious issues in the campaign.

It is also true that viewers and readers can exercise a degree of control over what they watch and read. For instance, a conservative Reagan supporter, if bombarded with pro-Democratic, liberal messages on television, can either switch channels or find a more compatible source of information. Moreover, while the public generally trusts the mass media, they are not given a blank check. A statement by a commentator characterizing Ronald Reagan as sympathetic to Communist expansion would probably not be believed. Finally, a number of studies suggest that people are limited in just how much they can absorb from the media: only a small portion of what is viewed or read may ever sink in.[18]

To return to our question of whether the mass media have too much power, it should be clear that the answer is no. Certainly they have great penetration of American life, they shape much of how we view the world, and they can affect voting. Nevertheless, they do not control politics. In addition, media abuses can be corrected. Over the years the federal government has issued many rules regarding access to the broadcast media, editing of political messages, and fees the media can charge candidates for commercials. (Otherwise, a television station might try to ban a particular view by charging overly high advertising rates.) In short, the media, though powerful, are not an unlimited or unchecked power.

Check Your Understanding

1. What kinds of approaches to political events do the mass media favor?

2. How can the mass media define a particular political situation?

3. What role can the media play in the outcome of an election?

4. What are some of the limits on the mass media's political influence?

THE POLITICS OF ELECTIONS AND CITIZENS' CONTROL OF GOVERNMENT

Taken together, all the material we have presented does not show the American public in the most flattering light. Many citizens do not vote; voting choices are not always careful, issue-based decisions; and numerous factors can prevent voters from reaching the best decisions. The election process has occasionally been likened to a three-ring circus, where candidates compete by using slogans and stunts.

People who accept this negative view usually have an idealistic view of what elections are supposed to accomplish. For them, elections are a means by which citizens shape the actions of government. If, for example, a majority of citizens want government to emphasize rebuilding American industries, keeping unemployment low, and eliminating pollution, it is through elections that the message is to be sent. Nonvoting or voting on the basis of a candidate's good looks and nice family thus hurts the political communication process.

There is, however, a different perspective on the role of elections in a democracy. Elections can be viewed as the means by which leaders are accepted or rejected on the basis of a large number of factors—past performance in office, promises of future action, evaluations of character and ability, leadership style, or moral virtue. The process can be likened to a marketplace—sellers (candidates) compete for buyers (voters), and buying decisions reflect a varying emphasis on quality, prestige, durability, and so on. There is no one product, buyers themselves decide what is important, and mistakes are correctable (you don't buy again). Put into election terms, voters shop around for leaders and, under conditions of limited information and uncertainty, make choices that seem best for them.

This view of elections has much to recommend it. It is a view consistent with our constitutional system of government. As noted in Chapter 2, those who wrote the Constitution did not expect citizens to dictate policy through the electoral process. Elections permitted citizens to hold officials accountable for their actions, not to choose these actions themselves. It is also a perspective that does not place a burden on the average citizen. To criticize citizens for not knowing where each and every candidate stands is unfair, given other demands on their time and the complexity of politics.

In sum, how you view nonvoting, mass-media-based "new politics," and the merchandising of candidates depends on how you view the role of elections. If elections are supposed to allow citizens to decide policy questions, such phenomena are problems. On the other hand, if elections are merely ways that citizens choose leaders, then they can be thought of as part of the political marketplace. Apathy and media influence are obstacles only when they undermine fair and open competition.

CHAPTER SUMMARY

Who participates in elections? Compared to many other Western democracies, voting participation is low in the United States. In general, wealthier, better-educated groups are more likely to vote. Apathy has its roots in legal, personal, and political factors. People disagree over the consequences of extensive apathy—some view it as a threat to democracy; others see it as largely unimportant.

What determines how people vote? There is no single accepted explanation of voting behavior. The party-identification approach stresses the early learning of party loyalty and the way this loyalty shapes later responses. However, many people do not identify with a political party, and changes can occur among those who do. The issue-voting explanation sees voters as choosing the candidate who comes closest to their own views. Closely related explanations focus on judgments made on past performance or evaluations of a person's character. From the group-voting perspective, voters make their choices on the basis of group identities and appeals. Each of these explanations has a degree of validity and may apply to different situations.

Are campaigns conducted fairly? In contemporary politics fears are often expressed regarding the role of money and political merchandising in campaigns. Despite several reforms limiting contributions and providing public funding of presidential races, money is still important. Modern campaigns are very expensive, but money is only one factor in success. In general, large contributors gain access, not special treatment. The use of professional campaign consultants has resulted in the clever selling of candidates to the public. However, such packaging is not always effective.

Do the mass media exercise too much power? The mass media are a widespread force in Ameri-

can society and politics. They affect politics in many ways. They help to create "reality," they define political situations, and under some circumstances they can sway voters. There are, however, limits on their impact. Voters may possess strong opinions, they may not believe the media, and they may refuse to listen to them. Equally important, no one source in the media has a monopoly, and many views have access. The media, overall, do not undermine a democratic electoral process.

IMPORTANT TERMS

Explain the following terms.

split ticket voting
retrospective voting
Australian ballot
political action committee (PAC)
exit poll

THINKING CRITICALLY

1. One possible solution to low voter turnout for elections is compulsory voting. Citizens would be fined for not voting. What might be some of the consequences of compulsory voting?
2. The present ballot used in elections does not offer the response "none of the above" for voters dissatisfied with the choices. Should such an alternative be included on ballots? Explain your answer.
3. Citizens are often told to vote on the basis of issues, not on the appearance of a candidate or on other personal characteristics. Can voting on the basis of race, sex, religion, or ethnicity be justified? Explain your answer.

4. Should there be minimum standards of political knowledge before a person can vote? Explain your answer.

5. Since incumbents often have advantages over opponents (in the amount of money they can raise, free publicity they receive, and so on), would a government-subsidized "bonus" to the challengers make elections more balanced? Why or why not?

6. Should there be a national law regulating how candidates for federal office can be "packaged"? Why or why not?

7. Do the mass media have an obligation to present in-depth treatments of political news even when the public might prefer more entertaining coverage? Explain your answer.

8. During past elections, TV news coverage often projected winners based on early voting results. This practice is not done as often now. Many officeholders proposed laws prohibiting such TV "calls" of election outcomes before all the votes are counted. They argued that such projections might change the results. Do you agree that TV "calls" of elections might effect election results? Why or why not? Would you support laws that ban such practices?

EXTENDING YOUR UNDERSTANDING

1. Compare U.S. voting turnout with figures from other Western democracies. What might explain the higher rates in other countries? Are there lessons to be learned for the United States? Present your conclusions in a report.

2. Investigate the legal qualifications for voting in elections in your town or city. You might find the information by calling the board of elections. What is the purpose of each of these restrictions? Explain your findings in a report.

3. Watch a national news program. Analyze the program in terms of (a) how many topics are covered; (b) how much time is spent on personalities rather than on issues; (c) the use of action "footage" rather than announcer description. Do you think the program is effective in presenting the news? Why or why not? What standards would you use to judge the effectiveness of the program?

4. Read articles on the same political issue appearing in several different magazines. Compare how the magazines treat this topic. Note any instances of biased reporting or viewpoint. Which of the articles do you find most convincing? Why? Write a report of your conclusions.

MAKING DECISIONS

In your library or local newspaper office, examine back issues of newspapers to find advertisements for a statewide or local candidate in a recent election. List the political issues that were mentioned. List the information included that refers to the candidates' past accomplishments. Do you think that the advertisements are helpful in persuading people how to vote? Based on the advertisements, for whom would you vote? On what factors would you base your decision?

Chapter 7
Political Parties

The existence of political parties in the United States is a paradox. On the one hand, the Democratic and Republican parties have had long and successful histories. Few political parties in other countries can match their longevity. Moreover, only on rare occasions do independent candidates win elections at the state and national level. On the other hand, many citizens dislike political parties, and proposals have been made to abolish or sharply curtail them. In many cities parties are prohibited from nominating candidates or conducting campaigns. Feelings toward parties are often negative. One survey conducted in 1980 found that 56 percent of the people interviewed believed that parties help to confuse, not clarify, the issues; 73 percent felt that a voter should ignore party affiliation. Only 22 percent thought that parties were doing a good job for the country. At the same time, however, only 32 percent said that we don't need parties in America.[1] Why do the two parties survive while so many people have mixed feelings about them? Are parties still relevant, or have they outlived their usefulness? In this chapter we will consider these four questions:

- What are political parties?
- Do the Democratic and Republican parties differ?
- Do political parties have any impact?
- Are political parties in decline?

PREVIEW

What are political parties? Parties are organizations that nominate candidates for office. There are several types of parties in the United States; the most important parties are the Democrats and the Republicans. These two parties are composed of three elements: citizens, party officials, and elected officeholders. Psychologically most people identify with either the Democratic party or the Republican party. The parties have no control over such affiliation, and as a result both include people of diverse backgrounds. The official party organization ranges from the precinct through the national committee. In principle, but not in practice, the parties are hierarchically organized and well coordinated. The third component of political parties, elected officials, includes governors, members of Congress, state legislators, and so on.

Do the Democratic and Republican parties differ? Differences between the parties exist, but they are usually moderate and do not extend to all issues. One difference is in the types of people attracted to the parties. Democrats have traditionally had support among poor people, blacks, Jews, Catholics, and Southerners. The Republicans are strongest among business and professional people. One major issue—the role government should play in the economy—provides the clearest illustration of the difference between the political philosophies of the parties. Differences also emerge when we examine preferences of party leaders, the policies endorsed in platforms, and votes in Congress.

Do political parties have any impact? Parties help citizens decide how to vote. Though a candidate's party affiliation is an imperfect guide to his or her position on issues, it permits reasonable guessing. Parties also simplify election conflict and provide campaign funds, technical help, and a certain number of "automatic" votes for candidates. They likewise help coordinate the actions of government officials. The tie of party loyalty helps overcome the separation of political power in our constitutional system. In addition, parties provide organized opposition to government policy by nominating candidates to run against incumbents and by serving as forums in which government policies can be discussed. Finally, because they contain diverse groups, provide entry into politics for new interests, and create broad electoral coalitions, parties help reduce political conflict.

Are political parties in decline? The two major parties seem to be weakening. Historically, however, the parties have gone through several periods of strength and weakness. Parties have also survived many challenges and have demonstrated their adaptability. The establishment of civil service, the popularity of primaries, the emergence of a campaign-for-hire industry, and a decline in party loyalty have posed threats to party survival. The collapse of parties would harm the poor most seriously, because this group is most dependent on the services provided by parties.

WHAT ARE POLITICAL PARTIES?

In principle, a political party is an organization that nominates candidates for public office. A group may work for a political goal by contributing to campaigns or voting for candidates, but it is not a party unless it puts forth candidates under its own name.

In the United States, political parties have taken a variety of forms. Some, like the Socialist Labor party, go through the motions of nominating and running candidates, but their goal is to promote their views, not to win elections. Others, such as the Independent party organized by John Anderson in his unsuccessful quest for the presidency in 1980, are little more than convenient vehicles for a single candidate, which disappear after the election. The Libertarian party, which advocates a minimal government, is yet a third type of party. Here a small group of people bound only by a common philosophy are committed to a lengthy process of gaining political power by running candidates for office. Their hope is that in each election they will show greater and greater strength.

The most important political parties in the United States are the Democrats and the Republicans. Describing these two major parties is not simple because each is itself composed of many citizens, organizations, and government officials. These components can be thought of as the party-in-the-electorate, the party-as-organization, and the party-in-government, in that order. Each of these elements is an integral part of the two major parties, yet each frequently acts independently of the others. Let us briefly characterize each of the three components of the Democrats and the Republicans.

Citizens: Party-in-the-Electorate

As mentioned in Chapter 6, psychologically most citizens identify with one of the two major parties. Just as they think of themselves as part of a religious or ethnic group, most people consider themselves Democrats or Republicans. In 1984, for example, about 64 percent of a national sample viewed themselves as either Democrats or Republicans.[2] Since the 1930s, when opinion polls began asking people their party affiliation, most Americans have identified with one of the two major parties. As Figure 7.1 shows, the proportion of those identifying with the two major parties has ebbed and flowed, but **independents**—those who do not identify with either party—have never been in a majority during this period.

Party "membership" is entirely an individual matter. There are no voting or issue position requirements for membership. If one decides to be a Republican, one becomes part of the Republican party. If other Republicans object to you, they can do little about it. The same is true, of course, of the Democrats. In some states there are legal obligations to declare one's party affiliation before

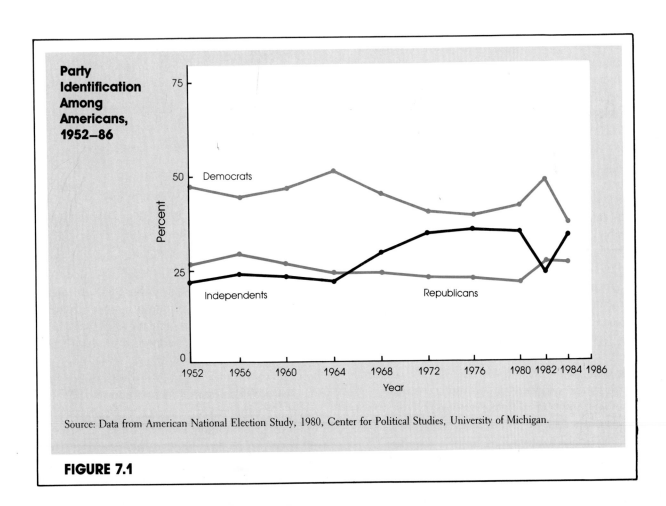

Party Identification Among Americans, 1952–86

Source: Data from American National Election Study, 1980, Center for Political Studies, University of Michigan.

FIGURE 7.1

being allowed to vote in a party primary, but there are no restrictions on who can join a party (primaries are discussed in more detail later in the chapter). Not surprisingly, the party-in-the-electorate is an extremely varied group. The Democratic party, for example, contains people who strongly favor civil rights and people who oppose government efforts to implement those rights. The Republican party includes both business executives and labor union members.

That political parties cannot control who affiliates with them is important. Both the Democrats and the Republicans have frequently been criticized for not taking distinct positions on issues or for trying to please contradictory interests. They have been characterized as "Tweedledum" and "Tweedledee," the nearly identical pair from *Alice in Wonderland*. Yet as long as the parties have no say in who becomes a member, lack of clarity on the issues will be unavoidable. As we saw in Chapter 6, parties rely heavily on their supporters for votes, so they must satisfy many different kinds of people who, entirely on their own, have decided to identify with them. This is not true in some European nations; parties there more closely resemble private organizations that set standards on who can join.

Party-as-Organization

The second element of American parties is their particular organizations at the national, state, and local levels, with their leaders and staffs. Psychological identification draws ordinary citizens to a party. To obtain a party leadership position, however, a person must follow some prescribed route. You cannot simply decide to become, say, a Democratic county chairperson. Becoming a party official typically requires winning elections among either citizens belonging to the party or fellow party officials.

The Organization of Political Parties

In principle, political parties are organized from the lowest official to the highest (see Figure 7.2). In practice, lines of authority are usually weak. As one study put it, "The political party organization in the United States can best be described as a network of committees which interact and cooperate when it is to their mutual benefit."[3] Since the chief goal of the party organization is to win elections, party structure generally follows the geographical boundaries of electoral districts.

Precinct. The smallest unit in the party is the **precinct**, which usually has fewer than a thousand voters. The precinct organization is headed by a precinct leader or precinct captain, who is either elected in the party primary or at a party precinct meeting, or appointed by higher party officials, depending on the state. The basic job of the precinct organization is to register sympathetic voters, distribute campaign literature, increase voter turnout on election day, and collect political information that will have a bearing on coming elections. In larger cities precinct leaders sometimes act as mediators between citizens and municipal agencies.

County organization. On the next rung up is the county organization. Considerable variation exists among states in how these officials are selected. In some states they are chosen by county voters in the party primary; in others they are elected from precincts or even chosen by party convention. The county party leader frequently plays a major role in making patronage appointments (government jobs given as rewards for campaign service), directing the campaign, and recruiting candidates for office. The county chairperson usually represents his or her area at the state level.

State organization. The third level is occupied by the state party committee. Again, there is a wide state-to-state variation in how these organizations are set up. Typically, state law requires that a certain number of men and women from each electoral district, such as a county, be represented on the state committee. County leaders and elected officials are also sometimes automatically included. The major responsibilities of the state party chairperson include raising money, coordinating state campaign activities, maintaining party organizations, and providing a channel of communication between national and state party offi-

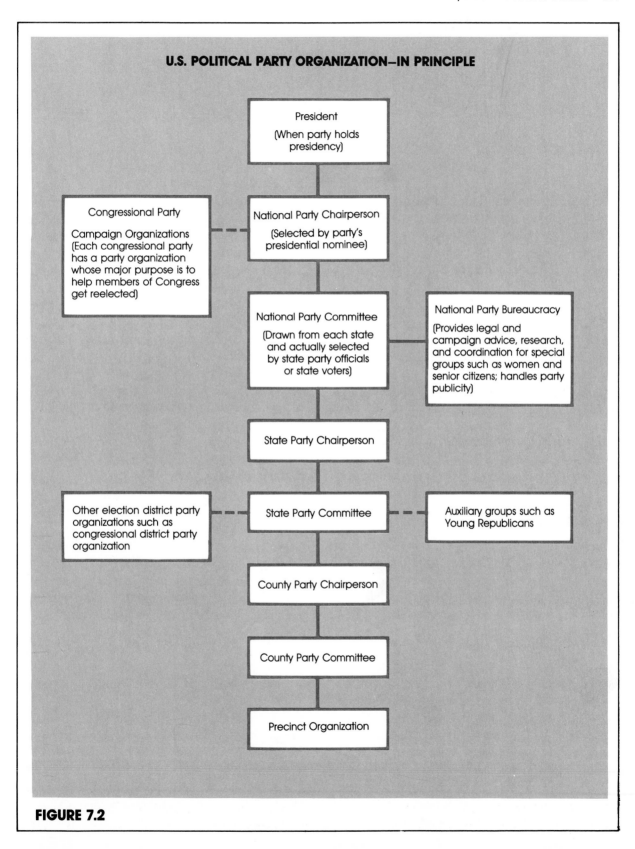

FIGURE 7.2

cials. Since states play a key role in American electoral politics (even at the presidential level, because of the electoral college), the state organization is usually the most important unit in party organization.

In many states several additional party organizations exist that do not fit into the pyramid-shaped organizational chart. Most parties have created special organizations to attract particular groups (for example, the Young Republicans). Other groups are created for fundraising purposes. In several states issue-oriented wings of the party have built a sort of party within a party to advance their causes. In 1953, for example, liberals in the California Democratic party formed the California Democratic Council (CDC) to work on behalf of liberal causes through campaign activity, forums, and social functions. The relationship between state organizations and these special groups varies considerably. Sometimes the offshoot groups are subordinate to the state party; in other cases disputes arise over resources and responsibilities.

National party organization. At the top of the Democratic and Republican party structures are the national party organizations, each having several parts. At the head is the national chairperson and his or her staff. These people come from a variety of backgrounds—members of Congress, campaign managers, business people—and their role has varied from quiet, behind-the-scenes manager to vigorous innovator. In principle, the national chairperson is selected by the delegates attending the presidential nominating convention, but in practice he or she is the choice of the party's presidential nominee.

The chairperson and his or her staff (which can grow to six hundred during a presidential election year) have many administrative responsibilities. The activities of numerous groups within the national party organization—groups dealing with women, blacks, Hispanics, and young people, among others—must be coordinated. There are also research services, associations of state and local party officials, speakers' bureaus, offices that deal with patronage, and several other specialized committees. On occasion the chairperson may be called on to give speeches defending the party's record, criticize the opposition, raise funds, and smooth over conflicts within the party.

The second major element of the national organization is the national committees. Both the Democratic and the Republican national committees consist of a number of party representatives from each state. Since the early 1970s the Democrats have also included elected officials and some representatives of party groups such as young Democrats. Because of their size and lack of day-to-day involvement in national party affairs, these national committees have limited responsibilities. Their most important task is to set the rules for the presidential nominating convention—its location, the procedures for selecting delegates, the apportionment of delegates among states, and actual convention arrangements. In many instances these rules have had a major impact on which candidate was selected. During the 1984 Democratic presidential primary, for example, Jesse Jackson and other contenders complained that the party's "threshold requirement"—a minimum percentage of a state's votes had to be gained before one could receive convention delegates—hurt their chances, since they often finished third or fourth in the primary.

In addition to these permanent organizational elements, the national parties sometimes create commissions and task forces to deal with special problems. For example, following the trouble-filled 1968 Democratic convention, a Commission on Party Structure and Delegate Selection was set up. Originally chaired by Senator George McGovern of South Dakota and then by Representative Donald Fraser of Minnesota, the McGovern-Fraser Commission (as it was called) proposed delegate selection rules that greatly opened up the presidential nominating process to women, young people, and minorities in 1972. This was followed by the Mikulski Commission in 1972, the Winegrad Commission in 1976, and the Hunt Commission in 1980, all of which dealt with delegate selection and convention voting procedures. The Republicans have also created national party commissions, though their proposals have not been as far-reaching as those of their Democratic counterparts.

Traditionally, the national party organizations were largely concerned with the presidential election; state and congressional races were the responsibility of state party organizations. Since the late 1970s, however, the national organizations have become much involved in the parties' overall electoral fate. From 1976 to 1981, the national Republican organization helped to recruit and train candidates for state legislatures, ran a Campaign Management College for congressional candidates, and recruited strong candidates in congressional races against Democratic incumbents who seemed relatively easy to defeat. The Democratic National Committee has also become a revitalized force, especially in raising funds and creating groups associated with the national organization. In anticipation of the 1984 election the Democratic party sponsored "training academies" for prospective candidates—four-day seminars at which candidates listened to pep talks, were advised on issues, and learned how to dress for television appearances.

Congressional Party Organization: Party-in-Government

Within both houses of Congress (and most state legislatures) there are organizations consisting of members of the same party (sometimes called caucuses). In Congress these include the elected leaders—Speaker of the House, majority leader, and so on—and their assistants, called whips. These leaders plan the party's overall legislative strategy and coordinate the President's program if the President is of the same party. Each party in each house has a committee with the important role of assigning members to congressional committees. Policy committees also exist to decide on party policy, but their decisions are not binding.

One element of the congressional party has recently grown in importance—the congressional campaign committees, which collect and distribute money for campaigns of party members. Though campaign committees have been in existence for some time, they did not become an

important source of funds until 1980. The Republican committees in particular have been well financed. Between January 1983 and the middle of October 1984, the Republican senatorial campaign committee raised $73.5 million; the equivalent Democratic committee raised only $8.2 million. Similar differences existed in House party campaign committees: the Republicans raised $54.2 million, the Democrats $9.3 million.

Coordination Among Party Groups

On paper, American political parties are neatly organized, well-coordinated organizations. This image is misleading. In practice, the national, state, and local groups function on their own and sometimes disagree with each other. In many states, such as New York and Illinois, conflicts often occur between big-city party officials and those in suburban or rural areas. During the 1960s many Democratic state party organizations in the South were split on the race issue and even sent separate delegations to presidential nominating conventions. The national party chairperson cannot set party policy in the state organizations. He or she must use persuasion, not coercion. In 1972 the powerful Chicago Democratic organization differed with the national organization and decided to "sit out" the election rather than wage its usual vigorous campaign. The national party could do little to overcome this decision. Perhaps the strongest weapons available to national leaders are to refuse to seat state party delegations at the presidential nominating convention and to deny national party campaign funds to state candidates. Such threats, however, are of limited value.

An important, though sometimes overlooked, reason for lack of central control is that activities are closely regulated by state law, not party rules. On such matters as scheduling of party elections, party membership requirements, and access to meetings, each state has its own complex laws. Attempts to set uniform national party policy or revise state party rules therefore run into legal obstacles imposed by the states. For example, in 1980 the National Democratic Committee prohibited the use of open primaries—primaries that do not require a person to be an enrolled member of the party in order to vote—in the selection of delegates to the presidential nominating convention: Nevertheless, consistent with their state law, Wisconsin Democrats used an open primary. Similar problems have occurred in the failure of the national committees to shorten the primary season by forcing states to move primaries up to March or April.

American parties also have very few ways of disciplining uncooperative groups or individual members. At one time a President or governor had control over thousands of government jobs—postmasterships, tariff collectors, and the like. Such patronage jobs were used to reward loyal party followers. In exchange for supporting the party's presidential candidates, for instance, a mayor might be given a federally funded construction project involving hundreds of jobs appointed by the mayor. Today, however, patronage jobs are far fewer. The inability of parties to impose their will was well illustrated following Reagan's 1980 victory. Reagan was elected on a platform of tax cuts. He faced strong opposition in the Democratic-controlled House. In 1981–82 much of Reagan's economic program was enacted with the help of conservative Democratic House members (so-called Boll Weevils). No Boll Weevil was expelled from the party, however.

Check Your Understanding

1. How is membership in the Republican and Democratic parties decided? What is the significance of this membership rule?

2. What is the typical structure of a political party organization?

3. What are some of the major responsibilities of the national party organizations?

4. What is the function of party caucuses within Congress?

DO THE DEMOCRATIC AND REPUBLICAN PARTIES DIFFER?

A frequent criticism of the Democratic and Republican parties is that they are the same. Many citizens probably believe that it makes little difference whether a Democrat or a Republican wins. *Are* the two parties different? The answer is yes, they are different—but not in every regard, and only occasionally are these differences significant.

Differences in Party Supporters

One way in which the parties differ is in the types of citizens who identify with them. Table 7.1 shows how the two parties differed in this regard in the middle of 1984. Democrats outnumbered Republicans in almost all groups, but the Republicans did better in some groups than in others. Overall, the Democrats draw their greatest strength from less-well-off groups or groups that are less "established" in American society. Note the clear Democratic edge among blacks, Hispanics, unskilled workers, the poor, and those with less than a high school education. Catholics, Jews, and those in families with union members are also more likely to be Democrats. The greatest sources of Republican strength are high-status groups—those with incomes greater than $40,000, professional and business people, and college graduates. Farmers are also a source of Republican strength.

It is important to realize that these patterns change over time. The most striking change has occurred among blacks. Before the elections of Franklin Roosevelt in 1932 and 1936, blacks were overwhelmingly loyal to the party of Lincoln, the Republican party. Gradually, however, this loyalty lessened as the Democrats vigorously appealed to black voters. Yet even during the 1950s, many blacks considered themselves Republicans. It was only in the 1960s that the black migration to the Democrats was almost complete. Meanwhile, there was a reverse trend among Southern white Protestants. In 1940, for example, 81 percent of

Group Differences in Party Affiliation, 1984		Democrats	Republicans	Independents
	National	41%	29%	30%
	Sex			
	Men	38	30	32
	Women	43	28	29
	Race			
	White	36	32	32
	Black	81	5	14
	Hispanic	49	24	27
	Education			
	College graduate	32	38	30
	Some college	34	31	35
	High school graduate	41	28	31
	Less than high school graduate	53	22	25
	Religion			
	Protestant	40	33	27
	Catholic	44	24	32
	Jewish	57	15	28
	Occupation of chief wage earner			
	Professional and business	33	37	30
	Clerical and sales	35	28	37
	Blue-collar	43	23	34
	Skilled	39	24	37
	Unskilled	46	22	32
	Farmer	32	42	26
	Family Income			
	$40,00 up	30	39	31
	$30,000–39,999	36	33	31
	$20,000–29,999	35	32	33
	$10,000–19,999	45	25	30
	Under $10,000	53	21	26
	One or more household members in a union			
	Union members	49	21	30
	Nonunion	39	31	30

Source: Gallup poll conducted June–July 1984.

TABLE 7.1

this group identified with the Democrats, 11 percent with the Republicans. By 1974, Democratic affiliation had fallen to 43 percent; Republican affiliation had risen to 24 percent.

Paralleling these differences are differences in the issue positions of Democratic and Republican supporters. In general, those who identify with the Democratic party usually take the liberal position on issues, while Republicans are most likely to support the conservative view. Table 7.2 shows how Democrats and Republicans describe themselves using such labels as "liberal," "middle of the

Particular groups in American society are traditionally regarded as loyal to one of the two major parties. Republicans usually do well among white, upper-class voters, while Democratic candidates direct their campaigns to middle-income and minority groups. At top, a cocktail party is held at the Republican National Convention, 1980; below, supporters show their enthusiasm at the 1984 Democratic National Convention.

road," and "conservative" (see Chapter 4). Note that less than a third of the Democrats (29 percent) consider themselves "conservatives," compared to more than two-thirds of the Republicans (69 percent). On the other hand, liberals make up a substantial group among Democrats. Only 8 percent of Republicans, however, would use this term to describe themselves.

The types of issues that most sharply divide Democrats and Republicans concern the federal government's role in regulating the economy and providing social services, a division that goes back to the 1930s and the Roosevelt New Deal. Under the New Deal, as Roosevelt called his policies to help the country recover from the Depression, the federal government set up such programs as Social Security, a national minimum wage, and protection for labor unions. Republican candidates for office attacked these programs as excessive government interference and contrary to the spirit of free

(Drawing by Lorenz; © 1985 The New Yorker Magazine)

"I can't explain it, but suddenly everything is beginning to look Republican."

enterprise. During the 1930s the Democrats gained many new voters who felt that government should provide economic assistance to the needy. Some Democrats opposing the **welfare state** switched their loyalty to the Republicans. (The term *welfare state*, which refers to the collection of government programs to help citizens of all ages, has a somewhat negative meaning in the United States.)

This division continues to this day. For example, in 1980, survey respondents were asked whether they thought the government should enact spending cuts or maintain existing levels of ser-

vices. Nearly 50 percent of the Democrats said that services should be maintained rather than cut; 23 percent of the Republicans expressed this view. On the other hand, Republicans were much more willing to cut services to save tax money. In 1983, respondents were asked whether they felt that the government had a responsibility to help people pay medical bills and that federal spending for health should be increased. In both cases Democrats favored greater government involvement. Democrats were also much more likely to say that the government should try to improve the living conditions of the poor.[4]

Party Affiliation and Liberal/ Conservative Self-Identification, 1980		Democrats	Republicans
	Liberal	37%	8%
	Middle of the Road	34	23
	Conservative	29	69
		100%	100%
	N =	378	259

Source: Data from American National Election Study, 1980, Center for Political Studies, University of Michigan.

TABLE 7.2

On noneconomic issues the pattern of differences is less clear. On matters involving race—the government's role in school integration, assistance to minority groups, and the like—Democrats are more likely to hold liberal views, in part because a large number of blacks identify with the Democratic party. On religious and moral issues (for example, abortion and prayer in public schools) party affiliation seems less important than religious affiliation.

The relationship between party identification and issue positions is most complex on foreign policy. As we might expect, Republicans are more likely to favor larger military expenditures and a more forceful stand against the Soviet Union. Democrats, on the other hand, tend to favor such measures as treaties limiting nuclear weapons. Often, however, attitudes seem to depend on which leader supports which policy. For example, in 1968, when the war in Vietnam was a "Democratic war," there were no differences in support for the war among Democrats and Republicans. However, in 1972, after four years of war under the Republican Nixon, support for the war among Democrats had substantially lessened—the war was now a "Republican war."

There are good reasons why many issues do not separate Democrats and Republicans. In some instances—U.S. resistance to Soviet aggression, for example—leaders of both parties basically have the same view. On other issues, especially highly controversial ones such as government aid to reli-

gious schools, there is nothing even close to an official party position because of the major differences within each party. On other issues—U.S. military involvement in Vietnam, for instance—there is not enough time for a distinct party perspective to emerge (this subject was debated only in the 1968 and 1972 presidential elections). On the whole, for an issue to divide Democrats and Republicans it must be one of fairly long duration and one on which the parties usually take distinct stands.

Differences Among Party Activists

Party differences also show up when we consider the typical characteristics of party officials—for example, county chairpersons and national committee members. According to a study conducted in 1980, 36 percent of the members of the Democratic National Committee called themselves liberal, compared to 1 percent of those on the National Republican Committee. On the other hand, 63 percent of the Republican National Committee were self-described conservatives, compared to 4 percent of the Democrats.[5] In general, issue differences between Democratic and Republican officials are sharper than those that exist between the Republican and Democrat rank and file (that is, members rather than leaders).

Differences between active participants in the two parties are perhaps most visible when we examine who attends presidential nominating conventions. A television viewer could probably quickly guess which convention was on the air. In 1984, for example, 15 percent of all delegates to the Democratic convention were black, as compared to 3 percent at the convention that renominated Reagan. More than half the delegates at the Democratic convention were women (53 percent), compared to 47 percent for the Republicans (up from 29 percent in 1980). The Democrats are also more likely to have young people (under thirty), Hispanics, and union members at their conventions. Delegates to both nominating conventions tend to be relatively well-off, but the Republicans are better off than the Democrats. In 1984, 46 percent of the Republican delegates earned $51,000 or more a year; only 30 percent of the Democratic delegates had this level of income. Overall, these differences are similar to the variations among party identifiers.

The differences between the parties at the activist level are frequently apparent in the **party platforms**—statements of the parties' programs and goals—adopted at presidential nominating conventions. Candidates are not required to support a

Points of View: The Other Parties in 1984

The Democratic and Republican parties dominate American politics, but they are not the only parties. In 1984 several other parties ran candidates for the presidency. Among these were:

Libertarian party. The party is committed to reducing drastically government's involvement in society. Its candidate—David Bergland—was on the ballot in thirty-eight states plus Washington, D.C.

Socialist Workers party. An enduring party calling for government ownership of all industry, it ran Mel Mason in twenty-three states.

American Communist party. Its candidate—Gus Hall—ran in twenty-two states plus Washing-

ton, D.C., in an effort to win Americans to communism.

Citizens party. A liberal party strongly committed to women's rights, higher taxes on corporations, a freeze on nuclear weapons, and a guaranteed income for all Americans. Sonia Johnson, its presidential candidate, qualified for federal matching funds in her campaign.

Populist party. A force in American politics during the late nineteenth century, the modern version was headed by Bob Richards, Gold Medal winner in the 1952 and 1956 Olympics. Its platform called for tax reform and protection from imports.

American party. The origins of this conservative party lie in George Wallace's 1968 bid for the presidency.

Prohibition party. This party is over one hundred years old and has added positions on abortion and religion to its traditional stand against alcohol.

Workers World party. This socialist-oriented party promotes full employment and free health care.

Big Deal party. Headed by Iowa typewriter salesman Gerald Baker, it was on the ballot only in Iowa. Baker opposed waste in the military and supply-side economics. He argued that the existing parties offer voters "no big deal."

Adapted from George B. Merry, "Why Those 'Other' Presidential Candidates Make the Effort," *Christian Science Monitor*, October 12, 1984.

platform, but it often reflects the views of active party leaders and members. Over the years the Democrats have routinely called for greater government efforts to create jobs, eliminate tax loopholes favoring business, and vigorously enforce antidiscrimination laws. Democrats have also endorsed the Equal Rights Amendment (ERA)—see Chapter 2. Republican platforms, on the other hand, typically stress the role of private enterprise in solving problems and the need to encourage investment; they may oppose some government-supported remedies, such as bussing, to help correct past discrimination. Both parties share many common goals—for example, a strong economy—but they often differ on how such goals are to be accomplished or which goals have the highest priority.

Difference Among Elected Officials

We can also compare the parties by looking at the actions of elected officials. Here again there are differences, though rarely do all Democratic officeholders differ from all Republicans. When interest groups rate the voting records of members of Congress, Democrats on average receive good marks from liberal groups such as the Americans for Democratic Action, while Republicans do better with the conservative Americans for Constitutional Action. One major study of Senate voting in 1981 found that on an economic liberalism scale that ranged from −107 (the most conservative) to +196 (the most liberal), Republicans averaged −68, compared to +79 for Democrats. In other words, Democrats are more likely to favor economic help for the poor, greater government regulation of business, and heavier taxes. Comparable differences also occurred on foreign policy issues.[6] In general, Republicans take a tougher position on such questions as arms control agreements with the Soviet Union and resistance to Communist expansion abroad.

Conclusions

We have seen that significant differences exist between the two political parties, especially among active party members and leaders and among members of Congress. However, these differences do not follow a sharp liberal–conservative dividing line. Both parties generally take moderate positions on issues, though each has a more ideologically committed wing, or section. In 1984, for example, some highly conservative Republicans spoke of making dramatic changes in tax policy, almost eliminating social welfare programs, and sharply reducing the size of government. Numerous Republicans in Congress and in state government, however, did not share these views. Also, rarely are positions totally different between the two parties. Most Democrats do not want government to take over private industry, while most Republicans do not want to eliminate all government regulation. There is also considerable overlap—some Democrats act as if they were Republicans, and the other way around.

Not everyone is satisfied with the overlap of issue positions and lack of significant differences between the parties. Some conservative Republicans have complained that some members of their party were too liberal to be "real" Republicans. Some Democrats, for their part, might consider some members of their party not liberal enough to be "true" Democrats. A number of critics of the two-party system would prefer, instead, a clearly liberal party and a clearly conservative party that would offer a genuine choice on election day. Such parties, they argue, would offer voters an easy way to express their views. The call for greater issue separation runs into two problems, however. First, when asked about party differences, survey respondents have indicated little desire for sharply divided parties. They certainly do not want a European-style system in which there are a number of parties, ranging from the extreme right (conservative) to the extreme left (liberal). Rather, they prefer having two parties whose positions occasionally overlap. Second, when a party has run a candidate who clearly differed from a middle-of-the-road opponent, the result has sometimes been an overwhelming electoral defeat. In 1964 the Republicans nominated Barry Goldwater, who advocated such highly conservative policies as abolishing the Social Security system and sharply

Commentary: Life Styles of Democrats and Republicans

The two major political parties in the United States differ from each other in some ways—mainly in terms of the people who identify with and work for each party. But drawing meaningful comparisons is difficult when it comes to basic philosophical positions, for members in both parties hold a range of widely divergent views. In their efforts to distinguish Democrats from Republicans, political writers have sometimes resorted to humorous stereotypes. Here are some of their tongue-in-cheek spoofs, presented as insights into differing life styles.

- Democrats read banned books in private. Republicans form censorship committees and read them in groups.
- Republicans employ exterminators. Democrats step on bugs.
- Republicans have governesses for their children. Democrats have grandmothers.

- Republicans study the financial pages of newspapers. Democrats put them in the bottom of bird cages.
- On Saturdays, the Republicans head for the hunting lodge or yacht club. Democrats wash the car and get a haircut.
- Democrats eat the fish they catch. Republicans hang them on the wall.
- Republicans have guest rooms. Democrats have spare rooms filled with old baby furniture.

---

reducing the government's role in many areas. He was soundly defeated by the more moderate Lyndon Johnson. A similar situation occurred in 1972, when the liberal wing of the Democratic party nominated George McGovern for President. He lost decisively to Richard Nixon. Of course, as Ronald Reagan's election proved, exceptions can occur.

Check Your Understanding

1. Overall, how do Democrats differ from Republicans in education and income?

2. Democratic supporters and Republican supporters differ most on which issues?

3. Democrats in Congress are likely to differ from Republicans on which types of issues?

4. What prevents the two major parties from being more different from each other?

DO POLITICAL PARTIES HAVE ANY IMPACT?

Does the existence of the Democratic and Republican parties make any significant difference? Even though parties are loosely organized, are made up of diverse groups, and basically agree on a number of issues, having parties *does* have an impact. Abolishing them would greatly affect many aspects of American politics. Specifically, political parties in the United States play an important role in five areas: (1) assisting citizens in voting, (2) helping candidates campaign, (3) coordinating policymaking of public officials, (4) providing organized opposition, and (5) reducing conflict.

Assisting Citizens in Voting

Chapter 6 showed that party identification is an important factor in many people's voting decisions. Most voters identify with either Democrats or Republicans, and most identifiers usually stick with their party. This is particularly true when they are choosing less important offices (for example, state senator) or when little information is

Biography: Robert La Follette

They called him "Battling Bob." Throughout his political life, he was indeed a fighter. His targets included corruption in government, unfair taxation, and big business. As a lifelong Republican, La Follette usually operated within the structure of the two-party system. But his goals frequently differed from those of the dominant, and more conservative, wing of the party. Thus, like many American political leaders, he turned to a minor party in order to make his voice heard.

Born in Wisconsin in 1855, La Follette graduated from the state university in 1879 and soon afterward became an attorney. Politics interested him far more than the law, however, and he ran successfully for three terms in the U.S. House of Representatives. At this point, La Follette was still a political conservative, seemingly content with the status quo. After being defeated in 1890, he returned to private life. Over the course of the next ten years, he adopted an increasingly reformist viewpoint, determined to make politics more responsive to the average citizen.

La Follette's growing concern with reform placed him in the ranks of the so-called progressives—members of both parties who wanted to curb the power of political bosses and enhance the rights of ordinary voters. The progressive movement is considered to have attained its fullest national expression when Theodore Roosevelt became President in 1901,

but many of the improvements it advocated had already been achieved earlier at the city and state levels.

La Follette ran successfully for governor of Wisconsin in 1900, and was soon able to put many progressive ideas into practice. The state passed laws to regulate railroad rates, and adopted the direct primary, initiative, and referendum. Other legislation limited campaign expenditures, expanded education, and set up a system of workers' compensation for on-the-job injuries. One innovation was the use of commissions of experts—many of them recruited from universities—to administer programs involving finance and taxation. All these reforms together became known as the "Wisconsin Idea," and many other states adopted similar measures. La Follette's followers continued to carry out his programs at the state level even after he was elected to the U.S. Senate.

During three terms as senator, La Follette continued his struggles for social justice. He worked to protect the rights of civil servants, to improve working conditions for labor (especially merchant seamen), and to win the vote for women.

Late in his life, La Follette became involved with a third party, the Progressives. The party had nominated Theodore Roosevelt as its unsuccessful presidential candidate in 1912, but became weaker during World War I. It revived briefly in the 1920s, in part be-

cause of the Teapot Dome scandals of the Harding administration. La Follette ran as the Progressive presidential candidate in 1924. Although he had no hopes of gaining the presidency through the popular vote, he hoped that the electoral college would be unable to decide on a winner and that the contest might be thrown into the House of Representatives, where fellow progressives could possibly turn the tide in his favor. This was not to be, although La Follette did win five million votes. He died the following year—worn out, it was said, by the physical exertions of campaigning.

available about the candidates. In other words, most Democrats and Republicans find party labels a convenient, time-saving method of deciding how to vote. In the 1982 congressional elections, for example, only about 17 percent of Republican and Democratic identifiers voted for the candidate of the other party.

Sticking with one's party may not seem very useful. Some people have argued that candidates should not be listed by party on the ballot so that citizens would be forced to judge each candidate on his or her own merits. In fact, party labels are prohibited in numerous local elections. On the other hand, a good case can be made for party voting in certain situations.

To appreciate the value of party voting, imagine that you had to make twenty-five voting choices, ranging from President to county judge, and that you had little or no information about most of the candidates for local office. What would you do? As we noted, the parties *do* differ in a number of predictable ways. Thus, choosing on the basis of party label is frequently the best bet when you have no other guide. If, for example, you preferred lower taxes and less government regulation of business, choosing Republicans would be a good move. Of course, party labels can be misleading, but they often provide at least some indication of a candidate's policy views.

Besides providing clues about candidates, parties can help voters by simplifying political conflict. The party rather than individual candidates becomes the target of voter disapproval. Suppose, for example, that you are upset with government policy. One effective way of expressing your discontent is to vote against the party in power. If the Republicans control the government, you can vote against every Republican on the ballot; Obviously, this strategy would be impossible if parties did not exist. And, in fact, many voters do seem to use it. Party punishment was well illustrated in the 1974 congressional elections, when many normally "safe" Republican members of Congress were defeated as a result of public outrage over the Watergate scandal. In this case it was impossible to vote against President Nixon directly, but voting out *other* Republicans helped get the message across.

Helping Candidates Campaign

Running for office can be expensive and difficult. Fortunately, the political parties, from the precinct organization to the national committee, can provide help to office seekers. At one time political parties were usually the most important source of campaign support. This is no longer true, as we saw in Chapter 6, but they can still be valuable. Without the assistance of political parties, politics would be much more of a rich person's activity.

The most useful service parties provide to candidates is the delivery of a certain amount of votes. Merely being a Democrat or a Republican ensures a candidate the votes of a significant number of party identifiers. Running as an independent is much harder. Most candidates probably get at least half of their support from partisan "automatic voters"—and at little cost or effort.

A second important way parties help individual candidates is by providing an overall **ticket**, or slate (list) of office seekers. Thus, instead of candidates running for office by themselves, they are part of the Democratic or the Republican ticket. The effect is most evident in presidential election years. A Republican candidate for the state legislature, for instance, would be part of a ticket that might include candidates for governor, Congress, and the presidency. Running on a ticket has several advantages. First, many states allow citizens to vote a **straight party ticket** by making a single choice. Because they are part of the ticket, office seekers get the votes of people who may never have heard of them but who are attracted to the slate by other candidates. In 1964, many Democrats were swept into office by the drawing power of Lyndon Johnson at the top of the ticket. In addition, individual candidates receive the benefits of a collective campaign. Advertisements such as "Support the team of Governor Frump—vote Democratic" are aimed at electing a party ticket. Especially when funds are limited, such advertising is efficient.

The party organization can also provide crucial services during the campaign. Political parties sometimes play a major role in conducting voter registration drives and getting supporters to the

Commentary: The Political Party as Welfare Agency

Political parties today devote themselves almost entirely to campaigning. This was not the case when big-city machines flourished in the late nineteenth and early twentieth centuries. Local party organizations often helped people find housing, get jobs, or simply make it from one payday to the next. The expectation, of course, was that grateful recipients of aid would show their appreciation on election day. A skillful practitioner of the strategy was George Washington Plunkitt, a New York City political boss active at the turn of the century. He described his approach to a reporter named William Riordan, who took notes on their conversations. Here is the secret of Plunkitt's success.

What tells in holdin' your grip on your district is to go right down among the poor families and help them in the different ways they need help. I've got a regular system for this. If there's a fire on Ninth, Tenth, or Eleventh Avenue, for example, any hour of the day or night, I'm usually there with some of my election district captains as soon as the fire engines. If a family is burned out I don't ask whether they are Republicans or Democrats, and I don't refer them to the Charity Organization Society, which would investigate their case in a month or two and decide they were worthy of help about the time they are dead from starvation. I just get quarters for them, buy clothes for them if their clothes were burned up, and fix them up till they get things runnin' again. It's philanthropy, but it's politics, too—mighty good politics. Who can tell how many votes one of these fires brings me? The poor are the most grateful people in the world, and, let me tell you, they have more friends in their neighborhoods than the rich have in theirs.

If there's a family in my district in want I know it before charitable societies do, and me and my men are first on the ground. I have a special corps to look up such cases. The consequence is that the poor look up to George W. Plunkitt as a father, come to him in trouble—and don't forget him on election day.

Another thing, I can always get a job for a deservin' man. I make it a point to keep on the track of good jobs, and it seldom happens that I don't have a few up my sleeve ready for use. I know every big employer in the district and in the whole city, for that matter, and they ain't in the habit of sayin' no to me when I ask them for a job.

And the children—the little roses of the district! Do I forget them? Oh, no! They know me, every one of them, and they know that a sight of Uncle George and candy means the same thing. Some of them are the best kind of vote-getters. I'll tell you a case. Last year a little Eleventh Avenue rosebud, whose father is a Republican, caught hold of his whiskers on election day and said she wouldn't let go till he'd promise to vote for me. And she didn't.

Source: William L. Riordan, *Plunkitt of Tammany Hall* (New York: Dutton, 1963), pp. 27–28.

polls on election day. The old-time party organizations in some big cities were called **party machines.** They controlled city or county politics by doing favors—giving out government jobs or reducing government regulations—in return for support. The machines were famous for their vigorous registration and turnout efforts (turnout sometimes exceeded 100 percent, since dead people "voted.") The Democratic party has traditionally sponsored registration drives. In recent years the Republican party has also been working to register its potential supporters.

Money is another form of assistance from political parties. Party organizations at all levels raise funds, which are then distributed to individual candidates. From January 1983 to just before the 1984 election, the national campaign committees of the two major parties raised a total of $267.4 million. The national Republican party organizations were particularly successful in raising

funds—they raised $207.7 million compared to $59.7 million for the Democrats. In addition, both national party organizations have initiated more general campaigns that are not tied to a particular candidate in order to improve their images. Parties can also offer numerous campaign services that many candidates cannot otherwise afford, including advice on how to campaign and on how election laws operate, help with the mass media, and data from public opinion polls. Though political parties may not be as powerful as the machines of yesteryear, they still give major assistance to candidates who need money, advice, and so on.

Coordinating Policy Making of Public Officials

The American political system is designed to prevent the consolidation of power. The Constitution limits the actions of public officials through the system of checks and balances, and federalism gives power to both the state and national governments.

If our system had been set up only to function as a brake on government activity, having political power dispersed, or spread out, would be perfectly acceptable. However, in modern times all levels of government are expected to play an active role. The contradiction between the dispersal of political power and modern demands for stronger government thus presents a conflict. How can we maintain our basic constitutional order and still achieve the coordination among government leaders that is necessary to carry out major policies?

To some extent political parties help meet this need. One important area in which parties overcome the decentralized character of our constitutional system is in Congress. Members of Congress are, in principle, completely independent of each other. They have no obligation to cooperate in making policy, drafting legislation, or administering the day-to-day work of Congress. However, if the 535 members of Congress acted more or less as independent ambassadors from congressional districts and states, the results would probably be inaction and confusion.

Political parties provide some degree of unity and leadership in Congress. First, parties furnish much of the organizational framework that allows Congress to conduct its business. Party committees—such as the House Republican Committee on Committees—have the responsibility of appointing members to committees (it is in committees that Congress does some of its most important work). The Speaker of the House is selected by a straight party vote. Second, parties provide leaders who help set the legislative agenda, decide the

In the 100th Congress, Robert Byrd of West Virginia, top, is Senate majority leader and Jim Wright of Texas is Speaker of the House. Both are Democrats.

rules of debate, establish lines of communication among differing groups, and otherwise run legislative business. Third, legislative parties serve as forums in which members from different backgrounds and with different interests can thrash out overall goals and strategies. Among House Democrats, for example, the Steering and Policy Committee functions as a private unit composed of key leaders and regional representatives to help in legislative planning. Both parties have such committees in both houses, though their precise roles can vary from mere instruments of party leaders to genuine forums for debate. Finally, parties allow Congress to speak with a more unified voice than would be possible without them. After Reagan's 1984 election, for example, it was the Speaker of the House—Tip O'Neil—who spoke for the Democrats. When Democrats controlled both Congress and the presidency, Republican leaders in Congress often presented their party's case to the public.

The relationship between Congress and the presidency is a second area in which political parties play a coordinating role. The potential for stalemate and conflict is considerable. Rarely can one branch impose its will on the other, and formal means of cooperation are minimal. On occasion, however, the bond of party affiliation can help promote cooperation. Shortly after his 1980 election, Ronald Reagan worked closely with Republican House and Senate leaders to ensure passage of major tax changes, budget cuts, and a controversial arms sale to Saudia Arabia. House leaders such as Robert Michel of Illinois served as the President's lobbyists by gathering support and providing information on who might be swayed by what arguments. Many Presidents have regularly consulted with top party leaders in Congress before

Political leaders generate support for their parties. Transportation Secretary Elizabeth Dole, left, addresses Republicans, 1986; former Representative Barbara Jordan delivers the keynote speech at the Democratic National Convention, 1976.

announcing major new policies. Such consultation is both a courtesy and a method of building support for the President's legislative program.

On many occasions legislative-executive cooperation is strengthened by the fact that a common party label puts members of Congress and the President in the same boat at election time. In the early 1980s, for example, many Senate Republicans had reservations about the budgetary policies of fellow Republican Reagan. They realized, however, that to oppose the President's program would be to discredit the ability of a Republican administration to govern. This, in turn, could be costly to their own chances. For better or worse, a degree of cooperation among Republicans was a necessity.

Political party ties may also provide a means of coordinating national, state, and local government activities. As is true in the executive-legislative relationship, the constitutional system is designed more to produce inaction or conflict than cooperation. Parties can promote cooperation in several ways. First, there are organizations of Democratic or Republican state and local officials (for example, the Republican Governors Association) to serve as channels of communication among people who might otherwise have no contact with each other. Second, because the President's election depends so much on the activities of state and local parties, a President is usually motivated to develop ties with these officials. Recent Presidents have usually assigned a senior aide to coordinate the President's schedule with the members of the party's national committee and numerous state and local party officials.

We must also recognize, however, the limits of political parties in overcoming the lack of unity and built-in conflict of our system. Presidents, for example, have rarely been able to punish fellow party members in Congress who resist their policies. Many members of Congress are not dependent on the national party for reelection, and resisting the President can sometimes be good politics back home, especially if the President is unpopular. In addition, the President's appeals to party loyalty among other officeholders can easily appear "unpresidential"—most citizens expect the President to be a national leader, not a party leader. Finally, state and local parties are often so varied that national gatherings of party members face serious obstacles in developing common goals and policies. What may be good politics for New York Democrats may be unacceptable to Democrats in Texas.

In short, political parties provide some help in overcoming constitutional hurdles to coordination, but they do not solve all the problem.

Providing Organized Opposition

An important element of a democratic government is the existence of organized opposition. Someone must be willing and able to criticize government policy and offer reasonable alternatives. Without constructive criticism and alternatives, elections would be a meaningless ritual. In the United States, political parties are an important source of reasonable opposition to those in power and of public examination of their policies. Although this is a valuable role, parties frequently do not get much credit for their work. In fact, parties are sometimes criticized for their "disruptive" behavior.

Parties offer constructive opposition in two important ways: (1) they serve as a forum for opponents of government policy, and (2) they provide candidates who will oppose incumbent officeholders.

A Forum for Opponents of Government Policy

Whether at the local, state, or federal level, governments are forever considering policies. Naturally, many citizens disagree with government actions. One convenient way to express this opposition is through the party currently out of power. The "out-party" typically sees such discontent as an opportunity to increase its own electoral strength and eventually become the "in-party." In the 1960s, for example, when the Republican party was a minority in the House, it created a House Republican Policy Committee, which conducted research and issued reports critical of many Democratic-sponsored programs. It developed alternatives and even gave its own "State of the

Union" message. When in 1981 President Reagan announced plans to reduce spending on social services, he immediately drew opposition from Democrats in Congress. Opposition was especially strong in the House, where the controlling Democrats could use their leadership positions as a forum. Democrats also used committee hearings and proposed legislation to stimulate public interest in what they called the unfairness of the Reagan program. Such opposition tactics not only provide alternative viewpoints on important issues but offer a potential rallying point for other dissatisfied individuals.

Of course, parties are not the only source of criticism or opposition. Newspaper columnists, television commentators, and ordinary citizens can all criticize government policy. But the political party is crucial because it can introduce alternative legislation and has the possibility of replacing the current leadership. While anyone can speak out against the government, the opposition of leaders of the "out-party" has to be taken far more seriously than complaints from ordinary citizens.

Opposition to Incumbents

In politics competition is central. Of course, competition itself does not guarantee the emergence of great leaders committed to the public well-being, but it can reduce the more severe abuses of office.

In many areas of the country, political parties recruit candidates for office and thus make most elections at least technically competitive. Especially when an incumbent is well established, the local party plays a key role in providing opposition. The party supports such "hopeless" causes because running as many candidates as possible helps the entire ticket, and every so often one of these candidates wins. What is most important, however, is that without the efforts of the party, voters would frequently not have a choice on election day.

Parties can aid candidates, even those who face strong opposition. Such aid helps make the election more of a contest and makes opposition more believable. Without the votes of party members, the existence of a ticket, and other resources pro-

vided by the parties, the idea of running against an incumbent would be extremely unattractive. Few citizens could afford to wage a campaign. Though many elections are not close, they would probably be even more lopsided without the efforts of political parties.

Reducing Conflict

Although parties play an important role in providing opposition, they also help reduce conflict. By serving as outlets for certain types of conflicts, American parties prevent more severe conflicts. Without parties, many of the conflicts that divide our society would be much more intense. The Democratic and Republican parties accomplish this in two ways: by recruiting supporters from differing social backgrounds and by providing easy entry into politics by new groups.

Recruiting

As we have seen, political party organizations are primarily concerned with electing candidates to office. Because of the winner-take-all election system and geographically based election districts, parties, in order to win, must appeal to a wide variety of groups. Rarely does any one group or interest constitute a majority in an electoral district, so victory depends on developing a **coalition,** a temporary alliance of two or more groups. Though each party may have a core of traditional supporters, it usually must reach out to other groups as well.

The need to create broad coalitions has important consequences in politics. Neither party can afford to advance the interests of one group at the expense of other groups. Though the Republican party has traditionally drawn a great deal of its strength from the business community, it must still appeal to union members if it is to win. In fact, President Reagan's 1980 and 1984 victories depended a great deal on such supporters. Likewise, though the Democrats have strong support among the poor, they cannot strongly support an antibusiness program, since many Democrats are wealthy. The need to appeal to groups outside the party, and divisions within the party, prevents many conflicts from becoming extreme. Divisions between rich and poor, North and South, black and white, urban and rural are reduced because no party can take only one side and consistently win.

The diversity of appeal is most visible in the special organizations established within the national party committees. In an effort to win blacks away from the Democrats, for instance, the Republicans have created the Black Community Involvement Program. Both parties have units dealing with Hispanics, women, young people, and various ethnic groups. Many state and local parties also follow this practice of creating groups to bolster traditional supporters—and bring in groups who have generally sided with the opposition.

Entry for New Groups

We saw in Chapter 5 that decisions help to channel public dissatisfaction into "safe" political activity. Political parties also contribute to this channeling process. Specifically, parties are sufficiently open to the public that almost any group of people can gain some influence.

A group can become politically involved in several ways. Perhaps the easiest way is to run candidates for party leadership positions or to get all of its supporters to attend the meetings at which party positions are filled. Under state law, parties are not private clubs that can exclude "undesirable" people. The requirements for voting in a local political club, for instance, may be minimal—to be a registered party member in the club's district, to pay inexpensive dues, and to attend a few meetings. A different route is to run candidates in a party primary. Here again, the efforts of a relatively small number of people can be successful. Both party organizational meetings and primary elections frequently draw light turnouts, and with many candidates running, a few hundred people can sometimes win a fairly large city or county organization. Finally, many people have simply formed their own branches of the Democratic or Republican party. In New York, Chicago, and Los Angeles during the 1960s, for example, some citizens felt that "old-fashioned" Democratic machine organizations were becoming corrupt. In

response, these citizens created "reform" Democratic clubs devoted to good government.

It is quite likely that the ease with which groups can acquire at least some influence in the two major parties has prevented the emergence of numerous strong third parties, especially parties advocating extreme positions. After all, why start a new party when one can play a role in an existing one? Rather than having the American Militant Black party, for instance, we have instead the Adam Clayton Powell Democratic Club, located in a black area of New York City. Practically every group that has wanted a piece of the political action has succeeded in finding a place in one of the two parties, so these groups are now part of the system.

Check Your Understanding

1. In what ways do political parties assist citizens in voting?

2. How can political parties help candidates campaign for office?

3. In what ways do political parties help coordinate the activities of government officials?

4. What are the two major ways political parties provide organized opposition in American politics?

ARE POLITICAL PARTIES IN DECLINE?

Since the 1960s some people have sensed that political parties are slowly on their way to extinction. Eventually, they believe, parties will consist of little more than a name and a weak organization with no power. This supposed decline has been viewed both positively and negatively. Those who favor the decline argue that parties have often placed winning ahead of principle and have discouraged candidates from seeking office. Defenders of political parties say that parties play a vital role in democratic government. Our concern is whether such a decline is, in fact, occurring, and what might happen if parties do become powerless. To answer these questions, let us begin by examining the complex evolution of American political parties.

The Evolution of Contemporary Political Parties

The Democratic and Republican parties have long and deep roots in American history. The emergence of the present system, however, has been marked by many changes, some fairly abrupt, rather than a gradual evolution. According to one analysis of party development, in American history there have been five distinct national party systems and six major party formations. In some instances, the whole **party system**—number of parties, their strength, bases of support, and degree of competition—has been transformed in a single decade.

The origins of American parties go back to the period between the battle over the ratification of the Constitution (1787–88) and 1800. As we saw in Chapter 2, the conflict between pro- and anti-ratification forces was widespread and intense. Bitter disagreements between Federalists and Anti-Federalists over economic policy continued into the administration of Washington and surfaced in the election for vice president in 1792. However, most of this conflict was **factional** rather than partisan. Each particular issue created short-lived new alliances, but these factions did not have party organizations to promote their cause. Starting around 1795, and the unpopular Alien and Sedition Acts passed by the Adams administration, two parties—the Federalists and the Republicans—began to emerge. In the election of 1800, the Republicans, led by Thomas Jefferson and using rather sophisticated techniques to attract voters, captured the presidency and the House. Parties now existed in the national government and in many state election districts.

Early Congresses were the scene of frequent brawls, as this etching from 1798 shows. Political parties have played an important role in bringing order to legislative bodies, as party leaders try to settle disputes through compromise and negotiation.

This first party system survived only briefly. Following its defeat in 1800, the Federalist party returned to its New England base and rapidly lost its appeal. In 1816 the Federalist presidential candidate carried only three states. By 1820 the United States had become a one-party system (a period commonly called the "Era of Good Feeling"). Again, politics was marked by factionalism.

Following the presidential election of 1824, in which Andrew Jackson won the popular vote but lost in the electoral college, the second political party system began to emerge. The 1824 election saw the creation of two groups—the National Republicans and the Democratic Republicans—that competed for their presidential candidates. This division was soon changed into the Democratic party—the party of Andrew Jackson—and the Whig party—a collection of conservative groups opposing Jackson. Both parties mobilized voters for their presidential and House candidates.

The growing controversy over slavery, however, soon destroyed the second party system. After 1850, the Whig party broke into Northern and Southern elements and soon disappeared as a national party. The Democratic party, which also had strong Northern and Southern components, won the presidency in 1856. By 1860, however, it was deeply divided and was doing poorly at the polls. In 1854 a new party—the Republicans— had been created out of elements of the old Whig party, Northern Democrats, and two other small parties—the Know-Nothings and the Free Soilers. The Republicans made dramatic gains in House elections of 1858; with Abraham Lincoln as its candidate, it won the presidency in 1860.

The period following the Civil War saw the Republicans emerge as the dominant party. But when regular elections returned to the South, the Democratic party began seriously challenging the Republican control of the presidency and frequently dominated Congress. From 1874 to 1892 there was a period of vigorous, well-balanced party competition.

In 1894 and 1896 the party system was again transformed. The Democrats lost badly in both elections. The immediate cause of their defeat was a severe economic depression in 1893, when the Democrats controlled both Congress and the White House. When the Democrats came under the domination of Western, pro-debtor, pro-easy-money forces in 1896, however, the momentary defeat became a dry spell lasting some thirty-six years. Only when the Republicans divided among themselves (as in 1912) could the Democrats win the presidency. Outside the South, the Republican party completely dominated and attracted support from many elements—cities, small towns, rural whites, blacks, workers, and the business community. The era from 1894 to 1932 might be called the one-and-a-half party system.

The election of Franklin D. Roosevelt in 1932 marked the reemergence of the Democratic party and a dramatic change in the types of supporters the party attracted. Though some movement toward the Democrats had occurred in the 1920s, especially among immigrant groups, the Great

European emigrants were among the groups whose support helped the Democrats make a comeback in 1932.

The Democratic candidate for President in 1932 was Franklin Roosevelt, Governor of New York. Here, throngs of well-wishers in Nebraska—traditionally a Republican state—great FDR during the campaign.

Depression that started in 1929 was the decisive force. Republicans, and citizens who had never before voted, supported Roosevelt by the millions against Herbert Hoover. New voters, and many of those who left the Republican party, became life-long Democrats. The changes brought about by the voting in 1932 and 1936 were so great and so enduring that these contests have been character-ized as **realigning elections.** The post-1930s period has been one of strong two-party competition, though the Democrats have usually dominated at the congressional and state levels.

The Lessons of Party History

We have touched on only some of the highlights of party history. What can this long and complex history tell us about contemporary parties? At least three lessons seem clear. First, the power and vitality of political parties has repeatedly ebbed and flowed. On a number of occasions, strong parties have collapsed into a number of squabbling and unimportant factions, only to reemerge later as strong parties with new names and leaders. Unforeseen events and issues such as the slavery controversy and the depression of 1893 can have relatively sudden impact. Dynamic, resourceful leaders—Jefferson, Jackson, Franklin Roosevelt—can also reshape party politics. History suggests, therefore, that it might be a mistake to project present trends far into the future.

Second, the present-day Democratic and Republican parties have demonstrated an ability to resist challenges. The most frequent type of challenge has been the appeal by other parties to voters unhappy with the major-party alternatives. In the last half of the nineteenth century, a number of third parties—particularly the Greenback and Populist parties—elected many members of Congress and won a respectable share of the presidential vote. Changing economic conditions or absorption by a major party ended these challenges, however. There have also been a number of more **doctrinaire** parties—the Socialist party, the Progressive party of 1948, and others that have placed commitment to doctrine, or ideology, ahead of electoral victory. These, too, have not been successful in challenging the two major parties. The Democrats and Republicans have also survived inept leaders and disastrous election campaigns. In 1964, when the Republican Goldwater was decisively defeated by the Democrat Johnson and the Democrats rolled up impressive numbers of House and Senate victories, some people predicted the end of the Republican party. Yet in 1968 the Republican Nixon won the presidency by a narrow margin, and in 1972 he was reelected by a landslide.

Finally, a close examination of parties over the last 100 years shows their adaptability to changing circumstances. For example, when rapid industrialization and large-scale immigration severely strained society at the turn of the century, parties responded by developing the machine organizations. The machines were centrally controlled—from the **boss** at the top to a small army of ward leaders, aldermen, and precinct captains at the bottom. Benefits, not issues, were central, and while corruption was common, the machine did provide many useful services and helped introduce many immigrants to electoral politics. However, when machines began to decline in the 1950s, reform party groups sprang up to replace them.

Members of such groups were often professionals—especially lawyers—more interested in issues of public policy than in getting a city job. In any case, parties did adjust to the needs of a changing population and new issues by rebuilding their organizational structure and developing incentives to attract new members.

Current Threats to Party Survival

As was true at the beginning of the Republic, parties must deal with numerous hostile forces. Madison, Franklin, Jefferson, Washington, and almost every other Founder stated their belief that parties are divisive and harmful. Many people today echo these views. Besides such long-standing anti-party sentiment, modern parties face four special problems.

The Growth of Civil Service

For most of our history, political parties at all levels of government have depended on government jobs and government favors for organizational vitality. Electoral victory would often mean thousands of jobs—from street sweeper to Justice Department attorney—for loyal campaign workers. However, beginning at the national level with the Civil Service Reform Act of 1883, followed by many similar acts at the state levels, more and more government jobs were filled through the civil service system: job qualifications are defined in advance, people are hired on the basis of objectively measured merit, and advancement is based on job performance. In addition, civil servants cannot be removed except for failure to do their work.

Today, especially in some states, parties still have favors to give out, but these are nowhere as plentiful or as important as they once were. At the national level a victorious President has approximately 2,000 *patronage jobs*—that is, jobs given to personal friends, political supporters, and so on—but they are all high-level policy-making positions requiring special training and ability. Members of Congress have even fewer positions available. Moreover, the awarding of government contracts is now regulated by rules covering bids, performance guarantees, and bans on conflict of interest. Thus, parties are no longer the most important supplier of thousands of campaigners and ready cash.

The Popularity of Primaries

During the nineteenth century, party organizations themselves decided who would run under their label in the general election. Sometimes candidates were chosen at a party *caucus*—all Democratic legislators would select the Democrats' nominee for President, for example. Party conventions were also popular. Delegates from county and state party organizations would assemble and nominate their candidate. There were no restrictions on how delegates would vote. Both caucuses and conventions were closed to the general public, and vote trading and secret deals were common.

Beginning in the early twentieth century, as one of the reforms supported by the Progressive movement, a third method of selecting the parties' nominees developed—the **primary,** which is an election held before the general election to decide who will be the party's nominee. The strongest supporters of primaries were reformers who believed that party bosses used their great power over the nominating process to select weak candidates completely under the control of corrupt party machines. By letting citizens, not party officials, choose candidates, the system would be more democratic, and better candidates would be nominated.

Though the popularity of primaries has ebbed and flowed, they are used today in all states and play a major role in the selection of delegates to presidential nominating conventions. The particular details of primary elections vary from state to state, but basically there are two types: open primaries and closed primaries. In an **open primary** any citizen, regardless of party affiliation, previous voting record, or issue positions, can participate. In **closed primaries,** prospective voters must make a declaration of party loyalty and may have to declare, months before the contest, their intention to vote in a particular party's primary. As of the end of 1986, twenty states used a closed primary.

Some time before the primary, a voter must declare his or her party affiliation. In sixteen states a voter must declare his or her affiliation, but this can be done on the day of the primary. Though this procedure technically makes a primary a closed primary, in actual practice it is an open primary. Nine states have pure open primaries— no declarations of affiliation is required. Four states—Alaska, Louisiana, Washington, and Virginia—have a **wide-open,** or **blanket, primary.** Here voters are not restricted to one or the other party's election. A voter, for example, could help choose the Democratic Senate nominee and the Republican House nominee. It should be noted, however, that state primary laws can easily change.

Table 7.3 shows the growing importance of presidential primaries in recent years. In 1968 only about a third of the presidential nominating convention delegates in both parties were selected by primaries. By 1972 this figure had risen to more than half. Presently, within the Democratic party only a relatively small number of convention delegates are "free" to choose whomever they want. Most are elected in *binding* presidential primaries—primaries in which the delegate is obligated to support the candidate he or she is pledged to (the precise nature of the obligation varies from state to state). A much larger proportion of delegates to the 1984 Republican convention were not selected in primaries, but this situation probably reflects the fact that Ronald Reagan's renomination was a certainty and therefore it was not necessary for party members to express their choices in primary contests. The increase in the number of primaries also means that presidential contenders must usually create large, well-financed campaign organizations in order to seek the party's nomination. As a consequence, the winner no longer has to depend so much on the party's campaign organization. Indeed, party officials often are less important than the nonparty people who supported the candidate from the very beginning.

In general, primaries weaken parties in two important ways. First, the party organization's loss of control over the nomination means that office-

The Growth of Presidential Primaries, 1968–1984	Democrats	1968	1972	1976	1980	1984
	Number of states using binding primaries	17	23	29	31	25 (plus Washington, D.C.)*
	Percentage of convention votes cast by delegates from binding primaries	37.5	60.5	72.6	74.7	66.1
	Republicans					
	Number of states using binding primaries	16	22	28	35	18 (plus Washington, D.C.)
	Percentage of convention votes cast by delegates from binding primaries	34.3	52.7	67.9	74.3	37.9

*In 1984, delegates to the Democratic National Convention were bound to vote only "in good conscience" for the candidate they were pledged to.

Source: Appendix E in Austin Ranney, ed., *The American Elections of 1980* (Washington, D.C.: American Enterprise Institute, 1981). Data for 1984 were supplied by the respective national committees.

TABLE 7.3

holders no longer "owe" their election to the organization. When the Democratic organization selected the mayoral or gubernatorial candidate through a caucus, the candidate knew that success in office and reelection required continued cooperation with party officials. The primary, however, allows those with no party ties to win the party label. Both Jimmy Carter and Ronald Reagan were outsiders in their parties. Also, office seekers can leave the party organization if they are denied an official endorsement and appeal for the nomination directly to the people. Control of the nomination was one of the most valuable party organization assets, and the primary has weakened this control.

Second, the primary can undermine a vigorous two-party system. When the two-party system is weakened, the likely result is not a strong one-party system, but a no-party system. Factionalism replaces party politics. This destructive impact of the primary is especially likely to occur when one party is stronger than the other. Members of the weaker party realize that, if their party regularly loses in the general election, winning their nomination means little. It makes more sense, therefore, to enter the dominant party's primary. In other words, if you are a Democrat in a heavily Republican area, you would be better off seeking the Republican nomination. Such action not only weakens the Democratic party, it can greatly confuse the meaning of a party label. The dominant party's primary attracts candidates of all different views, the winner may not represent the views of the party whose nomination he or she has won.

The Emergence of the Modern Campaign Industry

Until the 1960s, running a campaign required a great deal of work by campaign staff and volunteers. Rallies were held and doorbells were rung in an effort to gain supporters. Getting poorly motivated citizens to the polls on election day frequently took a small army of drivers, babysitters, and others to contact people one at a time. The use of the mass media was limited and very local. Simple billboards, radio commercials, and newspaper ads were the extent of the media campaign. Political parties, with their supply of workers and electoral know-how, were most active in electing public officials. Even a wealthy, well-known candidate would find it hard to match a party's electoral resources.

As we noted in Chapter 6, since the 1960s the situation has greatly changed. The presence of television in nearly every home has allowed candidates to deliver their message directly to large numbers of potential voters. Tedious clerical tasks and door-to-door campaigning have been replaced by thirty-second television commercials. Equally important, the elements necessary to run a large-scale campaign can be assembled with little or no party assistance. With sufficient funds, a would-be candidate can hire a polling organization to provide data on voters' thinking and feedback on candidate performance; additional money can be

In the days before television, parades and spectacles—as in this presidential campaign event in 1864—were essential for attracting voters.

raised by renting computerized mailing lists or hiring professional fundraisers; and paid consultants can offer expert advice on making speeches, dealing with ethnic groups, complying with the election law, and so forth.

The diminishing role of political parties in conducting campaigns is significant. Reaching top office once required a lengthy party apprenticeship; today it is relatively easy for a person with financial resources to begin at the top. Wealthy business people can use their personal fortunes to gain Senate seats despite little or no prior political experience. Nonparty organizations also now have a more direct line to candidates and public officials. Previously, well-heeled interest groups (such as corporations, unions, professional and trade associations) could contribute generously to a politician in office, but their power to elect or defeat candidates was limited. It was the political party that controlled the nomination and the army of campaign workers. Today, interest groups with money can help provide candidates with professional support (consultants, poll takers, and so on). Overall, the role of the mass media and of the campaign-for-hire industry has greatly weakened the party's most valuable resource—control over election to public office.

The Decline in Party Affiliation and Party Voting

The existence of widespread party affiliation is one of the foundations of the Democratic and Republican parties. Without significant rank-and-file loyalty, the parties would not have most of their "automatic" vote. Such enduring attachments also ensure party survival after major electoral defeats (for example, the Republican loss in 1964 and the Democratic defeat of 1972).

Before the 1970s, the widespread existence of party attachment was taken for granted. The number of people classifying themselves "independent, middle of the road" was rarely more than 25 percent on the surveys conducted by the University of Michigan, for instance. Equally important, voting tended to follow party loyalties closely. In the 1970s, however, fewer people identified with the parties. The proportion of people claiming to be independent rose, as did that of voters classifying themselves "independent-Democrat" or "independent-Republican."

The decline in party affiliation had several sources. The 1970s saw many young people—the "baby boomers" of the 1950s—enter the electorate for the first time. Young voters traditionally hold the weakest party loyalties and are most likely to label themselves as independents. In addition, the surfacing of long-standing conflicts within the parties led some people to abandon party loyalties. For example, many white Southerners left the Democrats in response to the party's strong support for civil rights. The Democrats' strong appeals to minorities, women, and antiwar groups in the late 1960s and early 1970s may also have contributed to a weakening of party loyalties among more conservative members. The Watergate crisis of 1974, in which President Nixon resigned when faced with possible impeachment, might have increased citizens' dissatisfaction with established political institutions, including parties.

One important indication of the weakening of party loyalty has been an increase in split ticket voting, which occurs when a voter selects candidates from both parties in a single election—for example, a Republican for president and a Democrat for Congress. In 1952 about 12 percent of voters divided their vote for President and member of the House; by 1980 this figure had risen to nearly 28 percent. According to a Gallup poll, some 54 percent of voters in the 1984 election chose candidates of different parties (43 percent stayed with the same party for every office). Split ticket voting has been especially evident in state and local elections. That is, a person might vote for a Republican mayor but a Democratic state senator. The abandonment of strict party loyalty in voting has meant that state and local parties can no longer easily deliver large blocs, or groups, of votes. For example, the Democratic parties in Virginia and Mississippi once could be counted on to keep their states within the Democratic party at the presidential level. Even though the Democrats

Issues: Do Third Parties Have Any Impact?

The impact of third parties on politics is difficult to determine. There has been much speculation, for example, about whether the candidacy of George Wallace in 1968 "gave" Richard Nixon his victory by taking away votes from Hubert H. Humphrey. Wallace, like Humphrey, was a Democrat but was running on the American party ticket. Similar controversy exists over whether Theodore Roosevelt's 1912 Progressive campaign resulted in the election of Woodrow Wilson, a Democrat. It seems likely that because of our winner-take-all system (see Chapter 5), third parties have sometimes held the balance of power by controlling a small percentage of the vote.

It has also been argued that minor parties frequently develop new policies that are eventually incorporated by the major parties. This argument is only partially true. Sometimes the program of a minor party does eventually become established policy. For example, the 1932 platform of the Socialist party called for:

- Programs of public employment for those out of work
- A six-hour day and a five-day work week without reduction in wages
- A comprehensive system of public employment agencies
- Unemployment insurance financed by the government and employers

- Old-age pensions

- Health and maternity insurance

- Workers' compensation and accident insurance

- Government aid to farmers and mortgage protection for home-owners

All of these policies (except the six-hour day) were eventually enacted into law or have become well-established customs. On the other hand, the Socialist party platform *also* called for:

- Public ownership of all mines, forests, oil companies, transportation systems, communications, and utilities

- Public ownership of the credit and banking system

- Proportional representation in elections

- Abolition of the Supreme Court's power to declare legislation unconstitutional

- Government ownership of the liquor industry

None of these programs has been enacted or even given serious attention in recent years.

Eugene V. Debs and Ben Hanford ran on the Socialist party ticket in 1904. Before the Russian Revolution of 1917, socialism was not necessarily considered un-American, and Debs did fairly well in his various presidential campaigns.

still dominate state politics, Republican candidates for the Senate and the White House have frequently carried those two states.

The Prospect of Partyless Politics

As we have suggested, the Democrats and Republican parties are resourceful organizations that have survived challenges before. Recent events indicate a degree of party revitalization. Party loyalties increased between 1980 and 1982. In the 1982 congressional election, party identifiers tended to stick with their party. Both national party organizations have raised substantial sums and are much more active in recruiting candidates and providing campaign support. Nevertheless, the possibility of further party decline cannot be dismissed. It is important, therefore, to ask what would happen if parties disappeared from the political scene. Would politics change for the better? Who would benefit?

Politics Without Parties

In the United States there are two situations in which political parties play no role. The first is **nonpartisan elections**. In nonpartisan elections candidates cannot use party labels, and parties may be prohibited from taking part in other election-related activities. Nonpartisan elections are popular in many cities (though some cities such as Chicago have parties, their elections are technically nonpartisan) and are used for selecting the state legislature in Nebraska. The second situation in which parties are irrelevant is in strong one-party areas. In this case, one party is so dominant that party labels are meaningless. For many years this was the case in the South: nearly everybody was a Democrat, and the "real" election was the Democratic primary.

Studies of nonpartisan elections and Southern one-party politics have shown that the poor suffer when party labels are not present. First, because they are often uneducated, unaware of issues, and unsure of how the election affects them, the poor are frequently not motivated to vote; without some push from an organization like a party, they will stay home on election day. Second, without par-

ties to recruit candidates for office, nominees are disproportionately drawn from the middle and upper classes. Parties sometimes provide important services to candidates—legal advice, campaign assistance, and a ticket; without such free services, a candidate who cannot afford to hire a professional staff probably will be unable to run for office.

Third, and perhaps most important for the less well-off, policies enacted by "partyless" government tend to be biased against them. For years the lack of a well-defined party system in the South gave special interests an enormous influence, because they could provide the resources necessary to campaign for elections. Groups representing highway contractors and utility companies were frequently major forces in state politics. A similar pattern is still found in nonpartisan California cities, where the influence of the business community favors the election of officeholders unwilling to use government to solve the problems of the disadvantaged. In short, without the parties to mobilize less well-off voters and to provide electoral resources, those already in positions of power tend to remain there.

Another important consequence of the absence of parties is an increase in "issueless" elections. Battles between Democrats and Republicans may not be great debates, but they typically have more issue content than when there are no parties. At a minimum, each of the two parties is traditionally associated with certain commitments (for instance, the Republicans favor less government regulation of business). Without parties, campaigns place even greater emphasis on personalities, friendships, places of residence, and other nonpolicy attributes. Candidates who are well known and personally attractive have a considerable advantage. In addition, without parties citizens find it more difficult to vote on the basis of issues. As we noted earlier, voting by party is frequently a good strategy if one's information about the candidates is limited. When voters have to choose from among many candidates but do not even know what party they represent, deciding according to the issues is even more difficult.

Finally, observers agree that the absence of political parties make it more difficult for voters to

Blacks have historically favored the Democrats, but in 1984 three prominent black athletes endorsed Reagan for reelection.

punish and reward leaders. One advantage of having parties is that they provide clearly labeled "ins" and "outs." In 1982, for example, with Ronald Reagan as President, the Republicans were the ins and Democrats were the outs. In the congressional elections of 1982, dissatisfied citizens could easily punish the ins by voting Democratic. Many, in fact, did. In nonpartisan and one-party politics, however, no clear in- or out-group usually exists. Alliances frequently shift, so that it is hard to tell who is acting with whom (it is as if two basketball teams constantly exchange players during a game). The average voter may find it impossible to register satisfaction or dissatisfaction at election time (it would be like deciding which basketball team won).

The Value of Partyless Politics

Whether the consequences of partyless politics are bad or not depends on your position and goals. If you are well-off, well educated, and satisfied with present conditions, the absence of political parties would probably be an advantage. After all, you do not need a party to motivate you, aid your candidates, or provide you with political information. Perhaps for this reason much of the support for nonpartisan elections has come from wealthy, established political interests. On the other hand, if you are not well-off, abolishing parties would probably be harmful to your cause. In many important ways political parties allow the have-nots to compete more effectively with the haves. Therefore, getting rid of parties would probably "improve" politics only for certain groups.

Check Your Understanding

1. When did the U.S. party system originate? What happened to these original parties?

2. How is the civil service system a threat to political parties?

3. In what ways do primaries weaken political parties?

4. What factors have contributed to the decline of party loyalty beginning in the 1970s?

5. Who benefits the most from partyless politics?

THE POLITICS OF POLITICAL PARTIES AND DEMOCRACY

Political parties have been criticized on many grounds, but the most important complaint is that they undermine democracy. The fact that party officials, frequently meeting in secret, decide such questions as who will run for what office, how campaigns will be fought, and what legislative programs will be pursued is usually viewed as undemocratic, "back-room" politics. The undemocratic image of political parties is given considerable support by the long tradition of party bosses who ran cities and states without much public interference or scrutiny. In their heyday, bosses such as Richard J. Daley of Chicago and Carmine De Sapio of New York controlled thousands of votes, gave out numerous patronage jobs, and even decided which laws would be enforced. Through their capacity to deliver the vote, their power extended to state and national levels.

The fear of government by the Daleys, the De Sapios, and other strong party leaders has had a major impact on politics. The widespread practice of filling some positions through civil service rather than by political appointments, as well as the use of primaries, nonpolitical municipal elections, and laws regulating internal party affairs, derives from the fear of party power. Many reformers have equated strong parties with corrupt government administered by party hacks. To weaken parties was to strengthen good government.

Antiparty sentiment is still very much alive. Recall the poll data presented at the beginning of the chapter showing that many people believe that parties confuse issues and do a poor job for the nation, and that party label should be unimportant in voting. Antiparty sentiment has also been common among politically active citizens. Following the trouble-filled 1968 Democratic presidential convention in Chicago, some politically active observers called for the replacement of established party leaders with citizens not drawn from the ranks of the party faithful. As a result, many party leaders were excluded from the 1972 Democratic convention. Running against the party bosses remains a useful campaign tactic in many areas. President Carter's successful 1976 campaign for the Democratic presidential nomination relied heavily on his image as a party outsider and thus (implicitly) a man of the people. Being closely identified as a party person is not a great asset in American politics. In 1984, Walter Mondale's close ties to Democratic party officials were as much a liability as an asset.

The frequent charge that parties are run undemocratically and therefore must be reformed rests on the assumption that a democratically run political party leads to greater democracy. This assumption can be challenged. An alternative argument is that democracy depends on conflict *between* the parties, and what goes on *within* parties is comparatively unimportant. According to this perspective, democracy is best served when voters are given a choice of candidates on election day and when all candidates can wage vigorous campaigns for public support. It is the opportunity to choose that is essential. Parties offer candidates and then help the candidates campaign. So long as voters are not coerced by the parties, how parties choose candidates, how money is raised, and so on is irrelevant. If voters do not like what a party offers, they don't support it.

The idea that competition between the parties rather than democracy within a party is basic to democracy is useful for evaluating proposed party reforms. A supporter of this view would argue that it is possible, in the name of attempting to "increase" democracy, to reform the parties out of existence. Allowing everyone to participate in internal party affairs, limiting party patronage, and weakening party control over public officials would destroy parties. To some people, this might make for more democracy, but the result might well be a reduced capacity of parties to compete for citizen support. Thus, from a different perspective, there would be less democracy.

In short, the relationship between democracy and parties is complex. The term "democracy" is used in a variety of ways in support of a particular vision of political parties. If one does not like parties or particular party officials, it is tempting to attack them in the name of democratic reform. On the other hand, strong parties can be defended as promoting democracy. We must be careful, therefore, not to endorse a program merely because its advocates call it democratic reform. A reform to one person might be a step backward to another. We should keep in mind that many of the features of parties that some people view as undemocratic (for example, control of nomination by nonelected party officials) are common in many European countries regarded as democratic.

CHAPTER SUMMARY

What are political parties? Parties are organizations that nominate candidates for political office. Parties take many forms in the United States. The most important parties are the Democrats and the Republicans. Both are loose collections of citizens, party officials, and officeholders. Power in the Democratic and Republican parties is dispersed, and neither party can strictly control its own membership.

Do the Democratic and Republican parties differ? In general, Democrats and Republicans differ in the people they attract, and these people diverge on some issues. Democrats draw primarily from less well-off groups; Republicans, from better-educated, wealthier groups. Democrats are more likely to consider themselves liberal; Republicans tend to think of themselves as conservative. Differences also occur among party activists and among officeholders, especially in the area of government involvement in the economy. These differences, however, are not extreme and agreement exists on many issues. Debate often occurs on whether the differences between the parties should be clarified and perhaps made more comprehensive.

Do political parties have any impact? Political parties perform several useful functions: they help people make voting decisions, help candidates campaign, coordinate the actions of public officials, provide organized opposition to government, and reduce political conflict.

Are political parties in decline? The power of political parties has varied considerably over the course of American history. Parties have disappeared only to reappear. They have met many challenges and adapted to diverse conditions. Contemporary factors working against parties include the growth of civil service, the popularity of primaries, the emergence of the campaign industry, and a weakening of party loyalty. The decline of parties would be most strongly felt by poorer people, since parties provide important campaign resources to counteract the advantages of wealthy interests.

IMPORTANT TERMS

Explain the following terms.

caucus	realigning election
welfare state	blanket primary
party platform	nonpartisan election
party machine	

THINKING CRITICALLY

1. In many other democracies, political parties have membership standards that help prevent outside groups from taking over control of the party. Should U.S. political parties be allowed to set qualifications for membership? Why or why not?

2. The national political party organization has little authority to see that a state party organization follows national party policy. What might be the consequences of such independence of the state organizations?

3. The United States has a two-party system, and many of our laws discourage the growth of minor parties. Because of the diversity of our society, should we encourage more parties—for instance, a women's party or a party for blacks? Explain your answer.

4. Many states allow citizens to vote a straight party ticket by marking a single choice on the ballot, which indicates that the vote is for the party's entire slate of candidates. What are the advantages and disadvantages of this procedure?

5. What effect has the growth of primaries had on the selection of candidates for national office?

6. What are the advantages and disadvantages, for a candidate for office, of having close ties to a party organization?

7. There are fewer party bosses today than several decades ago. What changes in party politics might take place that would help bring back the bosses?

EXTENDING YOUR UNDERSTANDING

1. Contact your local political organization (you may choose either party). Find out what kind of work it does and if it has any effect on your community. What effect does it have? Present your findings to the class.

2. Research the percentage of minority membership in both the Democratic and Republican parties. How do the percentages compare? Find out what attempts the parties are making to recruit minorities. Do you think they have been successful in recruiting minorities? What standards did you use to make this judgment? It may be helpful to contact the state or national party organization for information.

3. During the late nineteenth century, there were several fairly successful third parties. Make a chart showing these parties and indicating the major issues each supported. Why did these parties fail to replace either the Republican or the Democratic party? Why don't we have any successful third parties today? Write a report on your conclusions.

4. Research the political careers of such "bosses" as William Tweed, Richard Daley, or Carmine De Sapio. How were these bosses able to consolidate power? What conditions allowed them to maintain their authority?

MAKING DECISIONS

Obtain a copy of the 1984 Democratic and Republican party platforms (you might check in the library, or write to the national party offices in Washington). Select one important issue (civil rights, arms control, or the environment, for instance). Analyze the similarities and differences in the two platforms on that issue. What party would you vote for based on their stands on this issue? Prepare a speech aimed at convincing your classmates to support the party of your choice.

Chapter 8

Interest Groups and Pressure Politics

Like political parties, interest groups are viewed with mixed feelings. On the one hand, everyone accepts the right of citizens to organize politically and take their case to the government. The First Amendment specifically protects the right to petition government. If asked how they would influence a political decision, most people would say "join or organize a group." Thousands of groups have been created that have become politically involved. On the other hand, many people are uneasy about interest groups. A candidate who appealed strongly to each and every group would probably be widely criticized. In numerous instances government actions are condemned because they are the result of interest-group influence. "Special interests"—just another name for interest groups—are opposed by almost everyone. People are also concerned about the huge sums of money some of these groups spend and about some of their tactics (for example, giving expensive gifts to public officials). This chapter examines interest groups and their behavior by posing four key questions:

- What are interest groups and why are they so numerous?
- How do interest groups try to exert influence?
- How successful are interest groups?
- Do interest groups undermine democracy?

PREVIEW

What are interest groups and why are they so numerous? An interest group is a collection of people acting together to influence government. Interest groups vary considerably in how they are organized and in what tactics they employ. The most common are formally organized groups—typically those promoting a particular economic interest. Single-issue organizations have grown in popularity in recent years. Some interest groups take the form of a social movement. The professional advocate and nonpolitical interest groups are also means of influencing government.

Interest groups flourish under several conditions: a diverse society, a system of several branches and levels of government, guarantees of free speech, and weak political parties. The recent surge in group activity has resulted from increased government involvement in the economy, government encouragement of groups, the further decline of parties, and the emergence of a well-off, politically aware citizenry.

How do interest groups try to exert influence? Many groups try to influence public opinion so as to create pressure on government. Groups also support candidates for office, especially through political action committees (PACs). Influencing legislation by providing gifts to officials, rating legislators' votes, supplying information, and drafting bills is also common. Many groups focus their efforts on the administration of laws. Groups become involved in the legal system by influencing the selection of judges, bringing cases to court, and conducting legal research.

How successful are interest groups? Many people believe that interest groups are highly successful, considering all the money they spend and the extent to which they impose their goals on government. However, the evidence suggests that the power of groups is limited. Success is more likely when goals are narrow and aimed at preventing action and when the cause is socially acceptable. It also helps to have support in key places and not to have opposition from the President and the public. A group with close ties to government, particularly if it is involved in the actual decision making, is also likely to succeed. However, sometimes even groups with the opposite characteristic have been victorious.

Do interest groups undermine democracy? The most serious criticism of interest-group politics is that it is incompatible with democracy. Pluralist democracy, with its emphasis on numerous groups openly and fairly competing, attempts to reconcile special interests with the public interest. Groups provide the means by which citizens can influence government in large, complex societies. Pluralist democracy has been criticized on the grounds that not all citizens are equally represented, that group leaders are not always in tune with the membership, and that the push and pull of groups undermines the overall public interest. Defenders of pluralist democracy assert that "outsider" groups of limited resources can win and that the public interest is satisfied in the process of bargaining and compromise that groups participate in.

WHAT ARE INTEREST GROUPS AND WHY ARE THEY SO NUMEROUS?

In principle, a political **interest group** is easy to define. It is a collection of people acting together to influence government policy. Such groups, however, are not always easily identifiable. Interest groups vary considerably in their size, organization, and tactics. They might devote themselves to any issue, from highly specific technical matters to such broad concerns as world peace and global poverty. Some would even deny that they are politically motivated. Let us briefly examine some of the major types of organizations.

Formal Organizations

The classic interest group is a formal, permanent organization with a hired staff that advances well-defined political goals. Some groups—for example, the AFL-CIO in Washington—have impressive buildings; large, well-trained staffs; and ample resources. They employ many **lobbyists**—agents who deal with public officials on behalf of the group. Other groups might consist only of a director and a secretary operating out of a small office on a very limited budget.

The most common type of formal organization is one that represents a particular economic interest. These groups have grown in number as the government has become more involved in the economy. For example, because the federal government plays a major role in the banking industry, bankers have created the American Bankers Association, the Independent Bankers Association of America, and the Association of Bank Holding Companies. Every major economic interest—oil and gas, clothing manufacturers, restaurants, auto manufacturing, housing, and so on—is represented by a number of interest groups. Such groups believe that if government can tell them how to run their businesses, they should have some say in government.

Agricultural interests are especially well represented. Some are concerned with farmers generally—the American Agriculture Movement and the National Farm Organization are two examples. Most, however, focus on a fairly narrow commodity or type of farming—the American Seed Trade Association, the Cotton Council International, the United Egg Producers, and so on.

A large number of formal organizations also exist to advance broad political goals that involve several different issue areas. For example, the Americans for Constitutional Action is a conservative group interested in such issues as national defense, tax policy, and government regulation. On the liberal side is the Americans for Democratic Action, which focuses on social welfare policy, defense spending, and foreign policy, among other issues. A number of groups, usually referred to as **public-interest groups,** are also concerned with a variety of issues, but these groups say they are working for the overall public good, not for a particular liberal or conservative goal. Common Cause, which promotes honesty in government, is an example of a public-interest group.

Most ethnic, racial, and religious groups also have organizations that work on their behalf. Examples are the National Congress of American Indians, the Japanese American Citizens League, the Anti-Defamation League of B'nai B'rith, the National Association for the Advancement of Colored People, the National Council of Churches, and the United States Catholic Conference. In recent years even those sharing a common sexual preference have become organized—the Gay Activist Alliance and the National Coalition of Black Gays, for example.

Other governments, both within the United States and abroad, have established formal organizations to work on their behalf. Many cities and states now have Washington offices; they are also represented by such organizations as the U.S. Conference of Mayors or the National Conference of State Legislators. And because foreign governments can be vitally affected by U.S. government policies, organizations exist to represent their interests. For example, the European Community Information Service is the voice in Washington of the European member nations of the Common Market.

Many interests are represented by a number of separate groups. Large corporations typically have their own Washington office, belong to industry trade associations, and are members of general business groups, such as the U.S. Chamber of Commerce. Unions sometimes have their own office, in addition to AFL–CIO representation, to advance their interests. Some formal organizations consist of a number of groups that have joined forces to marshal resources and coordinate their actions. For example, the National Anti-Hunger Coalition was created by several groups to influence government programs dealing with food and nutrition.

Single-Issue Groups

Formal organizations, whether they represent business or labor, producer or consumer, usually see themselves as representing people with a number of concerns. The Pharmaceutical Manufacturers Association, for example, follows developments on behalf of drug makers in such areas as testing, product labeling, and licensing. Moreover, its activities change as situations evolve and new issues emerge. In contrast to this type of group are single-interest organizations that focus on one or two issues. Their purpose is not to look out for a business or ethnic group across numerous issues. Rather, they concentrate on one subject—saving the whales, legalizing marijuana, abolishing capital punishment, and so on. For example, the Children's Defense Fund, a traditional pro-children formal organization, focuses on such issues as disease-screening programs, health insurance for children, legal assistance for community child health programs, and many other child advocacy issues. In contrast, the National Right to Life Committee is a single-interest group exclusively concerned with abortion and the closely related issues of infanticide and euthanasia.

Single-issue groups tend to differ from the more traditional, formally organized groups in other ways as well. Whereas traditional formal organizations concentrate on developing close, lasting ties to government officials, single-issue groups are more likely to stress direct public pressure techniques, such as letter-writing campaigns and threats of boycotts (a mass action in which people deliberately avoid buying products of a company whose policies they believe are wrong). One such group is the National Federation for Decency (NFD), devoted to ridding television, radio, and magazines of sexual content and violence. The NFD rates shows and articles and then advises its 20,000 members to boycott products sponsoring the alleged indecency. Between January 1982 and May 1983, some 116 sponsors were targeted.

Single-issue groups are often less willing to compromise than traditional organizations, perhaps because of the religious or moral character of many of the issues they address, such as abortion, pornography, prayers in public school, homosexuality, sex on television, and Communist influence. Single-issue groups often see their mission more as a sacred cause than as a series of political negotiations involving compromises.

The line between traditional formal organizations and single-issue groups is not always precise, and groups can change. Some religious-oriented single-issue groups that focus mainly on nonpolitical moral concerns also take positions on economic and foreign-policy subjects. Many contemporary environmental and consumer groups began as one-issue groups but have been transformed into organizations concerned with a wider variety of issues and a more flexible style. "Nader's Raiders," the group created in the 1960s by Ralph Nader that dealt only with consumer product safety, has now become the Center for Study of Responsive Law and is involved with gas and electric rate reform, hazardous wastes, and other projects. Several civil rights associations have also gone from one-issue groups to more traditional organizations.

Social Movements

Quite different from formal organizations and even from single-issue groups are what might be called **social movement groups**—collections of people who work together for a political goal but who are only loosely bound together by organizational ties. Moreover, there is rarely a clear line separating movement members from nonmembers—people might decide to be involved, then drop out without taking formal action. There might be specific organized groups within a movement, but they rarely have the paid staffs and ample budgets of formal groups. Like single-issue organizations, social movement groups show a tendency to use so-called **direct action tactics**—boycotts, demonstrations, and so on—rather than rely on contact with officials.

In recent decades social movement groups have played a prominent and often highly visible political role. Beginning in the late 1950s, for example, blacks waged a vigorous campaign to achieve legal and economic equality. Although this movement had several notable leaders and organizations—for example, Martin Luther King, Jr., and the Congress of Racial Equality (CORE)—there was no one dominant group. Actions were often planned locally. The antiwar movement beginning in the mid-1960s had the same overall style. Dozens of local groups and millions of citizens worked in many ways to persuade the government to withdraw American troops from Vietnam. Anyone could be part of "the movement," and there was little coordination of strategy and resources. In

For interest groups, publicizing their cause is a major aim. Mothers Against Drunk Driving joined forces with a truckers' group, which donated the trailer, top. The Community for Creative Non-Violence placed a statue on Capitol Hill to alert Congress to the plight of the homeless, lower left. When budget cuts forced the Library of Congress to reduce its hours, students and scholars held a sit-in in the main reading room, lower right.

fact, as in the civil rights movement, differences among groups were common, and people would regularly join and leave the movement as circumstances changed.

Movements can become transformed into more conventional interest groups. For example, there has been an anti-nuclear-weapons movement in the United States since the 1950s. The movement has ebbed and flowed and is a loose coalition of groups and sympathizers. It originally emphasized such activities as placing newspaper advertisements against nuclear weapons rather than influencing legislators. In the early 1980s this focus began to shift. SANE, one of the leading anti-nuclear-weapons groups, has worked on increasing its formal membership and has hired lobbyists to try to influence members of Congress on such specific issues as cutting back funds for the MX missile. This lobbying effort has drawn support from well-established religious and political groups.

United in their desire for social justice, residents of a Northern suburban community join Martin Luther King, Jr., in a rally in 1965 under a banner that came to symbolize their cause.

Professional Advocates

The professional advocate might be described as a political "gun for hire"—an individual, a law firm, or a company that does public relations. These lobbyists might perform many of the same functions as formal organizations or single-issue groups, but their activities are done on a contract basis, and the advocate typically has many clients. Large corporations usually employ professional lobbyists in addition to having their own or industrywide groups.

Many former high-ranking government officials become lobbyists after they leave government. A number of large Washington-based law firms also specialize in helping people achieve their political goals. Often these lobbyists develop reputations for special competence, and a business or other group will hire them for a specific job (for example, some lobbyists have strong ties to a particular member of Congress or an executive branch agency). Foreign governments and corporations frequently make use of these advocates rather than set up a formal organization. The Jus-

tice Department calculated that in mid-1982 there were some 6,810 agents representing foreign clients. One advantage of using this approach is that it attracts less publicity than a formally established group.

"Nonpolitical" Interest Groups

The claim that nonpolitical groups engage in political pressure might seem a contradiction. There are, however, thousands of groups whose basic purpose is nonpolitical but that do, on occasion, engage in political action. Because these groups receive tax advantages for being nonpolitical, their activity must be conducted very carefully. In particular, a donation to an educational or charitable group is tax-deductible: a $10,000 donation to a college by a person in the 28-percent tax bracket thus costs "only" $7,200. But a donation to a political group is not deductible, so a $10,000 contribution costs $10,000. Hence, political activity on the part of these interest groups is sometimes so subtle that it is hardly viewed as political.

Lines of communication are kept open between lobbyists and legislators. For their efforts, lobbyists may gain favorable legislation—and they may reward those who helped them.

One of the best examples of such groups is provided by organized religions. On the abortion and birth control issues in particular, the Catholic hierarchy has made its presence felt in the lawmaking process. The Catholic Church has also become involved in foreign policy. Similarly, rabbis sometimes act as representatives of the American Jewish community on issues pertaining to Israel. On issues like prayers in public school, tuition tax credits for religious schools, and sex education, purely religious groups act as political groups. Another common nonpolitical interest group is the professional association. Such organizations as the American Political Science Association exist largely to promote scholarly activities (journals and meetings). Nevertheless, yearly membership fees help support a Washington office that occasionally tells the government why political scientists need more federal research grants and keeps members informed of relevant legislation. Charities also sometimes use their memberships and organizations to advance political causes. The United Cerebral Palsy Association, for instance, is not legally a lobby, but it nevertheless lobbies for federal funds for medical research.

The Growth of Interest Groups

There is an enormous number of interest groups in the United States, and new ones are being created all the time. There are perhaps between ten thousand and twenty thousand lobbyists working in Washington, D.C. Why are there so many groups and lobbyists? What keeps them all going?

Conditions Favorable to Interest Groups

Since its founding, the United States has been fertile soil for the emergence of interest groups. James Madison, in *The Federalist No. 10,* issued a warning against the dangers of "factions"—groups working toward self-serving political goals—and his warning has been regularly repeated (see Chapter 2). One major condition supporting the emergence of groups is the diversity of American society. Economically, geographically, socially, and politically we are an extremely varied society. This was true one hundred years ago; continued immigration and social and economic changes have, if anything, made contemporary society even more varied.

The nature of our political process also encourages numerous active groups. Our system of government is characterized by decentralized decision making. As we noted in Chapter 2, the Constitution created divisions in the national government and between national and state governments. Citizens concerned with, say, environmental policy might have to organize groups that operate at the local and state levels as well as in several parts of the national government—Congress, agencies within the executive branch, or even the courts. Moreover, public officials often use some discretion in administering programs. If all decisions were made centrally and laws allowed no leeway of interpretation, there would probably be fewer interest groups.

Constitutional guarantees of free speech and the right to free association also encourage groups. To ban some groups or to put limits on group activities would weaken both the First Amendment and our tradition regarding the rights of citizens to make their claims on government. In 1946, for example, Congress tried to place limited restrictions on lobbying activity by passing the Federal Regulation of Lobbying Act. This act defined a lobbyist as someone who collected money in order to influence legislation before Congress. Lobbyists were required to register with the Clerk of the House and file quarterly reports of income and expenditures. The maximum penalty for violation was one year in jail or a $5,000 fine. However, the Supreme Court considered even this modest regulation to be too severe. In the case of *United States v. Harriss* (1954), the Court ruled that the act applied only to groups that raised, collected, or received funds in an effort to influence Congress. "Educational" lobbyists were not covered, nor were grass-roots groups (such as local community-based groups). Overall, the 1946 act has had little impact.

Finally, the general weakness of American political parties has made interest groups an attractive way to influence government. As we saw in Chapter 7, the two major parties are loose coalitions of groups that approach issues from a perspective of bargaining and compromise. Moreover, parties rarely dominate the political process. If a particular interest has only a modest following, working through a party will probably mean that objectives will be watered down or lost altogether. Even if the cause is supported by the party, this is no guarantee of future success. Therefore, it usually is more advantageous to establish one's own organization rather than be one of several dozen competing groups within a diverse party. This situation does not occur in many European democracies, where there are several parties and each party can have a close relationship with groups such as labor unions or farmers.

Membership Value of Groups

Another reason for the importance of interest groups in the United States relates to the purpose of these groups. Obviously, many people join groups because of a desire for a specific, concrete benefit. Providing benefits is sometimes called the *instrumental purpose* of groups. For example, a business person who joins the U.S. Chamber of Commerce probably sees his or her dues as an investment in helping to create government policy favorable to business. Individuals who are worried about nuclear war might contribute to the nuclear freeze movement.

Less obvious are what have been called the *"expressive"* or *symbolic factors* encouraging group formation.[1] A collection of individuals create a group to give expression to their common identities. Many ethnic-related groups serve this purpose—for example, the Polish American Congress sponsors activities to enhance the image of Poles. NOW—the National Organization for Women—provides its members with a political identity. Often a profession that lacks public recognition will set up an organization to show both members and nonmembers that it has standing and resources. The American College of Nurse-Midwives, the American Society for Psychoprophylaxis, and the National Center for Homeopathy are examples of organizations created by specialized medical practitioners to provide themselves with a sense of identity.

Clearly, many groups simultaneously perform both instrumental and expressive services for members. The American Bar Association offers concrete benefits to lawyers while also giving them a professional identity. Groups might go through periods of differing emphasis on these services. A group like the Polish American Congress generally performs a largely expressive service for its members, but when domestic problems occurred in Poland during the early 1980s, it played an important instrumental role by helping its members provide aid to expatriate Poles.

Commentary: Too Much Success Can Lead to Failure

Successful lobbyists can do very well financially, but if they are *too* successful, they may eliminate their own jobs. Lobbyists are thus like doctors, who would become unemployed if they succeeded in banishing disease. This dilemma is illustrated in a story told by James Burke, a Democratic member of Congress from Massachusetts. Over the years Burke had co-sponsored a bill to restrict imports to the United States in order to protect the troubled New England shoe industry. Burke and his co-sponsor realized that the bill had little chance of passing, but they nevertheless kept it on the legislative agenda. A professional lobbyist, however, did not realize Burke's lack of commitment and invited him to a dinner party sponsored by industries opposed to the bill. At length the lobbyist berated Burke about his bill, claiming that it would ruin the economy. Burke admitted with a straight face that perhaps his bill was a disaster and stated that he would withdraw it. Confronted with the possibility of sudden unemployment, the lobbyist responded, "You wouldn't do that, would you?"

Cited in Austin H. Kiplinger and Knight A. Kiplinger, *Washington Now* (New York: Harper & Row, 1975), p. 214.

Recent Increase in Interest-Group Activity

The conditions we have described have existed for many years and help explain why groups have always played a vigorous role in American politics. However, since the 1960s there has been a dramatic increase in the number of groups. For example, in 1960 there were about sixteen groups that had a concern for American Indians; by 1980 this figure was forty-eight. In contemporary politics almost every business, ethnic group, political cause, or whatever has a group working on its behalf. To explain this upsurge requires yet another set of factors.

The most important reason for the rise in group efforts has been the enormous growth in government activity at all levels. Especially since the mid-1960s, governments have become deeply involved in such issues as health care, education, economic regulation, maintenance of the environment, disaster relief, and much, much more. Each time the government ventures into an area, it lays the groundwork for the creation of new groups to influence policy making. For example, when the federal government increased its responsibility in providing health care, one consequence was the emergence of numerous groups, both among the deliverers of medical services (for example, the Coalition for Health Funding) and among the recipients (for example, the National Council of Senior Citizens). The purpose of each group, of course, was to make sure that the interests and needs of the people it represented were not overlooked. One study reports that the number of groups representing the elderly doubled in 1965, when the federal government enacted Medicare (a government-funded health care program for those over sixty-five) and passed the Older Americans Act.[2] There would have been no need for so many groups if the government had continued its traditional role of leaving most social problems up to individuals and private industry.

The federal government itself has encouraged the creation of numerous groups. One reason is that many programs are more easily administered if people in the program are represented by a group. The government can then deal with a few group leaders rather than a multitude of individual constituents. The American Public Transit Association, an organization of rapid rail and bus system operators, is an example of a private body encouraged by government. The government frequently has provided funds to organizations, especially nonprofit "citizens' groups." Many government programs have included provisions requiring citizen participation, and this has generated a number of citizen councils, advisory boards, and neighborhood associations, all of which act as interest groups.

The further decline of political parties is a third factor contributing to the recent growth in group activity. Changes within parties (for example, the greater use of presidential primaries) as well as the lesser role of parties in campaigns have given groups that were once closely tied to parties a greater incentive to seek an independent course of action. As we noted earlier, modern media-oriented campaigns are very expensive, and candidates must seek financial support from numerous groups in addition to the parties. For example, unions, Jewish groups, and black groups once worked largely through the Democratic party to advance their goals. Today, these interests stress their own organizations instead of relying on party officials. After all, there is little value in trying to achieve your goals through a party coalition that no longer is a significant political force.

The growing number of well-educated, well-off people concerned with issues has provided many groups with a large potential membership. For such people a $25-a-year membership fee is not a burden; moreover, they might have the skills and the free time necessary to participate in vigorous grass-roots activity. Organizations such as Common Cause and the Sierra Club draw heavily from this well-educated, well-off part of the population.

Finally, several new technologies have invigorated interest-group activity. The computer, in particular, has helped organizations develop lists of potential joiners, send out millions of pieces of mail, and keep track of hundreds of issues. Budget-rate telephone systems give groups a relatively low-cost means of quick communication around the country. Some groups have become skillful at producing television and radio messages and distributing them by satellite. Such technology allows even a relatively modest organization with limited resources to enter the world of interest-group politics.

Maintaining Interest Groups

We have seen that many factors encourage people to create groups to advance their objectives. Nevertheless, it has been argued that groups face a major threat to their survival—the so-called **free-rider problem,** which is the task of keeping a group functioning after it has been set up. The free-rider problem was brought to the public's attention by Mancur Olson in his *Logic of Collective Action*, published in 1965. Basically, Olson argues that it is pointless for a person to give time and money to an existing group if he or she would receive the benefits of group action without any effort or expense. In other words, why should an older person pay to join a senior citizens' group if the objectives pursued by this group (for example, better medical facilities) will be enjoyed equally by both group members and nonmembers?

The existence of the free-rider problem helps to explain why organizations participate in many more activities than simply advancing their political goals. In particular, they provide numerous incentives to ensure that members will contine to pay their dues and give their support. Some of these incentives are material benefits—low cost insurance plans, merchandise discounts, or special convention rates. Group survival can depend on providing members with psychological benefits as well—feelings of common purpose, sense of importance, and prestige. Typically, in group newsletters and magazines, members are warned that some disaster is about to occur unless the group acts; past accomplishments are highlighted; and reduced-rate, "members only" vacation packages are offered.

Research on how groups survive has also pointed out the importance of wealthy sponsors, whether individuals, foundations, corporations, or the government.[3] Such funds frequently play a major role in creating and sustaining an organization. Moreover, the importance of sponsorship, as opposed to membership dues, seems to be growing. The role of this type of support is well illustrated by the relationship between the Students for a Democratic Society (SDS) and the United Auto Workers (UAW). The SDS began in the 1960s as a very liberal organization of young people

Issue: Who Speaks for the Public Interest?

Since the 1960s, a number of public-interest lobbies have emerged in the United States. They are devoted to such issues as consumer protection, exposure of corruption in government, protection of the environment, and access to legal assistance. Unlike traditional lobbies, they claim to represent the concerns of all citizens, not just of a "special interest."

Although public-interest lobbies claim to be broadly representative, their leadership reflects a fairly narrow element in American society. In the early 1980s S. Robert Lichter and Stanley Rothman examined the backgrounds and political outlooks of 157 leaders in 74 public-interest groups and law firms. Here are some of their major findings.

- Leaders are highly educated, with nearly half (45 percent) having attended a prestigious college or university. Almost 90 percent of them hold a post-graduate degree, mostly in law.
- As a group they are well-off. In 1981, 35 percent personally earned $50,000 or more; 58 percent had a family income of $50,000 or more.
- Ninety percent define themselves as "liberal"; since 1968, they have overwhelmingly supported the Democratic presidential candidate (only 2 percent voted for Reagan in 1980).
- In terms of issues, these public-interest-group leaders overwhelmingly endorse the idea of government redistribution of wealth, government guarantees of a good standard of living, a woman's right to abortion, and preference for minorities in hiring. They oppose a strong military and a forceful policy toward the Soviet Union.

It seems fair to say that, while the policies of public-interest lobbies may benefit society as a whole, the leaders of these groups are hardly representative of the average American citizen.

Adapted from S. Robert Lichter and Stanley Rothman, "What Interests the Public and What Interests the Public Interest," *Public Opinion*, April/May 1983, pp. 44–48.

and initially received extensive UAW financial assistance. However, as the SDS became increasingly revolutionary, UAW money was withdrawn and the SDS eventually collapsed into a small group of extremists. Evidence also suggests that the government sponsors groups that are sympathetic to its overall goals.

Conclusions

Our political system makes it relatively easy for interest groups to grow. The constitutional system, with decision making at the national, state, and local levels, enables groups to try to influence numerous elected and other officials. The Constitution also protects the right of organizations to exist. A weak party system likewise offers an incentive to use groups to influence government. The growing role of government has further encouraged the expansion of organized interests. When the government enters an area, new groups are created. In many instances, the government itself provides for the establishment of groups. Recently, the further weakening of parties and a well-off, politically aware citizenry have led to the formation of many new groups.

Check Your Understanding

1. What are the different types of interest groups? How do they differ in terms of goals and tactics?

2. How does the U.S. political system encourage the formation of interest groups?

3. What are some of the benefits interest groups provide members?

HOW DO INTEREST GROUPS TRY TO EXERT INFLUENCE?

All interest groups attempt to influence political decisions. However, because of differences in specific goals and resources, they do not all follow the same tactics. A well-off organization interested in a single piece of legislation will act differently from a small group with limited resources dedicated to world peace. Although most groups participate in several types of activities, we can distinguish four general techniques: (1) influencing public opinion, (2) influencing legislation, (3) influencing administrative decision making, and (4) influencing court decisions.

Influencing Public Opinion

Group representatives understand that public opinion does not determine government policy. Yet they realize that they should seek to make public opinion favorable to their cause. At a minimum, outright public hostility to one's objectives must be softened or neutralized. Even the most powerful interests recognize that political leaders will not make unpopular decisions that could jeopardize their reelection. The importance of public opinion is well demonstrated in the failure of Arab efforts to overcome American support for Israel. Even if billions were spent on their behalf, Arab interests would still face an uphill fight because of widespread public sympathy for Israel.

Favorable public opinion is sought through a variety of strategies. A familiar example is an advertising campaign to enhance the image of an entire industry. Over the years private electric companies have placed numerous magazine ads describing the advantages of private enterprise over public ownership of utilities. In recent years individual defense contractors have taken out full-page ads in national magazines and big-city newspapers, promoting the general idea of strong defense. The U.S. Chamber of Commerce has promoted the image of the business community with a television program, a radio show, and a number of educational packages for students. These campaigns are typically "soft-sell" programs designed

The purpose of this advertisement for the National Rifle Association is to give a positive public image of the organization— that its members are not social misfits but, ordinary people.

to create favorable climates of opinion. The technique is not limited to business interests. Many liberal groups (such as environmentalists) have used identical methods to generate support for their causes.

Interest groups also try to stimulate awareness of a topic in the hope that public concern will be translated into pressure on government. For example, in 1984 the nation's banks mobilized thousands of citizens to bombard Congress with letters opposing the automatic withholding of income tax on savings-account interest (they were successful). On a smaller scale, by meeting with newspaper editors in a particular legislative district, a lobbyist may generate editorials favorable to his or her client. Such editorials may then encourage citizens to write letters to a member of Congress. One company, which distributes brief news items and feature stories to newspapers and TV stations nationwide, claims that it can help mobilize "tons of letters" by putting a client's message in small-town newspapers and on television programs.

Sometimes campaigns are directed toward particular segments of the public. Interest-group leaders frequently reason that it is more effective to reach a few thousand influential citizens than to appeal to millions of people through the mass media. For example, some conservative groups send books highly favorable to their cause free of charge to political science professors. Their goal is to influence teachers who then might influence their students. Many political groups also advertise in the "prestige press"—magazines that are read by educators, writers, and others who occupy important public positions. The hope is that influential readers will pass on the messages.

Helping Candidates for Office

Besides creating pressure on leaders by shaping public opinion, interest groups can play a vigorous role in the election of public officials. Sometimes a group will encourage a person to seek office, but the most common interest-group election activity is to provide campaign funds. These funds are usually given through organizations called political action committees (PACs)—see Chapter 6. PACs have become important and highly controversial in recent years and deserve closer attention.

Until 1971, several laws banned corporations, labor unions, and those doing business with the government from making contributions to candidates for federal office. In general, most funds were obtained from individuals. Interest groups were not a major source of funds, because many groups received money from economic interests that did business with the government (the law even prohibited "indirect" contribution through a group). There were limits on the size of contributions, but these restrictions were easily avoided by a candidate creating several separate campaign committees ("Democrats for Frump," "Independents for Frump," etc.). Individuals, especially wealthy "fat cats," were the keys in financing campaigns.

In 1971 Congress passed the Federal Election Campaign Act, which allowed corporate or union money to be used to administer an organization that raised and distributed campaign funds. However, the election law put limits on how much could be given to these organizations and how much they could spend. In other words, General Motors could not give money to a candidate, but it could create an organization that would collect money from others for this purpose. The 1971 legislation paved the way for many unions and corporations to set up organizations to raise and distribute campaign funds. There was still legislation on the books that directly or indirectly prohibited businesses with federal contracts from making campaign contributions. Because thousands of businesses (and some unions) held federal contracts, the path to a political action committee was still not completely open. In 1974, Congress amended the 1971 act to allow businesses and unions doing business with the government to create PACs. When the Federal Election Commission in 1975 reaffirmed the right of corporations doing business with the government to establish PACs, the number of PACs rose sharply. In addition to businesses and labor unions, groups supporting issues—called **nonconnected PACs**—have come into existence. Some of these are offshoots of existing groups; others are completely new.

The laws allowing the creation of PACs also dealt with campaign contributions. As we described in Chapter 6, these laws greatly limited individual contributions to candidates for federal office. Now a person was limited to a $1,000 donation per candidate per election, with a maximum of $25,000 per year for all federal candidates. No total maximum was placed on contributions to groups and parties, but no more than $5,000 per year could be given to any one organization (the one exception was that $20,000 could be donated to the national committee of a political party). The only way that wealthy individuals could contribute huge sums was to spend money on *behalf* of candidates rather than to give it to them.

By allowing businesses, unions, and issue-oriented groups to create committees to raise and

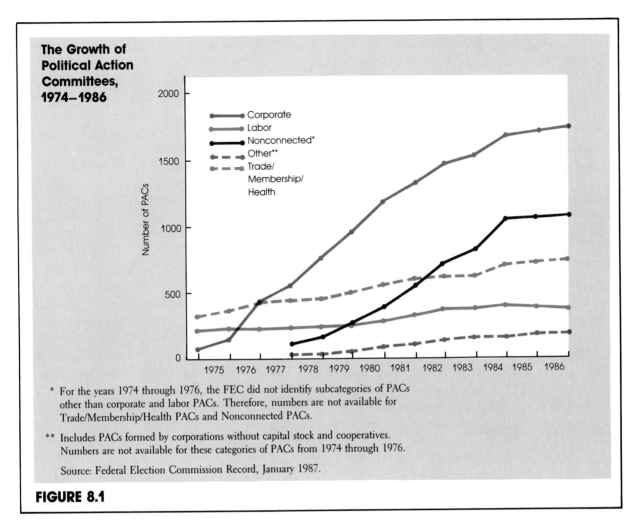

The Growth of Political Action Committees, 1974–1986

*   For the years 1974 through 1976, the FEC did not identify subcategories of PACs other than corporate and labor PACs. Therefore, numbers are not available for Trade/Membership/Health PACs and Nonconnected PACs.

**   Includes PACs formed by corporations without capital stock and cooperatives. Numbers are not available for these categories of PACs from 1974 through 1976.

Source: Federal Election Commission Record, January 1987.

FIGURE 8.1

spend money, and by limiting individual contributions, the 1971 and 1974 laws greatly altered the role of interest groups. The creation of political action committees started slowly, but their growth has become explosive. Figure 8.1 shows the growth of PACs between 1974 and 1986. At the end of 1974, there were 608 PACs officially registered with the Federal Election Commission; by the end of 1986, this figure had risen to 4,157. The key change has been the shift from the individual to the group—the PAC in particular—as the major force in campaign finance (and among groups, the corporate PAC has shown the greatest growth). Before the 1970s, groups were in the background when it came time to raise money. Now, with individual donations greatly limited,

groups have come to the forefront through the PAC.

Despite limits on individual donations to a single PAC and restrictions on PAC contributions to a particular candidate, PAC outlays to candidates have been considerable. In 1985–86, the total PAC contributions to all House candidates was $84.6 million. This figure would be much larger if PAC contributions on behalf of candidates, but not under candidates' control, were included. On average, House Democratic incumbents received $174,731 in PAC contributions; Republican incumbents, $157,087. It is not surprising that incumbents rather than challengers received the most PAC support—House Democratic challengers, for example, received an average of $45,188 in PAC donations, and Republican challengers got an average of $12,660. Obviously, because most incumbents were reelected, PACs like to make relatively safe investments.

Several PACs in particular have been major forces in funding campaigns. The two top PAC spenders in 1985–86 were the National Congressional Club and the National Conservative Political Action Committee. The former spent more than $8 million during 1985–86. During the same period nationwide, PACs spent a total of $254 million. The biggest spenders were issue-oriented nonconnected PACs. Groups whose livelihood is directly affected by legislation have especially active PACs. For example, the American Medical Association (AMA), a group representing doctors and traditionally concerned with government involvement in medical care, directly or indirectly gave some $6.6 million to congressional candidates between 1977 and 1982. In 1983, 87 percent of all senators and 84 percent of all House members received AMA contributions.

Influencing Legislation

Because one of the goals of interest groups is to persuade Congress and state and local legislatures to enact favorable laws, sooner or later all groups must face the problem of dealing with lawmakers. How do interest groups try to influence legislative policy making?

Money and Favors

One method is the outright buying of votes. Because the "right" government decision can be worth millions of dollars to certain individuals, it is not surprising that potential beneficiaries would invest a few thousand dollars in an effort to gain that outcome. Especially in the nineteenth century, and at the state and local levels until fairly recently, outright bribery was common and perhaps even acceptable, despite being illegal. For example, Senator Daniel Webster, widely viewed as incorruptible, received $32,000 from Nicholas Biddle for his support of the second Bank of the United States. Webster saw nothing wrong with this behavior. During the great economic expansion of the nineteenth century, whole state legislatures were purchased outright by railroad, lumber, or oil interests. Payoffs were so common that it was sometimes said that an honest politician was one who, when bought, stayed bought.

In contemporary politics such systematic buying of votes has almost disappeared. One reason is that the growth of the mass media and laws pertaining to outright bribery have made such practices risky. The custom of exchanging legislative influence for cash probably still continues, but it occurs in relatively minor matters—getting a government contract, blocking a deportation order—rather than on major politics. Large-scale vote-selling on major issues can easily backfire if discovered.

In today's politics attempts by interest groups to influence legislators have become more subtle. Often it is almost impossible to distinguish attempts at influence from useful assistance. Whereas a blatant vote-buyer provides a concrete payment for a specific vote, today's skillful lobbyists emphasize a more general feeling of good will between legislators and themselves. That is, the legislator develops a positive feeling toward the group, its leaders, and its goals. Such good will can be created in numerous ways. In the mid-1970s, for example, it was disclosed that some defense contractors had supplied congressional personnel with yacht trips, parties at hunting lodges, and free flights on corporate jets. A favorite tactic is for a group to sponsor an elegant fundraising event for a member of Congress. Groups can also invite members of Congress to address them for a fee plus expenses (though Congress has set limits on such outside income). Introductions to movie stars and sports celebrities can sometimes impress members of Congress. Campaign contributions made by lobbyists come closest to old-fashioned bribery, but as long as they are reported, they are perfectly legal.

Equally important as good will is access—the ability of a lobbyist to get a hearing from a legislator. Because public officials usually have very crowded schedules, being able to gain access is essential. Few lobbyists believe that an elaborate dinner or a large campaign contribution by itself will sway a vote. However, it eventually might open doors when the lobbyist has to make his or her case. Without regular access to decision makers, the lobbyist's job is extremely difficult. The reputation of many of Washington's top group advocates rests on their ability to gain instant access to those in power.

Rating Voting Records

In recent years more than seventy interest groups have developed ratings that show the degree to which a member of Congress agreed with a group's objectives. The ratings are publicized in newspapers and specialized magazines and are sometimes used in campaigns. Farm groups, labor unions, religious organizations, and many other associations all publish their own ratings. The Americans for Democratic Action (ADA) and the Americans for Constitutional Action (ACA) are the best-known examples of groups that issue ratings. Typically, only a relatively small number of votes are selected, and the types of votes selected by a group can vary from year to year. Hence, a legislator might receive a perfect score from the ADA (a liberal group), but he or she might not have taken the liberal position on all legislation.

Group ratings sometimes influence legislative votes. For example, a legislator desiring the support of elderly citizens in the next election might go out of his or her way to score high on the ratings provided by the National Alliance of Senior Citizens or the National Council of Senior Citizens. In the 1984 presidential race, Republicans used Geraldine Ferraro's high ADA scores to label the Democratic candidate for Vice President as an extreme liberal. Perhaps the most dramatic instance was the use of ratings in the 1970s by a group called Environmental Action. This group characterized members of Congress with the twelve lowest scores as the "Dirty Dozen." As a result of much publicity over five elections, nearly half of the dozen were defeated for reelection. For a period, many a legislator feared being put on Environmental Action's "hit list."

Supplying Information

Congress must deal with complex subjects daily. Legislators, no matter how intelligent or hardworking, cannot obtain all the information they need on their own. Congress has several agencies to provide information, but especially on highly technical matters these are of limited use. Into this picture steps the interest-group representative, who is more than willing to supply the needed data, frequently at public hearings conducted by legislative committees. When congressional com-

Public officials face competing demands from interest groups seeking favorable policy decisions. Providing expert testimony is one way of influencing government agencies. Here, Annie Wauneka, the leader of the Navajo Tribal Council's health committee, presents data to the U.S. Surgeon General. The public health needs of the Native American peoples have been a long-neglected social concern.

mittees considered energy legislation in 1977, they relied heavily on oil and gas data supplied by oil-industry associations. In other instances information is given directly to legislators and their staffs. Defense contractors frequently supply legislators with data showing the virtues of their products. Thus, many of our laws are based on data supplied by interests directly affected by the legislation.

Is it a wise idea to rely on information supplied by lobbyists? The evidence from lobbyists themselves indicates that no professional lobbyist would risk his or her reputation by providing faulty information. Inaccurate information, if exposed, might seriously undermine the lobbyist's career and cause. This is not to say that such lobbyists' information is unbiased. A report on acid rain prepared by the coal industry might stress certain types of data and reach conclusions favorable to its view, but this would not be considered falsification or lying. Also, legislators often receive information from different sides, so biases can cancel each other out. Thus, on transportation legislation, groups representing railroads and trucking companies can usually be counted on to supply information against each other. It is hoped that by evaluating biases and conflicting testimony, legislators can arrive at some degree of truth. Investigative agencies of Congress, like the General Accounting Office, can also be called upon to verify information.

Drafting Legislation

The third way that interest groups influence legislation is by drafting legislation. Here the line between lobbyist and legislator is nonexistent. According to some estimates, *half* of all the legislation proposed in Washington is drafted entirely or in part by interest groups. As in the supplying of information, this service results from limitations on congressional resources. Drafting bills usually requires expertise and time, and most legislators cannot do everything themselves. In addition, the lobbyist providing the bill will occasionally furnish draft speeches in support of the bill and advice on legislative strategy. Needless to say, a lobbyist's draft will be highly favorable to his or her client's interest.

Hiring Former Government Officials

Interest groups often ensure their access to the legislative process by hiring former government officials familiar with members of Congress, the ins and outs of law making, and their colleagues still in power. For example, when a company that wanted to influence the White House to guarantee

Commentary: Selling Out to the Russians

Although buying legislative votes has had a long history in the United States, the long-term impact of such bribery is not completely clear. While bribery itself is illegal, it need not necessarily result in disastrous public policy. This is well illustrated by events in Washington during 1868. At that time Congress was debating legislation of considerable financial value to the Russian government.

The Russian minister in Washington—a Mr. Stoekl—decided to help move things along by purchasing the support of leading public figures. N. P. Banks, chairman of the House Committee on Foreign Relations, was given $8,000 for his support. The "incorruptible" Thaddeus Stevens, a leading member of Congress, got $10,000. John W. Forney, a former public official and promi-

nent newspaper publisher, received $30,000 to publicize the Russian cause. Two well-known Washington lawyers received $20,000. Overall, about $200,000 was spent to bribe officials and sway public opinion. In the end, Stoekl and the Russian government were successful, and the United States agreed to pay for Alaska.

a large loan to produce synthetic oil, the firm hired a former member of Congress. The former congressman not only used his House friendships on behalf of the company but provided the company with analyses of previous legislation he had helped write.

Influencing Administrative Decision Making

Even if an interest group is successful in getting a law passed, its job is not over. The impact of a law frequently depends on its administration. Every law requires some degree of interpretation, and in many instances administrative agencies can use their judgment in preparing rules and regulations. Even when the law is specific, administrators make important decisions regarding how vigorously it will be enforced and what penalties should be sought for rule violators. Therefore, the passage of a favorable bill can mean that the battle simply shifts from Congress to the Department of Agriculture, the Interstate Commerce Commission, or some other agency responsible for enforcement.

Because administrative agencies, like legislatures, are responsible for making rules, many activities of lobbyists in Congress and the bureaucracies are similar. For example, most agencies are required to hold public hearings on proposed changes in regulations, and these are attended by group representatives. Thus, when the Interstate Commerce Commission considers a change in the maximum cargo that trucks can carry, representatives of the truckers, the trucking companies, highway safety groups, and the railroads all provide expert testimony on the impact of the proposed regulations. Moreover, especially when regulations are highly technical, interest groups can play a major role as the specific rules are worked out (on some topics not more than a few people understand all the complexities).

Influencing Administrative Appointments

Several activities of lobbyists are particularly relevant to administrative agencies. One of the most important is to make sure that administrative appointments are acceptable to the interest groups. It

is highly beneficial, for instance, for the National Association of Broadcasters to deal with a sympathetic Federal Communications Commission (FCC); therefore, broadcast representatives work long and hard with Congress and the executive branch to ensure the "right" appointments (the FCC makes regulations for TV and radio stations). Lobbying over administrative appointments is rarely well publicized, but it can become a major issue. When President Reagan took office with the strong backing of groups supporting greater economic development of public lands, he appointed James Watt as Secretary of the Interior. Groups dedicated to preserving public land began a long and vocal campaign to remove Watt. This controversy made Watt something of a political embarrassment to the Reagan administration. Eventually, over a relatively minor incident in 1983, Watt resigned.

Influencing Appropriations of Administrative Agencies

Another means to influence administrative decisions is the use of group influence on legislative appropriations. A working relationship often develops among interest groups, bureaucracies, and the congressional committees that help determine an agency's budget. Often, the interest groups, an agency in the executive branch, and congressional committee members share common goals, regularly meet with one another, and even might exchange jobs over a period of years. The relationship between an interest group, an executive branch agency, and a committee or subcommittee of Congress is commonly called an **iron triangle.** Veterans' groups, legislative committees dealing with veterans' benefits, and the Veterans Administration are an example of an iron triangle relationship.

Each member of the triangle helps the others. When the budget of the Veterans Administration is reviewed by the House Committee on Veterans' Affairs, the American Legion might testify on behalf of a budget increase. After all, the Legion is dedicated to the rights of veterans. The Veterans Administration in turn, will be sympathetic to the goals of the American Legion. Such sympathy is

"AT LAST! A WEAPONS SYSTEM ABSOLUTELY IMPERVIOUS TO ATTACK: IT HAS COMPONENTS MANUFACTURED IN ALL 435 CONGRESSIONAL DISTRICTS!"

appropriate for the VA, because the Legion might help the VA in carrying out its administrative responsibilities. Committee members might receive campaign funds from the Legion. It is also likely that legislators on veterans' committees view veterans' groups and the VA positively. Thus, triangle relationships allow groups to help smooth the relationship between Congress and the executive branch. Give-and-take relationships occur in almost every federal agency, whether the policies involve education or national defense.

Iron triangles pose special problems in making policy. As we have suggested, there are strong forces creating these close ties. And in principle, there is nothing immoral or illegal about these mutually supportive relationships. Nevertheless, their existence can create obstacles for Congress and the President in developing new policy. Suppose, for example, that Congress and the President decided to change the way the Defense Department did its purchasing. The proposed changes would have to go through House and Senate appropriations subcommittees, which have close ties to Defense Department procurement offices and defense contractors. If the changes were unfa-

vorable to the defense contractors, we might see an effort—publicity, specially commissioned reports, campaign contributions—to sway committee members. The Pentagon might lobby actively against change. And because Congress rarely acts against the wishes of a committee, a relatively small group of interests could prevail against Congress and the President—and the American public.

Co-opting Administrators

A third method of influencing administrative decision making is co-optation, or takeover. An interest group succeeds in transforming a potentially unfriendly government agency into an agent for its own cause. The interest group not only influences a few decisions but manages to run the entire show as well. Perhaps the classic case of co-optation occurred when the railroads "captured" the Interstate Commerce Commission (ICC) shortly after its creation in 1887. Originally designed to protect the public through the regulation of railroad rates, the ICC instead became the defender of the railroads against other transportation industries, Congress, and the public. The railroad-dominated

ICC acted to limit entry to the field and set artificially high shipping rates, on the grounds that unlimited competition would be harmful.

How can a private organization "capture" an administrative agency? One way is to encourage the interchange of personnel. It is not unusual for a member of an interest group to become part of the government and then later return to that group as a professional lobbyist. Dean Burch, for example, was chairperson of the Federal Communications Commission under President Nixon. He resigned and took a job for a law firm that represents clients involved in communication matters. When Reagan was elected in 1980, Burch helped select new FCC members.

In addition, agency appointees who at first are unfriendly to interest groups can be won over through persuasion, promises of future employment, or even lavish gifts. Interest groups also stress to administrators that they share the same basic values and goals. The American Farm Bureau Federation owes much of its success with various Agriculture Department agencies to the selling of an "all-of-us-farm-people-are-in-the-same-boat" philosophy. In short, a possible conflicting relationship between a lobbyist and an agency is changed into a cooperative relationship based on common purpose—as defined by the interest group.

Influencing Court Decisions

At first glance one might think that interest groups have little impact on the judicial process. After all, judges seem above day-to-day politics, strict rules of judicial procedure govern court decisions, and judges are not usually accessible to lobbyists for particular causes. Nevertheless, the formalities and apparent inaccessibility of the judicial process do not exclude interest-group activities. Especially as more and more important issues are decided by courts, interest groups have become deeply involved in the legal system.

Influencing Judicial Appointments

One important method that groups use to influence court decisions is to play a role in judicial appointments. Although judges must work within relatively narrow legal guidelines, interest groups are well aware that, particularly in complex cases, the personal opinions of judges can be crucial. Hence, whether the appointment is a city judge or the Chief Justice of the Supreme Court, citizens whose interests could be affected might lobby for a sympathetic judge. Over the years some of the most publicized efforts at getting "good" judges—especially on the Supreme Court—have been made by civil rights groups. They were helpful, for example, in blocking the Nixon appointments of Clement Haynsworth and Harrold Carswell, both of whom were viewed as unsympathetic to black interests. Numerous civil rights groups put intense pressure on several senators (because the Senate has to vote on the appointment of federal judges), and information discrediting the two nominees was publicized. When Ronald Reagan nominated Sandra Day O'Connor in 1981, there was vocal but unsuccessful opposition from groups opposing her position on abortion.

In 1986 two of President Reagan's conservative nominees—Daniel A. Manion, nominated to a court of appeals position, and William H. Rehnquist, nominated as Chief Justice of the Supreme Court, drew intense opposition from liberal groups. The Chicago Council of Lawyers, a liberal group, stated that Manion's legal briefs were poorly written, disorganized, and filled with spelling errors. Civil rights groups called attention to Rehnquist's past actions against black voters. Nevertheless, both Manion and Rehnquist received Senate confirmation.

Supporting Cases and Litigation

A second important method of exerting influence is to support cases as they move through the court system. In the U.S. judicial system, obtaining a legal ruling requires that a case be brought before a judge. Hypothetical cases will not be considered. Interest groups that are seeking legal changes are always on the lookout, therefore, for a court case that can be used to advance their cause. An interest group itself can bring a case (called *litigation*). The California Bankers Association once sued the government to block laws requiring banks to main-

Biography: Martin Luther King, Jr.

Martin Luther King, Jr., was born in 1929 and was assassinated by a sniper's bullet in 1968. During his relatively brief life he won fame both in the United States and abroad as a black leader who aroused the conscience of a nation against racial injustice, becoming, in 1964, the youngest man in history to win the Nobel Peace Prize. After his death he became the first black American to have a national holiday set aside in his honor.

King, the son and grandson of preachers, joined the Baptist ministry after graduating from Morehouse College and earning advanced degrees from Crozer Theological Seminary and Boston University. He had been living in Montgomery, Alabama, only a few months when, late in 1955, the local black community launched a boycott to protest segregated public buses. The boycott organizers asked King to head their association; a personable young man, he had not been in Montgomery long enough to make any enemies. King's confident presence and powerful oratory helped Montgomery blacks survive the thirteen-month struggle. Although a federal district court ruled in June that Montgomery's segregation laws violated the "equal protection" clause of the Fourteenth Amendment, the boycott continued until after the Supreme Court upheld the lower-court decision and Montgomery's buses were desegregated.

In 1957 King helped form the Southern Christian Leadership Conference, which served as his organizational base. Although the SCLC was only one of several civil rights groups, King soon dominated the movement. He won allies not only because of his charismatic personality but also because of his commitment to nonviolence, in the tradition of Mahatma Gandhi, the leader of India's struggle for independence from Britain. King believed in direct action: boycotts, marches, and other forms of public demonstration. Even though such tactics might lead to violence on the part of the authorities, King believe that he and his followers must respond "with the power of love." If need be, they would fill the jails; King himself was imprisoned several times. King's tactics were soon imitated by others, including feminists and opponents of the war in Vietnam.

King led sit-ins to desegregate public eating places and marches to encourage black voter registration. His campaign against segregation laws in Birmingham, Alabama, aroused nationwide attention. Television cameras recorded the violence as city police turned dogs and water hoses on youthful demonstrators. In 1963 King helped organize the massive March on Washington that culminated in his famous "I have a dream" speech. When President Lyndon B. Johnson lent his weight to the struggle for social justice, Congress responded with the Civil Rights Act of 1964, which banned racial discrimina-

tion in employment and public accommodations, and the Voting Rights Act of 1965 (see Chapter 5).

King's approach was highly successful in the early years of the movement because he encouraged all concerned Americans—whites as well as blacks—to join the crusade against racism. He felt that this strategy was necessary in a country where blacks were far outnumbered. As time went on, however, King's methods were attacked by more radical young blacks as being too slow and too dependent on whites. When, in 1966, King turned his attention to de facto school segregation (that is, based on residential patterns rather than on law) in Northern cities like Chicago, the tactics of nonviolence proved less successful. In his last years, King sought to organize the nation's poor. Although he was struck down before he could mobilize a strong campaign, he left an enduring legacy—an example of moral courage for a just cause—that no temporary setbacks could diminish.

tain certain records. Public Citizen, a group claiming to work on behalf of the entire public, used litigation to stop President Nixon from refusing to spend $5 million Congress had set aside for a water-quality program. By supporting cases, civil rights groups have managed to overturn many discriminatory laws. The National Association for the Advancement of Colored People (NAACP) provided the legal aid to help overturn a Kansas law requiring racial segregation in public schools (*Brown v. Board of Education*, 1954). The American Civil Liberties Union has played a major role in politics by supplying lawyers and financial support in cases involving free speech, censorship, and religion in public schools.

Even if not a direct participant in a case, an interest group can try to influence judicial decisions by supplying relevant information. The most common method is to file an **amicus curiae** (friend of the court) **brief,** in which a group with a stake in a case can offer arguments not offered by the immediate participants. Such briefs have played important roles in the results of several major cases. The 1978 *Bakke* case involved the use of racial quotas in a California medical school (that is, the medical school would admit a certain number of minority students each year). Some fifty *amicus curiae* briefs were filed. Interest groups can also encourage scholarly research that might ultimately prove valuable in preparing a case. This strategy has become important as some judges increasingly rely on sociological data, in addition to technical points of law, to reach a decision.

Conclusions

Lobbying is widespread, and lobbyists employ a great variety of techniques. Much lobbying follows the common stereotype—paid lobbyists will try to persuade legislators to vote for a particular bill. However, much of the activity of groups is less visible and more subtle. "Soft-sell" ads in prestige magazines, friendly "nonpolitical" dinners, group ratings of voting records, free legal assistance, and help in getting hard-to-find technical data are other ways of influencing government decisions. Interest groups will also try to ensure the appoint-

ment of sympathetic administrators and win over administrators already in power. Perhaps the least visible actions concern the judicial system. Groups lobby for the "right" judge to be appointed, support cases beneficial to their cause, and supply information in court cases.

Check Your Understanding

1. What are some of the ways an interest group can try to influence public opinion?

2. How can interest groups make a favorable impression on legislators?

3. Why are government officials willing to use information supplied by interest groups?

4. What can interest groups do to try to influence administrative decisions?

5. What can interest groups do to influence the judicial process?

HOW SUCCESSFUL ARE INTEREST GROUPS?

We have seen that interest groups are numerous and are involved in almost every aspect of politics. They employ a variety of strategies, everything from small dinners in expensive restaurants to marches and demonstrations. But how much do these groups affect public policy? Is government dominated by these groups? This section will examine the extent of interest-group power and consider when such groups are most likely to be successful.

Arguments Supporting the Power of Interest Groups

One of the most common arguments in support of the power of interest groups focuses on the money

In the 1980s family farmers were hard-hit by pro-business policies in Washington. Organizations like the American Agriculture Movement rely on membership solidarity rather than paid lobbyists.

they spend. Nobody knows for sure just how much is spent, but the figure is undoubtedly several hundred million dollars, for all the organizations' salaries, media campaigns, mass mailings, and direct campaign contributions. Would supporters of these groups throw their money away? Of course not, it is claimed, so it follows that contributors must be getting something for their money.

Studies of what groups get for their money suggest only a limited return on investment. For example, an analysis of how members of Congress voted on a 1975 bill to increase milk price supports shows that contributions by a milk products PAC had only a small impact on the outcome (however, the PAC did generously reward its supporters in the next election).[4] Diana Yiannakis, in her study of legislation guaranteeing loans to Chrysler and the windfall profits tax on oil, reached a similar conclusion—monetary contributions had only a small impact on legislative voting.[5] Several other studies on a variety of issues—support for the B-1 bomber, trucking deregulation, and the regulation of the used-car industry—generally confirm the conclusion of a modest relationship between contributions and voting.[6]

A second argument made regarding the strength of interest groups focuses on those cases in which a group prevailed despite the lack of merit of its cause and despite widespread opposition. One of the best-known examples has been the power of the National Rifle Association and other pro-gun groups to block gun control legislation in spite of the high incidence of crimes involving firearms, widespread public support for tougher gun laws, and frequent strong presidential support for gun control. Less well-known "sacred cows" that have survived because of intensive lobbying efforts involve various agricultural subsidy programs, money for schools on untaxed federal property, a number of military bases and weapons systems, and several other extensive programs of questionable value. Such programs seem to stand as monuments to the power of well-organized groups.

Here, too, as was true with the supposed power of lobby money, the success of interest groups might be somewhat exaggerated. For every story of a great lobbying victory, there undoubtedly is a story of a failure. The auto industry, for example, has generally been unable to get its way on laws dealing with antipollution devices, auto safety, mandatory gas economy standards, and requirements that defective cars be recalled and repaired at the manufacturer's expense. This is in spite of vast financial resources, access to top lawyers and lobbyists, and the advantage of plants and dealers scattered over many congressional districts. Similarly, the oil industry, once considered one of the strongest of all lobbies, has lost on a number of tax-related issues (for example, the government has cracked down on tax shelters involving exploration for oil). More generally, victory for one interest group often means defeat for another, so it cannot be said that groups dictate policy.

It is usually very difficult to evaluate precisely the impact of groups. In some instances even a small victory can have major consequences. When a legislative vote is close or when committee members cannot agree on a bill, the swaying of a few votes can turn defeat into victory. Thus, a group that tries to influence one hundred legislators, but influences only five, still might have accomplished its objective. Especially when the aim is to block action, winning the support of a single, powerful, strategically positioned legislator can be a great victory (for example, winning the support of the Speaker of the House, the most important leadership position in the House).

Perhaps the most difficult problem in measuring interest-group impact is sorting out the group influence versus other political forces. Take the situation in the early 1980s when the Federal Trade Commission (FTC) was considering issuing rules to require used-car dealers to list all known defects and warranty information on the window sticker. Such a requirement was bitterly opposed by car dealers, and the PAC of the National Association of Automobile Dealers distributed a million dollars to congressional candidates. These donations seemed to do the trick—the FTC action, originally authorized by Congress in 1975, was blocked. Nevertheless, it is conceivable that members of congress were also reflecting changes in public opinion between 1975 and the 1980s. When Congress originally acted, the issuing of rules in the name of consumer protection was widely accepted. by 1980, however, the public seemed to be less willing to accept such regulation. The automobile dealers just might have been riding a changing tide of public opinion in and out of Congress.

Finally, measuring the role of money is difficult, because in many instances financial rewards follow behavior rather than being given in advance. In other words, a member of Congress who supports the real estate lobby might receive a campaign contribution a year or more after his or her action. The legislator acted in anticipation of a reward, not for a specific "up-front" campaign contribution. Uncovering this type of influence relationship can be difficult because there might

be no contact at all between the legislator and the group when the favor is done. In fact, the group might never deliver its financial reward, and thus influence was exercised without any contact or exchange occurring. In short, conclusions about the power of particular groups must be treated cautiously.

Nevertheless, it is possible to consider some of the factors related to group success or failure. Three broad factors are especially relevant to the chances of group success: (1) the organization's goals, (2) the nature of the group's support and opposition, and (3) the group's relationship to government.

Organizational Goals

In any political struggle the likelihood of success depends in part on one's goals. Because interest groups vary considerably in what they try to achieve, some groups have a built-in advantage. One way to characterize goals is in terms of how specific and technical they are. Some groups—for example, civil rights organizations—are committed to broad social changes in numerous areas (such as eliminating discrimination in employment). Other groups, especially those representing specific economic interests, might focus all their attention on one or two narrow goals. In general, this second type of group might find success easier to achieve. Groups focusing on specific, detailed issues frequently develop close ties to the small number of government officials who make the key decisions. They also have great familiarity with the relevant technical data. (By way of contrast, a group concerned with racial discrimination in employment must deal with a large number of public officials, many of whom have different perspectives on what the problem is and how it should be addressed; the issues involved may also be widely debated and controversial.) On some occasions, because of their highly specialized goals, narrow groups are successful without the public realizing it.

This does *not* mean, however, that small groups with technical, limited goals have a greater overall impact on public policy. Even if a group like Trout Unlimited—which is dedicated to pre-

Points of View: Weighing the Benefits of Consumer Activism

Of all the people devoted to public-interest causes, few people enjoy greater respect for integrity and unselfishness than Ralph Nader. In the years since publication of his book attacking the auto industry, *Unsafe at Any Speed* (1965), he and his staff of "Nader's Raiders" have spearheaded the consumer advocacy movement, investigating everything from congressional reform to health care for the aged.

It has been argued that Nader and other public-interest lobbyists work not for the common good but primarily for the well-off, white, and college-educated. As a case in point, critics cite Nader's goal of a low-energy, slow-growth economy. Achieving such an economy would require the abandonment of nuclear power, the development of new sources of energy (such as solar energy), government regulation of oil prices, strict conservation measures, and high environmental standards for oil and coal production. This program would be of little benefit to the poor because it would not only make energy prohibitively expensive but would also prevent

people in need from improving their economic status; social and economic advancement depends on high energy use, not energy cutbacks.

Of course, this argument must be balanced against the very real accomplishments of Nader and his co-workers. In terms of legislation alone, they were at least partly responsible for the National Traffic and Motor Vehicle Safety Act (1966), the Clean Air Act (1970), the Clean Water Act

(1972), and the Freedom of Information Act (1974). To put it more concretely, it was through their efforts that such automobile safety devices as seat belts, padded dashboards, collapsible steering wheels, and shatter-resistant glass are now standard equipment. There is little doubt that thousands of Americans—rich, poor, and in-between—owe their lives to the public-interest movement in general and to Ralph Nader in particular.

serving trout habitats—always wins, its overall impact is far less than that of more generally oriented groups with lower success rates. Civil rights groups with far-reaching goals have experienced many failures, yet they have had a profound impact on society. Still, if a high batting average is what you want, make your group's goals as specific and technical as possible.

Whether a group wants government action or inaction is also relevant to success. Our constitu-

tional system of checks and balances and divided power makes it much easier to *block* action than to promote it. A single subcommittee, for example, can bury a bill. Success requires the support of many committees, Congress, and the President. Groups favoring the status quo therefore have the advantage.

A third way to characterize a group's goal is in terms of its social acceptability. Changes for success are better when an organization's aims are socially acceptable. For example, government officials, like most citizens, support the right of business to make decent profits, the right of farmers to earn a good living, and a strong national defense. Hence, lobbyists advancing proposals consistent with these principles will generally receive sympathetic hearings. On the other hand, groups advocating the legalization of cocaine will have a hard time making their case.

The importance of the overall acceptability of group goals is illustrated by the increased power of civil rights groups over the last twenty-five years. Prior to the 1960s, they faced an uphill struggle. The very idea of racially integrated schools struck some as contrary to the laws of nature. Eventually, however, the notion of racial equality became more accepted. Today, groups like the NAACP and the Urban League are part of the Washington "establishment," with access to many top officials. Women's groups still sometimes encounter opposition from legislators who cannot accept the idea of equal rights. Such groups realize that they must continue to promote their cause among both the public and members of government.

Nature of Group Support and Opposition

All interest groups have friends and enemies, but not all friends and enemies are of equal importance. One relevant factor is the location of support. Groups that can mobilize support in many states or congressional districts, for example, are more likely to be successful than are groups whose support is highly concentrated geographically. Many defense contractors understand this; when they take their case to Congress, they emphasize the project's economic benefits to many areas. When Rockwell promoted the B-1 bomber in the late 1970s, it stressed that the plane would be built by subcontractors in forty-seven states. On occasion, large defense contractors will even locate their plants with an eye to who represents what district (for example, in the 1950s Georgia was a favorite location because of the power wielded over the military budget by Georgia's Senator Richard Russell, chair of the Senate's Armed Services Committee). The fact that a group's supporters come from widely separated geographical areas is not always obvious. Advocates of foreign aid, for

instance, might enlist the support of all the legislators whose districts make the industrial and agricultural products to be shipped abroad.

Having supporters in key political positions can also help. Consider, for example, the long-standing debate over whether Amtrak—the government-run passenger railroad—should continue to receive large government subsidies. In his proposed 1982 budget President Reagan called for district cuts in Amtrak's funding, cuts that would have eliminated much of its service. Faced with a loss of railroad service, many small towns and cities turned to Congress for help. Fortunately for most of the localities, influential House and Senate members represented areas where Amtrak service was to be eliminated. The House Committee on Energy and Commerce, which reviewed the proposed cuts, was headed by John Dingell of Michigan; the Detroit–Chicago run was one of the routes to be cut. Senate Minority Leader Robert Byrd of West Virginia also made sure that the Chicago-to-Washington-via-West-Virginia route was kept. In the end, Congress gave Amtrak more than Reagan had proposed. In his proposed 1986 budget Reagan tried again, urging the elimination of all federal subsidies for Amtrak. But again, he was forced to compromise.

Whether a group's goals succeed or fail also depends on who is supporting or opposing those goals. One of the most important potential roadblocks to group success is the President. A President has several techniques to frustrate even the most well-organized lobby: the use of the media to stimulate public opposition to the group, the threat of a veto of a bill passed at the request of a group, and the use of the prestige of the office and the promise of rewards to help members of Congress resist group pressure. If group-sponsored legislation is enacted, the President still might have considerable discretion in administering the law. A good illustration of how a determined President can mobilize Congress against a well-established lobby occurred in 1982, when President Reagan proposed sharp reductions in aid to schools in areas where federal employees live on property not locally taxed (so-called federally impacted schools). This is an emotional issue in many localities, because a reduction of federal aid means higher local taxes. Despite the efforts of the National Association of Federally Impacted Schools, representing some one thousand school districts; state threats to charge tuition to military personnel and federal employees if cuts were made; and vigorous support from members of Congress, funds were cut from $725 million in fiscal 1981 to $475 million in 1982.

A second potential opponent of interest groups is a concerned public. Ultimately, the jobs of all legislators, the President, and top political appointees depend on public support. Few leaders will openly side with a group in the face of widespread public anger. This was well demonstrated in the debate in the late 1970s over federal price ceilings, or maximums, on natural gas. For years the price of natural gas shipped across state lines had been set by the federal government. Producers now argued that these prices were artificially low and therefore were preventing exploration for much-needed new supplies. Deregulation, it was argued, might raise prices temporarily, but in the long run there would be ample supplies at reasonable prices. Although there were many strong forces in favor of removing price controls—gas producers and legislators from gas-producing states—public concern over higher utility bills made Congress very cautious. Few members of Congress wanted the responsibility of sharply raising millions of utility bills. Natural gas remained regulated.

Frequently the fear of angering the public gives groups concerned with narrow, technical goals a definite advantage. A legislator discussing government step-ladder standards with a delegate from the American Ladder Institute does not have to worry about widespread public controversy. This is not the case when a lobbyist representing a nuclear disarmament group meets with the legislator. Even if the member of Congress were in full agreement with the group representative, the legislator would probably be very cautious in his or her support for fear of arousing public controversy.

The Organization's Relationship to Government

In principle, interest groups and government are separate. In practice, however, some groups are much closer to the center of power than others. Perhaps the best way of gaining direct access to policy making is to have one's "own" legislative committee or bureaucracy. We mentioned earlier that organizations can "capture" a government agency or develop close ties with congressional committees. In this way, for example, union leaders usually have easy access to government through the Department of Labor or congressional committees handling labor issues. Within the Justice Department there are specialized agencies dealing with the problems of blacks, women, Hispanics, Native Americans, and other groups.

Not all groups have equal access, however. Women's groups have frequently complained that they do not have their "own" bureaucracy in the same way that business executives have "their" agency in the Department of Commerce. Consumer-interest groups have also complained that they are less well represented within government than business groups are. The excluded groups argue that they cannot compete in the policy-making process because few officials share their perspectives and interests. The desire to have built-in representation was one of the major reasons behind the creation of the Department of Education in 1979. Although there were several agencies dealing with education in the Department of Health, Education and Welfare, education groups, especially the National Education Association, argued that education would be served best by a separate Cabinet-level education department.

Another way interest groups can increase their chance of success is to become closely involved with the administrators in policy-making decisions. The intermixing of government and interest group is illustrated by the role of the American Bar Association (ABA), an association of lawyers that looks out for the legal profession. The ABA plays a more direct role in government decisions than many other groups. Specifically, both at the state and the national levels, the ABA reviews the qualifications and legal backgrounds of potential judges. Candidates are rated from "highly qualified" to "not qualified." Even though these judgments are not official, the prestige of the ABA

When policy proposals are adopted by professional groups such as the American Medical Association, the organization will use its prestige and political clout to pressure state legislatures and Congress to enact its proposals into law.

often leads presidents and governors to go along with its recommendations. The mixing of public and private occurs in many other areas as well, because it is frequently much more efficient for the government to work through interest groups than to deal separately with each individual member. In 1974, for example, Congress created the Egg Board, which included representatives of the egg industry, to issue regulations that had the full force of federal law. Obviously, a group closely connected with actual decision making stands a better chance than one that is an outsider.

Conclusions

How successful are interest groups? The answer is, "It depends." Claims that interest groups *run* government are exaggerated. The degree of success depends on many factors. The most successful groups are likely to have narrow, socially approved goals that do not mobilize public or presidential opposition. Success is likely to be even greater if the group has a close relationship to government. This does not mean, however, that groups without these advantages always fail. More important,

even if they fail most of the time, a few victories can be very important politically. Just remember that the temperance movement, which opposed the use of alcoholic beverages, had few of the characteristics of the "successful" group, yet it succeeded for a time in prohibiting the legal sale of liquor in the United States.

Check Your Understanding

1. Describe the arguments claiming that interest groups exert a strong political influence.

2. Why is it difficult to evaluate the impact of interest groups?

3. In general, groups with what types of goals are likely to be most successful?

4. Groups with what types of support are most likely to succeed?

DO INTEREST GROUPS UNDERMINE DEMOCRACY?

Interest groups perform many valuable services. Without such groups, many opinions would not be heard, abuses of power might go unexposed, and public officials would lack important information. Nevertheless, despite these useful functions, interest groups have been severely criticized. Some of the criticism focuses on particular tactics, such as large campaign contributions or deceptive use of the mass media. Much more basic, however, is the charge that interest-group politics is incompatible with democratic politics. It is this view that is often behind calls for greatly limiting the power of the "special interests." We shall analyze this criticism by examining a type of democracy based on interest-group activity—**pluralist democracy**. Our analysis then will consider whether pluralist democracy really does facilitate public participation and policies in accord with the public interest.

Pluralist Democracy

Although many theories of democracy are based on hope and an idealized view of citizens, pluralistic democracy claims to be rooted in the "real" world of politics. It accepts the fact that people have selfish motives and will scheme and even deceive others to win at politics. The basic principles of pluralist democracy are as follows:

1. Society consists of a multitude of groups. Some are well organized, whereas others are **potential groups**—they might become organized if their interests are threatened (for example, college students might organize to defeat a proposed tuition increase). All interests can easily form groups.
2. Groups compete with each other in trying to influence government. There are many different tactics (campaign contributions, letter-writing campaigns, persuasion of leaders, demonstrations), and groups differ in their resources (numbers, money, prestige, skill).

Competition is regulated by the government to maintain fairness.

3. In this competition, no one group or coalition dominates across all issues. One group countervails, or neutralizes, another (truckers vs. railroads); groups fear arousing strong potential opposing groups (utility customers outraged over rate hikes); groups have overlapping membership (union members favoring high wages are also consumers who fear high prices); and elected public officials can limit groups.
4. Out of this fair and open competition, the will of the people emerges. It is a democratic process because all people can participate, resources are widely distributed, and decisions made by bargaining and compromise are enacted into law by officials accountable through elections.

Pluralist democracy is especially appealing to advocates of democracy worried about the survival of meaningful public participation in large, complex societies. How can people hope to understand all the issues and effectively make their voices heard in Washington? The answer, according to advocates of pluralist democracy, is by supporting groups. Interest groups, therefore, make democracy possible in modern society.

Criticisms of Pluralist Democracy

Unrepresentative Character of the Interest Group System

One of the most frequent criticisms of pluralist democracy is that not all interests and people are equally well represented. Although it might be true that organizations exist for everybody, some people are represented by stronger, more resourceful groups. According to one observer, when interest groups speak, they speak with an upper-class accent.[7]

The biased character of the interest-group system has been documented in a study conducted by Kay Lehman Schlozman that looked at the nearly seven thousand organizations listed in the 1981 *Washington Representatives* (a directory of interest groups).[8] Basically, Schlozman found that business groups, especially corporations, were heavily overrepresented. Seventy percent of groups having representation in Washington were business-oriented. Less than 5 percent could be considered as speaking for the "have-nots" of American politics (the elderly, blacks, people on welfare, workers, women, and so on). Similarly, only about 4 percent of all groups were concerned with overall policy objectives, such as consumer protection, world peace, and the environment. Moreover, an analysis of changes in interest-group representation suggests that the highly publicized emergence of public-interest organizations in the 1960s and 1970s has not changed the pro-business bias. Indeed, Schlozman notes, "For all newborn organizations representing the interests of diffuse publics, minorities, poor people, the elderly, and other disadvantaged groups, business actually is a more dominating presence in Washington now than it was two decades ago!"

Moreover, the nature of society encourages unequal group representation. It is much easier to organize for a particular economic interest than for a more general cause, such as women's rights or health care for the poor. For example, the banking industry has clear common goals, and the very nature of the business world brings bankers into contact with one another. On the other hand, it is difficult for a women's group to promote issues that can unite most women politically, because women are an economically and socially varied group. Business interests can also better provide the funds necessary to gain access to legislators, support lengthy litigation, and skillfully use the mass media. Representatives of blacks, Hispanics, and other "outsider" groups must worry about sustaining members' involvement during noncrisis periods. The free-rider problem described by Olson and noted earlier is especially troublesome for groups representing people with limited resources—a $25 yearly membership fee is a heavy cost if you will receive the benefits of success regardless of group membership.

Unresponsiveness of Group Leadership
A second criticism of pluralist democracy focuses on the relationship between a group's leaders and

group membership. In a pluralist democracy it is the group that expresses the preferences of individual citizens. It has been argued, however, that in many instances the policies advocated by group leaders are not the ones favored by group members. For example, the leadership of the Catholic Church has repeatedly taken strong anti-abortion and anti-birth-control positions, even though membership is divided on these questions. Several major unions, such as the United Auto Workers, have regularly given strong support to the civil rights movement despite some membership opposition to these goals. The American Medical Association leadership has not always reflected many members' feelings in its strong opposition to government-provided health care.

Such differences between leadership and membership have several sources. The day-to-day experiences of each can vary considerably. A top union lobbyist receives a large salary, lives in a nice neighborhood, regularly meets important people, and typically will develop a different perspective on union policy than a steelworker threatened with unemployment. Group leaders also can be far more sensitive to political realities and limitations. An environmental group member might desire strict pollution controls, but leaders based in Washington might know that an uncompromising stand has no chance of success. Leaders also might put their own job security ahead of membership goals. By avoiding tough conflicts, exaggerating minor successes, and providing biased reports, Washington leaders might ensure their jobs but frustrate membership goals.

Undermining of National Interest
That the interaction of thousands of groups, each in pursuit of its own objectives, undermines the overall public interest is perhaps the most serious criticism of pluralist democracy. This case against interest groups has been made most forcefully by Theodore Lowi in *The End of Liberalism*. For Lowi, contemporary government is characterized by **"interest group liberalism"**—a strong government exists to improve society, but private groups are ultimately responsible for the formation and implementation of government policy. In effect,

Much of the nation's farm policies are determined by well-established agricultural groups, not by representatives of the people. Here, wheat is harvested on a large farm.

Lowi argues, through its delegation of vast administrative powers to private groups, the government in Washington has abdicated, or handed over, its power to govern. This abdication has had three negative consequences: (1) elected officials, who represent citizens, are shut out of policy making; (2) numerous privileges are maintained and created; and (3) because existing groups gain so many benefits, there is considerable resistance to change and flexibility.

The consequences of interest-group liberalism can easily be seen in the area of agriculture. The government has developed close ties with farm interest groups, which, either through public officials or on their own, set policy. Rules on acreage allocations, price support levels, export subsidies, and even legally binding guarantees are made by concerned groups, not by representatives of the public. Such policies greatly favor established groups (for example, large producers), and the arrangement creating these policies has powerful defenders. The question "What is good policy?" has been replaced by "What policy will powerful, well-established groups and their allies in government allow the government to enact?"

The push and pull of these groups can frequently make for wasteful, contradictory policies. One well-known example is the government's policy of subsidizing tobacco growers while simulta-

neously spending millions of dollars to warn citizens about smoking. Less obvious are numerous military programs of questionable value, unnecessary public works projects, costly foreign trade regulations, and unneeded service programs that survive because of group influence. Eliminating even the most obviously wasteful programs is not easy. In the context of a $700 billion national budget, keeping a useless $250 million waterways project to make one particular group happy seems unimportant. Moreover, the project might receive full-time support from several groups, whereas a member of Congress or the President can devote only limited time to an effort to eliminate the program.

Defending Pluralist Democracy

Those who believe that interest groups provide the basis of democratic politics in a modern, complex society usually acknowledge the accuracy of these charges. Certainly, not every interest is represented exactly in proportion to its numbers, group leaders can disagree with followers, and group goals can conflict with the overall public interest. Nevertheless, the occasional problems do not invalidate the basic idea of pluralist democracy, they claim.

Consider the charge that group politics favors established economic interests. This charge ignores the numerous instances in which groups with limited resources representing less-well-off citizens had a clear impact. For example, when Ronald Reagan became President, he launched an ambitious program to reduce spending for social services, reduce government regulations on pollution standards, sell government-owned land, and limit government rules on workplace safety. The President was only partly successful, however, owing in large part to the mobilization of environmental groups, civil rights organizations, and groups representing the elderly, labor unions, and others of limited resources. "Outsider" groups did well against more established groups.

As for the very serious charge that "special interests" undermine the public interest, two arguments are usually made. First, there are some groups—Common Cause, the League of Women Voters, a number of public-interest organizations created by Ralph Nader, among others—that do take a general perspective on what is good policy. These groups typically have ample resources and large, highly educated memberships. Because they do not gain economically from government decisions, they frequently can provide unbiased evaluations and recommendations. Such groups have helped create policies in such areas as campaign finance disclosure, public access to government information, and tougher consumer protection; they have also exposed numerous abuses of power.

Second, it is a mistake to believe that some overall public interest exists apart from the sum total of all individual interests. When farmers, business executives, labor unions, defense contractors, and all others battle over policy, it can be argued that the result *is* the public interest, not some betrayal of an abstract public interest. The difficulty in trying to establish some overall abstract public interest can be seen if we consider farm prices. Consumer advocates claim that by abolishing government price supports and production restrictions, food prices would drop and the public would benefit. Farm organizations assert, however, that lowered prices would drive many farmers out of business. Eventually, shortages would occur, prices would skyrocket, and the public would be worse off. Both positions are reasonable interpretations of the public interest.

Conclusions

To return to our original question—Do interest groups undermine democracy?—the answer is still, "It depends." For those who view pluralist democracy as a valid form of democracy, one that is realistic in a large, modern society, interest groups are essential to democracy. Indeed, the existence of numerous, vigorously competing groups is a sign of a healthy democracy. Such activity means that more citizens are represented and that there is less chance of any one group dominating. On the other hand, if we look at the types of groups that usually do well and at the goals they pursue, it seems as if democracy is being betrayed. In this case we conclude that some interests receive weaker support and that the overall public interest is being ignored. Both perspectives have a degree of validity. Reaching a judgment on whether the system is good or bad perhaps depends on what we are willing to accept as possible. Advocates of pluralist democracy frequently argue that it is the best we can do under difficult circumstances. Opponents believe that the pluralist democracy argument merely transforms defects into acceptable facts of political life.

Check Your Understanding

1. What are the key elements in pluralist democracy?

2. What are the major criticisms of pluralist democracy?

3. What arguments support the idea of pluralistic democracy?

4. Why is it sometimes difficult to decide whether a policy is in the "public interest"?

THE POLITICS OF CONTROLLING INTEREST GROUPS

The history of lobbying in the United States has been characterized by two features: the fairly regular occurrence of scandals and a reluctance by Congress to do much about it. Such scandals have involved everything from outright bribery to extravagant gift-giving. In the late 1970s, for example, it was revealed that Tongsun Park, a Washington-based Korean business executive, had spent between $500,000 and $1 million on members of Congress to help the legislative cause of South Korea (as many as 115 members of Congress had received gifts from Park). More recently, several legislators were caught trying to peddle influence to an FBI informant disguised as a wealthy Arab. One senator—Harrison Williams of New Jersey—went to prison for taking money from the informants. Far more common than such outright buying of favors have been legal, though questionable, practices such as offering public officials inside business information, selling them stock at reduced prices, or providing free vacations, theater tickets, and the like.

Congress' responses to such activities have been limited, frequently not much more than an investigation. In 1876, in response to an investigation of a scandal, the House adopted a resolution requiring lobbyists to register with the Clerk of the House. This requirement was not renewed two years later. Laws regulating interest groups have usually focused only on some lobbyists and they concerned registration and disclosure, not lobby activities themselves. The Foreign Registration Act of 1938, for example, required those representing foreign governments to register with the government, disclose their status when contacting members of Congress, and report their activities. The most comprehensive federal law—the Federal Regulation of Lobbying Act of 1946—merely set up certain registration and disclosure requirements. For example, those who solicit or receive money for the purpose of influencing legislation must register with the Clerk of the House and show how the money was spent. Subsequent Supreme Court interpretations, however, greatly limited the impact of this law. This law also does not cover lobbying in the executive branch or lobbying involving no direct contact with Congress (for example, mass letter-writing campaigns). Today, much of the legislation has focused on lobbying by tax-exempt, nonprofit educational and charitable groups (Congress has sought to prevent groups receiving tax-deductible funds from extensively engaging in lobbying). Overall, Congress has done little about regulating interest groups.

Why has Congress taken such limited actions? In fact, on several occasions Congress has tried to act, but serious obstacles remain. One problem is the legal definition of a lobbyist. Because citizens have the right to contact public officials, drawing a precise line between the politically active citizen and the professional lobbyist is not simple. Unless the law can readily separate lobbyists from citizens who happen to be politically active, the result will be great confusion. Also, what exactly is lobbying—sending a postcard to Congress? talking to a legislator in person? sponsoring a television program to convey your message? Separating "lobbying" from many other political activities is difficult, especially when we realize that much lobbying occurs in social events like a golf game.

Perhaps the major obstacle to controlling "special interests" and "pressure politics" is that such restrictions can interfere with our political freedom. A law prohibiting a group from deceptively advocating selfish goals harmful to the public welfare could easily be used to suppress unpopular political views. As we saw in our analysis of the public interest, not everyone agrees on what is good for the public, and there is often a thin line between deception and clever advertising. Such a law would also likely violate the First Amendment's protection of free speech. As such, it would be invalidated by the Supreme Court. (As noted in Chapter 6, when Congress tried to limit the amount that individuals could spend in campaigns that are not subsidized by the government, this action was struck down as a violation of the First Amendment.)

Restrictive laws could also discourage political activity. A law requiring the complete disclosure of a group's financial sources could provide information useful for harassing those contributing to unpopular, controversial causes. For example, a person might not contribute to a homosexual rights group for fear of being publicly labeled a homosexual supporter. Extensive record-keeping requirements would probably discourage small, poorly financed groups from continuing. Legal fees alone could consume most of a group's budget. Finally, enforcing strict antilobbying laws could help create a police state. No doubt citizens, public officials, and group leaders would live

in fear that seemingly normal political activity could result in violation of the law, a fine, or imprisonment.

Clearly, then, occasional abuse is the necessary price for maintaining political freedom. This does not mean that any controls are harmful. Antibribery laws and minimal registration requirements certainly do not pose threats to freedom. However, to crack down on "bad" groups that "harm" the public interest would probably be a serious mistake if we want to promote an atmosphere of free political give-and-take.

CHAPTER SUMMARY

What are interest groups and why are they so numerous? An interest group is a collection of people trying to influence government. Groups in the United States take many forms—formal organizations, grass-roots single-issue groups, social movements, professional advocates, and even nonpolitical groups. There are many factors encouraging groups—the diversity of American society, the accessibility of our political system, legal guarantees of free speech, a weak party system, extensive government involvement in economics and welfare, direct government encouragement, and the existence of a large number of politically informed citizens.

How do interest groups try to exert influence? Groups may try to sway public opinion, contribute to election campaigns, and influence legislators by providing gifts, rating their votes, providing information, and drafting bills. Many groups attempt to gain input in the administration of laws. Groups may also seek a voice in the legal system by becoming involved in selecting judges, sponsoring cases, and providing information during trials.

How successful are interest groups? Although many groups spend a good deal of money and occasionally have well-known successes, overall their power is limited. There are, however, several problems in evaluating the precise impact of groups. Factors that influence a group's successes include group goals, the supporters and opponents

of the group, and the relationship of the group to government decision making.

Do interest groups undermine democracy? From the perspective of pluralist democracy, groups are essential because they allow meaningful citizen influence on government in a large, complex society. This view of democracy has been criticized, however, on the grounds that not all citizens are well represented in groups and groups can undermine the overall public interest.

IMPORTANT TERMS

Explain the following terms.

public-interest group   iron triangle
social movement group   *amicus curiae* brief
direct-action tactic   pluralist democracy
free-rider problem   interest group liberalism

THINKING CRITICALLY

1. In general, most interest groups advance the cause of members of society who are economically well-off. Should the government play a larger role in helping poor people organize their own interest groups?
2. Under the principles of our Constitution, there is a separation of church and state. Yet many religious groups lobby the government on vari-

ous issues. Should lobbying by religious groups be significantly restricted on the basis of the separation of church and state? Why or why not?

3. The great increase in the number of interest groups has disturbed many people. How might the strengthening of political parties discourage the growth of interest groups?

4. Should magazines and newspapers be required to give "equal time" to interest groups on both sides of an issue? Why or why not?

5. Do you think it is proper for a former government official to take a job with a company doing business with the government? Defend your answer.

6. Should individuals representing all interest groups, regardless of what they stand for, be allowed to organize and publicize their cause? Why or why not? What difficulties might arise in attempting to restrict certain groups from doing so?

EXTENDING YOUR UNDERSTANDING

1. Identify two national public policy issues you support and two you oppose. Locate a book listing and describing interest groups in the United States (for instance, *Washington Information Directory*). List the groups that might support the two policies you favor. Do the same for the policies you oppose. Compare the methods these groups use to achieve their goals. Which methods do you think are the most effective?

2. Examine several copies of magazines, such as *Time* and *Newsweek*. Identify one interest-group advertisement. At whom is the advertisement aimed? How are the arguments presented in the advertisement? Do you think it is successful? Defend your answer in a written report.

3. Contact a local interest group. Interview a leader or a member of the group. What are the group's goals? How successful has the group been in achieving its goal? What methods has the group found to be most successful in advancing its cause? Present your findings to the class.

4. Do research on a mass-action strategy of an interest group—for instance, the grape and lettuce boycotts of the United Farm Workers (1970s) or the letter-writing campaign sponsored by banks to repeal withholding of savings-account interest (1984). How did the interest group promote the action? How successful was the strategy in achieving the group's goals?

MAKING DECISIONS

You are the spokesperson for an interest group that thinks students should be paid to attend school. What problems would you face in creating such a group? What methods would you use to organize and publicize your cause? Prepare an action plan detailing the strategies, resources needed, and any other considerations for achieving your goal.

Unit 3
INSTITUTIONS

The word *institution* conveys an image of great stability and little activity. Indeed, it is tempting to view Congress, the President, and the Supreme Court as majestic buildings—the Capitol, the White House, and the Supreme Court building. This image is misleading. All three branches of government are changing constantly in character and in their relationship to each other. Congress in the 1980s is very different from Congress in the 1950s—it is no longer dominated by Southern conservatives, for example. The presidency has changed regularly, depending on the views and goals of the person in the White House. President Reagan has differed fundamentally from President Carter in what government is supposed to accomplish and how it is to be done. Change has been less abrupt in the judicial system, but the changes in the last hundred years have been enormous. The Supreme Court in particular has been transformed from a protector of established interests to a leading defender of the disadvantaged. Moreover, although each branch was created as a co-equal, the battle for supremacy is never-ending.

Chapter 9
Congressional Power and Representation

Demands on government have increased dramatically in recent years. At the center of much of the work of government is Congress. The 435 representatives and 100 senators must deal with problems that range from constituents' lost Social Security checks to nuclear disarmament. Congress must also balance a number of competing local and national interests. Even when it is able to act, it must often deal with an unsympathetic executive branch and judicial system. Because Congress is unable to handle all its tasks to everybody's satisfaction, it has been criticized variously as undemocratic, unresponsive, corrupt, incompetent, unrepresentative, lazy, self-serving, miserly, and overly generous. For as long as Congress has existed, people have talked about changing it.

Many of these attacks are based on an incomplete knowledge of what Congress can accomplish, how it operates, and what it has actually done. Before we can constructively criticize Congress, we must first understand how it operates. This is not always easy, because the official rules are not always strictly followed and not all lawmaking is out in the open. This chapter examines five important questions dealing with the powers and operations of Congress:

- How much power does Congress have?
- How does the legislative process work?
- Does Congress represent the people?
- Does Congress respond effectively to national problems?
- Should Congress be reformed?

PREVIEW

How much power does Congress have? The influence of Congress has varied over time. The Constitution provides Congress with several powers, the most important being those over taxation, spending, and commerce. These powers allow Congress to affect almost every aspect of our lives. Other powers involve foreign affairs, impeachment, confirmation of presidential appointments, amendments to the Constitution, and election of the President under certain conditions. Investigation and oversight (monitoring) of the executive bureaucracy are two other duties that have emerged over time. Major limits on Congress include constitutional restrictions, federalism, and the power of the other two branches.

How does the legislative process work? Once proposed, a bill faces a difficult obstacle course to passage. After being introduced, a bill is sent to a committee, where it may be examined in great detail. Because committees usually have life-or-death power over bills, committee membership and leadership are important. Party leaders help determine which bills receive a strong push toward passage. By the time a bill reaches the floor, much has already been decided. Floor debate can be important, especially in the Senate. But the crowded schedule and the complexity of many proposals prevent extended "great debates" over national issues.

Does Congress represent the people? Representation has several different meanings. One meaning involves the similarity or difference between Congress and the general public. Members of Congress tend not to be typical of the general population. But this fact does not mean that Congress cannot work on behalf of the American people. Congress responds to citizen demands in many ways: attending to casework, passing pork-barrel legislation, voting on matters important to the district, and providing a voice for many varied interests. It is difficult to say whether such responses constitute good representation. A legislator might pay attention to district desires for government benefits, yet such benefits might raise taxes.

Does Congress respond effectively to national problems? In recent years Congress has been criticized as an ineffective institution. In particular, it has been called slow-acting, uncoordinated, dominated by local interests, and poorly equipped to deal with complex problems. Congress can be defended, however. The Constitution never intended Congress to solve all our problems; a cautious approach is often appropriate; localism is necessary in a large, diverse nation; and many tasks are beyond the power of any government institution. On the issue of congressional effectiveness, your conclusions depend on how you interpret the evidence.

Should Congress be reformed? Three types of reforms have frequently been proposed. Some would strengthen the role of Congress. The increased resources now available to Congress and greater budgetary control reflect this kind of reform. A second type of reform emphasizes a greater equality of power within Congress. The power of committee heads would be weakened, and subcommittees would have greater independence. A third approach to reform stresses morality and ethics. Although each proposal has merits, each has drawbacks as well.

HOW MUCH POWER DOES CONGRESS HAVE?

The power of Congress has changed since April 1789, when the legislative body first convened. Article I of the Constitution creates Congress and spells out in some detail its powers and responsibilities, but "the First Branch of Government" cannot be described simply by looking at its constitutional roots. Congress has passed through several "strong" and several "weak" periods, depending on the personalities of its leaders, the ambition of the President, the philosophies of judges, and social and economic conditions. We begin our examination of Congress by reviewing the explicit powers granted to it by the Constitution. Following our analysis of specifically stated powers, we shall consider duties that have emerged over time and limits on congressional power.

Constitutionally Granted Powers

The Founders were deeply concerned about legislative power. Indeed, a major reason for calling the Constitutional Convention was to limit the actions of several state legislatures. As noted in Chapter 2, the legislature was the dominant political authority in many states, and there were few limits on its power. As a result, the powers (and restrictions) given to Congress, unlike those assigned to the presidency and the courts, are spelled out in detail in the Constitution. The most important of these can be organized into seven basic types.

1. Taxing and Spending

Article I, Section 8, paragraph 1, of the Constitution states: "The Congress shall have Power to lay and collect Taxes, Duties, Imports and Excises, to pay the Debts and provide for the common Defense and general Welfare of the United States." The power to tax and spend is one of Congress' most important duties. Many of the important decisions people make in their lives—buying a house or changing jobs—are greatly influenced by congressional taxing and spending policies. The prices of imported goods are affected by **tariffs**—taxes on imports—which are set by Congress. The explicitly granted congressional power over the **national debt**—the amount of money owed by the government—is significant. A substantial portion of government revenue comes from borrowed money. With some exceptions, the courts have allowed Congress considerable freedom in taxing and spending (for example, Congress *may not* tax state governments, their property, or their activities).

The power to spend can sometimes be used in a nonobvious way. In recent years Congress has often relied on a practice called **backdoor spending.** Basically this is the spending of government funds which do not appear in an annual *appropriations* bill (a bill granting money for specific purposes). In effect, Congress spends more than it appears to spend. Such spending can take several forms. One common tactic is to promise some group—the elderly, veterans, farmers, and others—

for instance—money that they will receive at a later time, in the form of a pension, subsidized health care, and so on. When enacted, the benefit might cost little, but future Congresses must pay the bills when they come in. Congress can also guarantee, or back up, private loans, ranging from those to a corporation to home mortgages. Again, there is no outlay, but if the loans are not paid back, higher appropriations will be needed later on. Finally, the least obvious form of backdoor spending is a **tax expenditure**—a reduction in the taxes for a specific group. Because such tax reductions result in loss of revenue, future Congresses must raise more money, as well as spend more on interest payments.

2. Foreign Affairs

Although the President usually plays the dominant role in foreign relations, Congress still has considerable power in this area. Many presidential actions involving other countries, such as waging war or providing economic assistance, require money raised and appropriated by Congress. Thus, by refusing to appropriate needed funds, Congress can limit the President's hand. Moreover, the Constitution grants Congress the right to regulate foreign commerce, declare war, and call up the military to repel invasion. In recent years, for example, Congress has formulated basic policy on such questions as limiting imports from foreign countries. With the requirement that all treaties be ratified by two-thirds of the Senate, the body is given a particular voice in foreign affairs.

3. Commerce

The Constitution explicitly grants Congress control over such commercial matters as regulating bankruptcies, fixing weights and measures, punishing counterfeiters, granting copyrights and patents, running the post office, and coining money. Much more significant, however, is the language in Article 1, Section 8, paragraph 3, which assigns to Congress the duty of regulating commerce among the several states. Recall from our discussion in Chapter 3 that this clause has been used as the basis for considerable government involvement in the lives of citizens, especially since the 1930s. For example, the government has banned interstate shipping of impure foods and drugs. In 1938 the Fair Labor Standards Act authorized Congress to set minimum wages in most private industries. Current regulations on oil and gas prices, telecommunications, banking, stock markets, television and radio broadcasting, and airline travel come from this power over commerce. (Much of the authority is exercised by regulatory commissions created by Congress.) Important civil rights laws also stem from this clause. The Civil Rights Act of 1964, for example banned racial discrimination in hotels, restaurants, and movie theaters on the grounds that discrimination harmed interstate commerce. There is hardly any aspect of contemporary life that remains untouched by Congress' authority to regulate interstate commerce.

4. Impeachment

The Constitution grants Congress the power to remove federal officials (but not members of Congress or military officers) from office through **impeachment**—a process in which the House and Senate act as judicial bodies to discover wrongdoing and hold a trial. The first step is for the House, by a majority vote, to pass "articles of impeachment"—a formal accusation of a crime or wrong-

doing. The Senate then conducts the trial, with members of the House acting as the prosecution and the Vice President presiding (unless he or she is being tried; then the Chief Justice of the Supreme Court presides). A two-thirds vote is required for conviction, which results in removal from office.

Impeachment has been used infrequently. Since 1789, only fourteen federal officials have been impeached by the House, and only five were convicted by the Senate. President Andrew Johnson was impeached by the House in 1868, but the Senate failed—by one vote—to convict him. Supreme Court Justice Samuel Chase was also impeached but not convicted. A more recent case, of course, stemmed from the Watergate scandal, when President Nixon was accused of authorizing illegal break-ins at the Democratic national headquarters. Impeachment proceedings were begun in 1974 against the President in the House, but President Nixon resigned before the full House could vote on articles of impeachment.

In 1986 the House voted four articles of impeachment against Harry E. Claiborne, a U.S. district judge who was in prison for tax fraud (Claiborne had not resigned his office despite being in jail). On October 9, 1986, the Senate by overwhelming margins convicted Claiborne on three of the four articles. He was removed from office as

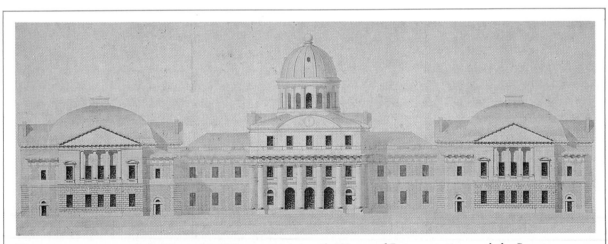

The present structure of the Capitol building, containing the House of Representatives and the Senate, has changed from the design shown in this early architechtural drawing.

soon as he was convicted. Despite its infrequent use, impeachment is a powerful weapon against abuse of office.

5. Confirming Appointments

The Constitution requires the Senate, by a two-thirds vote, to confirm (approve) or reject many presidential appointments—including Cabinet and sub-Cabinet positions, major diplomatic and military posts, all federal judgeships, and top positions on independent agencies within the executive branch and regulatory board. In 1981, for instance, the Senate received 106,616 nominations and confirmed 105,284 of them. As a result of their power, senators frequently have a strong say in who gets a nomination, especially in the case of federal judges and other judicial appointments, such as U.S. marshals. Under the custom of **senatorial courtesy,** a President nominating a federal judge to serve in a state clears the appointment with the senior senator of his or her party from that state. Even with nonjudicial nominees, senators can influence the appointment process by threatening long and difficult confirmation proceedings. On several occasions the Senate has used confirmation hearings to embarrass the President or to provide a forum for debating presidential policy. When President Reagan nominated William Clark as Secretary of the Interior in 1983, for example, many senators used the hearings as an opportunity to discuss publicly Reagan's environmental record. The Senate approved Clark as Secretary, however.

6. Amending the Constitution

The Constitution allows amendments to be proposed either by a convention called by two-thirds of all the states or by a vote of two-thirds of both houses of Congress. Up to now, all constitutional amendments have originated in Congress. In fact, given the technical and legal complexities of state conventions, it is very likely that if future amendments to the Constitution are to succeed, they first will have to be considered by Congress. Adopting amendments is not a congressional power, however. To be adopted, an amendment must be rat-

ified by three-quarters of all state legislatures or by conventions in three-quarters of all the states. Congress can specify which adoption process will be used. The Twenty-first Amendment, which repealed Prohibition in 1933, was ratified by state conventions as specified by Congress; all other amendments were ratified by the state legislatures.

7. Electing the President

If no candidate for President receives a majority of the electoral college vote, the House, with each state casting one vote, chooses the chief executive. The Senate elects the Vice President. Only twice—in 1801, when Thomas Jefferson was elected, and in 1825, when John Quincy Adams was chosen over Andrew Johnson—has the House actually used this power. Nevertheless, the very existence of the possibility has had an impact on campaign strategy. For example, in 1968, George Wallace ran as a candidate for the presidency even though he realized that he would not receive a majority. His third-party bid was based partially on the hope of throwing the election into the House; Wallace hoped to use his electoral votes to bargain for promises from the winner. In addition, the Twentieth and Twenty-fifth Amendments to the Constitution give Congress power to settle disputes arising from presidential incapacity or resignation.

A Perspective on Congress' Specified Powers

In reviewing the constitutionally delegated powers of Congress, we should not forget the "necessary and proper" clause described in Chapters 2 and 3. Article I, Section 8, of the Constitution enumerates many congressional duties. The article concludes by giving Congress the power to make all laws "necessary and proper" to carry out its previously listed responsibilities—a provision that gives Congress considerable freedom to pursue its legislative goals. Recall from Chapter 3 that the Supreme Court ruled in *McCulloch v. Maryland* (1819) that Congress could establish a national bank (a power not mentioned in the Constitution), on the grounds that such a bank was necessary for Congress to carry out its explicitly granted functions. Obviously, then, the formal powers enjoyed by Congress go well beyond those that are spelled out in the Constitution.

Other Powers

There is even more to congressional power than what is mentioned or implied in the Constitution. Over the years congressional power has grown considerably. We sometimes do not know the limits of congressional authority until Congress actually attempts to act. Nevertheless, observers agree that nonconstitutionally defined congressional power has developed in two important areas: (1) the power to investigate, and (2) the power to influence the bureaucracy.

The Power to Investigate

Nowhere in the Constitution is Congress given the explicit power to investigate. Nevertheless, since 1792, with the first congressional examination of an Army incident involving Indians, the power to investigate has played an important role in American politics; it has come to be considered essential if Congress is to make informed decisions. Investigations by Congress have helped illuminate the inner workings of the executive branch, called public attention to major social problems, and laid the basis for much legislation (for example, automobile safety requirements). Every year congressional committees and agencies within Congress conduct hundreds of investigations.

Most congressional investigations are businesslike inquiries that get little publicity. On occasion, however, these investigations can dominate national politics and have an impact far beyond Congress. In 1954 Senator Joseph McCarthy (Republican of Wisconsin) used the Government Operations Committee's Permanent Investigations Subcommittee to search for what McCarthy said were Communist sympathizers in government. McCarthy claimed that many top officials had close ties with the Communist party and the Soviet Union. Few, if any, pro-Communists were found, but McCarthy created an atmosphere of widespread hostility and suspicion toward those with unconventional political ideas. On occasion, merely being called to testify before the McCarthy

Senator Joseph McCarthy conducts a Senate hearing on alleged Communist subversion in the 1950s. Some people praised McCarthy, others accused him of using scare tactics to advance his political career.

When Congress demanded that Richard Nixon submit White House tapes to the Watergate investigation committee, the President refused. His refusal later led the House to enact three Articles of Impeachment.

committee could raise suspicions about a person's loyalty.

The importance of congressional investigations was illustrated in the inquiry into President Nixon's role in the Watergate scandal. Even before the House Judiciary Committee began its formal impeachment hearings in 1974, congressional committees in 1973 played a crucial role in bringing to light the pattern of break-ins, wiretaps, illegal political pressures, campaign fund misuse, and obstruction of justice on the part of certain White House staff members. This information played a major role in forcing the resignation of President Nixon.

Along with the power to investigate, Congress has also acquired the power to hold people in **contempt of Congress**—a formal declaration that a person's actions are contrary to the rules and authority of Congress. Although the Constitution does not explicitly mention this power, it is deeply rooted in English law, and court decisions have generally upheld it. Typical contempt cases involve individuals who try to bribe or obstruct Congress or witnesses in an investigation who fail to testify or to produce requested information. Congress can hold a person in contempt if a simple majority of either the House of the Senate so votes, and rarely are such motions opposed. The matter is then handed over to a U.S. attorney for presentation to a grand jury. If evidence of wrongdoing is found, the matter goes to trial in federal court. A fine or jail term is the usual punishment for conviction. Congress also has the power to issue a **subpoena**—a legal order compelling attendance in court—to force witnesses to testify.

Influence over the Bureaucracy

People sometimes assume that Congress passes laws and that the executive branch, with its large bureaucracy, then enforces them. This is not strictly true, because Congress frequently gets deeply involved in many aspects of day-to-day interpretation and implementation. This involvement in monitoring the executive branch is called administrative **oversight** and represents an important means of congressional influence over public policy.

Congressional oversight usually operates through the committee system. For example, not only does the House Ways and Means Committee write tax legislation, but it assumes some responsibility for ensuring that the Internal Revenue Service, which is the federal government's tax-collecting agency, follows its congressionally defined goals. Because Congress possesses an elaborate committee and subcommittee system, almost all agencies must deal with congressional intervention in their management. In both the House and the Senate several committees are even given *comprehensive policy oversight*, which allows them to investigate matters not necessarily in their specific jurisdiction, or usual type of work. Nor is such intervention limited to committee work. Especially when a constituent is in need of help, a representative or a senator can feel free to call a bureau official to find out what the agency is doing, make suggestions, or remedy a specific problem.

Techniques of Administrative Oversight. Congress employs a variety of techniques to oversee the executive branch. A widely used method is to conduct a hearing or an investigation. In 1982 and 1983, for example, when many members of Congress feared that President Reagan was involving the United States too deeply in Central America, various officials from the departments of State and Defense were called before committees to explain the scope and purpose of U.S. military aid and political support. Many of these hearings were widely publicized, and the President's policies were closely examined. This technique provides a convenient forum by which Congress can express its own opinion on executive branch policy. The General Accounting Office, an agency under congressional control responsible for making sure that federal agencies have spent money properly, may also conduct an investigation of an executive agency's activities.

Oversight can be conducted through informal channels as well. It is not unusual for congressional committee staff members to meet with executive department personnel to discuss a policy or a program. The staff then relays the information to members of Congress. Many legislators have close ties with executive branch officials who have testi-

Concerned about wasteful Pentagon spending, Senator William Roth displays a toilet seat for a naval aircraft. Under congressional pressure, the manufacturer reduced the price from $640 to $100.

fied frequently before a committee or otherwise supplied information to the lawmakers.

A third method of control is through personnel selection. We have already seen that the Constitution allows the Senate to influence the selection of top officials, but Congress also has a say in who occupies many lesser positions. By defining pay scales, job eligibility, working conditions, and job security, Congress can ensure that only certain types of people will fill certain agency positions. Equally important, Congress can decide how many employees an agency can hire, a power that can determine what the agency is able to accomplish. In the late 1960s, for instance, congressional opponents of integration attempted to undermine enforcement of civil rights legislation by cutting back on the number of Justice Department lawyers responsible for enforcing such laws.

Fourth, Congress controls the amount of money agencies receive. In some instances the threat of budgetary cuts influences which policies and projects an agency will pursue. In 1978, for example, the Federal Trade Commission (FTC) proposed strict limits on television commercials, directed at children, for highly sugared goods. These actions did not please all members of Congress. The House Appropriations Committee approved a bill forbidding the FTC from spending funds to regulate products classified as safe by the Food and Drug Administration (sugar is considered safe). Meanwhile, a senator threatened to cut the FTC's budget by an amount equal to the money it spent on investigating the television commercials. Faced with this pressure, the FTC backed down.

One important power of Congress is the **legislative veto.** This is a complex power, and considerable controversy exists over its constitutional status. Basically, the legislative veto is a provision of a law that allows Congress as a whole, or one house, or one legislative committee, to block an action in the executive branch. It was first used in 1933 when Congress specified that the President must receive congressional approval before reorganizing the executive branch. The insertion of legislative vetoes became popular in the 1970s and 1980s, and by 1983 there were 110 laws with such provi-

sions. A typical example was the Arms Control Export Act, which allowed Congress to stop a President from selling arms above a certain dollar amount overseas.

In 1983 the Supreme Court in the case of *Immigration and Naturalization Service v. Chadha* declared this procedure unconstitutional. According to the Court, such congressional power was a violation of the principle of separation of powers. Nevertheless, despite this ruling, the legislative veto to a significant extent has managed to survive. This has occurred in several ways.

First, laws have been amended so that the veto is made by a joint resolution of Congress, not by a concurrent resolution. To become law, **joint resolutions** follow the same procedures as a bill; a **concurrent resolution** is a measure passed by one house with the other house concurring, or agreeing. It does not need the President's signature but lacks the force of law. The President's approval makes the congressional action consistent with constitutional principles. A variation is for Congress to pass legislation canceling an executive action. If the President vetoes the legislation, Congress can override the veto. Both types of legislative actions are, in effect, legislative vetoes.

Second, a law can be drafted so that the President's authority to take a certain action automatically ends unless Congress says otherwise. For example, a section of the War Powers Act prohibits the President from keeping U.S. forces in hostile situations overseas for more than ninety days without a congressional declaration of war or specific authorization. In this way Congress can block a President without formally taking any action. In fact, this provision was employed when President Reagan sent the Marines to Lebanon in 1983 (Congress did, however, permit deployment for more than ninety days).

Finally, and perhaps most common, are informal agreements between the executive branch and congressional committees. In 1986, for example, an appropriations bill stated that the Treasury Department would need the approval of House and Senate appropriation committees to increase Secret Service expenditures beyond the amount specified in the bill. Although such action is prob-

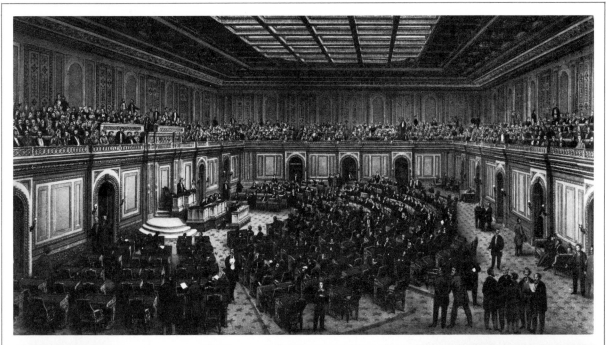

A lithograph shows the House of Representatives as it looked in 1866. Below, members of the House pose for a formal photograph in the 1980s.

ably unconstitutional in light of the *Chadha* decision, it is tolerated by officials in both branches. In particular, executive branch officials see legislative vetoes as a better, more flexible alternative to highly detailed legislation that might be too rigid.

Limits on Congressional Power

The drafters of the Constitution wanted a legislature that could act effectively in a number of areas, but they also feared that it might overstep its powers. To prevent abuses, numerous limits were explicitly placed on the exercise of congressional power. In addition, several limits on legislative power have developed outside the Constitution since the Constitution was drafted.

Constitutional Restrictions

Immediately following the explicit grants of power to Congress, Article I, Section 9 of the Constitution lists numerous legislative restrictions: Congress may not suspend the right to the *writ of habeas corpus*—a court order to explain why a person is being kept in jail—except in cases of rebellion or invasion. Congress is not allowed to pass a **bill of attainder** (a law directed at a specific person) or an *ex post facto law* (a law that makes an act illegal *after* it has been committed). Congress may not regulate commerce in such a way as to give one state an advantage, nor may it tax an article exported from one state to another. The First Amendment also prohibits Congress from establishing, forbidding, or governing religion, and from interfering with freedom of speech, freedom of the press, the right of peaceful assembly, and the right to petition government for a redress of grievances.

Less obvious than these restrictions are the limitations on congressional power that come from the very design of Congress. First, Congress is a two-house (**bicameral**) legislature. One-house legislatures existed when the Constitution was drafted, but the bicameral design was a useful solution to conflicts between large and small states over representation. As noted in Chapter 2, populous states wanted representation based on population but small states desired equal representation for each state. The significance of a bicameral legislature is that it often slows down work. Getting a bill through two houses rather than one not only is more time-consuming but also offers opponents two chances to defeat it.

Second, the frequency with which congressional elections take place works to limit the power of Congress. This is especially true for members of the House, who must run every two years. Although most House members are reelected, their success does not mean that they are free from restraints. In fact, one reason for the success rate is that many House members spend considerable time and energy campaigning. Even long-term House members must worry constantly about raising campaign funds and pleasing a number of diverse interests. On more than one occasion, members of Congress who have neglected their campaign responsibilities in favor of acquiring power within the House have been turned out of office. An often-heard complaint of House members is that they are always running for reelection and hardly have time to do their jobs properly. Because senators have six-year terms, they do not have to devote so much of their time to campaigning. Nevertheless, the fact that one-third of the Senate is up for reelection every two years means that the Senate also faces frequent changes in personnel. Such changes can disrupt relationships and alliances and otherwise hinder the accumulation of legislative power. In 1980, for example, the replacement of a few Democrats by Republicans gave the Republicans control of the Senate, which in turn meant dramatic changes in the exercise of power in that chamber. In the reshuffle, many powerful Democrats lost out who had not even been up for reelection.

Power of Other Government Officials

A key element in the design of the U.S. government is the principle of checks and balances. The drafters of the Constitution believed that when political power becomes concentrated in one office or body, abuse of power is likely to occur. Elaborate divisions of power and mechanisms of cooperation must therefore exist if abuses are to be prevented. The result of these checks and balances is that congressional actions are frequently limited by the powers and actions of other public officials.

Limits Imposed by Federalism. The principle of federalism is one such limiting force on congressional power. As we saw in Chapter 3, many important state and local matters are beyond the direct reach of congressional lawmaking. Congress may be able to declare war, but it may not directly tell New York City how to run its garbage service. On frequent occasions it has influenced state and local decisions by using its taxing power or its regulatory role in commerce (for example, the 55-mph speed limit). But Congress may not simply treat most state and local matters as its own domain.

Limits Imposed by the Courts. The judicial system also limits congressional power in several important ways. Before the passage of the Sixteenth Amendment in 1913, the courts halted congressional attempts to impose a national income tax by declaring income tax laws unconstitutional. The constant threat of rulings of unconstitutionality and the actual interpretations that judges give to laws are as important as the decisions themselves. These limits on congressional action are well illustrated by court decisions on religious observance in public schools. Despite widespread support in Congress for prayers in schools, no legislative action has been taken because members of Congress know that the courts will declare such acts unconstitutional.

The Power of the President. Perhaps the most important obstacles to congressional domination of government are the President and the executive agencies. A President can simply **veto**, or reject, congressional legislation, and only with great difficulty (a two-thirds vote by both houses) can a veto be overcome. Between 1789 and 1981, presidents vetoed a total of 2,393 bills. Congress overrode these vetoes only 92 times.

The President and the federal bureaucracy also play crucial roles in setting the legislative agenda. In the last twenty years, for example, 80 percent of all nonprivate bills originated in the executive branch, even though technically bills can be introduced only by members of Congress. The President's legislative role is especially important in setting national spending priorities. The Budget and Accounting Act of 1921 gives the President the power to draw up a national budget. This document is prepared by the Office of Management and Budget, and Congress is given nine months to review it. The executive branch also influences the review process, because much of the information Congress uses to evaluate expenditures comes from executive agencies. (The budget process is discussed in more detail later in the chapter.)

Even if Congress passes appropriations the President doesn't like, the President still has influence over actual spending. Presidents who want to withhold funds temporarily can do so. In 1974, Congress enacted the Congressional Budget and Impoundment Control Act which permitted Congress, by adopting a resolution, to require the President to spend the appropriated funds. However, in 1983 Congress' power to limit presidential action through the legislative veto was overturned by the Supreme Court on the grounds that it violated the principle of separation of powers. Presidents also have discovered that they can spend money not authorized by Congress through a system of "reprogramming" and "transfers." In 1971, for instance, President Nixon offered $52 million worth of military aid to Cambodia even though Congress had not approved funds for this purpose. He accomplished this by moving money from one account to another, issuing various "loans," and declaring army equipment "obsolete" and selling it cheaply to Cambodia. (The budget is discussed in more detail later in the chapter.)

Presidents have even managed to avoid the congressional requirement that all treaties with foreign governments must be approved by the Senate. Presidents have increasingly conducted foreign relations by making "executive agreements" with other nations. These agreements are not subject to Senate approval, because they are not actually treaties, but the courts have interpreted them to be as legally binding as Senate-approved treaties.

HOW DOES THE LEGISLATIVE PROCESS WORK?

During every legislative session thousands of bills and resolutions are introduced, but most sink into obscurity. In 1981, for example, 7,830 bills and joint resolutions were introduced, of which only 544, or 6.9 percent, were passed. Why do some bills survive? Who controls the fate of the thousands of bills?

To answer these questions we must examine both the difficult path a bill must travel and the individual legislators whose power determines whether a bill will survive. As we shall see, the

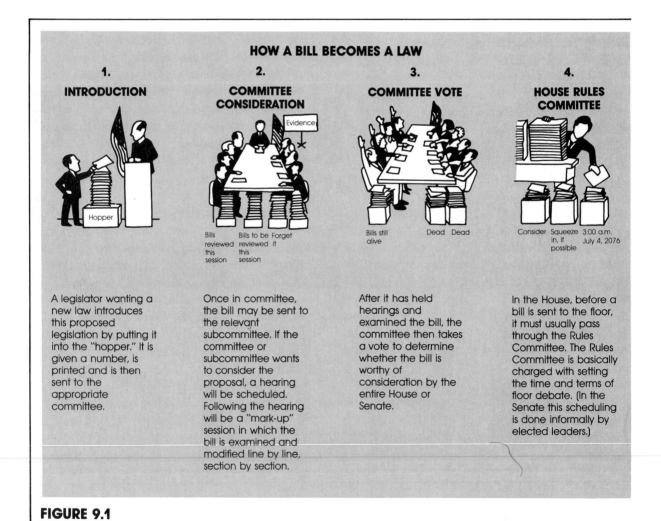

HOW A BILL BECOMES A LAW

1. INTRODUCTION

A legislator wanting a new law introduces this proposed legislation by putting it into the "hopper." It is given a number, is printed and is then sent to the appropriate committee.

2. COMMITTEE CONSIDERATION

Once in committee, the bill may be sent to the relevant subcommittee. If the committee or subcommittee wants to consider the proposal, a hearing will be scheduled. Following the hearing will be a "mark-up" session in which the bill is examined and modified line by line, section by section.

3. COMMITTEE VOTE

After it has held hearings and examined the bill, the committee then takes a vote to determine whether the bill is worthy of consideration by the entire House or Senate.

4. HOUSE RULES COMMITTEE

In the House, before a bill is sent to the floor, it must usually pass through the Rules Committee. The Rules Committee is basically charged with setting the time and terms of floor debate. (In the Senate this scheduling is done informally by elected leaders.)

FIGURE 9.1

how and the *who* of the legislative process greatly affect *what* is passed. We shall consider the process by examining the impact of three elements in legislative decision making: (1) the committee system, (2) elected leaders, and (3) floor decisions.

The Committee System

The first step for all legislation is its presentation to the Clerk of the House or the Secretary of the Senate. (See Figure 9.1.) The bill is given a number and promptly printed. The Speaker of the House or the presiding officer of the Senate then assigns the bill to the appropriate committee. Getting through the committee process in both houses is the first obstacle to a bill's passage.

The Organization of Congressional Committees

It is in congressional committees that much of the significant legislative decision making occurs. In the eighteenth century, Congress operated by creating an ad hoc committee to study each bill, but today committees are organized by general subject matter. There are four basic types of committees. The most important are the **standing committees,** which continue from session to session and deal with such key areas as tax policy, expenditures, defense, and foreign relations. The size of stand-

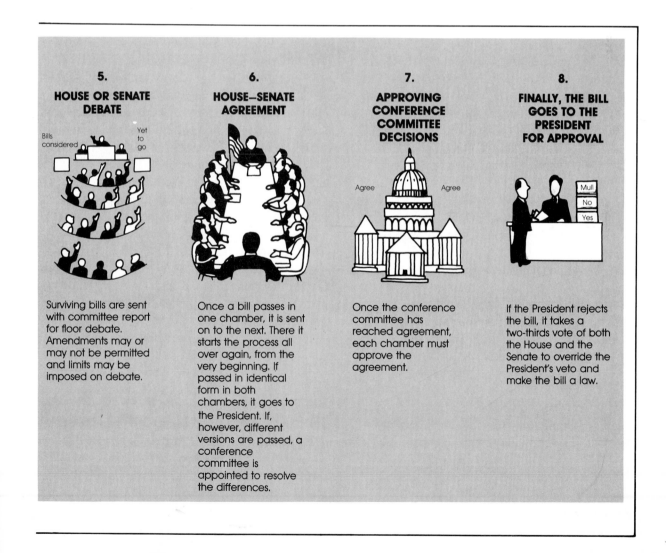

5.

HOUSE OR SENATE DEBATE

Surviving bills are sent with committee report for floor debate. Amendments may or may not be permitted and limits may be imposed on debate.

6.

HOUSE–SENATE AGREEMENT

Once a bill passes in one chamber, it is sent on to the next. There it starts the process all over again, from the very beginning. If passed in identical form in both chambers, it goes to the President. If, however, different versions are passed, a conference committee is appointed to resolve the differences.

7.

APPROVING CONFERENCE COMMITTEE DECISIONS

Once the conference committee has reached agreement, each chamber must approve the agreement.

8.

FINALLY, THE BILL GOES TO THE PRESIDENT FOR APPROVAL

If the President rejects the bill, it takes a two-thirds vote of both the House and the Senate to override the President's veto and make the bill a law.

ing and other committees is set at the beginning of each House session. The Senate uses its standing rules to define committee size. The number and roles of standing committees are not fixed. As issues and circumstances arise, Congress modifies its committee system to meet changing needs. In 1977, for example, the Senate created a standing committee on energy when the energy issue became important.

A second group of committees is made up of the **select and special committees,** which investigate either topics of nonpermanent concern or matters considered less important. Ordinarily, these committees are not allowed to report bills for a floor vote. A few, such as the House Select Committee on Aging, have continued for many years, but most of these committees are short-lived.

A third type, the **joint committee,** is composed of an equal number of representatives and senators. Some joint committees, such as the Joint Economic Committee, can have significant influence. Others, such as the Joint Committee on Printing, primarily handle administrative detail. Committee leadership alternates between the House and Senate. Like select and special committees, joint committees are rarely allowed to send legislation to the floor.

Finally, the most short-lived of all are the **conference committees.** When the House and Senate pass different versions of the same bill, a conference committee attempts to resolve the differences. These committees consist of members of both houses appointed by the presiding officers on the advice of the committee chairperson responsible for the bill (members of both political parties are represented). Delegations from each house vote as a unit, not individually. Conference committees end once their reports are accepted by both houses (which is usually the case). On occasion, conference committees can do far more than iron out minor differences in House and Senate versions of a bill. They substantially revise a bill or create an almost entirely new piece of legislation. In 1981, for example, the House voted to eliminate peanut and sugar support programs. In a conference committee that contained many senators from agricultural states, these programs were re-

stored to the bill and were later accepted by the House.

Committees, particularly standing committees, typically have several subcommittees (some committees use the term "task force" or "policy group"). In 1981, for example, there were 259 subcommittees of one kind or another in Congress. Subcommittees can have considerable influence, expecially in appropriating funds. Compared to standing committees, subcommittees are more likely to undergo changes in responsibilities, size, and resources as new issues develop.

Committee Procedures

Once in committee, a bill goes through several stages. First, if the committee thinks the bill is worth considering, a **hearing** is held on it. This is a forum, usually open to the public, in which members of Congress, lobbyists, concerned citizens, and other government officials can offer their opinions and make suggestions. Committee members then vote on the proposed law, section by section, in what is called a **mark-up session.** A heavily modified bill or several closely related bills must be redefined into a new, or "clean," bill. If it is satisfactory to a majority of the committee, the bill is reported out for discussion by the full chamber, accompanied by a summary report and supporting and opposing arguments. In the Senate, bills come up for discussion in the order they are reported out of committee.

In the House there is an extra step between committee approval and discussion from the floor. With only a few exceptions, all bills must first go through the Rules Committee, which decides when the bill will be considered and under what conditions (for example, whether amendments will be permitted and how much time will be allocated for debate). The Rules Committee is obviously a key point of legislative control, and it has often blocked legislation. Such blocking can be overcome if a House majority, after thirty days of Rules Committee inaction, signs a **discharge petition,** which brings the bill up for an immediate vote by the House. Discharge petitions are comparatively rare, however. Between 1973 and 1983, for example, fifty-nine discharge petitions were filed, but only one bill was discharged. It was later defeated by the full House.

Committee Membership

An important factor affecting a bill's survival is the perspective of the committee considering it. Defeat in committee almost always means legislative death, whereas a bill fully supported by a committee has an excellent chance of being passed by the whole House or Senate. Committee membership is therefore of great consequence.

Who determines the composition of the committees? Each political party in the House and Senate has special committees to make the assignments. In the Senate, the Democratic Steering Committee, consisting of party leaders and their appointees, make the choices, which then must be approved by all other Democrats. The Senate Republicans use a similar procedure, but *party caucus*—all legislators of the same party—approval is not required. House Democratic choices are made by the party's Steering and Policy Committee, which consists of the Speaker, party leaders, and other Democrats selected on a regional basis (the Rules Committee, however, is appointed only by the Speaker). Decisions—including appointment of the Rules Committee—are subject to approval by all party members. The Republican House members use a Committee on Committees, but as in the Senate, decisions do not require caucus approval. Such approval is required, however, in designating the **ranking**—the most senior—Republican member of each committee.

Legislators assigned to a committee can, if they so choose, almost always be reassigned to the committee in later sessions. Especially on important committees, legislators try to build up lengthy, continuous service, or **seniority,** which is very important in the selection of chairpersons. The initial committee assignment process is highly complex and involves several factors.

Seniority. The longer a legislator remains in the House or Senate (provided he or she stays in the same party), the greater the likelihood of receiving choice committee assignments. Overall, seniority is the most important, but not the only, factor in assignment decisions.

Interest and Experience. If a legislator represents a district with special needs or has an appropriate background, the chances of obtaining a relevant assignment are improved. Thus, a farmer from a rural district stands a better chance of getting on the Agricultural Committee than does an urban lawyer. Some committees also seek geographical representation—people are selected from different regions or from certain states. Recently there has been some effort to provide a balance of liberals and conservatives on some key committees.

These three actresses have played distressed farm wives in several movies. In testimony before a Democratic party task force in the House, they described the plight of hard-pressed family farmers.

David Boren, chair of the Senate intelligence committee, talks to reporters. Committee heads can determine the role their committee plays in Congress.

Acceptance by Congressional Leadership. Party leaders play a key role in committee assignment. Especially when it comes to appointments to important committees (for example, the House Appropriations Committee), party leaders favor "responsible" legislators. "Responsibility" means a willingness to compromise, to accept existing power arrangements, and, in general, not to rock the boat. Members of Congress who are too independent, favor extreme positions, or push too hard find it difficult to get ahead.

Politicking. Some members wage vigorous campaigns to gain choice assignments. Lobbies also occasionally campaign on behalf of a member of Congress. Over the years, for example, oil interests have tried to have someone sympathetic to the petroleum industry appointed to the House Ways and Means Committee, which controls tax rulings crucial to oil interests. Agricultural, labor, and other interest groups have conducted similar campaigns.

Party ratios within each committee also help determine the composition of committees. There are no formal rules specifying the ratio of Democrats to Republicans on committees. The party with the legislative majority always has more members on each committee, but the size of this majority is decided by party rather than according to some fixed formula. The Senate traditionally assigns committee seats in proportion to a party's strength—if the Democrats are in a minority, with 40 percent of the seats, they get about 40 percent of the seats on each committee. In the House, however, assignments often are not based on proportion, and Democrats generally benefit from the set-up. In recent years, when Republicans have had about 45 percent of the seats overall, they have been given disproportionately fewer seats. Especially on important House committees such as Rules, Budget, and Ways and Means, the Republicans have received far less than their "fair share" of seats.

Power in Committees

Because committees exercise considerable influence over legislation, the distribution of power within a committee is extremely important. Before the 1970s, most committees were dominated by their chairpersons, whose authority was especially significant in controlling subcommittee membership and jurisdiction, the enforcement of committee rules, scheduling, and the committee's budget. Some committees were run like dictatorships—opposition was pointless, and the only hope was that the chairperson would retire or lose an election. On occasion a committee head might refuse to report a bill to the full chamber despite the wishes of the committee majority.

Such great power was reduced in the 1970s, especially in the House, where many conservative Southern Democrats tended to monopolize committee power. In 1970, Congress passed the Legislative Reorganization Act, which required committees to have written rules (this act also required a record to be kept of committee proceedings and votes). In 1973, House Democrats, in what was called the "subcommittee bill of rights," required the committee head to share responsibility with committee members in establishing subcommittees, their jurisdictions, staff, and budgets. Subcommittees also were not required for all larger House committees, chairpersons could no longer "pocket" bills, and committees had to follow written rules. Because Democrats were limited to chairing one subcommittee, senior legislators could no longer control both the committee and many of its subcommittees. These changes allowed many less senior Democrats to gain a measure of legislative power. More important, appointments to committee leadership positions (and to the leadership of the Appropriations Committee subcommittees) were made subject to approval by House party colleagues. Becoming a chairperson is no longer automatic. Although seniority is still important in selecting committee heads, several chairpersons have been removed. Parallel though less dramatic changes have occurred in the Senate: committee chairpersons no longer exert powerful control over subcommittees, committee staff, and other resources. Here, too, since the early 1970s, committee leadership has been subject to party approval.

These changes do not mean, however, that all committee members are equal. A skilled chairperson still can have influence on committee proceedings, although this requires the cooperation of at least some other members. For example, chairpersons frequently have discretion over which subcommittees will be established and which bill will be sent to which subcommittee. Chairs also continue to have disproportionate power in the hiring and firing of staff—an important consideration, given the key role of staff in committee activities. The chairperson can reward allies. "Good" committee members might get their wishes on hearings and travel allowances and be appointed to manage the bill during floor debate. Equally important, much of the power once enjoyed by committee chairs has shifted to more specialized subcommittee leaders. In many situations "subcommittee government" has replaced rule by the once all-powerful committee heads.

The Role of Elected Party Leaders

The second important element in the legislative process is the elected party leadership. In the House this consists of the Speaker, the majority and minority party floor leaders, and the majority and minority party whips. The Senate, lacking an equivalent of Speaker of the House (the Vice President presides), has only majority and minority party floor leaders and their whips. As we shall see, these elected leaders, like members of important committees and key committee chairpersons, have a major say on which bills become law.

Speaker of the House

The House chooses a Speaker every two years. Traditionally, this is done by a straight party vote. Those elected have been among the most senior representatives, but seniority is not the only basis for selection. To win election by their party colleagues, candidates for Speaker must please many different groups and not be considered extreme or irresponsible. This was well illustrated when the House Democrats selected Jim Wright to replace Thomas P. O'Neill, who retired in late 1986. In the 1970s, Wright was among the more conservative Democrats, especially on military and foreign policy issues. But as the possibility of the Speaker's position drew nearer, Wright moved in a liberal direction, even supporting such measures as a one-year ban on testing nuclear weapons and reducing the funds for President Reagan's "Star Wars" plan. He also used his position on the House Public Works Committee to do favors for House colleagues. Once elected, Speakers usually are kept in office until death or retirement.

As presiding officer, the Speaker decides who shall address the House on which issues. Because the House is large, on any important issue there are frequently many more people wanting to speak, propose amendments, or engage in parliamentary tactics than can be allowed within a reasonable time. The power to recognize one legislator and ignore another can sometimes be crucial. Similarly, the Speaker is usually the final judge of parliamentary procedure. The Speaker also resolves disputes on important questions, such as the

Biography: Sam Rayburn

Sam Rayburn set two records. He was a continuous member of the House of Representatives for forty-eight years—longer than any other person in American history. And he served as Speaker of the House longer than anyone else—for over seventeen years. "Mr. Sam," as he liked to be called, was totally dedicated to the Democratic party and to the House of Representatives, which he refused to regard as the "lower house"; he preferred to call it the "popular branch."

Perhaps the major reason for Rayburn's congressional longevity was his moderation. He had an innate dislike of controversy, and a deep-seated desire to overlook differences. One of his favorite sayings, and his usual advice for younger colleagues, was "To get along, go along."

Rayburn was born in 1882 in Tennessee; his family moved to Texas when he was five, and he became a loyal Texan. He was never happier than when he was sitting on the porch of his Texas ranch, talking with old and trusted friends. Rayburn's values grew naturally out of his rural Southwest background. He had a strong belief in states' rights and the virtue of the small farmer, a lack of interest in—if not actual hostility toward—urban problems, and an attitude toward blacks and other minorities that might most charitably be termed paternalistic.

After graduating from college, Rayburn taught school, became a lawyer, and then ran successfully for the state legislature. In 1912 he was elected to the House of Representatives, in which he served until his death in 1961. (His Speakership began in 1940.)

Rayburn's career in Congress was helped by his friendship with an older Texan, John Nance Garner, who served as Speaker from 1931 to 1933 and was Franklin Roosevelt's Vice President from 1933 to 1941. During this period Rayburn helped develop and shepherd through the House several important New Deal measures, including the Securities Exchange Act of 1934 and the Rural Electrification Act of 1936. His powers of persuasion were especially significant in furthering FDR's policy of military preparedness before World War II. Through his ef-

forts, the House passed, in August 1941—by one vote—legislation to extend draftees' terms of service. After the war Rayburn supported President Harry Truman's domestic policies. When the Republicans controlled the House, in 1947–48 and 1953–54, Rayburn had to step aside as Speaker.

As Rayburn had been befriended by Garner, so he in turn served as the mentor of a younger Texan, Lyndon B. Johnson, who went on to become a powerful and capable congressional politician. The two men worked closely together, Rayburn as House Speaker and Johnson as Senate Democratic leader. Both were comfortable with the moderate conservatism of President Dwight Eisenhower' policies.

Rayburn worked to bring about the nomination of his protégé as Democratic candidate for President in 1960. But the Rayburn-Johnson moderate stance was unpopular with most liberal Democrats, and Johnson lost out to Massachusetts senator John F. Kennedy.

Sam Rayburn's long career had its ironies. Although he was devoted to the House of Representatives, the very support he gave to the many Presidents under whom he served tended to minimize congressional authority. By his stress on compromise, he weakened the independence of the "popular branch." By the end of his stewardship, the House had less autonomy than it had had when he first took over as leader.

relevance of an amendment to a bill, the presence of a quorum (required minimum number of legislators), or the interpretation of a bill.

Another major area of the Speaker's influence is the committee system. It is the Speaker who assigns a bill to a committee. When a bill is complex and relevant committees have different philosophies, the power of assignment can mean legislative life or death. The Speaker can also divide up a bill and send different sections to different committees. On occasion the Speaker can even refuse to assign a bill to a committee, a move that forces supporters of the bill to organize a time-consuming petition drive to get the bill released. In 1981, for instance, the Speaker used this power to stall a bill barring federal courts from issuing school busing orders. House members of conference committees (which iron out House-Senate differences) are also appointed by the Speaker in consultation with the relevant committee chairpersons. In addition, House Democratic party rules allow the Speaker (if he or she is a Democrat) to appoint nine members of the Democratic Steering and Policy Committee, which nominates Democrats for their committee assignments.

Finally, through these formal and informal powers, and the ability to give rewards, the Speaker can help shape overall legislative goals. Especially when the Speaker and the President are of the same party, the Speaker can provide overall direction and coordination of legislative efforts. During the Carter administration, for example, Speaker Tip O'Neill played an important role in keeping the President's programs alive in the face of congressional opposition. When Reagan was elected in 1980, O'Neill became a major spokesman for the Democratic party.

Party Floor Leadership

In both the House and the Senate, each party every two years elects a floor leader (called a majority or minority leader), who is, in turn, assisted by a party whip (for Senate Democrats this position is called assistant floor leader), whose main responsibility is to round up voting support for the party's positions. These officials are given a higher salary, additional expense money, and a special staff. Like other members of Congress in positions of power, floor leaders are almost always fairly senior, though seniority is not strictly followed in selecting them. In general, floor leaders are moderates in their policy stands and can get along with a variety of people and interests. An extremely liberal or conservative legislator unwilling to compromise and negotiate is unlikely to be elected a party leader.

Party leaders help shape the overall legislative program. Not every bill that is introduced or that gets through committee can be given equal consideration by the entire membership. Priorities must be established and appropriate strategies determined, especially when Congress and the presidency are controlled by the same party. Managing the flow of legislation involves such matters as deciding when a bill is to be brought to the floor, which versions of the bill will be considered, and how the bill is to be defended or attacked.

Party floor leaders can operate through a variety of techniques. Majority party leaders, in particular, are in a good position to grant favors to achieve their goals. A cooperative member might, for example, increase his or her chances of obtaining a favorable committee assignment or of getting his or her bills enacted. On occasion a party leader can be helpful in reelection campaigns by raising funds, making a personal appearance on a candidate's behalf, or arranging an event (for example, the appropriation of money for a local project) to make the candidate look good. The use of such techniques depends primarily on the skill and personality of the particular leaders, not on the formal powers of the office. Some, like Lyndon B. Johnson when he was Senate majority leader, are masters at using legislative rewards and threats to maneuver programs through the congressional obstacle course. Others, especially minority leaders, whose powers are limited, view their role as closer to that of a traffic officer attempting to keep order.

Floor Decisions

If a bill survives committee examination, it is ready to be considered by the full House or Senate.

This can be a complex process since many legislators know how to use parliamentary rules to their advantage. Moreover, there are differences between the formal procedures and actual practice. Let us begin our analysis of floor decisions by examining the rules used by the House and by the Senate in considering bills.

House Procedures

When a bill receives committee approval, it is assigned to a **legislative calendar**—a printed list used by the House to categorize proposed legislation by type and importance. There are four calendars. The **Union Calendar** lists all bills that directly or indirectly raise or spend money. The **House Calendar** covers general bills, frequently dealing with administrative or procedural matters, not involving finances. Bills on these two calendars receive the bulk of House attention.

Each year the House considers a large number of noncontroversial bills that require very limited attention. The **Consent Calendar** consists of bills originally put on the other two calendars but whose noncontroversial nature might allow for quick House approval. When the Clerk of the House calls a bill on the Consent Calendar, it is passed without debate unless two legislators object to it. To ensure that important legislation is not sneaked through, each party appoints three objectors to monitor this calendar. The **Private Calendar** deals with **private bills**—bills for the benefit of specific individuals or groups and usually dealing with immigration problems or claims against the government. These bills are reviewed by the Judiciary Committee; when a House vote is called, they are passed without debate unless there are two objections from legislators assigned to screen these bills.

Most bills except those from the Private Calendar then come to the House under a "rule" from the House Rules Committee. As we noted before, this states how long the debate can be, how debate time will be divided, and which types of amendments will be permitted. When the bill actually comes to the House for consideration, the House usually resolves itself into the **Committee of the Whole.** Unlike the whole House, this committee requires only 100 members for a quorum and is not presided over by the Speaker; moreover, it is governed by a different set of rules. If the bill survives the Committee of the Whole, the committee dissolves, the Speaker returns as the presiding officer, and the quorum returns to 218 members. Only the full House, not the Committee of the Whole, can pass legislation.

Senate Procedures

Senate procedures are simpler and more flexible. All legislation is considered under one calendar (*Calendar of the General Orders*)—although treaties and presidential nominations are assigned to the *Executive Calendar*. The Senate lacks a Rules Committee to schedule and define consideration of proposed legislation. In its place it frequently uses **unanimous consent agreements**—agree-

Two House of Representative pages, or assistants, sort through packages of documents on the budget. The packets will be delivered to the House and Senate committees that deal with the budget.

ments among majority and minority leaders, subject to approval by the entire Senate, that set the terms of debate on a bill. As in the House, the senate has provisions for dealing with noncontroversial and private bills that allow passage in a few minutes unless there are objections.

Individual senators enjoy greater freedom than House members in influencing the legislative agenda. A senator might try to get a bill considered by offering it as an amendment to legislation being considered (such unrelated amendments are called **nongermane amendments**). Also, by custom, a senator is permitted to speak on any subject as long as he or she wants, although limits can be imposed.

Debate

The debate over the merits of a proposal is an important, highly visible part of the legislative process, but rarely is it the crucial factor. As we have seen, committee decisions have a major impact on which bills survive and how they are modified. Most bills do not get out of committee. In addition, prior to floor consideration, elected party leaders have made key decisions about which version of a bill will be considered, whether it will be fully debated, and so on. Here again, a bill's fate can be decided without a floor vote. Nevertheless, on occasion the floor debate can make a difference.

One important aspect of the debate is the amending process. In some cases opponents will offer amendments that so weaken a bill that its passage becomes almost meaningless. An alternative tactic is to introduce amendments that so strengthen a bill that it becomes objectionable even to many of its supporters. Both tactics were used by opponents of civil rights legislation in the 1950s and early 1960s. Supporters of a bill can use the amendment process to "sweeten" a bill to pick up a few necessary additional votes. Sometimes the offering of dozens of amendments can obstruct, delay, and confuse legislative business. During the 1979 House debate on the establishment of a separate Department of Education, one unfriendly amendment was offered to rename the agency the Department of Public Education, or

DOPE. Amendments and other parliamentary requests for action intended to delay are called **dilatory motions** and are banned in the House (but not in the Senate).

A skilled legislator can sometimes use the amending process to great advantage by adding **riders**—additional provisions that do not directly relate to the bill. In some instances, legislation the President opposes is attached to a bill the President wants. Because the President lacks an **item veto**—the power to reject only part of a bill—the House may approve the whole package and thus force the White House to accept a measure it didn't want in order to get a provision it does want. Riders have been used to prevent federal funds from being used for abortions or for enforcement of court-ordered school busing. Riders can make for odd legislative combinations. In 1980, the House passed one bill that set nutritional standards for infant formula and increased penalties for selling marijuana.

The one place where floor debate can be crucial is the Senate. Because the Senate allows unlimited speechmaking, one or more lawmakers can block legislation by bringing business to a standstill. This practice, called a **filibuster,** has been used on many occasions. In the 1950s and 1960s, for example, several Southern senators gave marathon speeches on a wide variety of topics in order to block civil rights legislation. Between 1973 and 1983 there were 101 filibusters. A filibuster ends either when the speakers can no longer continue or when the Senate votes for **cloture,** a parliamentary move to end debate. A cloture motion can be introduced by a petition from sixteen senators and must be passed by a vote of three-fifths of the entire Senate (sixty senators if no vacancies exist). When a Senate rule is being debated, a two-thirds vote is needed for cloture. Since 1917, attempts to use cloture have succeeded only about 30 percent of the time.

Those who look to Congress as a forum in which the central issues of the day are publicly debated are frequently disappointed. Many floor discussions are poorly attended, not all legislators listen attentively, and the overall flow of the debate can be disjointed. Some important issues are given scant attention; it was not until 1970, for instance, that the House debated whether the United States should withdraw from Vietnam, and most speakers were given only one minute of time.

There are several good reasons for this state of affairs. First, members of Congress have so many responsibilities that it is difficult to spare much time for elaborate floor discussions. During a debate, a member of Congress might be greeting citizens from his or her district, meeting with aides to discuss future legislative proposals, talking with executive branch officials about a program, or otherwise participating in the business of Congress. Second, much of what occurs on the floor is of modest importance and of little relevance to most legislators. In 1982, for example, seventy-one bills were enacted declaring special days and weeks—Positive Mental Health Week, National Elvis Presley Day—and such issues can discourage serious legislators from attending floor sessions. Third, Congress today considers so much legislation that even fairly important matters must be taken care of in an hour or less. There are not enough hours in the day to give every bill a serious hearing. Finally, the complexity of much legislation does not permit informed public debate. Especially with tax and appropriations bills, it would require days of study for a legislator to understand all the issues. For this reason, many legislators will rely on the recommendations of the committees that spent weeks or months dealing with the bill.

The Vote

The final step in the life of a bill is the vote. This last action typically involves more than simply each legislator solemnly declaring his or her preferences. Because of their many responsibilities and the large number of bills, legislators sometimes enter the chamber without knowing which way they will vote. As a result, there might be considerable last-minute politicking. Party leaders stand at the doors to give the party's position as members enter; bill sponsors and opponents make last-ditch compromises and attempts to persuade; and frantic messages might be sent in from outsiders, such as the President or interest groups. An undecided member might seek out the opinion of close friends, trusted colleagues with a reputation in a bill's area, or someone from a similar district. On more than one occasion, the fate of important issues has been decided by legislators who made their choices by asking, "How will this vote look in my next campaign?"

The actual vote can take several forms. Many are simple **voice votes**—the presiding officer asks members to respond "aye" or "nay," and the chairperson decides which side wins. In a close vote the outcome might not be obvious, and presiding officers occasionally have been accused of biased interpretation (this procedure can, however, be appealed). In a **standing vote,** members favoring a bill stand up to be counted; opponents then stand and are counted. This procedure allows each legislator to vote without a record being kept. A **teller vote** is used only in the House and requires supporters and opponents of a bill to line up and file past recorders (called "tellers"). Here, too, members of Congress usually can avoid a record of their vote. Finally, there are formally recorded votes, called **role call votes.** In the upper house, members' names are called, and senators respond "yea" or "nay" (or simply "present" if they choose not to vote). In the House, the procedure is conducted electronically—a card is inserted into a recording device. A vote need not be final; both House and Senate members can change their recorded votes before the final tally is formally accepted. A legislator might, for example, join the winning side if this makes good political sense even if he or she strongly opposes that side. The reasoning is simple: "I lost but I might as well get some political gain from the loss." For example, a legislator from an agricultural area might oppose a bill helping farmers; if the bill is defeated by a wide margin, the lawmaker might change his or her vote to "yea" in order to look better in the next election. Also, a legislator might act quite differently on recorded votes and on voice votes or standing votes. For reasons such as these, recorded votes do not always reflect a legislator's true feelings.

The voting process is most hectic near the close of a legislative session, especially prior to a November election. Congress might have only a few days to consider dozens of bills that have been around for months. In the case of appropriations bills, agencies will be unable to operate after October 1 unless new funds are authorized. It is a time when hundreds of dams, reservoirs, and other pet projects are rushed through with no debate and little overall awareness of what is happening. With an election only weeks away, there is a strong incentive to add one more accomplishment to one's record. Leaders of the political parties often take advantage of the rush to get finished. For example, just before the end of the 98th Congress in late 1984, the Republicans successfully attached an unrelated anticrime bill to a general funding bill—with just ten minutes of debate and with few legislators aware of what was being done. The measure was approved in part because the funding bill included more than three hundred pet projects desired by numerous House members.

The Role of Congressional Staff

Behind all the committee hearings, mark-up sessions, leadership strategies, and floor votes are congressional staffers. Until fairly recently, staffs were small and unimportant in the legislative process. Their power has grown as a result of both the increased time demands on legislators and the technical complexity of the problems facing Con-

gress. In 1930 there were 1,150 staff members in Congress; by 1972 the number had risen to 7,706; and by 1981 it was 11,525. For better or worse, members of Congress have become dependent on their aides.

Staff members can have an influence at every stage of the lawmaking process. Often it is the job of committee staff members to compile lists of questions to be asked at hearings and to prepare background material. A staff member might even substitute for a legislator or a chairperson who is unable to attend a hearing. Especially when complex, technical issues are involved, the committee staff can be the authoritative voice on what can or cannot be done. Because staff members often participate in the actual drafting of a bill, some lobbyists pay particular attention to senior staff members. On occasion, staff members play a role in directing committees into new areas. For example, the idea of "sunset legislation" (under which a program or agency is automatically ended unless it is specifically renewed by Congress) was developed by committee staff in the late 1970s.

Much of the routine, but still important, legislative work is done by staff members. They draft reports, obtain the views of lobbyists and public officials, monitor support and opposition, and help implement legislative strategy. Aides can also exercise legislative power. In the summer of 1981, for example, when there were some three hundred

Before members of Congress can make overseas investigations—like this one to Grenada in 1983— their staff must handle many complex arrangements.

differences between the proposed House and Senate budgets, dozens of staff experts met to resolve these differences. A skilled staff can improve a legislator's reelection prospects by doing a good job with constituency requests and alerting the representative to potential problems. Finally, a trusted aide can influence legislative voting. Because no legislator can carefully study each bill, some members of Congress rely on their staff to evaluate a bill. On many occasions, the legislator's vote reflects what the staff believes is best for your legislator.

Check Your Understanding

1. What are the major types of congressional committees?

2. What are the most important factors in assigning legislators to a committee?

3. What are the major elected leadership positions in Congress and what are the key responsibilities of each?

4. What are the four types of House legislative calendars and what types of bills are assigned to each calendar?

5. Describe the major responsibilities of congressional staff members.

DOES CONGRESS REPRESENT THE PEOPLE?

Whether Congress is a representative institution is a complex question. First we should ask, What is "representation"? There is in fact no one accepted definition; citizens, experts, and members of Congress might interpret the word in different ways. We therefore shall approach this question by using two meanings of "representation:" (1) the similarity between Congress and the general public and (2) the responsiveness of Congress to citizen demands.

Similarity Between Congress and the General Public

The idea that representation means that leaders should reflect a cross section of the public is a common one in politics. Many blacks, for example, have claimed that they are not adequately represented by elected white officials. Similar arguments have been made by women's groups in their support of female candidates. In the 1960s many students demanded that fellow students be put on university committees to represent students.

Table 9.1 shows how Congress compared with the general population on numerous characteristics in 1981. It is clear that, as a group, Congress tends to be different from the citizenry as a whole. Members of Congress are older, more likely to be white males, and are much more likely to be in higher-status professions, such as law and business. In addition, because of their salaries, backgrounds, and business opportunities, members of Congress are substantially better-off than the average citizen.

Moreover, despite occasional changes brought about by retirements, deaths, and electoral defeats, the overall makeup of Congress changes little year after year. For example, in the 100th Congress, which convened in January 1987, 95.7 percent of the members were white, 95.3 percent were male, and law and business remained the two most popular prelegislative professions.

Although these differences are clear, their significance is less so. Some people might argue that Congress is biased against the poor, women, members of minority groups, and the young. It could also be claimed, however, that there is not necessarily a one-to-one relationship between people's personal traits and the policies they support. Many politicians born to great wealth (for example, Senator Edward Kennedy) have championed the interests of the poor.

Comparison of Members of Congress with General Public on Selected Characteristics, 1981	*Characteristic*	*Congress*	*General Public*
	Age	49.2 (mean)	30.3 (median)
	Sex (percent male)	95.9	48.6
	Race (percent white)	96.9	87.9
	Religion (percent)		
	Catholic	25.8	36.5
	Methodist	13.8	6.9
	Episcopalian	13.6	2.0
	Presbyterian	10.6	2.5
	Baptist	9.5	21.7
	Jewish	6.2	4.3
	Other	20.5	26.1
	Previous occupation*		
	Agriculture	6.9	
	Business/banking	30.3	
	Education	12.9	
	Journalism	5.2	
	Law	47.3	
	Public service/politics	12.1	
	Other	5.2	

* Adds up to more than 100 percent because some members give two professions prior to election.

Sources: Congressional data are from *Guide to Congress*, 3rd ed., p. 645. Population data are from the *Statistical Abstract of the United States, 1982–83.*

TABLE 9.1

The Responsiveness of Congress to Citizen Demands

A second approach to representation focuses on responsiveness. Representation in this sense implies a "looking-out-for" relationship. Congress could be said to represent the public if members were guided by the opinions and needs of citizens. Of all the questions asked about Congress, this is one of the most difficult to answer. Responding to citizens involves several different types of behavior. Let us consider four ways a member of Congress can "look out" for citizens: (1) attending to congressional casework, (2) providing legislative benefits to constituents, (3) voting on matters important to the district, and (4) serving as a voice for particular interests.

Attending to Congressional Casework

Because of the growth of government at all levels, many citizens encounter problems that must be resolved through contact with government officials. When in need of assistance, many citizens and local groups turn to their representative in Washington. Help provided to constituents is called **congressional casework**. On many occasions these problems have nothing to do with the national government or might not even involve legislation (for example, collecting an insurance claim). Because senators and members of Congress represent hundreds of thousands of citizens, the daily flow of requests can be overwhelming. More than one representative has complained that errand-running for troubled constituents takes precedence over lawmaking.

Senator Alfonse D'Amato of New York meets with students at a high school in the state. It is helpful for members of Congress to meet with their constituents, including future voters, to discuss their ideas and concerns.

The list of favors and services required of members of Congress is almost endless. Appeals for government jobs consume much time and energy. Government efforts to deal with community problems, reduce pollution, and so forth have resulted in constituent requests for government assistance in setting up local programs in urban renewal, small-business loans, or grants for water treatment plants. During her first four years in the House, for instance, Geraldine Ferraro's district caseworkers handled some 13,000 cases involving issues such as immigration and Social Security. Members of Congress occasionally are even asked for such nonpolitical favors as making hotel and airplane reservations, replacing china, and in one instance, asking Richard Nixon (when he was Vice President) to bring a spoon back from a visit to Russia for a constituent's collection. Another wanted a gold brick from Fort Knox.

Members of Congress actually encourage much of this casework. Some legislators seek out people with problems as a way of increasing their reputation for being concerned and hard-working. One lawmaker regularly mailed more than six thousand invitations to district residents asking them to bring their problems to a town meeting run by his staff or to his local office. Especially in diverse districts with many perspectives and controversies, emphasizing casework is an effective and noncontroversial way of building electoral support. According to one member of Congress, "My experience is that people don't care how I voted on foreign aid, federal aid to education and all those big issues, but they are very much interested in whether I answer their letters."

Impact of Casework. Can members of Congress really help ordinary citizens overcome problems with the federal bureaucracy? The answer seems to be that only about 10 percent of the problems are completely resolved by congressional help. We must remember, however, that many of the requests for help are hopeless or frivolous. By the time a legislator is contacted about something like collecting military disability pay or getting a government job, a citizen probably has met failure through ordinary channels. When the cause appears more reasonable, and especially when the member of Congress personally steps in to help, success rates are much higher. Here, perhaps, a third or half the cases are successfully resolved. Even when assistance on behalf of a constituent is unsuccessful, the ordinary citizen has at least received official attention and now knows that somebody will listen to his or her problem.

Providing Legislative Benefits to Constituents

Members of Congress can also provide their constituents with material benefits, through what are popularly called "**pork barrel**" **politics.** The name probably derives from the pre–Civil War custom of distributing salt pork from large barrels to slaves and became part of the language of politics in the 1870s. Unlike casework, in which help is given on request and on a person-by-person basis, "pork" need not be specifically requested by constituents and is intended to benefit large numbers of citizens. Its purpose is to promote reelection. Mem-

Commentary: "Like a Snowfall, Gently Falling"

One of the benefits enjoyed by members of Congress is the *franking privilege*—the right to send official mail free of charge. Because the Postal Service has been generous in interpreting the meaning of "official," legislators have been able to mail not only public documents and the *Congressional Record* but also questionnaires and a great variety of newsletters. Indeed, legend has it that one nineteenth-century senator "mailed" his horse home free by affixing his signature to the animal's bridle and declaring the animal to be official business.

The volume of franked mail has been increasing steadily in recent years. In 1976 the total number of pieces was 421 million; ten years later the annual total had soared to over a billion. The chief reason for the increase is computerized mailing systems, which can produce thousands of personalized letters an hour. "Mass mailings are like a snowfall, gently falling all over the country," one senator commented rather poetically. "You don't hear much, but it does begin to pile up."

What's free for legislators has to be paid for by somebody, of course. To cover the cost, Congress each year appropriates funds that, in turn, come from the taxpayers. Mass mailings, normally sent at the third-class bulk rate, cost $54 million in 1981, but the price tag had risen to almost $145 million by the mid-1980s.

Some of the nation's 535 legislators send much more franked mail than others. A 1985 study of the Senate revealed that twenty-one senators sent no franked mail at all, while the biggest spender mailed out 11.5 million pieces of mail in just three months, at a cost of $1.6 million. The discrepancy has little to do with the amount of mail a legislator receives. According to one estimate, only about 5 percent of franked mail is sent in response to incoming correspondence. Rather, some observers feel, constituents are most likely to receive mail from their representatives during a political campaign. Legislators up for reelection often send out significant quantities of mail; only two of the senators who sent no mail were campaigning in 1986. Public-interest lobbyists in particular are critical of the huge volume of franked mail, which they claim is nothing more than election-year propaganda. The franking privilege, they say, is one of the many advantages incumbents have over challengers—an advantage paid for by the taxpayer.

---

bers of Congress widely believe that providing such visible government benefits as a new highway will make people happy and will show that their legislator has accomplished something. As Clarence Long, once a representative from Maryland, put it: "A congressman is judged by the overwhelming mass of his constituents on the personal services he gives the home folks and the contracts he brings to the area."

Pork-barrel legislation is a long-established congressional tradition. For years, typical "goodies" included federally funded highways, post offices, dams, defense installations, harbor and river improvements, Army and Navy contracts, irrigation projects, and veterans' hospitals. As the government ventured into new domains, projects have been added to the pork barrel, including mass transit, scientific facilities, pollution treatment centers, job-training programs, and space travel facilities. Typically, legislators take considerable credit for these achievements and hope that each new building or job will pay dividends on election day.

A legislator will often go to great lengths to gain or protect pork-barrel benefits. Consider, for example, the battle that occurred when the National Oceanic and Atmospheric Administration (NOAA) of the Commerce Department tried to close a tiny weather station in Nebraska. NOAA claimed that the station, with few employees and no radar, contributed little to the store of weather information. In 1982, Congress agreed to close the station and seventeen similar ones. The member of Congress from the area fought back. At a hearing she accused the Secretary of Commerce of depriving local citizens of tornado protection, and she campaigned among House colleagues on committees that oversee NOAA to restore the funds. She was successful, but in 1983 NOAA tried again. Again the congresswoman rallied her colleagues, and the weather station was saved.

Even though many people, including several members of Congress, have criticized pork-barrel politics, the practice is well established. According to critics, Congress will authorize money for expensive projects of questionable value largely to impress constituents. Because these benefits raise taxes, they are hardly cost-free. To understand why legislators are so willing to shower their districts with material benefits, even when their value is questionable, we must consider two facts. First, members of Congress are forever worried about reelection, and pork-barrel politics seems to be a good reelection strategy. Second, the lawmaking style of Congress encourages pork-barrel legislation. On matters directly relating to particular district benefits, almost every legislator follows the rule, "I'll vote for your pet project if you'll vote for mine." This practice of mutual support is called **logrolling,** and the appropriations bills containing scores of river improvements, new post offices, and other special benefits are sometimes labeled **"Christmas tree" bills** because they contain presents for everybody.

The widespread acceptance of logrolling for the distribution of material benefits explains why everyone usually can get a piece of the action. Let us suppose that a representative wants increased federal funding for a local sewage treatment plant. To get backing for this project, the representative might agree to support numerous other locally oriented bills favored by fellow legislators. On occasion, legislators will find themselves voting for projects they do not want, but this is the price they must pay to get support for their own projects. Of course, there are limits to logrolling. Just so much money is available, and few legislators want to be considered irresponsible spenders. In addition, more than once a President has vetoed an expensive pork-barrel appropriations bill.

Voting on Matters Important to the District

A third view of responsiveness stresses the obligation of elected officials to follow the wishes of constituents. According to this view, a district is represented if the legislator supports those policies the citizens desire. Do representatives vote according to the wishes of their constituents? Are national legislators the means through which public opinion is transformed into government action?

The answer to these questions is that it depends. Sometimes members of Congress strictly follow the desires of the home folks. At other times, however, there is little relationship between how a legislator votes and what his or her district prefers. Individual members of Congress also vary in how closely they follow constituents' opinion. Why do legislators occasionally choose to ignore the preferences of those who elected them?

Observers of Congress have long noted that when the desires of the people at home are obvious and important, few legislators will oppose them. To do so would probably mean political suicide. For example, during the 1950s and 1960s, before the beginning of large-scale voting by blacks, Southern legislators vigorously followed the anti-civil-rights positions of their constituents. Even Southern members of Congress who privately supported many civil rights proposals (for example, Senator J. William Fulbright of Arkansas) would not risk voting against district opinion. Likewise, a legislator representing a district with large, well-organized unions will rarely antagonize these groups by supporting antilabor legislation.

Legislators are most likely to listen to district opinion on local economic matters. Members of Congress do not like to oppose publicly the economic interests of the people who elected them. Even a liberal legislator will take the conservative position (and vice versa) to defend the economic well-being of his or her constituents. Senator Alan Cranston of California, for example, has strongly opposed increases in defense spending but has supported the expensive B-1 bomber, which is being manufactured in California (and many people question the military value of manned bombers in nuclear warfare). Senator Edward Kennedy of

A homeless person on a bench in front of the Capitol serves as a reminder to members of Congress of a pressing issue confronting the nation.

all the matters considered by Congress. On numerous other issues there is no consistent relationship between the way legislators vote and majority opinions back home. More important, most members of Congress pretty much accept this difference. Why does the lack of agreement exist, and why is it tolerated?

Reasons Legislators Do Not Follow Constituency Opinion. One important reason why legislators do not always follow constituency opinion is that, on many issues, the citizens they represent do not possess clear, well-informed preferences. Each year Congress confronts hundreds of technical questions of little interest to many citizens. Obviously, it is impossible for a legislator to follow constituency opinion when it hardly exists.

A second explanation is that lawmakers in Washington frequently cannot get completely accurate information on what the people back home want. A member of Congress has several means available for determining opinions of constituents. Examining public opinion polls, conducting mailed questionnaires, tallying mail on issues, making trips home to talk with people, and reading local newspaper stories and editorials are common ways of learning about people's political feelings. Unfortunately, each technique is limited. Congressional opinion polls, for example, frequently have very low response rates (10–20 percent), and legislators lack the resources to conduct adequate surveys on the hundreds of issues they must vote on. Similarly, even though the mail is usually given careful attention, much of it arrives after an issue has been decided, and even then, letters might not faithfully reflect overall home opinion. Moreover, the incentive for gathering constituency opinion can be low because many citizens do not know (or seem to care) how legislators vote. One lawmaker offered to send any constitutent a copy of his entire voting record; not one copy was requested.

A third reason why members of Congress do not always vote according to the wishes of their constituents is that district opinion is so varied that regardless of how the legislator voted, the vote

Massachusetts, who normally opposes government regulation of foreign trade, makes an exception when it comes to protecting his state's shoe and bicycle industries. Legislators from farming areas are almost always strong supporters of high prices for agricultural goods.

That members of Congress follow their constituents' desires on certain key issues is important. If they stopped doing so, the result would probably be widespread public outcry and many defeated legislators. Nevertheless, issues on which constituents feel strongly make up only a small portion of

could not satisfy a majority. As noted in Chapter 5, elections are based on geographical divisions of the population, and geographically defined election districts frequently contain an enormous variety of people. A House district of 500,000 people can contain many opinions on controversial issues, with no one position being in the majority. It is not surprising that studies of legislative representation have found that legislator-constituency agreement is greatest when districts are relatively uniform in their preferences. [1]

The attitudes of national legislators themselves are a fourth factor contributing to imperfect agreement between legislators and district. All legislators want to service their districts, but not all legislators define service as simply transforming district opinion into legislative votes. In fact, a study of members of Congress in 1963–64 found that only 23 percent saw their role as that of a "delegate," an official whose main purpose was to transmit, without change, popular opinions to the legislature. Other members of Congress asserted that their constituents expected them to use their own judgment about what is best. Still other members stated that under some circumstances they might strictly follow district opinion, at other times they might ignore it, and sometimes they might "interpret" the political wishes of their constitutents. [2]

Finally, we must remember that constituency pressures are only one of many forces that affect legislative decisions. A lawmaker about to cast a vote often has to weigh pressure from party leaders, other committee members, the President, his or her staff, outside experts, and interest groups. In some circumstances, following the lead of other legislators or the President might be essential in order to take care of constituency interests in the future. We have seen that one important method of securing district benefits is by logrolling, or vote trading. A legislator might go along with the desires of others—even if they are contrary to district opinion—so that on certain really important matters he or she can cash in political IOUs. Even when there is no future payoff, a legislator might vote against district preferences because of party loyalty or support for a President's legislative program.

That lawmakers do not always follow the majority opinion in their districts does not necessarily mean that citizens' views are ignored. One study found that members of Congress view their constituencies as complex sets of groups. [3] Besides the district as a whole, most legislators perceive a **reelection constituency** (all people in the district who voted for the legislator) and a smaller **primary constituency** (voters who would support the candidate in a primary). A smart member of Congress knows that on certain issues loyalists in the primary constituency cannot be ignored. Satisfying this group, however, can sometimes mean opposing an overall majority in the entire district. Keeping one's most loyal supporters happy can thus lead to ignoring overall district opinion.

Serving as a Voice for Particular Interests

Our discussion thus far has considered whether a legislator from a particular area is responsive to the needs and interest of the constituency. There is another way of considering legislative responsiveness, however. We can ask whether citizens' opinions are represented in Congress as a whole, even if they are not expressed by their own House member or senators. For example, suppose a citizen favors the legalization of marijuana. Suppose also that that person's representative and two senators strongly oppose such legislation. Does this mean that that person is without representation on this issue? Not necessarily—since legislators from other areas might speak for those who share that person's views.

Over the years many citizens advocating political causes have been represented in Congress by legislators from outside their own districts. Long before Southern blacks could vote, many Northern legislators "looked out" for them. More recently, several women legislators have viewed their role not only as taking care of the citizens who elected them but also as promoting the interests of all women. Such nondistrict orientations are not unique. A 1963–64 study of House

Jesse Jackson, center front, talks to the media as members of the Congressional Black Caucus look on. Jackson was briefing the legislators on his recent trip overseas.

members found that only 42 percent considered themselves to be representing their own district exclusively.[4]

An important mechanism in this type of representation is the congressional committee and subcommittee system. Many congressional committees have subcommittees organized around a specific subject—for example, the cotton or tobacco industry. As we might expect, legislators with a particular interest may be placed on the appropriate subcommittees; these positions give them some influence. For example, in 1982 Charlie Rose of North Carolina represented a poor, rural district with a large number of tobacco farms. He was also the chairperson of the Agriculture Committee's Subcommittee on Tobacco and Peanuts. The many tobacco growers outside Rose's district knew that they had a powerful voice in Washington.

Along with an elaborate committee and subcommittee system are a large number of legislative caucuses. These are groups of legislators with a common interest or background who have created an organization—usually with a staff and budget—to advance this concern within Congress. Some caucuses are based on shared ethnicity—the Congressional Black Caucus, the Hispanic Caucus, and the Ad Hoc Committee for Irish Affairs, for example. Many industries are given representation through these legislative groups—the House Textile Caucus, the House Steel Caucus, the House Travel and Tourism Caucus, the Senate Coal Caucus, the Auto Task Force, and so on. Most geographical areas are also organized into caucuses—there are the Congressional Sunbelt Council, the New England Congressional Caucus, the Metropolitan Area Caucus (members from the Washington, D.C., area), and the Conference of Great Lakes Congressmen, among many others. Shared views are also a basis for caucus membership. Some, such as the Environmental Study Conference or the Arts Caucus, focus on a specific issue area. Others, such as the liberal Democratic Study Group or the Wednesday Group (a liberal Republican organization), address a broad range of issues.

These and the numerous other caucuses represent interests in many different ways. One important function is to collect and publicize information. For example, caucuses representing the Northeast and Midwest keep track of how federal programs affect their regions. Caucus-sponsored meetings publicize such information to ensure that these regions can compete successfully for federal funds. The Democratic Study Group provides analyses of bills; many caucuses publish newsletters and reports. Caucuses can also provide a legislative forum for an issue that has received little attention from established committees or party leaders. For example, the Steel Caucus has been successful in pushing the crisis in the steel industry onto the legislative agenda. A caucus can be especially helpful when an issue is not directly addressed by a single committee. The Alcohol Fuels Caucus, for example, has worked to coordinate legislative proposals, because gasohol is normally under the jurisdiction of two distinct committees.

Caucuses can sometimes play an important role in aiding widely scattered, diverse groups that do not dominate any one particular congressional district or state. For instance in the late 1970s, when high energy and credit costs cut tourism, the House Travel and Tourism Caucus acted as a broker among many different travel interests and publicized the problems of the travel industry. As a result of caucus efforts, the House in 1980 passed the National Tourism and Policy Act to encourage travel.

Conclusions

The answer to the question of whether Congress represents the people is highly complex. It greatly depends on how we define "representation" and how we evaluate the evidence. If we define representation as a similarity between Congress and the general population, Congress is not very representative. Young people, nonwhites, females, and the poor are underrepresented. If "representation" is defined as legislators' responsiveness in "looking out" for constituents through casework and pork-barrel benefits, representation is widespread. However, such representation might not be so beneficial or desirable as it first appears (for example, projects can raise taxes but yield few advantages). Furthermore, legislators often follow district preferences, especially when vital economic interests are at stake. Nevertheless legislators, are far from perfect channels of constituency opinion. Finally, many legislators, committees, and subcommittees provide representation to a multitude of interests.

Check Your Understanding

1. What is congressional casework and why is it so popular among members of Congress?

2. What is "pork-barrel" politics?

3. Under what conditions are members of Congress likely to follow district opinions? Why do they sometimes ignore such opinions?

4. In what ways do legislators look out for interests that go beyond their own constituencies?

DOES CONGRESS RESPOND EFFECTIVELY TO NATIONAL PROBLEMS?

During every session Congress passes hundreds of bills, spends thousands of hours questioning witnesses, launches dozens of investigations, and prints tons of reports. Moreover, most members of Congress bitterly complain that the work load is too heavy and that resources are stretched to the breaking point. Nevertheless, despite its hectic pace, Congress has been widely and persistently criticized for failing to respond to important national problems. To many people concerned with energy, ecology, women's rights, civil rights, economic growth, international relations, prices and inflation, and the like, congressional responses have not been effective. Critics have called the national legislature "ineffective" and "do-nothing."

Is Congress really incapable of responding effectively to the demands of modern society? As with so many important and controversial questions, there is no simple answer. Whether you see Congress as effective or ineffective depends a great deal on how you view the evidence. We will now examine both points of view.

Critics: Congress Is Ineffective

Whether the problem is inflation or pollution, critics of Congress claim that lawmaking in both houses is characterized as follows.

Congress Responds Very Slowly. Few significant pieces of legislation receive prompt consideration. Between the time a major policy is proposed and when it is finally voted upon, years can pass. It took over fifteen years for major health-care legislation, proposed during the Truman administration, to become law under the Johnson administration. A number of important issues—financing of Social Security, assistance for declining heavy industry, among others—seem to be stuck in the legislative process. Moreover, the very nature and organization of Congress encourages lengthy delays. The committee system, limitations on party leaders, and the bicameral (two-house) nature of the legislature all prevent swift action. A quick leg-

Commentary: What's a Couple of Billion Between Friends?

It is sometimes difficult to imagine the responsibilities that members of Congress face. This is especially true in financial matters, since the government deals in sums whose magnitude is well beyond ordinary experience. Most citizens fully understand the difference between $1,000 and $2,000, but how does one give meaning to the difference between $385 million and $389 million? Such differences are as abstract as the diameter of the solar system.

The implications are clear: members of Congress must decide questions for which they are ill-prepared in terms of their backgrounds and knowledge. This is il-

lustrated by the experiences of former Senator S. I. Hayakawa (Republican of California) on the Senate Budget Committee. At first, Hayakawa was worried because of his lack of financial background. He soon got over his worries, however. As he put it:

The numbers you work with on this committee turned out to be very simple. You are always dealing in hundreds of millions—or billions. Therefore, when we say 1.0, that means $1 billion. Then we have .1; that means $100 million—and that's the smallest figure we ever deal with in the Budget Committee.

A member of the committee will say, for instance, "Here's an appropriation for such-and-such. It was 1.7 for 1977. So for the 1978 budget we ought to make it 2.9." So all we do is add 1.2; that's not hard. The next item is 2.5. The members discuss it back and forth, and someone says, "Let's raise it to 3.7." They look around at each other. "Everyone in favor?" "Yes, sir. Okay." So in five minutes we have disposed of 2 *billion* bucks—2 billion, not 2 million. I never realized it could be so easy. It's all simple addition. *You don't even have to know subtraction.*

From S. I. Hayakawa, "Mr. Hayakawa Goes to Washington," *Harpers*, January 1978, p. 39.

islative response requires winning majorities in several committees and subcommittees, plus co-operation from key leaders. Even if most legislators want speedy action, the internal organization of Congress discourages a prompt response. No wonder that critics frequently describe congressional enactments as "too little, too late."

Legislative Responses Are Uncoordinated. Congress does not confront a major problem, such as poverty or energy, as a single issue. Rather, the problem is broken down into various pieces, and each piece is dealt with by different legislators or committees, with differing perspectives at different times. Take, for example, the House response to the energy question in the late 1970s. More than eighty committees and subcommittees had some jurisdiction over energy-related issues. This pattern is not unique. Almost every major social and economic problem cuts across several committees and subcommittees. Confusion is not surprising when we realize that the system operates so that one committee may authorize a program, a second committee appropriates the necessary funds, and a third is responsible for raising the funds through taxes.

Congress Approaches National Problems from a Local Perspective. Members of Congress know that to remain in office they must satisfy their constituents. A legislator who repeatedly ignores crucial district desires and seeks instead to further his or her own view of the national welfare will probably be looking for a job soon. On many issues, of course, no conflict exists between national and district interests. Nevertheless, when narrow district interests conflict with national interests, localism usually wins out. And because members of Congress accept each other's need to keep constituents happy, many nationally oriented policies become overwhelmed by purely local considerations and are thus greatly weakened. The impact of localism is well illustrated by the attempt of Congress to formulate a pollution policy. Tough antipollution laws commonly create economic hardships on industry. Rather than spend $50 million to clean up waste, a steel company might close down an old, inefficient plant. A legislator

representing the district where the mill is located faces a dilemma: enactment of antipollution legislation will hurt the economic well-being of his or her constituents. Many members of Congress reason that jobs are more important to their constituents than a clean environment and thus try to amend the antipollution bill to allow exceptions for the steel industry. These lawmakers might strike deals with other legislators worried over the impact of tough antipollution laws on *their* local industries. When everyone gets his or her particular loophole, the result will be a generally ineffective law. Of course, not every attempt to place local interests ahead of the national welfare succeeds, but localism remains a persistent congressional force.

Congress Is Ill-Prepared to Solve Major Problems. Many of the problems with which lawmakers must deal are complex, involve technical details, and require careful analysis. Critics argue that Congress is ill equipped to face such issues. First, they say, legislators are not chosen on the basis of their ability to understand complex social and economic problems. Different sets of skills are required for campaigning and for dealing with many contemporary issues. Second, most members of Congress, as we have seen, devote a large portion of their time to nonlegislative matters. Especially in the House, the average legislator spends considerable time helping constituents with their problems and engaging in many other nonpolicy activities. A review sponsored by the House staff stated "that members have too little time to concentrate on their important policy-making responsibilities, and that the House and its committees face challenges to competent and orderly performance because of work overload." As a result of these inadequacies, the argument goes, the executive branch has become the moving force in dealing with important national concerns. Congress at best deals with details, while the major policy leadership comes from the President or Cabinet officials. For this reason, the critics of Congress say, we frequently hear such statements as, "The White House has presented its comprehensive tax program and Congress hopes to consider it in due time." Then, a few months later, we hear, "The President's program is in trouble, according to congressional leaders," followed by, "The President calls for swift congressional action and an end to obstructionism."

Defenders: Congress Is Effective

Defenders of congressional effectiveness make the following points.

Congress Was Never Intended to Be an Institution Responsible for Promptly Solving the Nation's Problems. Certainly this was not the intent of those who wrote the Constitution. Many constitutional features are designed to *limit* legislative action. Congress is not supposed to act like a political fire department that jumps into action every time we face a crisis. If we want that type of response from our national legislature, we should have instead a parliamentary system with a single-house legislature at the instant call of a Prime Minister, as in Britain, for instance.

Congress Might Drag Its Feet on Important Legislation, but This Is Not Proof That It Undermines the National Welfare. Those who criticize Congress for lengthy delays assume that the bottled-up legislation is widely desired and represents a solution to a problem. Both assumptions are frequently false. In 1981, for example, Congress responded quickly to President Reagan's call for large tax cuts. A year or two later many supporters expressed serious doubts regarding the wisdom of rapid and drastic cuts. In addition, many legislators justify lengthy discussion on the grounds that much legislation is poorly formulated. Good legislation cannot be put together overnight and can require extensive hearings, research, and public debate. In August 1964, Congress, with little discussion or investigation, overwhelmingly passed the Gulf of Tonkin resolution, which authorized the President to "take all necessary measures" to stop aggression in Southeast Asia. The measure opened the door to a long series of military and political disasters in Vietnam. The piecemeal approach that Congress takes on major social and

Senate President Pro Tem Strom Thurmond says the Tax Reform Act of 1986 was the largest bill he ever signed. President Reagan signed the measure as well.

Members of the Senate gather for a formal photograph. Ordinarily the chamber is not filled, since much of the work of Congress is done in committee meetings and at legislative hearings.

economic problems is a reasonable and practical strategy. Specialization and an extensive committee system are essential to the efficient operation of Congress, the defenders maintain. Such problems as employment, race relations, and economic growth are too complex to be considered by a single committee or debated as a single issue. Imagine the result if 435 members of the House, as a group, sought to develop a coherent economic policy. After initial mass confusion, everyone would probably decide to split up into smaller groups to consider different pieces of legislation. In short, a step-by-step approach with uneven and sometimes contradictory outcomes is necessary when 435 representatives or 100 senators must decide major policy questions. The system might not be perfect, but it is better than any of the alternatives suggested by critics of Congress.

All Laws Designed to Cure National Problems Must Be Sensitive to Local Variations. This is especially true given the enormous regional and local differences that exist in the United States. We cannot expect a program that works well in New York City to work equally well in rural Mississippi. Moreover, it is sometimes difficult to distinguish between the local and the national interest. For example, proponents of a nationally oriented energy conservation program have called for high, federally enforced gas mileage standards to reduce American dependence on foreign oil. Legislators from Detroit and other auto-producing areas have generally opposed such requirements on the grounds that they would hurt the American automobile industry, damage to which, in turn, would have repercussions throughout the entire economy. Which position is in the national interest? Perhaps both.

Congress Is Just as Capable as Any Other Political Body of Dealing Intelligently with Complex National Problems. First, many legislators are extremely well informed on important aspects of public policy. Most legislators have spent years on specialized committees studying important national problems. In many cases, legislators are more experienced and knowledgeable than executive branch officials. It can also be argued that frequent elections and contact with citizens provide legislators with a useful perspective on national problems. A member of Congress voting on an energy bill might not have a Ph.D. in engineering, but he or she might have a better idea of public thinking than a technical expert in the executive branch. Each member of Congress, committee, and subcommittee maintains a staff that usually includes people with considerable expertise. The General Accounting Office, with more than five thousand employees, is a professional run "eyes and ears" of Congress in monitoring the executive branch. When Congress needed information on energy, the GAO provided more than one hundred reports in 1978 and 1979. The Congressional Research Service employs a large number of specialists to answer questions on everything from medical care to Soviet economics (in 1981, the CRS handled more than 200,000 requests for information). In 1974 the Congressional Budget Office was created to provide expert analysis of the President's proposed budget. All in all, either through hearings or through these supporting organizations, members of Congress have access to expertise in virtually every field. Finally, defenders of congressional effectiveness point out that although Congress does not possess solutions to the problems of education, social welfare, economic development, or any other pressing concerns, *neither does anyone else.* In fact, many of these problems are so complex that no all-encompassing solution exists. Congress might be only partially successful in dealing with the issues it confronts, but partial success might be the best we can expect.

Conclusions

It should be clear that the conclusion we reach about congressional effectiveness depends on our approach. If we define "effectiveness" as the rapid enactment of comprehensive programs that solve pressing problems, Congress usually comes up short. Congress rarely acts quickly, its responses are often partial, and major successes are not common. This standard, however, might be unrealistic and inappropriate. The Constitution does not provide Congress with the structure or authority to cure complex, deeply rooted social and economic ills. Moreover, the slow, piecemeal type of responses that Congress can offer might be all that is possible. Such solutions are reasonably informed and are politically feasible—no small accomplishment in a society like ours.

Check Your Understanding

1. What reasons have some critics given for calling Congress ineffective?

2. What responses to these criticisms do the defenders of Congress give?

3. What factors allow Congress to deal effectively with large-scale, complex projects?

SHOULD CONGRESS BE REFORMED?

Almost everyone who has observed Congress or served in it has suggested reforms. People disagree, however, on what in particular needs to be improved and how change should be accomplished. To understand the issues in reforming Congress, let us consider three types of reforms: (1) strengthening Congress' institutional role, (2) making Congress more democratic, and (3) improving congressional morality.

Strengthening Congress' Institutional Role

This reform rests on the belief that the President and the executive branch, contrary to constitutional design, have come to dominate Congress.

The shift in power has occurred for a number of reasons. First, since World War II, international affairs have become much more important, and it is the President who prevails in the making of foreign policy. Second, the growth of government involvement in society since the Roosevelt New Deal and Congress' willingness to delegate its authority in this area have resulted in a much larger executive branch. Many important decisions are now made by executive branch bureaucrats, not by legislators. Finally, the reduced authority of congressional party leaders in recent decades has meant that Congress cannot present a unified front. A divided, weakly led legislature is no match for a President with a well-defined program.

The desire to strengthen the legislative branch has resulted in important changes in recent years. More funds have been appropriated for support services, staff, and computerized information retrieval. Between 1960 and 1981, for example, the number of employees working for congressional committees more than tripled. Many of these support personnel are well paid and highly qualified. In 1972 Congress also created the Office of Technology Assessment to provide expert evaluations of legislation dealing with science and technology. The General Accounting Office (GAO), created in 1921, provides Congress with assessments of executive branch programs and expenditures. Members of Congress often rely heavily on the GAO for information on the way money actually is spent, the effectiveness of programs, and the legality of many government decisions.

Congress and the Budget: A Case Study in the Problem of a Stronger Congress

In recent years many of those wishing to strengthen the institutional role of Congress have focused on the federal budget. Basically, the federal budget describes what programs will get what money. Its impact cannot be overestimated. Such things as funding for the elderly and for education, our commitment to national defense, support for agriculture, and, indeed, every aspect of government are set by the budget. The overall size of the budget also has major consequences for the economy. For example, a very large budget with inadequate funding can result in high levels of inflation (see Chapter 15).

Until 1974 the President clearly dominated the budgetary process. The President prepared the initial budget, and the executive branch legitimately could claim greater familiarity with the facts and figures of government finance. At best, Congress would object to details and perhaps threaten delay to get a better deal for favorite projects. On occasion, the President might even refuse to inform Congress of how money was to be spent. Analysis of future revenue and the possible impact of programs also was prepared by executive branch officials.

The 1974 Reform. In 1974, to strengthen the budgetary role of Congress, the Congressional Budget and Impoundment Act was passed. This important act did several things. First, both the House and the Senate established standing Committees on the Budget to review the President's budget as a whole, to set up specific spending and revenue objectives, to decide on debt and surplus levels, and to apportion funds into broad categories (for example, defense, health care, and so on). These choices were to guide individual appropriations committees.

A Congressional Budget Office (CBO) was also created to assist both the budget committees and the rest of Congress in evaluating all the technical complexities of the national budget. The CBO is intended to be nonpartisan—it favors neither Democrats or Republicans. Even though the CBO does not make policy recommendations, its activities provide an important basis for congressional choices. Among its responsibilities are the estimation of the five-year costs of proposed legislation, the analysis of programs that affect the national budget, the analysis of economic trends, the consideration of the inflationary impact of proposals, keeping track of the total cost of budgetary proposals, and the preparation of a set of budget options for each year. The CBO had a staff of 222 in fiscal 1985, a budget of $17.4 million, and prepared numerous reports and memoranda on budget-related issues. For example, when President Reagan requested funding for the MX missile, the CBO prepared an independent analysis of the cost of the missile system.

The 1974 reform also gave Congress more time to review the President's proposed budget. The President would submit budgetary proposals in January, but the **fiscal year**—the twelve-month period used by the government in calculating its finances—would not begin until October 1. Thus Congress had nearly nine months for review. Various procedures to promote coordination between houses as well as ways to balance revenues and expenditures were also included in this reform. The Congressional Budget Office prepared an overall analysis of the budget before individual committees took their separate actions. The budget committee in each house then set overall targets for revenue and expenditures. If a difference existed between the appropriations called for by separate committees and these targets, a process called **reconciliation** was employed to ensure a match. This could involve expenditure reductions, revenue increases, or both.

The 1985 Reform. The 1974 reform strengthened the role of Congress, but it failed to resolve the problem of larger and larger budget deficits. It was as if Congress had drawn up a tough diet for itself, gone through the motions of following it, but then ignored it under pressure. To stop such "cheating," Congress in 1985 enacted legislation that would force it to impose greater restraint on its willingness to spend money it did not have.

The Balanced Budget and Emergency Deficit Control Act of 1985, commonly called Gramm-Rudman-Hollings, after its major sponsors in Congress, contained the following provisions.

1. The goal of zero deficits by fiscal 1991 was established, and maximum allowable deficits between 1986 and 1991 were specified.

2. The congressional budget review process established under the 1974 law was revised. The process was speeded up—for example, reconciliations would now occur on June 15, not September 25. This would allow more time to make cuts.

3. The Congressional Budget Office and the Office of Management and Budget (OMB), an executive branch agency, were given responsibility for reviewing congressional action in light of the maximum allowable deficits for that year. On the basis of economic forecasts, these two agencies would then recommend a percentage cut in expenditures.

4. The comptroller general, head of the General Accounting Office, would then suggest budget cuts based on the report prepared by the CBO and OMB. These would be sent to the President, who would be required to make the cuts without change.

5. Cuts were to be divided equally between national defense and nondefense programs. However certain programs were exempted from automatic cuts—Social Security, interest on the federal debt, and several welfare-related programs. Other programs had maximum cut limits. Such cuts could be suspended during an economic recession or a war. To a degree, the impact of these exemptions was lessened, because expenditures that previously were not part of the regular budget would now have to be considered with the rest of the budget. Making an expenditure not part of the budget had been a favorite congressional tactic for avoiding budgetary restraint.

This attempt to impose self-discipline was challenged immediately in federal court. Opponents believed that by giving the comptroller general, an official responsible to Congress, the power to tell the President what cuts must be made, Gramm-Rudman-Hollings violated the Constitution's principle of separation of powers. On February 7, 1986, a special three-judge panel agreed. On July 7, 1986, the Supreme Court concurred—an official of Congress cannot tell the President what cuts must be made.

This ruling then triggered a fallback procedure that had been included in Gramm-Rudman-Hollings in expectation of such a possibility. Now the report from the comptroller general would go to a special budget committee. Within five days this committee would report it as a joint resolu-

Meetings between the President and members of Congress are essential if the two branches are to work together. Here, four senators attend a White House briefing.

tion. If passed by both houses, the resolution would then go to the President for signature. In other words, Congress again would have to make decisions. It could not delegate authority in the hope of avoiding pressures for more and more spending.

What has been the overall impact of the 1985 reform? A clear agreement exists that Gramm-Rudman-Hollings has failed to impose an effective diet on Congress. Deficit targets have not been met; they are often ignored. Nor has this law encouraged Congress to be tougher in dealing with the President's budget. Indeed, the opposite might be true. The existence of a final review in August has often provided an incentive to avoid difficult decisions before the review. As in the past, critical choices might be made in a hectic, last-minute atmosphere. Moreover, because of the many exemptions and special rules, less than half of the budget is subject to the possibility of automatic cuts.

At the same time, however, there have been changes in the intended direction. The whole debate over the 1985 reform has made legislators more sensitive to the need for budgetary restraint and coordination. Some politically popular measures that in the past would have encountered little opposition have been blocked as too expensive (for example, a 1986 attempt to give $1 billion in aid to economically hard-hit farmers). Many legislative leaders have also used the deficit targets and budget reduction procedures in dealing with appropriations bills. In sum, however, Gramm-Rudman-Hollings has had only a modest impact as a means of controlling Congress' desire to spend more than it has.

Congressional experiences with the 1974 and 1985 budget reforms provide a number of lessons regarding any attempt to make Congress stronger in relation to the President. Basically, there are major limits on what can be done. First, a President facing tough, unified opposition in Congress might respond by making deals with particular legislators who face difficult reelection campaigns. Because congressional leaders have few powers over their colleagues, little can be done to stop someone from "selling out" to the executive branch.

Second, as a result of constitutional divisions of authority among branches of government, there are limits on the growth of congressional power. Congress may disagree with the way a President administers policy, but Congress cannot respond by trying to take away presidential authority. Such action would be strongly resisted by the executive and would likely be invalidated as unconstitutional by the federal courts. Unless a constitutional amendment is passed, Congress is going to have to accept presidential preeminence in many areas. Imagine what might happen if Congress decided that it, not the President, should negotiate treaties with foreign governments (this power is given to the President by the Constitution). Such action would have little chance of success, although Congress is certainly able to play a role in treaty making.

Finally, there is no guarantee that a stronger Congress will result in better overall policy. A stronger Congress might even encourage greater interbranch conflict and deadlock. The net result could be no action at all or one based upon last-minute negotiations to avoid catastrophes. Neither the 1974 nor the 1985 budget law reduced growing deficits or made the legislative appropriations process better organized. Opponents of greater congressional power might reasonably assert that presidential domination is necessary if there is to be a sense of direction and purpose. Put bluntly, the effort to strengthen Congress might not be worth it in terms of benefits received.

Making Congress More Democratic

A second type of reform of Congress focuses on the internal workings of the legislative process. This reform emphasizes the fact that some legislators—committee heads and party leaders—have too much influence over the agenda, staff appointments, and the types of bills that are passed. This inequality of power tends to favor certain interests over others. In the 1950s and 1960s, for example, Congress was dominated by conservative Southerners, even though they were outnumbered. To-day, legislators from **electorally safe districts** (districts in which the incumbent faces little or no opposition) can use their seniority to obtain choice committee assignments and other benefits. As a result, not all citizens are represented equally. A district that has sent the same legislator to Congress year after year is in a much better position than a district in which elections are more competitive.

As we mentioned earlier in the chapter, several steps were taken in the early 1970s to reduce the concentration of power in the House and Senate. Limits were placed on committee chairpersons, seniority was less rigidly followed in their selection, and the role of subcommittees was strengthened (this allowed more legislators to have an impact). Restrictions also were placed on the number of important committee positions one legislator could hold. These rule changes were reinforced by other factors that made legislators less dependent on party leadership: the rise of PACs to finance campaigns, a growing expectation among constituents that their representatives should be more concerned with district interests, and a declining interest among legislators in spending a lifetime to build a House or Senate career. The net impact of these changes has been the virtual disappearance of the "old guard" or "inner club" that once ran Congress. Indeed, since the mid-1970s several of these once-powerful leaders have voluntarily left Congress for private life.

Although the sharing of power might correct certain past abuses, there are possible negative consequences as well. In particular, the absence of centralized authority can increase the tendencies toward disunity and conflict that already exist in Congress. A legislative issue may now come under the examination of several committees and subcommittees, each headed by someone holding a different perspective, rather than of only one or two committees. For example, when in 1983 Congress looked into allegations of mismanagement at the Environmental Protection Agency, six separate House committees had jurisdiction in the area.

It has become increasingly common since the late 1970s for those inside and outside of Congress

Commentary: The Rewards and Costs of Serving in Congress

As a group, members of Congress are well paid and fairly well-off. Beginning in 1987, members of Congress received a salary of $89,500 plus a number of benefits (for example, reduced-cost meals) and opportunities to earn outside income (especially in the Senate, where there are no restrictions on outside income). It is misleading, however, to characterize Congress as a wealthy club.

In the first place, there are sizable variations in income and wealth, and many members rely heavily on spouse income to pay daily bills. In 1983 there were at least six senators whose outside income exceeded $1 million and a large number who earned a quarter of a million or more. At the other end of the scale were senators like Larry Pressler (Republican of South Dakota), who reported an outside income of $3,500, $18,300 in honorariums, and modest assets ($50,000) that matched his liabilities.

Second, even a total income of $200,000 may be inadequate to survive as a member of Congress; after all, members often maintain two residences, and Washington real estate is very expensive. Moreover, government funds are provided for only a certain amount of travel to and from a district—extra trips must be paid from personal funds. Another important consideration is that national legislators are expected to maintain a high-status life style. They must dress well, entertain frequently, and are often expected to pick up lunch and dinner checks for those of lesser status. It would be embarrassing to find senators buying their clothes at discount stores and eating lunch in fast-food restaurants. Legislators are also easy marks for worthy causes soliciting a contribution.

Finally, compared to the salaries and job security of high-level people in private industry, members of Congress are underpaid. A comparable private industry employee is likely to receive more than $200,000 in salary plus bonuses, and he or she does not have to win the position every two or six years. Even moderately successful Washington lawyers and lobbyists earn far more than members of Congress.

Under such circumstances, it is not surprising that a $2,000 fee for speaking before a group or a lavish meal paid for by a lobbyist can be very appealing.

to complain about the unwieldiness of the national legislature. As the journalist David Broder put it: "No one can lead men and women who refuse to be led. The House juniors have overthrown the old power centers. Yet they constantly refuse to heed even those they installed in power." A similar theme was echoed by C. Douglas Dillon, who had served as Secretary of the Treasury from 1961 to 1965: "When I was in government, Congress was well-enough organized so you could talk to a limited number of leaders and committee chairmen and have a good idea of what was going to be done, or come to agreements that would be kept. That's no longer possible." In other words, the price of greater equality of power is a loss of institutional capacity.

A second unintended, and to some, undesirable consequence of the spreading of authority is an enhancement of interest-group powers. Interest groups have many more points of access than before the mid-1970s. A group faced with a hostile committee chairperson can shift its focus to committee members and chairs of the various subcommittees—a tactic that would not have worked in the days when chairpersons more or less dominated their committees. Such access is particularly valuable to groups intent on stopping action, because it takes only a few legislators in key positions to block legislation.

Increasing Congressional Morality

The third type of commonly proposed reform focuses on the morality of individual members of Congress. There are two main reasons for this concern. First, as prominent public officials, members of Congress should be of good character and moral virtue in their personal and professional lives. Revelations of unethical business practices and the like can make the public less respectful of Congress. Second, because of their heavy public responsibilities, members of Congress have a particular obligation to behave honestly. It would be unthinkable to entrust hundreds of billions of dollars and choices involving life and death to officials who sold their votes to the highest bidder.

Over the years a number of incidents have led to calls for imposing stricter standards of conduct on members of Congress. An almost regular event has been the exposure of legislators taking advantage of their positions of power. In 1980, for example, an FBI informant posing as a wealthy Arab received assurances from six House members and one senator that their support could be gained for a price.

More complex ethical issues are raised when members of Congress accept fees, gifts, and campaign contributions from people needing assistance from government. Many legislators are lawyers, and it is not unusual for them or their law firms to perform services for clients doing business with government. The American Bar Association Code of Professional Responsibilities prohibits serious misconduct, but being "politically connected" is still an asset for a law firm. Legislators also regularly supplement their salaries by giving speeches or writing articles for organizations for a fee. Finally, as we noted in describing interest groups (Chapter 8), members of Congress frequently receive lavish dinners, free theater tickets, and many other benefits.

A number of mechanisms permit Congress to deal with impropriety. The Constitution (Article I, Section 5, paragraph 2) allows each house, by a two-thirds vote, to expel a member for "disorderly Behavior." As of 1984, four House members and fifteen senators had been expelled, even though many more efforts have been made (some legislators resigned rather than face expulsion). A second action that Congress can take is to **censure** a member guilty of improper conduct—to issue an official reprimand in accordance with the rules of each house. Censure has been used more com-

Harrison Williams announces his resignation from the Senate. He had been convicted of trying to sell legislative favors and was sent to prison.

monly than expulsion. As of 1984, eight senators and twenty-three House members had been censured. Congress has also used the terms "reprimand" and "denounce" to show its displeasure.

There are also criminal laws dealing with improper behavior. It is a federal crime to ask for or accept a bribe or receive "anything of value" for performing an official duty. Members of Congress have been convicted for violating this law. In 1981, for example, Senator Harrison Williams (Democrat of New Jersey) was convicted of bribery, conspiracy, aiding criminal activities, and accepting money for performing his official duties. In 1958 and 1977, Congress passed codes of ethics. The 1958 action had no force of law, but the

1977 code was given the full force of law in 1978. As it applies to Congress, this law requires detailed financial disclosures (value of property owned, outside income, gifts received), provides penalties for rule violations, permits public access to this information, and created an Office of Government Ethics to enforce these rules. The House also has imposed limits on the outside earnings of its members; the Senate has not.

As with all reforms, there are drawbacks as well as benefits. Holding lawmakers to very strict standards of personal conduct might drive many capable, reasonably moral people out of public life. Not everyone is willing to have his or her personal life and finances closely studied in public. There is also the issue of personal privacy—should a legislator's family life or personal business matters receive public attention in order to stop impropriety in government? Such attention is not given to those who occupy positions of power in private industry or even in other parts of the national government. Finally, by severely restricting the outside incomes and financial activities of legislators, Congress could become even more of a millionaires' club than it is. Without speaking fees or other benefits, many capable people would be forced to leave Congress in favor of people who are wealthy enough to rely on their own personal fortunes.

Conclusions

It is clear that reforming Congress is far more complex than ridding it of obvious evils. Reasonable people can disagree over what is an evil. For example, a weak, bickering Congress is a problem in need of reform if you believe in a balance of power between legislative and executive leadership. Moreover, solving one problem can create new problems. A tough anticorruption law can remedy some abuses, but too-vigorous enforcement of the law might create the misleading impression of widespread impropriety. A "good" reform, then, is one that is consistent with a certain set of values and whose benefits outweigh the disadvantages. Not all changes in the name of reform are necessarily changes for the better.

Check Your Understanding

1. What are three types of reforms of Congress that have been proposed?

2. What was the purpose of the 1985 budget reform act? What has been its impact?

3. Why is it difficult to strengthen Congress' role in relation to the President?

4. What are some of the problems in setting strict moral standards for members of Congress?

THE POLITICS OF EVALUATING CONGRESS

If we had to characterize the standards used to judge Congress, we could do so in one word: "contradictory." Hardly anyone wants a weak, ineffectual Congress. Yet if Congress does challenge presidential dominance, it is accused of hindering the President. We dislike the accumulation of power by a few leaders. But a situation of "nobody in charge" is equally undesirable. Congress is expected to deal with national problems. Yet a legislator who puts national goals ahead of district concerns will probably be defeated. No doubt there have been visitors to Washington who insisted on personally seeing their member of Congress for an hour, only to complain that legislators fail to spend enough time familiarizing themselves with important issues. Stories of legislators accepting free meals and lodging from businesses disturb the same people who complain when Congress votes itself a pay raise.

This conflicting view of Congress is reflected in public opinion polls and in the way citizens vote. Since the early 1960s, citizens have regularly been asked to rate the job done by Congress—excellent, pretty good, only fair, or poor. Since the late 1960s, only a minority of people have used the first two (positive) terms; overall, Congress is regularly given low marks. At the same time, however, most citizens are favorably inclined toward their own legislator. In a 1980 survey, for example, citizens gave their own representative a favorable rating by a three-to-one margin. More important, incumbent legislators have generally had excellent records in winning reelection, especially in the House, where 90 percent or more of the incumbents are usually reelected. Congress might be doing a poor job, but most people seem to like the job performed by their own legislator.

The difficulty of evaluating Congress should caution us about accepting any *one* evaluative standard. Requiring Congress to be able to respond effectively to national crises may also require us to accept strong leaders who may use questionable tactics to get things done. Creating a Congress that follows district opinion could set up an institution that puts local interests before national interests. Obviously, several evaluative standards are relevant, and they must be balanced against one another. Congress cannot be perfect on all standards because the standards themselves conflict.

It is also important to realize that the use of one standard over another can reflect specific political objectives. A plea for "responsiveness," "greater democracy," or "better lawmaking" could represent a call for a particular policy rather than an abstract commitment. Evaluative standards are not politically neutral. For example, in the 1960s many liberals criticized Congress as unresponsive and dominated by senior legislators who used their considerable power to defeat or delay liberal proposals. Especially after Lyndon Johnson's 1964 landslide victory, any sign of congressional hesitance in following the President's plans to increase spending on social services was harshly criticized as hindering the President. However, following President Reagan's 1980 victory, many of the same people called on Congress to assert its traditional authority and resist Reagan's proposed budget cuts in social welfare. What had once been called obstruction was now called protection of the less fortunate. In other words, the virtues of a strong Congress depended on just what it was trying to accomplish.

Chapter Summary

How much power does Congress have? The Constitution grants Congress important powers in the area of taxing and spending, foreign affairs, regulating commerce, impeachment, amending the Constitution, and choosing the President. By custom, Congress has acquired the power to investigate and influence the executive bureaucracy. Many factors, however, limit Congress: constitutional restrictions, federalism, and the other branches of government.

How does the legislative process work? Most proposed legislation does not survive the congressional obstacle course. Bills are first sent to committee, where they can be examined in detail. Because committees exercise major powers, decisions on committee memberships are important.

Proposed legislation rarely survives defeat in committee. Elected party officials also have an influence over which bills are passed. Because of the crush of business and the complexity of many bills, the final floor debate is rarely crucial in determining whether a bill passes. Increasingly, legislative staffs play an important role in Congress.

Does Congress represent the people? There are several different meanings of "representation." Congress does not reflect a cross section of the population and in this sense is unrepresentative, but the significance of this is unclear. Congress does respond to citizens through extensive casework, and it provides pork-barrel benefits. It can be argued that such activities detract from the effectiveness of Congress and do more harm than good. On important district issues, legislators generally follow constituency opinion. However, in many situations legislators do not follow the wishes of their districts. There are several understandable reasons for this—for example, when the district's views are not clear.

Does Congress respond effectively to national problems? Congress has often been criticized as being slow, uncoordinated, dominated by localism, and incapable of resolving pressing problems. But it can be argued that Congress was not designed to solve complex social problems and that a slow, cautious, locally oriented style is well suited to our society. Moreover, some problems might be beyond solution.

Should Congress be reformed? Three reforms have been frequently proposed. Congress should be strengthened, internal procedures should be more democratic, and stricter moral standards should be applied. All three reforms have been partly enacted. For example, in recent years power within Congress has been more widely shared and the congressional budgetary role has been strengthened. All three reforms have certain benefits, but each also creates problems.

Important Terms

Explain the following terms.

oversight
legislative veto
seniority
quorum
legislative calendar
item veto

filibuster
cloture
pork-barrel politics
reelection constituency
primary constituency

Thinking Critically

1. The role of Congress in dealing with the problems of our society has grown enormously since the government was established. Would the Founders have been likely to approve of this change? Discuss your answer in class.
2. The committee system in Congress has often been criticized. What might be an alternative? Who would benefit and who would lose by these changes?

3. The power of congressional party leaders has varied considerably during our country's history. What might be some of the consequences of stronger or weaker leaders?
4. Congressional debates are rarely national forums to discuss major policies. Should an effort be made to increase the importance of floor debates? Why or why not?
5. Elected representatives often vote for what they feel are the best interests of their district, not necessarily what the people of the district want. How responsive should a legislator be to the public opinion of his or her district? Explain your viewpoint.
6. If you were a member of Congress, would you vote for a bill that would put your district's largest employer out of business but significantly reduce the level of dangerous chemical waste? Give reasons for your answer.
7. Pork-barrel projects have often been criticized as wasteful and benefiting only certain special interests. Should a constitutional amendment be passed to limit the amount of money availale for such projects? Why or why not?

Extending Your Understanding

1. An often heard criticism of the committee system was that chairpersons were not typical of members of Congress in general. Using the *Congressional Directory* and other books describing members of Congress, make a chart showing the characteristics of current committee chairpersons in terms of age, sex, race, religion, and so on. Research these same characteristics for your senators and representative (if your senators or representative is a chairperson, you might select members of Congress from a nearby state for comparison). What differences do you find between chairpersons and other members of Congress? How representative of the general population do you think all members of Congress are? Present your views to the class.
2. Write your member of Congress and request information about the types of constituent (casework) services that are available. Find out

how someone would go about obtaining these services. Present your findings to the class.

3. Examine the roll call votes taken in the last session of the House of Representatives. You should be able to locate this information in the library. How many of the issues voted on are of interest to you personally? of interest to your congressional district? How does your representative's voting record compare with the way you would have voted? How does his or her voting record compare with that of the rest of the House? Prepare a report of your conclusions.

4. Select an important local issue that interests you. Write a letter to your member of Congress or to one or both senators expressing your views on the issue. Be sure to include information that supports your view.

5. Select an issue that interests the class. Examine this issue in a mock legislative meeting. Some class members can act as legislators and present their views on the issue. Other members of the class may act as "constituents" who notify their "legislators" of their views. The "legislature" should vote on the issue, after all presentations and arguments have been made.

Making Decisions

You are the head of a committee formed to draft a new code of ethics for members of Congress. Draw up your proposed list of standards. Prepare arguments to defend each proposal in terms of how it benefits the public and why it does not impose an unfair burden on members of Congress. Present your proposals to the class and have your classmates vote on the standards they wish to see adopted.

Chapter 10
Presidents and Presidential Power

The President of the United States occupies center stage in the drama of American politics. The process of selecting the President and the President's actions in office are often the top stories in the mass media. The President is many things to many different people. For some, the chief executive is a political knight on horseback riding off to do battle with evil forces in the name of the public interest—the great protector and world leader. Others, less positive, consider the President a potential tyrant capable of bringing about disaster in a quest for personal glory. They sometimes speak of the "imperial presidency," which they see as a threat to the democratic process. Still others deemphasize the importance of the individual occupying the office and stress that the President is only one person in a gigantic and frequently uncontrollable bureaucracy. Rather than governing, the President is a victim of modern government. All of these views are true to some degree. The presidency is complex, and what we can say about it depends in part on who occupies the office and what issues confront the nation. At times the President appears all-powerful, at other times powerless. We shall examine the President and the office by seeking answers to the following questions:

- How are Presidents selected?
- How much power does the President have?
- How are presidential decisions made?
- Should the presidency be reformed?

PREVIEW

How are Presidents selected? Becoming President requires overcoming numerous obstacles. The constitutional requirements are relatively simple. Public expectations favor white males with a conventional life style and morality. The electoral obstacle is the most difficult to overcome. Potential candidates must start with some political visibility and then win their party's nomination in a lengthy campaign in numerous primaries. Candidates must create a large campaign organization and prepare a strategy to build a coalition of support. The existing selection process is heavily biased toward those who campaign well.

How much power does the President have? Although the Constitution grants the President considerable power, disputes still exist over what the President can and cannot do. As a commander-in-chief of the armed forces, the President can make specific military decisions, use troops to handle domestic crises, and send troops overseas. The President is also a diplomatic leader. The power to shape legislation by proposing bills, vetoing bills, formulating the budget, and enforcing the laws is a third important power. The President likewise has influence over public opinion by being able to decide what issues will receive national attention, define the terms of debate, and change people's opinions through persuasion. Presidential power is limited by the other two branches of government, by the public, and by the mass media.

How are presidential decisions made? The Constitution and the existence of a vast executive branch bureaucracy can give the impression of great presidential decision-making power. This image is somewhat misleading. Agency officials sometimes can successfully resist the President. Presidents are also limited by their dependence on information and advice provided by others. How choices are actually made varies considerably. Some decisions are routine, based on careful analysis. In crisis situations, a course of action might be far less clear. Presidents have their own style of making decisions. The implementation of a decision is often a major problem. In many cases a President must rely more on persuasion than on legal authority.

Should the presidency be reformed? The presidency has undergone several changes since the Constitution was adopted. One currently debated set of reforms focuses on the selection process. The electoral reforms of the 1960s and 1970s are now being criticized as placing too much emphasis on campaigning and as being poorly suited to selecting experienced leaders. Another reform receiving attention is a single six-year term. Some critics say that this would better allow the President to pursue the overall national interest. Reformers concerned with improving the relationship between Congress and the President have argued in favor of the inclusion of legislative leaders in the Cabinet. Finally, proposals have been made to reduce the "presidential establishment" and strengthen the role of the Cabinet. All of these reforms, however, have disadvantages.

HOW ARE PRESIDENTS SELECTED?

The presidential selection process can be likened to a very difficult obstacle course. Even though most Americans, in principle, could become President, in reality only a few have a realistic chance. Not all types of citizens and political perspectives stand an equal chance of completing the obstacle course to the White House. We shall consider three hurdles in this process: constitutional requirements, public expectation, and electoral strategy.

Constitutional Requirements

Article II, Section 1, paragraph 5 of the Constitution requires that the President be a natural-born citizen (that is, born a U.S. citizen), be at least thirty-five years old, and have been a U.S. resident for at least fourteen years.

These are modest requirements, but they do exclude a fairly large number of people. In 1970, some 9.6 million people in the United States were foreign-born and thus excluded from the presidency. There were 133 million Americans in 1984 under the age of thirty-five. Although these numbers are large, the constitutional requirements are generally not considered highly restrictive. In recent years only one person—former Secretary of State Henry Kissinger—might be classified as a potential seeker of the presidency who could not run because of these requirements (Kissinger was originally a German citizen).

Public Expectations

Public expectations regarding who is "presidential" are a second hurdle. Such expectations can operate in indirect ways: a person with the "wrong" qualities is not taken seriously by the mass media and party leaders long before the election because "everybody knows" that the individual cannot become President. A person's sex and race are two important traits that limit who becomes President. Although some women have sought their party's nomination (Margaret Chase Smith in 1964), as well as a black (Jesse Jackson in 1984), only white males are generally given serious consideration. In 1984 the Democrats nominated a woman—Geraldine Ferraro—as their choice for Vice President, so the white male mo-

nopoly on the presidency might be weakening. Ethnic background and religion are also relevant, although they are no longer so crucial as in the past. Only two Catholics have run as major-party presidential candidates—Alfred Smith in 1928 and John Kennedy in 1960—and most serious contenders have been of Northern European descent. Another Catholic, Ferraro, ran for Vice President; her family was from Italy.

Less obvious than sex or race are expectations regarding morality and life style. Americans seem to want Presidents who are married, have families, and profess a traditional religion. Almost any hint of scandal or trouble with the law means disqualification. A Gallup poll conducted in 1979 reported that 70 percent of the public would "strongly object" if a President smoked marijuana occasionally; 43 percent would strongly object if the chief executive told an ethnic joke in private. Until Reagan's 1980 election, no divorced person had ever been elected, although Nelson Rockefeller, a divorcé had served as an appointed Vice President. In general, unconventional life styles or views on morality are seen as "unpresidential."

In 1872, as the candidate of the Equal Rights party, Victoria Woodhull, right, was the first woman to run for President. Because it was illegal for women to run for office, she spent election day in jail. Twelve years later Belva Ann Lockwood ran for President on the National Equal Rights party. Both women received a few thousand votes. It was not until 1920 that women were allowed to vote.

Electoral Strategy

Constitutional requirements and public expectations concerning suitablity reduce the number of potential chief executives considerably, but several million people still qualify. From here on, success depends on political qualifications.

Political Visibility

A first step for a potential President is to achieve a degree of political visibility, usually by winning election to a lower office, frequently the governorship of a major state or a Senate seat. John Kennedy, Lyndon Johnson, and Richard Nixon, for example, once served in the Senate. Jimmy Carter and Ronald Reagan are former governors. Only on very rare occasions can a complete newcomer to politics achieve the presidency. Dwight Eisenhower, elected in 1952 and 1956, had never run for office or held a political position before he became President (Eisenhower had, however, occupied the highly visible position of supreme commander of Allied troops in Europe during World War II).

Party Support

The second step toward the presidency is to win the nomination of either the Democratic or the Republican party. This is crucial—although some independent candidates (George Wallace in 1968 and John Anderson in 1980) have received millions of votes. Since the Civil War the winner has always been a nominee of one of the two major parties.

The way a person wins the party nomination has varied considerably. In the early nineteenth century, members of Congress chose their party's nominee. This procedure was replaced by a national convention in which delegates selected by state party leaders had complete freedom. In 1901 Florida became the first state to allow the use of party primaries to select convention delegates. Wisconsin followed in 1905. Before World War I, direct public involvement in delegate selection became fairly common. Enthusiasm for primaries soon weakened, however. In the late 1960s, the primaries experienced a comeback. Especially within the Democratic party, attempts were made to "open up" the party to allow voters, not just party officials, to make key decisions. It was argued that such an "opening up" of the presidential nominating process would promote greater democracy. (See Chapter 7 for a more complete analysis of presidential primaries.) In 1972 and 1976, about 70 percent of the delegates to the conventions of both parties were chosen in primaries, compared to about 35 percent in 1968.

In the 1980s both parties continued to emphasize primaries, although in 1984 the Republicans, and to a lesser extent the Democrats, reduced the number of primaries. Delegates can also be selected by state party caucuses and from among elected public officials. Winning a majority of convention delegates is a difficult process. Because so many delegates are chosen in primaries, all serious candidates—even an incumbent president—must run in almost all the primaries. Moreover, the need to become known to the public and raise funds now requires most candidates to start their preconvention campaigns very early. Jimmy Carter, for example, started his 1976 campaign two years before the convention; Walter Mondale began his 1984 campaign in 1981. Early contests—the February primary in New Hampshire, for instance—are especially significant. They attract great media attention, and doing well means gaining federal campaign matching funds. Winning a party's nomination can sometimes take as much campaigning as does the general election. No longer can a candidate win by making deals with powerful state party leaders.

The General Campaign

At one time, getting to the White House required relatively little personal campaign effort. The great burden of the campaign was on state and local party organizations. The campaign season was usually limited to September and October, and some successful candidates, such as Warren Harding in 1920, hardly ventured beyond their homes. Because of weakened parties, the growth of the mass media, and a more varied electorate, though, the situation has changed dramatically.

Commentary: The Presidential Campaign Can Be Cruel and Unusual Punishment

Campaigning for President is grueling. Not only is it physically demanding, but a candidate must always appear in command and guard against off-hand remarks that could prove disastrous. The problems of appearing enthusiastic when one is bored, thoughtful when one is reading a prepared speech for the tenth time, and informed when one is giving a superficial response to a silly question were well described by Adlai E. Stevenson, who campaigned unsuccessfully for the presidency in 1952 and 1956. As Stevenson put it:

At least for an inexperienced candidate, I suppose we have contrived few more exciting ordeals than a presidential campaign. You must emerge, bright and bubbling with wisdom and well-being, every morning at 8 o'clock, just in time for a charming and profound breakfast talk, shake hands with hundreds, often literally thousands, of people, make several inspiring, "newsworthy" speeches during the day, confer with political leaders along the way and with your staff all the time, write at every chance, think if possible, read mail and newspapers, talk on the telephone, talk to everybody, dictate, receive delegations, eat with decorum—and discretion!—and ride through city after city on the back of an open car, smiling until your mouth is dehydrated by the wind, waving until the blood runs out of your arm, and then bounce gaily, confidently, masterfully into great howling halls, shaved and all made up for television with the right color shirt and tie—I always forgot—and a manuscript so defaced with chicken tracks and last-minute jottings that you couldn't follow it, even if the spotlights weren't blinding and even if the still photographers didn't shoot you in the eye every time you looked at them. (I've often wondered what happened to all those pictures!) Then all you have to do is make a great, imperishable speech, get out through the pressing crowds with a few score autographs, your clothes intact, your hands bruised, and back to the hotel—in time to see a few important people.

But the real work has just commenced—two or three, sometimes four hours of frenzied writing and editing of the next day's immortal mouthings so you can get something to the stenographers, so they can get something to the mimeograph machines, so they can get something to the reporters, so they can get something to their papers by deadline time. (And I quickly concluded that all deadlines were yesterday!) Finally, sleep, sweet sleep, steals you away, unless you worry—which I do.

Adlai Stevenson reflects on his campaign after a whirlwind tour of five Michigan cities in twelve hours during the 1952 presidential race against Dwight Eisenhower.

Adlai E. Stevenson, *Major Campaign Speeches of Adlai E. Stevenson, 1952* (New York: Random House, 1953), pp. xii–xiii.

After winning the party's nomination in July or August, a potential President must put together an effective campaign organization. Although some organization exists from the primary election battles, as well as the political party apparatus, a national campaign requires a much larger effort. A candidate's organization has a multitude of responsibilities: establishing contacts with relevant groups (ethnic organizations, religious groups, unions), commissioning opinion polls, dealing with the mass media, complying with state election laws, distributing campaign funds, and scheduling the appearances of the candidate and his or her family. Considerable day-to-day decision making is often handled by staff people. But the candidate must still deal with the problems and tensions that emerge when people of different backgrounds and views work together. In his 1980 campaign, Reagan was occasionally caught in the middle between advisors who wanted him to play down his conservative views and conservatives who wanted greater recognition. In 1984, Walter Mondale spent considerable time seeking the endorsement of black leaders who had supported Jesse Jackson in the Democratic primary.

The overall goals of the campaign must also be defined. This involves several decisions. Typically, the campaign will attempt to convey some general theme. In 1980 the Reagan campaign promised strong, decisive leadership. In 1984, Reagan repeatedly asked if people were better off now than four years ago. Because of the winner-take-all role in the electoral college (see Chapter 5), candidates must decide in which states they will campaign most actively. In both of his campaigns Reagan emphasized the West, a few Southern states (Texas, Florida), and the large Midwestern states, such as Illinois and Ohio. Blocs of voters must also be targeted. The 1980 and 1984 Reagan campaigns assumed that they would win nearly all Republican votes, but to achieve majorities in key states, they placed greater emphasis on independents and certain dissatisfied Democrats (union members in areas of high unemployment in 1980; socially conservative Democrats in 1984).

Candidates for the presidency must decide how to allocate limited resources. If they choose, candidates in the general election can have their campaigns government-funded (although some private money for administrative costs may be collected). Nevertheless, federal money is not unlimited ($40.4 million in 1984 per candidate) and has to be divided carefully for advertising, travel, staff, research, and other essential expenses. There are difficult questions about when and where to place television ads and which issues to stress. In 1984, for example, Walter Mondale devoted considerable attention to the national deficit and its consequences. Reagan emphasized economic gains and the tax-increase plans of his opponent.

Consequences of the Selection Process

The way American campaigns are conducted helps to determine who wins. Not everyone stands an equal chance of surviving the process.

The procedure we now use gives a definite advantage to a person skilled in the arts of political campaigning. It is difficult to imagine, under the present system of multiple primaries, a clumsy campaigner winning a party's nomination. The inability of strong party organizations to deliver large blocs of votes also means that the candidate must campaign hard in the general election. Would-be Presidents must be willing to suffer a year-long physical ordeal—hurried meals, hundreds of repetitive speeches, disrupted family life, thousands of hours of traveling, and so on. No doubt many capable people are discouraged from seeking the presidency for this reason.

The importance of campaigning plus the nature of contemporary campaigns (see Chapter 6 for a discussion of the "new politics") gives a special advantage to the candidate who can use the mass media well. The ability to come across on television as honest, decisive, and sincere is crucial. During the preconvention period, when candidates compete for free publicity, it is important to have favorable media coverage. Jesse Jackson's campaign, for example, received considerable free media attention because a black was seriously seeking the nomination. Walter Mondale's selection of a woman as a running mate also generated much free publicity.

During presidential campaigns, voter interest is at its highest. In the 1984 race, Walter Mondale, top left, waves to a friendly audience. After their TV debate, seen by millions of viewers, vice presidential candidates George Bush and Geraldine Ferraro shake hands. Reaching out to the crowd, Ronald Reagan acknowledges the voters' support.

Finally, the openness of the present primary system and the availability of the mass media allow a political newcomer to achieve the presidency. A distinguished but not highly visible twenty-year Senate career is not necessarily an advantage in a contest with someone who is well known but lacks political experience. Political unknowns can now become household names in a few months, thanks to the media. Neither Jimmy Carter nor Ronald Reagan had had long political careers before running for President. Access to the party nominating process was less easy when state and local party leaders dominated the electoral system.

Not all democracies emphasize an ability to campaign as a key requirement for office. In Great Britain, for example, the Prime Minister is a member of Parliament and is selected by other party members. His or her campaign for the top position is relatively brief and the personal politicking is limited mostly to other political leaders. Someone who wants to be Prime Minister has only to win a seat in a parliamentary district. Much greater emphasis is placed on party alliances, positions on specific issues, and direct personal evaluations of a person's abilities by other elected officials. Over the years, British Prime Ministers have had qualities that might be disadvantages with the American electorate (Margaret Thatcher is female, Anthony Eden was a classics scholar, Edward Heath was unmarried, for example).

Selecting the Vice President

The selection of the President also involves that of the Vice President (the constitutional requirements for Vice President are the same as for President). In principle, the nominating convention chooses the vice presidential candidate. In practice, though, the presidential nominee makes the selection, often in the hurried atmosphere of the convention. Candidates for the presidency typically have a dozen or so possibilities in mind beforehand. The choice of Vice President is heavily influenced by electoral considerations and is usually an effort to "balance" the ticket. In 1976, for example, the relatively conservative Carter selected the more liberal Walter Mondale as his running mate. Regional coalition-building is also a consideration. Reagan, with his Western strength, selected George Bush in 1980 and 1984 in part because of Bush's ties to Eastern Republican leaders.

Part of the casualness of a running mate's selection can arise from the limited role of the vice presidency. The major constitutional responsibilities of the office are to preside over the Senate (and vote if there is a tie) and to help decide presidential disability. Presidents have given their Vice Presidents many other duties—chairing commissions, traveling abroad as the President's representative, defending the President's programs, and participating in Cabinet meetings. He or she is also a member of the National Security Council. Rarely, however, does the Vice President play a strong role in administering policy.

The major significance of the office is that it is a frequent stepping stone to the White House. In the twentieth century, six Vice Presidents have become President. Some—Theodore Roosevelt, Calvin Coolidge, Harry Truman, Lyndon Johnson—became President on the death of the President; Gerald Ford became President when Nixon resigned. Richard Nixon himself became nationally known when he served for eight years as Vice President under Eisenhower.

Presidential Succession

A key aspect of the presidential selection process involves the constitutional specifications for replacing a President who dies in office, resigns, is impeached and convicted, or is unable to perform the duties of the office. A quick look at American history shows how important a part of the selection process succession is. Eight Presidents have died in office and a number of others have had severe difficulty in performing their duties because of poor health. One President—Richard Nixon—resigned.

The Constitution as originally drafted simply states that if the President dies in office or is unable to discharge the duties of the office or is removed from office, the Vice President becomes President. Congress is given the power to enact legislation that establishes how presidential incapacity will be decided and the line of succession following the Vice President. There is no constitutionally specified line of succession beyond the Vice President.

Congress has dealt with the issue of presidential succession several times. The most recent resolu-

nbodied in the Twenty-fifth Amendment, in 1967. This says that if the presidency becomes vacant, the Vice President assumes the presidency and then nominates a new Vice President, subject to confirmation by majorities in both houses of Congress. (This provision was intended to avoid a repetition of the situation in 1963 and 1964, when President Johnson had no Vice President.) The President is also authorized to nominate a new Vice President if this office becomes vacant. The Twenty-fifth Amendment was used in 1973 when President Richard Nixon nominated Gerald Ford as Vice President to replace Spiro Agnew, who had resigned. When Nixon resigned in 1974, Vice President Ford became President and nominated Nelson Rockefeller as Vice President.

The Twenty-fifth Amendment gives the power to determine presidential disability to the Vice President and a majority of the principal officers of the executive departments or a group authorized by Congress. A President can reassume the presidency if he or she transmits to Congress a declaration that the disability no longer exists, although Congress retains the final power to settle disputes on this question. Evaluating disability can be a difficult question. Following the assassination attempt on President Reagan in 1982, there was some question as to whether he could fully perform his duties while hospitalized.

Check Your Understanding

1. What are the constitutional requirements to be President?

2. What are some of the basic steps a candidate for the presidency must take?

3. How are the candidates for the vice presidency selected?

4. What are the procedures for presidential succession?

HOW MUCH POWER DOES THE PRESIDENT HAVE?

The President is the most powerful public official in the United States, but there is no precise agreement on what powers the chief executive actually possesses. Presidents themselves have viewed presidential power very differently. Some, such as William Howard Taft and Dwight Eisenhower, saw themselves as strictly limited by Congress and the Constitution. Franklin Roosevelt and Lyndon Johnson, on the other hand, believed that the presidency requires vigorous leadership and that the only limitations on Presidents are explicit constitutional prohibitions.

Examination of the Constitution does not solve the problem. As noted in Chapter 2, the Founders were most concerned with legislative, not executive, power. In the words of one expert on the presidency, the constitutional description of presidential powers "is vague, disorganized, and misleading." Nevertheless, despite this vagueness, several important presidential powers are reasonably clear. Some are based on the written Constitution, others on constitutional interpretations, and still others on precedent and custom. Let us consider the power of the President in four important areas: (1) commander-in-chief of the armed forces, (2) diplomatic leader, (3) chief legislator, and (4) shaper of public opinion.

Commander-in-Chief of the Armed Forces

The principle of civilian control over the military is established by the Constitution in naming the President as commander-in-chief of the armed forces (Article II, Section 2). Just what the President can do in this role, however, the Constitution does not specify. When the document was drafted, it was generally accepted by the delegates to the Constitutional Convention that this power was limited to leadership of the military—the President would be the top general. Congress would be responsible for overall policy. Perhaps only in an emergency, such as a surprise invasion, would the President exercise unrestrained discretion. As the world has become more complex, though, the limitations on the use of the commander-in-chief power to make broad policy have become much less clear. Especially in the last fifty years, many Presidents have used their position as commander-in-chief as the basis for participating in a wide range of political actions.

Making Military Decisions

The President's military power is most firmly based on constitutional authority when Presidents make battlefield decisions. In 1794, for example, President Washington personally led an army against rebellious farmers. It was President Truman who decided to use the A-bomb against the Japanese in 1945. Presidents Johnson and Nixon made key military decisions during the Vietnam war. In addition, Presidents have frequently ordered U.S. troops overseas without a congressional declaration of war. President Jefferson, for example, dispatched the Navy against the Barbary pirates when they harassed American commerce. (Jefferson did request congressional authorization to go beyond defensive measures, and Congress approved these measures.) In 1926, President Calvin Coolidge sent 5,000 troops to intervene in the affairs of Nicaragua, without any congressional authorization and in the face of congressional opposition. More modern examples include Eisenhower's sending of 14,000 Marines to Lebanon in 1958, Johnson's dispatching of 32,000 Marines to the Dominican Republic in 1965, and Reagan's sending of the Marines to Lebanon in 1982 and Grenada in 1983.

As commander-in-chief, the President has significant leverage in foreign affairs. In the 1960s, Presidents John Kennedy and Lyndon Johnson sent troops to Vietnam, even though Congress had not declared war. Under President Reagan, in the 1980s, Marines were dispatched to Lebanon, the scene of civil war.

The President's military powers also have been exercised through **covert operations** (that is, secret activities) conducted by the Central Intelligence Agency (CIA), an executive branch agency. The CIA has conducted such operations as arranging assassination attempts against foreign leaders, providing aid to revolutionary groups in several African and South American nations, and even organizing whole armies to take part in secret wars. All in all, there have been some 125 instances in which Presidents sent U.S. troops into conflicts without approval from Congress. The two most important examples of presidential use of the commander-in-chief power were the Korean and Vietnam wars.

American involvement in Vietnam in particular illustrates the problem of precisely defining a President's military powers. Warfare in Vietnam began after World War II and involved conflicts between the French and the Vietnamese and among the Vietnamese themselves. Under Eisenhower, U.S. policy was to give military and economic aid to anti-Communist forces, but the use of American military personnel was kept to an absolute minimum.

The election of Kennedy in 1960 brought about a change. The President and his advisors believed that the proper type of military involvement could defeat the Communists. Based on this belief, plus a worsening military situation, the President sent 500 military personnel to Vietnam in May 1961. Although the advisors were in combat situations, and the action was not an emergency defense of the United States, Kennedy did not seek congressional authorization. By 1963, in response to worsening conditions, 16,000 U.S. troops and advisors had been shipped to South Vietnam. In February 1964, President Johnson concluded that direct, but highly secret, military actions against North Vietnam were necessary. In August 1964, North Vietnamese warships attacked two American destroyers in the Gulf of Tonkin, in international waters. At this point President Johnson sought congressional authorization for further military involvement. In an atmosphere characterized by a sense of urgency and outrage, Congress overwhelmingly passed the Gulf of Tonkin Resolution, which stated that "the Congress approves and supports the determination of the President, as Commander in Chief, to take all necessary measures to repel any armed attack against the forces of the United States and to prevent further aggression." This legislative measure provided the basis of massive, costly, and ineffective military intervention in Vietnam (the estimated cost was $153.8 billion). It was not until 1973 that the United States withdrew from Vietnam.

The Vietnam experience reveals several important features of the President's military powers. First, it is relatively easy for a President to get the United States involved in an armed conflict. By sending a few hundred military advisors, stationing U.S forces near a war zone, or permitting covert actions against a nation, a President can set the stage for events that can readily lead to stepped-up U.S. involvement. Suppose, for example, that an unarmed U.S. reconnaissance (information-gathering) plane were shot down by enemy forces. A "defensive" retaliatory air strike (that is, to punish the attacker) could lead to a full-scale war. Second, the President has considerable power over the information used by Congress and the public to assess the military situation. It has been claimed, for instance, that the Gulf of Tonkin attack was a North Vietnamese response to repeated covert U.S. military strikes launched from the area, not a totally unprovoked attack as claimed by the President. Third, the traditional distinction between defensive and offensive action has little meaning in a world of nuclear missiles and global conflicts. A President, arguing that even a minor skirmish in some remote area directly threatens vital U.S. security, can take immediate military action without consulting Congress.

Using the Military to Preserve Domestic Order

The President has also dispatched troops for domestic purposes. In 1894, President Grover Cleveland sent troops to Chicago to restore order during the strike against the Pullman railroad car company. (The American Railway Union was protesting the company's wage cuts.) During the 1950s and

A teenager hides her face as she is told by armed troops to move on. President Eisenhower had sent the troops to Little Rock, Arkansas, in 1957, to enforce recently enacted school desegregation laws.

1960s, some Southern communities used violence to protest the integration of the schools. U.S. troops were sent in to maintain order. Similarly, when Detroit police could no longer control the situation during the 1967 riots, President Johnson dispatched paratroopers. On many occasions the President has responded to potential violence or natural catastrophes by nationalizing state militias. The power to commandeer state troops is explicitly granted to the President in Article II, Section 2 of the Constitution.

Far-reaching Uses of Military Power

Several Presidents have interpreted their power as commander-in-chief as going well beyond the sending of troops. Especially in wartime, or when war is threatening, ambitious chief executives have used considerable powers, which they said came from the position of the President as military head. Acting as commander-in-chief in the period between the attack on Fort Sumter in April 1861 and the convening of Congress, Lincoln added more than 80,000 men to the armed forces, spent $2 million in unauthorized funds, banned "trea-

sonable correspondence" from the mails, suspended the writ of habeas corpus, and had people arrested for what he judged treasonable offenses. The Emancipation Proclamation, which freed more than four million slaves, was issued on the basis of Lincoln's position as commander-in-chief. In 1942, when a Japanese attack on the American mainland appeared to be a real possibility, President Franklin Roosevelt began procedures to forcibly uproot tens of thousands of Japanese-Americans (most of them U.S. citizens) from their homes and resettle them in "relocation centers." Six months *before* Pearl Harbor, Roosevelt, acting as commander-in-chief during an "unlimited national emergency" (which he had proclaimed), took over a strike-bound plant of the North American Aviation Company.

Diplomatic Leader

In foreign affairs the White House holds vast authority. Congress can cut into the President's authority by reducing appropriations or by failing to ratify treaties, but the President has greater freedom in foreign relations than in other areas of executive power.

Constitutional Sources of Presidential Power

The President's constitutional position as commander-in-chief of an enormous military organization automatically makes the chief executive an important diplomatic and world leader. Theodore Roosevelt became a major force in international affairs through his use of U.S. military might. Roosevelt's use of the Marines "solved" the diplomatic problem of obtaining the rights to build the Panama Canal. **Gunboat diplomacy**—the use of force for diplomatic purposes—has been common in U.S.–Latin American relations. In contemporary politics the President's ability to deploy military force, threaten its use, and decide strategy has had a major impact on international affairs. For example, in recent years the United States has played a major role in Middle Eastern affairs, and much of this influence is based on U.S. military commitments in the area and from an often-repeated willingness to intervene militarily in the area if vital U.S. interests are threatened.

An important constitutionally based source of power is the President's right to appoint and receive ambassadors. By formally accepting an ambassador from a nation, the President acknowledges the legitimacy of that government. The power of **diplomatic recognition,** as the formal acceptance of ambassadors is called, has significant consequences in international commercial relations. It is very difficult for American companies to deal with an "unrecognized" nation, and travel to and from that country is often greatly restricted. On many occasions Presidents have used the power of recognition to shape more general foreign policy. In 1948, for example, President Truman, by quickly accepting the Israeli ambassador to the United States, officially "recognized" the state of Israel. Truman's rapid response conveyed to the world that the United States would support Israel's right to exist; it also affected U.S. relations with most Arab nations in the region. Similarly, the decision to establish full diplomatic ties with China, at the end of 1978, was made by President Carter, not by Congress.

Another constitutionally based power concerns the President's role in treaty making. Even though the Senate by a two-thirds vote of all those present must approve all treaties, it is the President who almost always initiates and negotiates treaties. In addition, the President usually sets the terms and the time of debate. A President, for example, can delay sending a treaty to the Senate until the chances of passage are high. The President also can use the position and visibility of the White House to generate public pressure on Congress. With a few major exceptions, the Senate has endorsed presidential actions.

Even if the Senate resists, however, the President can act through **executive agreements,** or written understandings between the President and the head of a foreign nation. Most such agreements follow from treaties or statutes, but they can be important in their own right. Some of President Johnson's most important commitments to South Vietnam in the 1960s were secret executive agreements between him and the President of South Vietnam and were thus beyond congressional control. In 1973 peace with North Vietnam was made by executive agreement. The courts have treated executive agreements as nearly identical to Senate-confirmed treaties. In *Altman and Co. v. U.S.* (1912), the Court held that while executive agreements lacked the "dignity" of a treaty, they were valid international agreements. Executive agreements may not, however, violate the Constitution or laws passed by Congress. In fact, in several instances the courts have invalidated executive agreements with foreign nations for these reasons.

World Diplomatic Leader

The President not only plays a major role in directing American foreign policy but also helps shape world affairs. Since World War II, American Presidents have vigorously promoted a worldwide policy of containing Communist expansion, sometimes by creating military alliances among nations. NATO (North Atlantic Treaty Organization), established in 1949, is an example of an alliance initiated by an American President. NATO allies include many Western European countries. Chief executives have been instrumental in ensuring that countries, such as South Korea and the Philippines, are governed by leaders opposed to communism. Threats by Presidents to use force against Communist invasion have often kept nations such as Greece and Turkey from Soviet domination.

A contemporary President has many ways to influence world affairs. Traditionally, the President has played the dominant role in planning American foreign aid programs. Decisions on how much to give, to whom, and by what means can have far-reaching consequences for dozens of nations. For example, under the Marshall Plan, a program first proposed by President Truman's Secretary of State George C. Marshall, the United States gave Western European nations some $15 billion in aid between 1948 and 1952. This aid

helped save many nations from collapse and turmoil. Similarly, the President plays a pivotal role in setting American trade policy. Decisions on import limits, embargoes on exports, and the content of commercial treaties often determine the nature of international disputes. Presidents and their advisors can also involve themselves in disputes among foreign nations. When Israel and Egypt went to war in 1973, it was the U.S. President, Richard Nixon, and Secretary of State Henry Kissinger who helped bring about an end to hostilities.

Chief Legislator

We sometimes view Congress as the lawmaking branch of government and the executive branch as the law-enforcing arm. In reality, the division is less clear.

President Franklin Roosevelt, center, meets with Soviet leader Joseph Stalin, left, and British Prime Minister Winston Churchill at the Teheran Conference, 1943. The conference was one of several held near the end of World War II to plan Allied strategy against the Germans and Japanese.

Biography: Franklin D. Roosevelt

FDR, as he was almost universally known, is considered one of the greatest of all American Presidents and is a dominant figure in the history of the twentieth century. Elected to an unprecedented four terms in office, he left behind a vastly expanded federal government that, for the first time, became a real presence in the lives of ordinary citizens. Through his wartime leadership, he also helped make the United States a superpower in world affairs. Roosevelt's presidency offers insights into both the powers and the limits of the office.

Born in 1882 into a privileged New York family, Roosevelt graduated from Harvard University and practiced law before he began his political career as a state senator. His marriage to Eleanor Roosevelt—a distant cousin and the niece of Theodore Roosevelt—was to bring to the White House the most influential of all First Ladies.

FDR's rise up the political ladder continued, with several years as Assistant Secretary of the Navy under Woodrow Wilson and an unsuccessful campaign for the vice presidency in 1920, as the running mate of James M. Cox. His political career was interrupted in 1921 by an attack of polio that left Roosevelt's legs paralyzed but did not weaken his characteristic energy and optimism, nor dampen his interest in politics. (His handicap may have deepened his understanding of and sympathy for those less fortunate than he.) He returned to active politics in 1929,

serving two terms as governor of New York. In 1932 FDR ran for President and defeated Herbert Hoover, the incumbent, in a landslide.

When Roosevelt took office, the United States was in the depths of the Great Depression. His forceful inaugural speech, in which he asserted that "the only thing we have to fear is fear itself," did much to restore confidence. He quickly submitted, and Congress quickly passed, a host of measures launching the New Deal, which was designed to provide both short-term relief and long-term reform. Programs enacted in the first months of his administration aided banks, helped farmers, and established the Tennessee Valley Authority, which furnished low-cost electricity in rural areas of the South. Later legislation protected the rights of organized labor and set up the Social Security system.

When World War II broke out in Europe in 1939, Roosevelt turned the United States into an "Arsenal of Democracy" to help the Allies, especially Britain; he mobilized the country into an all-out war effort when it entered the conflict late in 1941, after the Japanese attack on Pearl Harbor.

FDR was effective in dealing with the other wartime leaders, particularly Winston Churchill of England, but his personal diplomacy has been criticized for its naïveté toward the Soviet leader, Joseph Stalin.

Although FDR was a popular President who relished political success, he was not invincible. The Supreme Court, for example, ruled some of the most significant New Deal measures unconstitutional. Congress, especially after FDR's initial "Hundred Days," refused to act on several New Deal programs and forced the abandonment of others. His biggest setback occurred in 1937, when he proposed expanding the Supreme Court by adding as many as six new justices. Roosevelt's "Court-packing" plan aroused a storm of controversy, and he had to back down.

Roosevelt was restrained not only by the checks and balances of the American system but by his own view of the presidency. As one historian has observed, "He dominated his countrymen without being domineering. . . . He never forgot that he was the repository of power, not its possessor; the representative of the people, not their ruler." Roosevelt's twelve-year presidency (he died in the spring of 1945) did not so much change the office of the chief executive as use its leadership possibilities to their fullest, in the tradition of Thomas Jefferson, Abraham Lincoln, and Theodore Roosevelt.

The Veto Power

One power that enables the President to influence lawmaking is granted explicitly in the Constitution—the veto power. Presidents can veto a bill in two ways. First, they can simply refuse to sign it, in which case it is returned with an explanation to Congress, where a two-thirds vote of each house is necessary to override the veto. Modern Presidents have been quite willing to use the veto power. In his four years in office, Jimmy Carter vetoed thirty-one bills. In his first six years in office, President Reagan used this power about fifty times. Congress overrode only six of those vetoes. Second, a chief executive can use the **pocket veto.** According to the Constitution, the President has ten days (excluding Sundays) to decide on a bill. If the ten days pass and the President has not signed or vetoed it, the bill automatically becomes law. If, however, Congress has adjourned during this period, the bill cannot be sent back to that legislative body. Thus after ten days the bill is "pocket-vetoed." Twenty-one of Reagan's vetoes in his first six years in office were pocket vetoes.

The *threat* of veto can influence legislation too. Presidents are not shy about telling legislators what they will accept. During his first term, for example, President Reagan repeatedly threatened to veto bills that increased spending for social programs. Hence, many bills are modified in advance to avoid a presidential veto. Congress is not completely defenseless, however, against a threatened veto. Unlike many state governors, the President lacks an *item veto*, or the power to reject a portion of a bill and accept the rest. As we noted in Chapter 9, Congress sometimes will take advantage of this situation. It will include in a bill the President desires very much various provisions the President opposes. To get what they want, Presidents frequently accept the entire package.

Proposing Legislation

A second way the President acts as legislator is by proposing legislation. The mixing of legislative and executive roles is traditional in American politics. As President, Thomas Jefferson personally drafted legislation to create a national university, protect harbors, change tariffs, and establish a naval militia. Jefferson also campaigned vigorously for his bills. It was not until the twentieth century, however, that Presidents routinely submitted large numbers of legislative proposals to Congress. In fact, it was only during the Truman administration (1945–52) that the President began submitting entire legislative packages of programs.

Most of the bills that originate in the executive branch are not personally drafted by the President. Through a process known as **central clearance,** the Office of Management and Budget controls the flow of legislative proposals from executive departments to Congress. These proposals represent the President's legislative program, which is usually conveyed to Congress through House and Senate leaders of the President's party. It has been estimated that beween 50 and 80 percent of all bills considered by Congress carry the stamp of the executive branch.

The President's role in lawmaking goes beyond drafting bills. In recent years the executive branch has become one of the major lobbying forces in Congress. Presidents now have special staff members whose only job is to advance the President's program in Congress. The White House can promote the legislative proposals by using many tactics. Presidential prestige is one such approach. Members of Congress will be told that a bill is part of "the President's program," or the President might personally call undecided legislators or invite them to the White House to discuss the bill. Many legislators will go along with the President in the belief that the administration, not the individual legislator, is the best judge of national needs. Others cannot resist the attention and flattery. When friendly persuasion fails, a President has available a wide range of more material rewards—appointments to government jobs, promises to support a legislator's pet project, and backing for contracts and facilities benefiting a legislator's district. A President can also offer to campaign for (or against) a member of Congress in the next election, as well as help raise campaign funds. Perhaps the most powerful weapon in a President's arsenal is a direct public appeal. By using the media, a skillful President can generate considerable public pressure on Congress. An avalanche of letters, calls, and visits endorsing the President's program can be a difficult force to resist. And an appeal to the public can involve mobilizing interest groups to pressure Congress. Especially since the 1960s, presidential aides have been assigned to develop close ties with important groups, and these ties can be used on behalf of the President's legislative proposals.

Power Over the Budget

The President's legislative role involves more than bombarding Congress with bills. In 1921, Congress passed the Budget and Accounting Act, creating the Bureau of the Budget, with a director appointed by the President. With this legislation, the President assumed primary responsibility for preparing the federal budget. The influence of the chief executive over expenditures was further enhanced in the 1970s, when President Nixon replaced the Bureau of the Budget with the Office of Management and Budget (OMB) and placed it more directly under White House control.

Naturally, Congress must approve the budget and is fully capable of making changes in it (see Chapter 9 for an analysis of the role Congress plays). Nevertheless, outlining federal expenditures is an important presidential advantage. The President and OMB have more staff resources, more detailed knowledge, and more time than Congress in the battle of the budget, so presidential priorities frequently dominate. Presidents can also achieve their policy goals by hiding or disguising budget items. When President Franklin Roosevelt wished to keep the atomic bomb project a secret, hundreds of millions of dollars were budgeted for "Engineer Service, Army" and "Expediting Production," and no members of Congress became suspicious. Presidents and executive branch agencies can also transfer funds from one account to another. For example, in 1970 President Nixon transferred $10 million Congress had authorized in aid to Turkey, Greece, Vietnam, and Taiwan to military assistance for Cambodia. Congress frequently authorizes various funds that Presidents can spend as they see fit. There are even so-called secret funds at the disposal of the President, for such activities as covert CIA operations, and Congress rarely has much knowledge of how this money will be spent.

Power Over Enforcement

Presidents determine the content of laws through their decisions on how laws will be administered. The chief executive affects the administration of laws in numerous ways. The power of appointment (often subject to Senate confirmation) allows Presidents to select people who share their views on running the federal bureaucracy. When President Reagan wanted the Interior Department to take a more pro-business perspective, he chose James Watt, who was sympathetic to developing public land, as Secretary. By increasing agency budgets, the President can reward administrators who make the "right" decisions and punish those who don't. Because so many of the government regulations that affect our lives originate in the executive branch, the power over administration is crucial. Furthermore, all Presidents have used their power to name federal judges as a means of advancing their economic and social philosophies, because judges have considerable leeway in interpreting laws. For example, a President who opposed vigorous enforcement of civil rights laws could nominate judges who shared this view.

The President also acts as lawmaker when an act passed by Congress allows the President a certain freedom of choice. For example, the Economic Stabilization Act of 1970 allows the President to issue orders freezing wages and prices—a step taken in 1971 by President Nixon in his attempt to reduce inflation. Foreign trade laws frequently give the President the right to adjust tariffs, within limits, as the occasion arises. Congress often delegates such authority to the President either because it lacks the expertise to write detailed legislation or wishes to avoid the controversy that occurs when specifics are spelled out.

Perhaps the most important legislative power a President has relates to national emergencies. The Constitution deals with national emergencies explicitly only by stating that the writ of habeas corpus may be suspended "when in Cases of Rebellion or Invasion the public Safety may require it" (Article I, Section 9, paragraph 2). Nevertheless,

Congress has shown a willingness to enact laws giving the President additional powers in emergency situations. Thus, when a President declares a national emergency, there are some 470 special laws that go into effect. The President can, for example, restrict the movement of American citizens, compel certain people to register with the government, establish means to censor public and private communications, and withhold from Congress information that would harm U.S. security. Several Presidents have declared national emergencies—the last two were by President Nixon and involved a postal strike and a problem with the U.S. **balance of payments** (the net balance between what the United States spends and what it receives from foreign nations).

The sheer number of emergency powers, plus uncertainties regarding how much leeway the President should have in this area, led Congress to consider the entire issue in the early 1970s (this review was further encouraged when it was discovered that one emergency statute passed in 1799 was still in force despite the ending of the original emergency!). In 1976 Congress enacted the National Emergencies Act, which (1) ended in 1978 all emergency provisions still in effect; (2) gave Congress the power to end presidentially declared emergencies by a concurrent resolution (which cannot be vetoed)—see Chapter 9; (3) mandated that a national emergency be ended after one year

by the President unless Congress is informed that it is still in effect; and (4) required the President, in declaring an emergency, to specify under what laws the action was taken and to keep records of all emergency orders and expenditures. Because no national emergency has been declared since the passage of this law, its impact cannot be evaluated.

The Use of Executive Orders and Proclamations

Finally, Presidents can make law by issuing **executive orders,** which have the full force of the law, and proclamations. In most instances the President is merely filling in the details of a previously enacted law or treaty. Such "details" can be significant, however. During World War II, President Franklin Roosevelt issued executive orders that allowed the federal government to take over shipbuilding companies, a cable company, and nearly 4,000 coal companies. None of these seizures was based on laws passed by Congress. Many Presidents have used executive orders to achieve civil rights objectives—such as banning job discrimination—because they knew that Congress would never pass such laws. By executive order, President Kennedy established an Equal Employment Opportunity Commission that had far more power

As a result of President Kennedy's executive order, many jobs were opened to minorities for the first time.

than a similar agency by an act of Congress. The ease with which executive orders and proclamations can be issued has made them popular means of lawmaking. Between 1907 (when they were first numbered) and November 1983, Presidents have issued more than 12,500 numbered executive orders. The actual number of executive orders is much higher, because many are not numbered and some have labels like Executive Order 106½ or Executive Order 103A.

Presidential proclamations are a related way in which a President can "make law." Some proclamations are mere declarations honoring people, events, industries, movements, and so on. Presidents have proclaimed Earth Week, Law Day, National Farm Safety Week, and so on. Other proclamations are virtually identical to executive orders. In 1971, for example, President Nixon used a proclamation to put a 10-percent surcharge on all imported goods. After a long and complex series of court cases in which importers claimed the President lacked authority to take such action, the President's decision was upheld by the Supreme Court.

Shaper of Public Opinion

As chief executive of the United States, the President is the center of attention. Almost everything the President does or says is reported, conveyed to millions of citizens, and widely discussed. This attention can also be the basis for considerable influence on public opinion.

Influencing the Public Agenda

One important presidential power is the ability to place an issue on the public agenda—that is, to decide what issues will receive national attention. At any one moment there are perhaps hundreds of important issues that might receive public attention. Most of these issues—even if important—will stay in the background. On several occasions the President has taken a relatively neglected issue and made it one of great public concern. For example, poverty has always existed in the United States, but it was not prominently discussed until Lyndon B. Johnson focused attention on the sub-

ject in 1964. Poverty then became a widely discussed topic and generated hundreds of books, magazine articles, television shows, and reports. Johnson, with the aid of Congress, established the War on Poverty. It almost seemed as if poverty had not existed before 1964. President Carter tried, somewhat less successfully, to use his position to heighten the public's awareness of worldwide human rights.

Presidents also influence public opinion by defining or specifying the issues. Their ability to outline policy choices is sometimes as important as the actual choice. This was strikingly illustrated by President Johnson's handling of the debate over American involvement in Vietnam. The war between North and South Vietnam, before extensive U.S. intervention in 1965, could have been characterized as purely a civil conflict or as an ethnic-religious dispute. Once the United States became heavily committed militarily, however, President Johnson successfully defined the war as a battle between the free world, led by the United States, and world communism. Opponents of American involvement thus were put on the defensive. Johnson seemed to be suggesting that they were Communist sympathizers. Counterclaims that the war did not represent a struggle between the United States and the Communists made little headway against Johnson's definition of the debate.

Changing Opinion

Table 10.1 indicates public opinion on nine issues *before* and *after* presidential action. In each case more people agreed with the President after he had taken a public stand than agreed with him before. For example, before President Nixon's May 1969 announcement of phased withdrawal of troops from Vietnam, 49 percent of those polled favored this policy. After the announcement, 67 percent favored it. Note also the dramatic turnabout in public support for the 1970 U.S. invasion of Cambodia—only 7 percent favored invasion before Nixon's action, compared to 50 percent afterward.

The emergence of the modern mass media (especially television) and of public relations experts has added to the President's ability to shape public

The Impact of Presidential Actions on Public Opinion

Date	Presidential Action	Poll Results
July 26, 1963	Kennedy announces nuclear test ban treaty	Before: 73 percent favored After: 81 percent favored
June 7, 1968	Johnson endorses stronger gun-control legislation	Before: 71 percent favored After: 81 percent favored
April 30, 1970	Nixon announces invasion of Cambodia	Before: 7 percent favored After: 50 percent favored
April 1980	Carter administration attempts unsuccessful military release of hostages in Iran	Before: 49 percent favored After: 47 percent favored
February 7, 1984	Reagan announces that U.S. will withdraw its forces from Beirut, Lebanon	Before: 57 percent favored After: 74 percent favored

Source: "Public Service Time for the Legislative Branch," Hearings Before the Communications Subcommittee of the Committee on Commerce, 91st Cong., 2nd sess. pp. 20–21. Data for 1980 and 1984 are from the Gallup poll.

TABLE 10.1

opinion. In recent years the White House has resembled an advertising agency with a single client—the President. Under President Nixon, for example, a special office of communications was created to help embellish the President's image by promoting books and articles about him and his family. This office also organized media events, such as press conferences and interviews, to show off administration accomplishments. Presidential activities are often carefully staged with the media in mind. When doubts were raised about the competence of President Ford, he conducted a special budget briefing arranged to make him look professional. When President Reagan decided to stress economic issues during his first years in office, the administration arranged for its members to appear on numerous Sunday interview shows as well as the *MacNeil-Lehrer Report* and ABC's *Nightline* program.

On many occasions Presidents have used the media deliberately as a way of drumming up support for themselves and their programs. President Nixon once vetoed a bill in front of a television

camera. When President Nixon returned from his highly publicized trip to China in 1972, Air Force One, the presidential airplane, sat on the ground nine hours in Anchorage, Alaska, so that the President's triumphant return to Washington could be broadcast live on prime-time television. President Carter traveled to New York City just to sign an aid bill for the city. During the 1984 presidential campaign, President Reagan made well-publicized visits to nursing homes and schools to show millions of Americans his concern for the elderly and the young (even though in practice he had fought against measures passed by Congress to aid the elderly).

Although the President's impact on public opinion is strong, we should not jump to the conclusion that the White House always calls the shots. The chief executive usually has the greatest influence on issues that are completely new or have little direct bearing on people's everyday lives—for example, the invasion of Cambodia. When citizens hold strong opinions on issues, say the court-ordered busing of children to achieve

"Photo opportunities" capture Presidents in highly visible, dramatic roles. Wearing protective footwear, President Carter tours the site of the accident at the Three Mile Island nuclear plant, 1977. On his 1972 visit to China, President Nixon shakes hands with a shy child.

racial integration, the President's impact is much smaller.

The figures in Table 10.1 raise an interesting and important question about the manipulation of public opinion. On the one hand, we expect the President to inform the public through speeches, press conferences, and direct addresses to the nation. This action can shape—intentionally or unintentionally—public opinion. Not surprisingly, then, Presidents frequently have been accused of using public opinion for their own advantage. During the 1930s, for example, Roosevelt's opponents claimed that the President's "fireside chats" over the radio were not neutral descriptions of public policy but attempts to undermine Republican opposition. During the Vietnam war, President Johnson's well-publicized television pronouncements during prime-time viewing hours were sometimes criticized as attempts to increase his popular standing. Obviously, it is difficult for Presidents to strike a balance between their obligation to keep the public informed and their inclination to use the presidency as a platform from which to control public opinion.

Limits on Presidential Power

Contemporary Presidents can exercise enormous political power, which is likely to increase as the federal government gets larger and world crises necessitate even more rapid executive action. Nevertheless, although Presidents can act with considerable freedom, important limits exist. Three factors are particularly crucial: (1) the power of Congress and of the courts, (2) public opinion, and (3) the mass media.

The Power of Congress

Our constitutional system allows each branch of government some power over the others. As noted earlier, the Senate must vote on whether to confirm or reject many presidential appointments. The vast majority of appointments are confirmed, but on occasion one is rejected. President Nixon's efforts to appoint two Southern conservatives—Clement F. Haynsworth, Jr., and G. Harrold

Carswell—to the Supreme Court were unsuccessful, despite presidential pressure. In most instances the President anticipates potential congressional opposition and nominates someone likely to be approved. Supposedly, when Spiro Agnew resigned as Vice President, Nixon wanted to appoint ex-governor of Texas John Connally to replace Agnew. Nixon was convinced, however, that Connally would never be approved, so he nominated Gerald R. Ford instead.

Congress can also limit presidential power by refusing to consider or pass legislative proposals originating in the executive branch. Although the President has many resources to ensure success with Congress, the White House cannot dictate to Congress. To appreciate the power of Congress, consider Lyndon B. Johnson's legislative success rate in 1965. President Johnson had won a landslide victory in 1964, he had overwhelming Democratic majorities in both houses, and he was a master at congressional bargaining—yet 31 percent of his legislative proposals never became law. In 1981, following his victory, Reagan had a success rate of 82.4 percent with Congress. By 1982, however, in spite of the President's popularity and skillful lobbying of Congress, this had dropped to 72.4 percent. By 1984, his success rate had fallen to 65.8 percent.

The nature of modern Congresses makes a degree of presidential failure almost inevitable. As noted in Chapter 9, members of Congress take local perspectives on many issues. The President, on the other hand, must have a more national outlook. These differing perspectives increasingly collide as election time draws near. For example, just before the 1984 election, President Reagan and Congress were unable to agree on key appropriations bills. Legislators backed numerous local projects to help their campaigns, while the President argued that such programs would increase an already large budget deficit. It is not surprising, then, that Presidents usually have their greatest legislative success at the beginning of a congressional session, when their popularity is high and reelection is not the pressing problem for members of Congress.

The fact that, particularly since the 1970s, power in Congress is spread among a number of members helps prevent domination by the President. (Congressional reform is discussed in Chapter 9.) Presidents and their legislative lobbyists cannot always strike bargains with a few top party leaders or chairpersons of powerful committees. Instead they must often deal with dozens of independent-minded committees and subcommittees, all of which jealously guard their jurisdictions and privileges. Moving a President's program through Congress is therefore time-consuming and costly in terms of commitments and favors. This helps explain why Presidents are unable to achieve major legislative success in more than a few policy areas during their administrations.

Because of the way our electoral system works, Congress is frequently controlled by one political party while the White House is controlled by the other party. This, too, can hinder presidential domination. Since 1960, three of six Presidents—Nixon, Ford, and Reagan—have had to deal with at least one house of Congress dominated by the opposing political party. During his six years in office, for example, President Nixon was confronted with a Democratic leadership in Congress that not only opposed many of his policies on philosophical grounds but also was motivated to make Republican programs and policies appear less attractive to voters in coming elections. President Reagan has had mixed success with a Democratic-controlled House. Beginning in 1987, the Democrats were also the majority party in the Senate.

Congress' power to expose through investigation and its oversight role work as additional major checks on executive power. During the 1960s, when President Johnson gradually escalated U.S. involvement in Vietnam, the Senate Foreign Relations Committee, chaired by J. William Fulbright, provided a visible forum for opponents of presidential actions. As we discussed in Chapter 9, one of the responsibilities of congressional committees is to monitor the activities of executive branch agencies. This oversight role can involve requiring agency heads to testify before Congress, having agencies prepare reports on their activities, or even conducting a congressional investigation. In the early 1980s, Congress used its investigatory and oversight powers to publicize the Reagan administration's policies in Central America.

Commentary: Of Mice and Presidents

The problem of managing the bureaucracy can be illustrated by President Carter's battle against White House mice. When two mice scampered across Carter's office, the General Services Administration (GSA), the federal housekeeping agency, was ordered into action. Its efforts were less than 100 percent effective, however, because one mouse had gotten into a White House wall, died, and filled the Oval Office with a terrible stench. The GSA was again called to the rescue. It now claimed that because it had previously disposed of all mice within the White House, the dead mouse must be an "outside" mouse and thus the responsibility of the Interior Department, which maintains White House grounds. The interagency deadlock was finally broken when Carter called officials of both agencies to his office to smell the dead mouse.

Perhaps the real reason for the stalemate was not a bureaucratic dispute but had to do with getting a better mousetrap. At about the same time that Carter was trying to get rid of White House mice, the federal government had drawn up specifications on how to build a mousetrap. The specs ran to 20,000 words on 700 pages and weighed 3.3 pounds. With the usual delays in setting up government projects, cost overruns, and so on, the lack of quick action was understandable.

The ultimate legislative restraint on presidential power is impeachment. The Constitution states that the House by a majority vote can bring charges of misconduct against the chief executive and that the Senate by a two-thirds vote can convict and thus remove a President from office (Article II, Section IV, lists impeachable offenses as "Treason, Bribery, or other high Crimes and Misdemeanors"). Only one President—Andrew Johnson—has ever been impeached, but the Senate fell one vote short of convicting him. President Nixon would probably have been the second President impeached (and probably the first convicted) if he had not resigned in August 1974 just before the House vote. (The House Judiciary Committee had voted three articles of impeachment against him.)

Finally, there is the *legislative veto*. As we noted in Chapter 9, this is the power of Congress, one house of Congress, or even a congressional committee to block action within the executive branch. For example, the 1974 Congressional Budget and Impoundment Control Act gave the President the power to delay expenditures for programs authorized by Congress. But the law also allowed one house of Congress to veto presidential action. However, the Supreme Court in the 1983 case of *Immigration and Naturalization Service v. Chadha* struck down the legislative veto as a violation of the separation of powers principle. Nevertheless, this power has managed to survive. In some instances laws containing legislative vetoes were redrafted; in other cases informal agreements replaced legal requirements. Overall, then, Presidents must still worry that Congress might invalidate exective branch actions.

Court Limitations on Presidential Power

The courts have been far more willing to give the President free rein than has Congress. Especially when the President acts in the capacity of commander-in-chief or chief of state or makes decisions on how the executive branch should be run, the courts have usually upheld presidential action. The judicial branch has interpreted favorably the President's power to issue executive orders and proclamations. In the case of *Dames and Moore v. Regan* (1981), for example, the Supreme Court held that President Carter had been within his legal power when, as part of the agreement for the release of Americans held hostage in Iran, he canceled all federal court orders taking property in the

Under the chairmanship of Senator Sam Ervin, center at left, the 1973 Watergate hearings investigated illegal activities by Richard Nixon's 1972 reelection committee. The proceedings focused on the mishandling of campaign funds and questioned the men accused of burglarizing the Democratic headquarters, including James McCord, back to camera.

United States away from Iranians. On the whole, the burden of proof has been on those challenging presidential authority, not on the President.

Nevertheless, in some important situations the courts have blocked presidential action. One important case involved President Truman's 1952 seizure of the steel mills in order to head off a strike. Truman argued that because we were at war in Korea he could, as commander-in-chief, act to prevent a national emergency. In its landmark decision, *Youngstown Sheet and Tube Co. v. Sawyer*, the Supreme Court ruled that because there was no official declaration of war and Congress had not specifically legislated such action, the President had overstepped his authority. The Court admitted that Truman might have had a good practical reason for seizing the mills but ruled that protection against tyrannical power overshadowed the needs of the moment.

A more recent and highly dramatic confrontation between the chief executive and the Court occurred when President Nixon refused to release various White House tape recordings and documents in connection with the Watergate affair (the 1972 break-in at the Democratic national party headquarters located in the Watergate building in Washington). When congressional committees, the Watergate special prosecutor, and judges in several Watergate-related cases requested this material as evidence, Nixon refused. The President claimed that records of his confidential conversations were protected by the principle of **executive privilege**—the right of the President and White House aides to keep their discussions from the other branches of government. To allow other branches of government access to this material, Nixon claimed, would effectively destroy the separation of powers and weaken the presidency. Presidents would no longer be able to discuss matters openly and freely with their advisors. He also argued that the principle of executive privilege was well established by the actions of numerous other Presidents. However, the Supreme Court, in *United States v. Nixon* (1974), ruled otherwise and ordered the tapes and documents released.

The release of the tape recordings meant that Nixon would almost surely have to resign. The

Court acknowledged, however, that the principle of executive privilege had a constitutional basis. Expecially when military, diplomatic, or national security issues are involved, complete confidentiality is protected. When no such issue is at stake, presidential records may be requested in criminal cases.

Public Opinion

Although it cannot, like Congress or the courts, directly block a President, public opinion nevertheless limits the President. It is a force that is rarely visible, but it is crucial.

Public Expectations About Presidential Behavior.

One important, though subtle, way in which public opinion limits the President concerns the high expectations most citizens have about "proper" presidential conduct. The President is more than just the chief public official. A President is also the head of state, a living symbol of the United States, and as such is supposedly above day-to-day politics. We expect Presidents to act with fairness, behave in a dignified manner, and uphold traditional moral values. By being on a public pedestal, the President cannot always do the things other, less-exalted politicians can do (or at least, cannot do them publicly). It would be very unpresidential for the chief executive to accept dinner invitations from lobbyists or to appear before business groups for a fee. Likewise, citizens would be outraged if Presidents used their position to reward their home state with a very large share of benefits or to gain financially from secret information or contacts made in office. Such actions are, however, tolerated for members of Congress. In some instances, the President may find it convenient to let the Vice President engage in "unpresidential" activities. During President Nixon's first term, Vice President Agnew played the role of the President's "heavy," as he strongly criticized opponents of Nixon's policies. The same speeches coming directly from the President would have been a cause of great concern, because we do not expect the head of state and the symbol of national unity to label enemies as an "effete corps of impudent snobs" or "unwashed hippies," as Agnew did.

Fear of Electoral Defeat. Public opinion also limits the President much more directly—through the power of voters at the polls. A first-term President must pay attention to opinion poll results as the reelection campaign nears. Controversial or unpopular proposals may thus be offered early, in the hope that voters will eventually forget them, or be held off until after the election, when it won't matter quite so much if the President is less popular. To ignore public opinion until just before election day would be almost unthinkable. That poll takers have now become key presidential advisors indicates the importance of public opinion. Public opinion is also important to second-term Presidents, who do not have to worry about reelection. Certainly no President wants to go down in history as having been the object of widespread public dislike. Presidents also try to avoid sinking too low in opinion polls so as not to bring electoral disaster upon fellow party members in state and congressional races. During President Nixon's last months in office, when his popularity was at its lowest, some of the pressure for resignation came from other Republicans, who argued that his unpopularity would mean the defeat of many Republican candidates.

Public Opinion and Presidential Prestige. Finally high regard in public opinion polls can increase a chief executive's prestige. Because a President's ability to persuade rests partially on personal prestige at a given moment, the importance of this factor cannot be discounted. A highly popular, well-respected President will find it easier to convince others of the value of a program. Government officials find it difficult to resist a leader who enjoys overwhelming public confidence. On the other hand, when public opinion starts to run heavily against a President, White House power may be reduced. Members of Congress can vote against the President's program without fear of electoral defeat. Indeed, opposing the unpopular President may be good politics. Top aides and members of the White House staff might resign rather than be linked to an unpopular chief executive. Bargaining with foreign nations can become more difficult if foreign leaders assume that the President, because of a low standing, cannot deliver on promises or get the public to accept an agreement.

The President and the Media

As the mass media have become a significant force in our society (see Chapter 6), their ability to help reduce presidential power has also grown. Though George Washington bitterly complained that the press misrepresented his policies and damaged his reputation, today journalists have an even greater opportunity to analyze and often criticize Presidents and their policies.

To understand how the media can help limit the President, we must first note that, to a significant extent, the relationship between the media

President Reagan is besieged by reporters to answer questions. Because of the prestige of the office, even a President's casual remarks are closely analyzed and debated.

and the President is one of conflict—a relationship between foes. Presidential complaints of unfairness, bias, and vengefulness in the media, as well as of individual reporters "out to get them," have become commonplace. For a multitude of reasons—desire for electoral gain, need to appear competent, desire for approval of past actions—Presidents want to have their views of reality accepted. In the 1960s, for example, President Johnson tried to convince the public that thanks to his leadership the United States was succeeding in Vietnam. President Reagan in the early 1980s repeatedly asserted that Americans were better off than before. In contrast, the media believe that they must present a more balanced view. Thus, presidential claims of military success are counterpointed by stories of failure; claims of prosperity are followed by stories of greater poverty. The media generally maintain that this role is both proper and essential in a free society.

In addition, individual journalists and media sometimes define themselves as opponents of the President and of White House policies. Some magazines—*National Review, The New Republic, The Washington Monthly*—and some reporters have an acknowledged bias in favor of certain policies and political figures. It is to be expected, for instance, that a Democratic President will be heavily criticized by conservative, Republican-oriented magazines, such as the *National Review.* Furthermore, some reporters from magazines, newspapers, and television stations might try to be objective and stress criticism of the President as a way of advancing their careers. Dan Rather, for example, gained considerable fame as a reporter from his antagonistic relationship with President Nixon.

The result of the unfriendly relationship between the media and the President is a constant state of low-level warfare. One common tactic is for the media to develop sources of information within the executive branch that can be used to contradict presidential assertions. When, in the early 1980s, President Reagan tried to assure the public that mounting budget deficits were not a serious problem, reporters sometimes offered contradictory statements from the President's own advisors. The media have also shown an inclination to expose presidential misconduct, the questionable activities of high executive branch officials, and the mismanagement of programs administered by the President. The whole Watergate scandal emerged as the result of the efforts of two reporters working for the *Washington Post* (the story is told in the book and the movie *All the President's Men*). During the Carter administration, the Washington press helped force one of the President's closest advisors—Bert Lance—from office by focusing attention on Lance's questionable financial practices. While President Reagan called for larger and larger defense budgets, the media caught the public fancy with stories of Defense Department waste—$400 hammers, $7,000 coffee makers, and the like.

It is difficult to say whether this relationship is good and, if desirable in principle, just how far it should go in practice. It can be argued that the powers of the modern presidency are so vast that strong media are a necessary restraint on abuses of office. Contemporary Presidents could easily use submissive mass media to immobilize all opposition to their policies. The public would believe only the President's views, and opposition would be conveniently ignored. On the other hand, Presidents and other officeholders have complained frequently that the media stress problems over accomplishments and shortcomings over strengths. In their attempt to gain attention, boost readership or number of viewers, and advance careers, the media—it is alleged—only undermine public confidence in our institutions and leaders. In the long run, this hostility does more harm than good, media critics assert.

Conclusions

It should be clear from our analysis that presidential power is a highly complex subject. Constitutionally granted powers, such as the commander-in-chief role, describe only a small part of the President's authority. In most instances presidential power has evolved; individual Presidents and the particular situation they faced have shaped their ability to dominate events. The Founders did not anticipate a President as chief legislator; in contemporary politics this role has come to be accepted as both proper and necessary. The President's place in diplomatic affairs and in influencing public opinion has emerged relatively recently, in response to changes that were unimaginable when the Constitution was written. Limits on presidential power are equally complex and ever-changing. Congress has traditionally served to block Presidents, but the capacity and willingness of Congress to resist has varied considerably. Public opinion can hinder a President, yet a skillful chief executive sometimes can use public opinion for political advantage. A similar contradiction exists with the mass media. Newspapers, magazines, television, and the like can inhibit abuses of power and expose incompetence, yet the mass media also allow the President to create an image of the all-knowing leader beyond criticism. Presidential power, then, is fluid and complex in nature, not a set of powers chiseled in stone.

Check Your Understanding

1. What are some of the actions a President can take as commander-in-chief of the military?

2. How can a president influence the kind of legislation Congress passes?

3. How can Congress limit the President's power?

4. How can the Courts limit the President?

HOW ARE PRESIDENTIAL DECISIONS MADE?

The Constitution, in Article II, gives the President "the executive Power" and directs the President to "take Care that the Laws be faithfully executed." Over the years an enormous bureaucracy has been created to assist the President in carrying out the laws (the bureaucracy will be described further in Chapter 11).

This considerable grant of legal power, plus all the resources of the executive branch, can give the impression that Presidents, like monarchs, command an army of assistants who faithfully carry out the President's will. Presidents simply decide on a course of action and then use the vast bureaucracy to do whatever is necessary to carry out the decision.

The image of a President as the all-powerful conductor of a willing orchestra of bureaucrats is not completely accurate. In some instances, of course, especially during a crisis in foreign affairs, the image has a degree of validity. The President might order U.S. military forces deployed in the Middle East. However, in most situations, decisions are handled quite differently. In fact, one expert has described the President as a "nonexecutive chief" rather than a chief executive. Presidents routinely complain that their power to get things done is greatly overestimated. To understand the discrepancy between the image of a powerful executive and the more modest reality, let us examine four aspects of presidential decision making: (1) the size and complexity of the executive branch, (2) the transmission of information and advice to the President, (3) the way choices are made; and (4) problems of implementing these choices.

Size and Complexity of the Executive Branch

The executive branch has some 2.7 million civilian employees organized into thirteen Cabinet-level departments and a large number of executive agencies. In principle, all the Cabinet secretaries and undersecretaries, bureau chiefs, and so on are accountable to the President and are responsible for carrying out White House programs. However, no modern President has been completely able to control the bureaucracy. Rather than increase presidential power, executive branch agencies and departments have often become a power unto themselves. In numerous instances, a "decision by the executive branch" is not a decision by the

President. In fact, the President might even oppose it.

One reason is that no President, even if assisted by a large staff, can possibly be aware of all the important decisions made each day in all the departments. No President has the time, energy, and knowledge to monitor hundreds of important decisions. On occasion, Presidents have tried to increase their personal involvement in agency decision making (for example, John Kennedy learned speed-reading, Carter worked extra-long hours). Almost always, however, the effort fails and Presidents emphasize setting overall policy objectives, not direct involvement. Even the strategy of establishing general goals is not always successful in ensuring that presidential objectives will be followed.

Presidential authority is also limited by policy differences between the President and both appointed and career officials. Although Presidents have considerable power over executive branch appointments, it is not easy to find capable aides who completely share a President's views. Even when they do, their responsibilities and position can encourage disagreement over just how a goal should be pursued. A President determined to reduce health-care expenditures, for example, might have to deal with a Secretary of Health and Human Services and other staff committed to maintaining the agency's existing programs. These people might argue that such reductions cannot be legally justified and would take years to bring about. Skilled bureaucrats have many tools to resist presidential control. They can mobilize interest-group pressure, generate pro-agency publicity, create alliances with members of Congress, find ways to delay, and so on.

A third factor limiting the White House is that many Presidents and their top aides begin their terms unfamiliar with the way Washington agencies work and the complexities of government programs. As we noted near the beginning of the chapter, becoming President requires a demonstration of campaign skills, not of administrative competence, and the electoral system based on primaries allows political newcomers to become President. Presidents cannot effectively use the machinery of government when they are still learning which agency does what or how to bring about change in policy. A frequent criticism of the Carter presidency was that Carter and his staff were unschooled in the complexities of Washington politics and thus could not exert much leadership. Decisions often were made by bureaucrats, not by the President.

Transmission of Information and Advice to the President

The President does not make policy by sitting at a desk and thinking about such general issues as reforming Social Security or ending the arms race. Rather, large problems are broken down into many smaller choices regarding specific objectives, how and when these objectives might be achieved, and how much effort should be allocated to the goals. In dealing with Social Security, for example, a President may spend a great deal of time deciding on whether to ask Congress to include federal employees in the system, how to accomplish this task, what its political costs would be, and how potential opposition will be handled.

Because of the sheer number of decisions and time pressures, the President is dependent on how choices and recommendations are presented by aides, Cabinet members, and so on. Rarely is the President able to gain extensive first-hand knowledge of a situation. By the time a problem reaches the President, it has passed through several hands, and important information and interpretations have been added or subtracted. This filtering process is crucial—faulty information and unrealistic evaluations of situations can prevent even competent Presidents from making wise decisions.

The President's need for adequate information and advice has resulted in the creation of several special agencies and an increase in the number of advisors. The emergence of an "institutional presidency" has been relatively recent. Lincoln, for example, had a staff of only four, and Grover Cleveland answered the White House telephone himself. In 1939, President Franklin Roosevelt created the Executive Office of the President

(EOP) to help him. The EOP was intended to be relatively small, but with time, both the number of advisory bodies within the EOP and the staff have grown in size. Compared to other parts of the federal bureaucracy, the President exercises considerable judgment in the size and structure of the Executive Office of the President. As a result, its make-up has undergone change with each new President. For example, under Reagan the Domestic Policy Staff was reorganized into the Office of Policy Development, and the Council on Wage and Price Stability was eliminated altogether. Overall staff size has also been reduced from the levels in the Carter administration.

Although the precise make-up of the EOP changes over time, several of its elements are durable and often provide the President with important advice (Figure 10.1 depicts the full EOP). The

White House office might be described as the President's most personal bureaucracy. It usually includes the President's closest advisors, top speechwriters, the press secretary, as well as liaisons with the Cabinet, Congress, state and local officials and important groups, and a host of experts on various matters who may act as general troubleshooters. The Office of Management and Budget (OMB) is perhaps the most important bureaucracy within the EOP. The OMB helps the President draw up the national budget, coordinates the President's overall legislative program, and reviews both the structure and administration of the executive branch to ensure that the President's programs are producing the intended results. The OMB, especially when headed by a capable person trusted by the President, can use its power over the budget to exercise considerable

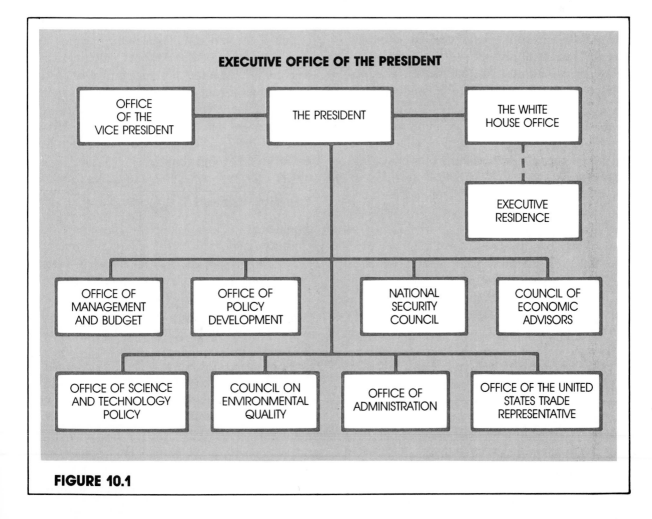

FIGURE 10.1

influence (perhaps for this reason the head of the OMB, unlike other EOP officials, must be confirmed by the Senate).

The roles played by other elements in the EOP have varied, depending on conditions and the personalities of the President and relationships among top aides. For example, the National Security Council (NSC) was created in 1947 to provide advice and policy coordination on national security. It was intended to be a strong body, and both Truman and Eisenhower relied on it extensively. Under subsequent Presidents, the NSC staff, more than NSC appointees, played a vital role in the formation of the president's national security policy. The role intended for the NSC was taken over by the president's advisor for national security. A similar situation has occurred with the Council of Economic Advisors (CEA). Some Presidents have sought its advice, whereas others have largely ignored it. During 1983–84 the CEA was often in the news because of the conflicts between its economic assessments and those of the President.

It is important to realize that the official lines of authority and roles within the EOP might not correspond to what actually occurs on a day-to-day basis. In particular, modern Presidents have relied more heavily on some advisors regardless of their official positions or even whether they held a position in government. For example, during the Nixon years H. R. Haldeman, White House chief of staff, exercised considerable power over who saw the President, while directly involving himself in policy areas formally handled by Cabinet secretaries. Haldeman actually made many presidential decisions. President Johnson regularly consulted with Abe Fortas when Fortas was a justice on the Supreme Court. President Carter often sought the advice of an Atlanta attorney not in government service at all.

The power of these advisors derives from several sources. Some have long personal ties to the President. Hamilton Jordan, an influential Carter advisor, for example, had been with Carter from the very beginning of the President's political career. Many advisors spend a great deal of time with the President, even when the President goes on vacation. The spouses of Presidents often can play an important political role—they can raise issues not on the official agenda and talk frankly about controversial topics. Other top officials, though, might receive only an hour or two per month in a regularly scheduled, tightly structured audience. Finally, Presidents frequently delegate considerable authority to these advisors regarding who and what should receive presidential attention. Some, like Richard Nixon, were uncomfortable with visitors; others, like Ronald Reagan, have a distaste for complex, detailed material. On many occasions, a presidential advisor actually makes the key decisions simply by determining that the President should not be bothered with a particular problem.

Because Presidents have considerable leeway in choosing top personnel in the Executive Office of the President, the information and advice they receive usually reflect their own views. No doubt the staff provides valuable assistance as well. Nevertheless, the very complexity of these support services plus the huge flow of information can overwhelm a President. A President must often deal with numerous advisors seeking attention, each with a different version of political reality. The actual choice can be to decide which advisors should be trusted, because the details of each decision may be overwhelming.

The Way Choices Are Made

Presidents are responsible for decisions ranging from the inconsequential to the most fundamental. There is no *one* way in which Presidents choose one policy over the other. Presidential decision making depends considerably on what is being decided, on the conditions surrounding the decisions, and on the particular style and personality of each President.

Some decisions are routine choices made on the basis of considerable information and advice. This is especially true when law or custom requires some action at some fixed time. A President's budget decisions are of this type. The timing of the submission of the budget and much of its content and organization are set by law. Each executive department has a deadline in making

At political and diplomatic functions, presidential spouses seek to generate support. Nancy Reagan greets Republicans, top left. Jimmy and Rosalynn Carter walk to his inauguration, 1977. Betty Ford, right, below, meets the wife of the United Nations Chief of Protocol.

requests to the OMB; these, in turn, are presented to the President with recommendations. The President must choose among a limited range of alternatives; because the process occurs each year, many problems and issues can be anticipated. Moreover, it is the President, not some assistant, who takes public responsibility for these decisions.

In addition, the President often faces choices in which only the most limited action can be taken. A policy that has existed for decades and is supported by powerful groups and large government bureaucracies can rarely be changed by a single presidential act. Political reality forces the President to focus on relatively small issues rather than raise broader questions. For example, when Ronald Reagan became President, one of his prime goals was to overhaul Social Security, a group of aid programs that had become very expensive. Because of strong support for these programs among the elderly, their allies in Congress, and a large government bureaucracy opposed to any changes, the President was forced to deal only with such issues as the timing of automatic cost-of-living increases; he would not tamper with the basic structure and objectives of the program. There was no way the President could make a choice to turn over the retirement program to private industry.

A very different decision-making process occurs during a crisis, especially one in international relations. Here the unique character and suddenness of events can make it difficult for a President to choose among carefully defined alternatives, each accompanied by research. The nonroutine nature of such decisions frequently means that the President will seek advice from an ad hoc group of advisors in addition to those with responsibilities in that area. For example, during the 1962 Cuban missile crisis, when the United States confronted the Soviet Union over the placement of missiles in Cuba, President Kennedy consulted a group of advisors that included several people with no background in foreign policy—the Attorney General (his brother), the Secretary of the Treasury, his appointments secretary, and a close legal advisor. Often, a decision must be made within a few days, and uncertainty can exist about the consequences

of each action. The President is much more likely to have a free hand, because the choices are not limited by established programs and well-defined interest groups. Compare, for example, the choices available to a President in responding to a Middle East crisis and in dealing with the Social Security laws. And unless the crisis directly threatens U.S. national security, a President even might choose to do very little. When the American embassy in Iran was seized in 1979, President Carter took a restrained position, despite strong public demands for action.

Decision making is greatly influenced by the personal styles of those who occupy the White House. Franklin D. Roosevelt, for example, would look at each choice from many angles, consider all possible advantages and disadvantages, and then think about all the information in an "unconscious calculation." Because decisions were rarely clear-cut, Roosevelt often delayed in the hope that pressing problems would disappear. On relatively minor issues, however, he frequently made well-defined, dramatic decisions.

President Kennedy's style can be described as the **multiple advocacy** model of decision making. He made choices only after extensive consultation with people of different backgrounds, positions, and points of view. Rather than have an aide or committee reduce the choice to a few specific alternatives, Kennedy would involve several people in the process and would define the alternatives. This approach to making decisions, however, resulted in lengthy delays while the President tried to sort out a vast quantity of conflicting views. Although he frequently spoke of decisive action, in fact his decisions reflected a cautious attempt to reconcile differing perspectives.

The President's personality and values also help determine how decisions are made. President Carter, for example, greatly valued hard work, discipline, morality, and excellence. According to one of his former speechwriters, the President stressed stability and harmony over originality. Each person had an assigned task and was held responsible for staying within the bounds of this job. This view of the world, plus Carter's engineering background, led the President to approach decisions as

In times of crisis, Presidents seek from their staff both advice and support. Here, President John Kennedy shares a tense moment with his brother Robert, the Attorney General, during the Cuban missile crisis, 1962.

technical problems to be overcome by hard work and careful analysis. In many instances, the result was an emphasis on details rather than on overall policy development. Moreover, unlike Kennedy and Roosevelt, Carter preferred to burden himself with long, complex reports and memoranda instead of consulting with others.

The Reagan approach seems to be very different from the Carter style. As President, Reagan has delegated considerable decision-making authority to aides and top administrators, who share his overall philosophy on a strong defense and cuts in social programs. And as we mentioned before, Reagan has shown a distaste for details. Instead, he views issues, such as arms control, taxes, federalism, the environment, and energy, at a general level and in terms of such principles as the dangers of world communism, the evil of government intervention in people's lives, and the virtues of traditional morality. Whereas President Carter

would personally evaluate detailed evidence to make the best choice, President Reagan sees his role as leading a comprehensive redirection of government toward a different set of political values.

Implementation of the Choices

Once a President has made a choice, it must be implemented. Some decisions are self-implementing, including such actions as vetoing legislation, nominating judges and executive branch officials, calling meetings, or submitting legally required reports and messages. There is little question that the President's decision will be faithfully carried out.

However, in many situations much more is required. Having made a decision, a President must follow it up to ensure that the necessary work is being done. If it is not, a President might have to increase pressure, seek alternatives, or assign the task to someone else. A President even might have to judge whether the decision *can* be fully implemented. It is one thing for the President to decide, say, that the Defense Department ought to rely more on competitive bidding in assigning contracts; it is quite another to ensure that this happens. As Harry Truman put it in describing what would occur when Eisenhower took office: "He will sit here and he'll say, 'Do this! Do this!' *and nothing will happen.* Poor Ike—it won't be a bit like the Army! He'll find it very frustrating."

Problems of implementing decisions result from several causes. As we have seen, people in the departments and bureaus responsible for carrying out an order might have their own goals, and they possess a number of tools to block the President's wishes. In response to the President's request, a Defense Department official might say that a committee will soon be created to look into the legal aspects of a change in procurement procedures. This can take months or even a year. Similar problems exist in getting aides and assis-

tants to follow presidential instructions. An assistant who opposes a particular order might ignore it for a while, then convey it to subordinates as a low-priority item, and if the President asks about it, write a vague memo showing "some progress" but "many unsolved problems."

The sheer number of people and agencies involved even in many fairly simple decisions also results in problems. The national government is not organized as a collection of departments, each of which has complete control over a policy area. Rather, an issue might have to be worked on at all three levels of government, in many agencies and offices. Each of these has its own perspective about what should be done. When President Reagan called for the reshaping of federalism by giving control to the states over certain nationally administered programs, the full implementation of the program required action from at least two Cabinet departments—Treasury and Health and Human Services—dozens of agencies within these departments (for example, the Health Care Financing Administration and the Social Security Adminis-

At the height of the cold war, in the 1950s, President Eisenhower, center, and his aides walk to the White House air raid shelter. The event may have been an effort to increase support for the nation's atomic weapons policy.

tration), aides within the EOP, a number of congressional committees and subcommittees, as well as fifty governors and the relevant agencies in each state.

A Perspective on Presidential Decision Making

The President is not, of course, completely defenseless against those who resist implementing White House decisions. One tactic occasionally used is to assign the same task to more than one person or agency. Though sometimes effective, this tactic can create staff conflicts and the appearance of disorganization, because responsibilities are not well defined. Another solution is to fill key positions with trusted aides whose personal loyalty ensures that decisions will be carried out. Presidents do this in varying degrees, but it can result in the appointment of people ill suited to their positions and all too willing to do the President's bidding out of a sense of loyalty. A President is more likely to be effective when precise orders are given and it is made clear that the policy is the President's and not that of some aide. Presidents can also use their position to generate publicity about a decision, in the hope that public attention will discourage resistance. Of course, bureaucrats can sometimes devise ways to mislead the media and the public about the President's program.

In general, the President rarely can completely dominate the executive branch. As one-time Eisenhower aide Emmet J. Hughes put it: "The sheer size and intricacy of government conspire to taunt and to thwart all brisk pretentions to set sensationally new directions. The vast machinery of national leadership—the tens of thousands of levers and switches and gears—simply do not respond to the impatient jab of a finger or the angry pounding of a fist." Moreover, even when the President is acting on the basis of clear legal authority, presidential power, according to one expert, is the power to persuade. The President has many rewards and punishments to use in persuading others, but only rarely can a President govern by simply commanding things to be done.

Conclusions

Our analysis makes it clear that there is no simple way to describe presidential decision making. Much depends on the particular President and on the type of decision to be made. Some Presidents thrive on administrative detail, have clearly organized chains of command, and act decisively. Others limit themselves to providing overall direction and delegating day-to-day matters to trusted assistants. Some decisions—for example, submitting the annual budget—follow predictable, well-defined patterns. In this case the President operates under fairly clear guidelines regarding the possible choices and how to act. In crisis situations there are fewer guidelines. Presidents can face a wide range of choices and uncertain outcomes. Whoever is in the White House and whatever the decision, however, the President can rarely command. Chief executives must use persuasion and skill to accomplish their objectives, and the opportunities for rapid, systematic changes are limited.

Check Your Understanding

1. What are some of the important agencies assigned to provide information to the President? How can the flow of information from these agencies affect the choices made?

2. Describe some of the different styles of decision making in the White House.

3. What are some of the problems faced by Presidents in getting their decisions implemented?

SHOULD THE PRESIDENCY BE REFORMED?

When the Constitution was drafted, there was considerable disagreement about the length of the President's term, the selection process, and the powers of the office. The final version of Article II represented a collection of compromises. Moreover, the evaluation of the presidency did not stop with the ratification of the Constitution. Four constitutional amendments—the Twelfth, the Twentieth, the Twenty-second, and the Twenty-fifth—concern the presidency. Congress has also passed several important laws dealing with presidential power.

There have been many proposed reforms of the presidency. Let us briefly consider four types of reforms that are discussed most frequently: (1) changing the selection process; (2) modifying the President's term of office, (3) involving Congress in the executive branch, and (4) revitalizing Cabinet government.

Changing the Selection Process

The selection process has been one of the most frequently changed aspects of the presidency. Originally, the President was selected by presidential electors chosen by state legislators. The change to popular election of presidential electors occurred largely during the first third of the nineteenth century. The process by which parties have nominated presidential candidates has also changed. For much of American history, state and local party leaders met once every four years at a nominating convention. Citizens had little say over who ran for President. There were primaries, but most delegates were not selected in the primaries. Overall, the system was dominated by party professionals. In the late 1960s and early 1970s, the nominating process was "opened up" through greater reliance on *binding primaries*—that is, primaries in which delegates are chosen and are bound, or obligated, to support the candidate they are committed to. New delegate selection rules encouraged newcomers to participate in the nominating process. To become President one had to wage a vigorous campaign for delegates in numerous states. As we observed near the beginning of the chapter, these reforms have allowed "outsiders" with limited political experience and party support—such as Jimmy Carter—to gain the nomination.

For some people, the pendulum has swung too far in the direction of openness. Opponents of the current system argue that too much emphasis is put on a long and demanding campaign. The prospect of beginning a campaign years before the general election and having to win a dozen or more races can easily discourage capable people. More important, voters in primaries are not typical of the party's rank and file. Therefore, the nominee will likely be more representative of one wing, or special viewpoint, of a party than of the average party member. Moreover, critics of the present system say, voters are incapable of deciding which of six or seven potential nominees (many of whom are unknowns) is best suited to the presidency. Under such conditions, having a familiar name can make a candidate a winner. Faced with a group of unknowns and one person named Kennedy, many votes would gravitate to the Kennedy. Or the political composition of the group of candidates can be crucial. One conservative in a field of six liberals will probably win an inflated share of the vote (or vice versa). In addition, the mass media, through their capacity to provide publicity and interpret events, are given far too much power. We observed in Chapter 6 that the mass media were able to make Edmund Muskie the "loser" in the 1972 New Hampshire Democratic primary even though he had received the most votes. Finally, the present scheduling of primaries can play havoc with a campaign. Currently, failure to do well in early primaries can destroy a candidate, even if the number of votes involved is fairly small. In 1980, for example, several prominent Republicans dropped out early because of poor showings. Or a candidate who comes on strong at the end might not be able to overcome a late start.

To deal with these problems, a set of reforms have been advocated. These include greatly restricting the campaign for the party nomination, grouping primaries rather than having a long series of them, giving convention delegates more freedom to choose candidates, and having a larger number of experienced, professional political leaders at the nominating convention. In other words, the campaign for the nomination would begin only a few months before the convention,

A campaign worker seeks support for Walter Mondale in the presidential primary, New Hampshire, 1984.

there would be fewer primaries (and all would be held in the space of two or three months), and state and national officials would automatically be given votes at the convention. The basic premise underlying these reforms is that the Democratic and Republican parties are more likely to nominate capable leaders when professional politicians, rather than primary voters or the mass media, have the strongest say. Such politicians are better able to judge a candidate's administrative skill, personal integrity, and ability to reach compromises under difficult conditions. Complete unknowns would have a much harder time winning the nomination. Nominees, moreover, would draw their support from a broader base. Such a practice, in turn, would enable the President to govern more effectively, supporters of this type of reform say.

Changing the President's Term

A President is limited to two four-year terms (or a total of ten years if he or she assumes the presidency as Vice President). A number of people, including Presidents Eisenhower, Johnson, Nixon, and Carter, have suggested a single six-year term. Advocates of this change believe that lengthening the term of office and eliminating the possibility of reelection would ensure that the President could better pursue the overall national interest. Rather than judge actions in terms of their electoral consequences, Presidents could evaluate policies on their objective merits. If a tax increase were necessary, it would be proposed even if it were unpopular. An incumbent President would no longer have to devote valuable time to planning election strategy and campaigning. Instead of flying around generating news stories and drumming up support, a chief executive could tackle complex policy issues and problems of implementation.

Reformers also advocate a six-year term on the grounds that it provides sufficient time for the President to learn a highly complex job. Too often, it is claimed, a President learns the intricacies of the office only near the end of the term, especially if the chief executive has had limited political experience. Even more important, the present system encourages Presidents to think largely of short-range results. If their terms were longer, they would have more time to evaluate the impact of their policies. A President elected in November 1988 will assume office in January 1989; proposals made in the first year of office generally will not take effect until after October 1989. The consequences of some of these programs may not be realized until 1990 or later. Presidents might choose relatively easy short-term solutions that in fact could lead to other problems later on. The public gets only the appearance of vigorous leadership, not effective leadership for the long haul.

Involving Congress in the Executive Branch

A fundamental constitutional principle is the separation of powers—the legislative, executive, and judicial functions of government are performed by different officials. As originally intended, this principle, along with the system of checks and balances, has produced regular conflicts between Congress and the President. In many situations the result has been stalemate or a policy of too little, too late.

Built-in conflict, some say, might have been desirable in the eighteenth and nineteenth centuries, but it is unacceptable in a highly complex society. Today, because government must often act quickly, coordination, not conflict, should be encouraged. To remedy this problem, it is proposed that a limited number of congressional leaders be made part of the Cabinet and that the new Cabinet be more deeply involved in presidential decision making. Such a change would supposedly have two advantages. First, since members of Congress are not dependent on the President for their position or power, they would provide a check on potential presidential wrongdoing. They

could provide the type of honest, independent advice that presidential aides are unwilling or unable to offer. Second, including congressional leaders in decisions would encourage a more harmonious and productive congressional–presidential relationship. Cooperation and shared responsibility would replace antagonism and deadlock.

Revitalizing Cabinet Government

This reform involves two related changes. The first would be a reduction in the number and influence of what has been called the presidential establishment—the chief executive's personal aides and advisory groups that are part of the Executive Office of the President. It has been claimed that this establishment has become "a powerful inner sanctum of government isolated from the traditional constitutional checks and balances." Personal aides are not elected, and many of them do not have to be confirmed by the Senate; yet they

Ronald Reagan presides at a Cabinet meeting during his first term. At such sessions, White House policy is mapped out and policy differences smoothed over.

exercise enormous power. During the Reagan presidency, for example, aides like Michael K. Deaver, deputy chief of staff and assistant to the President, played a critical role in shaping the President's agenda and choices.

Not only is this "inner sanctum" largely unaccountable, but also its members usually approach problems from a short-term perspective that emphasizes political gain over long-range, systematic planning. In 1983, for example, President Reagan had to decide whether to sign or veto a bill that would pay farmers not to produce milk. Despite the high cost of this legislation, mounting budget deficits, and the fact that it contradicted the President's free-market philosophy, he signed it. A major reason was the strong advocacy of Edwin Meese, then counselor to the President and later Attorney General. Meese was acting on behalf of Senator Jesse Helms of North Carolina, who feared that a veto would hurt his forthcoming reelection chances (the bill also contained provisions for tobacco growers). In many instances the presidential staff takes over the actual operations of domestic and foreign policy making from Cabinet secretaries.

To reduce the role of this behind-the-scenes presidential establishment, three remedies have been suggested. First, the size of the Executive Office should be reduced. Second, Congress should more closely monitor the appointments and powers of the White House establishment. Most important, the role of the Cabinet in decision making should be strengthened. A greater Cabinet role would narrow the gap between making a decision and administering it. As things now stand, the President's aides can help decide agricultural policy but have no responsibility for making the policy work. The quality of advice given to the President should also improve, since Cabinet officials tend to be experienced professionals familiar with the issue in their departments. Finally, greater Cabinet involvement would help clarify who is supposed to make which decision. Currently, it is unclear who is involved in which policy areas. With a stronger Cabinet role, a Secretary of Agriculture could not claim that he or she had nothing to do with a disastrous farm policy that had been made by a White House aide. Both Congress and the public would be well served by such clearer responsibility.

Evaluating Reforms of the Presidency

Although each of the proposals has its merits, they are not without faults either. Consider the case for returning to the older system of selecting Presidents. Although there is much to be said for giving them a greater say in nominating Presidents, the judgment of political professionals can be wrong. For example, in 1920, professionals selected Warren G. Harding—one of the most corrupt Presidents. Similar problems occur with regard to a single, six-year term. Six years gives the President ample time to learn the job, but there is no guarantee that the President will use the time well. Again, the reform offers only the possibility, not the certainty, of improvement. Breaking down the wall between Congress and the President by including members of Congress in the Cabinet may merely shift the location of conflict and deadlock, not resolve it. Disputes might then occur within the Cabinet rather than between the President and Congress. Finally, Cabinet government sounds fine in principle, but several modern Presidents who experimented with it early in their terms eventually dropped it as unworkable. Most Presidents seem to be more comfortable with a few close advisors than with a dozen or more Cabinet officials, who must often divide their loyalty between the President and their department.

The important lesson to be drawn from the experience of reforming the presidency is that each remedy has its own problems. There is no one all-purpose "cure" for the headaches of the presidency. In the 1930s the cure for a too-heavy burden on the President was to create various advisory boards and positions to help the President make more informed decisions. Today, at least for some people, having too many advisors is itself "the problem." The presidential bureaucracy, they argue, overwhelms and isolates the chief executive. In short, the real choice is which problems should be tolerated. Improvements undoubtedly can be made, but many problems defy solution, and some remedies merely exchange one set of difficulties for another.

Check Your Understanding

1. What are some of the proposed changes in the presidential selection process?

2. Why do some people want to have greater congressional involvement in the executive branch?

3. What are the arguments in favor of greater Cabinet government?

THE POLITICS OF PRESIDENTIAL POWER

Over the years a running debate has gone on over presidential power. As we mentioned earlier, there is no clear agreement on which powers the chief executive actually has. Moreover, changing world conditions have altered public expectations about how Presidents should act. Disputes have surfaced regularly over whether or not the President is exercising too much or too little power. When Franklin Roosevelt in the 1930s took vigorous actions, such as creating many agencies, proposing hundreds of bills, and making frequent use of executive orders in dealing with the Great Depression, many people claimed that the presidency was showing signs of becoming a monarchy. They feared that a forceful president, because of the position and the control over a vast bureaucracy, could easily dominate Congress. A few years later, under the less-active Dwight D. Eisenhower, experts debated ways to make Presidents more effective and stronger national leaders. Members of Congress even complained about the lack of White House leadership in proposing legislation. President Nixon's actions, such as the secret bombings of Cambodia and the illegal break-ins, again reawakened interest in the questions of presidential power. Now many questioned whether constitutional checks on the presidency were adequate.

Obviously, there is no simple answer to the question of whether the President has too much power. Nor is it likely that people will ever be able to agree on such a complex issue. Nevertheless, we can consider some of the basic reasoning underlying the two different points of view. Essentially, people disagreeing on whether the presidency should be made stronger or weaker usually differ in what political risks they think are worth taking and what the likely benefits of making changes would be. Let us first examine the case for greater limits on executive power.

People who are fearful of executive power usually argue that the possible abuses of power are not worth the supposed benefits of having strong chief executives. Such critics typically make the following points:

1. Our constitutional system is not designed to have an all-powerful leader responsible for dealing with every national problem. The Founders had in mind a chief executive who was to be strong only in some areas (for example, commanding the military). To allow Presidents greater and greater power in every policy area is to undermine a form of government whose checks and balances and separation of powers have been successful in preventing tyranny.

2. Even if we did grant them more powers, why should the actions of Presidents be more intelligent or more effective than, say, responses made by Congress or by state governments? Presidents, like everyone else, can make mistakes. There is no guarantee that providing Presidents with more staff and expert advisory bodies will solve the problem. Moreover, why put such a great political burden on a single person?

3. Even if the President did come up with better programs to solve national ills, there still is no guarantee that the programs would be implemented effectively. Bureaucratic foul-ups, staff incompetence, and the like are probably incurable. Legal grants of more power would not solve these headaches.

4. Therefore, strengthening the presidency would only increase the risk of wrongdoing in office while not improving the national welfare. A more powerful President could get away with more misconduct, such as illegal wiretapping of political opponents or irresponsible foreign adventures, and we would be no closer to solving such enduring problems as deficits, world conflicts, energy shortages, racial tensions, and pollution. Greater concentration of power is not an automatic solution to anything, and it almost always brings grave risks.

Other people see a stronger President as a necessary response to the numerous and growing problems of the contemporary world. In answer to the above arguments, they assert:

1. The likelihood that a stronger, more vigorous President would try to run the country by personal whim is exaggerated. Certainly an occasional abuse of power will occur—as in the past—but given our political tradition, free elections, the power of the other branches of government, and the existence of a free press, widespread and persistent patterns of wrongdoing are unlikely. A would-be dictator could be stopped easily. The real lesson of Watergate, for instance, is *not* that Presidents can overstep their limits but rather that such abuses will be uncovered and corrected.

2. The main issue underlying whether presidential power should be expanded or reduced concerns policies, not the corrupting influences of greater power. Specifically, vigorous uses of presidential power traditionally (though not exclusively, as the Reagan administrations have shown) have been associated with promoting *liberal* causes. For example, Franklin D. Roosevelt used his power on behalf of programs like Social Security, the minimum wage, and pro-union legislation. President Lyndon Johnson took full advantage of presidential authority to push through civil rights and antipoverty programs. This tendency is understandable, because the President, more than any other political official, must represent all the people, not just well-organized interests.

3. To limit the President further is to limit the one leader most capable of helping ordinary citizens. The overwhelming majority of Americans cannot directly influence congressional committees, hire public relations experts, or employ expensive lawyers to argue their cases. The President, more than anyone else, can be the defender of underrepresented groups, such as young people, the poor, and minorities.

4. The real choice, therefore, is not between possible excesses of power and no excesses of power, but between a government responsive to the needs of ordinary citizens and a government unable to deal with social and economic unjustice. Conservatives fear a stronger executive because of the liberal policies that would be enacted. The fear of tyrannical power is merely a convenient and respectable way of opposing these policies.

Both views on presidential power have considerable merit. It is important to understand, however, that a person's stand at a given moment can depend on particular political circumstances. For example, in the 1950s the conservative Senator Joseph McCarthy was vigorously investigating allegations of Communist subversion in the executive branch. To protect the executive branch from this intrusion, President Eisenhower invoked the doctrine of executive privilege and instructed Defense Department officials not to testify before a congressional committee. Liberals applauded this show of presidential strength. Twenty years later, liberals were angered when President Nixon invoked executive privilege as part of his defense against Congress. Similarly, liberals held President Kennedy in high esteem for ignoring congressional pleas for a military invasion during the Cuban missile crisis of 1962. During the war in Vietnam, liberals often condemned the President's independence from a Congress that was more supportive of a withdrawal of American troops. A strong, conservative President, obviously, is viewed differently from a strong, liberal President.

One's own position in this debate should probably depend on one's satisfaction with the current balance of political power. If one is doing well under the existing system, why take a chance by giving more power to the chief executive? Such power could be used to upset present policies. The worry over abuses of power is, of course, less relevant to, say, poor people who look to the government to solve their economic problems. Checks and balances and other controls against strong presidential action only keep a not very satisfying system going.

CHAPTER SUMMARY

How are Presidents elected? To become President, a person must meet certain constitutional requirements and satisfy public expectations regarding background and behavior. The greatest obstacle to the White House is electoral. A would-be President must achieve a degree of political visibility and gain either the Democratic or the Republican party nomination. The general campaign is a long ordeal that involves building an organization, creating a strategy, and putting together a winning coalition of voters.

How much power does the President have? The important constitutionally prescribed power of commander-in-chief has been used to enforce the law at home and to commit U.S. troops overseas. The President is also the diplomatic leader of the United States. Because of the veto power, the submitting of bills, budgetary power, and leeway allowed in enforcement, the President is also a legislative leader. Finally, the chief executive can mold public opinion. The power of the other two branches, public expectations, and the mass media can limit presidential influence.

How are presidential decisions made? Despite their great legal authority and a large bureaucracy responsible to them, Presidents cannot always have their way. The bureaucracy is not always controllable, and the President must depend on others for information. How final choices are made varies considerably, depending on the type of decision and on the President's personality. Implementing the choice can depend on the ability of the President to persuade others.

Should the presidency be reformed? One commonly suggested reform is to return to the previous method of selecting Presidents, which gave a greater role to professional politicians. A single,

six-year term is a second proposed reform. To reduce interbranch conflict, some people would include congressional leaders in the Cabinet. Finally, it has been suggested that the "presidential establishment" be reduced and the Cabinet strengthened. All four reforms have their advantages and disadvantages.

IMPORTANT TERMS

Explain the following terms.
gunboat diplomacy
diplomatic recognition
executive agreement
pocket veto
executive privilege

THINKING CRITICALLY

1. Many other democracies—Israel, Great Britain, and India, for example—have had women chief executives. Why do you think the United States has not had a woman President?

2. Would it be possible to pass a constitutional amendment limiting the length of the presidential campaign without restricting political freedom? Discuss your answer.

3. Because of the importance of the vice presidency as a stepping stone to the presidency, should there be a separate primary election system for this position? Why or why not?

4. The President's military power has become very important in recent years. The Constitution does not specifically define the military power of the President. Do we need more precise constitutional language on the military

role of the commander-in-chief? Why or why not? What limits, if any, should be placed on this role? Discuss your answer.

5. Presidents have considerable access to the mass media. What are the advantages and disadvantages of this access? Should there be a law regulating this access? For example, should the President be limited in the use of television to help persuade public opinion? Should the networks be required to give Congress equal time on television? Discuss your answer.

6. Presidents often surround themselves with advisors who have views similar to their own. Should chief executives make a greater effort to include staff members who might hold differing views? Why or why not?

7. The President spends a good deal of time on ceremonial duties—for example, awarding medals. Do you think this is an efficient use of the President's time? What purpose does it serve? Should our government have a separate head of state who could handle these ceremonial tasks? Why or why not?

EXTENDING YOUR UNDERSTANDING

1. Draw up a list of what you believe are the traits of an ideal President. Devise a system—consistent with democracy—that will encourage the selection of such people. How would your system differ from the present system?

2. Listen to the President's speech to the nation (or read the text of the speech in a newspaper). Summarize the major points the President has made. List the facts the President has used to support these points. What opinions are presented? Does the speech seem persuasive to you? Write a report to explain your views.

3. Many of the decision-making problems faced by the President are probably common to many administrators. Ask a local official, such as the mayor or school superintendent, to describe the types of problems he or she faces in making decisions. How do these problems compare with the problems you face when making a decision? How does the local official solve the problems? Present your findings to the class.

4. Research the roles of the Prime Minister and Parliament in Great Britain. Compare the relationship of the President and Congress with that of the Prime Minister and Parliament. How do the two systems of government differ? Prepare a chart to illustrate your findings.

MAKING DECISIONS

Select a problem of importance in your school or community. Assume that the chief executive—mayor, school board president, or other leader—must choose between alternative solutions to the problem. As an advisor, what solution would you recommend? Prepare a statement of your proposed solution, including reasons why this solution is the best.

Chapter 11
The Federal Bureaucracy

$\mathbf{F}$ew political words have so negative a connotation as "bureaucracy." Whereas reformers once pointed to pressure groups as the source of political evil, today the federal bureaucracy is the villain. Almost every politician—Democratic or Republican, conservative or liberal—promises to do something about the bureaucracy. The federal bureaucracy is regularly criticized as being too large, ineffective, and unresponsive. Nevertheless, the federal bureaucracy continues to survive and grow. New agencies are regularly created, and few old agencies ever go out of business. When Ronald Reagan ran for election in 1980, he promised to eliminate the departments of Education and of Energy, yet both have managed to survive. Moreover, the impact of the bureaucracy on people's lives seems to be increasing. Indeed, almost every significant activity is regulated by a government agency. Whether it concerns the food we eat or the shows we see on television, there is a federal agency that issues lengthy, complex rules. How can there be so much public ill-feeling toward an institution that continues to thrive? This chapter examines four questions that relate to these issues:

- What is the federal bureaucracy?
- Why has the federal bureaucracy grown so large?
- Is the federal bureaucracy effective?
- Does the federal bureaucracy pose a threat to democratic government?

PREVIEW

What is the federal bureaucracy? The term "bureaucracy" refers to both a way of doing business and a large number of federal government organizations performing certain tasks. The bureaucratic approach is characterized by (1) a clear division of labor, (2) hierarchical authority patterns, with increasing responsibility from bottom to top, (3) specified job qualifications, and (4) the objective administration of rules. Bureaucratic organizations are designed primarily to accomplish general goals rather than to attend to the special problems of individuals. As a result, bureaucratic procedures sometimes are viewed as impersonal and unresponsive.

The government organizations that make up the federal bureaucracy employ some 2.8 million people, the vast majority of whom are chosen on the basis of merit and enjoy considerable job security. The federal bureaucracy consists of thirteen Cabinet-level departments, independent executive agencies and corporations, and independent regulatory commissions.

Why has the federal bureaucracy grown so large? The federal bureaucracy has grown considerably since the ratification of the Constitution. Some major reasons for the increase in personnel are a growing U.S. population, domestic and international crises, demands for new government services, and the desire of many public officials to expand their power. There also has been a great increase in paperwork. One reason for this is that we now expect government to resolve complex social and economic problems. This necessitates the collection of a great deal of information and the issuing of many rules. Increased red tape, as these rules are called, also results from a concern for legal due process in administration.

Is the federal bureaucracy effective? Some critics of the federal bureaucracy have called it wasteful, ineffective, irresponsible, and dehumanizing. Yet it has been successful in many areas, especially in carrying out technical tasks. There has been relatively little corruption, and most citizens say they are satisfied with the way government agencies handled their problems. When tasks have been complex or involved difficult social problems, however, bureaucratic success has been more limited.

Does the federal bureaucracy pose a threat to democratic government? It has been claimed that the bureaucracy is unaccountable to elected political leaders. Critics argue that agencies have considerable rule-making authority, that civil servants have their own perspectives on policy matters, and that elected officials have only limited control over government agencies. However, defenders of the present system assert that Congress and the President have ways of exerting influence over the bureaucracy; the budgetary process, legislative oversight, reorganization, and the appointment process are especially useful. The relationship between elected officials and bureaucrats is highly complex, and it is not always obvious who best represents the public. On occasion, administrative technicians have thwarted the will of the people and thus undermined democracy. On other occasions, however, the bureaucracy has acted to check undemocratic abuses of power.

WHAT IS THE FEDERAL BUREAUCRACY?

There are two distinct meanings of the term "bureaucracy." The first refers to a way of conducting business, whether in government or in private enterprise. We have this meaning in mind when we make a statement like, "This university is run bureaucratically." The second use of "bureaucracy" refers to a government organization whose staff is nonelected and that performs a set of specific tasks—for example, the Department of Defense. Employees of these agencies are known as "bureaucrats." To understand the controversies surrounding the federal bureaucracy, we must understand both of these meanings.

The Bureaucratic Approach

Any large task—fighting a war, cleaning city streets, or whatever—can be approached in several ways. For example, we could ask for volunteers, who would all choose their own activities, hours of work, procedural methods, and so forth. Or we could create a bureaucracy to coordinate the job. A bureaucratic approach would have the following characteristics.

Clear Division of Labor. A large project is broken down into a series of specific tasks, and each person is responsible for a particular task. In football, for example, a defense is "bureaucratized" when it has designated positions, such as left outside linebacker or right defensive end, instead of eleven players milling around in hopes of stopping the opposing team. Large corporations have departments that specialize in sales, marketing, finance, personnel, and so on.

Hierarchical Authority Patterns. Each employee fits into a chain of command, and orders are sent through established channels. The organization of positions looks like a pyramid, with one chief at the top, who gives orders to, say, three assistants, who in turn direct twelve aides, and so on. The organization of a football team, with a hierarchy ranging from head coach to offensive coordinators to line coaches to player-captain, illustrates the bureaucratic authority pattern. In business there are titles, such as president, division manager, and department head.

Specified Job Qualifications. Because each job in a bureaucracy is a small part of a large organization, the job occupant might need special training and qualifications. Typically, people in bureaucracies are chosen on the basis of a written examination, completion of a training program, or specified previous experience. Bureaucratic jobs in government and business usually lead to long careers; advancement is on the basis of merit.

Objective Administration of Rules. Each official follows written rules that are applied uniformly. The use of personal reactions or opinions in decision making is minimized or eliminated. Therefore, at least in principle, everyone knows what to expect, and a written record is kept of previous decisions. Such procedures ensure fairness and predictability. Professional football teams, for example, have adopted the bureaucratic approach by

having specific penalties for players who violate training and practice rules.

A Perspective on Bureaucratic Organization

Obviously, no organization perfectly fits these ideal characteristics all the time, but these four traits are standard. Government makes a significant effort to follow the model because, in large organizations like those in the federal government, the benefits of a division of labor, a hierarchical authority pattern, standardized job qualifications, and objective rules are considerable. What would happen if, for example, thousands of officials in the Social Security Administration all used different rules in determining benefits? Without a reasonably high degree of bureaucratization, modern government would disintegrate into chaos. Bribery, threats of force, favoritism, and erratic decision making would be commonplace. Max Weber (1864–1920), a German sociologist, argued that compared to any other way of conducting business, bureaucracy is more precise, faster, less confusing, more knowledgeable, more unified, and it generates less conflict and costs less in material and personnel. All industrialized nations have large bureaucracies.

Unfortunately, if one wants quick action and personalized treatment, the bureaucratic approach is not ideal. Bureaucracies exist to handle large numbers of cases in an orderly, predetermined way; they are not geared to treating the special problems of individuals. When dealing with the federal government, the problem of complex rules, rigid interpretations, and tasks handled by a multitude of people can be far worse. We shall have more to say about these bureaucratic drawbacks.

Organizations of the Federal Bureaucracy

The people of the United States elect 535 national legislators and one President, who in turn appoints the nine Supreme Court justices (who are subject to confirmation by the Senate). This is only the tip of the federal iceberg. In addition to these policy makers, there were, as of September 1984, some 2,935,000 paid civilian employees in the federal

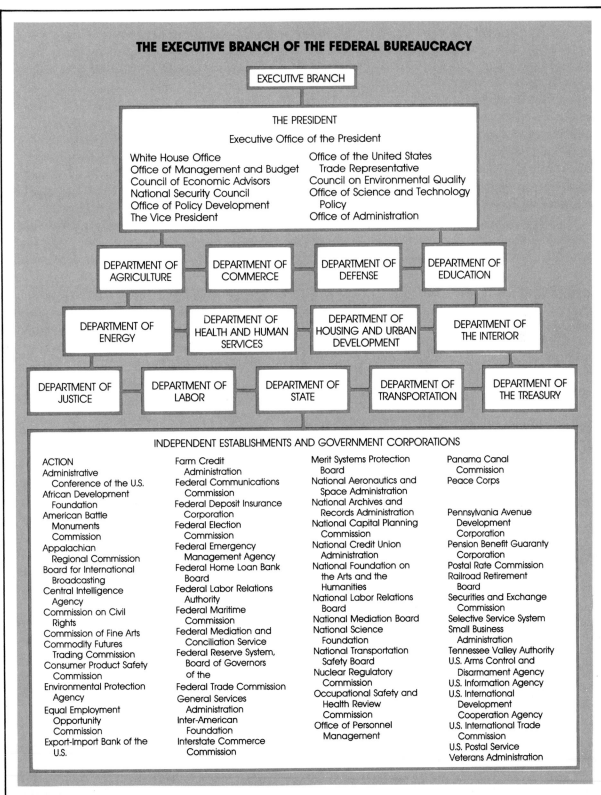

THE EXECUTIVE BRANCH OF THE FEDERAL BUREAUCRACY

EXECUTIVE BRANCH

THE PRESIDENT

Executive Office of the President

White House Office
Office of Management and Budget
Council of Economic Advisors
National Security Council
Office of Policy Development
The Vice President

Office of the United States
  Trade Representative
Council on Environmental Quality
Office of Science and Technology
  Policy
Office of Administration

DEPARTMENT OF AGRICULTURE

DEPARTMENT OF COMMERCE

DEPARTMENT OF DEFENSE

DEPARTMENT OF EDUCATION

DEPARTMENT OF ENERGY

DEPARTMENT OF HEALTH AND HUMAN SERVICES

DEPARTMENT OF HOUSING AND URBAN DEVELOPMENT

DEPARTMENT OF THE INTERIOR

DEPARTMENT OF JUSTICE

DEPARTMENT OF LABOR

DEPARTMENT OF STATE

DEPARTMENT OF TRANSPORTATION

DEPARTMENT OF THE TREASURY

INDEPENDENT ESTABLISHMENTS AND GOVERNMENT CORPORATIONS

ACTION
Administrative
  Conference of the U.S.
African Development
  Foundation
American Battle
  Monuments
  Commission
Appalachian
  Regional Commission
Board for International
  Broadcasting
Central Intelligence
  Agency
Commission on Civil
  Rights
Commission of Fine Arts
Commodity Futures
  Trading Commission
Consumer Product Safety
  Commission
Environmental Protection
  Agency
Equal Employment
  Opportunity
  Commission
Export-Import Bank of the
  U.S.

Farm Credit
  Administration
Federal Communications
  Commission
Federal Deposit Insurance
  Corporation
Federal Election
  Commission
Federal Emergency
  Management Agency
Federal Home Loan Bank
  Board
Federal Labor Relations
  Authority
Federal Maritime
  Commission
Federal Mediation and
  Conciliation Service
Federal Reserve System,
  Board of Governors
  of the
Federal Trade Commission
General Services
  Administration
Inter-American
  Foundation
Interstate Commerce
  Commission

Merit Systems Protection
  Board
National Aeronautics and
  Space Administration
National Archives and
  Records Administration
National Capital Planning
  Commission
National Credit Union
  Administration
National Foundation on
  the Arts and the
  Humanities
National Labor Relations
  Board
National Mediation Board
National Science
  Foundation
National Transportation
  Safety Board
Nuclear Regulatory
  Commission
Occupational Safety and
  Health Review
  Commission
Office of Personnel
  Management

Panama Canal
  Commission
Peace Corps

Pennsylvania Avenue
  Development
  Corporation
Pension Benefit Guaranty
  Corporation
Postal Rate Commission
Railroad Retirement
  Board
Securities and Exchange
  Commission
Selective Service System
Small Business
  Administration
Tennessee Valley Authority
U.S. Arms Control and
  Disarmament Agency
U.S. Information Agency
U.S. International
  Development
  Cooperation Agency
U.S. International Trade
  Commission
U.S. Postal Service
Veterans Administration

FIGURE 11.1

government, most of whom worked in the executive branch. This, then, is the size of the thing called the federal bureaucracy. What do these 2.9 million people do?

The types of jobs performed by employees of the federal bureaucracy are highly varied. Some employees fit the popular image of a federal government bureaucrat. That is, they work in Washington at a desk job in a large building and deal with some fairly detailed administrative matter— for example, helping to collect and interpret information for the World Agricultural Outlook Board, one small element in the Department of Agriculture. Many employees do not, however, fit the stereotype. A large number of federal employees are blue-collar workers—carpenters, truck drivers, and so on. Another large portion are clerical workers—secretaries, typists, and so on—whose duties are identical to those of similar employees in private industry. There are also thousands of highly trained professional and technical workers—physicians, veterinarians, biologists, lawyers, and computer programmers. Despite the popular image of the federal bureaucracy as being concentrated in the nation's capital, only a small percentage of all federal civilian employees work in the Washington metropolitan area (there were almost as many federal employees in California as in Washington, in fact).

Figure 11.1 shows a simplified organizational chart of the executive branch of the federal bureaucracy. In Chapter 10 we examined one of these elements—the Executive Office of the President. Let us now consider four other types of agencies: the Cabinet departments, independent executive agencies, government corporations, and regulatory commissions.

Cabinet-Level Departments

Originally there were only four Cabinet-level departments—State, Treasury, War (later named Defense), and Justice. As government grew, additional Cabinet-level departments were created. Today there are thirteen: State, Treasury, Defense, Justice, Interior, Agriculture, Commerce, Labor, Health and Human Services, Housing and Urban Development, Transportation, Energy,

and the most recent addition, Education. These departments represent some of the largest components of the federal bureaucracy. In 1984, for example, the Defense Department employed 1,043,785 *civilian* workers. The Department of Education, the smallest of these giants, employed some 5,350 people in 1984.

Each Cabinet-level department is headed by a Secretary appointed by the President and confirmed by the Senate. The Secretary is assisted by several other appointed officials who have titles such as "special assistant to the Secretary" or "Deputy Secretary." Within these Cabinet-level departments there are many more specialized agencies. For example, well-known divisions of the Department of Transportation include the U.S. Coast Guard, the Federal Aviation Administration, and the Federal Highway Administration. Some of these sub-Cabinet organizations have considerable independence, despite the fact that they are subordinate to the Secretary. Especially when it was headed by J. Edgar Hoover, for instance, the FBI was almost a power unto itself within the Justice Department.

Cabinet secretaries are appointed for a variety of reasons. Sometimes a President will appoint a long-standing advisor to head an especially important department. William French Smith, President Reagan's first Attorney General, had been close to the President for many years, in addition to being a prominent lawyer. Such an appointment encourages a good working relationship on sensitive matters, such as the way civil rights or antitrust laws are to be enforced. In other instances the appointee is unknown to the President but has close ties to groups involved with departmental business. For example, Presidents have traditionally selected individuals with good ties to the trade unions as Secretary of Labor. Treasury secretaries are always respected figures in the business community.

The designation of a bureaucracy as a Cabinet-level department does not necessarily imply great power. For many years education groups lobbied for a separate Department of Education (education had been included in the Department of Health, Education and Welfare). President Carter created

The federal bureaucracy has many faces. It includes, for instance, thousands of clerical workers at the Pentagon and the Internal Revenue Service, National Park Service Rangers, and Department of Agriculture inspectors.

a separate Education Department with congressional approval in 1979, but under President Reagan it has not become a major force for education. The Department of Housing and Urban Development, created in 1965, has rarely been among the most influential bureaucracies, despite the importance of its work.

Independent Executive Agencies and Government Corporations

A second type of federal bureaucracy is the independent executive agency. Although executive agencies do not enjoy Cabinet status, the largest ones are quite important. In 1984, the Veterans Administration employed almost 240,000 people and spent over $25 billion. Other well-known agencies are the National Science Foundation (NSF), the National Aeronautics and Space Administration (NASA), the Central Intelligence Agency (CIA), the Commission on Civil Rights, and the Consumer Product Safety Commission.

As in Cabinet-level departments, the top administrators of executive agencies are appointed by the President but must be confirmed by the Senate. Such appointments can sometimes generate as much controversy as Cabinet appointments. President Reagan's nominations to the Environmental Protection Agency and the Commission on Civil Rights in the early 1980s aroused intense debate in the Senate, because some people, inside and outside government, viewed the appointments as attempts to undermine the purposes of these agencies. The reasons for top appointments can vary considerably. When the Post Office was a Cabinet department, the postmaster general's position was a reward for loyal campaigning; today the head of the Postal Service is selected by nine members of the Board of Governors of the Postal Service. An individual is more likely to be chosen for his or her expertise than for political activity. However, in other executive agencies, top positions might be decided on the basis of political loyalty and philosophy.

Some executive agencies are legally established as government corporations and are intended to be run more like private businesses, although they are still responsible to Congress and to the President. These corporations provide services for a fee and even compete with private enterprises. The U.S. Postal Service is the largest government corporation. Others are the Tennessee Valley Authority (TVA), which supplies electricity to the Tennessee Valley region, and the Federal Deposit Insurance Corporation (the familiar FDIC seen on bank advertisements).

Independent Regulatory Commissions

The agencies farthest removed from direct presidential influence are the independent regulatory commissions. As in other agencies in the federal bureaucracy, top administrators are appointed by the President subject to Senate approval. However, unlike other top appointees, members of independent regulatory commissions cannot be removed by the President simply because they disagree with the White House. An appointee may be removed only for a specific cause that is authorized by law. Presidential control is further reduced by the fact that top appointees serve long terms and appointments are not all made at the same time. For example, the Federal Communications Commission has seven commissioners, each serving a separate seven-year term; a President can make only one new appointment a year. An additional requirement in some agencies is that a balance between Democrats and Republicans must be maintained, and the top position alternates between a Democrat and a Republican.

The basic purpose of the independent regulatory agencies is to promote open, fair, and competitive economic practices. Table 11.1 lists the major regulatory agencies and their areas of responsibility. The Interstate Commerce Commission (ICC), created in 1887 to ensure fair railroad rates, was the first of these agencies, although it was originally a part of the Interior Department (it was made independent two years later). The Federal Reserve System, which regulates banks, followed in 1913. In 1914 the Federal Trade Commission (FTC) was established to investigate and stop unfair business practices. Several other independent regulatory commissions were created under the administration of Franklin D. Roosevelt, including the Federal Communications Commission (FCC), which regulates all interstate and foreign communications, and the Securities and Exchange Commission (SEC), which regulates stock trading. The 1970s saw another flurry of agency creation; several were particularly concerned with health and safety, a change from the previous economic mission. Among these new agencies were the Occupational Safety and Health Administration (OSHA), the Consumer Product Safety Commission, and the Nuclear Regulatory Commission.

Political controversy has often surrounded these commissions. A long-standing charge has been that many agencies intended to protect the

Major Regulatory Agencies and Their Responsibilities

Agency (Year Created)	Size	Term of Appointment	Responsibilities
Interstate Commerce Commission (1887)	5	7 years	Regulates surface and water transportation and certain types of pipelines. Also deals with consumer complaints regarding these services.
Federal Trade Commission (1914)	5	7 years	Promotes economic competition, eliminates illegal restraint of trade, and regulates advertising to eliminate deception.
Federal Communications Commission (1934)	7	7 years, staggered terms	Regulates interstate and foreign radio, television, wire, telegraph, cable, and satellite communications.
Securities and Exchange Commission (1934)	5	5 years	Regulates the trading of stocks and bonds and related matters. Investigates securities fraud and enforces penalties.
Consumer Product Safety Commission (1972)	5	7 years, staggered terms	Sets safety standards for the design, construction, content, labeling, and performance of consumer products. Has power to enforce standards.
Nuclear Regulatory Commission (1974)	5	5 years	Licenses nuclear reactors and other users of nuclear materials, including disposal. Also licenses exporting and importing of radioactive materials.
Federal Election Commission (1971)	6	6 years, staggered terms	Administers federal election law. Issues rules concerning campaign contributions and expenditures and provides limited federal campaign subsidies.
Federal Energy Regulatory Commission (1977)	5	4 years	Regulates the prices of natural gas, oil pipelines, and electricity at wholesale level and licenses hydroelectric projects.

TABLE 11.1

public have been taken over by the regulated industries. For example, it has been claimed that railroads used the ICC to maintain artificially high prices and restrict competition. Another source of conflict has been agency independence. While Congress and Presidents often say they are in favor of agency independence, on many occasions they have tried to influence agency decisions. In recent years intense disputes have arisen over the rules and regulations issued by these agencies. We shall have more to say on this topic later in the chapter.

How Bureaucrats Are Selected

The selection of over 2.8 million employees is a complex process. Over the years a number of methods have been used for hiring government workers. In the nineteenth century a **patronage** or "spoils" system was used. The victorious presidential candidate would appoint tens of thousands of supporters to government positions to reward campaign services. The patronage system was full of scandal and wrongdoing. After the assassination of President Garfield by a disappointed office seeker, Congress passed the Civil Service Act of 1883 (called the Pendleton Act), which created the **civil service** system. The Pendleton Act required some jobs to be filled on the basis of merit and protected federal employees from being removed for political reasons. Over time, more and more federal jobs have been brought into the civil service system. Today, most government employees, from laborers to forest rangers, are hired on the basis of such standards as test scores, special training, education, and experience. After a one-year probationary period, a federal employee may be dismissed only for cause—that is, not at the whim of a politician or bureaucrat (though the position itself may be abolished). In practice, firing for poor performance is relatively rare. Advancement also is based on established standards, and many senior civil servants have risen through agency ranks.

Since the late 1970s, selection procedure has been affected by the issue of the racial, ethnic, and gender make-up of the federal bureaucracy. As the data in Table 11.2 show, blacks, Hispanics, and women are found disproportionately in lower posi-

tions; top bureaucrats are almost all white males. Several steps have been taken to change this situation. For example, many agencies actively recruit blacks, Hispanics, and women for higher level positions; job examinations have been revised to eliminate racial bias; and numerous pronouncements have been issued. Nevertheless, despite these efforts, changes have come slowly. It is not easy to find thousands of qualified minorities and women willing to work for the federal government, especially given opportunities in the private sector. Also, with the expansion of the federal work force greatly slowed or even reversed, openings are largely the result of retirement and resignation. Significant changes would be much easier if government were expanding rapidly.

Balancing Bureaucratic Independence and Responsiveness

There is a delicate balance between maintaining a bureaucracy that is protected from unreasonable political pressure and keeping it responsive to the demands of elected leaders. Until fairly recently, the emphasis has been on protecting federal employees from pressure. In 1912 the Civil Service Commission was established to formulate rules to shield government workers from unfair dismissal. The commission was replaced in 1979 by the Office of Personnel Management, which is responsible for maintaining the **merit system,** which ensures that the hiring, firing, and promotion of civil servants will be based on fair and objective regulations. The agency also develops more effective personnel policies. In 1939 Congress passed the Hatch Act, which forbids federal employees from participating in partisan elections except by voting (they cannot make financial contributions, run for office, assist in campaigns, conduct voter registration drives, and so on). The purpose of the Hatch Act is to prevent elected officials from forcing civil servants to participate in campaign activities on their behalf. Decisions by the Supreme Court have strengthened the independence of civil service employees by requiring that procedures for dismissing workers follow due process of law, a requirement making it difficult to fire someone

Minorities and Women in the Federal Bureaucracy, 1980	In 1980 there were some 1.5 million employees in the General Schedule classification system (this excluded the postal system and certain other types of employees). Among the 1.5 million employees:

211,300 were black (14.5 percent of all GS employees)
51,900 were Hispanic (3.6 percent of all GS employees)
664,000 were women (45.1 percent of all GS employees)

Blacks, Hispanics, and women were heavily concentrated at the lowest levels in the federal bureaucracy (laborers, clerks, messengers, etc):

65,800, or 31.1 percent, of all blacks were in GS grades 1–4
13,400, or 25.8 percent, of all Hispanics were in GS grades 1–4
501,000, or 74.1 percent, of all women were in GS grades 1–6

Blacks, Hispanics, and women were relatively rare at the upper level of the federal bureaucracy:

Blacks held only 4.8 percent of "executive level" positions.
There were fewer than 50 Hispanics in the 8,400 "executive level" positions.
Women held only 4.4 percent of "executive level" positions.

Source: Statistical Abstract of the United States, 1982–83, pp. 268–269.

TABLE 11.2

(due process is discussed later in the chapter). The existence of a strong civil service union willing to protect federal employees increases employee protection (and the right to join this union is guaranteed by the 1978 Civil Service Reform Act).

As we have noted, political factors nevertheless remain relevant for many positions. The very top bureaucrats—department secretaries, undersecretaries, and certain other officials—are appointed by the President subject to Senate confirmation. The White House also appoints, but without Senate confirmation, numerous top officials in the Executive Office of the President, Cabinet-level departments, other agencies, and various boards and commissions. These officials have a policy-making role and are entirely outside the civil service system. Below this top level are a group of between 1,000 and 2,000 top bureaucrats who hold civil service positions but, in practice, serve at the pleasure of the President. These officials have titles such as "executive assistant to the Un-

der-Secretary for . . ." and have some degree of job protection; they, too, must obey civil service rules that limit their political involvement.

Political factors can also play a role farther down the bureaucratic hierarchy. A job description can be written so specifically that only one person could fill it. An agency can request that a certain person be appointed to a job even though in principle the position is to be filled through open competition. Finally, thanks to the efforts of President Carter, in 1978, Congress established a new class of civil servant—the **Senior Executive Service** (SES). Members are top bureaucrats who are part of the civil service system, yet they can be shifted from department to department at the discretion of the President. To make up for the loss of job security, they are eligible for substantial salary bonuses. The purpose of the SES is to increase presidential control of the bureaucracy and to give bureaucrats a broader perspective on government operations.

Biography: Frances Perkins

The first woman to attain Cabinet rank, Frances Perkins served President Franklin Roosevelt—as his Secretary of Labor—longer than any other department head. Because she was a woman and had not risen through the ranks of organized labor, she aroused little initial enthusiasm among labor leaders. She did, however, have many years of experience working for private organizations and government agencies involved in labor relations. This background taught her not only a great deal about the working world but also how to use the bureaucracy to get things done.

Perkins, born in 1880, grew up in New England and graduated from Mount Holyoke College. She taught in girls' schools from 1903 to 1907 and headed a Philadelphia organization that aided young single women. In 1910 she moved to New York City to become executive secretary of the Consumers' League. The following year she witnessed the Triangle Shirtwaist Company fire, which claimed the lives of 146 sweatshop employees. Along with other horrified onlookers, she watched helplessly as workers unable to escape through locked fire doors jumped to their deaths. Her affiliation with the Consumers' League had given her prominence in the movement for social justice, and in 1912 Perkins was named director of a citizens' group that investigated the tragedy and recommended legislation to improve factory safety.

Perkins' lobbying work for this citizens' commission brought her into close contact with political leaders in New York State. In 1918 New York Governor Alfred E. Smith appointed her to the state's industrial commission, the governing board of the state's Labor Department. Then, under Smith's successor, Franklin Roosevelt, she became the chief administrator of the Labor Department. During her tenure, New York State gained a reputation for its progressive laws regulating wages, hours, and workers' compensation for employees injured on the job.

When FDR became President, he wanted Perkins as his Secretary of Labor. She resisted at first, feeling that the post should go to someone with stronger ties to organized labor, but finally she gave in. "I had been taught long ago by my grandmother," she later said, "that if anybody opens a door, one should always go through."

As Secretary of Labor, Perkins helped draft many New Deal measures, including those that established the Civilian Conservation Corps, the National Labor Relations Board, and the Social Security system. She also helped write many of Roosevelt's speeches dealing with labor and advised the President on numerous appointments. Her interest in efficient administration prompted her to strengthen the Department of Labor itself. Among other things, she got rid of racketeers in the Immigration and Naturalization Service and set up a Division of Labor Standards.

Throughout her career—she taught and lectured until the time of her death, in 1965—Perkins refused to be daunted by the patronizing and outright discriminatory

treatment to which she was often subjected. (At formal occasions, when Cabinet members were seated according to rank, she was usually placed with the wives of her male colleagues.) Keenly aware of her pioneering role, she once said: "I have always felt that it was not I alone who was appointed to the Cabinet, but that it was all the women in America."

<hr>

Check Your Understanding

1. What are the key elements in the bureaucratic approach to conducting business?

2. What are four major types of agencies within the federal bureaucracy?

3. In general, how are federal bureaucrats selected for their jobs?

4. What role do political factors play in filling jobs in the federal bureaucracy?

<hr>

WHY HAS THE FEDERAL BUREAUCRACY GROWN SO LARGE?

The federal bureaucracy has grown considerably since the ratification of the Constitution. When President Washington took office, the entire federal bureaucracy consisted of about 350 people. Even after the hiring of innumerable Revolutionary War veterans, worthy men in need of jobs, and friends and relatives of government officials, there were still only 2,100 federal employees in 1801. If early Presidents had hired bureaucrats at the ratio of public servants to population that we now have, the United States would have begun with a public payroll of some 45,000.

The Growth of the Federal Bureaucracy

Public employment at the federal level, however, soon became a growth industry. Especially after Andrew Jackson's election in 1828, a government job became a major way of rewarding supporters for help during an election campaign. By 1901, the executive branch employed 256,000 people, and by 1930, over 580,000. Between 1960 and 1980, some 425,000 workers were added to the federal payroll. Under the Reagan administration, however, the number of employees declined slightly for the first time in decades.

Reasons for Bureaucratic Growth

The rapid growth of offices and staffs in the executive department is relatively easy to understand. Obviously, population increases are a factor. A nation of nearly 240 million people cannot be run by the same number of officials who ran a country of 50 million. Compounding this increase in size is a dramatic change in the nature of contemporary life. Because of technological advances, we now face complexities undreamed of a hundred years ago. As a result, agencies such as the Office of Science and Technology, the Nuclear Regulatory Commission, and the National Science Foundation have come into existence. The launching of communications satellites or the regulation of atomic energy, for example, requires some degree of government involvement.

The cold war with the Soviet Union, conflicts in Korea and Vietnam, and a succession of world crises have also contributed to bureaucratic growth. Since the beginning of America's conflict with the Soviet Union (at the end of World War II), a sizable Defense Department has become an accepted fact. Other agencies have emerged in response to continued global tension, including the Central Intelligence Agency, the Arms Control and Disarmament Agency, the U.S. Information Agency, and even the Peace Corps, which is designed to generate good will abroad. The wars in Korea and South Vietnam have helped maintain a large Veterans Administration.

Domestic economic crises likewise have contributed to the swelling government payroll. During the Depression of the 1930s, President Franklin D. Roosevelt added more than 100,000 federal jobs in his first year in office to combat unemployment and economic stagnation. Many of Roosevelt's Great Depression remedies have been extended (for example, Social Security), as people have come to expect the federal government to help citizens in many different areas. Whereas the ill, the neglected, the retired, and the disabled once had to depend on family or private charity, the federal government now runs a vast number of assistance programs. Similarly, victims of earthquakes, floods, and other natural disasters are now eligible for government aid. Once a government

Peace corps volunteers teach homemaking and agricultural skills in Latin America, Asia, and Africa. In return, the volunteers gain an understanding of the needs of peoples in less-developed nations.

bureaucracy has been established to deal with a problem, even a temporary one, it is difficult to shut it down.

A fourth reason for bureaucratic growth involves the relationship between interest groups and government agencies. As we saw in Chapter 8, many bureaucracies develop close relationships with interest groups and others outside the government. These groups usually are referred to as an **agency client** (or **clientele**). The existence of one clientele relationship encourages the creation of opposing clientele bureaucracies. If business leaders can have "their" people in the Department of Commerce, trade union officials want to have "their" supporters in the Department of Labor. These same clientele groups become strong protectors of a bureaucracy once it is created. Often an agency facing a reduction in size can mobilize friendly interest groups to lobby Congress on its behalf. (Agency clients are discussed in more detail later in the chapter.)

Finally, once established, some agencies experience strong internal pressures for expansion. Because power and prestige within government are frequently measured by size, many high agency officials seek to add more people to their staffs. An administrator who willingly allows his or her agency to be reduced in size is likely to be viewed as disloyal to the agency or politically ineffectual. The pressure to grow is encouraged by the budgetary process in government: last year's expenses are accepted as the new standard, so one might as well ask for more money this year. A skillful administrator can sometimes find ways of adding employees without appearing to increase an agency's regular staff. People can be hired on a "temporary,"

Points of View: "But What About All of the Above or None of the Above?"

Government forms are sometimes highly complex in order to ensure that requests for information will be precisely understood. The need to be exact is well illustrated by the case of a young job applicant who filled out Form 57, which was once required for government employment. The question was, "Do you favor the overthrow of the Government by force, subversion, or violence?" The applicant, obviously experienced with undergraduate multiple choice examinations, answered: "violence."

Cited in Norval Morris and Gordon Hawkins, *The Honest Politician's Guide to Crime Control* (Chicago: University of Chicago Press, 1970), p. 55.

eleven-month basis, part-timers can be taken on, or employees can be put on someone else's payroll and paid through an agency contract.

Growth in Paperwork and Regulation

These factors help us to understand the growth of the executive bureaucracies. There is, however, another aspect of bureaucratic growth, far more controversial and complex—the increase in rules and regulations issued by federal departments and agencies, or **red tape,** as it is often called. The federal government generates an enormous quantity of regulations. In 1983, for example, *The Federal Register,* a document that lists all the proposed and final rules put out by government agencies for one year, ran 57,703 pages. According to one estimate, the federal government has 9,800 forms that might be completed; those forms generate 556 million responses each year. There were some

"*Granted the public has a right to know what's in a hot dog, but does the public really want to know what's in a hot dog?*"

(Drawing by Richter; © 1978 The New Yorker Magazine, Inc.)

To protect subjects who participate in psychological experiments from possible harm, the federal government issues guidelines that researchers receiving public funds must follow.

76,500 employees in fifty-seven agencies responsible for issuing rules on the economy, business, the environment, and health and safety.

For businesses and the self-employed, the burden of federal forms can be overwhelming. The chairman of the board of a large drug company claimed that his firm prepared 27,000 government forms a year, at a cost of $5 million. He also asserted that, in the United States, more company time is spent filling out forms than is spent on cancer and heart disease research combined. Government rules also require private firms, universities, and other organizations to generate a multitude of their own forms. In recent years, for example, university researchers whose work involves human subjects must follow government guidelines, even though the actual form might be issued by the university.

In addition, the nature of the requested information is frequently exasperating. Many businesses, in particular, complain that they cannot see the importance of numerous regulations. Confusing rules add to the psychological burden. How would you react if you, like the Scottdale Savings and Trust Company of Scottdale, Pennsylvania, answered a question on a government report with the word "none," only to have the report returned with the request that "-0-" be used instead of "none"?

Although much of the paperwork may be a nuisance, there is a good reason for the increase in government rules. The fact is that regulations are designed primarily to create efficiency while protecting citizens. What ends up as red tape usually starts out with the best of intentions. To understand why good intentions can easily lead to numerous complex rules and hundreds of detailed forms to be filled out, we must understand three facts about the national government: (1) government is increasingly responsible for preventing harm before it occurs, (2) government must function in accordance with laws and standards of fairness, and (3) government needs extensive information.

Preventing Harm Before It Occurs

A good example of this role can be found in the growth of consumer protection regulation. In the old days if you found a rat in your peanut butter, your response would be to stop buying that brand of peanut butter. If the rat bit you, you might take the company to court—a long, costly, and gener-

Commentary: "In Case of Fire, Proceed Immediately to That Portion of a Means of Egress . . ."

Perhaps the most exasperating aspect of bureaucratic procedure is the language that is often used in communications. Everything has to be spelled out in overly complex detail. Here, for example, is the definition of *exit* used by the Occupational Safety and Health Administration (OSHA). An *exit* is:

> that portion of a means of egress which is separated from all other spaces of the building or structure by construction or equipment as required in this subpart to provide a protected

way of travel to the exit discharge.

An *exit discharge* in turn is defined as:

> that portion of a means of egress between the termination of an exit and a public way.

A *means of egress* is:

> a continuous and unobstructed way of exit travel from any point in a building or structure to a public way and consists of three separate and distinct parts: the way of exit access, the exit,

and the way of exit discharge. A means of egress comprises the vertical and horizontal ways of travel and shall include intervening room spaces, doorways, hallways, corridors, passageways, balconies, ramps, stairs, enclosures, exits, escalators, horizontal exits, courts, and yards.

Not all definitions are as complicated however. OSHA tells us that "hazards are one of the main causes of accidents. A hazard is anything that is dangerous."

Reported in Murray L. Weidenbaum, "The Cost of Overregulating Business," *Tax Foundation's Tax Review* 36 (August 1975): 34–35.

---

ally inefficient solution. The attitude of the government toward products sold in the marketplace was, "Let the buyer beware." The federal government offered the consumer no protection in advance against faulty products or misleading advertising.

Today, however, Americans expect the government to protect them against such evils *before* they occur. We want the government to guarantee in advance that we will find no surprises in our peanut butter or automobiles or household appliances. This responsibility might require a small army of federal officials, and thousands of forms, to monitor the production of peanut butter in hundreds of factories. Manufacturers have to comply with dozens of rules on plant sanitation, methods of production, security of storage and shipping facilities, and the like. Meanwhile, the Food and Drug Administration might conduct an investigation into whether eating too many rats causes cancer. The Federal Trade Commission might con-

sider whether it is deceptive to advertise peanut butter mixed with rats as "peanut butter with whole natural protein." (Although our illustration is an exaggeration, the Food and Drug Administration does indeed regulate such matters. For example, 10 ounces of popcorn may contain up to one rodent hair or one rodent pellet and still not be considered legally contaminated. On the other hand, the fig paste in fig newtons may contain thirteen insect heads per 100 grams and still be allowed.) More and more complex rules and regulations are clearly the alternative to "let the buyer beware."

Government makes enormous efforts to protect consumers and prevent harm before it happens. Loan contracts must be written in plain English so that borrowers will not be misled by difficult legal language; regulations explain how clothing is to be labeled with washing instructions; and truth-in-advertising standards govern the kinds of claims manufacturers may make about their products.

There are a multitude of rules covering the content of food products, so that consumers will know what they are buying. The federal government has also become deeply involved in workplace safety, the design of automobiles, and the testing and selling of prescription medicines. Each effort at consumer protection is accomplished by the issuing of rules, standards, and forms.

Ensuring That Government Operates Fairly

Red tape also increases as a result of government efforts to operate legally and fairly. Consider the problem of providing Social Security benefits for disabled citizens. We want to make sure that those who legally deserve aid receive it and that the undeserving cannot defraud, or cheat, the government. To make sure that the program functions as intended by Congress and the President, many details must be spelled out. In fact, within the Social Security program it takes *fifteen* pages of rules and regulations just to define "disability." The rules even state exactly how "blindness" is to be measured ("usual perimetric methods, utilizing a 3 mm white disk target at a distance of 330 mm under illumination of not less than 7 foot-candles"). Unless rules and standards are stated clearly, a disabled person might be refused benefits or an ineligible person given public aid. Imagine what might happen if a program designed to assist poor people allowed each government employee to decide on his or her own who was or was not "poor."

Red tape is also generated by the requirement that bureaucracy operate according to **due process.** Here again, the desire to be fair creates complexity. Under the principle of due process, decisions must be made in accordance with set procedures, and people who will be affected by the final decision must be allowed to participate or defend themselves. An illustration of how due process creates red tape is provided by the environmental impact studies that must be conducted on many major building projects. In the old days if the state of Illinois wanted to build a dam on the Dirty River, the project basically involved engineering and financing problems. Decisions, made by a few individuals with little publicity, were often based on their limited personal knowledge. Today, the dam builders must first conduct extensive studies on the impact of the dam on the environment, hold hearings to learn the preferences of local citizens, and in other ways ensure that the final decision is reached fairly and openly. The types of studies, timing of public hearings, nature of reports to be filed, and so on are spelled out in administrative guidelines, and violation of these regulations can be the basis of court suits. The costs of operating according to due process can be lengthy delays and mountains of paperwork.

Due process in the bureaucracy also means providing the opportunity to review decisions. If, for example, taxpayers believe that the Internal Revenue Service, the federal government's tax-collecting agency, treated them unfairly, they can appeal their case and get a second (or third or fourth) evaluation. A special tax court eventually might settle the issue. This review process is intended as a check on possible abuses of office or faulty judgments. Because a decision ultimately might be reviewed, an agency must keep extensive records, have specific rules governing the review process, spell out the rights of all parties, and make sure that no regulation is unclear or contradictory. All these precautions grant protection to the citizen, but they can be confusing, frustrating and time-consuming.

The Need for Extensive Information

The need for information is yet another reason for the quantities of paperwork that flow from federal agencies. Dealing effectively with complex issues, as we expect our government to do, requires large amounts of data. Thus farmers must fill out forms describing their planting, businesses must provide payroll information, and so on. Without such data, how would Congress and the President know whether their economic policies are working? How could they plan for the future? One important lesson of the Depression of the 1930s was that economic (and social) problems cannot be analyzed correctly without a great deal of citizen-supplied data. Suppose the government is committed to abolishing sex discrimination in employment. In order to carry out this task, government must gather extensive information about the progress made and the problems encountered. Paperwork is

Commentary: The Politics of Pizza

The regulatory process is deceptively complex and fraught with potential political controversy. Consider, for example, the problem of regulating pizza. Pizza is a big business in the United States. In 1983 some $8 billion was spent on restaurant pizza, another $1 billion on the frozen supermarket variety. What goes into a pizza affects not only the pizza industry but the dairy industry and, of course, consumers.

In 1983 the dairy industry suffered from huge product surpluses. The government was spending several billion dollars each year buying and storing surplus dairy products. To help solve the problem, the Department of Agriculture—a traditional dairy industry ally—issued a regulation increasing the required percentage of real cheese in frozen pizzas. The use of cheese substitutes would have to be clearly labeled. This ruling, however, applied only to pizzas that contained meat. All cheese, mushroom, olive, and green pepper pizzas are regulated by the separate Food and Drug Administration.

Opposition, as expected, has come from pizza manufacturers, who argued that such regulations are unnecessary interference and would substantially raise the price of their product. Many consumers cannot tell the difference between real cheese, "cheese food," and imitation cheese. Some purchasers have even come to prefer the imitation product. Especially among poor families, cheap frozen pizza has become a dietary staple. There are other reasons why shoppers may choose to avoid the genuine article. A woman from Milwaukee wrote the Agriculture Department to say that her child was allergic to milk and pizza with artificial cheese was a real treat.

Allied with the dairy industry and the Department of Agriculture are many consumers. A frequent theme of letters in support of the increased cheese requirement is that it would make pizza more nutritious and eliminate mislabeling of phony cheese as cheese. As the issues become more complex, the controversy will probably grow from small to X-tra large.

Adapted from "Pizza Rule: Matter of Cheese, Dough," *USA Today*, April 16, 1984; and Ward Sinclair, "'Truth in Pizza' Draws Crusty Response," *Washington Post National Weekly Edition*, December 26, 1983.

also essential if the public is to evaluate the success of a government program. Holding government accountable for implementing its policies—a widely approved goal—generates seemingly endless forms and regulations.

A Perspective on Red Tape

To return to our original question of why there is so much red tape, the answer seems to be that many people want it even if they dislike the idea of big government and paperwork. People want the government to prevent harm before it occurs, to act fairly, and to collect enough data to allow public officials to make informed decisions. Of course, some people might favor the elimination of *some* government agencies—as long as the offices and departments *they* depend on aren't affected. For many farmers, for example, the Agricultural Research Service is a valuable government agency. To a city dweller this agency, its employees, and its regulations might be just another part of the giant bureaucracy. A farmer, of course, might feel the same way about programs in the Department of Housing and Urban Development. Fulfilling all the needs of a complex society ensures the existence of a large bureaucracy with many rules and regulations.

Check Your Understanding

1. What are some of the reasons for the rapid growth of the federal bureaucracy in the last fifty years?

2. Why is there so much "red tape" in government today?

3. What three factors account for the large number of regulations in government?

IS THE FEDERAL BUREAUCRACY EFFECTIVE?

Many citizens who disagree on other political issues share a negative view of "big government," especially big bureaucracy. At the center of their criticism is the belief that government agencies frequently do not accomplish their missions. Critics do differ, however, on the specific problems involved. Some conservatives, for example, assert that huge federal agencies waste taxpayers' money, move at a snail's pace, and create more problems than they solve. They argue that problems involving energy, housing, transportation, and agriculture, to name just a few, should be left to free enterprise, which could do a better job faster and less expensively. Even worse, they assert, the federal bureaucracy undermines individual initiative and thus might harm the nation's economic structure.

Many liberals also see big bureaucracy as ineffective—that tasks such as eliminating poverty or providing adequate health care are not performed well. They maintain that the bureaucratic process is often unresponsive to the needs of individuals. Huge agencies with tens of thousands of employees and volumes of regulations are frequently ill-suited to address problems such as drug abuse, family conflicts, and crime, which require a more individualized approach. In addition, they say, massive Washington-based bureaucracies can turn their employees into mere cogs in giant machines, more worried about petty rules and job security than about helping people. Such organizations, critics claim, must be made more sensitive to human needs or be replaced by smaller, community-based agencies.

Whether or not the federal bureaucracy works effectively is a tough question. Disagreements frequently occur over just what an agency is supposed to accomplish. For example, if we believe that the Environmental Protection Agency (EPA) is supposed to eliminate pollution, its present policy of reducing only some pollution can be judged a failure. There is also the question of cost. Not everyone would agree that the elimination of all pollu-

tion, at a cost of $500 billion and the loss of millions of jobs, is a success. In some cases an agency might be given a responsibility that it cannot handle. Depriving the EPA of sufficient funds, staff, and legal authority, for instance, probably would doom it to failure. A related issue is whether a task is technically possible—there might be no way to eliminate some types of pollution despite the existence of well-run, sufficiently funded programs.

Let us begin our analysis of the effectiveness of the federal bureaucracy by examining some of its clear successes.

Bureaucratic Successes

Many federal agencies have excellent records of public service. A familiar example is the Internal Revenue Service (IRS), which is able to collect hundreds of billions of dollars in taxes cheaply and with very few administrative difficulties. In 1985, for example, the IRS processed more than 172 million individual tax returns. Its staff of 88,000 helped to collect $737 billion that year. Of course, citizens complain about high taxes and complex tax forms, but given the enormous job it faces, the IRS has performed an essential function well. Stories of lost tax returns, excessive delays, incompetent employees, corruption, and breakdowns in service are the exception. Similarly, between World War II and the war in Vietnam, the Selective Service System (the agency in charge of military enlistment and the draft) was highly effective in raising a large military force. Here again, bureaucratic organization managed to do a competent job despite enormous potential problems. Most recently, thanks to the efforts of government agencies, workplace accidents in dangerous occupations have been reduced. Progress has also been made in cutting down worker exposure to unsafe chemicals, such as asbestos and vinyl chloride. The food stamp program has helped to reduce hunger and malnutrition.

Government bureaucracies have also had a long history of success in technical projects. Government agencies built the world's first atomic

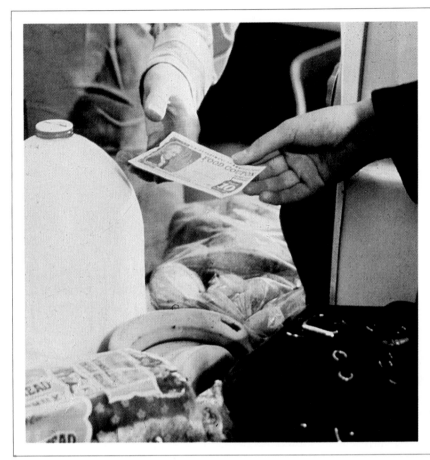

Supermarkets across the nation accept food stamps as payment for groceries. The program has helped millions of parents feed their families.

bomb, constructed the extensive interstate highway system, brought electricity to millions of rural Americans through the Rural Electrification Administration, and put a man on the moon. Much of our system of ports, canals, dams, bridges, airports, and scientific laboratories were created by federal, state, and local bureaucracies. A great deal of highly useful research has been conducted or initiated by bureaucracies, such as the National Science Foundation and the National Institute of Mental Health.

It is widely acknowledged that the federal bureaucracy is relatively free of the corruption so characteristic of bureaucracies in many other nations and in some states and communities. Federal bureaucrats do not buy their jobs and then make up the expense by taking bribes. Nor, typically, do they use their power to punish their political ene-

mies and reward their friends. It would be unthinkable, for example, if Republicans in the Social Security Administration used their positions to deny benefits to Democrats. Of course, some scandals occur, but despite all the opportunities for abuses of power, surprisingly few have taken place. Moreover, thanks in part to the merit system, civil servants tend to be well trained and well qualified for their positions.

Finally, most people who have dealt with government bureaucracy seem satisfied with their experience. In one study of citizen contacts with a variety of programs involving both state and federal rules, only 14 percent of the sample reported dissatisfaction with the service they received. Many respondents did not necessarily enjoy the experience, but they accepted the forms and delays philosophically. This study suggests that the brib-

During this lunar probe, in 1971—the sixth in a series conducted by the nation's space agency, NASA—astronauts Alan Shepard, Edgar Mitchell, and Stuart Roosa conducted valuable scientific experiments.

ery, inefficiency, and discourtesy characteristic of many bureaucracies in other nations seem to be relatively rare in the United States.

Limits on Bureaucratic Effectiveness

Although the federal bureaucracy has had successes in some areas, it has been less successful in others, especially in trying to carry out programs to correct deeply rooted social problems. The Justice Department, despite enormous expenditures and many special bureaus, task forces, experimental programs, and research projects, has had only limited success in reducing the crime rate. Similarly, the Medicare program, once believed to be the solution to health-care problems for the elderly, has generated huge cost overruns, driven up the price of medical care, and been the source of numerous scandals and frauds. During President Lyndon Johnson's administration (1963–69), a number of antipoverty programs, generally called the Great Society Program, were enacted. Some of these programs were poorly administered, wasteful, and achieved only meager accomplishments. Agencies designed to improve the quality of life (for example, the Environmental Protection Agency) have been accused of exhibiting "waste, bias, stupidity, concentration on trivia, conflicts among the regulators, and worst of all, arbitrary and uncontrolled power."

The Oakland Project as a Case Study

The types of problems the federal bureaucracy encounters are well illustrated by what happened in Oakland, California, in the 1960s. As part of the Great Society, the Economic Development Administration (EDA) of the Department of Commerce decided to help revitalize Oakland. In the 1960s, Oakland was a city with a large number of poor people, high unemployment, and a deteriorating economic base. On April 29, 1966, the Assistant Secretary of Commerce in charge of the EDA announced a $23.3-million plan to build various projects, such as a new airline terminal and a marine terminal in Oakland, to create three thousand jobs for the unemployed. Government, the business community, and local residents were all to be involved.

As described by Jeffrey L. Pressman and Aaron Wildavsky in their book *Implementation* (1973), the best of bureaucratic intentions plus $23.3 million can produce more frustrations than accomplishments. First, because many key decisions had to be approved by several layers of bureaucracy, there was considerable confusion and delay. For example, when one Oakland business wanted to initiate a job-training program, the proposal had to pass through eight separate and time-consuming bureaucratic reviews. The review process involved three separate federal agencies, which ultimately disagreed over the plan. Second, participants in the project frequently disagreed over priorities. Whereas black leaders emphasized the creation of new jobs, business groups were more interested in stimulating the local economy and in building facilities. Labor leaders wanted union members given preference; black leaders wanted jobs for blacks. These differences were understandable, given the scope of the Oakland project, but they led to delay and uncertainty. Finally, the desire to maximize participation and consultation frequently meant that nobody had the power to take action. Officials in Washington, local bureaucrats, community leaders, local elected officials, and Oakland business people all had some influence, but no single person or group could produce a solution. It is not surprising, then, that after three years and thousands of meetings, hundreds of memos, and millions of dollars, a grand total of only twenty jobs for minorities had been created.

Perhaps the clearest lesson from the failure of the Oakland project is that success is hard to achieve when problems are complex. When a bureaucracy is devoted to one goal—even an expensive one—the chance of success is likely to be higher than when several goals must be accomplished simultaneously. To see how this works, let us briefly consider two approaches to slum housing that show that as the standards for bureaucratic success become increasingly complex, effectiveness becomes more difficult to achieve.

The Difficulty of Achieving Complex Goals

Imagine a largely black inner-city slum. If the government's goal were only to build decent housing for the fewest dollars, the task would be relatively simple—contractors would bid on the project, and officials would accept the lowest bid. This was the traditional way slums were cleared until the 1960s, and success, as measured by living units built for each dollar, was usually high. Then things became more complex. Because of the civil rights movement, federal laws, and court decisions, racially segregated housing was no longer acceptable. People also became concerned that public housing tended to breed crime and social disorganization. Agencies charged with rebuilding slums were now given the added responsibility of creating a good environment for the new housing. Attention had to be given to recreation and shopping facilities, protection against crime, nearness to transportation, and so on.

The redevelopment agency had to consult with the tenants moving into the new housing about what they wanted. Architects and engineers had to be found who could meet these varying needs within budgetary limitations. In many instances the housing developer became responsible for the "human ecology" of the project—the ratio of blacks to whites, the ratio of middle-income to lower-income residents, the number of children allowed, and so forth.

Beginning in the 1970s, a new set of requirements was added—the social composition of the work force building the housing. An agency had to find contractors with sufficient numbers of minority employees to work on the project, and some building contracts were given to minority-owned businesses. These rules sometimes necessitated special training programs or led to court suits to enforce hiring agreements, both of which meant costly delays. The agency also had to be prepared to follow Environmental Protection Agency standards, another potential source of increased expense and delay. During the project, hearings would be held to enable groups and individuals to respond to agency plans. It was possible that several years after the housing project was begun, there would be little to show except plans, administrative salaries, legal fees, delays, and unresolved disputes.

Obviously, it is relatively easy for a federal agency to be effective if it wants only to construct good, inexpensive buildings. If it seeks to provide a good environment, with the right balance of tenants, that meets the needs of the community and that furthers minority employment, effectiveness is more difficult to achieve. As government moves into more difficult areas (for example, crime prevention and poverty) and bureaucracies are held accountable for more, and sometimes contradictory, goals, effectiveness will probably decline.

Check Your Understanding

1. Describe some of the major accomplishments of the federal bureaucracy.

2. What types of problems are likely to be especially troublesome to federal bureaucracies?

DOES THE FEDERAL BUREAUCRACY POSE A THREAT TO DEMOCRATIC GOVERNMENT?

The federal bureaucracy has been criticized for its size and inefficiency. Perhaps the most serious criticism, however, concerns whether a huge bureaucracy should exist in a democratic government. A commonly expressed fear is that the bureaucracy, sometimes called the fourth branch of government, will pursue its own goals rather than those of the elected Congress and the President. That is, a program desired by the people and enacted into law by Congress and the President might be harmed by bureaucrats who oppose the program. Let us briefly review the problems of bureaucratic accountability.

Factors Reducing Control over the Bureaucracy
Delegation of Power

A once-popular view of the relationship between elected officials and bureaucrats was that elected officials enacted the laws and bureaucrats merely enforced them. In contemporary government, however, the line between "making law" and "administering law" has almost disappeared. Many, if not most, laws are written in broad terms that delegate considerable discretionary power to the agencies that administer the law. A law dealing with environmental pollution may express the broad intent of Congress, but it typically allows the agency to fill in important details by issuing regulations that have the power of law. Such regulations might, for example, specify the permissible levels of pollution or how a toxic waste site is to be cleaned up. In some cases, federal courts have permitted agencies to establish broad policy even when Congress did not specifically give them this authority. Such delegation of power is necessary. Congress cannot write detailed, complex legislation that anticipates every new development, nor can Congress closely monitor the ongoing administration of the law.

On the other hand, delegation of power can provide bureaucrats with an open invitation to create their own programs. Theodore Lowi offers an excellent analysis of the process in his description of the role given to the Consumer Product Safety Commission (CPSC). Congress gave the CPSC the responsibility to protect consumers, but the legislation does not specify what risks are to be eliminated, what constitutes a "risk" to consumers, or how the agency should remove any dangers it finds. As a result, the CPSC has been able to pursue an independent, and somewhat unpredictable, policy of banning certain consumer goods and issuing product design standards. It has used its powers extensively. For example, one study found that between 1973 and 1980, the CPSC initiated some 2,600 recalls of defective products involving some 120 million items. Between 1966 and 1980, some 86 million motor vehicles were recalled. Lowi describes the CPSC, which is not

Issue: The Public and Government Regulation

We saw in Chapter 4 that gauging public opinion on major issues is often difficult. This is especially true if people are asked what they think about government regulation.

In the first place, the whole issue of regulation is so broad that there is no one way to assess public sentiment. We could ask questions about the general idea of regulation, regulation of specific industries, the enforcement of regulations, the acceptable costs of regulation, and so on. Responses to each question would shed light on a portion of the public's thinking on regulation, but not on the whole picture.

Second, since regulation often involves important but highly complex topics, the significance of the public response is always open to question. That is, public opinion might be based on faulty information or a misunderstanding of government policy. If this were the case, the messages conveyed by polls would be of little value.

Those who have examined public thinking on regulation find a complicated collection of prefer-

ences. Since the 1930s, the public seems opposed to government regulation in general. For example, a 1935 Gallup poll reported that by a 53–47 margin, the public opposed further government economic regulation. Nearly a half-century later, a 1981 CBS/*New York Times* poll reported that nearly two-thirds of the American people felt that government regulation of business had gone too far. A 1981 Harris poll found 59 percent agreeing with the idea that the best government is the one that governs least.

Does this mean that the public wants to roll back regulatory efforts? Not quite. It seems that while people oppose government regulation in the abstract, they are willing to accept existing (and high) levels of regulation when confronting actual situations. In opinion polls that offer respondents the alternative of "less regulation," that is rarely the most popular choice. Acceptance of regulation is especially visible when people are asked about specific industries. A 1976 Harris poll, for example, found 80 per-

cent in favor of regulating the drug industry; 66 percent, the banking industry; 67 percent, the airlines. In fact, a majority of respondents endorsed regulation for each of the thirteen industries mentioned in the poll. (However, majorities also opposed further industry regulation.) A 1978 poll found that in areas such as occupational safety, consumer products, and environmental protection, more people accepted than rejected the additional costs of regulation.

When these and many other poll results are compared, it is not easy to decipher a single loud and clear message on regulation. Regulation in the abstract is not popular, but the public does not want to eliminate it. Majorities often accept the idea that regulation is needed for the public welfare, yet the same majorities object to the idea that government can tell businesses how to run their affairs. Obviously, it is difficult for public officials to use public opinion as a precise guideline in grappling with the problem of regulation.

unique in its authority, as "an example of pure administrative power."

Differing Perspectives

The ability of elected leaders to control the bureaucracy is also hindered by the different perspectives of each type of official. A member of Congress and a civil servant do not always see eye to eye on problems and solutions. This difference in

perspective has its roots in two factors: (1) the people with whom elected officials and bureaucrats regularly interact and (2) different administrative styles.

Members of Congress, the President, and top political appointees must deal with a large variety of interests. A typical legislator might have to accommodate the demands of farmers, labor unions, unemployed workers, local business

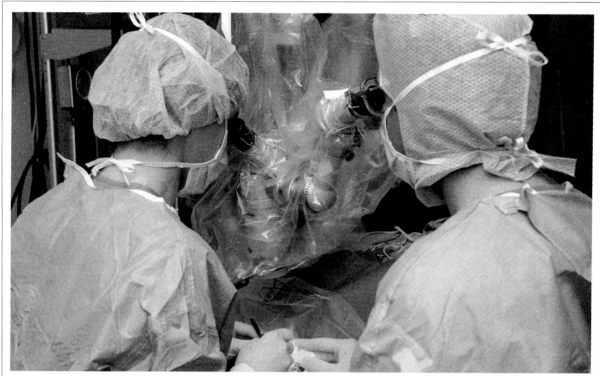

The Veterans Administration, the agency devoted to the needs of the nation's millions of veterans and their dependents, was established in 1930. At thousands of VA hospitals like this one around the country, veterans receive comprehensive, free medical care.

groups, and many others. Moreover, the prominence of different interests varies over time as issues come and go. The President has to satisfy an even greater range of groups, many of whom oppose each other. Thus elected officials generally have to develop a broad view.

Career civil servants, on the other hand, deal with fewer interests and a narrower range of demands. For example, top officials at the Veterans Administration deal primarily with leaders of veterans' groups, people doing business with the VA, and the relevant committees in Congress. Frequently, agency bureaucrats develop a common viewpoint with the agency's clients. That an agency and its clients should have a shared perspective is understandable, given the regular contacts between the two. Moreover, there is often a "revolving door" between top agency officials and private groups—those active in veterans' affairs might be appointed to government positions and

vice versa. As a result of these common ties, when the President or Congress wants to institute a new policy unfavorable to an agency's clientele, agency bureaucrats are likely to resist. Loyalty to the clientele can override loyalty to elected officials.

This resistance can take a number of forms. One common tactic is simply to delay implementing the new policy. Postponement can be justified on the grounds that more research is needed, unexpected problems have occurred, and the like. A long delay could cause elected officials to lose interest in the policy, or the officials might retire or be defeated at the polls. An agency can protect its clients by threatening to implement the policy in such a way as to harm the interests of the official who proposed the change. For example, if President Reagan insisted that the Veterans Administration eliminate underused hospitals, the VA could propose shutting down hospitals in the districts of the President's close congressional allies.

Because the hospitals are often valuable to the local economy, the President would be under pressure from his allies to cancel the cutbacks.

Career bureaucrats and elected officials also differ in how they approach and solve problems. Because of the pressures of reelection and the need to accomplish something that will receive publicity, elected leaders prefer rapid, large-scale action. A President, for example, might direct a Cabinet Secretary to initiate a program to apply high technology to older industries. The President and top appointed officials would expect the program to be functioning in two or three years at most—a relatively fast pace for a government program. This style of action frequently goes against the inclinations of career bureaucrats. Hugh Heclo, in his study of Washington bureaucracy, observes that civil servants prefer gradual to rapid action. This, claims Heclo, is understandable: in the context of a ten- or fifteen-year carrer, even a small change each year means long-term change. What a political leader wants, from the perspective of a civil servant, appears to be an upheaval. A President might say, "I want the United States self-sufficient in energy within three years," but a career bureaucrat might say, "It will take three years to establish an agency to handle the problem of energy self-sufficiency." In addition, many career civil servants are more attuned to the professional standards of their work than to the goals of political officials. A professional city planner and a top political appointee at Housing and Urban Development, for instance, would probably differ in the way they viewed a problem.

The bureaucratic style is also characterized by careful, indirect approaches to problems rather than a direct frontal attack. Unlike elected officials and the people they appoint, career civil servants must consider their long-term survival in the system. It makes sense, therefore, to avoid antagonizing others and not become identified too closely with a single policy or philosophy. A bureaucrat who, for example, vigorously championed the policies of a particular President would have problems if the administration changed its views or after the President left office. A wise civil servant ˜also knows that maintaining good relations with fellow

civil servants can be far more important than satisfying the desires of political appointees, who usually last in office only two or three years. From the perspective of an elected official with a desire for quick action, this caution appears to be unnecessary.

Problems of Managing the Agencies

Elected officials and their appointees often find it difficult to manage career bureaucrats, for several reasons. First, Cabinet secretaries, undersecretaries, and even the President usually begin their jobs unfamiliar with the inner workings of government bureaucracy and with the complex problems for which they are responsible. Being a governor, corporate lawyer, or successful business person does not always provide the knowledge and experience necessary to manage a federal government bureau. Running Ford Motor Company is not the same as running the Defense Department (the president of Ford does not, for example, deal with an organization like Congress in deciding policy).

Second, even though elected officials and political appointees can "learn on the job," top political appointees frequently don't stay on the job very long; therefore, many bureaucracies are headed by people who are still learning. One study of the Nixon administration, for example, found an annual turnover rate among presidential and executive-level appointments of between 27 and 30 percent. The average Cabinet official stayed a mere eighteen months on the job. This rate of change is typical and predictable. The more responsible government jobs are not well paid in comparison with those in private industry, the pressures are intense, and there is not much time or opportunity to make a permanent impact. In Congress the rate of turnover in membership is less rapid, but legislators rarely have the time to become well acquainted with the bureaucracies they must monitor. Turnover also makes coordination among policy-oriented appointees or elected officials more difficult. Each resignation by a Cabinet Secretary or Undersecretary or change in Congress means that new working relationships must be established. In contrast, career bureaucrats have spent years dealing with each other and the system. The upshot is that career civil servants frequently have greater expertise, experience, and established working relationships. A President or Cabinet Secretary often must rely on permanent civil servants for guidance in planning and implementing policies.

Finally, removing a career bureaucrat is extremely difficult, even when the employee is guilty of insubordination. The rules for firing civil servants require considerable specific evidence of misconduct and provide numerous opportunities for review, creating long delays. The time and energy it takes to remove a government employee and the possibility of lengthy lawsuits frequently far exceed the potential benefits. A Cabinet Secretary who insists on removing uncooperative staff people might find that such action detracts from more important matters. On occasion, even the President has been frustrated in managing personnel within the Executive Office, the one bureaucracy specifically intended to be more under presidential control.

Limitations on Bureaucratic Power

We have seen that although the federal bureaucracy was created to administer laws passed by elected officials, this "fourth branch" is not always in agreement with the first two branches of government. What prevents the federal bureaucracy from dominating the political process? Let us examine how Congress and the President can exercise a degree of control over the bureaucracy.

Congress and the Bureaucracy

Although Congress lacks direct administrative responsibility for most of the federal bureaucracy, it nevertheless has a way, known as congressional *oversight*, of ensuring that its laws will be carried out as intended (oversight is also discussed in Chapter 9). One way is through the appropriations process—cooperative agencies are rewarded, and uncooperative ones punished. Sometimes Congress will state specifically, in a law, how an agency is to spend its money. An agency may be told how to allocate its funds among programs and be prohibited from spending its money on other pro-

jects. Congress also can review the funding for an agency annually rather than authorize longer-term funding. Well-known agencies that must justify their programs each year include the National Aeronautics and Space Administration (NASA), Amtrak, and the National Science Foundation.

In addition, Congress can request an agency to submit a report on its activities and programs. It even can force an agency to consider a problem it has avoided, by requesting an agency report on the topic, together with legislative proposals. Congress also has its own investigative agencies, especially the General Accounting Office (GAO), that can review the work of executive branch bureaucracies. If, for example, Congress wished to know how the Interior Department was managing federally owned land, the GAO could be asked to investigate the program, its financial practices, and its compliance with the law. The GAO can help draft legislation to remedy problems. Congressional committee hearings in which agency personnel are required to explain and defend their activities serve a similar purpose. The possibility of being asked embarrassing questions at highly publicized hearings can be an important limitation on bureaucratic behavior.

During the 1970s and early 1980s, as noted in Chapter 9, Congress had a *legislative veto* over agencies in the executive branch. The legislative veto was a provision within a law that required an agency to receive congressional approval for some action. The veto could be exercised by both houses, a single house, or a single committee of one house, depending on the particular law. In 1981 some two hundred laws had provisions for legislative vetoes. The legislative veto was an important congressional check on executive branch agencies. It was employed fairly frequently and had involved everything from giving permission to build a science laboratory to sending U.S. troops overseas in military actions. In 1983 the Supreme Court held that the legislative veto was unconstitutional because it conflicted with the President's authority to approve and veto legislation. However, some doubt still remains within Congress as to whether the Court's action bans legislative vetoes entirely or just greatly restricts them.

The Department of the Interior is responsible for the preservation of millions of acres of wilderness, like this forestland in Alaska.

The President and the Bureaucracy

Like Congress, the President has several important powers relevant to managing the bureaucracy—especially the authority to prepare the national budget. The President's budget, which must be approved by Congress, sets funding levels for each department. Financial appropriations can be strong rewards and punishments in achieving a President's goals. In 1982 President Reagan used this power to further his goal of reducing economic regulation. For example, to reduce regulations on mining, Reagan's budget cut some 360 positions from the Department of Interior's office of surface mining, eliminated five regional offices, and decreased the number of federal mining inspectors. Overall, in order to lower the bureaucracy's regulatory capacity, the 1982 budget imposed cuts averaging 10 percent on funds and 9 percent on staff for fifty-seven regulatory agencies.

The power to reorganize the bureaucracy is another possible means of presidential control. Since 1949, the President has usually had the legal power to make organizational modifications subject to congressional approval; Congress usually goes along with the President. In 1970 President Nixon used this authority to replace the Bureau of the Budget with the Office of Management and Budget and thereby strengthen his control over the budgetary process. We have already mentioned that at the request of President Carter, Congress in 1978 created a new type of civil service position—the Senior Executive Service—which gives the President greater power over civil service assignments.

A third general approach available to a President is to build what might be called a **counter-bureaucracy,** in which decision-making power is given to close presidential aids in order to bypass career bureaucrats who have formal responsibility in that area. This was a favorite tactic of President Nixon during his first administration. For example, many key decisions on welfare policy were made by a White House group headed by John Ehrlichman. The purpose was to prevent decisions from being influenced by career civil servants in the Department of Health, Education and Welfare, who were seen as unsympathetic to the conservative goals of the Nixon administration. As the White House group grew in size and power, it began to ignore the top Cabinet officials and to deal with routine administrative matters rather than just general policy. Eventually, however, as the counter-bureaucracy became larger and more deeply involved in details, it became an unwieldy method of control and was abandoned.

Finally, the White House can influence the bureaucracy by taking great care to appoint people who share the President's political philosophy. Finding a thousand capable, politically "in-tune" people willing to take government jobs is not easy, but it can be done. Ronald Reagan has stressed this approach in controlling the bureaucracy. Because Reagan wanted the Interior Department to place less emphasis on conservation and more on developing natural resources, he appointed James Watt, a proponent of resource development, to head the agency. Watt in turn filled numerous lesser jobs with people who shared his prodevelopment view of the department's mission. Steps were taken to ensure that conservative appointees unfamiliar with agency procedures would not be "captured" by more liberal, permanent civil servants. Conservative task forces were created to help acquaint conservative Cabinet officials with their agencies so that they would not be dependent on the advice of those who opposed their programs. Reagan made an effort to meet *his* appointees and stress the importance of implementing *his* program, not the programs of the bureaucrats.

Other Restrictions on the Bureaucracy

Besides the power of Congress and the President, there are several other limitations on the bureaucracy. Especially in recent years, the federal courts have come to play a major role in checking the arbitrary or even unlawful actions of federal agencies. The Administrative Procedure Act of 1946 allows an individual who has been adversely affected by an agency regulation to seek assistance in the courts. Under current legal doctrine, an individual need not suffer serious and direct harm from an agency's actions in order to bring suit. For example, in 1973 the Supreme Court reviewed a

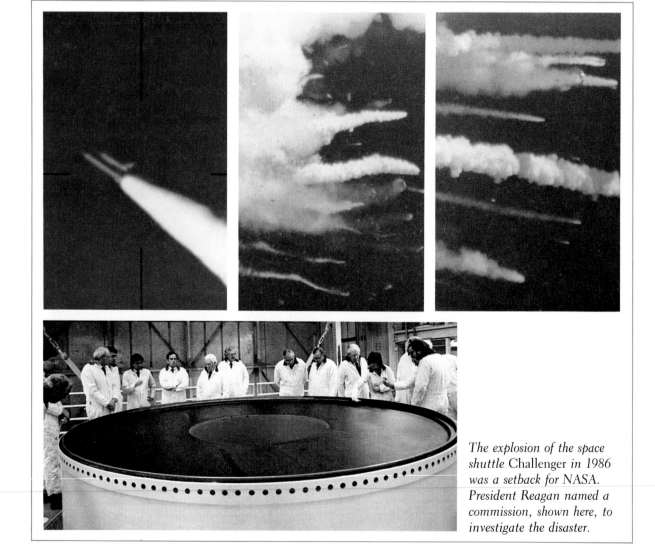

The explosion of the space shuttle Challenger *in 1986 was a setback for NASA. President Reagan named a commission, shown here, to investigate the disaster.*

case in which a group of law school students challenged an Interstate Commerce Commission decision that gave railroads a temporary rate increase of 2.5 percent. The students asserted that because this increase made recyclable products more expensive, the ICC should have conducted an environmental impact study, as required by the National Environmental Impact Policy Act of 1969. The students lost, but only because the Court ruled that it lacked jurisdiction over temporary rate increases.

Individual civil servants who are willing to come forth to expose agency problems and abuses are another source of restraint. These "whistleblowers" often provide inside information to members of Congress or the mass media, to the displeasure of their bosses in the agencies. One well-known whistleblower in recent years was A. Ernest Fitzgerald, an employee of the Department of Defense. On several occasions he testified before Congress about inefficient Pentagon purchasing policies that add unnecessary billions to the cost of national defense. The threat of an employee to "go public" with information that might embarrass an agency can be an important means to promote agency compliance with the law. To ensure that whistleblowers will not be harassed, the 1978 Civil Service Reform Act created an Office of Special Counsel to investigate possible punishments against whistleblowers and to provide protection against dismissal.

Who Does Control the Bureaucracy?

At the beginning of this section we raised the possibility that the bureaucracy poses a threat to democratic government because it can thwart the will of the people acting through their elected leaders. We have seen that this is a genuine possibility, despite the many powers available to elected leaders to control the federal bureaucracy. On more than one occasion, legislation enacted by Congress and the President has come to little because of resistance or incompetence within a federal agency. Recently, for example, both President Reagan and Congress campaigned against wasteful

Defense Department purchasing procedures. Changes have been slow, however, despite the publicity and pressure.

The issue of bureaucracy is more complex, however, than figuring out who wins in making policy. Obviously, if government agencies systematically ignored elected officials, we would have to conclude that the will of the people was being subverted. In day-to-day "real world" politics, such conflict is rarely so clear-cut. More often, there are differences among elected officials on the proper role of a government agency, and bureaucratic resistance to presidential orders might be justified as a means of following the will of the people. In other words, the conflict between the bureaucracy and elected leaders is not always a simple battle between good and evil.

To appreciate the complexity of the conflict, think of the controversy involving the Environmental Protection Agency during the early 1980s. President Reagan viewed his election in 1980 as a mandate for less government regulation—in the case of the EPA, a less vigorous enforcement of antipollution laws. Reagan did not want the agency to violate existing laws; rather, he believed that in the past, the agency's policies had been unwise and too antibusiness. Often, he believed, jobs and economic development had been sacrificed to achieve small reductions in pollution. Through the appointment and budgetary processes the President attempted to redirect the EPA more toward his own philosophy. He named as administrator Anne Gorsuch Burford, a strong critic of existing environmental protection laws. Between 1981 and 1982, the agency's operating budget was cut 29 percent and the staff was reduced substantially. For a period, an elected official was controlling a Washington bureaucracy—the "new" EPA—to achieve goals clearly stated in an election campaign.

Reagan's approach, however, greatly disturbed environmentalists, who believed that the EPA should vigorously enforce antipollution laws. Some of these critics were bureaucrats within the EPA itself, and they soon gained allies among members of Congress and various interest groups, like the Sierra Club, to reverse Reagan's redirection of the EPA. After many highly publicized congressional hearings, charges of law-breaking and cover-ups, and investigations of mismanagement, Burford and several other Reagan appointees were forced to resign. Congress also refused to accept Reagan's budgetary cutbacks and added $10 million more to the EPA's budget than the President requested. A new director without close ties to Reagan—William Ruckleshaus—was appointed. Ruckleshaus immediately announced that the EPA would return to a policy of more vigorous enforcement of antipollution laws.

Several lessons can be drawn from this example and similar political conflicts. First, elected officials frequently disagree among themselves about what policies ought to be pursued. Thus, rarely is the battle a simple one of elected officials versus the bureaucrats. The President might pressure the Interior Department to reduce expenditures for national parks, but members of Congress might want to increase spending for the parks. Elected leaders might agree that something ought to be done but disagree on how much to spend on the specifics. Second, bureaucratic resistance to elected officials need not mean that the public will is violated. A President might complain about the difficulty of creating new programs, but programs already established might have widespread public support. Officials of the EPA who resisted President Reagan certainly could claim strong public backing for their position. Finally, the cautious, rule-oriented character of the bureaucracy can provide a valuable check against abuses of power and illegal actions by elected officials and their appointees. This possibility was well illustrated when President Nixon and some of his aides devised a plan to harass their enemies with illegal wiretaps, burglaries, and other "dirty tricks." When FBI director J. Edgar Hoover refused to cooperate, the plan was dropped. Bureaucratic obstruction can thus be a vice or a virtue, depending on what elected officials want to accomplish.

To return to the question of whether the vast federal bureaucracy poses a threat to democratic government, the answer is that a potential threat exists. It is possible that the public will be thwarted by the agencies responsible for administering the policies enacted by Congress and the President. But the unresponsiveness of the bureaucracy to Congress or the President does not automatically mean that public preferences are being undermined. Often agencies are pressured in different directions by elected officials and groups representing the public. Under such circumstances no single course of action will satisfy everyone. In addition, elected leaders can misjudge what the public wants. In such cases, career bureaucrats may be more in tune with the public. In short, the potential for undermining democracy does not necessarily mean that democracy *will* be undermined.

Check Your Understanding

1. Why do career bureaucrats and elected officials often differ in the way they view problems and solutions?

2. What types of problems do political appointees typically face in managing bureaucracies?

3. How can Congress attempt to control the bureaucracy? How can the President try to control it?

4. In what way can bureaucratic independence help maintain democracy?

THE POLITICS OF THE BURDENS OF BUREAUCRACY

That something ought to be done about bureaucratic growth and the expansion of regulation has become widely accepted. In the 1980 election both Reagan and Carter agreed on this issue.

Moreover, changes are occurring. In recent years bureaucratic involvement in the airline, trucking, bus, and banking industries has been reduced. Airlines, for example, now have much more freedom in their fares, routes, merger opportunities, and the operation of charters. President Reagan issued numerous executive orders to streamline the bureaucracy, and these efforts have had an impact. In 1982 the Reagan administration claimed that paperwork had been reduced by 13 percent from the Carter presidency, (saving 200 million hours per year). Between 1980 and 1981 the number of rules issued by federal agencies declined from 7,755 to 6,481. Even the size of the federal work force has been reduced slightly.

It would be a serious mistake, however, to believe that the federal bureaucracy can be significantly shut down and regulations sharply reduced. Cries for less bureaucracy are usually general demands; it is much more difficult to say what agency should be abolished or what rules eliminated. As the former EPA administrator put it: "People are fed up with regulations, but that begins to fall apart the minute you start asking about specific regulations." The Western rancher whose livelihood depends on several federal bureaucracies to supply water, control the spread of disease, prevent soil erosion, and market U.S. agricultural products overseas might judge the government's effort to ensure workplace safety as meddling and a waste of tax money. A cotton mill worker worried over dust has a different perspective, however. The lack of agreement on "unnecessary bureaucracy" means that it will be difficult to make significant cuts.

Advocates of a "let's get the government off our backs" approach also fail to realize that many citizens and leaders want the results of such bureaucratic interference. Almost everyone wants clean water, safe automobiles, standards for commercial aircraft construction, health-care programs, and many other benefits. Groups will sometimes exert considerable pressure to maintain the "heavy burden" of government. For example, deregulation of the trucking and airline industries has been resisted by unions and smaller companies, who fear unrestricted competition. Opponents of bureaucratic regulation sometimes want programs with all benefits at no cost, an impossible demand.

It is important to remember that an attack on "bloated bureaucracy" might disguise an attack on the program itself, not on its administration. An unscrupulous loan company that regularly swindles its customers will probably focus on the "unnecessary paperwork" of government rules protecting borrowers, not on the program itself. Criticizing the costs of abiding by government regulations is often a far better tactic than defending questionable business practices.

In short, the debate over the burdens of bureaucracy is more than a debate over good versus evil. Hundreds of bureaucratic agencies exist to accomplish goals believed to be desirable by at least some elected officials and citizens. These agencies might not always operate efficiently, but eliminating them is no guarantee of improving the system. In some respects this situation is comparable to a medicine and its unpleasant side effects—as long as the benefits outweigh the costs, take the medicine.

Anne Gorsuch Burford, then head of the Environmental Protection Agency, testifies in 1983 before a House committee investigating charges of mismanagement at the EPA.

CHAPTER SUMMARY

What is the federal bureaucracy? "Bureaucracy" refers to both a method of doing business and a large number of organizations that do the work of the federal government. As a way of doing business, bureaucracies emphasize a clear division of labor, hierarchical authority patterns, specific job qualifications, and administrative objectivity. Bureaucratic agencies are the organizations that do the work of government. The bureaucratic approach is used because of its comparative effectiveness in dealing with large-scale problems. Some of the major elements of the federal bureaucracy are Cabinet-level departments, independent executive agencies and corporations, and independent regulatory commissions.

Why has the federal bureaucracy grown so large? Population increases, technological developments, and growth in government responsibility have contributed greatly to bureaucratic expansion. Since the 1960s, the rise in bureaucratic regulation has been especially pronounced. Attempts to solve complex problems in a fair manner have helped generate enormous quantities of red tape. The need for extensive information has also contributed to government paperwork.

Is the federal bureaucracy effective? It has been relatively effective in many areas, especially in projects that involve a single, clear goal. The bureaucracy is also comparatively free of corruption, and most of its clients seem to be satisfied. However, when agencies attempt projects with numerous, complex goals, success is less likely. In many instances, goals come into conflict and problems are beyond the capabilities of government to solve.

Does the federal bureaucracy pose a threat to democratic government? Because of bureaucratic resistance, elected officials cannot always enact their programs. In many cases agencies possess the power to issue their own rules, loyalty might be given to agency clients rather than to public officials, and bureaucrats differ from elected officials in how they approach problems. Means by which bureaucracies can be controlled include congressional oversight, the budgetary process, and personnel decisions. In practice, control is highly complex, because elected officials differ among themselves and bureaucrats may respond to groups outside government. The potential for thwarting the will of the public exists; but it is often difficult to say whether this occurs.

IMPORTANT TERMS

Explain the following terms.

bureaucratic approach
dismissal for cause
civil service system
merit system
agency client
red tape
due process
delegation of power
counter-bureaucracy
whistleblower

THINKING CRITICALLY

1. One suggestion for improving the quality of federal bureaucrats is to create a special college to train civil servants (a West Point of the bureaucracy). What might be the advantages and disadvantages of recruiting most top officials from a single school or college? Discuss your answer.

2. Do you agree that the federal government has an obligation to protect citizens in advance from faulty products? Why or why not? How much responsibility should citizens assume in protecting themselves?

3. Would it be more effective to turn over to private industry many of the large, complex projects now handled by the government? Discuss your answer.

4. In 1980 the Department of Education became a new Cabinet-level office. Do you think education should have its own Cabinet department? Why or why not?

5. What should government policy be toward whistleblowers—civil servants who expose agency problems? Discuss your answer.

6. Do you agree or disagree with the idea that a bureaucracy should be set up only when it can provide services, such as national defense, that individuals or corporations cannot provide? Explain your answer.

EXTENDING YOUR UNDERSTANDING

1. How is a bureaucratic approach applied to your school? Prepare a chart that shows which administrators, teachers, or others are responsible for which tasks.

2. Contact the office of a federal agency in your locality. Find out what kind of work the office does and what services it provides. Explain how this agency applies a bureaucratic approach to its operation. Write your findings in a report.

3. Contact the Student Financial Assistance office of the Department of Education in your locality. Ask about the procedures for obtaining federal money to help pay for college. Examine the regulations involved. What are the purposes of the various rules? Are they clear? Could any be eliminated? Present your findings to the class.

4. Choose one of the departments or agencies in the executive branch of the federal government that interests you. Contact the nearest office of that agency. Find out what types of jobs the agency has and the qualifications for obtaining those jobs.

MAKING DECISIONS

You are an official charged with improving the operation of a government program you head, such as Social Security, unemployment insurance, Medicare, food stamps, and so on. Do research on the qualifications for receiving program benefits and on the procedures for applying for these benefits. Decide how the program could be improved. Prepare a proposal outlining your recommendations and your reasons for making them.

Chapter 12

The Supreme Court and the Judicial System

Compared to Congress and the President, the judicial branch of government seems to be the weakest partner. Unlike Congress, it lacks the broad constitutional authority to involve itself directly in many important areas. The courts cannot rule on an issue unless a case involving that issue comes before them. Even then, judges are usually limited by the specific facts of the case and by elaborate legal codes and procedural guidelines. In the face of the executive bureaucracy and contemporary presidential power, the federal courts appear almost overwhelmed. It might take years before the courts have the opportunity to deal with executive branch decisions. Moreover, the appointment of judges and much of their work are determined by the legislative and executive branches. Congress, for example, can restrict the type of cases that may be heard by federal courts. Yet, despite these handicaps, the court system has been able to hold its own. In fact, certain critics of the federal judiciary have asserted that judges have become too powerful. Critics fear that nonelected judges can even undermine democracy. Especially in sensitive matters involving racial and economic policy, federal judges—not elected officials—are making and enforcing public policy. Despite opposition from Congress, the President, and much of the public, judges often have had the final say. This chapter examines three questions on the role of the federal court system in the political process:

- What is the federal court system, and how does it function?
- How do Supreme Court justices decide cases?
- What has been the political impact of the Supreme Court?

PREVIEW

What is the federal court system, and how does it function? Beyond creating the Supreme Court, the Constitution is vague about the judiciary. The organization of the federal court system has changed several times in our history. Currently its major elements are federal district courts, courts of appeals, the Supreme Court, and specialized courts, such as the U.S. Claims Court. Court jurisdiction (that is, the types of cases that a court can decide) is set both by the Constitution and by Congress. Especially when constitutional questions, acts of foreign nations, or issues of federal law are involved, cases are handled in federal courts. Federal judges are appointed by the President and are confirmed (or rejected) by the Senate. For federal district judgeships, political connections and support are necessary; at the Supreme Court level, philosophical agreement with the President is important. Almost all appointed judges are members of the President's political party. A potential federal judge must also meet legal training and ethical standards.

How do Supreme Court justices decide cases? Cases from the district courts and appeals courts may be sent to the Supreme Court. A case is considered if it raises important legal issues, if lower courts have given conflicting opinions, or if lower-court decisions conflict with previous Supreme Court rulings. Reaching the high Court also requires much time and money.

One description of the way Supreme Court justices approach voting is that they simply compare the Constitution and the case. Usually, however, cases are too complex for this technique. Following precedent (previous rulings) is another possible way. If precedent were clear, though, the case would probably not have reached the Court in the first place (and precedents can conflict). The attitudes of justices are good predictors of how they will vote, although judges are not supposed to enact their personal biases into law. Finally, the interactions of the nine justices and outside pressures can affect the final decision.

What has been the political impact of the Supreme Court? The Court can affect public policy through its power to declare laws and executive actions unconstitutional. It can also reinterpret existing legislation. Recently, for instance, lower courts have actually administered school districts and hospitals.

The Court has been criticized, at times in our history, for the types of rulings it makes. During the second half of the nineteenth century, the Court's rulings tended to favor the interests of businesses rather than of individual workers. At other times—especially during the Warren Court (1953–69)—the Court has played a strong role in protecting less powerful groups.

There are a number of limitations on the power of the judicial system. The Supreme Court must wait for cases to be brought to it—it cannot seek them out. The courts are reluctant, generally, to become involved in "political questions." The courts cannot, on their own, ensure that their rulings are obeyed. Finally, both Congress and the President play a role in determining the courts' jurisdictions, enforcing court orders, rewriting laws, and supporting possible constitutional amendments to reverse a Court ruling.

WHAT IS THE FEDERAL COURT SYSTEM, AND HOW DOES IT FUNCTION?

Despite the importance of the courts, even well-informed citizens know little about the judicial system or its operation. Because federal judges do not run for office and many of their activities are technical, the public's lack of familiarity with the judiciary is to be expected. Only on rare occasions—for example, when the Supreme Court makes a controversial or unpopular decision—does the judicial process receive widespread attention. To understand how the federal judicial system operates, let us consider three basic aspects of that system: (1) the federal court system, (2) federal court jurisdiction, and (3) the selection of judges.

The Federal Court System

The Constitution does not specify how the federal courts are to be organized. The Constitution says simply, in Article III, Section 1, "The judicial Power of the United States, shall be vested in one supreme Court, and in such inferior Courts as the Congress may from time to time ordain and establish." The court system is mentioned also in Article I, Section 8, in which Congress is given the power "To constitute Tribunals inferior to the supreme Court." There is no mention in the Constitution of the Supreme Court's size or of the size and number of lesser courts. The first Congress filled in some details in the Judiciary Act of 1789, which formally created the first Supreme Court, thirteen district courts (one for each state), and three circuit (or appeals) courts.

The Development of the Judicial System

This was only the first of several versions of the federal court system. The most obvious changes have been in the size of the Supreme Court. The number has varied between five and ten and is currently nine. The most important changes in the federal judicial system have occurred below the Supreme Court level. Immediately beneath the Supreme Court are the United States courts of appeals, created in 1891 to consider appeals from federal trial courts, review final decisions of these courts, and review and enforce orders of administrative bodies. (In an *appeal*, the losing side in a case asks a higher-level court to reconsider and reverse the lower court's ruling.) The United States and its territories are divided into twelve judicial circuits, with one appeals court in each circuit. Depending on the work load, between four and twenty-three judges are assigned to each court of appeals (in 1984 there were 144 judges in all). One justice of the Supreme Court is also assigned to each circuit to handle emergencies and special motions (for example, an appeal from a prisoner awaiting execution). Usually cases are tried by three-judge panels, although on special occasions all the judges in the judicial circuit will hear a case.

The courts that do most of the federal judicial work are the district courts. It is here—with very few exceptions—that cases involving federal law begin and usually end. Each state, plus the District of Columbia and the Commonwealth of Puerto Rico, has at least one federal district court, and some of the larger states have four. The federal district courts have between three and twenty-seven judges each. Most cases are tried by a single judge, although certain cases require a trial by a three-judge panel. In 1968 Congress created the Judicial Panel on Multidistrict Litigation, which provides for seven federal judges, who can be transferred temporarily to a single district for pretrial proceedings involving cases that cut across district lines. There are also federal district courts in U.S. territories, such as Guam and the Virgin Islands. Besides dealing with federal laws, the territorial courts take up many matters handled by state courts (for example, violations of local criminal law).

Special Courts

The Supreme Court, the courts of appeals, and district courts are the basic elements of the federal court system. Additionally, there are several special courts. In 1855 the United States Court of Claims was established; in 1982 it was reconstituted as the United States Claims Court. It has **original jurisdiction**—it hears cases when they first come to trial—in matters involving claims against the U.S. government. A typical case might involve a defense contractor suing the government for unpaid bills. In 1984 there were sixteen judges on the court, appointed for fifteen-year terms.

A second special court is the United States Court of Appeals for the Federal Circuit. This court was also created in 1982, to replace the United States Court of Customs and Patent Appeals. It handles appeals from district and territorial courts involving patent ownership, trademarks, certain laws regulating customs duties, and several other matters.

A third special court is the United States Court of International Trade, created in 1980 to deal mainly with tariff and trade matters. If you imported a woolen work of art (art works are duty-free) and the customs agent believed it to be a mere rug (on which there is a duty), you could take your case to this court. An American company seeking

Commentary: "OK, Team, Let's Go Out There and Win an Injunction for the Gipper"

The growth in the number of court cases has been especially pronounced in civil litigation. In 1970, about 87,300 civil cases were brought to federal district court; by 1984 this figure had risen to 261,485. By comparison, the number of criminal actions had decreased from 38,100 to 35,900. Such litigation has burdened federal judges, slowed the speed of justice, and frequently made proceedings more expensive for all parties. Equally important, the willingness of people to sue has influenced many aspects of society. Employers will often keep very detailed records of disputes with employees in anticipation of lawsuits if the employee is fired. Unmarried people living together may draw up contracts as a way of avoiding "palimony" suits. Doctors may order extra tests to pro-

tect themselves against future malpractice suits. Legal contracts have become more complex. Some companies are now reluctant to invest in new medical technologies because a single product failure, such as unanticipated side effects from a drug, can mean a devastating legal action.

Even sports disputes, once a totally private area, are now being settled by the courts. Litigation over municipal franchise agreements, the legality of player drafts, television rights to games, and the like has become commonplace. Players have even sued coaches and trainers in personal injury suits. Courts have become involved in the actual contests. In one 1977 Illinois high school game, for example, the scorekeeper forgot to remove a first-half last-second disallowed basket from the

official score. Only after the one-point game was the error discovered. Because the one disallowed basket marked the difference between victory and defeat, the losing team took its case to court and won. The second half was replayed with a new scorekeeper and no spectators.

The growing recourse to litigation in sports has considerable implications. Teams in the future may include lawyers on their coaching staffs. Football games may begin after a coin is flipped and players are read their legal rights. An unsportsmanlike conduct infraction in a football game may result in a 15-yard penalty and a million-dollar personal injury suit. A championship team may be the one that wins more lawsuits than it loses.

relief from the unfair trade practices of foreign firms importing goods to the United States could also appeal to this court.

For court-martialed military personnel there is a fourth type of special federal court, the Court of Military Appeals, which can recommend improvements in military law as well.

Finally, a taxpayer who believes that the Internal Revenue Service made an unfair ruling concerning his or her income tax can take the case to the United States Tax Court. This court can also issue advisory opinions on tax matters relating to retirement programs. The overall organization of the federal court system is shown in Figure 12.1.

Staff and Work Load of Federal Courts

Associated with each of these courts are various officials who assist in judicial administration. The major aides of the Supreme Court are the clerk, the reporter of decisions, the marshal, and the librarian. All told, about three hundred people work for the Court, from typists to legal specialists. Of particular importance in the Court's operation are the law clerks assigned to each justice (three or four for each judge). Law clerks are generally top graduates from prestigious law schools who serve for one to two years and play an important role in the Court's day-to-day business—screening cases, summarizing information, conducting research, and drafting preliminary opinions. On rare occa-

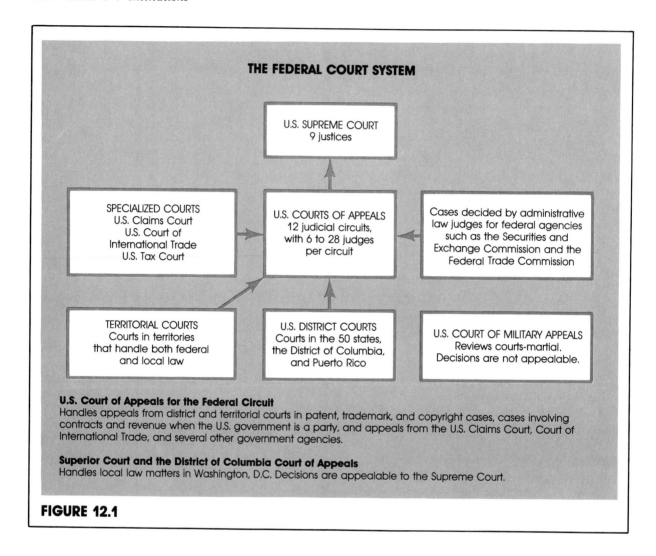

THE FEDERAL COURT SYSTEM

U.S. SUPREME COURT
9 justices

SPECIALIZED COURTS
U.S. Claims Court
U.S. Court of
International Trade
U.S. Tax Court

U.S. COURTS OF APPEALS
12 judicial circuits,
with 6 to 28 judges
per circuit

Cases decided by administrative
law judges for federal agencies
such as the Securities and
Exchange Commission and the
Federal Trade Commission

TERRITORIAL COURTS
Courts in territories
that handle both federal
and local law

U.S. DISTRICT COURTS
Courts in the 50 states,
the District of Columbia,
and Puerto Rico

U.S. COURT OF MILITARY APPEALS
Reviews courts-martial.
Decisions are not appealable.

U.S. Court of Appeals for the Federal Circuit
Handles appeals from district and territorial courts in patent, trademark, and copyright cases, cases involving contracts and revenue when the U.S. government is a party, and appeals from the U.S. Claims Court, Court of International Trade, and several other government agencies.

Superior Court and the District of Columbia Court of Appeals
Handles local law matters in Washington, D.C. Decisions are appealable to the Supreme Court.

FIGURE 12.1

sions a clerk can provide information and arguments that affect the content of written opinions or even the way a justice votes on a case.

The federal district courts have larger staffs, each consisting of a clerk, a U.S. marshal (who carries out court orders but is formally employed by the Justice Department), one or more U.S. magistrates (appointed officials who act as judges on many relatively minor disputes), probation officers, court reporters, and clerical aides. In 1939, Congress created the Administrative Office of the United States Courts to oversee the personnel, finances, and other aspects of courts below the Supreme Court level. In 1984 the entire federal judicial system employed about 17,000 people (compared to more than 2.8 million employees in the executive branch and nearly 39,000 in the legislative branch). Compared to the overall cost of running the national government, the judicial system's share is modest. In 1984, for example, the total expenditures of the judicial system were about $900 million, out of a total budget outlay of well over $800 *billion*.

The case load of the federal courts varies considerably, although the increased willingness of citizens to use the courts has placed a heavy burden on nearly all judges. The Supreme Court handles the smallest number of cases. By law, the Court begins a "term" on the first Monday in October; the term usually runs until early summer of the following year (the justices do, however, meet before the official opening to consider petitions, or requests, for review). The Court also operates on a system of alternating "sittings" and "recesses." During a sitting, which usually lasts about two weeks, the Court hears spoken arguments and holds regular conferences on cases. During recesses the justices research and write opinions, evaluate cases, discuss opinions with other justices; occasionally a conference of all the justices will be held. In 1984 a grand total of 5,006 cases came before the Court, but the vast majority were denied review—that is, the Court refused to consider them. Only 175 cases were argued before the Court; signed opinions were given in 159 of these.

By comparison, in 1984 there were 31,490 cases considered in the U.S. courts of appeals. This figure was nearly triple the number heard in 1970. The federal courts that had the heaviest load were the U.S. district courts. In 1984 a total of about 296,000 cases were begun in these courts. Only a fraction of the trials involved federal crimes, such as forgery, drug smuggling, and embezzlement. The overwhelming number of cases were **civil cases**—disputes among individuals involving contracts, (written agreements between individuals or businesses), real estate transactions, and other matters regulated by law.

Federal Court Jurisdiction

In the United States there are two court systems: the federal courts and the courts in each of the fifty states. What makes a case a "federal case"? What determines whether a case will be tried in a federal rather than in a state court? These are important questions, because *who* decides a case and according to *what* rules can have an impact on *how* a case is decided. During the 1960s, for example, many civil rights lawyers in the South sought to have their cases tried in federal rather than state courts in the hope of receiving more sympathetic treatment. Rules of evidence and procedures can also differ in the two court systems. Whether a case becomes a federal case is largely prescribed by the Constitution and by acts of Congress regulating federal court jurisdiction, or the types of cases that may come before a court.

Article III of the Constitution describes the jurisdiction of the federal, as opposed to state, courts. A case can become a federal case depending on what type of law it involves or who is involved. Regarding the *type of law* involved, an issue enters the federal system when

1. *The Constitution itself is involved.* If you challenge a federal or state law on the explicit grounds that it violates the Constitution, you might have a federal case.
2. *Laws and treaties enacted by the federal government are involved.* If Congress has made the importation of heroin illegal and you are caught importing it, you go directly to federal court. Cases involving treaties with foreign nations or with Indian tribes are less common.
3. *Cases involve admiralty and maritime jurisdiction.* These refer to crimes committed on the high seas or other navigable waters, as well as maritime-related commercial transactions.

The Constitution also gives the federal courts jurisdiction when certain *types of people* are involved. Specifically, a federal court can become involved when

1. *The U.S. government is a party, or participant, in the case.* If the federal government is suing a private citizen or is being sued by an individual for damages, the case is tried in federal court.
2. *Controversies arise between two or more states.* Such disputes would include, for example, cases in which an agency of one state was polluting water that flowed into a second state. Here, and in other instances in which a state is involved, the Supreme Court has original jurisdiction—the case starts off in the Supreme Court. However, on occasion the Supreme Court has ruled that the case first be tried in state courts, with appeal possible to the Supreme Court (see, for example, *Arizona v. New Mexico* [1976], in which one state sued another over a tax on electricity).
3. *Civil (as opposed to criminal) controversies arise between a state and citizens of another state.* In the *Georgia v. Pennsylvania R. Co.* (1945), for

instance, the state of Georgia, in federal court, sued twenty railroads for price-fixing, even though the railroads were not located in Georgia. However, the Eleventh Amendment generally forbids citizens of one state from suing another state without its permission (states may sue citizens, however).

4. *Conflict arises between citizens of different states.* If a citizen of New York sues a citizen of, say, New Jersey (or a corporation chartered in New Jersey), one of the parties can require that the trial be held in federal court. However, in the key decision in *Erie Railroad v. Tompkins* (1938), the Supreme Court ruled that federal courts must follow appropriate state (not federal) law in such circumstances. In 1982 about a quarter of all civil cases in federal district courts involved this jurisdiction.

5. *Cases involve foreign states and citizens.* If a foreign government sues a U.S. citizen, or a state sues a foreign citizen, or if a foreign and a U.S. citizen are involved, the case, at the request of one of the parties, is decided in federal court.

6. *Cases involve ambassadors, ministers, and consuls.* Under international law, ambassadors, ministers, and others representing foreign governments are exempt from U.S. jurisdiction. That is, a foreign representative may not be prosecuted for violating our criminal law. Nevertheless, a foreign ambassador suing a U.S. citizen in a civil suit would take the case to the Supreme Court, which has original jurisdiction in such matters.

The other branches of government have also used their constitutional power to regulate court jurisdiction. In the Judiciary Act of 1925, for example, Congress gave the Supreme Court considerable leeway in accepting cases appealed from the lower courts. The Administrative Procedures Act of 1946 allows decisions made by many regulatory and executive agencies to be appealed in federal courts. In 1958, Congress sought to reduce the number of cases in the federal system by requiring that a civil suit between citizens of different states involve at least $10,000 before it can be tried in federal court (cases involving workers' compensation laws are also excluded from federal courts).

Federal–State Court Relationships

Thus far, the operation of the federal system is relatively clear. What occasionally makes the situation complex is the relationship of the federal courts to the state courts. Federal courts coexist with courts in all fifty states, and an act simultaneously might violate both federal and state law. There is also the problem of federal and state courts making different decisions in similar cases. To understand the federal court–state court relationship, we must make three points. First, Article VI, paragraph 2 of the Constitution, the supremacy clause, makes federal law supreme (see Chapter 3). When state law conflicts with federal law, judges (federal and state) must enforce federal law. If an act is a crime under federal but not state law, the accused cannot win simply by taking the case to a state court. Second, when no such conflict exists, state law, as interpreted by state courts, is supreme. A state law making something a criminal act is valid even if federal law is silent on the subject. Third, state judicial decisions may be appealed in the federal system only when disputes involve federal law or the Constitution. For example, a person convicted under state law who believes that the conviction was obtained by violating the constitutionally protected right against unlawful searches may appeal on constitutional grounds. The appeal must proceed through the state court system before it may be taken directly to the Supreme Court (bypassing the lower federal courts). On the whole, Supreme Court justices are cautious in reviewing cases appealed from state courts.

Selection of Federal Judges

Who can become a Supreme Court justice or a district or circuit judge? The formal requirements for these positions are simple: nomination by the President and confirmation by a Senate majority. There are no age, training, or residency requirements (you must live within the jurisdiction of

In 1889, when the top photo was taken, the Supreme Court's decisions generally favored business interests. Nearly a century later, the Court's rulings have ranged from conservative to liberal on a number of issues—including affirmative action and capital punishment—that the earlier Court never even addressed. The lower photo shows the Court in 1987.

your court when in office, but not before). There are, however, several informal requirements, the most important of which are political associations, legal training, and "judicial temperament."

Political Requirements

Federal judges must almost always satisfy certain political requirements. Although they are not legal requirements, they are nevertheless rarely violated. Being of the same political party as the President is very important. At least 90 percent of presidential appointees have come from the ranks of the President's own party. Even a President such as Dwight Eisenhower, who was not widely regarded as a strong party leader, drew 94.8 percent of his judicial appointments from the Republican party.

A second political requirement, especially important for federal district judges, is created by the custom of *senatorial courtesy.* According to this custom, the senior senator of the President's party from the state in which the appointment is to be made usually has veto power over the nomination. In other words, a Republican President would consult the senior Republican senator from California before nominating a federal district judge for California. When there are no senators of the same party, the President has a freer hand, although the state political party organization might be consulted.

Philosophical agreement between the President and the prospective nominee is a third important political consideration. This a particularly important factor in Supreme Court appointments, because these judicial decisions can have a major impact on public policy. In the 1930s Franklin D. Roosevelt used his appointment power to create a Supreme Court more sympathetic to his goals of greater government regulation of the economy. President Nixon had campaigned on a strong "law and order" platform in 1968, and his nominees to the Supreme Court were lower-court judges who had demonstrated their toughness on criminals. In 1981 President Reagan fulfilled his 1980 campaign promise of appointing a woman justice (Sandra Day O'Connor), but she also shared many of the President's conservative political values.

Similarly, when a Supreme Court vacancy occurred in 1986, President Reagan appointed another conservative judge—Antonin Scalia. In numerous lower-court votes and opinions, Judge Scalia had made it clear that he supported the Reagan administration on such issues as affirmative action, deregulation, consumer protection, the limits of free expression, and perhaps most important, the role of the courts in making broad policy.

Although Presidents try to create a Supreme Court that closely reflects their own political views, there are obstacles to this goal. Finding a nominee who is qualified, is willing to serve, can survive Senate confirmation, *and* is in tune with the President's political goals is not always easy. As of 1986, 26 of 139 Supreme Court nominations made by Presidents had been defeated by the Senate. Moreover, many justices, once appointed, follow an independent path. There are numerous examples of conservative Presidents appointing justices who then pursued liberal objectives, and vice versa. Calvin Coolidge, a conservative, appointed Harlan Stone, who turned out to be more liberal than expected. Dwight Eisenhower was determined to appoint conservative justices, yet two of the court's most liberal members—Earl Warren and William Brennan—were his choices.

A fourth political consideration is whether or not a judicial nominee has offended a significant political group. Many groups take a strong interest in judicial appointments (see Chapter 8). In most instances nominees who are totally unacceptable to important groups are eliminated in the initial screening process by the Attorney General. These groups usually have allies in the Senate, and Presidents typically wish to avoid long and possibly unsuccessful confirmation debates. For example, it is unlikely that a lawyer known for his or her outspoken antiblack views would survive Senate confirmation hearings, and so the nomination of such an individual would be unlikely. This does not mean that a potential nominee must please everyone. The American Civil Liberties Union opposed the 1971 nomination of William Rehnquist, yet Rehnquist had little trouble being con-

Sandra Day O'Connor was appointed to the Supreme Court by Ronald Reagan in 1981. Although she is the first woman to serve on the Court, her views have generally not been profeminist.

firmed by the Senate. In 1986, Rehnquist again faced opposition from civil rights and civil liberties groups when he was nominated for the Chief Justice position after Warren Burger retired. Following several rather heated hearings, however, Rehnquist was confirmed 65 to 33 by the Senate.

Legal Training

Federal judges in practice must meet certain standards of legal training. At one time, graduation from law school was not a requirement—of all the federal district judges sitting in 1930, 46.2 percent did *not* have law degrees. Most had learned their law through on-the-job experience and then studying for the bar examination. James Byrnes, nominated in 1944, was the last Supreme Court

justice who had not graduated from law school. Today, however, a law degree is not only essential, but it also must come from an established law school. This was illustrated in the conflict over President Kennedy's nomination of Francis X. Morrissey to a district judgeship. Strong objections were raised when it was discovered that Morrissey's law degree came from a three-month extension course (nevertheless, he was approved by the Senate Judiciary Committee, but he ultimately withdrew). A prospective federal judge usually must have a good reputation among his or her colleagues and the bar association. Many federal judges are drawn from political life or are lawyers who were active in political campaigns. Some Presidents have even appointed law school professors as judges. At the Supreme Court level, one type of legal training that is not crucial is prior experience as a judge—about half the appointees in recent years have had no past experience as judges.

Judicial Temperament

The third broad requirement—**judicial temperament**—is perhaps the most difficult to define. At a minimum it means being a law-abiding, upstanding citizen. This issue is usually settled by an FBI investigation during the preliminary stages of the nomination process. Nominees with criminal records or with problems that might interfere with their work (for example, alcoholism) are eliminated.

Other important traits—impartiality, caution, legal knowledge, ethics, and propriety—are more difficult to determine. The American Bar Association (ABA), through its Committee on the Federal Judiciary, has on occasion played an important role in making these evaluations. Since 1947, the committee has been rating judicial nominees. In general, the ABA ratings have been most influential for positions below the Supreme Court level. Based on its own investigations, potential federal judges are rated qualified or unqualified (the exact terms used by the ABA have varied over time). Presidents have differed considerably in their use of these ratings. Presidents Dwight Eisenhower and Gerald Ford gave ABA ratings careful attention; Presidents Kennedy and Johnson often disregarded them. At first, President Nixon directly involved the ABA's Committee on the Federal Judiciary in evaluating appointments. When its decisions were at odds with his own views, he later excluded the committee from making evaluations. On occasion, other members of the legal profession—prominent attorneys, deans of law schools—have played roles in evaluating the qualifications of potential judges.

Such "impartial ratings," might conceal political biases. One of the most distinguished Supreme Court justices of all time—Louis Brandeis—was bitterly opposed by almost the entire organized legal profession when he was nominated in 1916. He was declared "unqualified" because of his liberal philosophy (and some people would say, because of his Jewish religion as well). For many years the ABA was dominated by establishment lawyers who found it relatively easy to say that a nominee with whom they felt uncomfortable somehow lacked "judicial temperament" or "impartiality." Such biases are not limited to conservatives. Liberals in the ABA might question the "ethics" of candidates sympathetic to business interests.

Louis D. Brandeis was a public interest lawyer before President Wilson named him to the Supreme Court. Both as an attorney and as a justice, Brandeis sided with the working class and the poor.

Check Your Understanding

1. How does the Constitution define the federal court system?

2. Which courts, including the special courts, make up the present federal judicial system?

3. Under what conditions does a legal case come under federal jurisdiction?

4. What are the constitutional requirements for federal judges?

5. In actual practice, what are the political and legal-training requirements for federal judges?

HOW DO SUPREME COURT JUSTICES DECIDE CASES?

Every year the Supreme Court makes decisions that have far-reaching and often controversial consequences. Decisions on abortion, school busing, and pornography made during the last two decades are still debated and studied. What determines how the justices arrive at their decisions? This is a difficult question to answer because only a very small part of the Court's activities take place in public, and behind-the-scenes activity occurs in secrecy. In fact, the Court's public side is visible only about six or seven days per month and then only from 10:00 A.M. to 3:00 P.M., with an hour off for lunch.

Two separate issues actually are involved in the decision process. The first concerns what particular cases the Court will examine, or place on the agenda. Only a small portion of cases appealed to the Court are ever given serious consideration, so this step is crucial. Not to consider a case is actually a decision to leave matters unchanged. The second question is: Once a case is on the agenda, what influences the outcome? How do judges weigh the evidence and make up their minds? Let us begin by considering which cases the Supreme Court considers.

How Cases Reach the Supreme Court

In 1984, of the 5,006 total cases in the docket, only 175 were actually put on the agenda. Some of these reviewed cases received little attention. No oral arguments were heard and brief *per curiam* (by the Court) decisions were issued, giving no details of how the decision was made. Many of the cases not taken for review involved matters of life and death, serious prison sentences, and huge sums of money. Why does one case make it to the Supreme Court when dozens of others do not?

Formally, cases can generally be placed on the Court agenda in one of two ways. First, the Constitution or laws passed by Congress give certain cases a right to Court consideration. As noted earlier, cases involving a conflict between two states fall under the original jurisdiction of the Court. For example, if Colorado and Arizona disagree over water rights, the case will be taken directly to the Supreme Court. And Congress has specified that certain types of cases—particularly cases in which lower federal or state courts have ruled that federal laws are unconstitutional—receive a Supreme Court review as a matter of right. The requirement that the Supreme Court take a case does not, however, mean that the case will be given an in-depth treatment. On many occasions such cases receive only minimal attention.

Most cases involve appeals from the lower courts on matters that do not require a Court review. The Supreme Court justices can exercise almost complete discretion. For both the types of cases legally guaranteed a review and all other cases, getting a full hearing involves a long and difficult path few cases survive. The clerks of the

Chief Justice do most of the early selection of cases, although other justices and their clerks participate in the process. Obviously frivolous and inappropriate cases are rejected. About one-third of the appeals survive the early selection process and are put on a "discuss list," to be reviewed in more detail at a conference of the other justices.

At this conference the Chief Justice provides a summary of the cases. Each justice, in order of length of service on the court, then offers comments. If four justices agree that the case is worth considering at length, the case is granted a **writ of certiorari**—the technical name for the Court's decision to call for the records of a case from a lower court so that it can evaluate the case in detail. As is true of the "discuss list," most requests for full consideration are denied. When a decision is made to grant certiorari, the justices will also decide whether the case deserves oral arguments or whether a final determination can be made on the basis of the available written record.

The reasons why one case is granted a full review and another is dismissed with little attention are highly complex. In some instances, the person seeking a review has not satisfied certain technical requirements. A petitioner might not have filed the proper number of copies of records, or the case might involve largely hypothetical issues (*moot questions* are discussed later in the chapter). In other instances the Court might decide that a case is outside its jurisdiction—no violation of federal law or the Constitution is involved, for example.

The Supreme Court itself has tried to address the matter in its Rule 17, which states when it will grant certiorari. Basically, Rule 17 says that a writ of certiorari exists at the discretion of the Court rather than as a right. The rule goes on to say that a review is most likely to be granted in two general circumstances: lower courts have given conflicting decisions, or lower courts have made an important decision that should be made by the Supreme Court or is in conflict with a prior decision of the Court. An example of the first category—conflict among courts—might be a case in which two federal district courts made very different decisions on how a tax law is to be interpreted. A well-known

Biography: Earl Warren

The fourteenth Chief Justice of the United States, Earl Warren was vilified as few of his predecessors had been. Bumper stickers and billboards urged his impeachment. President Dwight Eisenhower, who had nominated him, called his appointment "the biggest . . . mistake I ever made." The Warren Court had equally vehement defenders, however, who saw it as a bastion of the individual against the powers of the state.

Warren, the son of Scandinavian immigrants, was born in 1891 in Los Angeles. After graduating from the University of California, he became a lawyer and served in the infantry in World War I. In the 1920s he went to work in the Alameda County district attorney's office, where he gained a reputation as a tough prosecutor; this reputation was enhanced by a term as the state's attorney general. Warren, a bluff six-footer with an outgoint manner, was then elected a record three terms as California governor. He also ran for Vice President on the Republican ticket in 1948, when Thomas E. Dewey was narrowly defeated by Harry S. Truman.

During his California years, Warren was noted more for his conservative acceptance of prevailing attitudes than for progressive or liberal tendencies. For instance, he joined the whites-only Order of Elks. He also strongly supported the federal measure moving Japanese-Americans to re-location camps during World War II. When Eisenhower appointed Warren to the Supreme Court in 1953, most people expected a noncontroversial emphasis on the status quo. Less than a year passed before these expectations were shattered by the landmark school desegregation decision in *Brown v. Board of Education of Topeka* (1954), which sparked the civil rights movement.

Actually, Warren himself ranked *Brown* and similar cases second in importance to the Court decisions involving legislative redistricting, especially *Baker v. Carr* (1962) and *Reynolds v. Sims* (1964). He believed that if the United States had adopted a "one-man, one-vote" principle earlier in its history, racial problems would have been solved by the political process.

It was a third category of Warren Court decisions, those protecting the rights of the accused, that aroused the most fury, especially among right-wing conservatives. They thought that the decisions in such cases as *Gideon* (1963) and *Miranda* (1966) "coddled" criminals and tied the hands of law-enforcement agencies. When attacked for these rulings, Warren replied that the Court was simply "expressing the concepts of the Constitution in common language."

After the assassination of President John F. Kennedy in 1963, Warren headed a commission that investigated the crime. The Chief Justice called his

ten-month chairmanship "the unhappiest time in my life," necessitating as it did an intense concentration on the events surrounding the tragedy.

When Warren retired in 1969 (five years before his death), he remarked that "I would like the Court to be remembered as the people's court"—a sentiment he would never have expressed twenty years earlier. For Warren had moved in an unusual direction, from the conservative right to the liberal left, as he grew older. In the view of many legal scholars, it was the Court that formed Warren, not Warren that formed the Court. As he himself put it, "No man can sit on the Court over 16 years and remain parochial, for he must look out over all the United States."

example of an important issue granted a full review—the second possibility under Rule 17—was the 1974 case involving President Nixon's right to withhold taped White House conversations from Congress' Watergate investigation.

It should be noted, though, that even Rule 17 provides considerable leeway in accepting cases. It is not always clear just what constitutes a "conflict" between decisions; and even when it exists, it might not require immediate attention. Nor has the Court always demonstrated a willingness to consider important questions. If the Court so desires, a case raising fundamental issues can be avoided by asserting that the issues are best resolved by the other branches of government, that the case fails to satisfy certain technical requirements, that it is not a good case upon which to base general rules, or that the case is not a truly important one. In the 1960s, for example, the Court used several such justifications in refusing to consider the constitutionality of U.S. military involvement in Vietnam.

Because of this leeway in accepting cases, it is not surprising that the personal preferences of judges seem to play a role in their decisions. For example, a justice who strongly believes that accused criminals should be granted all possible rights will probably be sympathetic to a petition claiming that certain rights of the accused were violated. It also seems to be true that the identity of the person or organization requesting review makes a difference. In particular, when the request is from the federal government itself, the Court is more likely to act favorably than if a private citizen requests a review. Some organizations, such as the National Association for the Advancement of Colored People (NAACP), have traditionally done fairly well. Whether petitioners seeking a hearing will be successful depends, in part, on their legal skill as well as their ability to choose, from among several cases, the one that stands the best chance of being accepted.

To receive a full hearing from the Supreme Court, however, meeting the technical requirements is not enough. Time and money are also necessary. A $200 filing fee is required, although poor people and prisoners usually do not have to pay the fee. A case commonly takes between two and five years to get to the Supreme Court, and the cost for legal fees and paperwork can easily be more than $100,000. Not surprisingly, then, cases heard by the Supreme Court tend to involve either the government itself or citizens who can afford expensive legal help. For many ordinary people, the only real hope is that their plight will receive the support of some group, such as the American Civil Liberties Union (ACLU) or the NAACP. For example, the ACLU supported the suit of Stephen Wisenfeld in his long and ultimately successful quest for Social Security benefits after his wife died. The NAACP has financed a large number of key civil rights cases on behalf of citizens unable to pay their own legal fees. Only rarely do

Lawyers on the staffs of civil rights and civil liberties organizations often handle cases dealing with major constitutional issues. Here, an attorney presents papers to a judge.

we find instances like that of a Louisville, Kentucky, handyman with virtually no money or influence who took his $20 local police court fine directly to the Supreme Court and won a unanimous reversal (*Thompson v. Louisville* [1960]). However, if individuals without resources manage to reach the Court, the Court will appoint a well-qualified lawyer to represent them free of charge.

Deciding a Case

What factors determine how the Supreme Court decides a case? Do the justices carefully follow the letter of the law? Do they respond to the political climate of the day? Let us consider some of the more popular explanations of judicial decision making and the supporting evidence.

The Constitution and Federal Law as the Sole Standard

Perhaps the simplest explanation is that judge decide by mechanically comparing the facts of the case with the Constitution or federal law. In *United States v. Butler* (1936), for example, Justice Owen J. Roberts stated that the one duty of the judicial branch is "to lay the article of the Constitution which is involved beside the statute which is challenging and to decide whether the latter squares with the former." Thus, if you want to know how the Supreme Court would rule in a particular case, you need only consult the Constitution or the relevant federal statute, or law.

This explanation has many drawbacks. First, even when the Constitution or statute is fairly explicit, reasonable people can disagree over what it means. For example, the Constitution explicitly allows Congress to regulate commerce between the states, yet one of the lengthiest debates in constitutional law concerns the meaning of "interstate commmerce." The Constitution prohibits "cruel and unusual punishments," but is the electric chair cruel and unusual? Second, in many important instances the Constitution is vague or says nothing. For example, the Constitution does not mention the congressional power to investigate or oversee executive bureaucracies. What does a jus-

tice do if a case involves an investigation conducted by a congressional committee?

Problems can also occur when judges try to follow the letter of the law and the law itself is vague. A classic instance was the Sherman Antitrust Act (1890), a congressional law, which never provided clear definition of the key term "monopoly." Such vagueness can be intentional and necessary, because in complex areas Congress might realize that spelling out all the details is impossible. Another problem is that Congress might have enacted contradictory laws. Congress has passed laws promoting economic competition (the Clayton Antitrust Act) and legislation restricting vigorous competition (the Robinson-Patman Act). How can justices strictly apply conflicting laws?

An extension of applying the Constitution or federal law in a literal way is to look behind constitutional and statutory language to find the intent of those who drafted the law. In the case of the Constitution, this can mean a review of the debates of the original Constitutional Convention, the writings of the Founders in *The Federalist*, or more general analyses of what words and concepts meant in late eighteenth-century America. Debates over the adoption of amendments can also be examined. In the case of laws passed by Congress, intent can be learned by reading the reports that usually accompany bills, committee hearings testimony, legislative debate, and even public statements by those who drafted the legislation. As was true in literally interpreting the Constitution or statute, the objective is to stick faithfully to established principles.

Although it has been used by justices, this approach does have limitations. The intent of those who drafted legislation is not always clear, or a law might have been motivated by many different factors. Even when intent is crystal-clear, many of the concepts used cannot be defined precisely (for example, discrimination, rights, reasonable, due process). There is also the problem of "translating" past intention into modern situations. How would those who wrote the constitutional prohibition against unlawful searches handle a wiretapping case? In practice, given the uncertainty surrounding past enactments, this approach to deciding cases offers justices considerable leeway.

Precedent

Another explanation of judicial decision making emphasizes the role of precedent. Like English law, U.S. law operates on the principle of **stare decisis** ("let the decision stand"). The concept of stare decisis means that if two essentially similar cases arise, the decision on the second case should be based on the principles of the first. (A different system is **code law**—in which a judge applies a written code to a particular case without regard to previous decisions in similar cases.) According to the stare decisis explanation, a Supreme Court justice confronted with a new case will simply make a choice consistent with previous decisions in similar cases.

As an explanation of routine court decisions handed down in district courts, this is a good account. When it comes to Supreme Court decisions, however, stare decisis is only partially applicable. One reason is obvious. If a case could have been decided easily on the basis of precedent, the case would probably not have reached the Supreme Court in the first place. A factor that helps bring a case before the Court is an absence of clear precedent, so we cannot expect justices to follow the stare decisis rule in such instances.

Also, complex cases can involve numerous, sometimes conflicting, precedents. Which of the past cases is the most relevant? In other instances, doubts might be raised about the relevance of precedent to a new issue. Can one apply a precedent based on steamship travel to an airline case? Also, no two cases are ever exactly alike. On occasion justices simply might reject precedent as no longer relevant to contemporary values. Many of the Supreme Court's most famous rulings in recent decades in the fields of civil rights, legislative redistricting, and the rights of the accused have been clear reversals of earlier decisions. One study of the Court between 1961 and 1980 found that on average the Court reversed itself about four times per year. Overall, stare decisis cannot be ignored when precedent is overwhelming, but Supreme Court justices cannot rely on it entirely.

Political Preferences of Justices

A third major explanation of Supreme Court decision making emphasizes the political preferences of the justices. According to this view, every justice, consciously or unconsciously, holds an opinion on controversial issues. Because cases before the Court are usually complex and ambiguous, personal preferences will influence decisions. Liberal justices will decide cases in favor of liberal interests, and conservatives will decide on behalf of the conservative position. Of course, justices might claim complete objectivity and impartiality and support their decisions with evidence and judicial precedent.

Do Supreme Court justices vote their personal opinions? Much evidence suggests that they do, although this is not proof that the law and precedent are entirely disregarded. Observers of the Court note that most justices follow a highly predictable pattern in certain types of cases. For example, William O. Douglas, who served on the Court between 1939 and 1975, consistently sup-

Justice William O. Douglas, who served on the Supreme Court from 1939 to 1975, was often a controversial figure. His commitment to freedom of speech is particularly notable.

ported liberal positions on free speech and civil rights; he also advocated these positions in his public speeches and writing. By contrast, John Marshall Harlan, who served from 1955 to 1971, could almost always be counted on to oppose Douglas and take a conservative perspective on free speech and civil rights. Such consistency suggests that these justices were strongly committed to their beliefs.

That Supreme Court justices are guided by their political preferences should not be interpreted to mean that each judge mechanically decide a case strictly according to the philosophical concepts of liberalism or conservatism. In the first place, justices hold complex sets of political values rather than a simple, all-encompassing viewpoint. One study of Court members' views distinguished three dimensions of liberalism–conservatism: (1) support for or opposition to "freedom"—the rights of criminals, expression of free speech, and so on; (2) support for or opposition to "equality"—the role of law in eliminating inequalities between men and women, blacks and whites, and so on; and (3) support for or opposition to government economic intervention—the right of government to regulate business. Although some judges are liberal or conservative on all three dimensions, others take more varied positions. For example, Justice Byron White consistently has taken the liberal position on equality based on sex and race but is less liberal on the rights of criminals.

The views of justices can change with time and circumstances. For example, for many years one of the strongest defenders of individual freedom was Justice Hugo Black. Later on, however, Black became more conservative; he ended his career as one of the most conservative justices. Outside events can act as counterforces against personal beliefs. It is quite likely that the civil rights movement of the 1960s gave many justices a more sympathetic view of blacks, a view that was probably not deeply rooted in their own political philosophies. As we noted earlier in the chapter, many justices have altered their views once appointed.

Despite the importance of personal preferences, it would be a mistake to claim that justices advance their views in complete disregard of the

law. In most of the decisions before the Court, the justices—liberal, moderate, and conservative—essentially concur in their legal interpretations, so that cases are decided quickly without publicity. A justice's personal values are important, but they are most relevant when a case cannot easily be decided on clear legal grounds. And even when legal grounds are unclear, justices hold professional standards regarding what is "fact" and what is "interpretation." Supreme Court justices know that their written opinions will be widely examined within the legal profession and that strong biases will be harshly criticized.

Group Interaction of Justices

Observers claim that we cannot fully understand the behavior of the Court unless we consider the interaction of the nine individuals as they decide cases. Although justices spend most of their time alone or with their personal staffs, the need to reach a collective decision makes interaction important. Justices usually circulate draft opinions to learn the reactions of the other justices, hold meetings to discuss differences, and try to persuade their colleagues. Law clerks discussing matters among themselves also provide channels of communication. Personality conflicts and differences of opinion on the competence of colleagues regularly occur and can easily spill over into legal disputes. Some justices have refused to have anything to do with each other, and others have formed close personal friendships.

Viewing the Court as a small group of people who discuss issues helps us understand why decisions are not always the sum total of each individual justice's first response. A justice might believe that a case should be decided in a certain way, yet because of social pressure from a trusted colleague eventually might change his or her mind. Examination of the private papers of several justices has shown that judges can behave just like ordinary people trying to get their way in group decisions. Some will use flattery and friendliness to win over potential opponents. Outright vote-trading can occur. Even a justice in the minority on a case can affect the majority decision by threatening to write a strong disenting opinion unless certain changes are made in the written opinion of the majority (in *dissenting opinions* justices who voted on the losing side of a case explain their reasons). In extreme cases justices can threaten to air their differences in public. In short, like any group working on a common goal, there is give-and-take, accommodation, and bargaining.

The Chief Justice sometimes can play an especially influential role in court interaction. When drawing up the "discuss list" for granting writs of certiorari, it is the Chief Justice who by custom always speaks first and thus can set the tone of debate and describe the alternatives. The Chief Justice can also shape group interaction by the power to assign opinions. By custom, a Chief Justice who is with the majority on a decision decides who will speak for the Court if a written opinion is to be offered. If harmony is to be emphasized, the opinion might be assigned to a justice with a moderate view who is especially skilled at compromise. At other times the Chief Justice might want a more forceful message to be conveyed by an opinion. Then a justice with more pronounced views—either liberal or conservative, depending on the case—would be chosen to write the opinion. Chief Justices can also use opinion-writing assignments as rewards to promote a sense of unity and to enhance the smooth operation of the Court.

Such bargaining and accommodation on the final vote and the written opinion can greatly affect the meaning of a decision. Let us look at two important civil rights cases. In *Brown v. Board of Education* (1954), the Court held that state-required segregation in public schools was unconstitutional. The nine justices differed on the issue, but the forceful leadership of Chief Justice Earl Warren resulted in a 9–0 decision and a strongly worded, single majority opinion (sometimes more than one written majority opinion is offered). This action clearly conveyed the Court's stand. If the decision had been 5–4, with a strongly worded dissent, opponents of the decision would have been encouraged to challenge it in the hope of later changing a vote or two. In contrast, consider the case of *Regents of the University of California v. Bakke* (1978). The case concerned a white (Allan Bakke) who was denied admission to medical

school and charged discrimination because, he said, the school had accepted less-qualified minority group members (through a special admissions program). Potentially, the case involved the highly controversial issue of racial quotas. The Court ruled in favor of Bakke's admission but also held that race could be a factor in school admission. In the *Bakke* case the division in the Court was highly visible—six separate and differing opinions were given. Moreover, because the written opinion dealt only with one specific school program, the narrow 5–4 majority ruling did not consider the general issue of racial quotas in school admissions policy. Compared to the *Brown* case, the Court was conveying a weak message. The meaning of the *Bakke* case would have been very different if one side had managed to persuade the minority to join it and issue a clear, unanimous opinion on the constitutionality of racial quotas.

Outside Pressures on the Court

Outside pressures on individual justices represent yet another factor that can play a role in how a decision is reached. In principle, because they are appointed for life and there are strict rules against lobbying, or influencing, justices, a Supreme Court justice cannot be pressured. In practice, because justices do not live in a vacuum, outside forces do have an impact. It often has been said that judges read election returns. A landslide victory for a conservative President, for instance, can send a message that eventually will surface in the Court's rulings. A justice might reason that moving along with the public, as expressed by the vote, will help ensure public support for the judicial system and facilitate enforcement. Justices also might consider the results of public opinion polls—in the controversial decision upholding the death penalty (*Gregg v. Georgia* [1976]), opinion poll results were cited in the written opinion.

Although it might be hard to document, it is likely that justices are sensitive to attacks by private citizens, the media, and public officials. Decisions on such emotion-laden issues as school prayer, abortion, busing, and obscenity have often generated "hate mail," ugly anti-Court demonstrations, and outpourings of anti-Court editorials. Members of Congress have traditionally felt free to criticize the Court's rulings. Following the *Brown* decision, some members of Congress personally told Chief Justice Warren that he had stabbed them in the back. In *Jencks v. United States* (1957), the Court ruled that a person accused of subversive activities that might severely harm the government should have access to information provided by an undercover FBI informant. Many members of Congress were outraged. One representative from Georgia stated: "[The Court] in great measure destroyed the effectiveness of the Federal Bureau of Investigation." Another added: "The decision encourages crime. It encourages the underworld, and it is a blow to law enforcement." A third called it "a victory greater than any achieved by the Soviets in any battlefield since World War II." Although it seems unlikely that hate mail, critical editorials, and anti-Court speeches by members of Congress could sway a particular decision, such attacks could contribute to an overall atmosphere in which some issues were avoided and actual compromises were made on others.

Conclusions

How, then, do Supreme Court justices decide cases? Many factors—legislation, precedents, the political values of the justices, group interaction among the justices, and outside pressures contribute to the final outcome. If a case involves clear-cut law and has adequate precedent, it is unlikely to reach the Supreme Court. The outcome of cases that the Court fully considers depends to a great extent on the personal viewpoints of individual justices. A justice's attitudes might influence him or her in one direction when the conflict is close, but no justice would disregard the facts entirely. On such matters as writing the opinion, the size of the majority—and even the actual justification of the decision—the social interactions of the justices themselves can be important. Finally, outside factors, such as election results and personal attacks, also can help determine what cases are considered by the Court and what decisions justices make.

Check Your Understanding

1. What steps must a case go through in order to be considered by the Supreme Court?

2. Why is precedent not always a useful guide in deciding a case?

3. What role does group interaction among Supreme Court justices play in deciding a case?

4. What are some important sources of outside influence on Supreme Court justices?

WHAT HAS BEEN THE POLITICAL IMPACT OF THE SUPREME COURT?

A frequent question of American politics concerns the impact of the Supreme Court. Some people regard the Court as the weakest of the three branches of government, capable only of making high-sounding but unenforceable pronouncements. On the other side are those who believe that the Court is too much involved in making policy. They see the Court as a group of unelected officials determined to impose their values on the public. To understand the impact of the Court, let us consider three aspects of Court behavior: (1) the methods by which the Court can influence public policy; (2) the goals the Court has sought to achieve; and (3) the limits on the Court's political impact.

Methods for Influencing Public Policy

Most judicial decisions have little impact beyond the parties involved. One party wins, one loses, and life is unchanged for everyone else. On occasion, however, judicial actions have far-reaching implications. Then the courts are engaged in policy making: a decision contains orders or guide-

Points of View: The Public Face of the Court

Although most of the work of the Supreme Court is settled in private, on certain important cases the Court hears arguments from lawyers. These public proceedings are not like the familiar courtroom trial. There are no witnesses, and justices can and do play an active role in questioning lawyers. Especially when a significant, long-awaited case is to be heard, the drama can be intense.

The workings of the Court were observed closely by J. Harvie Wilkinson III, who was a law clerk to Justice Lewis F. Powell, Jr., during the 1971 and 1972 terms. Here is Wilkinson's first-hand description of arguments before the Court.

It is on days of oral argument that the Supreme Court is most alive. The small first-floor cafeteria becomes a hub of activity, with its swarms of tourists and dark-suited lawyers huddling intently at their tables. Members of the press . . . might stroll through. Occasionally, Solicitor General Griswold would appear, bedecked in formal tux and tails. Eating breakfast there, I would sometimes be interrupted by friends dropping by and wanting to know what seats in the courtroom were available that day.

The courtroom itself, where arguments take place, is elegant in its simplicity. It is of clean, rectangular composition, somewhat higher than it is wide, and ringed about with twenty-four columns of Italian marble. It is imposing but at the same time sufficiently intimate to give dialogue between counsel and Court a conversational tone, not one of formal debate. Institutions of government, even in a democracy, require an aura of drama and ceremony, and the Supreme Court, on a day of argument, is no exception. The courtroom is a theatrical creation, with its high, ornate ceiling, its bench of rich, deep mahogany behind which are the highbacked black leather chairs of the Justices and the red velvet curtain from which they emerge, blackrobed, as the marshal bangs his gavel and announces solemnly,

The Honorable, the Chief Justice, and the Associate Justices of the Supreme Court of the United States. Oyez! Oyez! Oyez! All persons having business before the Honorable, the Supreme Court of the United States, are admonished to draw near and give their attention, for the Court is now sitting. God save the United States and this Honorable Court.

Again the gavel falls, the Justices and all others take their seats, and the day's business begins. . . . Argument at its best is an illuminating and rapid-paced exercise, at its worst pedantic and unprofitable, sending spectators and judges alike into bouts of drowsiness. Argument before the Court can also take a more unpredictable bent, such as when one celebrated lawyer, after several evasions, finally answered, "I don't know, your honor," to a question on a critical fact of his case; or when an Assistant Attorney General from a Midwestern state failed to cite, when asked, a single federal precedent for his position; or, more pleasantly, when a young, green-looking attorney still in his twenties gave a plucky argument in the face of stiff questioning by the Justices in a significant search and seizure case.

I never sat long in that courtroom, however, without recognizing that effective oral arguments before the Supreme Court of the United States demand the very best from a lawyer. Personally, he has to communicate candor and directness, confidence but not arrogance, and, in the case of the great advocates, an appropriate touch of humor and eloquence. Intellectually, he needs a determined instinct for the jugular of his case, and the agility of mind to take advantage of play as it develops, to synchronize the questions of the Justices with the logic and momentum of his own argument. Model appellate advocates are exceedingly rare; when one does perform, it is a thing of exquisite grace and power, a view of a master artist at work.

Harvie Wilkinson III, *Serving Justice: A Supreme Court Clerk's View* (New York: Charterhouse, 1974), pp. 31–34.

lines that affect people not directly involved in the case. In the last thirty years, for example, the Supreme Court has had a profound impact on our education system, the administration of criminal justice, the availability of abortion, the banning of pornography, and the quality of our physical environment. How has the Supreme Court made its presence felt?

The Power of Judicial Review

One important way the courts affect policy is through the power of **judicial review**—the authority of a court to declare both national and state laws (and executive actions) unconstitutional. The capacity to declare an act of Congress or a state law null and void is such an important judicial power that it deserves special attention.

The question of who ultimately interprets the laws—the executive, the legislative, the judiciary, or the people—is an old and perhaps unanswerable one. What happens if Congress interprets a law one way and judges take exactly the opposite view? The framers of the Constitution inherited the problem of ultimate legal authority from English law, and for a while, attempted to resolve it. James Madison, for example, proposed to the delegates at the Constitutional Convention that the President and a "convenient number" of Supreme Court justices form a council that could veto congressional legislation. The council would thus be the final legal authority. This plan and similar ones were defeated, and the whole matter was conveniently avoided by not including in the Constitution anything about who has the last word in interpreting the Constitution.

Here the matter stood until 1803. The question of who was the "ultimate" constitutional interpreter began to be resolved as the result of events during the last week of President John Adams' term (February 24 to March 4, 1801). Adams made a last-minute appointment of forty-two justices of the peace for Washington, D.C. However, Adams' Secretary of State, John Marshall, neglected to deliver seventeen of the formal notifications of appointment before he left office. When Thomas Jefferson became President, on March 4, 1801, he ordered *his* Secretary of State (James Madison) not to deliver the appointments. William Marbury and three other Adams appointees, under Section 13 of the Judiciary Act of 1789, petitioned the Supreme Court for a **writ of mandamus** ("we command") to force Madison to deliver the commissions. The case of *Marbury v. Madison* (1803) thus came before the Supreme Court, which was now led by Chief Justice John Marshall (who had been appointed by John Adams and who had caused the problem in the first place).

The Court had several reasonable alternatives before it. On technical grounds it could have claimed that it lacked jurisdiction and thrown out Marbury's claim. Or the Court could have ruled that Madison's withholding of the commissions was illegal and that Marbury deserved his justice of the peace commission. What Marshall did instead was to use this conflict over a government appointment to raise the broad issue of court power over an act of Congress.

Marshall conceded that Marbury had a right to the appointment. But, asked Marshall, was it proper for Marbury to use Section 13 of the Judiciary Act of 1789 to enforce this right? Section 13 gave the Supreme Court the power to issue writs of mandamus. This power, reasoned Marshall, was a grant of original jurisdiction to the Court. But according to Article III, Section 2 of the Constitution, Congress can change only the appellate, not the original, jurisdiction of the Court. Therefore, Marshall reasoned, Section 13 of the Judiciary Act was in conflict with the Constitution. Given a choice between legislation and the Constitution, Marshall concluded that the congressional law must be invalidated—and the Supreme Court had a right to declare the act invalid. Marbury could not get his appointment because the means to get it—Section 13 of the 1789 act—was unconstitutional.

Some legal scholars have said that Marshall's claim of Supreme Court authority (and, by implication, that of other federal courts) to declare laws unconstitutional was a weak argument. The *Marbury v. Madison* decision itself is open to question. For example, many of the legislators who drafted the Judiciary Act of 1789 were once delegates to the Constitutional Convention, so it is hard to argue that Congress consciously passed an unconstitutional act. Twice before, moreover, the Court had issued writs of mandamus without questioning the constitutional basis of the 1789 act. The whole idea of judicial review under our Constitution can be questioned. Even if Section 13 conflicted with the Constitution, there was no logical reason for the Court to assert that it could declare *any* law unconstitutional. The Court could claim the power of judicial review only on matters affecting the judicial branch of government. Nevertheless, although the reasoning in *Marbury v. Madison* is controversial, the custom of judicial review is now firmly established.

The controversial basis of judicial review has not interfered with the Court's use of this important power. Between 1789 and 1978, the Court struck down 136 provisions of federal law and almost 800 state laws as unconstitutional. Some of these decisions were well publicized and involved important policies. For example, in the famous *Dred Scott v. Sanford* case (1857), congressional prohibition of slavery in portions of territory belonging to the United States was declared unconstitutional. This decision, which invalidated the Missouri Compromise, heightened controversy over slavery and provoked public outrage in the antislavery North. In 1894 the Court struck down an attempt to introduce a national income tax; a constitutional amendment (the Sixteenth) was needed to reverse this decision. Between 1935 and 1936, the Court declared that twelve New Deal laws involving the economic powers of the federal government violated the Constitution. In 1970 the Court invalidated Congress' attempt to allow eighteen-year-olds to vote in state elections. Here, too, it took a constitutional amendment (the Twenty-sixth) to reverse this exercise of judicial review.

Reinterpreting the Law

Judicial review is not the only weapon available to the Court, however. Equally effective, though less dramatic, is the Court's power to create policy through new interpretations of existing law. The Court may reinterpret the Constitution or a **statute** (a law enacted by a legislature) and thus change its meaning or coverage. A famous, but by

no means unique, illustration of this interpretive power occurred in the *Brown v. Board of Education* case (1954), in which the Supreme Court struck down state-imposed racial segregation in schools. In taking this action, the Court did two things. First, it used its power of judicial review to invalidate a Kansas law; second, it offered a new meaning of the Fourteenth Amendment. Let us consider this second, reinterpretive, action.

In the 1896 case of *Plessy v. Ferguson*, the Court had ruled that a state could require racial segregation in public facilities (specifically railway cars) provided that the facilities, though separate, were equal. State-imposed racial segregation, the Court ruled, did not necessarily amount to discrimination. At first glance the acceptance of state-required racial segregation would seem to

A *fugitive slave, Harriet Tubman helped some 300 other slaves find freedom. Her dream of equality became the law of the land in the Supreme Court's 1954* Brown v. Board of Education *ruling.*

violate Section 1 of the Fourteenth Amendment, which says: "No state shall make or enforce any law which shall abridge the privileges or immunities of citizens . . . nor deny to any person within its jurisdiction the equal protection of the laws." This was not, however, the conclusion the Court reached. Speaking of the Fourteenth Amendment, Justice Henry B. Brown wrote: "The object of the amendment was undoubtedly to enforce the absolute equality of the two races before the law, but in the nature of things it could not have been intended to abolish distinction based upon color, or to enforce social, as distinguished from political, equality." In other words, the amendment meant absolute legal but not social equality.

In 1954 the Supreme Court again took up the issue of a state law requiring racial segregation, but this time it viewed the Fourteenth Amendment differently. Chief Justice Earl Warren, writing for a 9–0 majority, raised the question of whether segregated education violated the amendment's guarantee of equal protection of the laws. He acknowledged that the amendment did not speak directly to the issue of segregated schools and that the evidence about its original intention was inconclusive. Warren nevertheless forcefully ruled that the black children on behalf of whom the lawsuit was brought had been "deprived of the equal protection of the laws guaranteed by the Fourteenth Amendment."

In other words, the meaning of the Fourteenth Amendment had undergone a significant change in the space of fifty-eight years, without a single word being altered. A narrow interpretation—a guarantee of legal equality, no more—was replaced by a much broader one. The change in interpretation helped open the door to a flood of decisions on civil rights, sexual discrimination, and the drawing of election district boundaries.

Court Administration of Institutions

In recent years the Court has had a political impact by the use of a third method: administering public institutions. Judges assume duties normally performed by lower-level elected officials or professional administrators. For the present this involves only the federal district courts, but such actions occur with the knowledge and support of the Supreme Court. To understand how a federal judge can take on the role of a hospital or school administrator, consider the case of *Wyatt v. Stickney* (1972). The story began with a suit in federal court charging that the care patients received in Bryce Hospital (run by the state of Alabama) was so poor that it violated their constitutional rights. The judge agreed, but the ruling went beyond the usual proclamation of who was right and who was wrong. Instead the judge issued detailed orders to remedy the problems. Among other specifications, the court ordered that "thermostatically controlled hot water shall be provided in adequate quantities and maintained at the required temperature for patient or residential use (110 degrees F at the fixture) and for mechanical dishwashing and laundry use (180 degrees F at the equipment)." Not only had the federal judge become the chief administrator of Bryce Hospital, but indirectly he also had compelled the Alabama state legislature to issue bonds and impose taxes to pay for these changes. Moreover, in several cities federal judges have taken an active role in helping to desegregate public schools—drawing school boundary lines, establishing ratios of black to white students, making teacher assignments, and so on. Correctional facilities are another area in which federal judges have acted as administrators. On occasion, judges have made decisions on how many prisoners may be kept in a cell and how much time should be set aside for prisoner recreation.

Supreme Court Goals

We have seen that the Supreme Court can play a major role in formulating the law of the land. An important related question is, Whom does the Court serve? What are the justices trying to accomplish with their decisions? There are two main schools of thought on this question.

One view is that the Court functions mainly for the benefit of those who already have power, money, or privilege. This view emphasizes the role of personal values in the selection process for the Court. One does not usually get appointed to the Supreme Court by challenging those in power. In

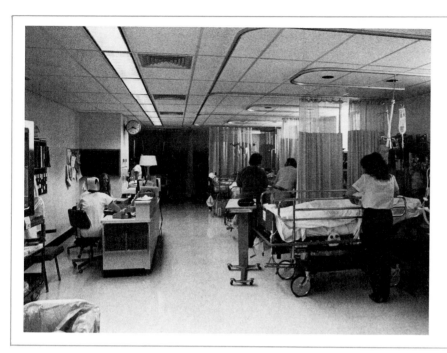

Well-run public hospitals are unlikely to require judicial intervention. When such facilities violate patients' rights, federal judges may step in as overseers.

contemporary politics, for example, a person who favored a policy that would heavily tax the wealthy and turn the money over to the poor would have little chance of being appointed to the Court. Generally, according to this view, Supreme Court justices reflect the values of those people in society who have the most authority and influence. The justices, for this reason, are opposed to significant changes in the social structure. If, for example, business interests are the most important in society, the Court will protect those interests in the name of "freedom," "liberty," and so on.

An opposing view is that the Court is the guardian of freedom. Because justices serve for life, according to this view, the Court is above day-to-day politics and pressures. Thus the Court can uphold the rights of the weak against the strong, protect the unpopular against the conventional, and prevent the majority from tyrannizing the minority.

Which of these two views is correct? The most reasonable answer seems to be that neither description is completely valid for the entire history of the Court, but that during some historical periods one description has been much more applicable than the other.

The Court as Protector of Established Interests

Scholars do not question the fact that the Court has aligned itself with powerful interests for most of its history. Robert G. McCloskey, in *The American Supreme Court*, notes that the early Court, largely under the direction of John Marshall (Chief Justice 1801–35), worked long and successfully on behalf of established commercial and property interests. Marshall had been a Federalist (rather than a Jeffersonian Republican) and as such was committed to a strong national government. He also believed that the protection of private property and contracts was essential in maintaining the social order. In several landmark decisions—for example, *McCulloch v. Maryland* (1819) and *Dartmouth College v. Woodward* (1819)—Marshall achieved important victories on behalf of established Federalist interests.

When Chief Justice Marshall died in 1835, and with Andrew Jackson in the White House, wealthy interests feared the worst. Jackson, after all, was something of a populist, who championed the cause of ordinary people. For Chief Justice, the President appointed Roger B. Taney, who joined four other Jackson appointees already on the Court. But those who hoped that the Court would now favor ordinary citizens and more democratically oriented state legislatures were disappointed. While the Taney Court lacked the vigor of the Marshall Court, it nevertheless continued to uphold the rights of property. Even the one notion dearest to the hearts of wealthy interests—the importance of contracts—was upheld by the Jackson appointees.

At the end of the Civil War, in 1865, two major social problems emerged that forced the Court to confront difficult legal questions. The first involved the plight of freed slaves. Immediately following the Civil War, Congress passed the Thirteenth, Fourteenth, and Fifteenth Amendments and several civil rights acts, to help blacks obtain political equality. The end of Reconstruction in the 1870s placed many of the newly won rights in jeopardy. The reaction of the Court was essentially to avoid the problem. Laws calling for outright racial discrimination were struck down, but indirect segregation (which was just as effec-

Roger Taney was Chief Justice from 1836 to 1864. Although appointed by Andrew Jackson, Taney disappointed the President in his rulings favoring the national government over the states.

tive) was usually tolerated. In a number of cases, key provisions of the Fourteenth Amendment and other civil rights laws were weakened.

The strategy of judicial avoidance did not, however, apply to the other great issue of the day—the regulation of business. The post-Civil War era saw an expansion of industry accompanied by numerous attempts on the part of the states and federal government to control private enterprises. Little by little, precedent by precedent, the Court became the defender of *laissez-faire*, the principle that government should not interfere with or regulate business. As Congress and state legislatures made more and more attempts to regulate industry, the Court "discovered" new ways to protect business from what the justices felt was interference.

When states tried to regulate railroad rates, the Court ruled that the national government is supreme in matters involving interstate commerce; therefore such regulations were unconstitutional. Between 1877 and 1886, fourteen separate instances of state regulation were nullified. More important, the Supreme Court gradually began to interpret Section 1—frequently called the **due process clause**—of the Fourteenth Amendment (no state may deprive a person of life, liberty, or property without due process of law) as applying to protection not only of persons but of property from government control (*Allgeyer v. Louisiana* [1897]). In *Santa Clara County v. Southern Pacific Railroad* (1886), the Court even ruled that corporations are "persons" and are entitled to the full protection of the Fourteenth Amendment. The protection of business from government regulation often was based on the doctrine of **substantive due process**—the principle that the Court could decide what the government could and could not regulate. In some instances the Court had to stretch the law considerably to protect free enterprise. In 1895, for example, it ruled that the Sherman Antitrust Act, intended by Congress to prevent monopolies, did not forbid monopolies in manufacturing, because manufacturing was not an interstate business.

The underlying bias in favor of established interests remained pretty much intact between the

Two children harvest cotton. Until the 1930s, efforts by the federal government to ban child labor were repeatedly invalidated by the courts.

1890s and 1936. It was during this period that the Court ruled that the personal income tax and the ban on child labor were unconstitutional. As part of its overall attack on the "welfare state" and "creeping socialism," the Court also struck down state attempts to set a minimum wage. The civil rights of blacks remained a judicial nonissue. Perhaps the only major decision of this era in support of free speech was a 1925 ruling that the due process clause of the Fourteenth Amendment protects free speech from state interference. Even here, however, the conviction of the person making the speech was upheld, and this point was not central to the decision.

Writing in 1943, the historian Henry Steele Commager drew this conclusion on the record of the Supreme Court:

> [T]he record . . . discloses not a single case, in a century and a half, where the Supreme Court has protected freedom of speech, press, assembly, or petition against congressional attack. It reveals no instance [save one possible exception] where the court has intervened on behalf of the underprivileged—the Negro, the alien, women, children, workers, tenant farmers.

In 1937, in a series of close decisions, the Court reversed much of its long-standing opposition to government regulation of the economy. In many respects this date also marked a new era in Court policy. Especially as appointees of Franklin

D. Roosevelt made their presence felt, the Court began to reexamine some of the previously avoided questions regarding civil rights, free speech, criminal justice, and the rights of employees in labor disputes. The Court had yet to become the great protector of the oppressed, but it was no longer the champion of the economic establishment.

The Supreme Court as the Guardian of Freedom

The Supreme Court began to emerge as the "guardian of freedom" during the era of the Warren Court (1953–69). The changes brought about by the Warren Court were monumental, particularly in four areas: (1) political equality, (2) civil rights, (3) free speech and free association, and (4) criminal justice.

Political equality. Laws requiring that voters must pay a fee (poll tax) or property tax were struck down. The principle of "one person, one vote" was extended to congressional, state, and local legislative districts so as to prevent a minority of citizens from electing a majority of legislators (*Gray v. Sanders* [1963] and other cases). (One person, one vote is discussed in Chapter 5.) The Court also held that a state legislator could not be denied a seat solely because the legislature objected to his or her political views.

Civil rights. The Warren Court outlawed state-enforced racial segregation in public schools. In other decisions it invalidated racial discrimination in public facilities, such as swimming pools, parks, transportation, and courthouses. In 1967 the Court ruled that state laws forbidding racial intermarriage were unconstitutional (*Loving v. Virginia*). The Warren Court took vigorous action to prevent unreasonable delay in the implementation of civil rights rulings. Moreover, the Court was sympathetic to those engaging in such activities as protests and boycotts to overcome racial injustice.

Free speech and free association. The Court extended the meaning of free speech to include symbolic speech, such as the burning of an American flag and the wearing of black armbands to protest the war in Vietnam. The Court also took steps to protect from economic retribution citizens using their right of free speech. For example, it ruled that a teacher could not be fired for criticizing the school board. Local ordinances limiting demonstrations were overturned, and laws making it a crime to be a Communist were made almost unenforceable. State-required "loyalty oaths" were declared unconstitutional. Newspapers were given considerably more freedom in what they could say about public figures.

Criminal justice. The Warren Court greatly expanded the rights of those accused of a crime. In *Mapp v. Ohio* (1961), the Court ruled that evidence obtained illegally could not be used in state courts (the *exclusionary rule*). In *Gideon v. Wainwright* (1963), the right to a lawyer was extended to all criminal trials. Perhaps the most controversial decision of all was *Miranda v. Arizona* (1966), in which the Court ruled that suspects must be told (1) that they have a right to remain silent, (2) that anything they say may be held against them, and (3) that they have a right to a lawyer before and during police interrogation (these conditions are generally known as the *Miranda rules*). The Court also has set limits on the use of searches, surveillance techniques, and police discretion in stopping people for suspected crimes. The Warren Court extended protection of the right against *self-incrimination* (the act of implicating oneself in a crime) and *double jeopardy* (being tried for the same crime twice) to state court proceedings. (The rights are described in more detail in Chapter 13.)

Decisions on behalf of the less powerful continued, but with some exceptions, under Earl Warren's successor as Chief Justice, Warren E. Burger. Although Burger and several subsequent justices were appointed by Presidents who hoped for a more conservative Court, the Warren Court's actions have not been reversed. In the area of civil rights, for example, the Burger Court has repeatedly encouraged strong measures to eliminate racial discrimination in education and employment. In *Bob Jones University v. United States* (1983), for example, the Court denied tax-exempt status to a college that practiced segregation (schools ordinarily don't have to pay taxes, unless they violate certain laws). In another 1983 case the Court held that women could not be given reduced retirement benefits just because, as a group, they live longer than men. During the 1986 term the Court made rulings favorable to the interests of blacks in the area of voting rights, jury selection, and employment. The Court also differed from the more conservative Reagan administration in such matters as abortion, prayers in public school, and workers' safety and health. The Burger Court also upheld such controversial rights of accused criminals as the exclusionary rule, although some exceptions have been allowed.

A Perspective on the Court's Goals

Our brief review of policy making shows that the Court has played different roles at different times. In the early 1900s, for instance, the Court ruled on behalf of established economic interests against demands for change. On other occasions, especially from the 1950s onward, the Court acted to protect the less fortunate. It is difficult to say what the proper role of the Court ought to be. The Constitution says nothing about whether the Court should protect the advantaged or the disadvantaged. Nor are there any universally accepted stan-

The legend above the imposing columns of the Supreme Court building, "Equal Justice Under Law," expresses the goal of the judicial branch of government.

dards for the way justices ought to behave. Justices who upheld state-required racial segregation believed they were honestly upholding the Constitution. As they explained in their decisions, it was not their intention to be agents of economic or social privilege. When later justices declared segregation unconstitutional, they also argued that they were upholding the Constitution, not acting as social reformers. No doubt most justices have believed that their decisions were in the best interests of the nation. Perhaps all we can say is that the Supreme Court has no one set role to play in American politics.

The Limits on the Court's Political Impact

Justices have considerable leeway in reaching decisions, and it is nearly impossible to remove a Supreme Court justice simply on the basis of unpopular decisions. We might ask, then, how an ambitious Court can be prevented from having too much political influence. After all, justices do not have to worry about reelection, campaign support, or disgruntled constituents. What prevents gov-

ernment by the Supreme Court? Three important checks limit the power of the judicial system and the Supreme Court: (1) the types of issues the judicial system will or may consider, (2) limits on enforcement power, and (3) the power of Congress and the President.

Types of Issues Federal Courts Will or May Consider

Compared to the other branches of government, the federal courts are more limited in the scope of their actions. Certain doctrines and customs limit the involvement of the Court. Understanding these limits is enormously helpful in understanding why courts sometimes appear to do little to resolve urgent legal issues.

Courts may not consider hypothetical cases. An important restriction that federal courts impose on themselves is the exclusion of **moot cases** from consideration. That is, judges will not decide a hypothetical case. You cannot, for example, get a judicial decision in anticipation of some government action or what might happen to you if you violated the law. The Court is therefore limited in making pronouncements on many political issues of the day. This point was illustrated in a suit over a New Jersey law requiring that Old Testament verses be read in school. The Supreme Court refused to make a ruling on the grounds that the child whose parent brought the suit had already graduated. In other words, because the child was no longer being forced to hear Bible verses, the whole issue was hypothetical. A crucial case testing reverse discrimination—*DeFunis v. Odegaard* (1974)—was dismissed because the law student claiming discrimination had graduated by the time the Court was to hear the case (the issue of racial quotas eventually did generate a "real" case—see *Bakke*, discussed earlier in the chapter). In criminal cases, however, the Supreme Court has been somewhat less strict in applying mootness. A degree of mootness has been tolerated also when a situation is likely to be repeated—for example, pregnancy. As a result, the Court ruled, long after her baby was born, that Jane Roe had a right to an abortion. Moreover, unlike some state courts, the U.S. Supreme Court will not offer advisory opinions on the constitutionality of proposed legislation. President Washington once asked for such an opinion and was refused. Thus, Congress can enact an unconstitutional statute, the law can shape people's behavior, and it can be on the books forever unless it generates a Court case.

Court cases must have real consequences.

The courts have been unwilling to consider cases in which no harm to an individual has occurred. Here, too, the range of issues that can be decided is limited. This was illustrated in a series of decisions regarding the constitutionality of a Connecticut law prohibiting the use or sale of birth-control devices. In one case (*Poe v. Ullman* [1961]), a physician claimed that his liberty and freedom were being unconstitutionally restricted by the ban on contraceptives. A married couple also claimed in the suit that the woman's health and well-being were being jeopardized. The Supreme Court nevertheless refused to decide the case, on the grounds that the Connecticut law was not being enforced, and therefore no real or immediate threat of prosecution existed. (Ultimately, in 1965, the Court did declare the law unconstitutional, but only after it had been enforced.) Nor will the Court hear a case if the justices believe that the legal action was "made up" just to create a case. For a case to be heard, there must be a genuine conflict between the parties.

A closely related principle is that the Court will not consider a case unless the party bringing suit has suffered some personal harm, not a general harm that any citizen might experience. If a government official deprives you of a right, the courts will consider your suit. In legal terms, you are considered to have **standing to sue.** However, if the government action affects all citizens, you may not sue as one adversely affected citizen. The inability of individual citizens to bring court action unless they personally are harmed was illustrated in the case of *United States v. Richardson* (1974), in which the Court ruled that a citizen wanting to force the government to publish the secret budget of the CIA lacked standing. All citizens—not just the one desiring the information—were in the same situation. Thus a law that harms everyone more or less equally might never come before the courts. The only possible exceptions are **class action suits.** An individual who, along with many others, has suffered harm may sue on behalf of the others, but the courts have placed restrictions on such action (for example, the amount of harm suffered must be fairly significant). Class action suits have involved such issues as overcharges on stock purchases and faulty consumer products.

Courts will not consider "political questions."

Another, self-imposed Court restraint is the tradition of refusing to deal with "political questions." On several occasions the Supreme Court has refused to become involved in controversies on the grounds that it would be imposing its views improperly on questions better left to the executive or legislative branch. Included in this category have been such questions as whether the President acted correctly in recognizing a foreign government or whether military action, like the war in Vietnam, was legal. In the nineteenth century the Court refused to rule on whether the executive branch had honored its treaty obligations with the Indians. No hard-and-fast line separates nonpolitical from political questions, and much seems to depend on the climate of public opinion. For example, in *Colegove v. Green* (1946), the Court used the political-question doctrine to refuse to rule on population inequalities in congressional districts. Sixteen years later, in *Baker v. Carr* (1962), it changed its mind and decided to consider the apportionment issue. More recently, political questions have largely dealt with the conduct of foreign affairs, but in principle the doctrine can still be applied to difficult issues in general. Overall, the practice of avoiding political questions appears to be a convenient way of bypassing complex, thorny issues. As one federal judge put it, "[Political questions] encompass all questions outside the sphere of judicial power" (*Velvel v. Johnson* [1968]).

Courts have limited power over their agendas.

Finally, it is the nature of the judicial system that courts have little power to place specific cases and issues on their agendas. Courts may decide only cases that someone else brings to them. By contrast, Congress and the President have the freedom to address almost any issue. In some situations, major constitutional controversies with important consequences remain unresolved until a suitable case works its way to the Supreme Court's agenda. The inability to place items on its agenda was illustrated by the case over the *legislative veto*—the power of Congress to invalidate an executive action (legislative veto is discussed in Chapters 9, 10, and 11). For many years the constitutionality of the legislative veto was widely debated but could not be considered. Then, in a very minor action based on a legislative veto provision of a federal immigration law, the House reversed a Justice Department deportation ruling. The person to be deported sued the government to overrule the House. This action resulted in a case (*Immigration and Naturalization Service v. Chadha* [1983]) that finally brought the constitutional question to the Court. Without this lawsuit by a private individual, the constitutionality of the legislative veto might still be the subject of abstract debate. In addition, the Justice Department, in the executive branch, handles the government side of cases and thus influences such key questions as what cases to take to the Court, which arguments to make, and whether a decision will be appealed. Because all violations of federal criminal law and many civil cases involve the federal government, this is an important power over the flow of cases into the court system. In particular, the Solicitor General, in the Justice Department, plays a vital role in deciding which cases to take to the Supreme Court. On the other hand, a federal judge wishing to rule on a particular case might have to wait years before the right case in the right context comes up (if it ever does).

Limits on Enforcement Power

The federal courts—including the Supreme Court—possess limited direct enforcement power. It is one thing to rule that something is illegal, quite another to ensure compliance. Whether court decisions are carried out depends on the actions of other public officials or the general public. The courts are far from powerless, but a gap often exists between the decision and what actually happens next. Perhaps the classic statement regarding judicial dependence on the other branches was President Andrew Jackson's famous remark: "John Marshall has made his decision; now let him enforce it." (This case—*Worcester v. Georgia* [1832]—held that the federal government, not the states, exercised exclusive power over Indians on Indian territory. But Jackson refused to use U.S. troops to enforce the decision.)

Lower courts and officials can ignore Supreme Court decisions. Noncompliance with Supreme Court decisions can occur in a number of ways. Once the Supreme Court has stated a doctrine, lower-court judges can simply ignore it. Inattention often results from poor communication rather than from outright defiance. In many instances lower-court judges and the attorneys who bring cases are unaware of the relevant Supreme Court rulings, or if aware of them, are unclear on how to interpret them. This is especially likely in state courts were records of Court decisions are not readily available. On occasion, however, there is an element of resistance in lower-court disregard of Supreme Court decisions. This occurred in the early 1960s when the Court banned mandatory religious observances in public schools. Even though the decision of the Court was unambiguous—for example, no Bible readings were to be permitted—many state court judges refused to adhere to it. Perhaps they felt that a Bible reading is in the area of history and not religion. Eventually, though, lower-court decisions were brought into line with the Supreme Court ruling. One study of a ten-year period found eight instances in which state courts had clearly operated in ways contrary to Supreme Court intent.

Problems of implementing Supreme Court rulings become more severe when officials—such as district attorneys, prosecuting attorneys, police, and state and local administrators—are involved. Major gaps often occur in up-to-date knowledge of Court rulings. One study of Wisconsin district attorneys found that some did not understand the Court's ruling on obscenity and thus were treating as obscene some books and magazines judged not to be obscene. Although some big cities have arrangements by which police can be adequately informed of complex Court rulings on criminal justice matters, in smaller communities information might be sketchier. Even when they are aware of the Court's decisions, lawyers, police officers, and administrators might not give them high priority in their day-to-day activities.

On occasion, strong forces encourage the noncompliance of those responsible for putting Court decisions into practice. The Supreme Court's 1954 ruling against state-required segregation in public schools was extremely unpopular in the South. Federal judges who tried to enforce the decision sometimes encountered intense personal hostility and even threats against their lives. Similar situations occurred in such cities as Boston and Detroit when federal judges ordered busing and other unpopular measures to integrate the schools. Many police departments face strong community "law and order" sentiment, which can hinder adherence to rulings intended to protect those accused of crimes. School administrators also face community pressure to ignore controversial Court rulings in such areas as prayers in the classroom, the rights of students to express unpopular ideas, and obscenity.

Supreme Court justices have some tools available to ensure enforcement of their decisions by lower-court judges and other officials. Justices attempt to present their written opinions in a clear fashion in order to encourage compliance by the lower courts. On occasion a justice has even employed personal persuasion or flattery to promote compliance. Sometimes pressure can be brought through the Judicial Conference of the United States, an annual meeting of the chief judge of each circuit (the senior judge in each circuit under sixty-five who has served for more than one year) and one district judge from each circuit, with the Chief Justice of the United States presiding. The Judicial Conference helps administer the federal court system—for example, it deals with increased caseload and formulates procedures—but it also provides a channel by which the Chief Justice can communicate the Court's position to lower-court judges, who often must enforce Court rulings.

In front of the Supreme Court, a young woman displays a newspaper headline announcing the historical Brown v. Board of Education *decision. The ruling mandated the desegregation of the public schools.*

Because the Supreme Court has considerable prestige, almost all law enforcement officials from federal district judges to police officers accept its authority. It is hard to imagine a public official systematically ignoring Court orders. Only rarely will lower-level officials openly challenge the Court's authority when they personally disagree with a ruling. Reinforcing this respect is the power of the Court to overrule actions by lower-court judges and to invalidate the actions of administrators, district attorneys, and police officers. Members of the legal profession suffer a loss of prestige if their actions are repeatedly appealed or overruled by a higher authority. Questions of competence will inevitably be raised, for instance, if a state judge frequently is reversed or if the cases an attorney prosecutes are eventually found to be faulty.

The Court cannot monitor all violations. The difficulties of obtaining compliance are especially severe when thousands of people and millions of small decisions are involved. It is here that the Court's lack of its own enforcement staff is especially important. The Supreme Court might rule that racial or religious discrimination in apartment rentals is unconstitutional, but monitoring all such occurrences is impossible. The enforcement of school desegregation orders in the South was particularly susceptible to this problem. The Court would issue one order after another, yet officials, ranging from school principals to governors and senators (and even the President occasionally), would find ways to undermine court orders—sometimes by withholding funds for enforcement or by making misleading claims about compliance.

Power of Congress and the President

Perhaps the most important limit on the Supreme Court is the power of the other two branches of government. The appellate jurisdiction of the Supreme Court is set by Congress, not the Constitution, and thus can be modified to strip the Court of its power to hear certain types of cases. This happened once in American history, in the case of *Ex parte McCardle* (1869). In 1868 an individual contested, in federal court, an arrest and trial by a military tribunal. Congress feared that if the case reached the Supreme Court, the Court would have an opportunity to declare unconstitutional several laws dealing with Southern Reconstruction. One day before the Court's decision, Congress stripped the Court of its power to hear appeals for this type of case. There have been many other such efforts, none of them successful. In the late 1950s, for example, congressional displeasure over Court decisions on "subversive activity" led to proposals to prohibit Court jurisdiction in such cases. In the 1960s, Congress sought to limit the Court's jurisdiction in matters involving the apportionment of state legislatures. During the 1980s, a similar attempt was made in the areas of abortion, school prayer, and racial balance in schools. Congress can also pass legislation concerning the types of orders that the Court may issue. On civil rights matters, for example, some of the Court's enforcement options have been reduced by specific laws.

On at least one occasion Congress has pressured the Supreme Court through its control of the salary of the justices. In 1964 Congress voted a pay raise of $7,500 for all federal judges, but because many members of Congress were feeling unsympathetic toward the high Court, Supreme Court justices received only a $4,500 increase.

Because it is the President and the Senate who choose Supreme Court justices, a contrary Court can be brought into line, although it might take a few years. President Nixon's use of the appointment power well demonstrated this mode of control. In the space of three years Nixon nominated one Chief Justice and three associate justices and was thus able to bring the Court closer to his own moderate–conservative philosophy. Sometimes a change of one or two votes can have a major impact on the direction of the Court. Congress and the President can also use their constitutional authority to create courts below the Supreme Court level—they may add or abolish courts as well as change the number of judges. A liberal President facing an unsympathetic federal judiciary could, for example, with the cooperation of Congress create new federal district and appeals courts and appoint liberal judges to fill the new positions. Both Carter and Reagan had ample opportunity to appoint lower federal court judges, and these appointments clearly reflected their respective political views.

Congress' power over appropriations, and the President's use of personal judgment in enforcing the law, can also limit the Supreme Court, as the responses of Congresses and Presidents to the *Brown* decision illustrate. When the ruling was made, in 1954, President Eisenhower exhibited little sympathy, and his administration took no steps to implement it. Only in 1957, when mob violence over integration threatened Little Rock, Arkansas, did Eisenhower take vigorous enforcement action (he dispatched federal troops to maintain order). By way of contrast, President Johnson used the full powers of the presidency to bring about desegregation—the Justice Department filed numerous suits, the Department of Health, Education and Welfare (HEW) closely monitored desegregation efforts, and the White House wholeheartedly endorsed pro-integration legislation. The role of Congress in support of the *Brown* ruling has also varied. In 1964 Congress gave HEW the power to withhold federal funds from schools that would not integrate. In 1975, however, Congress prohibited HEW from withholding federal aid to schools that refused to use busing to desegregate.

Finally, a President and Congress can legislate around the Court. In 1920, for example, the Supreme Court invalidated an act that required employers to compensate dock and harbor workers injured on the job. In 1922, Congress passed another compensation bill for workers, and again

the Court struck it down. In 1927, Congress tried a third time, and this time it succeeded. In the mid-1930s the Court invalidated six laws dealing with government involvement in the economy. Five of these were rewritten and eventually became law. State governments have legislated around Court decisions too. In 1972, for example, the Court declared unconstitutional the death penalty in thirty-nine states on the grounds that the penalty was exercised in an arbitrary way. Most of these states later redrafted their capital punishment laws to be more specific; the revised laws were upheld as constitutional.

The most extreme way of overcoming the Court is to pass a constitutional amendment. This strategy has succeeded three times in American history. When the Court ruled that a state could be sued in federal court by a citizen from another state, Congress and the states passed the Eleventh Amendment, prohibiting such action. When the Court refused to rule the income tax constitutional, the result was the Sixteenth Amendment. The Twenty-sixth Amendment, giving eighteen-year-olds the vote in all elections, was enacted after the Supreme Court ruled that Congress could not set eighteen as the minimum age for state elections. In recent times, unpopular Court decisions on prayers in public schools, abortion, and school busing have resulted in campaigns for constitutional amendments.

A Perspective on the Court's Impact

To return to our basic question: What has been the political impact of the Supreme Court? One conclusion we can draw is that the Supreme Court and the federal judiciary *cannot* dominate the political process. Despite an occasional unpopular decision, we have never had government by judiciary. At the same time, however, the courts are not rubber stamps. Numerous instances of judicial defiance of Congress and the President have occurred on such important issues as tax policy, civil rights, freedom of speech, and political equality. Overall, it appears that the court system has had its greatest impact when it has cooperated with the other branches of government. If the executive

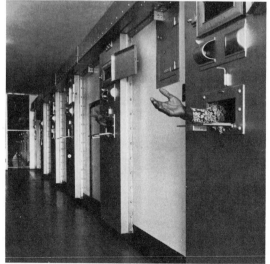

Congress and the states have acted in response to Court rulings on industrial safety and the death penalty. Above, workers lay railroad cable; below, a prisoner reaches out from the cell.

branch vigorously enforces a ruling, and Congress backs it up with supportive legislation, judges indeed become powerful. This was demonstrated in the mid-1960s, when the three branches of government made a concerted effort to advance civil rights. On the other hand, when disagreements occur, the judicial system is limited.

Check Your Understanding

1. In what ways is the principle of judicial review an important power of the Supreme Court?

2. To what extent has the Supreme Court been the protector of established economic interests?

3. What shift in the Court's role occurred under Chief Justice Earl Warren?

4. What types of cases will the Supreme Court not review?

5. What are the major limits on the Supreme Court's enforcement power?

THE POLITICS OF COURT POWER

We have seen that the judicial system is an important part of the political process. Judges might wear black robes, base their actions on complex legal principles, and claim impartiality, but they are not neutral computers processing law into court rulings. The court system is just as "political" as Congress and the executive branch. Federal judges are chosen on political grounds, their decisions are often guided by political objectives, and the results can have major political consequences (many of which are intentional).

Nobody disputes the political character of judicial decision making, but considerable conflict surrounds the question of how politically involved the courts *ought* to be. Should the courts attempt to deal with the general policy issues underlying such controversial subjects as abortion, private sexual behavior, discriminatory practices by private citizens, and the like? Or should the courts limit themselves to the particulars of each case and leave general policy making to Congress and the President? Put somewhat differently, should the courts emphasize or minimize their role in the political process? In one form or another, this debate has been going on since the early days of the Republic.

It is probably impossible to settle the conflict objectively. We can, however, outline the basic elements and underlying political goals of each view. Supporters of the **judicial restraint** position hold that the proper role of the courts is to settle disputes, not to make policy. The Constitution, they argue, is clear on this matter. As the late Senator Sam J. Ervin, Jr., put it:

> There is not a syllable in [the Constitution] which gives the Supreme Court any discretionary power to fashion policies based on such considerations as expediency or prudence to guide the course of action of the government of our country. On the contrary, the Constitution provides in plain and positive terms that the role of the Supreme Court is that of adjudicator, which determines judicially legal controversies between adverse litigants.

Advocates of judicial restraint believe that modern-era courts, especially the Supreme Court under Chief Justice Earl Warren, have violated this constitutional intention. The misguided venture into policy making, critics maintain, has had several unfortunate consequences. First, the courts have taken over the constitutional role of the other two branches of government. Congress might pass a law and the President might try to enforce it, but such execution of duty can come to nothing if the courts intervene. Second, the willingness of the courts, particularly the Supreme Court, to use constitutional language to accomplish policy objectives adds harmful uncertainty. How are public officials and private citizens to behave if such phrases as "equal protection of the laws" undergo repeated changes of meaning to suit momentary policy preferences?

Supporters of judicial restraint also believe that involvement in controversial issues interferes with the integrity of the judicial process. Judges derive their power from adherence to the law; when they go beyond narrow legal interpretation and deal with broad policy questions, they lose their special standing. Moreover, the argument continues, judges are less qualified to make public policy than elected leaders. Law school and years of practicing law can isolate judges from the pressures and problems that elected leaders confront. Nor are judges accountable for their actions at election time. Mistakes by elected officials might not be reversible, but at least it is possible to defeat incompetent leaders at the polls. Supreme Court justices, on the other hand, are appointed for life. Overall, the use of constitutional interpretation as a foundation for policy making can only undermine the very Constitution that judges are sworn to uphold.

Defenders of **judicial activism,** by contrast, argue that the Constitution must be adapted to contemporary needs if it is to maintain its relevance. It is impossible for a judge to rely completely on words written in 1787 to decide complex cases in the 1980s—the words themselves can be vague, the intention behind them unclear, and situations can change drastically. The principles in the Constitution are enduring and are to be preserved, but judges must have some freedom in applying them. Without such flexibility, the Constitution becomes merely a historical document. Just because the Constitution does not mention school busing, for example, does not mean that judges cannot rule on the issue. Busing might be needed to ensure that the principle of equal protection of the laws (Fourteenth Amendment) is followed.

Moreover, there really is no such thing as "abstract" law. Cases deal with real situations involving costs and benefits. Because law cannot be separated from its social context, judges must deal with economic and social factors in their decisions. It would be a neglect of judicial duty, for example, to claim that a poor person and a millionaire are equally "free" to hire a first-rate lawyer. In dealing with social and economic realities, judges must address more controversial questions.

We can observe the difference between the judicial restraint and the judicial activism positions by considering the problem of racially segregated schools. As noted earlier, in 1954 the Supreme Court held that state-required segregation violated the equal protection clause of the Fourteenth Amendment. From the perspective of judicial restraint, the decision itself is open to question, because this amendment does not specifically deal with school segregation. Moreover, according to this view, the reasoning behind the decision was faulty, because it relied heavily on nonlegal factors, such as the supposed feeling of inferiority among blacks who attended segregated schools and the social value of an education. Even if the decision were accepted as legitimate, it should have gone no further than the cases at hand—certain schoolchildren in a particular state with a particular law. Other disputes would be handled on a case-by-case basis. Questions involving enforcement of the decision and standards for evaluating success would be left to Congress and the President.

In its rulings requiring school integration, the Supreme Court has had an impact, since the 1950s, on the lives of millions of schoolchildren around the nation.

From the activist perspective, the *Brown* and later decisions were the correct ones. First, the written opinion itself considered the broader social aspects of the issue—the importance of education, the impact of segregation, and so on—in addition to the case's specifics. Second, the Court in its later rulings addressed the implementation of the decision—how fast integration was to proceed, who had responsibility for achieving this goal, how progress was to be measured, and the like. Third, the Court eventually examined aspects of the case that went beyond its original ruling—for example, whether schools segregated as a result of neighborhood housing patterns should be treated the same as schools segregated by law. Fourth, when the other branches of government proved reluctant to integrate schools, the Court in the 1970s took vigorous action—issued orders, permitted judicial administration of noncompliant schools, and imposed penalties, among other measures. In short, the Court established general policy on a number of education issues as part of its responsibility to interpret the Constitution.

If we cannot resolve this conflict, at least we can understand why most people tend toward one side or the other: one's stance depends on whether one favors or opposes the judicial outcomes. Abstract principles generally seem less important than who wins or loses. When economically conservative judges in the nineteenth century used the Fourteenth Amendment to protect free enterprise from government regulation, the business community applauded, whereas people who supported regulation asserted that Supreme Court justices should stick to a narrow interpretation of the law. When, in the 1960s, justices employed the same provision to protect civil rights in public accommodations, many business leaders accused the Court of going too far. The position of liberals and conservatives on activism/restraint were now reversed. Considerable evidence exists that neither interpretation is consistent with the intentions of those who drafted the Fourteenth Amendment. Perhaps the moral of this is to be beware of people who claim the sanctity of judicial decisions; they possibly have just won their case.

CHAPTER SUMMARY

What is the federal court system, and how does it function? The three basic elements of the federal court system are the district courts, courts of appeals, and the Supreme Court. There are also a number of special courts. The cases handled by the courts are defined in the Constitution and by congressional laws. Whether a case is heard in federal or state court depends on what type of law is involved and on who the parties to the case are. Most cases involve violation of federal laws or suits between citizens of different states. The appointment of federal judges is made on the basis of considerations such as party affiliation and political philosophy as well as legal background.

How do Supreme Court justices decide cases? Of the five thousand or so cases that are brought to the Court every year, only a very small number are reviewed in depth. Cases that have relatively clear precedents or do not raise important legal questions are unlikely to receive Court attention. In

the cases reviewed by the Court, decisions usually reflect the political values of the justices. The interaction of judges is also important in the outcome. Supreme Court justices do not, however, have a completely free hand. They cannot ignore significant legal principles and precedents and can be subject to outside pressures.

What has been the political impact of the Supreme Court? The Court has a variety of procedures it can use, perhaps the most important of which are its powers to declare a law unconstitutional (judicial review) and to give new meaning to existing laws. Before Earl Warren was Chief Justice, the Court usually reinforced the values of a business-oriented society. Since the 1950s, it has taken numerous actions to protect disadvantaged citizens and to ensure greater political equality. However, numerous limits on Supreme Court power prevent it from dominating the political process. The Court does not hear many types of cases, and Congress and the President are sometimes able to get around Court rulings.

IMPORTANT TERMS

Explain the following terms.

jurisdiction
judicial temperament
precedent
dissenting opinion
judicial review

due process clause
substantive due process
class action suit
judicial restraint
judicial activism

THINKING CRITICALLY

1. The Supreme Court and other federal courts have often made decisions that a majority of U.S. citizens oppose. Should the courts be responsive to majority opinion? Why or why not? Should federal judges, like legislators and Presidents, be held accountable for their actions? Explain your answers.

2. The Supreme Court consists of only nine justices, including the Chief Justice. Yet the burden on the Court is enormous and is growing. Should the number of justices be increased? Why or why not? How might increasing the number of justices affect the work of the Court?

3. In recent years the federal courts have been overwhelmed with cases involving civil suits. Do you think a system can be set up outside the courts for resolving civil suits such as disputes between individuals or businesses? What type of system would this be? How would this system affect the judicial process? Discuss your answer.

4. Do you think it is justifiable to use social, religious, or gender qualifications in appointing federal judges? Why or why not?

5. Should Presidents appoint only judges with moderate, "middle-of-the road" values and reject any potential appointees who hold more pronounced views, either liberal or conservative? Discuss your answer.

6. Is the principle of judicial review undemocratic, because it is exercised by officials who are not elected? Discuss your answer.

7. Is the principle of judicial restraint relevant to a modern society, in which almost all issues, sooner or later, find their way to the courts? Discuss your answer.

EXTENDING YOUR UNDERSTANDING

1. Do research on the British judicial system. Compare the structure and responsibilities of the British system with the U.S. judicial system. Can British judges exercise judicial review? Do they decide issues of broad social impact? Present your research findings in a report.

2. Contact a local court or judge in your area and ask about several recent court cases. Select and describe one case—the issues, the participants, and the outcome. Could this case qualify for appeal to the Supreme Court? Why or why not?

3. Using a source such as *Supreme Court Reporter* or *United States Reports*, examine a recent Supreme Court decision. What arguments are used in the majority's decision? Is the Constitution cited? What evidence is used to support the decision? How do the dissenting justices (if any) make their arguments? Write your findings in a report.

4. Choose one of the special federal courts, other than district court, appeals court, or Supreme Court. Find out what kinds of cases it handles. Present your findings to the class.

5. Prepare a mock class action suit. For instance, you might present a case against the Sharpy Pencil Company for manufacturing faulty products. Prepare the case you will present in court. Choose other students in your class to take the roles of attorneys, jurors, and judges. Present your case in a mock trial.

MAKING DECISIONS

You are the chairperson of a group investigating the use of busing to achieve racial integration in public schools. The Supreme Court has ruled that such busing is permissible. Prepare a proposal that describes what actions can be taken to implement this ruling.

Unit 4
POLICY

Policy is what the government does. In contemporary society the government does a great many things. Chapter 13 looks at the rights enjoyed by American citizens. We shall see that the meaning of these rights is determined by government actions—decisions by judges, laws passed by Congress, and even choices made by the local police. Chapter 14 provides an overall framework for understanding policy in general. Whether we are dealing with tax rates or civil rights, government actions can be better understood if we ask certain questions about how problems are defined, how choices are made, and how results are evaluated. The final three chapters address three broad issues—economic policy, foreign policy, and state and local government. These chapters show that there are no simple, mechanical means to achieve the best policy. Citizens and officials must make difficult choices based on competing values under conditions of uncertainty or limited knowledge.

Chapter 13
Civil Liberties and the Politics of Rights

In many ways the political history of the United States is the history of conflict over rights. The American Revolution, the writing of the Constitution, the battle over slavery, and the contemporary struggle of women and minorities for equality have all involved the rights of Americans. The issue of rights can be incredibly complex. It is not always easy to decide who has which rights or which right takes priority. For example, a mother and father decided to forgo medical treatment for an infant born irreversibly disabled. Doctors, clergy, and the state court supported the decision. However, the federal government took steps to ensure that the baby—called Baby Jane Doe—survived. According to the government, the parents' decision ignored the rights of the infant. Whose rights come first—the parents' or the child's? Who decides the issue—citizens themselves or the government? Does the right to be nurtured prevail even in the case of an incurable deformity? Issues such as these often make disputes over rights highly emotional and bitter. Our analysis will address three important questions:

- What are rights?
- What political rights do citizens have?
- What sustains our rights?

PREVIEW

What are rights? A *right* is a legal or moral claim to some benefit. Rights differ from privileges, which can be restricted more easily. The line separating rights and privileges is not always clear, though. One view holds that the rights we enjoy are those spelled out in the Constitution or in law. A different approach claims that rights exist independently of written law—that they derive from natural law, or are inherent. Deciding who has which rights raises several key issues. Should everyone have equal rights? Are some rights more basic than others? What is the government's responsibility for implementing rights? Who resolves conflicts over rights?

What political rights do citizens have? Several rights are viewed as fundamental in American politics. The right to free speech is guaranteed in the First Amendment, but the guarantee is not absolute. Definitions of "free speech" vary, and some types of speech are not protected by the First Amendment. Freedom of the press is also spelled out in the First Amendment. The freedom enjoyed by the electronic media, such as television, is more limited than that of newspapers or magazines. The press may not be told in advance what it *may not* print unless such *prior restraint* is justified by exceptional circumstances. Newspapers also have considerable freedom in what they can say about public figures. Although the First Amendment does not specifically mention freedom of association, it has been viewed as a corollary of freedom of speech. Freedom of association has frequently conflicted with the need to protect national security.

The First Amendment's religious freedom guarantee prohibits government from establishing an official religion or passing laws limiting the exercise of religion. The government has tried to maintain a "wall of separation" between it and religious organizations. When religious practices conflict with the law, it is the law that prevails.

Equal protection of the laws means that the laws must apply to all citizens equally. This doctrine has helped minorities and women in their struggles to achieve equality. However, the Supreme Court has allowed people to be treated differently under certain circumstances. Numerous rights exist in the criminal justice system. Citizens are protected against unreasonable searches, imprisonment without charges, and secret trials without legal counsel. A person may not be tried twice for the same offense.

What sustains our rights? One argument is that our liberties require strong support among citizens for their survival, yet studies show that many citizens are indifferent to the protection of rights—especially the rights of unpopular groups. And the argument that political activists help maintain our freedoms is weakened by the fact that blacks and women have been discriminated against for so long without much public outcry. Finally, evidence exists that our safeguards are not strongly established. Government has occasionally violated our rights, and constitutional provisions are little protection against the behavior of private individuals.

WHAT ARE RIGHTS?

A **right** is a legal or moral claim to some benefit. Legal claims are spelled out in some laws—for example, the Constitution gives citizens the right to fair compensation if their property is taken for public use. Other rights can be considered moral rights—expectations of benefits not expressly stated in a law. Being treated with respect by government officials is an example of a moral right. In contrast to rights are **privileges.** Whereas rights can be ignored or violated only under unusual circumstances, a privilege is a benefit that can be given to some citizens for a limited time and is more easily taken away. For example, a fair trial is a right, but a veteran's pension or a license to practice medicine is a privilege granted by the government. Also, some privileges—for example, a license to practice medicine—may be granted only after demonstrating a special skill or having certain experiences. Even though a license to practice medicine cannot be removed without adherence to certain standards, it is considered less fundamental than a right to a fair trial. Rights and privileges also exist outside the political realm. High school students, for instance, have a right to be treated fairly by their teachers. However, the opportunity to make up a missed test is usually considered a privilege that teachers *may* grant at their discretion.

The distinction between rights and privileges can be fuzzy. In fact, some privileges have been transformed into rights. For example, having a lawyer defend you in criminal court is now a right, but it was once merely a privilege. As we shall see at the end of this chapter, much of the politics surrounding rights involves the transformation of privileges into rights.

Sources of Rights

The Constitution and Statutes

Under the Constitution citizens possess many different types of specifically stated rights. Some—the right of *habeas corpus* (the right of individuals to a court hearing to learn why they have been held in detention), the right to a speedy and public trial, the right to due process of law—deal with criminal justice. Other rights, called **civil liberties,** protect the individual from arbitrary government interference. Many civil liberties are stated in the First Amendment, including protection against government abridgment, or restriction, of free speech; government censorship of the press; and government restrictions on the right to assemble peaceably. There are also civil liberties involving criminal law—the Fourth Amendment, for example, prohibits unreasonable searches.

Civil liberties are sometimes distinguished from **civil rights.** Although civil rights, like civil liberties, protect citizens from discrimination and the arbitrary actions of others, civil rights usually go two steps further. First, they protect citizens from other citizens (besides protecting citizens from government). Second, they provide for a government remedy to correct the harm done when civil rights are violated. For example, the 1964 Civil Rights Act forbids citizens from discriminating against other citizens in public accommodations on the grounds of race, color, religion, or national origin. The act also authorizes the federal government to bring suits to accomplish this goal.

The Notion of Natural, or Inherent, Rights

Defining the rights of citizens in terms of the Constitution or specific laws is only one approach. A second perspective holds that certain liberties exist independently of government guarantees. The rights possessed by individuals are inherent because they are **natural rights** given to human beings by God or some higher authority other than government. As John Dickinson, a writer of the Revolutionary period, put it: "Our liberties do not come from charters; for these are only the declaration of preexisting rights. They do not depend on parchments or seals; but come from the King of Kings and the Lord of all the earth." Although this position has a long history, there is no agreement on what constitutes natural rights. In the Declaration of Independence, Jefferson suggested that natural rights include the right to life, liberty, and the pursuit of happiness. Other writers have included religious freedom, the right to disobey unjust laws, and freedom from arbitrary searches as natural rights beyond the reach of government.

Although the natural-rights argument received its strongest support during the colonial period, it remains a politically relevant idea. Many groups have claimed an inherent right to engage in certain behavior, not on constitutional or statutory ground but on the basis of natural law. When Southern civil rights activists consciously violated racial segregation laws in the 1960s, many asserted that higher natural authority gave them the right to disobey unjust laws. In recent years the idea of inherent natural rights has surfaced in several life-and-death situations. Some supporters of abortion believe that women have a natural right to control their own bodies. The freedom to end one's life through suicide has also been defined as a natural right.

Equality of Rights

Defining the precise rights of individuals is only one issue that has troubled experts over the years. Another major question is whether everyone should enjoy the same rights. At first glance, most people would answer yes. In specific situations, however, many would be willing to make exceptions. For example, should the right to public education be extended to illegal aliens? Should citizens of foreign countries permanently residing in the United States have the same voting rights as U.S. citizens? On occasion the Supreme Court has ruled that not every citizen should enjoy equal rights. In 1974, in *Richardson v. Ramirez*, for example, the Court ruled on the constitutionality of a California law prohibiting felons from voting. Based on Section 2 of the Fourteenth Amendment—which says that states can deny the right to vote for participation in rebellion or other crime— the Court held that the voting rights of criminals could be limited. And, by tradition, certain rights of children and the mentally disabled have been restricted. Children, for example, may not participate in certain types of commercial transactions.

The Question of Whether Some Rights Are More Fundamental Than Others

Another problem concerning rights is whether some are more "untouchable," or more fundamental, than others. Are some rights so basic that they can never be abridged, whereas others can be violated under certain circumstances? Article I, Section 9 of the Constitution, which guarantees the right to a writ of habeas corpus, also specifies that this right may be suspended when the public safety is endangered during rebellion or invasion. The framers of the Constitution clearly placed public safety above the rights of criminals. Some people would argue that the right to free speech, guaranteed in the First Amendment, is more fundamental to our liberty than the right to bear arms, provided in the Second Amendment. Conservatives have sometimes claimed that the right to private property (which is not explicitly mentioned in the Constitution) is the most fundamental of all human rights and thus takes precedence over every other right.

The issue of which rights are more fundamental than others usually surfaces when different rights conflict. The area of national security, in particular, has involved repeated clashes between the personal freedom of citizens and the right of government to protect the nation. Perhaps the most famous of all such conflicts occurred in early 1942, when tens of thousands of people of Japanese ancestry (many of whom were U.S. citizens) were forcibly relocated, on the grounds of military

During World War II, Japanese-Americans were evacuated to internment camps. The U.S. government justified the action—which many civil libertarians have condemned—on grounds of national security.

In 1939, a man drinks from a segregated fountain at a street car station. Before the 1960s, "separate but equal" public facilities were common in many parts of the country.

necessity, to isolated areas. Many of these individuals lost their homes and businesses and lived under strict regimentation, all without the due process guaranteed under the Fifth and Fourteenth Amendments. In 1944, in the case of *Korematsu v. United States*, a divided Supreme Court ruled that military necessity made such gross violation of rights acceptable. One dissenting justice charged, however, that military necessity was never proved, and even if it had been demonstrated, such necessity did not override constitutional guarantees.

The civil rights struggle has raised numerous questions concerning which rights are most basic. The Civil Rights Act of 1964, for example, prohibits discrimination on the basis of race, color, religion, or national origin in the sale or rental of housing (as well as in certain types of public accommodations). Many property owners believed that such laws violated their more basic right to do with their property as they pleased. Civil rights leaders answered these claims by asserting that the right to live wherever one could afford to live was more basic than property rights. The conflict between control of one's property and freedom from discrimination surfaced again in California in 1968. Before 1968, California state laws prohibited racial discrimination in private dwellings of more than four units. In 1968 an amendment to the state constitution giving owners "absolute discretion" over renting or selling their property was approved overwhelmingly by voters in a referendum. Both the California Supreme Court and the national Supreme Court ruled, however, that the amendment was void because it gave state approval to discriminatory behavior. In other words, given a choice between supporting owner control over property and banning discrimination, most California voters preferred owner control. The courts, however, ruled that freedom from racial discrimination should take precedence.

The Government's Responsibility to Implement Rights

A different type of issue involves the government's responsibility in implementing the rights of citizens. As we noted, a right is a claim to a benefit. For example, if you are arrested, you have a right to a lawyer. What is the government's responsibility in this situation? Does this right merely mean that you may have a lawyer if you want one? Or must the government supply a lawyer free of charge? Or going a step further, must the lawyer supplied by the government satisfy your personal standards of what constitutes a good lawyer? All three positions are consistent with the "right to legal counsel." A similar uncertainty has occurred over the meaning of a woman's right to an abortion. Does this right imply that the government must provide or finance the abortion or only that it must permit an abortion to be performed?

The question of how far government should go to ensure the rights of citizens has generated widespread controversy. For some people, the existence of rights is meaningless without a strong effort to implement them. What is the meaning of free speech, they might ask, if individuals with unpopular views cannot gain access to the mass media to present their ideas? Nor would a right to equal pay for equal work be more than a "paper right" without tough government enforcement. The classic example of such "paper rights" prevailed in the South. Although blacks were guaranteed the right to vote by the Constitution and laws, they often were prevented from doing so by such devices as the poll tax (see Chapter 5).

The question of just how far the government must go in protecting rights has emerged on the issue of equal opportunity to an education. Most people accept the principle that all citizens should have an equal right to an education. But what if blacks, women, or other groups, perhaps because of past discrimination, are less able to enter professional schools? Does the presence of comparatively few women in medical school mean that the right of women to equal opportunity has been abridged? Some people would answer yes and therefore require government action to make schools accept a larger proportion of women. Such efforts frequently take the form of **affirmative action** programs, which encourage schools to make an extra effort to recruit women, blacks, or members of other groups. Critics of this reasoning argue that so long as schools do not overly discriminate against women, blacks, or others as a group, their rights have not been infringed. To go beyond non-

discrimination is to practice "**reverse discrimination,**" which violates the rights of individuals not given special treatment.

Resolving Conflicts Over Rights

Obviously, deciding who has which rights under which conditions is difficult and perhaps impossible. Almost any action can somehow be justified on the grounds of some right. Who determines, for example, whether possessing a gun is a state-regulated privilege, or a right that is secondary to other rights, or a fundamental right that can never be abridged?

The Supreme Court as Interpreter of Rights

Should the Supreme Court be the interpreter of our rights? If one believes that our rights consist solely of those claims enumerated in the Constitution (and related legislation) and that the Supreme Court is the final arbiter of the Constitution, this approach makes sense. Nevertheless, while the Court does exercise considerable power over rights questions, its mandate to interpret the Constitution does not automatically make it the final interpreter of our rights. First, the Constitution *itself* says that it does *not* contain all the rights of citizens. According to the Ninth Amendment, "The enumeration in the Constitution, of certain rights, shall not be construed to deny or disparage others retained by the people" (what these "others" are is the subject of controversy). Hence, even if the Court were the final arbiter of the Constitution (and many people would deny this claim), our rights are not limited to those cited in the document.

Second, in determining what is or is not a fundamental right, Supreme Court justices have disagreed among themselves. This was illustrated in the case of *San Antonio Independent School District v. Rodrigues* (1973). The question was whether students living in less well-off school districts were being denied the same rights pupils had in wealthy districts. It was argued that poorer communities could not afford the type of education that wealthier areas could provide. Thus there existed an inequality in the right to education,

Commentary: The Right to Your Name

Your right to call yourself whatever you want is long established, under both common law and the existing legal system. The only general restriction is that name changes cannot be used to defraud (for example, you could not call yourself "Marlon Brando" to help your film career). The issue of name changes has recently received attention because of the desire of many women to keep their original names after marriage or to make their names less sexist (for example, one woman changed her name from Zimmerman to Zimmerperson). All states except Hawaii (and the Commonwealth of Puerto Rico) allow women to keep their parental names, although it may involve some legal paperwork.

Like most other rights, however, this freedom is not absolute. As Michael Herbert Dengler, a short-order cook and ex-teacher, learned, you cannot call yourself a number. Dengler legally tried to rename himself 1069 (or "One-Zero" to his friends). When he lived in North Dakota, he took his case all the way to the state supreme court, but he lost. 1069 then moved to Minneapolis to renew the legal battle. His campaign had mixed results. The state of Minnesota and the telephone company refused to accept 1069 as Dengler's name. He does, however, have a Social Security card and a checking account in the name of 1069.

The case of 1069 is reported in "He Says He's One-Zero but Court is Unconvinced," *New York Times*, November 27, 1977, p. 33.

---

which, it was asserted, is a fundamental right. The Court, in a 5–4 vote, held that because education is neither implicitly nor explicitly guaranteed in the Constitution, it cannot be considered "fundamental." The minority opinion observed, however, that in the past the Court had ruled that several nonconstitutionally listed rights—for example, the right to appeal criminal convictions—were "fundamental." In short, a one-vote margin prevented education from becoming a fundamental right, and the justices themselves acknowledged that no clear guidelines exist to resolve this dispute.

Public Officials as Interpreters of Rights

Public officials also play an important role in interpreting rights, because the meaning of many rights is defined concretely by national, state, and local laws. We all might have the constitutionally guaranteed right of assembly to petition our government, but many crucial aspects of this right are decided by public officials. For example, legislators pass laws that define peaceful assembly, specify penalties for violations, and decide how much effort will be made to enforce the law. Often legislators leave it up to the police, who enforce the law, to decide what a right means.

That the actual meaning of a right depends on the behavior of public officials does, however, present one problem: the purpose of many rights is to protect citizens from government. Our protection of free speech, for example, is supposed to prevent government from abridging the speech of citizens. The existence of numerous rights protecting criminals is intended to shield innocent citizens from overzealous public authorities. To give government the ultimate power to decide our rights is like giving foxes the power to regulate the chicken coop.

The People as Interpreters of Rights

Finally, a long tradition exists that the people themselves are the ultimate guardians and interpreters of their rights. The people might allow government to administer these rights, but this does not mean that the rights are surrendered. When the government enforces civil rights laws, for example, it is acting on behalf of the people; it is not giving the people something they do not have. If the government violates these rights, the people are justified in changing their government.

The idea that the people are the ultimate interpreters of their rights was a guiding principle of the American Revolution. In resolving problems of interpretation and conflict, however, this approach provides little help. How can society operate if each individual decides on his or her own such questions as which rights are most important or whether everyone will have identical rights? Nor would putting such questions to a vote necessarily provide the answers. A majority vote might extend or restrict a *privilege*, but many people would claim that it may not define an *inalienable right*, which exists regardless of the actions of others. It is argued also that a right has little meaning if it can be abolished by a simple majority of citizens. The belief that the people themselves define and interpret their rights is perhaps more of a philosophical position than a solution to the problem of who decides which rights we possess.

Conclusions

It should be clear from our analysis that rights generate numerous controversies. Disputes occur over which rights we enjoy, whether some rights are more fundamental, how rights should be enforced, and who settles conflicts over interpretation. Different answers to these questions can profoundly affect the lives of all citizens.

Check Your Understanding

1. What is a *right* and how does it differ from a *privilege*?

2. What are some possible sources of rights?

3. What is the difference between *civil liberties* and *civil rights*?

4. Why is it sometimes difficult for the Supreme Court to resolve conflicts over rights?

WHAT POLITICAL RIGHTS DO CITIZENS HAVE?

We have seen that defining rights is a complex process. Nevertheless, several kinds of rights are widely viewed as "fundamental" in American politics. We shall describe six types of rights that constitute key safeguards of our freedom: (1) freedom of speech, (2) freedom of the press, (3) freedom of association, (4) religious freedom, (5) equal protection of the laws, and (6) the rights of suspected criminals. We shall see that even though these rights are deeply established, they are not immune from many of the problems previously described.

Freedom of Speech

The First Amendment states that "Congress shall make no law . . . abridging the freedom of speech. . . ." At first glance this prohibition seems clear. Nevertheless, only a few people—most notably former Supreme Court justices Hugo Black and William O. Douglas—have interpreted the phrase "no law" literally. This view frequently is called the **absolutist position**. In practice, the right has been limited, and free speech has generated many interpretations, doctrines, and unresolved questions.

The Meaning of "Speech"
A good place to begin our examination of this right is to consider the meaning of "speech." What, precisely, comes under the heading of speech? Scholars have frequently distinguished three types of speech that can be protected. The most obvious is called **pure speech**—the peaceful expression of ideas before an audience that has chosen voluntarily to listen. If students give a lecture entitled "Students: The Oppressed Minority" before the International Downtrodden Association, they are engaging, or participating, in pure speech and are protected by the First Amendment.

However, suppose these students decided to picket a local movie house, which they said played too many poor-quality films. They carried posters that read, "We want better movies!" Are these students engaging in speech? Because they are *communicating* their ideas, a protest like theirs would be interpreted as being a form of speech (even if no word is ever spoken). Such activity is sometimes called **speech plus.** Because the students' behavior goes beyond mere speech, however, their actions can be subject to various restrictions that would not apply to pure speech. For example, the Supreme Court has ruled that such "speech" may not obstruct traffic, block sidewalks, or endanger public safety.

Defining "speech" becomes more troublesome when we enter the realm of what is usually called **symbolic speech,** in which individuals use symbols to express their opinions. During the U.S. involvement in Vietnam, symbolic expressions included burning draft cards and pouring blood on draft board records. The Court accepted some of these actions as exercises in free speech but rejected others. In *Tinker v. Des Moines School District* (1969) the Court ruled that wearing black armbands to protest the war in Vietnam was within the bounds of freedom of expression. The burning of draft cards, however, was rejected.

Extension of Free Speech Protection to the State Level

A second important aspect of free speech concerns *who* may not make laws abridging free speech. The First Amendment states only that *Congress* shall make no such law. There is no mention of what states, local government, or private individuals may do.

The question of who is bound by the First Amendment (and the rest of the Bill of Rights) is a crucial one. Imagine a society in which state and local governments were not covered by these protections. Some states might, for example, ban controversial types of speech, establish an official religion, or employ cruel and unusual punishment. It makes quite a difference, in other words, that all governments—national, state, and local—must abide by the Bill of Rights. The question of coverage deserves elaboration.

When the Bill of Rights was passed on December 15, 1791, it was intended to apply only to the national government. There was some talk of placing similar restrictions on state governments, but the plan was rejected. The Supreme Court in

---

Points of View: But What If They Talk in Their Sleep?

The notion of "symbolic speech" is filled with complexities. What might be ordinary behavior in one context can be the communication of a political idea in another. Consider the so-called free sleep case that occurred in 1983. To protest the conditions of the poor under the Reagan administration, a group called the Community for Creative Non-Violence camped out in Lafayette Park, directly across from the White House.

The use of Lafayette Park for political protests was not in question. It has been the traditional site of rallies, silent vigils, and other political activities. The issue was whether sleeping could be included as a protected activity that can occur on park grounds. The government argued that protesters could remain in the park as long as they chose, even overnight, but that they could not sleep there. If they did go to sleep, then they would be using the park as a place to live, a violation of Park Service rules. Once they started sleeping, they were no longer protected by

the First Amendment.

A 6–5 majority of the District of Columbia Court of Appeals took a different view. In protecting sleep as a communication of an idea, Judge Harry Edwards wrote: "These destitute men and women can express with their bodies the poignancy of their plight. They can physically demonstrate the neglect from which they suffer with an articulateness even Dickens could not match."

Adapted from Nat Hentoff, "The Free Sleep Case," *Washington Post*, March 10, 1984.

A member of the Young Lords, a Puerto Rican group, marches in a New York City Puerto Rican Day parade. The Supreme Court has interpreted such acts as flag burning as "symbolic speech."

1833 reaffirmed this limit when it held that the state of Maryland was not bound by the Fifth Amendment's guarantee of fair compensation for private property taken for public purposes *(Barron v. Baltimore)*. States were free to ignore the amendment's provisions, and many did. Both Connecticut and Massachusetts, for example, used tax money to support an official state religion, a forbidden activity for national government.

In 1868 the Fourteenth Amendment was adopted. Based on its language and on the intent of those who drafted it, the amendment appeared to apply the Bill of Rights to the states. It says, in part: "No state shall make or enforce any law which shall abridge the privileges or immunities of citizens of the United States; nor shall any State deprive any person of life, liberty, or property, without due process of law; nor deny to any person within its jurisdiction the equal protection of the laws." In other words, because citizens already possessed guarantees granted by the Bill of Rights,

and because the states could not deprive citizens of their rights, it would seem to follow that states were now bound by these restrictions as well.

In an 1873 case in which the state of Louisiana was accused of depriving butchers of their right to do business, however, the Supreme Court held that state laws depriving citizens of a right guaranteed by the Bill of Rights did *not* violate the Fourteenth Amendment. The Court rejected the reasoning that due process was guaranteed by the Fifth Amendment and that the Fourteenth Amendment applied the Fifth Amendment to state action. The Court's view was strengthened in a series of decisions involving discrimination against blacks ten years later. The overall thrust of these and many other rulings was that the Bill of Rights did not apply to states. Indeed, in one 1876 case *(United States v. Cruikshank)*, the Court ruled that the national government was powerless to act against states that violated a person's right to peaceful assembly, the right to petition for redress of grievances, and the right to bear arms—all explicit Bill of Rights guarantees. States were generally free to do as they pleased.

The first change occurred in 1925. In the case of *Gitlow v. New York*, a member of the Socialist Party (Gitlow) had been convicted of advocating the overthrow of the government. Gitlow argued that the New York law under which he was convicted violated his right to due process, because the law did not require the state to demonstrate any harmful effects of his speech. The Court did not declare the New York law unconstitutional, and it upheld Gitlow's conviction. However, the Court said that the due process guarantee of the Fourteenth Amendment—"nor shall any State deprive any person of life, liberty, or property, without due process of law"—meant that the states could be bound by the Bill of Rights. In particular, if a right is fundamental—and the decision singled out freedom of speech and of the press as fundamental—states, as well as the national government, must respect it.

In a series of later decisions, almost all Bill of Rights protections against the national government were extended, one by one, to state action. In a process called **incorporation,** Bill of Rights guarantees have been incorporated into the due process clause of the Fourteenth Amendment to apply to the states. Today, just a few comparatively unimportant provisions apply only to the national government: states do not have to provide jury trials in civil cases, and grand jury indictments are not required in state criminal proceedings (the role of the grand jury is discussed later in the chapter).

Speech Not Protected by the First Amendment

A third aspect of freedom of speech involves the types of speech that are *not* protected by the First Amendment. Could students in their speech to the International Downtrodden Association say or do *anything* that comes to mind? The answer is a clear no, despite our guarantee of free speech.

One important limitation involves the issue of obscenity. There are two issues here: (1) may obscene speech be limited? and (2) what makes something "obscene"? The first question has usually been answered yes. A long tradition going back to English common law holds that free speech does not mean that obscenity is permitted. (English common law is based on centuries of custom and precedent rather than on written legislation.)

The second issue has caused great difficulty, as judges and officials have tried to separate obscene from nonobscene material. State and federal statutes have often banned material that is "lewd" or "filthy" or involves nudity. This has proved troublesome, because many books, paintings, and other works of art might be interpreted as "lewd" despite having artistic intent.

Over the years the Supreme Court has offered several solutions to this problem. A number of modern rulings have tried, with only partial success, to grapple with this issue. In *Roth v. United States* (1957), the Court held that something is obscene if "to the average person, applying contemporary community standards, the dominant theme of the material taken as a whole appeals to the prurient interest." Because this ruling emphasized "community standards," not the most corruptible person in the community, and the "material taken as a whole," not isolated passages, the *Roth* decision was a liberalizing one. No longer could a prosecutor claim that one word in a book might corrupt a child and therefore the entire book was obscene. As a result of this case, several legal actions against books and movies were dismissed. The Court also ruled that mere advocacy of an idea like adultery cannot be obscene. Nevertheless, many problems of defining and dealing with obscenity remained. In *Miller v. California* (1973), the Court again tried to separate obscene from nonobscene. Something would be obscene if (1) the average person applying community standards decides that the material (2) "depicts or describes, in a patently offensive way, sexual conduct specifically defined by the applicable state law," and (3) the work "taken as a whole, lacks serious literary, artistic, political or scientific value."

Overall, these and other Court decisions have resulted in a liberalization of obscenity standards. Although in principle the *Miller* case gave local communities greater power to regulate obscenity, it is no longer true that nudity, profane language,

Police stand in front of an "adult" theater. Because of unclear definitions of "obscenity," enforcement of antipornography laws is controversial.

or explicit sexual conduct automatically makes something obscene. The Court has ruled, for example, that it may not be made illegal to possess obscene material (*Stanley v. Georgia*, 1969), nor do juries have total discretion in censoring films (*Jenkins v. Georgia*, 1974). Limits remain, however. In *New York v. Ferber* (1982), the Court ruled that the pornographic depiction of children is not protected by the First Amendment.

A second type of speech not protected by the Constitution is known as **fighting words**—speech that incites, or arouses, others to violence. Fighting words are not necessarily the same thing as controversial or insulting language. This principle was established in the 1942 case of *Chaplinsky v. New Hampshire*. The defendant, Chaplinsky, had caused a public disturbance by, among other things calling the Rochester, New Hampshire, city marshal "a God-damned racketeer." Under a state law he was convicted of calling someone "offensive and derisive" names in public. His conviction was upheld on the grounds that such fighting words could bring an immediate breach of the peace. Writing for the majority, Justice Frank Murphy said that such utterances "are of such slight social value that any benefit that may be derived from them is clearly outweighed by the social interest in order and morality." However, the Court has since insisted that laws restricting "fighting words" be precise. For example, in a 1972 case the Court overturned the conviction of a man who used profanity against a policeman and threatened him with violence. The Court ruled that the Georgia law under which he was convicted was not specific enough.

The conflict between the right to free speech and the need to protect public order has been a troublesome constitutional issue. If we desire to maintain public order at all costs, anyone willing to cause a public disturbance can exercise veto power over another person's right to free expression. In the late 1960s and early 1970s, a few individuals were, in fact, frequently successful in preventing public debates on such controversial issues as Vietnam or South Africa's racial policy merely by threatening disruptions.

During the mid-1960s, officials opposed to the activities of civil rights groups used the "fear of violence" to prevent rallies and marches. Since that time, the Supreme Court has formulated strict rules regarding the abridgment of free speech because of the expectation of violence. Restrictions have been permitted only when (1) more was involved than just "pure speech" (for example, occupying a building), (2) the state or local law authorizing the abridgment was specific, and (3) the likelihood of public disorder was very clear. The willingness of the courts to protect free speech in the face of potential violence was illustrated when the American Nazi party organized several Chicago demonstrations in the summer of 1978. Despite the fear of Chicago city officials that riots might occur (and many explicit threats of violence

Biography: William O. Douglas

William O. Douglas served as a U.S. Supreme Court justice longer than anyone else in history—from 1936 to 1975. Noted for his uncompromising defense of civil liberties, he once said that "our Constitution was framed to keep government off the backs of the people."

Born in Minnesota in 1898, Douglas grew up in Washington State. He worked as a migrant farmhand to put himself through Whitman College and "rode the rails" as a hobo when traveling east to attend Columbia University Law School. These and other early experiences with poverty made him sympathetic to the poor and friendless.

After graduating from Columbia University in 1925, Douglas worked briefly for a prestigious New York City law firm and then taught at Yale Law School. His specialty, corporation law, made him a natural appointee for the Securities and Exchange Commission, on which he served from 1934 to 1936, when President Franklin D. Roosevelt named him to the Supreme Court.

During his thirty-nine years on the Court, Douglas, whether in the majority or as a dissenting voice, never wavered in his defense of individual liberty. In the realm of free speech, for example, he was an absolutist, believing that all forms of speech, including symbolic speech such as draft card burning, should be unrestricted and were protected by the First Amendment. In other areas of civil liberties Douglas was just as

outspoken in his feeling that government could not trample on the rights of the individual. In the landmark *Pentagon Papers* case (1971), for instance, he stood with the majority, noting that "secrecy in government is fundamentally undemocratic." Moreover, he felt that publishers should not be restrained in the name of protection against obscenity. His defense of the right of association reflected his advocacy of the "full and free discussion even of ideas we hate." When, in *Dennis v. United States* (1951), the Supreme Court upheld

the Smith Act, which made it a crime to belong to an organization advocating the overthrow of the government, Douglas dissented. He was equally assertive in championing the legal rights of accused criminals: "It is no answer that a man is doubtlessly guilty. The Bill of Rights was designed to protect every accused against practices of the police which history showed were oppressive." Finally, Douglas felt, individuals have a constitutional right to privacy. He spoke for the majority in *Griswold v. Connecticut* (1965), which overturned a Connecticut law forbidding the sale of contraceptives. "The First Amendment has a penumbra [a surrounding shadow]," he wrote, "where privacy is protected from governmental intrusion."

Douglas' views aroused strong opposition from many groups, and there were threats to impeach him (see Chapter 12). One of his most unpopular moves was to grant a stay of execution for convicted spies Ethel and Julius Rosenberg. The stay was overruled, however, and the two were electrocuted in 1953.

An active person, Douglas exhibited an extraordinary energy until a stroke forced him to retire from the Supreme Court in 1975. He died five years later. Douglas' longevity on the Court and his consistent approach to matters of individual rights—characterized by one scholar as "a gut reaction to injustice"—had the effect of broadening previously held ideas of civil liberties.

came from anti-Nazi groups), the Court upheld the right of Nazis to march.

Different Rules Regulating Free Speech

Over the years, judges and scholars have attempted to bring order to the many varied rules governing the exercise and abridgment of free expression. Several general principles have been suggested. The so-called **clear and present danger test** was first formulated by Justice Oliver Wendell Holmes in the *Schenck v. United States* case (1919). This case involved the mailing of material to men subject to the draft during World War I urging them to resist induction into the army. One of those doing the mailing—Schenck—was convicted under a federal law that made it a crime to incite resistance to the United States or to promote the cause of its enemies. Holmes and the rest of the Court ruled that Schenck's action was not protected free speech. The basic question, according to Holmes, was whether the words would directly bring about an evil that "government has the right to prevent." Holmes used the analogy of someone falsely shouting "fire" in a crowded theater. Such speech is not permissible because it would immediately result in a dangerous panic.

A second doctrine that attempts to bring logical order to limitations on free speech emphasizes the "reasonableness" of legislatively imposed restrictions. The basic presumption is that a restriction—for example, that demonstrators may not block automobile traffic—is acceptable if a "reasonable" person would accept such limitations. In practice, this doctrine allows legislatures vast discretion in abridging free speech. Only when restrictions are clearly unfair or unreasonable are they to be struck down.

Finally, some Supreme Court justices have formulated what has been called the **preferred position doctrine.** According to this principle, freedoms of speech, the press, and religion are more fundamental than other freedoms because they provide the basis of all our liberties. Because they enjoy a preferred position, they can be infringed upon, or interfered with, only under special conditions. As Justice Wiley B. Rutledge put it in *Thomas v. Collings* (1945): "Only the gravest

Justice Oliver Wendell Holmes believed that some speech was not protected by the First Amendment.

abuses, endangering paramount interests, give occasion for permissible limitations."

The three doctrines we have discussed and several variations have all received substantial support from respected judges and scholars. Nevertheless, no general approach has succeeded very well. Each might seem appropriate for certain cases and in certain historical periods, but none provides a clear guide to be used in all circumstances. Moreover, each ultimately rests on interpretations of indefinite terms. For example, how "clear" must a danger be before it is a "clear and present" danger? What if two supposedly reasonable people differ on what is "reasonable"? Even if freedom of speech enjoys a preferred status, under what precise conditions can it be abridged? Obviously, although free speech is a crucial right and its existence is unchallenged, considerable leeway exists in its actual interpretation.

Freedom of the Press

Like free speech, freedom of the press is expressly protected by the First Amendment. And as was true for free speech, the interpretation of this protection is not simple. Let us begin by considering the freedoms enjoyed by the press. We shall then examine limits on these freedoms. Finally, we shall discuss the application of the First Amendment to the mass media.

Freedom Enjoyed by Newspapers, Books, and Magazines

Just how much freedom do magazines and books enjoy? Can the *Daily Planet* publish anything? Despite the importance of this question, guidelines were never spelled out clearly until 1931 in the *Near v. Minnesota* decision. This case involved a Minnesota weekly newspaper that local law enforcement officials had prevented from publishing, on the grounds that its malicious and scandalous attacks on city officials were a public nuisance. In a 5–4 decision, the Court held that Minnesota's public nuisance law was a violation of the First Amendment. Chief Justice Charles Evans Hughes, speaking for the majority, affirmed the crucial doctrine prohibiting **prior restraint** of publication. The ruling did not mean that newspapers could print just anything; rather, punishment could occur only *after* publication, not before. The doctrine of no prior restraint is deeply rooted in English common law. Without this principle, government officials could easily censor newspapers with arguments about what *might* happen if something were published.

The Supreme Court did, however, stop short of saying that prior restraint was never permitted. It specified four situations in which it would be permissible: (1) military necessity, (2) obscenity, (3) incitements to violence, and (4) the protection of private rights. In several later cases the Supreme Court employed these standards to provide considerable leeway to newspapers printing controversial material. Perhaps the toughest case involved the publication of the so-called *Pentagon Papers* by the *New York Times*, the *Washington Post*, and other newspapers in June 1971. The *Pentagon Papers* were part of a Department of Defense study (classified as "secret") of U.S. involvement in Vietnam and contained some highly embarrassing military information, such as reports of early secret raids against North Vietnam that had been officially denied. These documents were made available to the newspapers illegally, and the government sought to stop publication on the grounds of national security (the war in Vietnam was still in progress). In a 6–3 vote, the Supreme Court ruled that the government had not proved its claim of military necessity and thus had not met the "heavy burden" needed to justify prior restraint.

In more recent decisions the Supreme Court has taken steps also to protect commercial messages found in newspapers. In *Bigelow v. Virginia* (1975), for example, the Court reversed the conviction of a newspaper editor for violating a state law by encouraging abortions. The editor had merely accepted an advertisement that offered information on legal abortions in New York. In 1977 the Court struck down an Arizona law that prevented attorneys from advertising in newspapers (*Bates v. Arizona State Bar*).

Libel

Historically, the First Amendment has been interpreted to exclude libel and slander from its protection. **Libel** is defamation of character (false statements that are malicious) in print or by other visual means. **Slander** is oral, or spoken, defamation. Libel can be punished as a criminal offense or privately through a civil suit. The laws on libel also have deep roots in English common law and generally are considered necessary to the social order. For many years the existence of libel laws greatly limited the freedom of newspapers. If a story described an officeholder as dishonest, the newspapers could be sued for libel unless there was overwhelming proof of the charge.

The question of whether newspapers were to be governed by strict libel laws emerged in the landmark case of *New York Times Co. v. Sullivan* (1964). The *New York Times* had published an advertisement by a civil rights group critical of the treatment blacks received in Montgomery, Alabama. The *Times* was convicted of libel by an Ala-

The first installment of the Pentagon Papers *appeared on June 13, 1971. Publication of the material raised issues of whether national security can be the basis of censorship of the press.*

bama court and fined $500,000, to be paid to the Montgomery police commissioner. The Supreme Court, however, overruled the lower-court decision on the grounds that free and open communication is an essential right, and the exercise of this right can include unpleasant or even fierce attacks on government officials. Even if such attacks involve inaccuracies, they are still not necessarily libelous, the Court maintained. To require absolute accuracy in a public debate, ruled the Court, would tend to eliminate all public discussion. Action could be taken against a newspaper for printing malicious falsehoods about public officials *if* such statements were known to be false and there was a total disregard for the truth. Even then, however, the burden of proof is on the official being attacked.

Limits on Free Expression in Newspapers

The *New York Times* case provides protection against libel actions for public figures. However, a private citizen defamed by a newspaper or magazine still might collect substantial damages (money awarded by a court). When *Time* incorrectly called a divorcee an "adulteress," the magazine was taken to court and had to pay damages of $100,000 (*Time, Inc. v. Firestone* [1976]). Moreover, on numerous occasions the Court has upheld the banning of obscene books and magazines. As mentioned earlier, the definition of *obscenity* has undergone change, but the principle that obscenity (however defined) is not constitutionally protected generally remains unchallenged. The circulation of newspapers and magazines can also be controlled through postal regulations. Even though the Court has struck down laws allowing postal employees to open and read other people's mail, it has not ruled that the use of the mail is protected by the First Amendment. Thus, as it did in the Espionage Act of 1917, the government can prohibit the mailing of newspapers or other printed material urging treason, insurrection, or forcible resistance to the law.

One of the most controversial restraints on newspaper freedom concerns the confidentiality, or privacy, of reporters' news sources. Some journalists maintain that if they can be forced to reveal their sources to law enforcement officials, their ability to pursue the truth will be seriously weakened. (People might be afraid to talk freely to reporters, because their names could be given to the government.) In addition, government access to their private information would transform the news media into an investigative arm of the government. Many states have accepted this argument and have enacted so-called **shield laws** that permit reporters to withhold from police and courts information on criminal behavior that they have gathered. There is no equivalent of the shield law at the federal level. In the case of *Branzburg v. Hayes* (1972), the Supreme Court said that reporters aware of illegal activities may be compelled to testify. Many reporters, choosing to defy this ruling, have been held in contempt of court (contempt of court is discussed later in the chapter).

Finally, the freedom of newspapers has been abridged when it conflicted with a person's right to a fair trial, guaranteed by the Sixth Amendment. Here the courts applied what has been called a **balancing test** in limiting a right. In such a test, the government's restriction of a right is balanced against competing private and public interests in a particular situation. This approach has often been used since the 1950s. In several cases the Supreme Court has reversed convictions in which intense pretrial newspaper coverage made it almost impossible to select unbiased jurors. New trials have been ordered when reporters have influenced judicial proceedings by publicizing evidence, confessions, and comments by lawyers and witnesses. These rulings are an indirect warning to newspapers to practice self-restraint on behalf of those

accused of a crime. In some cases, judges have issued so-called **gag orders** to prevent newspapers and other media from even mentioning certain trial-related facts. One gag order, forbidding reporters from mentioning a confession for eleven weeks, was struck down by the Supreme Court, but the principle of prior restraint by judges was accepted, although it must be clearly justified (*Nebraska Press Association v. Stuart* [1976]).

The Mass Media

A major problem in applying the First Amendment's protection of newspapers involves the relevance of such protection to electronic journalism. What if a television newscaster reads, word for word, a newspaper story? Is this act protected by the Constitution? Is a film about politics equivalent to a magazine article on the identical subject? There are also questions as to whether the print media include billboards, leaflets, and the like.

In general, the courts have been less protective of radio, television, and film than of newspapers. The broadcast media have been viewed as a privilege granted by the government, not a right. For technical reasons, not everyone can be allowed to transmit radio or television signals. By allowing a small number of people to engage in this activity, the government has granted them a privilege. As with all government-granted privileges, strict rules can be established. The Federal Communications Commission, for example, imposes rules prohibiting cigarette and hard liquor advertising on television, as well as offensive language.

The technical considerations that make broadcasting a privilege rather than a right do not apply to films. For many years, though, the courts held that the movies were a form of entertainment and thus could be regulated the same way as circuses or amusement parks. However, in *Burstyn v. Wilson* (1952), the Court recognized the informational role of movies. In later decisions the Court has extended some (but not complete) First Amendment protection to films. Essentially, films *may* be censored before they are shown, but the burden of proof is on the censor and there must be a judicial remedy for appeals.

Freedom of Association

Unlike free speech and freedom of the press, freedom of association does not rest on an explicit constitutional guarantee. Nevertheless, the Supreme Court has held that this right is a natural corollary of the right of free speech and the right of assembly. Especially when controversial issues are at stake or one's goals involve many people (for example, equality for women), the freedom to associate with like-minded citizens is essential. What would be the value of free speech if those who share an idea could not legally associate with one another?

Freedom of Association and National Security

Like many of our rights, freedom of association becomes less absolute in actual practice. In particular, how do you balance the right of association with the government's responsibility to protect itself from secret organizations that would overthrow it by illegal or violent means? Must government wait until violence occurs, or can it act to stop conspiracy at the planning stage?

This issue has surfaced periodically since World War I, when the threat of a secret Communist conspiracy to overthrow our government appeared very real to many people. The frequent reaction of courts at both the state and federal levels was to limit freedom of association in the name of national security. In *Whitney v. California* (1927), the Supreme Court upheld the conviction of Charlotte Anita Whitney for participating in a meeting that established the Communist Labor Party of California. Her conviction was based on a California law that made it a crime to belong to an organization that advocated, taught, or aided and abetted criminal **syndicalism** (the idea that industry should be owned by the workers). Merely belonging to such a group, regardless of one's actions, was a crime.

In 1940, Congress passed the Alien Registration Act (widely known as the Smith Act). The act made it a crime to belong to any organization that advocated the overthrow of the U.S. government, *regardless of what an individual said or did.* In effect, membership in the Communist party be-

came a federal crime. The constitutionality of this statute was upheld in *Dennis v. United States* (1951) by a 6–2 vote. A further attack on the Communist party was launched with the Internal Security Act of 1950. This act (commonly known as the McCarran Act) required that all subversive organizations register with the government. Once registered, organization members had to identify their public messages as subversive propaganda, they could not hold nonelective federal office, they were forbidden to apply for or use a U.S. passport, and their right to work in defense plants was curtailed.

During the 1940s and 1950s, most states also required their employees (including teachers) to sign **loyalty oaths** affirming that they had never been members of the Communist party or otherwise plotted the violent overthrow of the U.S. government. The purpose of such oaths was not to prevent subversives from getting government jobs (a true subversive could lie). Rather, any employee who had been associated at some time with a Communist-run organization but who signed the oath to get a job could be charged with perjury (lying under oath). The oaths gave a kind of hunting license to anti-Communists, who would investigate the backgrounds of public employees in search of past association with one of the many supposed Communist-dominated organizations popular during the 1930s. (Many of these groups were never publicly identified as "**Communist fronts**" until years after their creation.)

Gradually, however, the Supreme Court began to restrain government efforts to make it a crime to be associated with the Communist party. In *Yates v. United States* (1957), the Court held that advocating an abstract, or theoretical, doctrine is very different from directly promoting unlawful actions. The Smith Act, according to the Court, could make only direct advocacy of unlawful actions illegal; belief in an abstract doctine (for example, the inevitable collapse of capitalism) was protected by the right of free speech. Several later Court decisions further weakened the Smith Act, and in *Brandenburg v. Ohio* (1969) the whole idea of guilt by (Communist) association was thrown out. A similar fate befell the Internal Security Act of 1950, as the courts ruled that having to declare oneself a Communist, which was automatically a crime, violated the protection from self-incrimination guaranteed by the Fifth Amendment. The Supreme Court also reduced the scope of loyalty oaths. In *Elfbrandt v. Russell* (1966), for example, it held that membership in a subversive organization was punishable only if there had been a "specific intent" to further the illegal aims of the organization.

Other Limits on Freedom of Association

The anti-Communist laws of the 1940s and 1950s are gone or are greatly weakened today. Nor is there much "witch hunting," or public exposure and punishment of those with past Communist associaitons. Nevertheless, individuals are not completely free to associate with whomever they choose. **Criminal conspiracy**—that is, agreement among two or more people to commit an unlawful act or to commit a lawful act through unlawful means—still remains a serious offense. Because

criminal conspiracy generally involves secrecy, normal rules of evidence for proving guilt are usually loosened. On several occasions the charge of criminal conspiracy has been a useful government weapon to prosecute individuals who have been associated with unpopular groups. In 1968, for example, several anti–Vietnam war leaders were prosecuted for criminal conspiracy following the widespread disorders at the Democratic presidential nominating convention in Chicago. In general, the government has had little success in convicting political activists of criminal conspiracy, but the threat of being taken to court merely because one is publicly identified with some group remains real.

Religious Freedom

The issue of religious freedom is perhaps, the oldest controversy in American history. By today's standards religious freedom might not seem an important right, because people may choose their

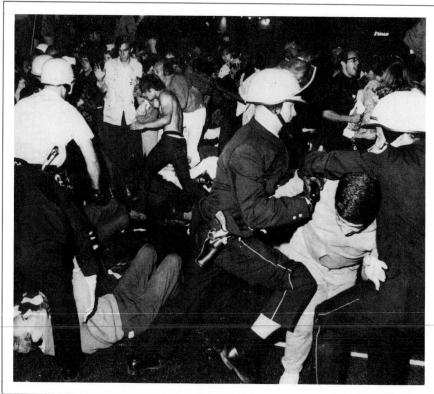

In 1968, angry that the Democratic party did not nominate an antiwar presidential candidate, demonstrators protest outside the convention and are restrained by the police. Some people criticized the actions of law enforcement authorities as excessive.

religions and worship as they please. We must remember, however, that a **theocracy**—government by a religious group—can be one of the most oppressive types of society, because no aspect of one's life is beyond its reach.

The right of religious freedom is spelled out in the Constitution in two places. Article VI bans religious qualifications, or requirements, for public office, and the First Amendment states that "Congress shall make no law respecting an establishment of religion, or prohibiting the free exercise thereof. . . ." This First Amendment right contains two separate though related provisions: (1) government may not "establish" a religion, and (2) laws may not be enacted that limit the free exercise of religion. Because the provisions have involved somewhat different sets of issues, we shall consider them separately.

Free Exercise of Religion

When the Constitution says that no law may abridge one's religious practices, does this mean that a person may do *anything* he or she wants so long as it is "religious" in nature? Defining "religion" is not easy, and many people disagree sharply over what constitutes a religion. Can a philosophy reject the existence of God and still qualify as a religion? Does a religion need more than one believer, or can each person believe in his or her unique brand of religion?

In the nineteenth century, the Supreme Court held a restricted view of what constituted a religion. In *Davis v. Beason* (1890), the Court stated that "the term 'religon' has reference to one's views of his relations to his Creator, and to the obligation they impose of reverence for his being and character, and of obedience to his will." Under this definition many contemporary religions, especially those with a mystical orientation, would not qualify for constitutional protection. More recent decisions, however, have emphasized the right of people to define religion for themselves. In 1963, for example, the Court ruled that the Black Muslims were a legitimate religious group, not a political and racist organization, as prison authorities had argued. In several decisions affecting the right to refuse military service on religious grounds, the

Court interpreted religious beliefs as being identical to ethical or moral codes. There are limits, however. In one case the Church of the New-Song, founded by two prison inmates, did not win federal court recognition as a legitimate religion. Perhaps its requirement of steak and sherry meals, monthly fruit baskets, and movies had something to do with its rejection.

A second issue in the "free exercise" guarantee concerns what happens when religious practices conflict with the laws of the community. Can you claim, for example, that your religious beliefs forbid the making of war and you therefore refuse to pay all your taxes, on the grounds that some of your tax money would be spent for war? More generally, are religious practices entitled to some special protection not given to the identical behavior performed in a nonreligious context?

Over the years the courts have attempted to resolve this issue through the use of the **secular regulation rule,** which says that the free exercise provision does not mean that any kind of behavior or conduct is exempt from the law. The right to hold unorthodox *beliefs* is absolute; the right to engage in unorthodox *behavior*, however, may be limited. An exemption may be provided, but a religious group cannot make a constitutionally protected claim to this right. This conflict surfaced in the case of *Wisconsin v. Yoder* (1972), which involved the refusal of some Amish parents to send their children to school past the eighth grade despite the state's compulsory education law. The Amish claimed that additional education would undermine their traditional religious values. The Court supported the Amish parents and agreed that in this particular instance religious beliefs could override state law.

Resolving the conflict between laws that supposedly apply to everyone and special religious practices has not always been so easy. On several occasions the Supreme Court had to decide whether members of the Jehovah's Witnesses could be forced to salute the flag in school despite their religion's ban on worshipping "graven images." In a 1940 decision the Court ruled that a state flag-saluting requirement did not infringe on the freedom of religion. Three years later, the

A young Amish man waits with friends to plead not guilty to a charge of draft evasion. The Amish have challenged many public laws that they say conflict with their religious, pacifist way of life.

Court reversed itself and said that no child could be forced to salute the flag against his or her religious convictions. Other religious activities permitted by state and federal courts include the right not to serve on a jury, the right not to stand during the playing of the national anthem, and the right of Navajo members of the North American Church to use peyote in their rituals. However, when religious principles might result in death—for example, the Jehovah's Witnesses' refusal of blood transfusions because of the biblical prohibition against "eating blood"—the courts have usually ruled against religous practices (especially when the life of a child is in danger).

Prohibition Against the Establishment of Religion

Besides guaranteeing the free exercise of religion, the First Amendment prohibits government from establishing a religion. Disagreement exists on exactly what is meant by "establishment." Some people view the ban on "establishment" as prohibiting the government from creating an official, government-financed church. In Great Britain, the Anglican Church is the official church, and high church officials receive government salaries. From this perspective, government financial aid to religion would be constitutional so long as there was no one official church. Others go much further and view "establishment" as *any* government support of religious institutions, regardless of whether benefits apply equally to all religions. Advocates of this position (including Thomas Jefferson) have called for a "high wall" between church and state. From the **"high-wall" perspective,** any government aid would violate the First Amendment because public money would be used to promote religion.

In principle, Congress, the President, and the courts have generally endorsed the "high-wall" position. In practice, however, disagreements have occurred over the exact boundary line between church and state. Sometimes it is almost impossible to separate benefits extended to churches from those pertaining to the general population. For example, public money provides houses of worship with such elementary services as police and fire protection, sidewalks, postal delivery, and many other benefits (consider the complexities if churches had to have their own separate water and sewage systems). Moreover, religious practices are so deeply embedded in our lives that eliminating them completely would be almost impossible. Imagine the outcry if Congress did away with military chaplains or the "In God We Trust" motto on coins.

The major area in which the "establishment" principle has generated legal problems is that of government aid to religious schools. The "high-wall" doctrine says there should be no aid to religion, but religious schools engage in an important public function (education) in addition to their religious activities. Is it constitutionally possible to assist the purely educational aspect of these schools without aiding the religious part as well? The Supreme Court has generally given a very limited yes to this question. For example, in *Committee for Public Education and Religious Liberty v. Regan* (1980), the Court said that no First Amendment violation occurs when the state reimburses a church-related school for administering certain standardized tests and keeping state-required records. More recently the Court has upheld a Minnesota law that allows parents to take tax deductions for tuition to private schools, a decision that assists religious schools because many private schools are church-affiliated. However, laws allowing religious instruction in public schools, public money for religious-school guidance activities, and state subsidies for parochial school teachers have been overturned. Standards have been less strict for public money given to religious colleges, however.

Perhaps the strongest action taken by the Supreme Court to maintain the "high wall" occurred when, in *Engel v. Vitale* (1962) and *School District of Abington Township v. Schempp* (1963), mandatory religious prayers and Bible readings in schools were declared unconstitutional. Later lower-court decisions have banned even mild, nondenominational prayers. In *DeSpain v. DeKalb County School District* (1967), the United States Court of Appeals ruled that in-school recitation of the poem "We thank you for the flowers so sweet; we thank you for the food we eat; we thank you for the birds that sing; we thank you for everything" was unconstitutional. In some schools throughout the nation, however, prayers and Bible readings still exist despite the judicial decisions.

In recent years there has been an upsurge in religion, and the courts have had to confront new complexities in what constitutes "establishment." One such issue is the "moment of silence" that several states allow in schools as a way to avoid the ban on prayer. Even though the periods of silence have no obvious religious content, the federal courts have repeatedly struck down laws authorizing them. Nevertheless, states have persisted in allowing the practice. The Court in 1985 confronted the constitutionality of the issue in a suit brought by an Alabama parent who believed that the moment of silence restores organized religion

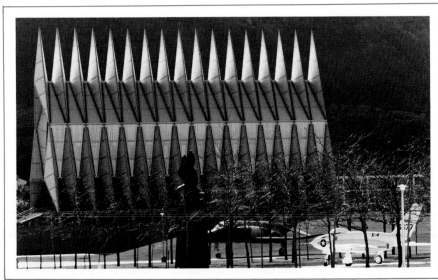

The U.S. Air Force Academy has several chapels where cadets may attend services. Despite separation of church and state, government funds support these religious facilities.

to the classroom. One interesting aspect of this case is that the Justice Department filed a friend-of-the-Court brief on behalf of the Alabama practice. The Court later ruled that the "moment of silence" was unconstitutional.

A second issue that has generated controversy concerns religious displays and observances on public property. This situation is filled with ironies. For example, although the Court has struck down classroom images of the Ten Commandments, those same Commandments are displayed in the building that houses the Court. The Supreme Court also allows Christmas festivities on its own property, yet lower federal courts have banned similar events on public property. But the Court has occasionally relaxed this strict ban on Christmas activities. In 1984 the Court upheld a Christmas display sponsored by the Pawtucket, Rhode Island, local government; the singing of carols in Sioux Falls, South Dakota, schools has also been upheld. Such actions suggest that the Court might be seeking to accommodate those desiring a stronger religious flavor in public life.

Equal Protection of the Laws

Equality before the law means that laws apply to all citizens equally unless there is a clear reason for a distinction (for example, a law setting a minimum age for holding a driver's license). This principle is made explicit in the Fourteenth Amendment, which prohibits states from enacting or enforcing measures that deny persons equal protection of the laws. The Supreme Court in the decision of *Bolling v. Sharpe* (1954) said that the guarantee of equal protection of the laws applies to the federal government as well, through the due process clause of the Fifth Amendment.

Equal Protection and Civil Rights in the Post–Civil War Period

Like many other important rights, the equal-protection-of-the-laws guarantee has generated controversy and differing interpretations. Many of those who drafted this provision of the Fourteenth Amendment immediately following the Civil War intended it to protect newly freed blacks and all

other citizens from discriminatory laws regarding property and commerce. (Some states had made it illegal for blacks to buy or sell property or to engage in certain businesses and occupations.) The Civil Rights Act of 1875, based on the Fourteenth Amendment, took a broad view of this guarantee and prohibited racial segregation in hotels, schools, theaters, jury selection, and transportation. In the *Civil Rights Cases* of 1883, however, the Supreme Court took a very narrow view of equal protection of the laws. The Court reasoned that the purpose of the Fourteenth Amendment and the Civil Rights Act of 1875 was to invalidate discriminatory state laws. If *private* individuals and companies discriminated against blacks, the national government was powerless to interfere.

Although the Court's 1883 decisions appeared to offer blacks some degree of protection—states could not pass discriminatory laws—even this progress fell by the wayside. In 1896 a case came before the Court—*Plessy v. Ferguson*—involving a Louisiana law that *required* racial segregation on railroads. The Court found that state-required segregation did *not* violate the Fourteenth Amendment's equal-protection clause. The majority said that because the Louisiana law reflected only social distinctions, not political inequality, there was no conflict between the provision and the Fourteenth Amendment's mandate of equal political treatment. So long as blacks had more-or-less equal facilities, states could require segregation.

The doctrine of "separate but equal" provided the basis of numerous **Jim Crow laws.** These laws, which were common in the South, required separate facilities for blacks and whites in schools, public transportation, restaurants, places of entertainment, and many other areas. Laws were passed making it a crime for whites and blacks to marry. The second-class status of blacks now had the full backing of the legal system.

Changing Interpretation of Equal Protection of the Laws

The emergence of the equal-protection-of-the-laws guarantee as a meaningful right was a slow process. Beginning in the 1930s, the question was

Rosa Parks, whose refusal to move to the back of the bus touched off a bus boycott in Alabama in 1955, is fingerprinted. The boycott eventually led to desegregation of the buses.

whether separate facilities were indeed equal, not whether the principle of separation was fair or unlawful. In *Missouri ex rel. Gaines v. Canada* (1938) the Court held that Missouri could not send its black residents out of state to attend law school; it had a state-supported law school for whites, it must have one for blacks as well. In *Mitchell v. United States* (1941), the Court ruled that a black member of Congress from Illinois traveling in Arkansas had a right to railroad sleeping accommodations if such facilities were available to whites. In 1950 the Court, in *Sweatt v. Painter*, closely examined the facilities of the black and white law schools established by Texas and concluded that the inferiority of the black school made the whole arrangement unconstitutional.

The case of *Brown v. Board of Education of Topeka* (1954) directly attacked the principle of "separate but equal." A Kansas law required school segregation, and a child was denied admission to her neighborhood school because it was for whites only. In a 9–0 precedent-shattering ruling, the Court held that racial separation generated feelings of inferiority and was thus inherently unequal. The *Brown* decision destroyed the legal foundation of the Jim Crow laws and of many other less obvious attempts to enforce a second-class status for blacks.

Other Applications of the Equal-Protection Principle

The equal-protection-of-the-laws provision, however, has broader implications beyond civil rights. In 1962, for example, in the historic *Baker v. Carr* decision, the Supreme Court ruled that state laws allowing legislative districts of unequal population could be challenged as a denial of the Fourteenth Amendment's equal-protection clause. The "one-person, one-vote" decision (and later elaborations) has produced major political changes. No longer can voting districts containing a small portion of the population of a state elect a majority of the legislature. Nor may state legislative houses be based on factors other than population. All state and local legislatures must be based on the "one-person, one-vote" rule. At the federal level the equal-protection clause has been interpreted to mean that congressional districts must be of approximately equal population and that state election laws may not give unequal weight to votes in Senate primaries.

The Fourteenth Amendment's equal-protection guarantee has been employed in the battle for women's rights. In a series of decisions, the Court has struck down laws discriminating against women in such matters as the administration of the estates of deceased children, selection for jury duty, Social Security benefits, pension fund contributions, and unemployment benefits. While the courts have allowed some distinctions to be kept—for example, separate men's and women's state-supported schools—they have generally applied the Fourteenth Amendment to outlaw discrimination against women. A lower federal court, for instance, has used the amendment to outlaw bars that serve only men. Men, too, have received several benefits from recent interpretations of the Fourteenth Amendment. In *Craig v. Boren* (1976), for example, the Court said that a state may not have a higher drinking age for men than for women. Men have also won rights in child custody and alimony matters.

Limits on the Equal-Protection Principle

The right of equal protection of the laws, like all other rights, is not unlimited. The principle does *not* guarantee that all citizens will always receive equal treatment. One important limitation on the guarantee of equal protection is that many private actions are not covered. A number of measures, of course, forbid discrimination in public transactions: the Civil Rights Act of 1866 prohibits racial discrimination in real estate dealings; the Civil Rights Act of 1964 bans discrimination based on race, color, religion, sex, or national origin in employment and discrimination based on race, color, religion, or national origin in public accommodations, such as hotels, movie theaters, and restaurants. Discrimination in any program receiving federal funds—schools, hospitals, businesses, and so on—is also outlawed. Nevertheless, such legislation does not cover certain types of behavior on the part of individuals. A federal or

state law forbidding women to become doctors would undoubtedly be declared unconstitutional. It would also be illegal for a state-funded medical school to discriminate against women applicants. However, if citizens refused to visit women doctors, such actions would be purely private and thus beyond the scope of the equal-protection principle. Of course, the line between private and government involvement can be difficult to distinguish. For example, in 1964 the Supreme Court ruled that a private amusement park practicing racial discrimination violated the Fourteenth Amendment because the segregation was enforced by an off-duty sheriff who wore his badge.

Even if discrimination results directly from federal or state laws, there is still no guarantee that strict equality will be enforced. Laws treating the rich differently from the poor, blacks differently from whites, women differently from men, and so on, *can* be consistent with the equal-protection principle. Over the years the Supreme Court has elaborated two doctrines that have allowed laws to make distinctions among groups of citizens— "reasonableness" and "suspect classification."

Reasonableness. Under the reasonableness standard, the key question is whether a legislature had a reasonable purpose in passing a law. This standard frequently has involved an attempt to protect women and children from alleged evils. For example, in 1948 the Court upheld a Michigan law prohibiting women from being bartenders unless they were wives or daughters of proprietors *(Goesaert v. Cleary)*. The Court argued that because women bartenders can create "moral and social problems" and because states have the right to prevent such problems, discriminatory legislation is permissible. By a 5–4 vote in *Michael M. v. Superior Court of Sonoma County, Calif.* (1981), the Court accepted a California practice of prosecuting unmarried men, but not women, under eighteen for having sexual relations. Writing for the majority, Justice William Rehnquist argued that prosecuting only men is fair because men are not deterred by the fear of pregnancy. "A criminal sanction imposed solely on males thus serves to roughly 'equalize' the deterrent on the sexes," said

Rehnquist. Needless to say, the difference between what is reasonable and what is unfair discrimination is not always clear. In general, the principle gives legislatures considerable leeway, because most laws have some degree of "reasonable" purpose.

Suspect Classification. The second, and currently popular, doctrine is that of **suspect classification.** The Court has ruled that if race or nationality is explicitly taken into account in the law, a compelling state interest must be established by rigid study of the legislation. Unless state interest can be proved, the courts would assume that equal protection is being denied. Examination of the law involves two questions: (1) Does the state have a compelling interest in the law? and (2) Is the suspect classification necessary to accomplish its purpose? This approach was illustrated in the case of *Loving v. Virginia* (1967), which involved a Virginia law prohibiting marriages between people of different races. The Court ruled that Virginia had no compelling interest in passing such a law and that "the freedom to marry has long been recognized as one of the vital personal rights essential to the orderly pursuit of happiness of free men." Although states may regulate marriages, the standard of race in this regulation was not essential. The Virginia law therefore was declared unconstitutional.

The Rights of Suspected Criminals

The rights of suspected criminals have been an important political issue since the adoption of the Constitution. Criminal law is complex and controversial, and interpretations are always changing, but the following discussion outlines some of the major rights enjoyed by suspects. Let us begin with the initial police contact and then examine the subsequent procedures.

Freedom from Unreasonable Searches

A basic right of U.S. citizens is protection against overenthusiastic police who will stop at nothing to get evidence of criminal behavior. The fear of surprise, of midnight raids in pursuit of wrongdoing,

led to the Fourth Amendment, which bans "unreasonable searches and seizures" and requires that search warrants be specific and be based on "probable cause." What, however, is "unreasonable"? How specific must a search warrant be? Are all police limited by the Fourth Amendment?

The easiest of these questions is the last one, which concerns the scope of the Fourth Amendment. Originally, the prohibition against unreasonable searches and seizures applied solely to federal actions; the states were bound only by the broader requirement of due process stated in the Fourth Amendment. In 1949, however, the Supreme Court ruled, in *Wolf v. Colorado*, that the provisions of the Fourth Amendment were applicable to state courts (under the doctrine of *incorporation* discussed earlier in the chapter).

In general, contemporary Court interpretation holds that citizens and their possessions, such as houses or automobiles, may be searched if (1) the individual being searched consents, or (2) the search is part of a lawful arrest, or (3) there is a warrant for the search. In practice, of course, things can get complicated, and numerous rules exist to handle different situations. For example, police with a warrant are normally required to announce themselves before conducting a search. If an announcement could jeopardize the case (for instance, illegal drugs can be flushed down the toilet), **"no-knock" entry** may be permitted. The courts have also upheld **"stop-and-frisk" laws,** which allow the police to search people legally if there is a reasonable suspicion of wrongdoing, even if no arrest occurs. The advent of electronic surveillance has complicated the meaning of properly authorized searches. Originally such techniques were not covered by the Fourth Amendment. Gradually, however, the courts have held that wiretapping and the like must be justified in advance and be strictly limited.

The legality of a search is a crucial question because the courts have ruled that illegally obtained evidence usually may not be used at the trial (such evidence, however, may be used in grand jury proceedings). The **exclusionary rule** was first applied by the Supreme Court to federal cases in 1914 *(Weeks v. United States)*. (This rule is discussed also in Chapter 12.) In the landmark case of *Mapp v. Ohio* (1961), the Supreme Court said that the exclusionary rule applied equally to federal and state courts (but not in civil cases). Since then, many cases have been dismissed when the defendant successfully argued that the evidence had been obtained without a proper search warrant or without his or her permission. (However, a 1985 Court decision held that evidence could be used even if the warrant was not properly drafted by a judge.)

Rights Prior to Trial

A second set of rights possessed by a suspect applies to the period after arrest but before trial. One important provision is the right to be promptly informed of the charges against you. The police cannot legally lock you up for a few weeks while they decide what crime you committed. Federal statutes require a charge to be made "without unnecessary delay," but state regulations vary from "promptly" to as long as seventy-two hours in Georgia under some circumstances. If, as sometimes happens, you are not charged promptly with a crime, you may file a writ of habeas corpus, which requires a judge to hold a hearing to inform you of the charge (or otherwise change the conditions of your confinement.)

The Supreme Court has taken vigorous action to protect suspects during the pretrial period, especially during police interrogation. The best known of these are the so-called **Miranda rules** (from the *Miranda v. Arizona* [1966] decision). In the *Miranda* case, the Court said that suspects must be told that they have a right to remain silent, that anything they say may be held against them, and that they have the right to an attorney before and during police interrogation. If the suspect cannot afford a lawyer, one will be appointed. The *Miranda* rule also covers interrogation during and after a trial. In 1972 the right to an attorney was extended to misdemeanors or petty offenses for which imprisonment was possible. The Court has held, however, that a lawyer need not be present at every stage of the process—for example, during a line-up or in grand jury testimony. In general, confessions obtained through the use of physical or psychological force have been thrown out of court.

Finally, in all federal cases, but in only about half the states, a person must be *indicted* by a **grand jury** before he or she may be tried. Grand juries usually have between twelve and twenty-three people who are charged with determining whether there is enough evidence of a crime to warrant a full trial. Grand juries are supposed to

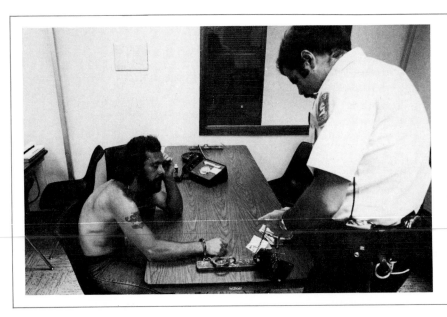

A police officer reads the Miranda *rules to an arrested person. The rules inform suspects of their rights, including the right to remain silent and to have an attorney.*

prevent time-consuming trials based on flimsy evidence or trials that could be used to embarrass defendants. If a reasonable amount of evidence exists, the grand jury votes to indict, or issues a "true bill."

The Right to Bail

Between arraignment (the procedure by which a defendant pleads guilty or not guilty) and trial, most suspects have the opportunity to post *bail*. The defendant gives the court a certain amount of money, determined by the judge within certain guidelines, which will be forfeited if the defendant does not show up for trial. Because bail can be high—for example, $20,000 or more—most defendants make use of a bail bondsman, who puts up the money in exchange for a fee (usually 10 percent). The Eighth Amendment guarantees only that bail must not be "excessive," but a defendant has no constitutional right to bail (without bail, the defendant would go to prison before the trial). Federal courts and some states will deny bail in **capital cases**—crimes punishable by death—or when the defendant has previously fled to avoid prosecution. Because "excessive" is a difficult word to define, the bail system has occasionally been used to imprison people without a trial. A group of civil rights workers in Americus, Georgia, were once charged with "attempted insurrection," which was a capital offense and thus not subject to bail.

Rights During the Trial

In the trial itself, the defendant has several other important rights. The Fifth Amendment provides that persons shall not be forced to give testimony against themselves (self-incrimination). This protection has always applied to federal cases, and in 1964, in *Malloy v. Hogan*, the principle was extended to state courts. Essentially, the prosecution must be able to prove its case without the cooperation of the suspect. There is, however, a way to pressure defendants into testifying. Prosecutors can require that defendants be granted *immunity from prosecution*—that is, charges against the defendants will be dropped or reduced if they cooperate. Failure to testify after a proper grant of

immunity can result in a defendant being held in **contempt of court**—an act to obstruct court proceedings that is punishable by a fine or jail term. (Immunity is often used to get small-time criminals to testify against bigger criminals.)

Another key guarantee during a trial is the right to a lawyer. The Sixth Amendment provides that a defendant in a criminal trial shall enjoy "the Assistance of Counsel for his defence." Nevertheless, this right was implemented only gradually. Until 1938, it applied only to federal cases involving capital crimes. In 1938, the right to an attorney, even if the defendant could not afford one, was extended to all federal, but not state, trials. Gradually, however, the Supreme Court said that under various special circumstances state courts must provide a defense lawyer. Ultimately, in *Gideon v. Wainwright* (1963), the Supreme Court ruled that representation by counsel was constitutionally required in all criminal cases.

A third important trial right is to have a jury trial. Although the provision is guaranteed in the Constitution (Article III, Section 2, paragraph 3) and by the Sixth Amendment, it has not been viewed as an absolute requirement, and a defendant may waive, or set aside, his or her right to a trial by jury. The courts have also ruled that jury trials are not constitutionally required for minor offenses. For many years the right to a jury trial applied only to federal cases, but in 1968 the Supreme Court extended the guarantee to state criminal trials.

If tried before a jury, a defendant usually has the protection of the **unanimity rule**—each juror has to vote conviction for the prosecution to convict. Because there are usually twelve jurors, this is an important safeguard to ensure that the evidence for conviction is beyond a reasonable doubt. In recent years, however, the Supreme Court has upheld guilty convictions by less-than-unanimous votes (for example, 9–3 and 10–2) for state, but not federal, cases. In *Burch v. Louisiana* (1979), the Supreme Court said that it was constitutional for a state to use a six-person jury but that a conviction verdict had to be unanimous.

The Sixth Amendment provides several other important protections during the trial. The proceedings must be "speedy and public"; thus prosecutors cannot drag a trial on for years if they have no real case, nor can the trial be conducted in secret. At the federal level and in many states there are laws specifying deadlines for trials. The defendant also may confront and cross-examine witnesses. The prosecutor cannot normally introduce written testimony from witnesses or prevent the defendant from challenging the person directly. Defendants also may have the court compel favorable witnesses to testify on their behalf (in both federal and state courts).

Rights After the Trial

The most important post-trial right is the Fifth Amendment ban on **double jeopardy.** That is, the government may not try a person twice for the same crime (thus, the government may not appeal an acquittal). Prior to 1969, the ban on double jeopardy applied only in federal cases, but in *Benton v. Maryland* (1969), by a 6–2 vote, the Supreme Court applied this ban to the states. There are some exceptions, however. A convicted person may waive this right and demand a new trial. If the jury cannot reach a decision, there may be a second trial. Or if a conviction is overturned on appeal, the government may request a new trial on the original offense. Occasionally, one crime can result in separate state and federal trials. In some state courts (but not in federal court, generally) a defendant who has committed several crimes can be tried separately for each offense, even if all the crimes were the result of one incident. (However, in the case of *Ashe v. Swenson* [1970], the Supreme Court outlawed separate trials based on the same evidence.)

Another important protection is the Eighth Amendment's ban on "cruel and unusual punishments." For example, punishments that were overly severe for the crimes committed have been struck down. A California law sentencing individuals to ninety days in jail merely because they are drug addicts illustrates the type of judicial "overkill" forbidden by the Eighth Amendment. Death by torture or slow dismemberment would also be voided as unconstitutional.

The major recent use of the Eighth Amend-

The death penalty—symbolized by the electric chair—has generated intense controversy. Recent rulings by the Supreme Court have widened the use of capital punishment.

ment concerns the death penalty. Is electrocution, hanging, or gassing inherently "cruel and unusual"? In 1972, in *Furman v. Georgia,* the Supreme Court struck down the Georgia death penalty as cruel and unusual. However, of the five-justice majority, three said that the cruel and unusual aspect was not the death penalty itself but rather the *unevenness* of its application. The two remaining justices believed that capital punishment is, by its very nature, barbaric and uncivilized. Following the *Furman* decision, numerous states reinstituted the death penalty with new, tighter procedures granting less judicial leeway. In 1976 the Supreme Court, in *Gregg v. Georgia,* by a 7–2 margin, again said that the death penalty was *not* inherently cruel and unusual. The Court, however, has limited the use of the death penalty. In *Emmund v. Florida* (1982), the Court held that those convicted of murder may not be sentenced to death unless they themselves killed someone. In other words, the death penalty could not be given to an accomplice in a murder.

The Emergence of New Rights

The rights we have described might be characterized as the major traditional safeguards that Americans enjoy. It is important to realize, however, that as conditions change, new types of rights become part of the public agenda.

One emerging area concerns the right of privacy. Although our concept of limited government incorporates the idea that some personal behavior is "off limits" to government, the privacy issue remained in the background until the 1960s. The matter was brought to public attention by state laws regulating contraceptives. In *Griswold v. Connecticut* (1965), the Court overturned a Connecticut law banning the sale or use of birth control devices, on the grounds that it interfered with "a right of privacy older than the Bill of Rights." Even though the Constitution does not mention privacy, various justices have found that the First, Third, Fourth, Fifth, and Ninth Amendments all contain some implied protection of this right.

In recent years, the privacy right has surfaced in the collection and storage of information in electronic data banks. Congress has passed several laws to protect the rights of citizens, but many complex issues remain to be resolved. One conflict involves the right of citizens to keep their financial affairs private versus the government's need to combat criminal activity. In *California Bankers Association v. Shultz* (1974), the Court ruled on the side of the government. The case involved a federal law—the Bank Secrecy Act of 1970—that required financial institutions to keep certain records on depositors and report certain large transactions to the government. The Court said that the law was necessary in the government's war on crime and did not violate constitutional safeguards against unreasonable searches and self-incrimination. A related issue concerns citizens' access to information about themselves. In 1974 Congress passed the Family Education and Privacy Act, which gives parents access to their children's school records. The Privacy Act of 1974 allows citizens to examine information about themselves in federal files and to correct any wrong information; it also provides limits on the use the government may make of the data.

Other guarantees that have achieved prominence recently are the so-called body rights—the right to abortion, the right to die. A woman's right to an abortion without restriction during the first three months of pregnancy was affirmed in *Roe v. Wade* (1973) and *Doe v. Bolton* (1973). The Court has protected this safeguard further by striking down laws that required a husband's consent to an abortion and that gave parents sole power over a minor's abortion. At the same time, however, both the Court and Congress have rejected the argument that the right to an abortion implies a government obligation to pay for the procedure if the woman cannot afford it (*Harris v. McRae* [1980] and others).

The emergence of the privacy issue in the 1960s and the "body rights" issue in the 1970s shows that rights are not dictums etched in stone for all eternity. The meaning of a right and the rights that we possess both change over time.

Check Your Understanding

1. What types of speech are not protected by the First Amendment?

2. In what situations is prior restraint permitted against newspapers and magazines?

3. What two provisions concerning freedom of religion does the First Amendment contain?

4. What does "equal protection of the laws" mean and how has it changed since the Civil War?

5. What are some important rights of suspected criminals?

6. What are some new types of rights that have emerged in recent years?

WHAT SUSTAINS OUR RIGHTS?

American citizens possess a long list of important rights. It is one thing to have a right in the abstract but quite another to enjoy the right in practice. Many dictators have claimed that their people are completely "free" because a written constitution protects everyone's fundamental rights. In analyzing the rights of citizens, we thus face a crucial question: What ensures that our rights are real instead of meaningless "paper rights"? What prevents, say, the guarantee of free speech from being transformed into the right to express only approved ideas at the approved time and place?

Citizens as Guardians of Rights

One possible answer is the people themselves. It has been argued that all rights are meaningless unless ordinary citizens are willing to defend them. If the government decides that people with radical beliefs ought to be prevented from organizing a political group, the surest check on such abuse is for citizens to vote out of office those who enacted such unconstitutional laws. If the local police prevent controversial speakers from expressing their opinions, according to this view, citizen outrage at such violation of the First Amendment is much more powerful than a lengthy and costly court battle. Advocates of this position believe that the lack of popular support for fundamental rights was responsible for several countries (for example, Germany in the 1930s) becoming dictatorships despite strong written protections of rights.

This argument undoubtedly has some truth. It is difficult to imagine the survival of the free exercise of religion if most citizens deeply believed that there is only one true faith and that everyone should accept it. Nevertheless, to claim that the people themselves are the primary protectors of their basic rights is probably an exaggeration. In the last two or three decades, a number of public opinion polls have asked citizens about their support for the rights of controversial groups. The overall results do not show overwhelming support. Table 13.1 shows that only 64 percent of the pop-

ulation would allow someone opposed to religion to speak in their community, and only 46 percent would allow such a person to teach in college. A significant minority would keep books written by Communists and homosexuals out of public libraries. In general, studies of attitudes toward the rights of unpopular groups suggest that people's feelings toward a group greatly influence their willingness to extend basic, constitutionally protected rights to that group. In other words, you might believe in the right of free speech, but if you oppose communism, there is a good chance that you would oppose letting a Communist speak freely.

Political Activists as Guardians of Rights

A second explanation for the survival of our rights emphasizes the role of well-educated, politically active individuals. This argument goes as follows. Well-educated, politically active citizens are much more likely to uphold the right of free speech, the right of free association, and other important safeguards. These citizens occupy important leadership positions both in and out of government. Besides public officials, this category includes newspaper editors, civic leaders, and supporters of organizations, such as the American Civil Liberties Union, that pay special attention to the possible violations of rights. Because of their relatively important positions in society, their pro-rights views have greater weight in policy making. These individuals act as guardians who can alert the public to government abuses as well as check the occasional abuses of less enlightened citizens. Whereas the first argument emphasizes the role of the average citizen in maintaining our rights, this view says that it is the elite (that is, well-educated, powerful citizens) who protect our guarantees.

This second argument has had considerable popularity. Its principal advantage is that it reconciles the apparent contradiction between the existence of many rights and only lukewarm (or negative) public support for such rights. Nevertheless, though this view might be correct, it has not been completely verified. There is little doubt that well-educated, politically involved citizens are more likely to support important rights, but the transla-

Public Support for Rights of Controversial Groups, 1982 Group	*Percent that would allow speech in community by member of the group*	*Percent that would allow member of the group to teach in college*	*Percent that would allow book in library by member of the group*
People opposed to churches and religion	64%	46%	61%
People who believed that blacks were genetically inferior to whites	59	43	60
An admitted Communist	55	43	57
An admitted homosexual	65	55	56

Source: National Opinion Research Center, University of Chicago. The respondents represented a cross section of the U.S. population.

TABLE 13.1

tion of verbal endorsement into concrete action is not always clear. Recall that for decades black Americans were systematically denied equal protection of the laws, but there was little complaint from many public officials, civic leaders, newspaper editors, and other so-called guardians of our rights. Only when blacks themselves forced the issue did the elite show much concern. Critics of this position maintain that such indifference is typical. To be sure, these "guardians" do play an important role in protecting our rights, but to claim that they guard against each and every abuse is an exaggeration.

The Argument That Our Rights Are Not Well Protected

A third, and quite different, response to the question of what sustains our rights is that our rights are *not* well sustained. Put bluntly, for most citizens and during most periods, many of our rights *are* "paper rights." After all, merely because the Supreme Court declares that a specific government abridgment of a right is unconstitutional does not necessarily mean that one now may exercise that right freely. This argument does not claim that we live in an oppressive dictatorship with no rights whatsoever, but rather that there is a significant gap between our actual rights and our "abstract" rights. This assertion can be supported on two grounds.

Lack of Protection from Private Abuses

First, many of the rights widely accepted as "fundamental" concern citizens' protection *against* government action. The Bill of Rights (the first ten amendments) prevents government abridgment of free speech, requires that government provide a speedy trial, and prohibits government violations of due process. Other laws ban discrimination in

THE POLLS.

"MOVE ON!"

HAS THE NATIVE AMERICAN NO RIGHTS THAT THE NATURALIZED AMERICAN IS BOUND TO RESPECT?—[See Page 868.]

An 1871 print advocating suffrage for American Indians suggests that concern for the rights of native peoples is not a new issue.

real estate transactions, employment, and public accommodations. Nevertheless, despite these guarantees, there are few protections against numerous private violations of rights. Such violations can be as oppressive as government actions. For example, the Supreme Court may protect a newspaper from government censorship. However, for most newspapers, a threat from a major advertiser that the advertising will go elsewhere if certain stories are printed is far more relevant. Americans might have a theoretical right to advocate communism, but the penalty for doing so could be high— loss of job and friends, for instance.

The deprivation of basic rights through the actions of private individuals or corporations poses a difficult problem. On the one hand, it may be tempting to extend many of our rights to such private matters. For example, we could make it a crime for advertisers to censor newspapers by threatening to remove their ads. A law could be enacted to protect those with unpopular views from social harassment. In fact, the courts did take steps in this direction when they prevented public employees from being fired for making public, non–job-related statements. In *Pickering v. Board*

of Education (1968), the Court held that the right of free speech meant that a teacher could not be fired for writing a letter to the local newspaper criticizing the school board. Even the private conversations of public employees now seem protected by the First Amendment. In *Givhan v. Western Line Consolidated School District* (1979), the Court ruled that schoolteachers and other public employees could not be fired for criticizing school policy in their private conversations. In other words, both public and private speech is constitutionally protected, the Court said.

It is not obvious, however, that the steps taken in the *Pickering* and *Givhan* decisions are truly in the direction of a freer and more open society. To enforce numerous rights in strictly private relationships would raise enormous problems. More important, involving government in day-to-day private actions could provide the basis of a *totalitarian state*—a government committed in principle to controlling every aspect of citizens' lives. Imagine a society in which, for example, government would establish comprehensive "proper relationships" between parents and children, worker and boss, teacher and student, and so on. This might be far more oppressive than the occasional abuse that occurs in society today.

Ability of Modern Governments to Violate Our Rights

The second argument supporting the view that our rights are not well protected claims that even when strong legal protections exist, government can get away with extensive violations, in part because of technological innovations. When the Bill of Rights was written, government action against free speech was comparatively open. If you made a public speech that the state objected to, you could be locked up or fined. Private behavior was generally beyond the reach of government. Today, however, sophisticated electronic surveillance techniques, computers capable of maintaining millions of records, and extensive intelligence networks have given governments extraordinary capacity to invade our privacy. The willingness of public officials to violate rights has been reinforced by the threat of Communist subversion and other threats against law and order by militant political groups.

The precise extent of government abuse of our rights is impossible to measure. We do know, however, that on numerous occasions the government has overstepped the fine line between a legitimate concern for preventing subversion and interfering with fundamental rights. For example, for years the FBI has kept political intelligence files on thousands of citizens without authority from Congress or the President—in addition to the legal security index set up in the 1950s to identify citizens who could be politically dangerous during a national emergency. Some 26,000 people were at one time listed on this index (much of this information is still kept, despite the repeal of the original law in 1971). Moreover, since 1939 the FBI has compiled more than 500,000 dossiers on citizens with "dangerous" ideas. During a fifteen-year period, the FBI admitted carrying out 2,370 "dirty tricks" against U.S. citizens and foreigners living in the United States. Of course, a number of these actions were legitimate attempts to protect national security, but in many other instances there was little evidence of a threat.

Another government agency that has gone after those with unpopular political beliefs is the Internal Revenue Service (IRS). Unlike other government agencies, it can *legally* investigate any citizen without a warrant and without solid evidence that a crime has been committed. It also has the power to obtain records on its own authority. The IRS' ability to intimidate people is considerable. Intensive analysis of tax returns can result in heavy financial penalties, criminal charges, and a significant expenditure of time, money, and effort in defending oneself. Organizations can lose their tax-exempt status, which means that donations to them no longer are tax-deductible (which, in turn, will reduce donations). Like the FBI and the Central Intelligence Agency (CIA), the IRS maintains a large investigative staff, and these three agencies frequently share information.

The basic purpose of IRS investigations is to uncover tax cheating, and targets of investigation are supposed to be chosen according to the amount of money that can be recovered. Nevertheless, the IRS occasionally has used this power for other purposes. For example, the notorious gangster Al Capone went to jail in 1931 for tax evasion, not for murder or bootlegging. During the 1960s, seventy-two civil rights leaders had their tax returns audited, or examined, to embarrass and distract them. The most ambitious IRS effort was the creation of the Special Service Staff (SSS), specifically designed to investigate political groups. Between 1969 and 1973, the SSS maintained financial and political files on 8,585 individuals and 2,873 organizations (well-known people in the SSS files included New York mayor John Lindsay and Nobel Prize-winner Linus Pauling; organizations ranged from the Ku Klux Klan to the National Student Association).

The Watergate scandal revealed that government sponsorship of illegal break-ins, wiretaps, and "enemies lists" had become increasingly common. Even some respected and hardly radical journalists had their telephones bugged. Even though such actions might be defended as isolated exceptions or reasonable mistakes, they probably inhibit many citizens from fully utilizing their rights. After all, why take a chance by joining an unpopular group or getting involved in a demonstration when such action *might* get one on a list of subversives?

A Perspective

In response to our original question of what sustains our rights, it is clear that simply possessing written guarantees of liberties is not enough. The people themselves must be willing, when necessary, to speak out against abuses, while public officials, including legislators and judges, also have a responsibility to protect citizens from unbridled government. The role of the mass media in exposing and investigating abuses is important. On the other hand, there are tremendous pressures to restrict rights: fear of Communist subversion, a desire to reduce crime, and more. Finally, possession of political safeguards is not eternal; because of government abuse or public indifference, some liberties will exist only in the abstract.

Check Your Understanding

1. What evidence exists that would contradict the view that political activists are the guardians of our rights?

2. What problems are likely to result from laws against *private* violations of rights?

3. What factors make modern governments especially capable of violating the rights of citizens?

4. How has the federal government used its power to harass those with unpopular or controversial ideas?

THE POLITICS OF RIGHTS

It is tempting to analyze rights purely from a philosophical or legal perspective. We could discuss the distinctions among different types of rights, the origins of rights, and whether some rights are more basic than others. Many descriptions of the liberties enjoyed by citizens do, in fact, take this approach. We argue, instead, that rights are basically no different from other benefits (money, status) obtained through the political process. To treat rights as one might treat abstract philosophical doctrine is to misunderstand the meaning of "right."

To appreciate the political nature of a right, consider the evolution of rights in the area of education. In the eighteenth century, when thinkers debated the issue of inalienable rights, human rights, and the like, the right to an education at public expense was not mentioned. Education was a privilege available only to the wealthy. If you had insisted that twelve years of publicly supported education was a right no different from the right to private property, you would have been considered quite strange. The Declaration of Independence, the Constitution, the Bill of Rights, and other early statements of our liberties make no mention of education.

In the twentieth century, public education has emerged as a right, as opposed to a privilege, of U.S. citizens. Legal scholars did not suddenly discover that education was an accidentally overlooked guarantee. Rather, various interests successfully asserted claims to government-supported education. A privilege for a few wealthy citizens gradually became available to a larger number and eventually became a right for all citizens. Nor has this process ended with universal, publicly supported education. Some people today claim that the right to public schooling should include the right to a college education, to a high-quality education, and to career training, as well as to a wide variety of opportunities within the educational process (for example, open hearings in disciplinary actions). Some of these demands might become basic rights; others might disappear without a trace.

The moral of the transformation of education from a privilege to a right is clear: liberties are achieved through the political process. The basis for a right need not be self-evident: it can be implicit in the Constitution, a corollary of an existing right, or a natural, obvious right of each human being. Once the guarantee is widely recognized, it can be defended on the grounds that anything undermining it would also undermine the foundations of our political system. Through this process women have won the right to abortion, workers the right to join unions, and many students the right to publicly funded college educations.

CHAPTER SUMMARY

What are rights? A right is a legal or moral claim to a benefit. Unlike a privilege, a right may be abridged only under unusual circumstances. Considerable controversy exists over what our fundamental rights are, the relative importance of different rights, the role of government in enforcing rights, and who decides who has which rights.

What political rights do citizens have? Among the most important constitutional guarantees are freedom of speech, freedom of the press, freedom of association, religious freedom, the right to equal protection of the laws, and safeguards in the administration of criminal justice. Few people, however, believe that these liberties are without limitations. Enormous differences of opinion exist on how they are to be interpreted. In addition, new types of rights, such as the right to privacy, can emerge.

What sustains our rights? Although agreement exists that rights on paper are insufficient by themselves, experts disagree on what makes our rights "real." The support of basic liberties by ordinary citizens, or more specifically, by better-educated, influential citizens, are two possible explanations. It has also been argued that a significant gap exists between our "paper rights" and the rights we actually enjoy.

IMPORTANT TERMS

Explain the following terms.

civil liberties
civil rights
fundamental right
affirmative action
reverse discrimination

THINKING CRITICALLY

1. When the thirteen colonies declared their independence from Britain, in 1776, they claimed that the natural rights of individuals were being violated. What might happen today if you refused to obey the government on the grounds that it was violating "certain unalienable Rights"?

2. Should people from other nations living in the United States who are not U.S. citizens be protected by all the rights that U.S. citizens have? Why or why not?

3. Some people have suggested an "Economic Bill of Rights" for all Americans—for example, the right to a decent job, protection against unfair dismissal from a job, and so on. Do you agree with this proposal? Discuss your answer.

4. The separation of church and state is an important principle of the U.S. Constitution. Should there be any limits in regard to how this principle is applied to the laws of our country? Explain your answer.

5. The electronic media have become an important means by which views are expressed. Should TV and radio stations be required to provide equal air time for all conflicting opinions? Why or why not? Should there be any limitations on the type of opinions expressed on radio or TV? Explain your answer.

6. Some critics have claimed that criminals have more rights than their victims. Should the government guarantee certain rights for victims of crimes? Why or why not? If you think there should be such a provision, what guarantees should it contain?

7. There is much disagreement over just what rights Americans have. Would it be helpful to create a government commission to study the issue and list all the rights we have? Discuss your answer.

EXTENDING YOUR UNDERSTANDING

1. Research the arguments on both sides of the issue of affirmative action (look at newspaper or magazine articles on the topic). Write a report in which you present the pros and cons of affirmative action. State your views on the subject, supported by convincing evidence.

2. What would happen if the people themselves interpreted rights? To see some of the possibilities, ask ten students in other classes (a) to define "free speech" and (b) to decide whether free speech applies to high school publications. Tabulate your findings.

3. Contact the editor of your local newspaper. Ask him or her about the limits faced in reporting the news. Are there pressures from important advertisers or from local politicians who want to make the community "look good"? Do such limits infringe upon the principle of freedom of the press? Present your findings to the class.

4. Contact the department of your local government that is in charge of managing public property. Ask what the department's policy is in regard to the use of public land for religious displays (Nativity scenes at Christmas, for example). How has the policy been affected by recent court cases? Has there been public pressure for or against the use of public property for such displays? Prepare an argument either for or against the use of public property in this way.

5. Contact an organization that works for the rights of a particular group—for instance, women, senior citizens, or the handicapped. Find out what problems the organization faces in working toward its goals. Does it meet resistance from citizens or from the government? How does it handle the problems it faces? Write your findings in a report.

MAKING DECISIONS

A controversy has erupted in your community over the issue of requiring all businesses to remain closed on Sundays. Petitions from both sides in the controversy have been submitted to the local government. As a member of the local governing board, you must evaluate these petitions and recommend what policy should be established. What rights are involved in this controversy? What will your decision be? Prepare a statement outlining the reasons for your decision.

Chapter 14
Public Policy: A Framework for Analysis

Our analysis thus far has stressed the institutions of government. We have, for example, examined presidential power, the organization of the federal bureaucracy, and the way the Supreme Court makes its decisions. The focus of our analysis will now shift to the outcome of these activities, powers, and responsibilities. What does government accomplish when legislators enact laws, Presidents bargain, and bureaucrats and judges interpret laws? Are their actions effective and fair? The study of the results of government activity—sometimes technically called *outputs*—generally is called the study of public policy. In chapters 15 and 16 we shall examine two policy areas—economic policy and foreign policy. In this chapter we provide an analytical framework—that is, a set of categories and questions to help organize the bewildering collection of facts, assumptions, claims, and counterclaims associated with public policy in general. We might not be able to tell you, for instance, which tax policy government *should* pursue, but we can offer assistance in analyzing why a given policy might be chosen and in evaluating its impact and usefulness. Our discussion of public policy is divided into three questions:

- What is public policy?
- How is public policy made?
- How do we evaluate public policy?

PREVIEW

What is public policy? Public policy is the collective response of government to the problems within a society, but this definition does not capture the complexity of public policy. There are different ways to view government response. One interpretation focuses on the government's general commitments and goals—for example, a desire to eliminate unemployment. Or public policy can be defined in terms of what the government actually does—its programs, expenditures, and so on. A third meaning stresses the impact of a policy. A related issue concerns the separation of private from public policy—that is, some public decisions may actually be made by private individuals.

How is public policy made? No two policies are created in the same way, but all share common traits. Before a problem can be addressed by public policy, it must first be on the government's agenda; not all problems necessarily require a government response. The government must also formulate the precise nature of the policy, because most problems can be characterized in several ways. Finally, a policy must be implemented, because its actual significance depends on just how it is carried out. There are many explanations of how policy is made. The rational choice approach emphasizes the selection of policies that provide the greatest benefit-to-cost ratio for the largest number of people. Incrementalism sees policy as a series of step-by-step adjustments of existing programs. According to group theory, policy results from the interplay of competing groups. The elite theory holds that elites, usually economic elites impose policy on society.

How do we evaluate public policy? Although policy must be evaluated, there is no one set of evaluative standards. Process evaluation compares the administration of the policy with guidelines specifying how the policy should be enacted. An alternative is impact evaluation to determine whether the policy has had the desired impact. In cost-benefit analysis, a policy is deemed worthwhile if the benefits outweigh the costs. The analysis can be made either by examining one policy at a time or by considering the total mix of policies. According to the political value approach, a policy is good if it satisfies a social or economic goal, such as equality. Different people employ different standards, which often yield conflicting conclusions.

WHAT IS PUBLIC POLICY?

Defining public policy is both simple and complex. Most people who use the term "public policy" generally are referring to the response of government to society's problems. When Congress requires automobile manufacturers to meet certain mileage standards, it is responding to the need to conserve energy. When a state trooper stops a motorist for exceeding the speed limit on an interstate highway, the trooper is enforcing a public policy. A citizen might choose to waste gasoline and to drive too fast, but such private actions are not public policy. The notion that government seeks solutions in response to problems is the simple definition of "public policy." The more difficult task is to determine just what is being done, and by whom, in the name of public policy.

Different Aspects of Public Policy

If you were to ask what the public policy was in an area such as education or agriculture, an answer might deal with three different aspects of policy. One aspect concerns the government's stated commitment and goals, as expressed in speeches by public officials, legislative proclamations, endorsements of advisory committee reports, pronouncements in judicial decisions, and statements in laws. Consider, for example, how the public policy on employment was phrased in an act of Congress passed in 1946: "All Americans able to work and seeking to work have the right to useful, remunerative, regular and full-time employment, and it is the policy of the United States to assure the existence at all times of sufficient employment opportunities to enable all Americans to freely exercise this right."

Can it therefore be said that full employment is public policy in the United States? Not quite. A more accurate characterization would be that the government's policy is to make an effort to achieve full employment. The effort might involve creating government jobs and providing tax incentives to corporations to hire the unemployed, but the government will not actually offer a job to anyone who lacks work. The effort to reach a goal, not the goal itself, is what constitutes public policy. A gap between a government's abstract commitment and its actual behavior is common. For years the public policy of the national government has been to eliminate racially segregated schools, yet extensive segregation remains. Discrepancies occur as well in the areas of environmental protection, elimination of poverty, reduction in crime, rebuilding of decaying cities, and so on.

A second, more realistic, approach to defining public policy is to focus on what government does. In other words, we should examine behavior, not read proclamations of intentions. Thus, if the question were "What is public policy in providing employment to those without a job?" an answer would be that the national government, with such legislation as the Comprehensive Employment and Training Act of 1973 (CETA), gave city and county governments millions of dollars to create public jobs and provide vocational skills to the unemployed. (This program was subsequently ended by the Reagan administration). How this money was distributed, what programs were created, and who received what benefits constituted the "real" public policy on unemployment. Likewise, the real public policy on school integration is revealed by court orders, school board decisions, the imposition of penalties to enforce laws and court orders, and similar actions that government takes to implement its programs.

A third definition of public policy stresses the consequences of government actions. Rather than examine program goals or day-to-day administration, we should look at the results in order to determine what our government's public policy is. Consider again the issue of government policy on full employment. It could be argued that under the CETA program government only seemed to be finding jobs for the unemployed; the reality was quite different. In particular, pressures to make the

President Lyndon Johnson, addressing a joint session of Congress, often used this national forum to generate support for his policies.

program a "success" encouraged administrators to find jobs for those with marketable skills, who would have found work easily without government help. The real beneficiaries of CETA were the well-off—aid program administrators, businesses that used government-subsidized employees, and local governments that substituted CETA money for local tax revenue. In short, the program did not create many new jobs; it merely gave government money to those who were likely to get jobs on their own.

The third approach to public policy is the most difficult to apply. In many instances, the consequences of government action may not be known for years or may be highly complex. For instance, a multibillion-dollar job program has wide-ranging effects in such areas as the tax rate and the careers that participants select. It might take a decade before analysts can demonstrate whether the job program was a success. Perhaps the need for higher taxes decreased employment and steered young people away from higher paying jobs. Assessing the consequences of a policy is not easy, and controversies almost always occur.

Is one of these approaches better than the others? Not necessarily. It is more useful to think of the three approaches as differing aspects of public policy, not as competing definitions. Each is appropriate for certain types of analyses and situations. If, for instance, we want to know how the government views inequalities in income among groups of citizens, statements by public officials on the objectives of tax policy would indicate public policy. On the other hand, if we want to know how the government's tax program actually works, we must examine such data as tax rates and taxes paid. Both types of information reflect government public policy—the first represents goals, the second, actual administration.

As we have suggested, differences can occur between goals, administration, and impact. Congress might enact a law committing the government to eliminating poverty. Funds are then authorized, people hired, and programs begun, and some people become better off. Ten years later, however, experts might conclude that the effort actually worsened poverty. Inconsistencies can also occur within the government itself. A well-known illustration is the policy of providing tobacco growers with government subsidies while simultaneously discouraging smoking. Such contradictions probably will always occur, because of the many areas of government involvement and the competing pressures that public officials face.

Separating Public Policy from Private Policy

Thus far we have focused on the different meanings of "policy" in "public policy." The "public" component of public policy also requires some explanation. Usually when we speak of public policy we are referring to the actions of public officials—elected or appointed, the President of the United States or some unknown bureaucrat, they are all part of government. The definition of policy becomes more complex when nongovernmental officials make decisions normally reserved for public officials. Under such circumstances, public policy really is better described as private policy made for the public.

The Head Start program provides educational enrichment for disadvantaged children. It is one of the most successful programs begun during the War on Poverty in the 1960s.

The blurring of the line between public and private is easiest to see in the way many states regulate professions, such as medicine, real estate, accounting, and law. In principle, it is the government that establishes the rules on training and certification. In practice, however, the rules are made and enforced by nongovernmental professional associations. The American Medical Association decides what constitutes a proper medical education, what types of businesses doctors may own, and whether a school is qualified to graduate doctors. The delegation of power from public to private hands occurs also in the operation of numerous government agencies. For example, several agricultural programs dealing with price supports and acreage allotments are managed by farmers themselves. Moreover, a portion of the federal government's grant-in-aid program is administered through private organizations.

The existence of large, powerful unions, corporations, and economic associations has frequently meant that private individuals make decisions of national significance. This was dramatically demonstrated in the mid-1970s, when the energy shortage suddenly emerged. Many important choices—the amount of oil to be imported, the negotiation of prices, exploration for new oil, and so on—were made by a few top officials of the major oil companies, not by government officials. Such decisions had major ramifications for auto sales, the travel industry, employment, inflation, and almost every other aspect of society. Likewise, decisions made by union officials on wage increases, working conditions, and strikes play a major role in public economic policy.

Some people have even argued that many important government decisions are not really made by government officials at all, but instead by a behind-the-scenes **power elite** composed of the economically powerful. According to this view, the heads of large corporations and private foundations decide policy, and their decisions are carried out by public officials acting as errand runners. However, while there is some evidence that a few decisions have been initiated by powerful economic interests, overall support for this view is lacking. Nevertheless, this view cannot be entirely dismissed.

As politicians with differing policy orientations have taken office, programs like Medicare—providing health insurance for the aged—have undergone changes in direction and funding.

Conclusions

Although defining public policy is simple, determining what constitutes public policy in an area is much more complex. Public policy is the government's response to a problem, but the response can have different aspects, and the line between government and nongovernment action can be unclear. Thus, while the government might be committed to providing full employment, its commitment does not necessarily mean that it will actively pursue its goal. Moreover, the implementation of the policy might be in the hands of private employers and union leaders rather than government officials.

Check Your Understanding

1. Define *public policy*.

2. In actual practice, what are the three different meanings of *public policy*?

3. What types of private groups or individuals are more likely to make public policy?

HOW IS PUBLIC POLICY MADE?

At first glance, the making of public policy seems beyond any general description. Policies are made in a wide variety of settings—the floor of the House, bureaucratic committees, rural county boards—and involve everything from choosing a state bird to declaring war. Determining common elements of policy making is not easy. Nevertheless, although it is impossible to provide a complete description of every policy, we can offer a general perspective on how public policy comes into being. We shall deal with two aspects of how policy is made: the stages of policy creation and explanations of the creation process.

The Stages of Policy Creation
The Policy Agenda

Before government—whether Congress, the state legislature, or a local official—can respond to an issue, a "problem" must become a "problem to be addressed by government." When public officials decide that something ought to be done, the problem is now on the agenda. It is crucial to realize that only a small portion of potential problems ever work their way onto the government agenda. In the first place, troublesome situations can exist but not necessarily be viewed as "problems." During the eighteenth century, for instance, the ruling class did not consider the subordinate position of women as a social ill needing a solution—those in power believed that inferiority was "natural" and inevitable. In the second place, even when a problem is acknowledged, citizens need not turn to government for a solution. Families might worry about inadequate child-care facilities, but not every family would want government to resolve the problem.

Assuming that there are numerous problems that the government could try to solve, why are only some dealt with by the government? Several factors seem to be relevant. The nature of the problem is obviously one factor. In particular, events of wide scope and great impact will be put on the agenda more readily than less important ones. Large-scale unemployment, catastrophic accidents, dramatic increases in crime, and crippling labor disputes in key industries are all likely to receive prompt attention. Sometimes a relatively small event can trigger a major government reaction because of its important implications. In 1957, for example, the Soviet Union's unexpected launching of the first orbiting satellite—Sputnik I—galvanized a major government response in both education and military policy.

A second set of factors concerns the skillful marshaling of resources in support of an issue. Many problems that *could* receive government attention do not necessarily *require* such attention. A government must respond to the need for national defense; it does not have to prevent racial discrimination in hotels. An issue like racial conflict can be put on the agenda by group efforts. In

At hearings during the 1970s, United Farm Workers president César Chávez, left, urged Congress to legislate collective bargaining for farm workers. At right is Senator Edward Kennedy.

the mid-1960s, for example, voter registration drives, mass demonstrations, boycotts, use of the mass media, lawsuits, and letter-writing campaigns forced the issue of racial inequality onto the agenda. Many programs in environmental protection, health care for the elderly, restrictions on the use of nuclear power, and consumer product safety originated in the demands of groups. Advocacy by a group does not automatically place an issue on the agenda, but unless individuals or organizations spend time, money, and energy in promoting such causes, the likelihood of government action is small.

In some cases the media can play a key role in bringing a problem to the attention of the public. This was illustrated when the U.S. mass media "rediscovered" the widespread and terrible famine in Ethiopia following the 1984 presidential elec-

tion. Severe drought and hunger had been going on for years, but they were pushed out of the news by campaign coverage. With the campaign over, news magazines, such as *Newsweek,* and television news programs turned starvation in Africa into one of the big stories of the day. The sudden publicity encouraged both the national government and private citizens to offer aid to famine victims.

The responsiveness of government to different demands is a third factor that helps explain what gets on the agenda. Although every citizen has an equal right to make demands on government, governments are not organized to give everyone an equal hearing. Some interests have "built-in" representation—for example, the Department of Agriculture and agricultural committees in Congress are sympathetic to the plight of farmers. Other groups with ready access include veterans, labor unions, professional educators, and numerous business groups. The electoral system can also determine whose demands get attention. For example, because illegal immigrants cannot vote, it is unlikely that many legislators will be motivated to champion their cause.

Finally, traditions and customs of government can influence which problems are deemed worthy of attention. Consider, for example, how government has come to respond to demands for disease control. At one time personal illness was not a government responsibility. Gradually, however, the control of some diseases (for example, tuberculosis) became a government function. Once the principle of government responsibility was established, other diseases were included. In the early 1980s, for example, there was relatively little resistance to the government's undertaking a commitment to combat acquired immune deficiency syndrome (AIDS). Likewise, once the issue of discrimination against blacks in schools was on the agenda, it was easier to place discrimination in employment on the agenda. More generally, new problems that resemble those already on the agenda are likely to receive attention. On the other hand, unfamiliar problems (for example, the control of genetic engineering) might wait much longer before officials decide that a government response is in order.

Sometimes concerned citizens take action when governmental authorities refuse to step in. Here, a member of the group Life of the Land plants a warning sign on the beach, because the Health Department did not consider the pollution level of the water high enough to pose a hazard to the public.

Formulating Policy

Once a problem is on the agenda, the next step is to decide what should be done about it. In other words, a policy or set of policies must be formulated. Usually a wide range of possible approaches exists. If a government, for instance, decided that it would provide recreational areas for children, possible solutions would range from posting "Caution. Children at Play" highway signs to constructing a multimillion-dollar recreation center.

An important first step in formulating a policy response is to define the precise character of the problem. Because many problems are complex and closely related to other issues, a definition rarely is self-evident. Consider a sudden rise in unemployment in heavy industries, such as steel and automobiles. Some people might view this as a foreign trade matter—because cheap imports are putting Americans out of work, higher tariffs are in order. Alternatively, some observers might focus on what they consider to be a problem with the unions—because excessive wage demands make American products uncompetitive, union power ought to be curbed. Still others might see it as a tax problem—the tax code provides too few incentives to modernize antiquated industry. All of these are plausible explanations.

How a problem is defined can have major consequences. If a problem is viewed as a short-term, individual one, the appropriate government response might be little more than to pass a resolution offering sympathy and encouragement. If the identical problem is judged a potential catastrophe, it would receive the full attention of government. Changing views of poverty illustrate the importance of definition. In the nineteenth century, poverty was considered largely an individual matter; very limited government aid was available. It was up to individuals, through hard work, thrift, and persistence, to solve their own problems. By the mid-1960s, poverty had become a social problem whose solution required major legal and economic reforms.

A second step in the formulation process is the determination of the appropriate government body to deal with the problem. Should it be a state matter? Should the states and Washington cooperate? If it is to be solved at the national level, who

Points of View: Think Tanks and Public Policy

A major force in the making of public policy is what has been called the "think tank." Basically, a think tank is a group of scholars who conduct research, write, and publish. Some scholars study long-term abstract questions, while others seek immediate practical solutions to urgent problems. Think tanks resemble small universities but without students. Financial support is provided by private contributions, corporate and government grants, sales of books, and, in a few cases, investment income from endowments.

The general goal of think tanks is to provide the intellectual basis for public policy. In some cases the motivation is clearly ideological, in others it is more altruistic. Findings are distributed by publishing research, conducting seminars for public officials, arranging testimony before Congress, and offering forums for the expression of new ideas. One example of a policy that received its impetus from think tanks was the movement toward deregulation. During the 1960s and 1970s, the Brookings Institution, the Hoover Institution on War, Revolution and Peace, and the American Enterprise Institute for Public Policy Research (AEI) provided the research and justification for the extensive deregulation of the transportation, banking, and communications industries enacted in the late 1970s.

One think tank that has had particular influence in the Reagan administration is the Heritage Foundation. This conservative organization produces between sixty and one hundred studies a year; each is hand-delivered to about a thousand high-ranking officials and mailed to six thousand journalists, educators, and others in positions of influence. When Reagan was elected in 1980, it published a 1,093-page report, "Mandate for Leadership," which served as an important source of ideas in the President's administration. As the President himself said: "The Heritage Foundation research continues to be useful to us and our policy-making process." A number of people once associated with the Heritage Foundation have served in the Reagan administration.

Think tanks vary considerably in their interests and political orientation. Some of the better-known ones include the following:

Brookings Institution. Highly respected, well-financed, Washington-based organization that publishes numerous political and economic studies by leading scholars. Generally liberal and Democratic, it has made an effort to add a conservative viewpoint to its offerings.

American Enterprise Institute for Public Policy Research. A moderately conservative think tank in Washington that has grown dramatically in the last decade. It publishes numerous books, pamphlets, magazines, and position papers as well as organizing conferences for scholars and officials. The AEI has close ties to the Reagan administration.

Hoover Institution on War, Revolution and Peace. Located in Palo Alto, California, it provides a detached, university-like environment where leading scholars can work with great freedom. It is less involved in specific policy debates than most other think tanks. Once decidedly conservative, it has become more diverse in recent years.

Cato Institute. A relatively small organization committed to "classical liberalism"—minimal government intervention in the economy and society.

Joint Center for Policy Studies. A very liberal organization that concentrates on matters of relevance to blacks. It sponsors research on black political participation, the economic conditions of blacks, and the general area of civil rights law enforcement.

Resources for the Future. A large (staff of one hundred; $5.5-million yearly budget) group that conducts research on the economics of energy, conservation, and natural resources.

Center for Strategic and International Studies. A well-endowed, well-staffed think tank that focuses on questions dealing with international military matters, national resources, regional problems, and energy. It tries to avoid political bias.

Urban Institute. Washington-based organization with a staff of 150 and budget of nearly $10 million that conducts research on urban problems—neighborhood rehabilitation, housing, taxes, and the like.

should have the responsibility? Here again, considerable choice usually exists. On an issue like unemployment, Congress itself might try to take control of the situation, enacting specific laws and closely monitoring its programs through the oversight process. Or it could delegate responsibility to any number of executive branch agencies—the Labor Department, the Department of Health and Human Services, and the Commerce Department are all possible administrators. Alternatively, a whole new government bureaucracy could be created to deal with the problem (the Department of Energy was established to handle the interrelated challenges of fuel conservation, nuclear power, and so forth).

The delegation of responsibility can be important. Suppose, for example, that the states rather than Washington are assigned the task of solving unemployment. Because states differ in their industrial base, tax capacity, population mix, and many other characteristics, some states would have ambitious programs, while others would take minimal action. A program administered by Congress itself would probably distribute funds differently from a program directed by officials in the Labor Department. Both programs would be unlike one run by private industry.

Finally, a proposed solution to a problem requires a commitment of resources. This is far more complicated than appropriating a certain sum of money. Financial commitment can vary from a yearly reviewed appropriation to the creation of a program's own source of revenue, with an open-ended guarantee of adequate funding. A program's operations can depend on whether administrators have to request funds from Congress annually or whether, as in the construction of the interstate highway system, money automatically arrives through a special tax set aside for the program. If Congress gives program beneficiaries a legal right to their benefits regardless of the amount of revenue collected (as with Social Security), there is little chance that the program will run out of money.

The "who pays?" issue is as important as how much is committed. The costs can be distributed in many different ways. In some programs users help pay for a service (for example, toll roads and the gasoline tax pay for highways). In other cases, a tax is levied on a particular group (employers and employees, for example, pay a tax to finance Social Security). States and cities sometimes give agencies the power to raise revenue by selling bonds. The most common sources of program funding are general revenues—the taxes collected by government not set aside for a specific program. How a program is financed can affect its survival and the political controversy it generates. A retraining program funded by a one-time 25-percent tax on corporate income probably will raise greater opposition than one financed by a permanent 2-percent increase in tariffs.

Implementing Policy

Enacting a law and setting aside funds rarely bring a program into existence. A law on the books, or a judicial decision, unless it is implemented, is an empty gesture. **Implementation**—the period between the enactment of a policy and its completion—has an enormous impact on the actual meaning of a policy. In 1954, for example, the Supreme Court, in *Brown v. Board of Education*, declared that state-required segregation in public schools was unconstitutional. In 1955 the Court ordered the lower courts to ensure "a prompt and reasonable start toward full compliance." Nevertheless, for nearly ten years almost nothing was done about segregated schools. In practice, the lack of implementation undermined the Court's actions.

The implementation process may be highly complex or quite simple. In some cases—for example, the War on Poverty in the 1960s—implementation involved thousands of people, hundreds of millions of dollars, and the creation of numerous government agencies. Personnel had to be assigned to the program, organizational responsibilities defined, information collected, methods for giving out funds decided on, and numerous specific rules and regulations had to be written. In other cases, implementation involves no more than changing a rule or adjusting a statistical formula.

The success of government programs often depends on the actions of thousands of workers providing many types of services.

It is crucial to understand that implementation is not a mechanical, predetermined process. Congress does not pass a law and, lo and behold, six months later an agency does precisely what Congress intended. Many factors affect just how a program will be implemented. One key factor is the degree of independence given policy administrators. Though Congress can be very specific when it enacts legislation, it frequently leaves many important decisions to the implementing agencies. Such delegation of authority is often necessary if administrators are to adapt programs to new and complex situations. Independence can, however, allow administrators to change the meaning of a program. A program intended to train the hard-core unemployed can be restructured through implementation to provide summer jobs for students.

Even when a program is formulated in precise terms, some administrative leeway is inevitable. Program administrators cannot possibly give full attention to every detail. For example, when the President orders the Justice Department to enforce laws prohibiting the dumping of toxic wastes, the attorneys in charge must decide, in particular, on who will be prosecuted, how much evidence will be collected, how the cases will be argued, and so on. Each of these choices will influence the implementation process. A decision to prosecute thousands of small companies could mean years of trials and very slow progress in eliminating pollution. An alternative would be to concentrate on a few prominent violators. The pace might be quicker but the impact less widespread.

Implementation also is affected by how closely the resources committed to a program reflect the program's objectives. If an agency is assigned a task but is given inadequate legal powers to set standards, request information, and enforce orders, policy goals are unlikely to be realized. Agencies must possess sufficient personnel, expertise, and facilities if a program is to operate as intended. Furthermore, an agency's organization must be appropriate. An agency that operates almost entirely in Washington and moves slowly would probably have little success in running a local high school antidrug program. Essential cooperation with other public officials and private groups must be arranged. Ways must also exist for overcoming obstacles, such as resistance to program goals within the agency or public misunderstanding.

Clearly, proper implementation of a program is difficult. Many mistakes can occur, and failures seem to outnumber successes. A few critics have even suggested that a discrepancy between intention and results is to be expected, because of the many different ways a program's goals can be sidetracked. Moreover, even the best of intentions do not guarantee success. An offical deeply committed to reducing the cost of administering government might put so much pressure on subordinates that failures are hidden; later decisions then are based on faulty data. In 1985, for example, it was claimed that employees of the Internal Revenue Service were pressured to be more efficient—a goal of the Reagan administration—that they destroyed thousands of tax returns rather than process them. Agencies can also develop a purpose at odds with their original mission. Several independent regulatory commissions, for example, were created to help consumers but were eventually used to advance the cause of the industry they were supposed to regulate. The Interstate Commerce Commission, set up to protect consumers from excessive charges by railroads, was often used by the railroads to enforce artificially high rates.

Explanations of Policy Making

Thus far we have described the stages of the policy process—from the way a problem gets on the agenda to the implementation of a solution. We shall now consider different explanations of how and why issues move through these stages. In other words, how do public officials decide to tackle problems such as inflation, unemployment, or pollution? How do officials decide which solution to try and how much money to spend? To answer questions like these, we shall examine several alternative descriptions (sometimes called policy making models) that political scientists use. These descriptions, or models, are not offered as complete, proven accounts. Rather, they constitute different perspectives on the way decision makers translate problems into public policy.

Rational Choice Approach

According to the rational choice perspective, policies are selected and strategies implemented that, in comparison with all other choices, maximize benefits over costs. A policy maker first determines what people want and how they rank their preferences and then considers the available policy options and their consequences. From this analysis emerges a policy that is most effective—that is, there are more benefits than costs for more people than in any other likely policy.

Consider how this approach might be applied to unemployment. Information on the personal, social, and economic costs of unemployment is collected, along with people's views on what economic conditions are desirable. We might find, for example, that most people will tolerate some unemployment in order to reduce labor costs, but they object to unemployment above a certain level. Several solutions are considered—temporary government jobs, cash payments, tax incentives to hire the unemployed, or even doing nothing. The chosen solution is cash payments, because, judged against the alternatives, their virtues—ease of administration, adaptability to change, and quick implementation—far outweigh the principal cost—higher taxes on the employed. When unemployment reaches a certain level, the program of cash payments is put into effect.

Although the rational choice approach might be an accurate description in some instances, many differences exist between it and real-world politics. Rarely do decision makers have the needed information about people's preferences and the consequences of policy alternatives. It is not always easy to determine what people really want. People might say they want lower taxes but be unwilling to give up government benefits. Or public officials simply might lack the resources to obtain all the needed data. Experts also can disagree on which facts are the most important and on the consequences of different methods of operation. In addition, the need for immediate action sometimes outweighs the desirability of basing a decision on the careful analysis of mountains of data. The solutions generated by rational decision making also might conflict with democratic procedures, political feasibility, tradition, and the Constitution. For example, solving the unemployment problem by forcing the unemployed to take unpleasant jobs against their will would hardly be acceptable, even if it were the most rational, efficient solution. Finally, political decision makers are not always motivated by a willingness to enact the most rational solution. The desire for fame, prestige, personal enrichment, bureaucratic power, and innumerable "nonrational" factors can result in decisions that are known to have greater costs than benefits. A member of Congress might, for example, favor wasteful public works projects in his or her district to solve local unemployment because these projects are a good reelection strategy. In short, although many analysts have praised this approach, it is of limited usefulness in explaining most policy making.

Incrementalism

Incrementalism, which is almost the mirror image of the rational choice view, is an approach to policy making in which previous policies are generally accepted as they stand and new policies are limited to small, or incremental, changes. When confronted with a problem, the policy maker says, "How can we adjust existing policies to meet a new situation?" There is no systematic attempt to collect all the relevant information or evaluate the differing costs of alternatives. Instead of maximum efficiency, policy makers seek limited change and adaptation.

If the government were facing large-scale unemployment, a policy maker using the incremental approach would stick to past solutions, administered within agencies that have traditionally dealt with the problem. Changes would be restricted to such responses as raising expenditures somewhat, hiring more staff, opening more local offices, and eliminating organizational inefficiencies. Sharp breaks with the past or new approaches would receive low priority. Change would occur, however, and over a period of time the program might be transformed completely.

The incremental method accurately describes much policy making. Many legislators and officials in the executive branch do, in fact, approach

Points of View: What Price Deregulation?

The flip side of government economic regulation is *deregulation*—the reduction or elimination of government controls. Beginning in the late 1970s, deregulation became the watchword in federal dealings with a host of industries, including airlines, trucking, railroads, oil, and banking. With its promise of increased competition, deregulation achieved a favored place on the public policy agenda because it seemed desirable to both conservatives and liberals. It appealed to the former because it would lessen burdensome government restraints, and to the latter because it seemed likely to help consumers by lowering prices and improving service.

One landmark piece of legislation was the Airline Deregulation Act of 1978, which removed the government controls that had formerly set prices and determined the routes for every airline operating in the United States. The law did not affect rules governing safety, however. What have been the effects of deregulation on the airline industry?

Competition certainly increased. Between 1978 and the mid-1980s, the number of airlines jumped from 44 to 114. Competition became so intense, in fact,

that there were several bankruptcies and a great deal of consolidation. For example, Pan Am sold its Pacific routes to United Airlines, while Texas Air bought Eastern Airlines.

Competition, in turn, had the effect of lowering fares. This occurred mainly because many of the new lines were not unionized and thus had relatively low operating costs. Meanwhile, the number of passengers soared—from 11.3 million in 1978 to over 26 million by the mid-1980s.

The effect of deregulation on service was complex. For cities like Chicago and Atlanta, whose airports were among the nation's busiest, loosened controls brought more carriers and a bigger choice of flights. In many other cities, however, service declined. In some localities passengers had fewer choices, while in other areas airline service was discontinued altogether. Overall, the number of cities receiving scheduled airline service shrank from around 630 in 1978 to around 540 by the mid-1980s. Ironically, cities in which airline service was increased faced a problem, too: a growing number of delays in takeoffs and landings. At some busy airports, planes waiting on the runways or

"stacked' in flight patterns around the airports became commonplace, and complaints of missed connections increased sharply.

One trend that worried some observers was the scramble for qualified pilots and a consequent lowering of requirements for their employment. According to a survey by the National Transportation Safety Board, the number of hours of jetliner experience for the average pilot dropped from over 2,000 in 1983 to under 1,000 just two years later. It was during this period, too, that many experienced air traffic controllers lost their jobs as a result of a strike. Fortunately, the number of air fatalities actually decreased in relation to passenger miles. There was, however, an alarming increase in the number of "near midairs"—collisions that almost happened.

After almost ten years of airline deregulation, opinions about it were mixed. Proponents praised the lower fares, while opponents noted the decline in service and the increased possibility of accidents. The main point on which both sides agreed was that the airline industry was still in a period of transition, with the full effects of deregulation still to be known.

---

problems from an incremental prospective. The use of incrementalism reflects the pressures on officials that prevent them from developing new policies. Only very rarely can a bureaucrat collect all the information needed for the best possible choice. Incrementalism usually makes good political sense. Because existing programs typically have many supporters in and outside government, a major change is likely to draw opposition. Recall from our discussion of Congress and the bureaucracy that public officials often have close ties with interest groups that benefit from existing programs (Chapters 9 and 11). Frequent large-scale change would heighten political conflict. Moreover, most officials know that it is often better to keep a partially successful program than to risk a crisis if a replacement program fails. Finally, gradual change and periodic modification are better suited to modern bureaucracies, with their need for predictability and stability, than are constant fresh starts. The problem of running government would be overwhelming if programs were continually in a state of flux.

Incrementalism does, of course, have its drawbacks as an explanation of how policy is made. Changes can and do occur in government policy that are inconsistent with incrementalism. For example, between 1965 and 1970, the federal government's expenditures for human services (health care, education, and so on) more than doubled—from $35.4 billion to $72.7 billion. Such changes are hardly incremental. Incrementalism also can be of limited value during crisis periods, like the energy shortage of the mid-1970s or the dramatic rise in inflation and interest rates in the late 1970s. Nor can incrementalism explain the emergence of whole new issues on the agenda. The development of women's issues in recent years, for example, was fairly sudden and largely unexpected.

Group Theory

This approach sees the policy process as the result of group interactions. Society is composed of a multitude of groups that make claims on government. Some of these groups are well organized—the American Medical Association, labor unions, the Sierra Club, for instance. Others consist of individuals who share a common interest, but no organization or common course of action exists. These are sometimes called **latent** or **potential groups** (for example, customers of a certain power company) that can be mobilized into action if their interests are threatened. Government sets the rules of conflict, and the outcome of this group struggle becomes public policy.

From the perspective of group theory, here is how the making of a policy on unemployment might look. In response to increased unemployment, a coalition of organizations—labor unions, business associations, new coalitions of the unemployed themselves—pressure government for more benefits and government jobs. Their demands are challenged by opponents of increased government spending and by private companies who believe that the easy availability of government jobs will make it difficult for them to hire needed workers. Groups on both sides have their allies in government. Officials in the Labor Department might, for example, push for greater unemployment benefits, whereas pro-business members of Congress might try to stop the appropriations. Even though Congress and the President are inclined to increase unemployment benefits, they don't want to antagonize taxpayers and employers who contribute to these benefits. Tactics in this conflict might include demonstrations, threats of work stoppages, contributions to election campaigns, letters to Congress, television commercials, and testimony at government hearings. Eventually, as a result of bargains and compro-

THE WIZARD OF ID   by Brant parker and Johnny hart

By permission of Johnny Hart and News America Syndicate

mises, the government provides a modest number of short-term jobs for the unemployed.

Like incrementalism, the group approach makes some sense. Many policies are greatly influenced by the push and pull of group conflict. In recent years, for example, environmental groups have put issues like water pollution on the agenda and have vigorously monitored implementation. Their efforts have usually been opposed by industry associations, which claim that antipollution programs are too expensive, are technically impossible, and result in unemployment. Nevertheless, the group theory is far from a complete description. Many major programs—for example the War on Poverty in the 1960s—were begun largely by political leaders themselves with little group pressure (this policy mobilized groups, not the other way around). The group approach also suffers from imprecision in predicting which groups will push which policies. Why, for example, did antipollution groups become active only in the early 1970s, even though pollution problems had existed for decades?

Elite Theory

According to elite theory, public policy is made by a small group, the elite. There are several versions of elite theory, but most assert that the elite consists of the very wealthy who control the large banks, insurance companies, and corporations. This elite does not govern directly—it rules instead through public officials, government advisors, and private foundations and universities that supply ideas to government. By avoiding publicity and active involvement, the elite creates the illusion of government by the people.

Explaining policy with the elite model is relatively simple. Whether or not unemployment should become an issue requiring government response is decided by the elite. The elite would also formulate the policy and use its influence to ensure that the program was properly carried out. The basic objective of any policy would be to preserve the elite's power. The elite might, for example, support generous unemployment benefits if it believed that such aid would help prevent a serious challenge to its authority. Or the elite might

decide that nothing ought to be done; the policy of inaction would be presented to the public through numerous stories in the mass media about the excessive cost of such benefits, their ineffectiveness, and why people should not rely on government handouts. The elite would ensure that its wishes were carried out by making donations to political campaigns, sponsoring research, and even encouraging government harassment of opponents.

This perspective enjoys a degree of popularity, but it lacks much supporting evidence. Although we can document the existence of an elite, it is far more difficult to prove manipulation of policy making. Attempts to do so have had only limited success, and the issues were not crucial (for example, the role of the elite in encouraging the government to make a commitment to stabilizing population growth). It is one thing to show that top corporate officials have exercised a degree of influence in politics, quite another to demonstrate their domination of government. Evidence showing that the elite prevailed in the face of widespread opposition from public officials and private citizens is particularly weak. This would be the true test of domination, yet no example of it has been offered by elite theorists. Perhaps more than anything else, elite theory is a way of explaining certain situations and events (for example, continued large differences in income) that lack a more direct explanation. It is more of a "behind-the-scenes" explanation of social forces in general than an account of a specific government action.

A Perspective

It should be clear that no one of these four approaches offers an accurate, complete account of the way policy is made. Incrementalism and group theory have considerable relevance, but not in all situations. Rational choice and elite theory generally are less appropriate, but they are reasonable in some situations. Rather than choose one over the other, it is perhaps more useful to think of these models as applying to different policy areas at different times. In some situations, rational choice might provide the best account of policy making; in others incrementalism is more useful.

HOW DO WE EVALUATE PUBLIC POLICY?

Contemporary governments produce a steady stream of public policies. Almost every aspect of our lives is directly or indirectly influenced by such policies. It is essential for a society to have standards for evaluating whether such laws, regulations, and programs are desirable. Because almost every policy has some advantages (otherwise it would not be considered) and some disadvantages, deciding which policies are best, most effective, or most useful is difficult. Numerous approaches to evaluation exist, but disagreement occurs over their relevance and usefulness. It is as if a group were trying to decide which restaurant is best, but could not decide what standards to use (food? price? service? variety? decor? and so on). Our analysis begins with relatively narrow approaches to policy evaluation and moves to more inclusive frameworks.

Process Evaluation

Process evaluation is the assessment of a policy in terms of its stated guidelines. When Congress enacts a program that is administered by an executive branch agency, numerous guidelines must be followed, some of which might be included in the legislation itself. A program to aid the poor, for example, might specify who was to run the program, where the money was to be spent, and what the maximum program outlays were to be. The administrative agency would prepare further guidelines—methods for selecting recipients, rules for hiring and firing staff, and procedures for settling conflicts. In addition, thousands of regulations exist covering all federal programs—funds may not be used where racial, sexual, or religious discrimination occurs, proper records must be kept, meetings usually may not be held in secret, and so on.

Many program evaluations, especially those conducted by government itself, judge a program against these stated criteria. In other words, has the program been carried out as legally intended and required? Have the right people received aid? Have contracts been given out according to established guidelines? Process evaluation is most visible in congressional oversight hearings, when members of Congress interrogate bureaucrats about unaccounted-for funds, cost overruns, and failure to take required actions. Whether the program itself, even if administered according to every rule and regulation, is worthwhile is not an issue in process evaluation.

Impact Evaluation

Impact evaluation is the determination of whether a policy has produced results in the intended direction. Policy intent is usually made clear in the legislation itself, in debates surrounding the passage of a bill, in the testimony of bill sponsors, and in the pronouncements of public officials. If a program is created to reduce poverty, impact evaluation asks, "Has poverty been reduced as a result of this program?" There is no specific concern about whether the program was carried out as legally intended; it is not crucial whether or not proper records were kept or nondiscriminatory guidelines followed.

Impact evaluation is much more complex than process evaluation. It is rarely easy to show conclusively the impact of a program. For example,

Commentary: Life and Death, Dollars and Cents

The problems of evaluating a policy are especially evident when human life is at stake. What price do you place on a human being? Should financial factors govern choices about who lives and who dies?

Consider the problem of permanent kidney failure, or ESRD (end stage renal disease). Until the 1960s there was no hope for people with ESRD. With the invention of the dialysis machine, however, ESRD sufferers could be kept alive by periodic filtering of their blood. But treatment was very expensive, there were too few machines, and hospitals often had to let people die who might otherwise have lived.

The situation generated widespread debate. In 1965, NBC-TV ran a dramatic story about how the government was spending billions for space exploration but would not invest millions to save lives. A dialysis machine was even demonstrated to a congressional committee.

In 1972 Congress acted by an overwhelming majority to provide government assistance via the Medicare program to sufferers of ESRD. The federal government pays a sizable portion of the yearly cost of dialysis for each patient, and a number of states also help defray the expenses. Congress originally believed that the total yearly cost would be small—$90 to 100 million—and would decline as technology improved. This estimate was far off—the 1985 outlay was more than $1 billion—and costs are rising sharply. Even worse, this well-intentioned program has had negative medical consequences and encourages fraud.

First, government's guarantee of funds for treatment created a boom in hospital-run dialysis. While some of the increase was legitimate, in many instances treatment was questionable. Often terminally ill patients or those who would not benefit from it were nevertheless given dialysis because it is "free" and doctors collect handsome fees for having patients on the machine.

Second, the guaranteed availability of government money for dialysis encouraged hospitals and doctors to run up costs. All types of "free" or heavily subsidized equipment, supplies, and services could be included as part of the dialysis treatment (there were ceilings on permitted costs, but exceptions were liberally granted). One government audit even found that items such as theater tickets and vacations were being billed as part of ESRD treatment. Few incentives existed to control soaring costs, since many increased costs could simply be passed along to the taxpayer.

Finally, and most important, government financial assistance has discouraged alternative, more effective, and less costly treatments. Kidney transplants, a much cheaper and far better medical solution to ESRD, became relatively less popular. The development of much more convenient portable, at-home machines has also been discouraged. Why should the medical profession give up a steady, government-supplied income?

In sum, though the government policy of financing dialysis machines has had many benefits and saved thousands of lives, it has not been trouble-free. It has given hospitals and doctors a strong incentive to raise costs and avoid alternative treatments. The program has also cost many more billions than originally anticipated.

Our analysis is drawn from Michael Kronman, "Dialyzing for Dollars," *Reason*, August 1984.

even if a program to combat crime does not lower the crime rate, the program was not necessarily a failure: crime might have increased even more without the program. Impact studies commonly use complicated statistical methods to reach their conclusions. Many programs have been studied under experimental conditions in which one group participates in a program and other individuals do not. Comparisons between the period before a law and following a law are also used in impact evaluation.

Although impact evaluation has become popular, it is still a limited technique. Many policies—for example, an arms control agreement—cannot

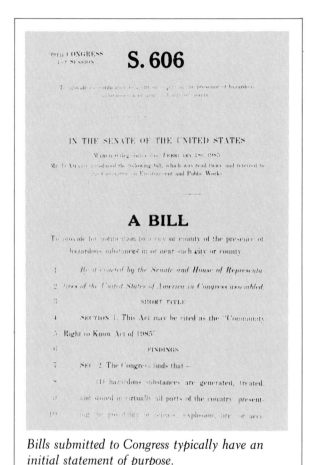

99TH CONGRESS
1ST SESSION

S. 606

IN THE SENATE OF THE UNITED STATES

A BILL

Bills submitted to Congress typically have an initial statement of purpose.

be evaluated easily. One could not say that because no war followed the agreement, peace was therefore a direct result of the agreement. Peace might have continued without the agreement. In other cases—for example, laws prohibiting racial and sexual discrimination—the impact is very difficult to measure (millions of actions are involved, decisions are often hidden from public view, and reasonable people may differ on the meaning of "discrimination"). Separating the impact of a program from ongoing social and economic changes is also difficult. A program to provide jobs for the unskilled may yield dramatic results, but the success may really be a consequence of economic growth, not of the program itself. Confusion can also exist over just what a program is supposed to accomplish. A law may be intended to provide jobs for everyone, yet legislators and administra-

tors may privately realize that the program can offer only limited help for a brief period.

Cost-Benefit Analysis

In **cost-benefit analysis** the costs of a policy are judged against its benefits. Policies are judged favorably when benefits outweigh costs. The cost-benefit approach can be used in different ways. The costs and benefits might be calculated solely in terms of a single policy. For a water-pollution-control program, costs would include the salaries of program employees, increased burdens on the legal system as a result of litigation, higher prices of manufactured goods, and greater unemployment when polluting industries are closed. Benefits might include a healthier public, improved fishing, lower costs for drinking water, and a more picturesque environment.

Costs and benefits can also be calculated more broadly when numerous policy areas are involved. The decision to tackle one problem might mean that another problem will have to be tolerated. Economists call this the **opportunity cost** of a decision—the benefits of one policy are lost when another policy is chosen. Put in ordinary terms, the opportunity cost of going to a movie includes the pleasure lost by not staying home and watching television. Opportunity costs exist because no government has the time, money, or personnel to deal with every problem. Thus the decision to stress environmental protection might mean that other areas—education, bridge and highway maintenance, inflation control, for example—will receive less attention. Hence, even if the environmental protection program is a great success in terms of its own costs and benefits, high opportunity costs can lead to other serious problems.

Like impact evaluation, cost-benefit analysis has attracted much praise, but it remains limited in its application. For one thing, many costs and benefits are difficult to quantify. On the issue of burning coal to reduce oil consumption, for example, experts differ on such matters as health problems created by burning coal, the true energy costs of generating electricity from coal, and the supposed benefits of lower oil consumption. More-

Biography: Rachel Carson

Rachel Carson was a reluctant crusader. This reserved, soft-spoken woman, who combined the knowledge of a scientist with the talents of a writer, was happiest when she was exploring the world of nature. But when she became interested in what chemicals were doing to that world—and to humanity—she could not rest until she had researched the subject thoroughly and presented her findings to the public. The result was *Silent Spring*, a book that placed concern for the environment on the government's agenda as a major public policy issue.

Born in 1907 and reared in Pennsylvania, Carson obtained degrees in both biology and zoology before becoming a teacher at Johns Hopkins University. Later she spent several years working for the government's Fish and Wildlife Service, where she combined her interests by writing about scientific subjects. Carson's first book, *Under the Sea-Wind* (1941), had only modest sales. But her second one, *The Sea Around Us* (1951), won a National Book Award and became a best seller. Next, in 1955, came *The Edge of the Sea*, an attempt, in the author's words, "to take the seashore out of the category of scenery and make it come alive."

The impetus for *Silent Spring* came from personal friends, whose small wildlife refuge in Massachusetts had been devastated after the state sprayed it with DDT as part of a mosquito-control program.

This powerful chemical insecticide, introduced into the United States in 1942, had been widely sprayed on farms, forest lands, and home lawns and gardens. Its long-term effects, however, had received little attention.

The more Carson learned, the more concerned she became. There was evidence that indiscriminate spraying of DDT and other chemicals was destroying wildlife by killing off links in the food chain. People also appeared to be at risk because pesticides left reisdues (perhaps carcinogenic) in the human body.

Silent Spring was published in 1962; its title referred to some future season when songbirds would fail to return to their usual haunts. The book touched off a tremendous furor. The chemical industry attacked Carson, claiming that insects, not pesticides, were the real enemy. But her views found many influential supporters, including Supreme Court Justice William O. Douglas and the *New York Times*.

Public concern in turn sparked action by the federal government. President John F. Kennedy formed a Scientific Advisory Committee, which issued a report warning against indiscriminate pesticide use and calling for further research on potential health hazards. Congress held hearings, at which Carson testified, and passed legislation regulating pesticide use. Although Carson died just two years after publication of *Silent Spring*, the crusade continued. Among its milestones were the formation of the Environmental Protection Agency in 1970, the banning of DDT in 1972, and a host of laws aimed at reducing air and water pollution.

Why did Carson's book have such a profound influence on public policy? There were probably many different factors at work, including her own eloquence and the fact that environmental hazards affect almost everyone in society. Whatever the reasons, few doubted Carson's impact. "A few thousand words from her," as one newspaper put it, "and the world took a new direction."

over, many benefits and costs do not become fully visible until years or decades after a policy comes into existence. In the 1950s, for instance, building large-scale urban public housing projects seemed to be a cost-effective solution to the housing shortage, because the maximum number of people were given adequate housing at the lowest possible cost. In the 1980s, such projects are viewed as breeding grounds for crime and other social ills with very high costs. What was originally a cheap solution turned out to be very expensive. Finally, even if costs and benefits could be measured accurately, it is not always simple to decide whether benefits exceed costs. Should $10 million be spent to improve a highway to save two lives per year? Is $200 billion a year a bargain if it prevents Soviet aggression? What if crime could be reduced only by violating the rights of citizens? Such questions are not easily answered.

Political Value Approach

The final standard we can use for judging the worth of a policy is the way the policy fits with political values—access to government, legal equality, democratic decision making, and freedom to express our ideas. Some values are widely accepted (for example, the right of people to participate in politics), and others are more controversial (say, the elimination of economic inequality). Each individual has his or her own set of political values and therefore may ask: "How does a policy fit with my own values?" Policies are evaluated against such criteria as whether they promote justice and democracy, not whether they are administered correctly or whether benefits outweigh costs.

From this perspective an individual might support a policy of generous financial aid to the unemployed because such a policy was consistent with the principles of humane treatment of the less fortunate, a society based on compassion, and a belief that society's wealth and resources should be distributed as equally as possible. On the other hand, someone who opposes government interference in the economy and believes that self-reli-

Boy Scouts organize a recycling drive in their town. Local programs often begin through individual or group effort; they may later become public policy.

ance ought to be encouraged would not favor payments to the unemployed.

In practice, this is the way much public policy gets evaluated. Such topics as abortion, divorce, or even day care for children are likely to arouse heated debate among those who believe that these are moral issues outside the domain of government. Programs to help the poor are sometimes criticized on the grounds that they encourage immorality. The principal drawback of the political value approach is that judgments may be rooted in ignorance of what a policy actually accomplishes. Policies that may seem to uphold certain values may not do so in practice. Money given to the poor in the name of economic equality may instead only enrich the people who administer aid programs and thereby increase inequality. Banning pornography to promote public virtue could provide huge profits to suppliers of illegal pornographic films. In addition, many policies involve several, often conflicting, political values. An expensive program to stop crime poses a dilemma to someone who favors both low taxes and a crime-free society.

Perspective

It is apparent that there is no one way to judge political policy. All of the evaluative approaches we have discussed have their advantages and disadvantages, and all have their relevant applications. Because in most situations any of the approaches might work, the decision about *how* to judge a program can influence *what* evaluation is reached. A policy to combat unemployment that is a "failure" in terms of process evaluation might be a great success if measured by impact evaluation or cost-benefit analysis. Moreover, no method provides an automatic, foolproof way to judge the success or failure of a policy. Reasonable people can disagree over whether certain rules have been followed, what impact a program has had, what the dollar value of a program is, and whether a program in practice is consistent with a political value. Finally, the evaluation process is not politically neutral. Because information is often complex and incomplete, the final judgment of a program can depend on the evaluator's own policy preferences. It is no accident that those who favor a policy can usually find evidence that the policy is a success. This is not to say that evaluation is always a sham. Rather, judgments can be reached in many different ways, and there is no single way that is universally accepted.

Check Your Understanding

1. What is process evaluation?

2. What are some of the disadvantages of impact evaluation?

3. What are some of the disadvantages of cost-benefit analysis?

4. Which type of policy evaluation is probably most often used?

5. What difficulties are involved in choosing the type of policy evaluation to use?

CHAPTER SUMMARY

What is public policy? Public policy is the government's response to a problem. This response can be stated in terms of the government's goals, the actual content of a program (laws, personnel, expenditures), or the impact of the program. Also, the line between private action and public policy is not always clear—some public decisions can be made by private citizens.

How is public policy made? Even though policies vary considerably, they follow a similar pattern. They first must be put on the government's agenda; the particular solution to a problem must be formulated; and the program must be implemented. Many key choices exist at each stage. Explanations of policy making include rational choice, incrementalism, group theory, and elite theory. No one explanation is completely valid.

How do we evaluate public policy? There is no single standard for deciding whether a policy is good or bad. It can be judged according to whether it meets proper standards of administration, whether it has accomplished its goal, whether benefits outweigh costs, or whether the results are consistent with an individual's values. Different criteria can produce different conclusions.

IMPORTANT TERMS

Explain the following terms.

power elite
policy agenda
implementation
rational choice approach
incrementalism
latent *or* potential groups

elite theory
process evaluation
impact evaluation
cost-benefit analysis
opportunity cost

THINKING CRITICALLY

1. What should the federal government do to attempt to resolve deeply rooted social and economic problems such as poverty and inequality? What role should private organizations and individuals have in helping to solve these problems?

2. Large corporations must often make choices with far-reaching public consequences. Do corporations have an obligation to the community in general? Why or why not? What might happen if a company's obligations to the community conflict with the interests of company stockholders?

3. Are there certain issues—for example, the religious views of citizens—that should never be on the public agenda? Explain your answer.

4. Periodically there are calls for a "government of experts, not politicians." Suppose choices in such areas as energy, environmental protection, and international trade were made entirely by experts instead of by political leaders. How might this affect our system of government?

5. Evaluation of public policy often requires that a price be put on the value of human life (for instance, a $1 million highway repair might save five lives per year; thus each life "costs" $40,000 in a five-year period). Is it useful to place a dollar value on human life in evaluating public policy? Would there be other ways of evaluating the worth of the highway repair program? Explain your answer.

6. What might be some of the consequences of allowing a public program to be handled by a private organization?

7. What is likely to happen when powerful interest groups take opposing positions on public policy?

EXTENDING YOUR UNDERSTANDING

1. Contact your local school board. What is the public policy on education in your community? What are the local school board's goals for supporting and improving education in the schools? Are there any other goals that you think should be included? Write a report on your conclusions.

2. Contact the local association representing lawyers or the association representing doctors. Describe the codes of ethics the organization sets for its members. How are these standards of professional behavior enforced? Are these codes in the best interest of the community or the state? Present your findings to the class.

3. Conduct an opinion poll among friends or family members about what issue(s) they would like to see placed on the public agenda in your community. Tabulate the results and present them to the class.

4. Attend a meeting of the local government that is deciding on the merits of a public policy. Which method—if any—of policy evaluation is used? What are the major points raised for and against the policy? Present your findings to the class.

MAKING DECISIONS

You are a member of a committee set up to analyze local problems. Choose a community problem that interests you. Prepare a report for your committee outlining the following: (a) How should the problem be defined? (b) What groups have become or should become involved in the issue? (c) What role, if any, should the local media play? (d) What standards should be used in evaluating a proposed solution to the problem? (e) What solution to the problem would you recommend?

Chapter 15
The Politics of Economic Policy

It was once customary to draw a sharp line between politics and economics. At one time the idea that economics and government were interrelated was deemed un-American. Even today, many people are unaware of the close connections between their jobs, the overall economy, and government action. Politics and economics are two separate departments in almost all universities. The fact is, however, that politics and economics in the United States have traditionally been closely intertwined. No economic decision is completely separated from politics. The value of the dollar, interest rates, the use of courts to enforce agreements, distinctions between private and public property, and the types of economic activities permitted ultimately come from political decisions. Moreover, some of the most heated political conflicts involve economics. In both the 1980 and 1984 presidential elections, the state of the economy was a central issue. Few issues can mobilize citizens to action so quickly as increased taxes or the elimination of their government aid. This chapter examines three important questions dealing with the relationship between politics and economics:

- How does the government affect the economy?
- How is economic policy made?
- Has the federal government become too involved in the economy?

PREVIEW

How does the government affect the economy?
First, the government influences the economy
through its policies to encourage economic development. Taxes and subsidies are a second source
of impact. Federal taxes take a large share of the
gross national product (GNP), and they can determine many noneconomic behaviors. Important
subsidies include cash payments, reduced tax liability, and low-cost loans. Regulations, a third
form of government involvement, not only affect
prices but also influence who can compete economically and what goods and services are available. Government consumption, or use, of goods
and services also plays a role, as does government
production of goods and services. All of these
activities can create controversy. Some current
debates involving the government's economic role
include the elimination of poverty, reducing inequalities of wealth, reindustrialization, deregulation, and control of waste in government.

How is economic policy made? Economic policy is made by a large number of people: the President, White House advisors, other executive
branch officials, the Federal Reserve Board, Congress, the private sector, and the general public.
The interaction among these participants is complex. In general, the process is decentralized, it is
characterized by conflict, and policy develops incrementally. How policy is evaluated depends on
the assessment standards used. The policy-making
process can be criticized or defended, depending
on what alternative is considered desirable and
possible. Policy makers face many problems. For
example, economic policy can conflict with noneconomic goals, events can be unpredictable, and
our knowledge of economics is inexact.

*Has the federal government become too involved
in the economy?* The government's extensive economic involvement has come under attack in the
last few years. Critics assert that individual freedom and economic efficiency would be increased
if government played only a limited role. This perspective has been critized for ignoring the power of
wealthy interests to dominate society unless they
are restricted by government. Moreover, history
shows that uncontrolled free enterprise can lead to
economic problems. The conflict between free
enterprise and government regulation, then, is not
easily solved.

HOW DOES THE GOVERNMENT AFFECT THE ECONOMY?

In contemporary society almost every government
action has economic consequences. Government
requirements that airplanes provide no-smoking
sections might reduce the income of North Carolina and Virginia tobacco farmers. When President Reagan decided to increase defense spending
sharply, he set off a whole chain of economic
events affecting nearly every industry and citizen.
We can distinguish among five different types of
government economic involvement: (1) economic
development, (2) taxes and subsidies, (3) regulation, (4) government consumption, and (5) government-owned enterprises.

Economic Development
Early Economic Activity
The obligation of the government to promote
economic development can be traced to pre-Revolutionary times. Colonial governments frequently used tax incentives, government loans,
land grants, and monopolies to encourage prosperity. Part of the government's early commitment to
the economy was spelled out in the Constitution.
In Article I, Section 8, Congress is given the right
to coin money and to regulate commerce, to
establish post offices, to punish counterfeiting,
and to issue patents and copyrights to protect
inventors and authors. Section 9 of Article I also
encouraged growth by prohibiting taxes on exports
and preventing laws that give one port preference
over another. As we noted in Chapter 2, a major
impetus for drafting the Constitution was an ailing
economy created in part by rivalries among the
states and a weak central government incapable of
maintaining order.

The most important contribution to economic
development made by the national government

during the early Republic was to provide a stable and orderly commercial environment. Without a recognized system of money, enforceable laws regulating business transactions, a workable credit structure, and freedom from banditry and piracy, the economy would have been reduced to primitive local barter.

Once the basic political framework for a developing economy had been established, federal and state governments turned to more ambitious proposals. At the urging of Secretary of the Treasury Alexander Hamilton, the federal government instituted **tariffs**—taxes on imports—designed to protect newly created industries from foreign competition. Many states made major financial commitments to build bridges, roads, harbors, reservoirs, and railroads, all of which are necessary to economic development. Between 1815 and 1860, for example, more than $136 million was invested in canals. Some, like the famous Erie Canal in New York (which cost $7.1 million), were spectacular successes. Others, like the $16.5-million Pennsylvania Main Line Canal, were complete failures. To encourage the building of a transcontinental system, the national government gave the railroad companies 131 million acres of land (and

the states contributed 48 million more). A strong steamship industry was also promoted.

Another important, economically related factor was the development of free public education. Partly as a result of business demands for skilled, literate help in the late nineteenth century, state and local governments sharply increased their spending on education. In 1862 the federal government, through the Morrill Act, provided states with nearly eleven million acres of land for the support of colleges (the so-called **land-grant colleges**) to teach engineering, agriculture, and home economics. This was just the beginning of federal support for higher education. Land-grant universities have produced thousands of trained personnel essential to our economy.

Modern Government Economic Assistance

Almost every contemporary business enterprise owes some debt to the government for financial and technical assistance. For example, the independent family farm reaps enormous benefits from government-sponsored agricultural research, networks of government-paid county agents, and government-funded interstate highways and waterways that allow national distribution of prod-

In the nineteenth century, the railroad became a familiar sight as the federal government encouraged the development of transportation. Railroads helped promote industrialization and the settlement of the West.

ucts. Many of the commodities that made American agriculture so successful were originally designed and tested in state-supported experimental stations. The benefits of such research are usually given free as part of government's contribution to the general welfare.

Another industry that would not have survived without the encouragement of government during the lean years is the airlines. To get airlines started, the federal government provided extensive subsidies for airmail service. Much of the airlines' expenses, such as for airport facilities, navigation assistance, weather reporting, pilot training, and the design of new equipment, were heavily underwritten by government. Today the federal government bears a major portion of the start-up cost for such endeavors as solar energy, the extraction of minerals from the sea, satellite communications, and numerous other expensive technologies.

The government also plays a vigorous role in helping American businesses overseas. For example, the government has pressured the Japanese into opening their domestic markets to American industry. Foreign aid frequently is used to encourage consumption of American goods and services (in providing money for highways, the government may specify that the construction equipment must be purchased in the United States). The tax system provides financial incentives for American businesses to operate abroad. In some instances, U.S. military force has been deployed to open markets, to install governments sympathetic to American business interests, or to prevent foreign takeovers of American-owned assets (see Chapter 16).

The *principle* that government ought to create an environment permitting economic development has widespread support. In *practice*, however, the distinction between contributing to overall economic well-being and giving an unfair advantage to a special interest is not always clear. Consider the Jones Act of 1920, which required that all commerce between U.S. ports must travel in American ships built in American shipyards. Was the government simply "helping" American shippers and shipbuilders in the same way that it helped in the building of roads and canals? Or as

some critics believe, has the Jones Act resulted in higher shipping costs while preserving obsolete transportation and construction techniques? Would our economy benefit if our merchant fleet and shipbuilding capacity all but disappeared because of cheaper foreign competition?

Economic Development and Economic Equality

That the national government has a responsibility for promoting economic development is widely accepted, although analysts might disagree about the precise role of government in this area (for example, should the government subsidize research conducted by private firms?). A much more controversial issue is the distribution of economic benefits. If the government helps to enlarge the economic pie, should it also have a role in deciding who gets which slice of the pie? This distributive question has two separate, though related, aspects: (1) inequalities of wealth and (2) the persistence of poverty. Let us consider what these issues are and how government has dealt with them.

Economic Inequality. "Economic inequality" basically refers to the gap between the haves and the have-nots. Because some degree of inequality exists in all economic systems—even in Communist systems committed to equality—the real question is the extent of inequality. A society in which 10 percent of the population has $1 million each and the rest have $1,000 is obviously more unequal than one in which the top 10 percent has $100,000 each and everyone else $10,000. Economists have devised several measures of economic inequality, but most involve the proportion of wealth owned by the very rich compared to the proportion possessed by the less well-off. In other words, do a few very wealthy people own most of what there is to own?

Table 15.1 shows one indication of inequality—the proportion of all assets held by the wealthiest 1 percent of the population. In 1976 this group owned 18.3 percent of all assets. Much of the wealth stemmed from ownership of corporate stocks, bonds, and instruments, or means of

Government agricultural research increases soil productivity and enriches the nation's food supply.

dent Kennedy, Johnson's War on Poverty, and subsequent proposals have not been Robin Hood schemes to tax the rich for the benefit of the poor.

Perhaps the most important reason for the persistence of economic inequality is the public's acceptance of it. When George McGovern, the 1972 Democratic presidential candidate, suggested a guaranteed income for the poor to be financed by heavier taxes on the rich, the idea outraged the public and contributed to his overwhelming defeat by President Nixon. Most Americans tolerate inequality as unavoidable and even desirable. As James Tobin, a leading economist, put it: "Americans accept and approve a large measure of inequality; the differential earnings of effort, skill, foresight, and enterprise are seen as deserved, just so long as the earnings are legitimately and fairly won. Even lucky winnings are sanctioned by most Americans."[1]

Poverty. The second factor in government efforts to shape the distribution of economic benefits is poverty. The central question is what the government should do about those unable to support

collecting, debts, such as mortgages. Although the proportion of assets owned by the top 1 percent might appear to be very high, in the last several decades the figure has declined. Indeed, during the 1920s and 1930s, the top 1 percent owned about 30 percent of all personal wealth. Between 1962 and 1976, stock and bond ownership became somewhat more evenly distributed among the population. In 1962, for example, the top 1 percent owned 62.4 percent of all stocks; in 1976, only 46.0 percent.

In many respects, the existence of substantial inequalities of wealth has been a "nonissue" politically. Some aspects of the tax system—the income tax and inheritance taxes in particular—serve to reduce extreme inequality. The goal of tax policy, however, generally has not been to redistribute the nation's assets. In fact, the tax system has sometimes been accused of doing just the opposite: preserving the status quo by providing an unfair advantage to the wealthy through numerous loopholes and preferential tax treatments. When Presidents address economic inequality, they focus on the plight of the less fortunate, not the overall distribution of wealth. The job training and regional development programs offered by Presi-

---

Proportion of All Personal Wealth Held by Richest 1 Percent, 1976

Total Assets	18.3%*
Real estate	12.6
Corporate stock	46.0
Bonds	29.8
Cash	10.9
Debt instruments	36.9
Liabilities	14.2
Net worth	19.2

*The wealthiest 1 percent of the population possesses 18.3 percent of all assets. In a perfectly equal society, this group would possess only 1 percent of all assets.

Source: Statistical Abstract of the United States, 1984, p. 481.

TABLE 15.1

themselves and their families. This is a different issue from economic equality. Enormous variations in wealth can coexist with a policy of lavish benefits for the poor; conversely, perfect equality exists if everyone is equally poor.

Public policy toward the poor has undergone numerous changes. In the colonial period, counties sometimes provided minimal assistance to the needy, but the poor pretty much had to depend on themselves or relatives. Many localities "solved" poverty by escorting poor people out of the area. The almshouse—a government-run farm or factory employing the able-bodied poor—was also common. The nineteenth century saw the emergence of numerous private organizations dedicated to eliminating poverty: the Society for the Prevention of Pauperism and the Society for the Improvement of the Condition of the Poor, among others. Many believed that poverty could be overcome by religious education, abstinence from alcohol, and greater morality among the poor. Public responsibility for the poor continued to be minimal—programs were local and were directed at the incapacitated and, perhaps, at those suffering temporary misfortune.

A dramatic shift in policies toward poverty occurred during the Great Depression of the 1930s. Local government and private charitable groups were overwhelmed by the human suffering caused by economic collapse (in 1932 one in every four workers was unemployed). The Social Security Act, passed in 1935 as part of the Roosevelt New Deal, provided compulsory retirement insurance, assistance to the elderly, and aid to dependent children. The original goals and commitment were modest, because economic problems were viewed as temporary. Nevertheless, assistance to the less fortunate grew substantially in scope and size. Today there are government programs to help the blind, disabled or unemployed workers, and the medically needy, and to provide subsidized food, housing, and education. States and localities also have general assistance programs for those ineligible for more specialized federal aid programs.

Table 15.2 shows the rising cost of social welfare programs at all levels of government. Between 1960 and 1982 these expenditures increased by more than 1,000 percent. Even taking into account inflation and population growth, the rise is substantial. Several programs in particular have shown dramatic increases. Between 1971 and 1983, for example, expenditures for Medicare— the federally funded medical assistance program for the elderly—jumped from $7.5 billion to $48.4 billion. The cost of the Social Security pro-

Social Welfare Expenditures for All Governments, 1960–82	Year	Total (Billions)	Percent of GNP*	Percent of All Government Outlays	Per Capita in 1982 Dollars
	1960	52.3	10.3	38.4	$ 815
	1965	77.2	11.2	42.2	1,040
	1970	145.9	14.7	48.2	1,550
	1975	290.1	18.7	57.4	2,174
	1980	492.5	18.7	57.6	2,450
	1982 (preliminary)	594.4	19.4	55.7	2,527

*GNP = Gross national product, or total value of all goods and services produced in a year.

Source: Adapted from Tables 595 and 596, *Statistical Abstract of the United States, 1986,* p. 356.

TABLE 15.2

In the United States, victims of poverty include migrant farm workers, the neglected elderly, children in urban slums, and the homeless in many of the nation's cities.

gram overall rose from $34.2 billion in 1971 to $150.3 billion in 1983. Clearly, the government's commitment to help its citizens is a far cry from the past policy of giving minimal aid and preaching self-reliance.

Nevertheless, despite the vast expenditures for health care, food, shelter, education, and vocational training, poverty has not disappeared. In 1964 the federal government developed a **poverty index,** a measure of poverty based on a family's minimum needs. The index is adjusted regularly

to reflect changing prices. In 1984, for instance, the poverty line for a nonfarm family of four was $10,609 (the cash value of government benefits, such as free medical care, is not included). This means that a family whose income was below $10,609 was classified as being "poor." Table 15.3 shows some of the changes that have occurred in poverty between 1972 and 1984. The most obvious fact is that poverty still exists in large numbers. Moreover, there has not been a steady decline in poverty since 1959. Between 1959 and the early

Persons Below Poverty Level, by Race 1972–84			Race*		
	Year	Percent Below Poverty Level	White	Black	Hispanic
	1972	11.9	9.0	33.3	22.8
	1975	12.3	9.7	31.3	26.9
	1980	13.0	10.2	32.5	25.7
	1982	15.0	12.0	35.6	29.9
	1983	15.3	12.2	35.7	28.1
	1984	14.4	11.5	33.8	28.4

*These figures indicate for each race the percentage of individuals below the poverty line.

Source: *Statistical Abstract of the United States, 1986,* p. 457.

TABLE 15.3

1970s, the proportion of the population below the poverty level was cut in half. However, the decline then leveled off; with the economic slowdown of the late 1970s, poverty began to increase.

Perhaps equally striking about these data are the differences among whites, blacks, and Hispanics. Note that in 1984 the proportion of blacks below the poverty line was nearly triple the rate for whites (33.8 percent versus 11.5 percent). Similarly, the poverty rate for Hispanics was much higher than for whites. Indeed, since the mid-1960s, and despite antipoverty programs and numerous antidiscrimination laws, 30 percent or more of blacks continue to remain below the poverty line. Black poverty is especially pronounced in the South. In 1979 the proportion of blacks below the poverty line was 42.7 percent in Arkansas and 44.4 percent in Mississippi.

Conclusions

To return to the original question of government's role in the distribution of economic benefits, our discussion of equality and poverty clearly shows that government efforts, though successful in some areas, have not resulted in uniformly high levels of prosperity. Government economic assistance programs have been directed at almost all citizens, but the results have been mixed.

Taxes and Subsidies

A second important way the national government plays a direct economic role is through tax and subsidy policies—which involve far more than just taking money from some people and giving it to others. Taxes and subsidies can be a powerful influence on how people work, where they live, what they eat, how they travel, and nearly every other aspect of their lives. For most citizens, taxes and subsidies represent the most obvious and direct way the government affects their economic status. Let us begin by considering the impact of taxes.

Taxes

It is sometimes said that if the colonists thought that taxation without representation was bad, they should see taxation *with* representation. In fiscal 1982 the national government collected a total of $632 billion in taxes.

Types of Taxes. The largest single source of federal tax revenue is the individual income tax. When originally instituted in 1913, the federal income tax had a very low maximum rate (2 percent) and applied only to comparatively wealthy citizens (less than one-half of one percent had to file a return). Things have changed dramatically since

Commentary: Corporate Perks

As we noted in Chapter 11, the Internal Revenue Service—the nation's tax-collecting agency—has, generally speaking, been one of the more successful of the government's bureaucracies. Most citizens are reasonably honest in filling out their tax forms. At the same time, the IRS has a variety of means of enforcement at its disposal—of making sure that citizens pay what they owe. For instance, salary earned each year and the taxes the employer has withheld on that salary are reported to the IRS on the W-2 form.

Some areas of tax collecting may give the IRS a particular headache, however. One such area involves what are known as "perks." The word is short for "perquisites"—benefits or privileges associated with a certain type of job. In addition to handsome salaries, many corporate executives and other high-income people receive company-paid perks. Such benefits often enable employees to live much better than their salaries alone would allow. Here are some of the most common perks enjoyed by corporate employees:

- Season boxes for sporting events and free theater tickets
- Free trips on company planes to resorts
- Company-paid country club memberships
- Free use of company-maintained vacation homes
- Free use of company-maintained swimming pools, tennis courts, squash courts, and other recreational facilities
- Subsidized meals in company dining rooms.
- Free residences and hotel accommodations

By law, perks used for non-business purposes are taxable as income. For instance, time spent around a conference table at a company-owned country club discussing profit and loss is obviously business-related; time spent on the golf course or at the swimming pool would probably be considered nonbusiness—unless it was claimed that the employees talked shop as they swung their golf clubs or sat by the swimming pool.

Employers are required to report nonbusiness perks, generally on Form 1099, for what is called miscellaneous income—that is, not salary income. Companies may disregard the reporting requirement, however, because they can then deduct the entire cost of the perk as a business expense—thus reducing their own tax burden.

The problem may be one of enforcement. It is often difficult for the IRS to monitor the non-business use of company perks. Until the IRS sets up more strict reporting procedures, perks may continue to be a special tax privilege of the well-off.

---

then. In 1982, over 170 million individual tax returns were filed. The Treasury Department has estimated that in 1977 the American public spent some 613 million hours filling out various tax forms.

There are two important principles governing the individual income tax. The first is that the rate of taxation on personal income is **progressive**—the higher the income, the greater the proportion of income that goes to taxes. Millionaires are not only supposed to pay more money in taxes; they are also supposed to pay a greater proportion of their income in taxes. In 1982, for example, the effective tax rate for a single person earning $5,000 was 4.3 percent; for a person earning $75,000 it was 34.3 percent. Some taxes—for example, sales taxes—are called **regressive** because the proportion (but not necessarily the amount) of money going to taxes generally declines as income increases. That is, the lower your income, the greater the proportion of your total income you pay in taxes.

The second important principle is that taxes are adjusted to individual circumstances. Two people earning identical incomes do not always pay identical income taxes. Allowances are made for family size, age, medical expenses, charitable contributions, occupationally related expenses, and so on. Although the "individualization" of income taxes is widely accepted in principle, a number of allowances have been criticized as loopholes favoring the rich. We shall have more to say about this question.

A second type of taxation is the payroll tax. Like the personal income tax, it is usually subtracted from paychecks. There are several kinds of payroll taxes, with Social Security being the most important (other payroll taxes include unemployment compensation and various railroad-related programs). In 1982, payroll taxes generated $168.7 billion in federal revenue, making them the second most important source of federal revenue. The Social Security program, the largest of the payroll taxes, is paid by both the employee and the employer. When initially enacted in 1935, Social Security was designed to operate like private insurance—that is, eventual benefits were tied to previous contributions. However, because of the massive increase in the cost of benefits, Social Security now is simply a government program that transfers money from one group of citizens (those currently working), to another (those who are retired).

The third most important source of federal tax revenue is the corporate income tax. In 1982, corporate taxes contributed $65 billion to the federal treasury. Like the personal income tax, the corporate tax is computed on all income after deductions for various necessary expenses (salaries, equipment, rent, advertising, and so on). However, the rate of corporate taxation is much less progressive. Although the tax is substantial, economists are divided on who ultimately pays the tax bill. Some argue that it is merely passed along through higher prices to consumers. Others claim that a corporation's shareholders bear the burden, and still others assert that it is the corporation itself. The evidence so far remains inconclusive.

The last type of tax we shall describe is the **excise tax.** The federal government collects either a flat fee or a percentage every time a particular item or service is purchased. It is basically a selective **sales tax.** The most familiar excise taxes are on alcohol, gasoline, tobacco, and telephone service Overall, in 1982, $22.5 billion was raised through excise taxes. In general, this type of tax is regressive.

Administering Taxes. The billions of dollars raised through taxation can be generated in several ways. To paraphrase a well-known expression concerning cats, there are many ways to skin a taxpayer. Several European governments, for example, use the **value-added tax (VAT)**—a sales tax charged on a commodity at each stage of manufacture. It is a regressive tax whose real cost is hidden in higher purchase prices. Most states and communities rely more heavily on regressive property and sales taxes. There has been considerable talk of replacing the progressive income tax with a **flat tax**—a single tax rate for all income groups, with minimal adjustments for individual differences.

Equally important, the government has a great deal of leeway in how the various taxes will be administered. Although Congress and the President might agree that a progressive income tax is preferable to an excise tax, the actual operation of the income tax can be controversial. Decisions on tax rates, the legal definition of "income," what constitutes a legitimate business expense, when taxes must be paid, and dozens of similar questions are major political issues. Seemingly technical matters can have enormous financial consequences. For example, a persistent tax-related question is, "What is a business?" Until a few years ago people who worked at other jobs but who owned a few horses might declare themselves a horse-farming business and legally deduct all horse-related expenses from their personal incomes. Congress eventually decided that the government should not give such generous tax benefits to leisure-time farmers and required that to be a genuine business, one must follow certain guidelines, such as occasionally showing a profit.

Tax regulations can also motivate certain types of behavior. The interest paid on home mortgages and real estate taxes are deductible from income and therefore reduce the amount of money on which taxes are paid. Thus part of a monthly mort-

Local offices of the Internal Revenue Service offer assistance to taxpayers in completing their tax forms.

gage payment and local tax bill is "refunded" through tax benefits. However, if you pay rent, there is no such "refund," even though a portion of your rent goes to pay the landlord's interest and tax bill on the property. A $500-a-month house payment is therefore less expensive than a $500-a-month rent payment. Not surprisingly, then, many Americans have made large investments in private homes.

The Need for Tax Reform. Although everybody acknowledges government's need for money, hardly anybody likes the idea of paying taxes. On the whole, especially compared with citizens of many other nations, Americans do pay their taxes. Beginning in the mid-1970s, however, taxpayers began to grumble about sharp increases in taxes at all levels of government. For example, between 1965 and 1975, total tax revenue collected by states went from $26 billion to $80 billion; in 1983, the figure was $171 billion. Although tax rates at the national level have generally remained fairly constant, **inflation** (the process by which the value of the dollar drops and prices go up) during this period forced people into higher and higher

tax brackets—the percent of income they pay in taxes. As inflation increased, wages and salaries were raised so that workers could afford the higher costs of goods and services. Raises in salary, however, pushed taxpayers into higher tax brackets. Thus their taxes went up but their *spending power,* or ability to pay for the goods and services they needed, remained about the same. This process is called *bracket creep.* For example, in 1970 the average federal personal (as distinct from business) income tax was $1,415; by 1981 the figure had risen to $3,703. A 1976 CBS/*New York Times* poll asked people how they felt about the fairness of the tax system; 7 percent said it was fair and 38 percent said "reasonably fair," but 55 percent characterized it as unfair.[2] A 1985 *Washington Post*/ABC News poll showed similar sentiment: 72 percent felt that it was unfair to working people; 61 percent said taxes were too high.[3]

These feelings soon found expression in political action. Beginning with California's Proposition 13 in 1978, several states allowed residents to vote on measures to put ceilings, or maximums, on state and local taxes. Antitax groups, such as the National Taxpayers Union and the National

Biography: Andrew Carnegie

Few business leaders have exemplified the American rags-to-riches legend as dramatically as Andrew Carnegie. His climb from factory laborer earning $1.20 a week to steel tycoon with an annual income of $12 million was one of the most spectacular in an era of unrestrained economic development. In their rise to power, men like Carnegie—the so-called robber barons—used unscrupulous tactics that aroused public concern and eventually resulted in government regulation of business.

Carnegie, born in Scotland in 1835, immigrated to Pennsylvania with his family when he was twelve. The Carnegies were poor, and Andrew immediately went to work as a bobbin boy in a cotton factory. The progress of his career was rapid, for his small body (his height never exceeded 5 feet 3 inches) housed a burning ambition. He went on to get a job as a telegraph operator and then moved on to become the personal secretary of a Pennsylvania Railroad executive. After the Civil War, Carnegie made small but shrewd investments in varied enterprises: Pullman cars, railroad stock, bridges, and oil derricks. His investments paid off well in a time of tremendous industrial expansion.

In the 1870s Carnegie began to concentrate his energies on the steel industry, which he soon came to dominate. Among the reasons for his success in the steel industry were his insistence on the latest technology and a constant

effort to lower production costs. It was in order to achieve the latter goal that Carnegie pioneered the idea of vertical integration—that is, controlling all the steps in a manufacturing process. Thus Carnegie Steel bought iron mines in Minnesota, operated freighters on the Great Lakes, and turned out finished steel products in Pennsylvania.

Carnegie did not hesitate to use the standard business methods of his day in order to gain an ever bigger share of the steel market. With the railroads he arranged rebates—secret deals whereby Carnegie Steel shipments were charged lower rates than those offered the general public. With other steel manufacturers he agreed, when it suited him, on

various price-fixing tactics. He strongly opposed unions and condoned the violence used to break a strike at his Homestead steel plant in 1892.

In some ways, however, Carnegie was a maverick among the robber barons. He realized that unrestrained competition might well ruin the economy, and he believed that government action was a necessary counterbalance. He shocked the business world when, in response to labor's efforts to win an eight-hour day, he stated that "I believe we shall have more and more occasion for the state to legislate on behalf of workers." The federal government did indeed begin regulatory efforts with the establishment of the Interstate Commerce Commission in 1892, although many years were to pass before controls were effective.

Carnegie was also unusual in his determination to give away as much of his wealth as he could, believing it to be the obligation of the rich to assist the poor. In 1901 he sold Carnegie Steel to the newly formed United States Steel Corporation and devoted the rest of his life to philanthropy. By the time of his death, in 1919, he had given more than $350 million to, among other organizations, the Carnegie Endowment for International Peace, the Carnegie Foundation for the Advancement of Teaching, the Tuskegee Institute, and over 2,500 public libraries in the United States, Canada, and Great Britain.

Tax Limitation Committee, attracted many new members and publicity. In the 1980 presidential election, both Carter and Reagan acknowledged the need to reduce the burden of taxation, though they disagreed on how much was to be cut and on who should benefit the most.

Approaches to Tax Reform. Several approaches to tax reform have attracted a degree of support. One proposal endorsed by President Reagan and many others was the **balanced budget amendment,** the goal of which is to attack the source of higher taxes—higher and higher expenditures financed by the government's enormous borrowing power. Basically, this proposed amendment to the Constitution would (1) require Congress to adopt a balanced budget each year (revenue would match expenses), (2) allow a deficit only if approved by a three-fifths vote of Congress, and (3) prohibit Congress from raising the national debt or increasing revenue without raising taxes. These limits could be suspended only during a war. Supporters of the proposal believe that it would prevent the nation from running up huge deficits that ultimately must be paid off by the taxpayers. No longer would future generations be burdened with huge interest payments on the national debt or with tax increases to finance expensive but initially underfunded programs. Opponents of the balanced budget amendment argue that it would hinder the government's freedom of action unnecessarily and that a determined Congress could find ways to get around it (for example, by exaggerating revenue estimates).

A second tax reform measure with significant political appeal is **indexing,** which is basically a response to higher taxes resulting from bracket creep. In other words, because of the progressive tax rate, a person whose income doubles over a period of time simply through inflation will experience a disproportionate tax increase (in 1983 a single person who earned $10,000 had an effective tax rate of 9.5 percent; if income went to $20,000 because of inflation, the tax rate would jump to 15.4 percent). Bracket creep even provides government with an incentive to promote inflation and run up deficits: pumping more money into the economy by authorizing new programs will cause inflation, inflation will result in higher tax brackets for citizens, and the increase in revenue will pay for the new programs, so the program is really "free." Under indexing, taxable income is adjusted to eliminate inflationary increases. If your income goes from $10,000 to $15,000 as a result of inflation, the percentage of your income that you pay in taxes will remain the same. Like the balanced budget amendment, indexing is viewed as a way of promoting tax reform by limiting government involvement in various programs, especially domestic social programs.

A third, and perhaps the most popular, approach to tax reform focuses on the provisions of the existing tax code. It is incremental in character and concentrates on such factors as what business expenses can be deducted, what constitutes taxable income, and the like. When President Reagan, following his 1984 reelection, called tax reform one of his administration's highest priorities, he had this type of reform in mind. In October 1986, after months of intense political debate over numerous proposals and counterproposals, the President signed the Tax Reform Act of 1986 into law. Before we take a look at some of its key provisions, we will examine the general problems of enacting tax reform.

General Problems of Tax Reform. Almost any attempt to reform taxes faces serious problems. First, an existing system will always have defenders who see reform as a threat to their livelihoods. This problem is well illustrated by the 1986 Tax Reform Act. One of the aims of this law was to eliminate many **tax shelters**—investments intended primarily to reduce taxes owed rather than to produce income. Abolishing tax shelters, though, could put numerous bankers, accountants, lawyers, stockbrokers, and other professionals out of work. However, in response to the Tax Reform Act, these financial experts might simply devise new strategies. For example, interest on car loans is no longer deductible from income. To make up for this loss, banks can call the loan a second mortgage. The interest on that type of loan remains deductible. In actual practice, therefore,

Under the 1986 Tax Reform Act, credit card interest payments will no longer be deductible. Consumers may be less inclined to use credit cards in making major purchases, like this stereo system.

the tax reform is partially defeated by those, such as banks, who benefit from high levels of consumer borrowing.

Second, because the government's need for revenue will remain high, any tax reform that does not include expenditure reductions will impose new and heavier burdens on some taxpayers. Thus citizens might favor reform in the abstract but oppose all reforms that might harm them personally.

A third obstacle to tax reform is that people often disagree on what—besides raising revenue—a tax system is supposed to accomplish. Some believe that the most important goal is a fair distribution of burdens. In particular, the less fortunate should have a much lighter tax burden than the wealthy. Others stress the role of the tax system in encouraging economic growth. To accomplish this objective, businesses receive tax breaks to promote investment in new facilities. The incentives might be so favorable that a huge corporation pays less federal tax than a single poor family. Disagreements also arise on the tradeoff between simplicity and flexibility. A 25-percent flat tax plan with no deductions, exemptions, or tax credits might save taxpayers the hardship of filing numerous technical forms, but its very rigidity can penalize those

with special circumstances (for example, those with large families or exceptionally high medical expenses). Simplicity and fairness are not identical.

Finally, any tax reform proposal must address the problem of implementation. Sufficient revenue must be raised at the lowest possible cost and in a politically acceptable way. These goals are not always easy to accomplish. For example, a tax on assets—as opposed to income—might encourage people to undervalue their homes, cars, stocks, and the like. To ensure sufficient revenue collection, a small army of inspectors might have to check up on citizens. Hence, even if a tax on assets were a good idea in principle, it might be an unworkable, unacceptable idea in practice. Attempts to close loopholes and punish abuses often have implementation problems. How, for example, can the Internal Revenue Service know for sure that millions of meals and trips are legitimate business expenses rather than personal expenditures? Verification would be very costly and would be likely to outrage most citizens (the same citizens who oppose loopholes).

The Tax Reform Act of 1986. The Tax Reform Act of 1986 had two general objectives. First, the tax rate structure on personal income was greatly simplified. The fourteen different rates were reduced to two—15 percent and 28 percent. Second, several steps were taken to reduce or eliminate tax abuses and inequalities under the old system. A much lower top bracket (28 percent instead of the former 50 percent) would reduce the incentive to invest in tax shelters. The tax advantages enjoyed by investors in stocks, bonds, and similar assets was reduced substantially by abolishing lower taxes on **capital gains** income—that is, profit from buying and selling various types of property. In addition, the share of the total tax burden paid by corporations was increased under the legislation.

The Tax Reform Act of 1986 was a landmark bill, but talk of tax reform has not ended. Even as President Reagan signed the legislation, plans were being made to correct widely acknowledged technical errors that could not be resolved in last-minute legislative–executive negotiations. No doubt, major economic groups will continue to press for other changes if present policy proves harmful to their interests. Future events also could contribute to a reworking of the 1986 law. A growing deficit, for example, might require the maximum rate of 28 percent to be increased substantially. In sum, this tax reform is hardly a permanent cure for our tax problems.

Subsidies

The federal government both gives and takes away. Through taxation it takes and through subsidies it gives. A **subsidy** is economic assistance provided by the government in return for some specific economic behavior—either taking positive action (for example, a company hires inner-city youths) or not taking certain action (for example, a farmer doesn't plant soybeans).

Types of Subsidy Programs. Subsidy programs take several forms. The most obvious is direct cash payments or free services. Under the government's Payment in Kind (PIK) program, for example, farmers were paid not to produce crops. The program was justified on the grounds that if farmers planted all they could, the market would be glutted, the government would have to buy and store

much of the excess, and the resulting economic problems would be far more expensive than payments to limit production. Other government subsidy programs include payments to people to enroll in job training, free health care, and government-supplied transportation. The government has tried to encourage train travel by giving subsidies to Amtrak to keep fares low. Many municipal bus services also receive federal funds.

A second common form of subsidy is a reduction in taxes due. If the government wanted to encourage the construction of middle-income housing, for example, it might reduce taxes for companies that build reasonably priced apartments. These **tax expenditures,** as they are called, cost the government far more than gifts of money or services. In 1984, for example, the government lost $25 billion in revenue because of deductions of interest payments on home mortgages. Another $49.7 billion was lost by the exclusion of certain kinds of pensions from taxable income.

A third method of providing subsidies is to lend money at below-market interest rates or to guarantee loans made by private financial institutions. The primary beneficiaries of low-interest, long-term financing by the government are students, the elderly, and the poor. In 1984, for example, the federal government guaranteed some 3.4 million student loans. Another 680,000 students received direct low-interest government loans. Other pro-grams involve loans to farmers and agriculture-related facilities, such as schools, resource-conservation programs, and recreational facilities.

Reindustrialization. In the mid-1980s, a new subsidy-related issue received widespread public debate: **reindustrialization.** Basically, reindustrialization entails extensive cooperation between private businesses and government to revitalize American industries that have become less competitive in world markets. Reindustrialization would be directed at industries such as steel and automobile plants, shipbuilding, and other so-called mature or sundown industries. Reinvigoration would be accomplished by low-interest government loans, tax benefits for modernization,

A welder works on parts piled in a bin, left; assembly line operators fit tires onto tractors, right. Reindustrialization would be aimed at assisting the nation's less-competitive firms.

relaxation of some restrictive regulations, government subsidies for retraining workers and developing new production techniques, and import restrictions to provide temporary protection of home markets. In effect, the federal government would mobilize its vast financial resources to subsidize and reestablish world leadership for American manufacturers. Reindustrialization would be particularly attractive to the Northeast and upper Midwest (sometimes called the "Rustbelt"), where older, less efficient heavy industry has been hurt by foreign competition.

Like almost all government assistance programs, reindustrialization has generated sharp controversy. Its defenders assert that the United States merely would be doing what is standard operating procedure in Japan and much of Europe. That is, Japanese automakers receive generous government aid that allows them to sell cheaply in the United States (for example, Japa-

nese automakers are financially integrated with banks in ways that would violate U.S. monopoly laws). Moreover, reindustrialization investments would pay handsome dividends in future tax revenue, and in the long run, would be cheaper than continued unemployment insurance programs, public welfare, and other financial and human costs associated with economic stagnation. Building products in the United States also would help reduce the huge **trade deficit**—a negative dollar difference between the value of exported and imported goods. That is, more money leaves the country (to buy foreign goods) than enters the country (as foreigners purchase American goods or invest here). Finally, without a reindustrialization policy the United States would soon become heavily dependent on overseas suppliers for many vital industrial products. This could prove disastrous in wartime or even peacetime, if U.S. relations with an important industrial supplier

In Mexico, where labor is cheaper, young women assemble a TV set. The parts were made in America and the finished product will be sold in the United States.

worsened (this happened in 1973, when Middle Eastern oil-producing countries placed an embargo on oil exports to the United States).

Many people remain unconvinced of the need for massive government aid for declining industry. Political conservatives, in particular, believe that a reindustrialization plan administered by Congress would become a huge pork-barrel project used for political purposes, not economic development. In other words, grants, subsidized loans, technological assistance, and so on would be dispensed like new post office buildings, dams, and other goodies, whose real purpose is to ensure reelection of the incumbent (see Chapter 9). Conservatives say that private businesses and the free market system are better judges of where scarce resources should be invested. If it really makes sense to modernize steel mills in Youngstown, Ohio, private industry will do it. A much more basic criticism of reindustrialization is that it would redirect investment away from growth industries into declining industries that are going to die sooner or later. The billions spent on rebuilding an antiquated shipyard would be better invested in computer technology or perfecting solar energy. Rather than try to compete with foreign steel plants, government should focus on future industrial development, critics suggest,

Under the Reagan administration, reindustrialization has been kept off the political agenda. Nevertheless, it has several prominent supporters, especially within the Democratic party. It might emerge as a major response to a variety of economic problems, such as chronic unemployment, continued trade deficits, and revenue shortages in some states.

Regulation

A third means by which the government affects the economy is through regulation (see Chapter 11 for more on regulation). In some instances a regulation's impact is highly visible—for example, rules limiting interest rates on savings accounts. In most cases, however, the impact is less obvious— for example, safety standards that raise the price of microwave ovens. Issuing rules and regulations can often be an alternative to taxation, subsidies, or other government mechanisms for controlling economic behavior. Consider the problem of automobile safety. The current approach emphasizes numerous government regulations and standards. Another approach might be to place a high tax on unsafe cars to force them out of existence. Or government could provide a subsidy to manufacturers of safe automobiles—safe cars would be cheaper and therefore more popular. Still another approach would be for government itself to build and sell safer cars.

Federal economic regulations have always existed, but until recently they were usually fairly general. The nineteenth-century government coined money, set standard weights and measures, and provided certain minimal banking procedures but stopped well short of telling people how to run their businesses. Beginning in 1887, with the creation of the Interstate Commerce Commission (ICC), which was designed to monitor railroad rates, the federal government has played a more vigorous regulatory role. The ICC was followed by a number of other regulatory agencies—for example, the Federal Trade Commission (FTC), which, like the ICC, regulates specific industries. Since the mid-1960s, several new government regulatory agencies have been created. Unlike the ICC, FTC, and other agencies that regulate specific industries, new agencies, such as the Consumer Product Safety Commission and the Environmental Protection Agency (EPA), can involve themselves in a wide range of economic activities (the growth of government regulatory agencies is described more fully in Chapter 11).

Economic Impact of Government Regulation

One obvious economic impact of regulation concerns the goods and services available to the public. The Food and Drug Administration (FDA), in particular, has played a vigorous role in removing unclean and dangerous products from the market. The elimination of cyclamates from diet soft drinks and red dye number 2 from food was undertaken by the FDA. The Consumer Product Safety Commission has taken off the market items ranging from unsafe toys to chromosome-damaging aerosol adhesive sprays.

A related impact of regulation concerns what business people may and may not do. The Federal government in the 1970s and 1980s took steps to deregulate the transportation industry. Even so, entry into such businesses as trucking, air travel, railroads, and bus service remains restricted, and many rates are still regulated. Government restrictions also exist in banking, the stock and bond markets, television and radio, and most other fields. Government regulation may cover every phase of a business. For instance, builders must obey rules regarding land use, techniques of construction, and a project's environmental impact.

Like many industries, the railroads are regulated by the government, which may set rates and determine which companies can operate lines.

Once a facility is in operation, there are rules regarding worker safety, nondiscrimination in hiring, minimum wages and overtime, and pension plans. Packages must be properly labeled; products must meet fire and safety standards and must be sold according to federal laws dealing with fair competition. The financial operation of the business must conform to numerous complex rules.

Government regulations can add substantially to the cost of products (and increased costs have effects on investments, inflation, and employment). The best-known, but not the only, example of this process occurred in the automobile industry as a result of safety and antipollution requirements. Between 1968 and 1974, the addition of seat belts, head restraints, exhaust controls, and the like added $350 to the price of the average car. In 1974, the total cost of required equipment was $3 billion. The addition of the catalytic converter in 1975 raised costs even further. Recalls mandated by the Environmental Protection Agency or the National Highway Safety Administration also have become more expensive. According to noted economist Murray L. Weidenbaum, the cost of federal regulations in 1981 was more than $100 billion.[4]

Regulation and President Reagan

In 1980 Ronald Reagan campaigned on a program of "getting the government off the backs of the American people." He and his aides have made a major effort to reverse the growth in regulation (both President Ford and President Carter, however, had pressed for deregulation in some industries). As a first step, some 172 last-minute Carter regulations were delayed for further review and many were eventually toned down or dropped entirely. To head many regulatory departments, the President appointed people with a clear distaste for government intervention (for example, James Watt, Secretary of the Interior, once headed a prodevelopment group and had often sued the Interior Department over its regulatory policies). People with business backgrounds were named to such regulatory bodies as the Securities and Exchange Commission, the National Traffic Safety Administration, and the Occupational Safety and Health Administration. Major deregulation occurred in banking, intercity bus service, and telecommunications (for example, new rules encouraged the creation of numerous long-distance telephone companies).

Perhaps the strongest attempt to reduce regulation involved the reduction of enforcement personnel. For example, the EPA referred far fewer actions to the Justice Department for prosecution. The EPA enforcement section itself was abolished and its duties assigned to several offices. Federal regulatory inspectors made fewer visits and were instructed to work more closely with industry. Overall, between 1980 and 1984, the number of federal employees enforcing economic regulation declined by 11 percent (compared to an increase of 34 percent between 1970 and 1980). In 1983 the Task Force on Regulatory Relief, created by the President in 1981, declared itself a success, said it had saved American consumers $150 billion over the next ten years, and disbanded.

These efforts, however, did not signify the end of government regulation of the economy. At best, the President's program slowed a long-term trend. As we noted in Chapter 11, Reagan was only partially successful. Strong pressures to keep many of the regulations emerged in Congress, among the general public, and even within the agencies themselves. Several vocal opponents of regulation were forced to resign, and funds cut by the President were restored by Congress. The deregulation of natural gas, a priority goal of the Reagan program, was slowed considerably by public fears of higher heating costs. The courts also acted to limit deregulation. For example, in 1983 the Supreme Court held that the National Highway Transportation and Safety Administration could not eliminate a regulation requiring air bags or automatic seat belts on cars. Many businesses also had second thoughts about deregulation. Some, like many transportation companies, feared the possibility of unrestrained competition. Others, such as the drug and chemical industries, were worried that each of the fifty states would impose its own separate rules. Despite some publicized changes, then, most of the regulations set up before Reagan took office remain in effect.

Government Consumption of Goods and Services

The government itself is the number one spender in the economy. In fiscal 1983 the federal government had budget outlays of $803 billion, which bought a good many paper clips, rubber bands, atomic-powered aircraft carriers, supersonic jet fighters, and much more. Many industries, especially in national defense, exist solely to sell products and services to the government. The extent to which government purchases affect the economy sometimes staggers the imagination. For example, the Polaris missile carried in submarines involved some *thirty thousand* contractors and subcontractors in its development and production. Putting Neil Armstrong on the moon took three hundred thousand workers in forty-eight states. The survival of many communities depends on government purchases or government payrolls.

Government purchases are, however, far more than just another set of orders for goods or services. Because of its size and power, the government can have a much broader economic impact. Companies doing business with the government have often been required to pursue some noneconomic policy, such as banning racial discrimination in hiring, buying goods made by the blind, or establishing facilities in areas of high unemployment. During the Vietnam war, defense contractors were prohibited from using ships that had visited Cuban or North Vietnamese ports. The purpose of this policy was to make it difficult for these two Communist nations to engage in commerce. The government's considerable leeway in many of its purchases can generate intense political conflict. For example, between 1965 and 1970, the United Farm Workers union, led by César Chávez, called for a nationwide boycott of California grapes. Under pressure from grape growers, the Defense Department, however, decided that soldiers needed more grapes and thus bought up large quantities of the boycotted fruit.

The impact of government purchasing power can be more subtle—and more widespread. It has been claimed, for example, that large government outlays for defense materials can substantially affect almost every aspect of the economy. One claim is that such purchases encourage inflation. In particular, because defense items are not sold to the public, income produced by defense spending is used to buy other goods and services. Put somewhat differently, defense products—tanks, guns, and so on—create income but no goods for this income to purchase. The imbalance between available money and things to buy causes prices to rise. A second claim is that because the government is willing to pay top dollar for personnel and materials, prices are artificially bid up on nondefense items. Why should a good engineer settle for a $40,000-a-year job at an automobile company when a defense contractor can offer $60,000? Also, outlays for defense drain away money that otherwise might be spent on education, rebuilding industry, improving transportation, lowering taxes, and other important endeavors. It should be noted, however, that people disagree considerably over the size and impact of military spending, and many would say that huge defense expenditures are essential to national security.

Finally, an important, but not well-known, government purchasing program involves U.S. stockpiles of strategic materials. Beginning in 1946, the government began buying goods to ensure that we would be prepared in case of a one-year war fought simultaneously in Europe and Southeast Asia. These large-scale reserves include such commodities as chrome, industrial diamonds, silver, tin, tungsten, jewel bearings, and feathers. In 1982 the government had stockpiled some 137,506 ounces of silver with a market value of $1.4 billion. When the government buys and sells the stockpiled items, it can affect the prices of many key industrial goods.

Government-Owned Enterprises

Besides setting economic policy for private industry, the federal government itself operates many businesses. In fact, in several instances the government competes directly with private industry. For example, the national government owns millions of acres of forest and sells timber from the land. Large quantities of government land are also

In a deficit economy, outlays for military equipment may necessitate cutbacks in civilian goods and services, such as commuter and freight transportation.

leased or lent free for grazing and mining. What the government charges for its timber can help determine what lumber companies charge for their products. Even more important, the government competes with private industry in the credit market. When the government offers bonds at, say, 10 percent interest, private companies will have to pay higher rates, because government bonds are considered the least risky investments.

Most government-owned enterprises are organized as special agencies or corporations to perform certain tasks. The best-known and largest is the U.S. Postal Service, which had more than 682,000 employees in 1984. Several companies, such as United Parcel Service (UPS) and Federal Express, compete with the Postal Service, but thanks to various court rulings, the Postal Service has maintained its monopoly on the direct delivery of first-class mail. Another well-known government corporation is the Tennessee Valley Authority (TVA), which sells electricity to cities and industries in the Tennessee River basin.

In agriculture, the Commodity Credit Corporation and the Federal Crop Insurance Corporation provide services ranging from grain-storage facilities to farm loans. Housing is another area of government business involvement. Many citizens have been able to buy homes because the Federal Housing Administration guaranteed their mortgages. In transportation, the government operates the Panama Canal, the St. Lawrence Seaway (jointly owned with Canada), and various other waterways. Through COMSAT, the government, in conjunction with private companies, runs a communications satellite system.

These government enterprises can have consequences well beyond their immediate activities. Postal rates, for example, can spell life or death to magazine publishers and mail-order companies. Similarly, the Federal Housing Administration's policies have had a far-reaching impact on the construction and real estate industries.

Periodically, government's competition with private industry becomes an issue on the public agenda. Many businesses—for example, power and insurance—would benefit considerably if Washington left things to private enterprise. Some conservatives say that government ownership of businesses could lead to socialism. Perhaps the strongest case against government competition with private industry focuses on the inefficiency and costliness of government. The most recent example of this view was a report published in 1984 by the President's Private Sector Survey on Cost Containment (popularly known as the Grace Commission after its head, J. Peter Grace). Here are just a few of hundreds of comparisons:

- In managing building space, the General Services Administration spends 17 times as much as private industry.
- The Veterans Administration (VA) spends $61,250 to construct a bed in a nursing home, compared to $16,000 in private nursing homes.
- The VA spends $140 to process a claim for hospital insurance, compared to $3 to $6 in private industry.

Government facilities like this generating plant supply low-cost electricity to millions.

Such findings lead to the conclusion that the government should turn over many of its activities to the private sector. For instance, a local real estate agency, not the General Services Administration, could manage government buildings. If government enterprises are not turned over to private companies, they at least should be run in accordance with good business practices. Businesslike procedures, argued the Grace Commission, could save the government $424 billion over a three-year period.

This theme was stated strongly in the federal budget President Reagan prepared for 1987. The call for "privatization" was rooted not only in the President's conservative economic philosophy but also in the government's need to raise more revenue. Proposals included selling off naval petroleum reserves to the highest bidder, phasing out government involvement in crop insurance, and stepping up substantially the sale of surplus government property, as well as having private industry take over the railroad business, the marketing of electrical power, and numerous loan programs. Thus far, however, these proposals have had little concrete success.

The case against government competition with private industry has much truth to it, but there are limits. First, the government's goal is often to provide goods and services to a group regardless of cost. The VA, for example, offers quality medical care to the poor and the elderly, a group frequently shunned by "for profit" hospitals. This policy makes the VA look "cost-ineffective." Second, private industry rarely has to face powerful political pressures in making economic choices. When the Postal Service wants to eliminate thousands of inefficient rural post offices, the outcry is intense and members of Congress defend the waste. Third, the government's business decisions must frequently be made differently from those made by, say, an automobile company. To ensure fairness, reduce the possibility of corruption, provide uniform standards, and accomplish noneconomic goals, such as encouraging minority-owned businesses, government operates slowly and with a great deal of paperwork. A government worker needing a new typewriter cannot pick one up at a discount store during lunch hour; because of paperwork, overhead, and other procurement costs, the typewriter the government buys may end up costing five times as much as the discount store's machine. Finally, the annual appropriations process in Congress does not facilitate the long-term planning necessary for cost effectiveness. In private companies, for example, a huge investment in computers now might save money in the future. In the government, however, capital (long-term) budgets and operating budgets (day-to-day expenses) are combined; therefore, a big computer purchase might be delayed in order to maintain adequate funds for ongoing programs. This approach, it should be noted, is consistent with the general policy of annual control of agency expenditures rather than allowing agencies to tie up resources well into the future.

Perspective

Our analysis of government's involvement in the economy has revealed several points. Obviously, government has a profound and extensive impact, even though private enterprise maintains a high degree of independence. Tax rates, subsidy programs, regulations, and so on influence prices, marketplace availability, and competition. Second, although the goals of this involvement generally are accepted, the particulars can generate intense political conflict. We all agree on the need for taxes, but what type of tax? Who should pay it? How will it be administered? Rarely are there simple, clear-cut answers. Every alternative has pluses and minuses. Finally, many of the decisions we make are rooted in personal values. A person who wants government to eliminate poverty, reduce inequalities in wealth, provide subsidies to students, and operate hospitals rarely considers the economic merit of these desires. It is more common for economic analysis to be used as a justification for pursuing noneconomic goals than for noneconomic goals to be determined strictly by scientific economic reasoning. We shall have more to say on this point at the end of the chapter.

HOW IS ECONOMIC POLICY MADE?

The making of economic policy in the United States is complex. There is no Ministry of Economics with the power to decide all matters affecting business and industry. Indeed, it often appears that nobody is making economic policy. It more or less emerges from the interaction of thousands of officials, businesses, and citizens. Our description must therefore be fairly general. Let us begin by considering some of the major participants in the policy-making process.

Participants in Economic Policy-Making

The President

The President is probably the single most important person in setting government economic pol-

icy. Shaping policy is a traditional presidential role that goes back to Washington's support for Alexander Hamilton's plans to promote industry. All Presidents have put their own stamp on economic policy. Some Presidents, like Eisenhower, emphasized maintenance of the economic status quo. Others, such as Franklin D. Roosevelt, saw the presidency as a force for dramatic economic change. The New Deal established new regulatory agencies, vigorously enforced antitrust laws, and created programs, such as Social Security and the TVA. President Reagan has emphasized deregulation and cutbacks in government spending for social services.

The formulation and administration of economic policy involves several advisors and agencies within the Executive Office of the President. An important potential source of information is the Council of Economic Advisors (CEA). The CEA was created in 1946 and consists of three

If government revenue and spending are equal, the result, is a balanced budget.

members appointed by the President and confirmed by the Senate, plus a staff of about thirty-five. The CEA makes forecasts, collects and analyzes economic information, and prepares reports. The professional economists who are appointed to the CEA share the President's overall philosophy. In general, the CEA seems to have its greatest influence at the early stages of policy formation— providing expertise on alternatives, describing possible consequences of different policies, establishing reachable goals, and so on. The precise role of the CEA depends on the personalities of its members and the inclinations of the President.

A second important source of economic advice is the Office of Management and Budget (OMB). Basically, the OMB assists the President in preparing the national budget and coordinating administrative agencies within the executive branch. Especially in recent years, the director of the OMB has played a major role in allocating resources for different programs. When President Reagan decided to cut spending for social welfare programs, it was David Stockman, then director of the OMB, who made key decisions on just which programs to cut and by how much. As with the CEA, the precise influence of the OMB depends on personal relationships with the President.

Presidents have also created temporary groups to help develop economic policy. For example, in his first term President Nixon formed a Cabinet Committee on Economic Policy that included himself, the Vice president, several Cabinet secretaries, and other top officials. President Carter established the Economic Policy Group, co-chaired by the Secretary of the Treasury and the chairperson of the Council of Economic Advisors. The Reagan alternative has been the Council on Economic Affairs. Not only has the membership of these groups varied somewhat from President to President, but each, in addition, has had a somewhat different role, depending on such factors as the personalities of the members, the importance of economic issues, and the power of other agencies.

It is important to realize that the formulation of economic policy might not correspond to official, formal procedures. As noted in Chapter 10, each

President has several close personal aides, who offer advice on almost all subjects. President Reagan, for example, often relied on the advice of James A. Baker III, his chief of staff. When Baker was appointed in 1985 to head the Treasury Department, his economic advisory role became official.

Cabinet-Level Departments

Even though in principle each department in the executive branch is under presidential direction, the departments typically have their own economic responsibilities and perspectives, as well as a degree of independence. Of particular importance is the Treasury Department, which collects taxes, manages the national debt, controls the currency, and administers our international financial affairs. The Secretary of the Treasury also can provide the President with advice on a wide range of domestic and foreign economic matters.

The Department of Commerce, which is responsible for promoting economic growth, international trade, and technological development, is another important Cabinet-level participant. Commerce officials deal with small businesses, consumer affairs, trade policy, and so on. Each of the other Cabinet departments has a major voice in economic policy. Decisions by the Defense Department to seek expensive new weapons systems can affect tax policy and employment. The Justice Department's Antitrust Division influences patterns of business activity by preventing anti-competition practices.

The Federal Reserve Board

The Federal Reserve system was established in 1913 to act as the nation's central bank. It sets lending and investing guidelines for banks and handles many government financial dealings, especially the selling of government bonds and other securities to raise revenue. The "Fed" (as it is commonly called) is headed by a Board of Governors composed of seven members appointed by the President subject to Senate confirmation. One member serves as chair for four years. Terms are fourteen years and members cannot be removed by the President. In principle, the Fed is supposed to act independently to promote the overall public economic interest. The Fed's independence is further enhanced by the fact that it is self-supporting financially (its deposits in private banks earn interest).

The Fed possesses powerful tools to regulate the economy. Through its *open-market operation* it buys and sells government securities to regulate the supply of money in the economy. For example, if it sells a security for $1 million, there is $1 million less available in the economy to buy goods and services. The Fed also lends money to banks, and the interest rate charged—called the **rediscount rate**—greatly influences the availability of credit. When banks can borrow cheaply from the Fed, consumers can more easily finance homes, cars, and appliances. The amount of money available for loans is also governed by the Fed's reserve requirement—the cash that banks must keep on hand for customer withdrawals. Increasing the reserve requirement leaves less money for banks to lend. Management of the supply of money and credit is generally referred to as **monetary policy**,

whose overall goal is to promote a healthy, growing economy. If, for example, inflation occurs because too much money is chasing a limited supply of goods, the Fed might raise its rediscount rate, increase bank reserve requirements, and otherwise restrict the supply of money (a "tight" money policy). If the economy slows down too much, the restrictions can be relaxed (a "loose" money policy).

Independent Agencies

Important economic decisions are made by a number of independent regulatory agencies. For example, the Securities and Exchange Commission (SEC) broadly regulates trading in securities that deals with other business practices. SEC regulations can help determine stock prices and the ability of companies to raise capital, or money for investment. The Interstate Commerce Commission has regulatory powers over transportation. Because transportation expenses are part of the cost of almost all goods, ICC decisions can have far-reaching consequences. The Federal Trade

Behind the ornate facade of the New York Stock Exchange, the trading is fast-paced. The securities market is regulated by the SEC.

Commission is concerned principally with maintaining free and open competition as well as with protecting the public from deceptive trade practices. Other independent regulatory agencies deal with energy prices, banking, and labor practices.

As with the Federal Reserve Board, members of these commissions have a degree of independence. Though appointed by the President, subject to Senate confirmation, they serve for long terms and cannot be removed by the White House.

Congress

Congress is probably second only to the President in influencing economic policy. The Constitution gives Congress three important economic powers: the power to tax, the power to spend, and the power to borrow. There is perhaps no aspect of the economy that is beyond the reach of congressional authority.

However, whereas the President and White House advisors usually share a common perspective, members of Congress might not all see eye to eye on money matters. Recall from our analysis of Congress in Chapter 9 that in both houses there is an absence of strong leadership and a diversity of perspectives. Moreover, the committee and subcommittee system means that a general policy, such as management of the economy, is handled by several groups of legislators all eager to protect their own jurisdictions. For the most part, tax policy is made in two committees—the Ways and Means Committee in the House and the Senate Finance Committee. Their activities help determine the funds available, but they do not decide on expenditures. Each legislative chamber also has an Appropriations Committee responsible for allocating funds to the various government programs. Since 1974 and the passage of the Congressional Budget and Impoundment Act, there have also been separate House and Senate Budget Committees, which examine and reevaluate the President's proposed budget, and keep track of the relationship between future tax revenue and present financial commitments. Each of these six committees (and several subcommittees) has a significant, and somewhat different, voice in overall economic policy making. (This process is more fully developed in Chapter 9.)

Besides its direct control over taxing and spending, Congress makes other types of decisions with far-ranging economic implications. For example, Congress may set up **entitlement programs,** whose beneficiaries have a legal claim to benefits regardless of the amount of money available for the programs. Social Security and Medicare are well-known entitlement programs whose large costs have resulted in higher taxes and government borrowing. Congress also sometimes allows government agencies to make long-term contracts even if no money has been appropriated to meet such contracts. The practice of allowing certain agencies to borrow also obligates the government well into the future. In fiscal 1982 various federal agencies had some $5 billion in loans outstanding (in addition to regular Treasury borrowing).

The Private Sector

As we saw in Chapter 1, the United States has a mixed economy. Even though government is deeply involved in the economy, private enterprise maintains considerable freedom. The tens of thousands of economic decisions made by corporate officers, union officials, and business people in general help determine economic policy. An automobile company, not a government agency, decides how many automobiles to produce, how much to sell them for, where they will be manufactured, and where they will be sold. The government, of course, has some say in these decisions, but the company can take steps to resist government intervention. As our analysis of economic interest groups in Chapter 8 showed, businesses spend considerable time and money trying to influence government. Equally important, there is strong public support for the tradition of limited government involvement in regulating the conduct of private business.

Private economic decisions obviously influence overall economic policy. The federal government can rarely command the private sector, although it might try to use indirect methods of persuasion. If, for example, private industry refuses to invest in inner-city housing, the government might create a policy of tax incentives and spending programs to meet this need. Private industry still might refuse to invest. It would be unthinkable to pass a law requiring such investment. Decisions made by oil and gas companies will certainly have consequences in government regulation of energy prices. Government might want to influence these choices, but it cannot force the issue. Actions taken by private firms can also impose great costs on the government that it sometimes might be powerless to control. If a company closes its U.S. factory and moves overseas, government expenditures for unemployment benefits will probably increase, producing higher taxes, deficits, or cutbacks in other areas.

The General Public

Ordinary citizens obviously do not make economic policy in the same sense as, say, the chair of the Federal Reserve Board. Nevertheless, the public does play a vital role. Clearly, widespread public support for certain policies—low rates of inflation and economic growth, among others—is a factor in the decisions made by public officials. The voting public provides a powerful motivation for members of Congress and the President to seek acceptable solutions to economic problems. Considerable evidence suggests that the desire for reelection guides many political choices affecting the economy.

Citizens as consumers of goods and services also influence economic policy making. The public's fondness for Japanese cars, for example, has forced the U.S. government to negotiate import restrictions with the Japanese to protect American companies. As more Americans purchase Toyotas and Hondas, the U.S. trade deficit worsens, affecting policies ranging from subsidizing exports to maintaining the value of the dollar in international trading. In the early 1980s the government began to consider seriously the deregulation of the banking industry, largely because millions of Americans had withdrawn funds from banks during the period of high inflation in the late 1970s (banks could not offer more than 5.25 percent interest when the inflation rate was above 10 per-

cent). Only when banks were able to offer higher interest rates did funds return to banks.

Interaction Among Participants

It is evident that a large number of institutions, groups, and individuals are involved in creating economic policy. How do these participants interact? Does one individual or coalition dominate?

Decision Making Is Decentralized

One important characteristic of economic policy making is that it is decentralized. No single individual, institution, or comprehensive plan dictates overall policy. Decentralization is present at every step of the process. Consider the creation of the agenda following President Reagan's victory in 1980. In numerous public statements Reagan stressed economic growth, deregulation, less reliance on government, and greater involvement of private industry in solving the nation's problems. Despite his victory, however, the President could not impose his agenda completely or for a lengthy period as *the* national economic agenda. A number of groups and their congressional allies continued to push for generous government help to the needy and for extensive regulation, while some prominent Democrats promoted a policy of reindustrialization. Following his 1984 reelection, President Reagan again found his priorities—especially reductions in social spending—competing with those offered by members of Congress (for example, cutbacks in military spending).

Decentralization also characterizes the formulation of solutions. We can see how the process works by examining how the problem of inadequate funding for Social Security has been handled. Because of the growing number of elderly citizens, the soaring costs of benefits and insufficient revenue, the system faced a crisis beginning in the 1970s. Congress, the President, various agencies, the states, and numerous groups (senior citizens, doctors, insurance companies) all had a major stake in the outcome. A National Commission on Social Security Reform was created. Proposed solutions have run into the dozens—reducing benefits, raising the retirement age, including federal employees in the system, funding the program out of general revenue, and so on. Although everybody agreed that something had to be done to prevent the system's financial collapse, no one plan satisfied everyone. Eventually, only modest changes—not a fundamental reorganization—were acceptable to all parties.

Implementation of the nation's economic policy is also decentralized and even occasionally uncoordinated. This is most apparent in the complex relationship between fiscal and monetary policy. **Fiscal policy** is the use of the national budget to regulate the economy. By adjusting taxes, expenditures, and borrowing, the President and Congress can smooth out the ups and downs of the business cycle (the alteration of upswings and downswings in economic activity) and encourage a strong, stable economy. Monetary policy, as we discussed previously, involves the supply of money and credit and is established by the Federal Reserve Board. In many instances, the Board of Governors of the Fed have not seen eye to eye with the President and Congress. In both the Nixon and Carter administrations, for example, the Fed pursued a tight money policy while fiscal policies encouraged easy money. Disputes have also occurred under Reagan.

Another important decentralizing factor is that the government cannot usually command private industry to invest or change its prices. A key element of the early Reagan economic policy was to encourage industrial growth through tax incentives and more rapid **depreciation,** or tax deductions for old business equipment. The goal was to facilitate the purchase of new production equipment, to create manufacturing jobs and promote greater consumption through reduced prices. Although appropriate legislation was passed, many businesses did not use these incentives in the way government had intended. In particular, they believed that low consumer demand did not warrant expansion. Instead, tax incentives were frequently used to reduce corporate taxes while adding nothing to industrial capacity.

Decision Making is Marked by Conflict

Not only are important decisions made by different groups of people, but these decisions are typically characterized by conflict. A major source of conflict stems from differing perspectives. For ex-

Industrial modernization doesn't necessarily mean new jobs—at least not for humans. Here, robots work on an automobile assembly line.

ample, the President usually views economic choices in terms of fairly short-range political considerations—how they will affect reelection, whether they are acceptable to political allies, and so on. The chair of the Council of Economic Advisors, on the other hand, generally offers professionally oriented economic advice, even if it is politically unpopular. Meanwhile, key members of Congress might be under pressure to satisfy important economic interests in their districts. The executive departments themselves often disagree. The Secretary of the Treasury represents the opinions of financial institutions, but the Secretary of Labor worries that help to banks might harm workers who borrow.

Moreover, these conflicts are almost continuous, because no one group has the power to impose its will permanently. A victory is almost always short-lived. In recent years, for example, the Treasury announced that banks would be required to withhold a percentage of bank-deposit interest in order to ensure compliance with the tax law. Before the new rule could go into effect, however, intense lobbying from banks forced it to be canceled. Our political system encourages groups to keep fighting even if they lose a particular battle. After all, in a year or two the composition of Congress might be different, or a new person might be in the White House. Sometimes a change of one or two votes in a congressional committee can turn defeat into victory.

Policy Is Made Incrementally

Although there are occasional exceptions, economic policy generally is made incrementally. Existing policies are the basis of new policies, and changes are relatively small. Over several decades, policies can shift dramatically, but in the short run changes tend to be modest.

There are many reasons why change occurs incrementally. We have already mentioned that no one group or perspective is able to dominate. As a result, policies come into being through lengthy bargaining and compromises, not commands. A President wanting private industry to hold the line on prices might use what has been called **jawboning**—persuasion based on appeals to

the public good—rather than using laws that would impose controls. Fiscal policy in particular is incremental because it is shaped by several different congressional committees and executive branch agencies.

A second reason for incrementalism is that almost every existing economic policy has strong support. A drastic change, therefore, must overcome built-in resistance. For example, some argue that the policy of allowing interest on loans to be deducted from taxable income promotes inflation, discourages savings, and has other negative consequences. This provision of the tax code is unlikely to be altered, however, because it is defended by many industries. Real estate firms, the lumber industry, contractors, and banks all have a strong stake in the deductibility of interest on home mortgages. When President Reagan proposed an almost complete elimination of subsidies to farmers, in 1985, there was an enormous outcry from farmers and agricultural groups. The influence of groups protecting the status quo is reinforced by the bias against change built into the system—a group needs only to win in one or two key congressional committees to succeed in blocking change (see Chapter 9).

The absence of a widely accepted, comprehensive solution to economic problems also produces incrementalism. Public officials, professional economists, business people, and citizens differ in how they think economic problems, such as high unemployment or a large trade imbalance, are to be treated. According to the British economist John Maynard Keynes (1883–1946), for example, unemployment can be controlled by increasing government spending to stimulate economic growth. If too high levels of employment lead to inflation, higher taxes would "cool" the economy. Though the Keynesian approach has enjoyed wide popularity and respect since the 1930s, it has recently been challenged by those who view the money supply as the key element. Monetarists—economists who emphasize the importance of the money supply in the economy—would ease credit restrictions and increase the supply of money in circulation to stimulate the economy. Each of these two perspectives has many variations endorsed by reputable analysts. Neither one, however, dominates. The upshot of this lack of consensus is caution. Although a particular philosophy might offer a drastic response to a problem, only the few people who completely accept the philosophy would take the risk. Even if the President heavily promoted one viewpoint, it is unlikely that everyone would go along. Policy is therefore a cautious blend of differing approaches.

Finally, the interrelated nature of economic policy means that the pursuit of any one goal must be balanced against other goals. A policy that emphasized growth and nothing else would soon generate inflationary pressures. To respond to these pressures, growth might have to be slowed. In other words, a strong push in one direction can generate pulls in the opposite directions. The need to balance change so as to satisfy numerous economic objectives is well illustrated by President Reagan's attempts to slash federal taxes.

In 1978, two members of Congress—Jack Kemp (Republican of New York) and William Roth (Republican of Delaware)—proposed a 30-percent tax cut for everyone over a three-year period (corporate tax cuts were also proposed). The Kemp-Roth plan soon became official Republican policy, and following his 1981 inauguration, Reagan called for a 30-percent tax cut over three years, plus numerous tax cuts for businesses. Compared to past tax measures, this was a major change. The public and both Democrats and Republicans in Congress reacted with strong support. To ensure passage in the Democratic-controlled House, Reagan made several minor concessions—the cut was reduced to 25 percent over thirty-three months, benefits were extended to other groups, and promises of continued agricultural subsidies were made. The package passed by strong margins in both houses and was signed into law.

The tax cuts, plus sharply increased military spending, soon led to budget deficits. In fiscal 1980, for example, the budget deficit was $59.6 billion; by 1982 it had risen to $110.6 billion. Since deficits must be financed at high interest rates—over 10 percent—the new figures represented far more than a doubling of future obligations. The deficit grew even larger when the President was unsuccessful in persuading Congress to make drastic cuts in social welfare programs. The prospect of a $200-billion deficit in 1983 and 1984 convinced many tax cut supporters that Reagan's program had gone too far. Faced with widespread, vocal opposition as well as the possibility of even higher deficits, Reagan reversed his strong dislike of taxes. In 1982 the federal gasoline tax was raised and some corporate tax benefits were eliminated. In his 1984 proposed budget the President more or less admitted, when he proposed a standby 5-percent surtax on income, that the 1981 tax cuts had been too deep. Additional tax increases were proposed on oil. The President's call for massive increases in military spending were scaled back in the face of growing deficits. All in all, the dramatic 1981 cuts were reduced by competing demands. What started off as almost a revolutionary policy became, over a three-year period, a more modest though still substantial change.

Evaluating Economic Policy Making

Is the government doing a good job at making economic policy? This is a difficult question, because an answer depends both on what evaluation standard we are using and on what we believe constitutes a "good" job. Consider the process by which economic policy is made. It is easy to criticize it as fragmented and frequently marked by conflict. The President and Congress frequently are stalemated while pressing problems are ignored (for example, how to deal with deregulation of oil and natural gas). Numerous examples exist of executive agencies working at cross-purposes, while one committee of Congress is undoing the economic policy of another. Similarly, policies enacted by the government can be easily undermined by private industry and ordinary citizens (for example, by refusing to invest surplus income in economically productive activities). Obviously, the making of economic policy is not a coordinated, long-range process guided by an overall philosophy and set of objectives.

These characterizations do not necessarily mean, however, that the process can be substantially improved. Politically, it may be the best arrangement possible. Moreover, an alternative emphasizing central planning might not be an improvement. The American economy is far too complex to be run by a single, all-powerful agency. The failures of centralized planning in the Soviet Union are well known. Most important, a reorganization that, say, stripped Congress (or the White House) of most of its economic policy-making role would constitute a profound change in our system of government. Because the legislative and executive roles in the economy are rooted in the Constitution, greater centralization would run contrary to the principle of checks and balances. The use of coercion to implement a coordinated economic policy would also violate many traditional freedoms.

In evaluating the record of government policy makers, it is important to realize the problems that public officials face. The American economy is not like some giant machine with a detailed instruction manual and lots of controlling buttons and levers. Despite all our knowledge, events do not always go according to expectations. Consider, for example, the large budget deficits that emerged during President Reagan's first administration. These deficits led many economists and public officials to predict economic disaster. They believed that the government's need to borrow huge sums would "crowd out" private firms and individuals seeking credit. Interest rates would soar and industries that depend on credit—automobiles, home construction, appliances—would suffer. The resulting unemployment would reduce tax revenues, raise government welfare costs, and otherwise increase the deficit even more. As of 1987, this doomsday picture had not proved correct. Deficits continue to be large—about $200 billion per year—yet interest rates and unemployment levels generally have fallen since the early 1980s. Indeed, the period of the mid-1980s has been one of relative prosperity.

It should be noted also that public officials often reject a strict economic cost-benefit approach to policy making. A technically "good" economic choice might be rejected for any number of convincing reasons. A member of Congress might, for example, support an inefficient subsidy because its beneficiaries were important to his or her reelection. In Chapter 8 we saw that well-organized economic groups can defend themselves from attack even when their case is highly questionable. Even more important, humanitarian goals can sometimes override purely economic considerations. In the 1984 presidential election, for example, both Reagan and Mondale emphasized the needs of the elderly over the need to reduce growing budget deficit. Similarly, many political leaders believe that maintaining a strong national defense takes priority over sound economic policy making. What is the value of a healthy economy, they argue, if we cannot defend ourselves against Soviet aggression?

A final set of problems facing government officials concerns the unpredictability and uncontrollability of the world economy. U.S. economic policy is not made in a vacuum. Weather conditions in Europe and Asia can have a major impact on the demand for American agricultural products, and this has far-reaching consequences for American banks and heavy industry. Lower-cost manufacturing, especially in parts of Asia, has flooded the American market with less-expensive imports, a situation that will surely increase U.S. unemployment. Political events in a Middle Eastern nation can drastically affect the supply and price of oil. Even the wisest, best-informed, and most public-spirited leaders cannot anticipate and shape such events. At times, the best policy is the one that minimizes damage rather than increases benefits.

A different approach to evaluating economic policy making is to focus on the results. Here again, conclusions can vary. On the one hand, the United States has one of the most vigorous, productive economies in the world. The standard of living most citizens enjoy is high and will probably improve with time. Between 1970 and 1982, personal income rose 26.4 percent, even after inflation was taken into account. Between 1960 and 1982, the gross national product grew an average of 3.6 percent a year (and this figure does not include inflation). One-time luxuries—cars, indoor plumbing, telephones, refrigerators, and so on—are now taken for granted by most people.

Issues: Deficits and the National Debt

Since the early 1980s, a persistent and hotly debated issue has been the amount of money owed by the United States. Year after year, government expenditures exceed income, producing a *deficit* in the budget. Annual deficits in turn become part of the *national debt*—the total sum the United States owes. And as the debt increases, so does the cost, in interest payments, of borrowing more money and of repaying loans.

Many Americans probably see deficits and debt in terms of their own personal finances: it's as if the United States were experiencing the national equivalent of larger and larger bank loans, credit card charges, and end-of-the-month cash shortages. This parallel is somewhat simplistic and misleading, however. Indeed, the whole issue is surrounded by enormous complexities and serious disagreements. Let's consider some of these briefly.

How Big Are the Deficit and the Debt?

According to the Congressional Budget Office, the estimated deficit for 1987 was $174.5 billion. The total outstanding national debt at the end of 1986 was 2.2 trillion.

Although these numbers are huge, whether the deficit and debt are dangerously large is open to interpretation. The figures can be looked at in different ways. It could be argued, for instance, that the debt has merely kept up with the overall expansion of the econ-omy. The estimated total debt in late 1986 constituted about 50 percent of the gross national product (GNP). Although this figure was higher than the average for the 1970s, it was comparable to the 1960s average and lower than that for the 1950s.

Yearly budget deficits as a proportion of the GNP have grown since 1980. And, because of higher interest costs, the total debt is disproportionately expensive. In 1960, for example, interest on the national debt constituted 10 percent of all federal outlays; the figure was 18.1 percent in 1984. But again, this higher interest expense may be the temporary result of unusually high interest rates. The accounting methods by which the deficit has been calculated also help determine its size. All in all, evidence on the "how big" question is mixed. It depends on what standards are used.

Who Owns the Debt?

This is an important issue, although it has not received much public attention. In contrast to the national debt in Brazil, Argentina, Mexico, and many less-developed nations, the U.S. national debt is largely internal. In 1984, foreigners held only about 18 percent of it. This means that the money paid out in interest stays chiefly within the U.S. economy and is recycled. A person's interest income is taxed, and the remainder is spent on goods and services which, in turn, generate more taxable income.

Ownership of the debt is associated with the benefits and burdens of supporting it. Although small savings bonds continue to be issued to finance the debt, the government today relies on much larger types of borrowing by the public—$5,000 and $10,000 Treasury bills, for example. Portions of these can be purchased in various money market funds. In general, upper-income individuals tend to invest in the government debt and the interest income they receive is financed out of general revenue. In effect, this constitutes a transfer of wealth to the wealthier: taxes from the less well-off are routed to the well-off through interest on government securities.

Are the Debt and the Deficit Harmful?

This question is the most controversial. Many experts agree that the government *should* go into debt as a response to economic stagnation. Increased government spending, financed by borrowing, can be a cost-effective way of reducing unemployment, stimulating consumer demands, and otherwise creating a healthy economy—which will then produce enough tax revenue to pay for the previous borrowing. Likewise, agreement exists that heavy government borrowing during prosperity can be harmful: it promotes inflation and high interest rates, as industry and individuals must compete with the government for available dollars. It also deprives private industry of capital.

When it comes to assessing the situation in the late 1980s, there is less agreement. Some, like former Federal Reserve chairman Paul Volcker, see the huge deficit and debt as an economic time bomb. In a 1985 appearance before the Senate Budget Committee, Volcker argued that the deficit had attracted heavy foreign investment, which had strongly increased the value of the dollar. A strong dollar was causing a flood of cheap imports and severe difficulty for U.S. exports as well as a huge trade deficit. This situation, Volcker asserted, cannot last; we cannot continue to use money from Europe and Asia to keep the government running. This policy also deprives foreign economies of much-needed capital. Even if our prosperity survives, many have argued that we are maintaining ourselves by mortgaging the future.

The next generation may very well be spending all of its tax revenue to pay interest on past debt.

Other than securities dealers, who collect fees in financing the deficit, nobody advocates larger and larger deficits. But some people, like President Reagan, accept them as temporary measures that are the price to be paid for needed tax reductions and greater military spending. Eventually, according to this view, economic expansion will eliminate the yearly deficit by increasing tax revenue and reducing the need for many social welfare services. The overall national debt will also get smaller in comparison with an expanded economy.

Can the Debt and the Deficit Be Reduced?

Most deficit-reduction solutions call for cuts in federal spending. This is a very difficult solution to implement politically. Everyone wants somebody else's favorite programs cut, and existing programs almost always have strong support among interest groups and public officials. Sharp spending cuts might also cause economic hardship, which could eventually increase the deficit. For example, President Reagan repeatedly called for reduced farm subsidies as part of a reduction in federal spending. Agricultural leaders have asserted, however, that foreclosures, bankruptcies, and strain on social welfare would outweigh the savings. The government might even have to borrow to cover the cost of these "savings."

An alternative is to raise taxes. Several congressional leaders have proposed tax increases or at least tried to combine tax increases with cuts in federal spending. Opponents of tax increases not only stress their unpopularity but also assert that they are self-defeating. Higher taxes, they argue, will slow economic growth and thereby reduce tax revenue, further enlarging both the deficit and the debt.

A new administration in Washington, beginning in 1989, may make different political and economic choices from those dominating the Reagan presidency. Much of the debate surrounding the deficit and the debt is a matter of the policy preference. The decade of the 1990s will reveal what those priorities are.

The United States is a nation of contrasts—of inner-city slums and tidy suburban homes. Achieving economic equality would require commitment on the part of many Americans.

Problems such as inflation, unemployment, high interest rates, and shortages, are almost always short-term. Their effects are also cushioned by a wide variety of programs, such as unemployment insurance or food stamps. Even those who have not done well economically are probably better off than most of the world's peoples.

It is possible, however, to paint a different picture of the outcome of economic policy making. It could be argued that the present mixture of free markets and government intervention has failed to solve many important problems. In particular, many citizens—blacks, women, and certain rural people—have never really shared in prosperity (recall our earlier discussion of economic inequality). In addition, economic development historically has been built on cheap energy, abundant resources, a disregard of environmental damage, and exploitation of labor, conditions that no longer exist or are morally unacceptable. Economic success in the past has also depended heavily on regular disruptions in the world economy. For

example, the lingering effects of World War II in Europe and Asia contributed to America's prosperity in the 1950s. Finally, although the economy has provided citizens with many goods and services, the cost has been heavy: pollution, the waste of nonrenewable resources, a neglect of public facilities in favor of private consumption, and widespread labor dissatisfaction. Some might argue that the American economy has been built on artificial demand for more and more consumer goods of questionable value or usefulness. All in all, at best, the existing system has been adequate as a result of circumstances that might not continue.

Conclusions

To return to our original question of how economic policy is made, it should be clear that it is a complex process. Many people, groups, and institutions have some say, but nobody can impose a coherent, comprehensive policy. It is not surprising that policy often lacks coordination, conflicts regularly occur, and major problems are often dealt with piecemeal. The economy is not run in strict accordance with a specific philosophy. This situation is not easy to change, especially because it is almost a built-in feature of our constitutional system. Judged by its results, our system of economic policy making has had mixed results. It has produced greater prosperity, yet many problems remain—in particular, unequally distributed economic advantages and an inability to maintain prosperity without causing pollution, unemployment, and, sometimes, inflation.

Check Your Understanding

1. What are some sources of advice available to the President on economic policy making?

2. What agencies in the executive branch play a role in making economic policy?

3. How does Congress exert an influence over economic policy?

4. How do private sector and consumer choices affect the making of economic policy?

5. In what way is economic policy making decentralized?

6. Why is there conflict when economic decisions are made?

7. What problems do officials face in planning economic policy?

HAS THE FEDERAL GOVERNMENT BECOME TOO INVOLVED IN THE ECONOMY?

Despite the controversy surrounding economic policy making, most national political leaders ac-cept the principle of fairly significant government involvement. Controversies generally concern the amount and type of involvement, not involvement itself. For example, a President faced with a high level of unemployment might debate whether to spend more to create public jobs, lower taxes to increase purchasing, or pressure the Fed to pump more money into the economy. It would be a mistake, however, to conclude that extensive government economic involvement goes completely unchallenged. A long and distinguished intellectual tradition asserts that when government meddles in the economy, the ultimate result is economic ruin and loss of personal freedom. Especially in recent years, as the federal government has shown less ability to achieve its economic objectives, this position has received more attention. Let us briefly consider the arguments made by one of the best-known critics of government economic intervention, Milton Friedman.

Milton Friedman received the Nobel Prize in Economics in 1976.

Friedman's Economic Philosophy

According to Friedman, the most important element in politics and economics is individual freedom. For Friedman, the ability to do what one wants to do, subject to minimal restrictions (for example, laws against killing other people), is more important than any other value, including social equality or prosperity. However, he strongly rejects **anarchy**—the absence of all formal government. Government is essential if a free society is to exist. The major problem, according to Friedman, is how to maintain freedom while having a government strong enough to enforce the laws and provide essential services.

Limiting Government

The problem of controlling government is resolved in several ways. One is to limit severely the scope of government action. Government exists only to perform functions that citizens acting independently cannot perform themselves—maintaining national defense, keeping law and order, enforcing agreements between private individuals, fostering competitive markets, and collecting taxes to maintain public facilities, such as roads. The government, according to Friedman, should not tell a citizen how to live, what to eat, or otherwise interfere with individual freedom.

A second important way to balance government power with individual freedom is to spread the power of government as widely as possible. Specifically, political power is better concentrated at the local rather than the state level, and in turn, state political power is preferable to concentration at the national level. Friedman argues that if local government becomes oppressive, you can always leave. The same is true at the state level—if you don't like the politics of New York, you can always move to New Jersey. If you don't like the policies made in Washington, D.C., however, your freedom to choose is much more limited.

Capitalism and Freedom

Up to this point, much of Friedman's analysis is not very different from some of the principles found in the Constitution. What arouses controversy is the next step in Friedman's analysis. It is his linking of individual freedom to a particular economic system—**competitive capitalism.** Friedman defines competitive capitalism as a system in which exchanges are voluntary for all participants and people are informed in their actions. If you and your parents, freely and knowingly, agree that you may use the family car on Saturday in exchange for mowing the grass, you are operating under a system of competitive capitalism. Friedman argues that without competitive capitalism there can be *no* freedom, although the mere existence of competitive capitalism does not guarantee individual freedom.

Capitalism and freedom are linked in the following two ways. First, the economic freedom provided by capitalism is a crucial liberty in and of itself. You are not free, according to Friedman, if the government can determine such things as your conditions of employment or what you may purchase. Second, capitalism separates political and economical power, so that one can offset the other. In a capitalist system, you can hold antigovernment views or otherwise unpopular opinions, yet because the government does not control the economy, you can still find employment. Moreover, in a competitive system, characteristics such as political opinion, race, religion, sex, and the like are irrelevant to transactions. In fact, Friedman argues that historically there has been less racial, ethnic, and religious discrimination in economically competitive segments of society. The desire to make a profit drives out irrational prejudices.

Friedman's analysis of the relationship between economic freedom and political freedom leads him to oppose almost all government intervention in the economy. He would, among other things, abolish all government subsidies, remove all tariffs and import restrictions, eliminate compulsory Social Security contributions, and have toll roads, schools, libraries, hospitals, and most other public facilities run by private enterprise. All the regulations designed to protect consumers and business investors would also be abolished. Nor would government help regulate entry into professions, such as law and medicine. Friedman however, would

Issues: Keynesian Economics

Running parallel to conflicts over specific economic choices are debates over "schools" of economics. In recent times, for example, there have been supply-side economics, rational choice economics, and several other perspectives on how economies are organized, how people behave, and what the proper economic role of government is. Perhaps the most important school of thought has been Keynesian economics. Named after the English economist John Maynard Keynes, Keynesian economics has been politically and intellectually influential, defining the terms of debate even for those who reject it.

John Maynard Keynes (1883–1946) was born to a prominent English family. His father was also an eminent economist. He was educated at the most prestigious schools and had a long association with Cambridge University. Keynes also possessed considerable real-world experience. He served in several important government positions, spoke out on controversial issues, and became a wealthy businessman. Politically, he considered himself a defender of capitalism, though his ideas were sometimes judged radical by those who opposed government intervention in the economy.

The Keynesian approach can be understood as a reaction to the dominant, "classical" economic theory of his day. Basically, the "classical" approach saw the capitalist economy as a continuing set of actions that tended, on its own, toward full employment. People supply labor and capital to businesses, businesses produce goods, and these goods are consumed with income derived from labor and investments. If goods produced are not sold, prices are lowered until they are sold. If unemployment occurs, workers receive lower wages and businesses hire more workers. If a depression occurs, consumption is reduced and savings are increased. These savings generate more—and therefore cheaper—capital, which in turn stimulates economic activity. Classical theory stresses the role of prices—the relative price of labor, interest, and goods—in determining economic conditions.

Keynes argued that this view of economic behavior as self-correcting did not square with reality. In particular, high levels of unemployment could persist for years. A central element in the Keynesian approach is the overall level of society's demand for goods and services. Demand is a function of income: the higher the income, the greater the demand. Income levels also affect savings levels, because, as income increases, the amount and proportion saved also go up. Savings become the source of investment funds, which businesses will use to the extend that future demand is anticipated. In other words, no factory will be built to supply unwanted goods, even if it could be built with low-interest money.

Unlike classical economics, Keynesian theory does not see the system as automatically adjusting itself. If demand falls, income will fall, investments will decline, and the economy will stagnate. On the other hand, excessive demand will cause an overabundance of income and investment capital, with inflation as a result. It is up to the government, therefore, to play an active interventionist role by regu-

lating credit, adjusting taxes, and increasing or decreasing government spending. If demand falls, the government might spend more. When it pumps money into the economy, income rises and demand increases. If demand becomes too high, government can lower it by raising taxes and restricting credit. Without the proper government management of demand, the economy can go from one crisis to the next.

not give private enterprise an absolutely free hand. Because monopolies limit free choice, they should be prevented by government action—unless for technical reasons they are economically essential. Another limitation comes from what Friedman calls "neighborhood effects"—the effects of transactions on people who are not a party to those transactions. For example, a polluting steel mill can harm everyone in the area, and no one has a say in the situation. In such instances Friedman recommends case-by-case solutions, with a careful weighing of the costs and benefits of government intervention.

Friedman's defense of competitive capitalism is not based solely on its emphasis on individual freedom. He also believes that free enterprise is more effective than government intervention in solving social and economic problems. For example, Friedman argues that if we abolished government licensing of doctors, medical care for the population would be more plentiful, of better quality, and cheaper than under current rules. Currently, because entry into medicine is highly restricted, medical care is artificially expensive. Moreover, even a doctor who performs poorly is allowed to practice, except if he is grossly incompetent. If doctors had to compete more vigorously for patients, consumers would seek the most competent physicians rather than just relying on government certification. Similarly, racial and ethnic bias would decline faster if the government stopped issuing antidiscrimination rules and instead encouraged greater economic competition. Friedman claims that the economic costs of discriminatory behavior are a more powerful (and much cheaper) solution to discrimination than a multitude of complex, difficult-to-enforce regulations and court orders.

The arguments advanced by Friedman and his associates are not always viewed as unrealistic, "pie-in-the-sky" schemes. Increasingly, the case for getting government out of the economy is being stated and applauded. The issue of deregulation has now become part of the public agenda. In both 1980 and 1984, Ronald Reagan struck a responsive note when he called for less govern-ment. In the 1970s, major steps were taken to deregulate the transportation and financial industries. There is serious talk of a greater role for private enterprise in areas such as schools, prisons, and even space exploration. The question that now comes up is this: How far can we carry Friedman's analysis of capitalism and freedom? If it were politically possible to disengage government and the economy, would this be a goal worth pursuing? In other words, is Friedman correct in claiming that competitive capitalism, freedom, and effectiveness go hand in hand?

Criticisms of Minimal Government and Unrestricted Capitalism

A basic criticism of Friedman's position concerns his view of freedom. Recall that his definition of freedom includes the right to do what you want except for actions like committing murder or not fulfilling legal obligations. Critics point out that such "freedom" is meaningless without a certain amount of economic protection and equality. A poor person and a millionaire do not bargain in the marketplace as equals. Eventually, unrestrained economic competition will result in a large class of impoverished, exploited citizens, totally dependent on the wealthy. The United States would return to the robber baron era of the nineteenth century, when a small number of powerful industrialists had enormous control over the economy. Thus, if freedom is to be meaningful, some degree of economic equality must be assured, and this requires government intervention. Government policies, such as progressive taxation, social services for the needy, and protection of the right to join unions, are required to maintain (not reduce) individual freedom.

A second criticism focuses on Friedman's view of government as a kind of neutral police officer to enforce the rules and maintain physical safety. This view is unrealistic, according to Friedman's critics, because wealthy interests will soon gain control of government and use its coercive power for their own purposes. A government controlled by the rich would soon rewrite the laws to weaken the bargaining position of workers in order to increase free enterprise. The proper role of government in a free society is to redress the imbalance between rich and poor. At a minimum, it should protect the poor from exploitation. Government in a purely capitalist society would only deepen the differences of power and promote misery.

Finally, the assertion that capitalism can be an effective provider of goods and services has no historical foundation, according to Friedman's critics. Capitalist societies, such as nineteenth-century England, or the United States in the Great Depression, have experienced economic crises during which fortunes were wiped out and millions of people suffered severe hardship. Moreover, some critics of capitalism claim that the system by its very nature encourages war and exploitation to solve its economic problems. Without strong government planning and management, the economic system goes from one crisis to the next.

Resolving the Conflict Between Capitalism and Government Involvement

The debate between supporters of capitalism and of government involvement is unlikely ever to be resolved. One reason is that neither system has ever existed in its pure form, nor is it likely to do so in the future. Most, perhaps all, economies are mixtures of free enterprise and government control. Even the Communist economy of the Soviet Union contains a small class of officially tolerated capitalists, who provide essential services in agriculture and industry. Nor has any country ever been run solely on the principles of competitive capitalism. Moreover, the two sides disagree sharply on the meaning of key terms. Because of differing interpretations of words like "freedom" and "equality," participants in the debate usually talk past one another. Hence, it is unlikely that either side could convince the other of its arguments. This does not mean, however, that the discussion is meaningless. The idea of competitive capitalism has been influential; it has led economists and others to propose programs that have

some elements of competitive capitalism. Likewise, the case against competitive capitalism is more than just opposition to an unachievable goal. For instance, some analysts believe that the deregulatory policies of President Reagan represent a step toward competitive capitalism and oppose them on these grounds. In sum, the debate over competitive capitalism—even if inconclusive—is part of the debate over contemporary economic policy making.

Check your understanding

1. What is the proper role of government according to Milton Friedman?

2. According to Friedman, how are capitalism and freedom linked?

3. What are the major criticisms of Friedman's philosophy?

4. Why is it unlikely that the arguments between Friedman and his critics will be resolved?

THE POLITICS OF GOVERNMENT AND ECONOMICS

The American economy is complex. Almost everything is related somehow to everything else, and many important factors—for example, the responses of foreign nations—are difficult to predict. The technical and highly mathematical nature of contemporary economics reinforces the complexity. Although citizens can make economic decisions regarding where they will work and what they will buy, the language of professional economists leaves most people baffled.

This makes it tempting to leave economic policy making to trained experts. One could treat economic problems as one would treat a disabled automobile: you discover that something is wrong, but you leave it to an expert to diagnose and correct the problem. You pay the bill, but you don't tell the mechanic how to do the job.

We have argued in this chapter that political decisions affecting the economy are more important than purely technical decisions. The American economy is *not* like a car that has to be tuned correctly by master technicians following a service manual. Put bluntly, political considerations, not economics, are fundamental in economic policy making. There are many different ways, not a single "correct" way, of solving economic problems. Through the political process we establish our priorities and the particular solutions we shall employ. A professional economist could show us that production is exceeding demand and suggest a tax cut to stimulate consumption. However, the seriousness of the problem and the question of *who* will get the benefit of a tax reduction are political, not technical, questions. Similarly, an economist might claim that federal programs must be cut

back to reduce inflation, but which programs should be reduced? Should we prune the budget for the National Park Service or cut expenditures for medical care?

All solutions to economic problems have costs and benefits. An acceptable cost for one person might be an intolerable burden for another. A manual worker on a salary might not be affected by a 10-percent increase in the capital gains tax (a tax on profits from buying and selling property); for a real estate developer, however, such a tax might be a calamity. Naturally, the beneficiaries of a particular economic policy will probably argue their case on the basis of "sound economic policy as proven by experts." The actual decision about who will win and who will lose is a political one, not one to be made by an economist. We are not claiming that expert opinion is irrelevant or serves only to justify personal gain. Rather, basic questions regarding who is to benefit at whose expense are issues decided in the *political* process. They are not technical matters better left to trained experts.

CHAPTER SUMMARY

How does the government affect the economy? The major ways government affects the economy are through economic development, taxes and subsidies, regulation, government consumption, and government-owned enterprises. Each of these endeavors is surrounded by controversy. For example, should the government not only assist the economy but also ensure a more equal distribution of wealth? People also differ in their views of what constitutes legitimate aid as against unfair advantage.

How is economic policy made? The making of economic policy involves many participants: the President, executive department officials, members of Congress, the Federal Reserve Board, private industry and the public. The process is marked by decentralization, conflict, and incrementalism. The quality of the decision making is

open to debate. There are major limits on improving the decision-making process. Some problems almost are built into our political system; one economic goal can conflict with another, and both can conflict with noneconomic objectives.

Has the federal government become too involved in the economy? Most political leaders do not seriously question the existing role of government, although differences of opinion occur over specific policies. Recently, however, some long-held assumptions have been challenged. Such analysts as Milton Friedman argue that government economic intervention leads to a loss of individual freedom and greater inefficiency. Friedman, in turn, has been criticized for his view of personal freedom and his unrealistic expectations of what would happen to a government under competitive capitalism.

IMPORTANT TERMS

Explain the following terms.

economic inequality
progressive tax
regressive tax
subsidy
reindustrialization
trade deficit
privatization
Federal Reserve Board
supply-side economics

THINKING CRITICALLY

1. What are some of the problems that arise in government programs to help the needy? How might some of these problems be dealt with?
2. Should individuals and corporations share the nation's tax burden equally? Why or why not?
3. Agricultural subsidies are an especially controversial issue. Should the government try to implement policies to save so-called family farms? Should the government provide subsidies for other types of family-owned businesses? Discuss your answer.
4. Several industries have recently launched "buy American" campaigns. Should the U.S. government buy only goods made in the U.S.A.? What are the advantages and disadvantages of such a policy? Discuss your answer.
5. The Federal Reserve is a politically independent agency that has become a key economic policy maker. Should elected officials be given greater control over the Fed? Why or why not?
6. Is a pattern of highly decentralized economic decision making in the United States desirable? Why or why not?
7. Can there be such a thing as "objective" economic advice? Or is all expertise ultimately based on political values? Discuss your answer.

EXTENDING YOUR UNDERSTANDING

1. Contact the local government office dealing with unemployment assistance. What are the requirements for receiving aid? How much aid can individuals receive? For how long can they receive it? Present your findings in a report.
2. Consider alternatives to the present income tax system. Are there other methods of taxation that could raise the funds the government needs? Outline your plan for raising revenue. Present this plan to the class.
3. Conduct an analysis of your local post office in comparison with a private competitor, such as Federal Express. How do the two differ in terms of services offered? in terms of price? What services does the post office provide that the competitor does not offer? Does the competitor provide services the post office doesn't?
4. The Reagan administration has promoted the policies associated with "supply-side" economics. How are these policies similar to, or different from, Milton Friedman's economic theories? Present your conclusions in a report.
5. In what way did President Franklin Roosevelt's New Deal represent a break from traditional American economics? Choose one of the programs from the New Deal (for instance, the National Recovery Administration) and find out (a) what social and economic problems the program was set up to deal with; (b) what resistance, if any, the program faced, and (c) whether any of the program's provisions remain in effect today. Present your findings in a report.

MAKING DECISIONS

You are on a government committee charged with devising a plan to keep unsafe used cars off the market. What types of economic incentives would you use to achieve this goal? What political problems would you be likely to encounter? Prepare a proposal outlining your plan and presenting arguments that support your plan.

Chapter 16
Government and Foreign Policy

For most of American history, political leaders were far more concerned with domestic policy than with foreign policy. Until World War II, the policy of isolationism—a lack of involvement in the affairs of other nations except to protect national interests—was a reasonably accurate description of American foreign policy. Since the war, however, there has been a major change. Many of the most basic aspects of our lives—for example, energy, food, clothing, and security—are dependent on international agreements. The American farmer, once a symbol of isolationism, has become keenly interested in foreign trade. Foreign policy issues regarding military commitments, arms agreements, and trade frequently play a significant role in state and national elections. Even more important, nuclear weapons and the missile systems to deliver them have raised the stakes of foreign policy making dramatically. Whereas a domestic policy mistake may waste billions of dollars or outrage a segment of the population, foreign policy mistakes can bring nuclear disaster. In many ways the politics of national security is *the* high-stakes game in politics. American foreign policy is highly complex, but our analysis will consider three basic aspects.

- How is American foreign policy made?
- What are the goals of American foreign policy?
- Can the arms race be ended?

PREVIEW

How is American foreign policy made? Foreign policy involves the relations between the United States and foreign governments. The line between foreign and domestic policy is not always clear. Foreign policy decisions involve six major participants: the President, the executive branch advisors and departments, Congress, interest groups, multinational corporations, and public opinion. The roles they play usually depend on whether a situation is a crisis demanding an immediate response. Policy making during a crisis is directed by the President and involves a limited number of other participants, rapid decisions, and a heightened concern for the national interest. In contrast, noncrisis decision making is marked by many participants, a concern for public opinion, extensive bargaining, and differing views on overall policy goals. Noncrisis decision making usually resembles domestic policy making.

What are the goals of American foreign policy? The basic goal is to maintain national security, which, before World War II, did not require active involvement in world affairs. Since the war, the focus of national security has been the containment of Soviet expansion. Promoting peace and international stability is a second major objective. Supporting the United Nations, mediating armed conflicts, and most important, reaching agreements with the Soviet Union have contributed to this goal. Through such policies as foreign aid, technical assistance, and reduced trade restrictions, the United States has sought to promote a third goal: worldwide economic development. Furthering American economic interests is a fourth major foreign policy aim. This policy has been criticized as promoting American domination of less-developed nations. Achieving these four objectives is difficult, because events are often unpredictable, our knowledge is limited, and goals can conflict.

Can the arms race be ended? The United States and the Soviet Union, which spend enormous sums on arms, have huge stockpiles of destructive nuclear power. U.S. arms spending has many sources: a complex set of military objectives, the need to have a strong deterrent (defense against military attack), the technology of modern warfare, and political pressures. The arms race has been criticized on the grounds that it has negative economic impacts and will lead to World War III. However, it can be defended as a necessity, given an aggressive Soviet Union. Proposals to remedy the present situation have included arms reductions and changes in weapons and decision procedures. Each solution rests on different perceptions, assumptions, and acceptable costs.

HOW IS AMERICAN FOREIGN POLICY MADE?

Before we answer the question of how foreign policy is made, we must first define what exactly foreign policy is. In the past, the answer was clear—foreign policy consisted of those policies directly involving foreign governments. Foreign policy concerned declarations of war, military alliances, diplomatic recognition, and foreign trade.

Today the distinction between foreign and domestic policy frequently is less clear. Many domestic issues have important implications for American relations with other countries, and agreements with other nations can have immediate consequences in our country. For example, in 1973 the U.S. government decided to sell a substantial quantity of wheat to the Soviet Union. This decision affected world trade and was part of an overall U.S. policy of improving relations with the U.S.S.R. On the domestic side, by decreasing the supply of wheat, the sale increased the price of food and encouraged wheat farmers to expand production. This, in turn, had financial and political consequences when wheat prices eventually fell and farmers who had planted too much wheat sought government aid. Overall, it is more useful to think of a policy that ranges from the purely domestic (for example, building a highway) to the purely foreign (for example, a military alliance). In between are many policies—for example, energy-conversion programs designed to reduce oil imports—with both domestic and foreign consequences.

Let us begin our analysis of the making of foreign policy by considering the role of the six chief participants (or "actors," as they are frequently called): (1) the President, (2) executive branch advisors and departments, (3) Congress, (4) interest groups, (5) multinational corporations, and (6) public opinion.

The President

More than any other individual, the President is responsible for making American foreign policy. Although the President cannot dictate policy, our overall foreign policy orientation must have presidential approval. One observer has called the President "the ultimate decider."[1] In the mid-1980s, for example, the United States' policy of vigorously resisting Communist expansion in Central America clearly reflected President Reagan's personal views. In contrast, the Carter administration stressed greater cooperation with the Soviet Union and a concern for worldwide human rights.

The President's importance in foreign affairs derives in part from the Constitution. As commander-in-chief of the armed forces, the President can dispatch troops anywhere in the world. It was this constitutional provision that allowed President Truman to involve the United States in Korea in 1950 and President Reagan to send troops to Lebanon and Grenada in 1983. Article II, Section 2 also gives the President the power to make treaties and appoint ambassadors (both functions are subject to Senate approval). Section 3 of Article II further authorizes the President to receive ambassadors. This duty has generally been interpreted to mean the power of diplomatic recognition of foreign nations. Presidents Carter and Reagan, for example, refused diplomatic recognition to Vietnam, thus hindering trade and travel between the United States and Vietnam.

The President's constitutional authority is not limited to the powers explicitly granted. The Founders clearly realized that the system of checks and balances and separation of powers designed to prevent domestic tyranny was less appropriate for foreign relations. Thus the federal government was left relatively free to protect national sovereignty. By "federal government" the writers of the Constitution meant, in this instance, the President. In the words of Chief Justice John Marshall, the President is "the Nation's organ for foreign affairs." In the case of *United States v. Curtis-Wright Export Corporation* (1936), the Supreme Court affirmed that the President's power in foreign affairs does not depend upon constitutional grants of authority and that the principle of separation of powers does not apply when the President represents the nation abroad. In practice, a determined President can almost always push to their limits, without legislative or judicial interference, the constitutional grants of power relating to foreign policy. Even explicit limitations—for example, the congressional authority to declare war—can be overcome sometimes by a chief executive. For instance, the President can avoid congressional involvement in treaty making by using executive agreements and proclamations (Chapter 10).

The importance of the chief executive in foreign policy is also based on practical considerations. Dealing effectively with foreign countries requires a unified voice, and only the President can provide such unity. Congressional or Cabinet leaders, unless speaking on behalf of the President, would lack the prestige necessary for international negotiations. Another practical reason for presidential preeminence is the speed at which foreign affairs can move. Many international events requiring an American response must receive immediate attention. It is much easier for one person to act decisively than for a committee or two legislative houses. The special nature of many foreign policy decisions also helps the White House maintain its key position. Much of the information on which decisions are based cannot be stated openly, and the information is more likely to remain secret if it stays in the White House. Some data—for example, evaluations of Soviet missile strength—could be shared with key congressional leaders. But it would be extremely risky to release the material to all 535 members of Congress. Nor could the American bargaining position in international negotiations be widely discussed without serious risk.

Executive Branch Advisors and Departments

Even though Presidents dominate the foreign policy-making process, they do not act all by themselves. Surrounding the President are numerous advisors and heads of Cabinet-level departments and special agencies, who provide detailed technical information and serve as sounding boards for new policies. Advisors and Cabinet secretaries play a key role in arriving at policies and determining how they will be implemented. Many presidential directives came to nothing when top aides or middle-level bureaucrats chose to ignore or change them.

Every President has advisors who are especially important in the creation of foreign policy. Their precise titles vary from President to President and can change in the course of an administration. President Carter, for example, sought advice from many people, including Zbigniew Brzezinski (National Security Advisor) and Cyrus Vance (Secretary of State). President Reagan has relied heavily on his Secretary of Defense, Caspar Weinberger, and Secretary of State, George Shultz. Important foreign policy advisors may even come from domestic departments. President Nixon during his first term frequently consulted with his Attorney General, John Mitchell. In his first term Ronald Reagan relied heavily on the advice of James A. Baker, chief of staff, and Michael Deaver, deputy chief of staff. A key advisor may not even have an official position—men like former ambassador to the Soviet Union W. Averell Harriman and former Secretary of State Dean Acheson advised Presidents Kennedy and Johnson but never received formal titles in their role as advisors.

The closest thing to an "official" foreign policy advisory group is the National Security Council (NSC). A part of the Executive Office of the President, the NSC was created in 1947 to ensure coordination in national security policy making. Presidents have varied considerably in how they have used it. The original membership consisted of the President, Vice President, secretaries of Defense and State, the National Security Advisor, head of the Joint Chiefs of Staff, the director of

Central Intelligence, and the director of the Office of Emergency Preparedness. Most recently the Secretary of the Treasury and the head of the Council of Economic Advisors have been added. Generally, however, the group of "inner advisors" on whom the President relies are not on the National Security Council. Top appointees, such as the Treasury Secretary, sometimes gain their position because of their links to outside groups rather than close ties to the President. Such appointees may also feel closer to their departments than to the President.

Beyond the NSC and other White House advisors are several large bureaucracies that handle much of the routine (though highly important) business of foreign policy. The most significant is the Department of State, which drafts treaties, runs the worldwide network of U.S. embassies and consulates, and oversees relations with international organizations, such as the United Nations and the Organization of American States. The State Department also has numerous worldwide research and intelligence responsibilities. Embassy personnel regularly make reports on events in their host nations. Perhaps because of its sheer size and unwieldiness, however, in recent years the State Department has rarely played a significant role in major foreign policy decisions. President Kennedy once described it as a "bowl of jelly." Moreover, unlike many other executive departments, it lacks a strong domestic constituency to support it. In a dispute with, say, the Department of Agriculture, the State Department cannot count on the equivalent of millions of farmers, farm groups, and their allies in Congress.

Another large bureaucracy with a special foreign policy role is the Central Intelligence Agency (CIA). Established in 1947, it is charged with collecting intelligence and advising the President and the NSC on intelligence matters. On occasion, the CIA has engaged in more direct actions—for example, assassinating foreign leaders or inciting revolution—but it is unclear just how much of this behavior was explicitly authorized by the President. As with other government departments, the importance of the CIA's official functions does not automatically guarantee its influence with the President.

The Department of Defense is another important element in the making of foreign policy. Over the years top Defense officials have been among the President's closest advisors. The military services maintain their own intelligence organizations, and, as mentioned, the chairperson of the Joint Chiefs of Staff is a member of the NSC. The military has played a significant role in arms-control negotiations and in assessing both U.S. and foreign military capabilities. The lengthy and costly involvement of the United States in Vietnam resulted, in part, from overly optimistic evaluations by the Pentagon (and other executive branch agencies) of American intervention.

Other executive branch agencies with foreign policy responsibilities include the Arms Control and Disarmament Agency, the Agency for International Development (AID) (which administers economic aid to foreign nations), the United States Information Agency (USIA), the United States International Trade Commission, and the Export-Import Bank of the United States. In fact, because of the growing interrelationship of foreign and domestic policy, several departments traditionally concerned with domestic issues have become involved in overseas matters. For example, the Justice Department now stations several hundred people abroad to coordinate efforts against drug smuggling and international terrorism. The Department of Labor maintains ties with international trade union groups.

Congress

Like the President, Congress derives much of its role in foreign policy making from explicit constitutional grants of power. Article I, Section 8 gives Congress the power to regulate foreign commerce, declare war, and define and punish "Offenses against the Law of Nations." In Article II, which describes presidential power, the Senate is given responsibility for approving treaties (by a two-thirds vote) made by the President. Although the President negotiates a treaty, the Senate can leave its mark by adding "amendments," "reservations,"

and "understandings." The Senate also has the right to approve "Ambassadors, other public Ministers and Consuls." On occasion, confirmation hearings on appointments become public forums on the President's foreign policy. Equally significant to the conduct of foreign affairs is the power over appropriations. Because many foreign policies require money, refusing to authorize funds the President requests is a powerful weapon. Foreign aid appropriations bills have often contained congressional instructions on what recipients must do to qualify for aid—not violate human rights, refuse to shelter terrorists, not seize American property, and so on. Recently, for example, opponents of President Reagan's policy in Central America have tried to limit U.S. Financial aid. On several occasions Congress has refused to authorize funds to CIA-backed rebels in Nicaragua.

Many of the congressional powers that have evolved over the years contribute to Congress' role in foreign policy. Congressional oversight—legislative monitoring of the executive bureaucracy—has allowed lawmakers to keep an eye on the State Department, the CIA, and more specialized agencies, such as the Export-Import Bank. The House Permanent Select Committee on Intelligence, for example, has helped limit CIA covert operations in South America. Moreover, each legislative house has several committees with foreign policy jurisdiction. Finally, the congressional power to investigate can sometimes be a weapon. During much of the war in Vietnam the Senate Foreign Relations Committee's investigation of the war provided a public forum for those opposed to U.S. intervention. In the 1970s, congressional subcommittees uncovered numerous abuses of authority by the CIA.

Limits on Congressional Power over Foreign Policy

The formal foreign policy powers of Congress are considerable, but the gap between formal and actual authority is usually large. Congress can sometimes thwart presidential goals. Historically, however, Congress has been the junior partner to the President in making foreign policy. One study of twenty-one major policy decisions, found that

Congress had initiated only three of them.[2] In the area of treaty approval, the Senate usually accepts the President's position. If the Senate insists on modifying a treaty, the President can refuse to sign it or withdraw it. Many important international agreements have been enacted by executive agreements that do not require Senate approval but that have the same legal standing as treaties. In 1980 there were 7,142 agreements in force between the United States and foreign nations; only 980 involved treaties. Regarding confirmation of diplomatic appointments, the Senate almost always goes along with the President. Even if the Senate resists, Presidents have available such tactics as "interim" appointments (appointments made after Congress has adjourned that do not require Senate approval until forty days after the start of the next legislative session), or they can simply appoint a person not in the government as their "personal representative" to important diplomatic missions. Presidents have used their personal advisors to negotiate with foreign nations (for example, the

critical negotiations prior to U.S. recognition of Communist China were conducted by President Nixon's National Security Advisor, Henry Kissinger).

Perhaps the most significant area in which congressional foreign policy initiative has been weakened is that of the power to declare war. Two of the costliest wars in American history—the Korean and Vietnam conflicts—were never declared by Congress. In both instances the President relied on his powers as commander-in-chief to dispatch U.S. troops (see Chapter 10 for a more detailed description of presidential war-making power). As a result of what it perceived as excessive White House reliance on military intervention, Congress passed the War Powers Act of 1973 to curb undeclared wars. The heart of this act is a provision requiring a President to obtain congressional authorization of a troop commitment within sixty days; approval for an additional thirty days can be given without a formal declaration of war, but after ninety days Congress can require withdrawal

Three witnesses are sworn in at congressional hearings on the Iran-contra affair. White House aides and others were charged with illegally using profits from arms sales to Iran to aid the Nicaraguan rebels.

of all troops, and the action cannot be vetoed by the President. However, doubt remains as to whether Congress would actually resist presidential military initiatives if national security was clearly involved. Perhaps most important, the War Powers Act involves a legislative veto, and the Supreme Court has declared such measures to be unconstitutional (see Chapter 12).

Congressional control over appropriations has proved to be more of a limited weapon than a major instrument of control. On several occasions congressional efforts to use appropriations to set foreign policy have been met by presidential vetoes or outright refusal to spend the money. Even members of Congress who disagree with the President will often defer to the White House on foreign policy issues. Presidents have avoided legislative interference through the appropriations process by transferring funds from one program to another or by other strategies (for example, declaring military equipment "obsolete" so that it can be given away or sold without congressional authorization). In addition, the President has funds that can be used almost entirely as the White House wants to use them. Moreover, by its very nature Congress is ill equipped to offer a budget that reflects its own foreign policy goals. As we noted in Chapter 9, numerous committees often work at cross-purposes, and leaders cannot impose their will on independent-minded colleagues. Creating a policy on an issue like international trade means gaining the cooperation of several committees, many party leaders, and two separate legislative chambers. Overall, Congress acts more as a brake on the executive than as a creator of policy.

Congress' role in foreign policy making is limited also by its preoccupation with domestic issues. Legislators worry a great deal about being reelected. Although some lawmakers have a deep interest in foreign policy, most become involved in it only when it directly concerns their district. For example, senators from farm states must pay attention to international trade involving agriculture if they want to remain in office. A representative from a heavily Jewish area must follow U.S.–Israeli relations. However, Congress as a whole rarely has a set of goals on these foreign policy issues. A President has an international trade policy; Congress, on the other hand, contains advocates of dozens of often contradictory international trade programs. A farm state senator might face numerous colleagues who are indifferent or even opposed to the policy his or her constituents want.

Interest Groups

It was once customary to dismiss the role of interest groups in foreign policy. Foreign policy involved such momentous decisions as war, peace, treaties, and diplomatic alliances, whereas interest groups supposedly were concerned with more closer-to-home politics. It is perhaps still true that on "big" foreign policy decisions (for example, whether U.S. troops should be committed to a Middle East war), interest groups play a limited role.

Nevertheless, pressure groups do affect policy decisions. Moreover, if the trend of growing interdependence between foreign and domestic policy continues, the role of pressure groups will increase.

The Impact of Interest Groups on Foreign Policy

Interest-group behavior related to foreign policy takes several forms. The most obvious is probably in the area of international trade. Especially in recent years, with increased worldwide economic competition, numerous American industries depend on trade agreements for their survival. Businesses, through such trade associations as the Footwear Industries of America, the Corduroy Council of America, or the National Frozen Pizza Institute (which is concerned with cheese imports), can exert considerable pressure on Congress and the White House for favorable import duties, export subsidies, import quotas, and other details of trade. The Footwear Industries of America, for example, consists of companies that have dozens of large factories in many states. Protecting thousands of jobs and real estate tax revenue is an important priority for numerous state officials and members of Congress. Agricultural groups gener-

Vietnam veterans and their families examine medals placed at the foot of the Vietnam Memorial in Washington. Veterans protesting U.S. aid to Nicaraguan rebels had refused to accept the medals.

ated intense public pressure on President Reagan to cancel President Carter's embargo on grain shipments to the Soviet Union.

Often these battles involve far more than the price of television sets or pizzas. To a nation that depends heavily on exports to the United States—for example, Japan or Great Britain—increased import duties might be interpreted as a hostile action. Because the stakes are so high in trade policy, foreign governments and corporations are becoming active in Washington. In 1982, some 712 lobbyists had registered with the Justice Department as agents of foreign governments or firms (the actual number of people working on behalf of foreign interests, however, was close to eight thousand). Several of these agents were former members of Congress or other ex-government officials. In 1981, Japanese companies and government agencies paid $13.4 million to various law firms, consultants, and lobbyists to represent their case to the U.S. government. Japanese automobile manufacturers, for example, have mobilized thou-

sands of dealers and joined forces with American agricultural groups—which sell to Japan—and dock workers' unions to protect their U.S. market.

Other types of interest groups that have a voice in making American foreign policy are ethnic or nationality organizations. Millions of Americans have special ties to foreign nations, and groups representing these citizens frequently lobby government. Americans of German descent were among the many groups that tried to keep the United States out of World War I. When Turkey invaded the predominantly Greek island of Cyprus in 1974, Greek organizations waged a successful campaign to cut off American military aid to Turkey. Refugees from Castro's Cuba have strongly supported President Reagan's anti-Communist policies in Central America. Over the years numerous Jewish groups have lobbied in support of American aid to Israel.

A third type of interest group oriented toward foreign policy can best be described as the political-cause organization, which has no economic moti-

Points of View: The Hidden Side of Foreign Policy

Behind the visible world of diplomats, summit meetings, and international agreements lies another, secret world where foreign policy is also made and carried out. This is the world of *covert action*—attempts by governments to influence events in other nations or territories without revealing their involvement. Carrying out its policies by covert action allows a nation to deny its role in operations that may be unpopular, illegal, or immoral.

Covert action has been practiced throughout history. Moreover, almost everyone agrees that covert action is sometimes necessary. But there is wide disagreement about what kind of covert activities should be undertaken. This is especially true in the United States, where there is a strong dislike of "dirty tricks" in politics and diplomacy.

In the field of intelligence gathering alone, the United States maintains several agencies, including the Central Intelligence Agency (CIA), the National Security Agency (NSA), the Federal Bureau of Investigation (FBI), the Bureau of Intelligence of the State Department, and the Defense Intelligence Agency of the Defense Department. When they are revealed, covert actions by these agencies tend to arouse strong opposition.

It should be emphasized that almost every nation engages in covert action. American agencies have their counterparts in MI-5 and MI-6 of Britain, the KGB of the Soviet Union, and Israel's Shin Bet. The wide variety of covert activities is only suggested by the examples that follow.

Covert Military Operations

Most covert activities in the military sphere are *paramilitary*—that is, they are carried out not by a nation's own armed forces but in more unconventional ways, such as through aid to a rebel army in another country. In recent times, undercover operations have frequently pitted the Soviet Union and other Communist regimes against the United States and its allies. In Angola, for instance, the government has been supported by Russia and Cuba, while guerrilla forces have received aid from the United States and South Africa.

One of the best-known examples of a covert military action occurred in the Middle East during World War I. Britain wanted to encourage the breakup of the Ottoman Empire (present-day Turkey), one of its enemies in the war. So when Arabs in the empire revolted, the British aided them through an extraordinary organizer of guerrilla troops, Colonel T. E. Lawrence ("Lawrence of Arabia"). Among other things, Lawrence carried out a successful undercover operation against Turkish railroad supply lines.

A recent example of covert action involved France and the environmental organization known as Greenpeace. In the summer of 1985, the Greenpeace ship *Rainbow Warrior* was in New Zealand preparing to sail northward to protest French nuclear exercises in the Pacific Ocean. A sudden and suspicious explosion destroyed the ship in Auckland harbor, killing one man, a photographer for Greenpeace. After New Zealand police arrested two French nationals in connection with the incident, the French government was forced to admit that the *Rainbow Warrior* had been sunk by a team of French military advisors.

Covert military activity by the United States has often been directed by the CIA. When the people of Tibet rebelled against China in 1959, the CIA not only trained and equipped Tibetan troops but also operated planes that helped organize raids over China. Tibetans were also secretly brought to Colorado for more extensive training.

U.S. covert military operations have been especially common in Latin America. In 1954 the CIA was largely responsible for a successful coup d'état that overthrew the Socialist government of Guatemala. The CIA was also involved in the disastrous Bay of Pigs invasion of Cuba in 1961, which failed to overthrow the Castro regime. In 1967, CIA agents were dispatched to Bolivia to help hunt down the Cuban revolutionary leader Che Guevara; he was captured by the Bolivian army and executed. The CIA likewise played a major role in the "destabilization" of the leftist Salvador Allende regime in Chile in the early 1970s. Since the early 1980s, the intelligence agency has directed U.S. aid to the contras—the Nicaraguan forces waging a re-

bellion against the Marxist government of that country.

Espionage

In 1987 the United States and the Soviet Union traded charges over the "bugging" of embassies in Moscow and Washington. Each country accused the other of using electronic surveillance to penetrate its security.

These charges were only the most recent in the long history of espionage and counterespionage. A certain glamour surrounds the secret agent: Nathan Hale, who gave his life as a spy for the Revolutionary cause; Belle Boyd, who spied for the Confederacy during the Civil War; Mata Hari, executed by the French for aiding the Germans in World War I. Modern espionage, however, is much more apt to rely on the painstaking gathering of intelligence from relatively public sources, such as news broadcasts and government reports. Governments also routinely monitor the communications of other nations (including their allies). In many foreign countries, the CIA intercepts tele-

phone messages between officials. In Washington, the FBI, working with the telephone company, regularly taps the phones of foreign embassies.

Since many communications are coded, governments are constantly working to break foreign codes. In the United States, most of this work is done by computers at the NSA, but the CIA has stolen foreign codebooks, bugged embassy radio rooms, and secretly enlisted the aid of foreign code clerks. The United States, which sells encoding and cryptographic devices abroad, uses them to break the codes of the very nations that have bought them. Other sophisticated technologies used to gather foreign intelligence include tiny radio transmitters, infrared sensors, and spy satellites that photograph military installations from miles overhead.

Attacks on Foreign Leaders

Of all the "dirty tricks" in international relations, the most controversial are assassination attempts on foreign leaders. Cuban Prime Minister Fidel Castro was the object of repeated CIA-organized as-

sassination attempts during the Eisenhower, Kennedy, and Johnson administrations. Evidence points to American involvement in several successful assassinations as well. Victims included Patrice Lumumba, a leftist leader in the Congo (now Zaire), killed in 1961; Rafael Trujillo, dictator of the Dominican Republic, also killed in 1961; and President Ngo Dinh Diem of South Vietnam, assassinated in 1963.

One of the most blatant "covert" assassinations was carried out by Russia's KGB against Hafizullah Amin, president of Afghanistan, in 1979. First the Russians installed a Farsi-speaking agent in the palace kitchen. When his attempts to poison Amin failed, a Russian assassination team stormed the palace and massacred the president and all of his palace guards. Even the Russian who commanded the action was killed. When he ran out to call for reinforcements, his own troops—under orders not to let anyone leave the palace alive—mistook him for an Afghan and shot him. The overthrow of the Amin government offered a pretext for the Soviet invasion of the country shortly afterward.

Covert activities and assorted dirty tricks come to light from time to time and may be condemned by members of Congress, editorial writers, and ordinary citizens. Yet it is unlikely that public exposure will put an end to undercover operations. Spying has been going on throughout history, and, if anything, international tensions in the nuclear era have only increased nations' reliance on it.

vation or feeling of ethnic sympathy. Rather, these groups concentrate on policies, such as nuclear disarmament, world hunger, human rights, religious freedom, or an international treaty protecting whales from extinction. These groups have varied in organization and tactics. Some, like the American Friends Service Committee, maintain low-key Washington-based operations devoted to such noncontroversial issues as world hunger or the plight of refugees. Others view their role as that of marshaling public pressure on Congress or the President. In recent years advocates of a nuclear freeze have organized numerous demonstrations to promote their cause. Civil rights groups, religious organizations, and other groups have sought to change U.S. policy on South Africa because of its policy of apartheid, or racial discrimination.

Multinational Corporations

Another group of participants in the foreign policy-making process that deserve mention are the **multinational corporations,** or firms that have substantial operations in several countries. Shell Oil, Exxon, and International Telephone and Telegraph (ITT) are well-known multinationals. Like domestic corporations, multinationals can use their influence to affect tariff and trade policies.

However, because of their extensive dealings in several countries, multinationals can become especially involved in foreign policy issues. For example, several oil companies have a strong concern for American Middle East policy, because they are dependent on Arab nations for their oil. These companies thus will work to ensure friendly relations between the United States and countries like Saudi Arabia.

It has been charged that some multinationals behave as if they were sovereign nations with their own foreign policy. In the early 1970s, for example, ITT waged a vigorous campaign against the democratically elected Marxist government of Salvador Allende of Chile. Besides taking anti-Allende actions within Chile, ITT tried to create an anti-Allende U.S. foreign policy. When the State Department and top officials rejected ITT's view of the situation in Chile, the company sought CIA assistance to encourage other American corporations to join the battle. In general, the foreign policy that ITT, a U.S.-based firm, was trying to impose on the U.S. government involved far more than specific commercial matters and was contrary to official U.S. government policy. Ultimately, ITT was successful when Allende was assassinated and the leftist government was replaced by a right-wing dictatorship.

U.S. universities that invest in firms doing business in South Africa have become frequent targets of student demonstrations, like this one in Berkeley, California.

Public Opinion

The remaining actor that we shall consider in foreign policy making is public opinion. Evaluating the role of public opinion is not as simple a task as our analysis of the other participants in foreign policy making. The role of the President, members of Congress, or interest-group leaders can be observed or otherwise taken into account. The impact of public opinion is less easy to measure.

Public Opinion and Broad Foreign Policy Objective

Does public opinion have an impact on American foreign policy? Most experts would probably agree that the greatest impact the public has is in defining broad policy boundaries. That is, the public holds leaders responsible for meeting general foreign policy objectives, and leaders understand that to ignore these objectives is to risk almost certain electoral defeat. Among these objectives are maintenance of our national sovereignty, preventing the spread of Communism, promoting world peace, protecting traditional allies, such as Great Britain, and upholding America's prestige and influence. In both the 1980 and 1984 elections, Ronald Reagan's style of standing up to the Russians and using patriotic rhetoric was warmly received by many voters. Of course, a variety of policies can be consistent with these broad goals. One President, for example, might pursue world peace by intervening militarily in the affairs of other nations. Another might emphasize the peacekeeping role of the United Nations. Although the goals valued by the public might be vague, they are important.

Public Opinion and Specific Policy

When it comes to more specific foreign policy choices, however, public opinion plays a less important role. One study of top-ranking government officials concluded that public opinion polls were almost never taken into consideration in formulating foreign policy. Perhaps only among members of Congress was public opinion given weight, and even then it was rarely of great priority. Public opinion *was* given attention in the *selling* of foreign policy decisions to the public. A President's speechwriter might, for example, use poll results to determine the best way to explain or defend a White House decision. Opponents of a policy also could use poll results as ammunition in their attacks.

Even though the public rarely determines the final decision, it can set certain limits on what will be acceptable. Consider, for example, the situation in El Salvador in the early 1980s. Basically, President Reagan had committed the United States to supporting the established government against insurgents who were alleged to be receiving Communist aid. To accomplish this goal, the President had several alternatives—diplomatic pressure, military and economic aid, personal persuasion—that he could employ without reference to public opinion. Each of these policies was broadly compatible with public sentiment. But some alternatives—sending U.S. combat troops to El Salvador or threatening nuclear weapons, for example—were probably "off-limits" because of anticipated negative public reaction. The public provided the range of acceptable responses; the President selected the particular policy.

It should also be remembered that some foreign policy choices have major domestic implications. For example, a decision not to sell farm goods to the Soviet Union would greatly anger agricultural interests. Only a very determined President would risk generating such intense negative opinion. During the war in Vietnam, the role of public opinion grew as the United States became more deeply involved and as casualty rates soared.

The Relationship Among Foreign Policy Actors

Thus far we have described the six major participants in the foreign policy process. The question we now face is how these various participants interact. If the President, presidential advisors, Congress, pressure groups, multinationals, and public opinion are the actors, what are the scripts? Those who have observed the making of American foreign policy have distinguished between two basic policy-making patterns; crisis and noncrisis de-

Commentary: When Good Friends Disagree

The United States and Canada are proud of the fact that theirs is the longest unfortified border in the world. The two nations share a common heritage of English law and political traditions; each is the major trading partner of the other. The relationship is not without its tensions, however, and one foreign policy disagreement—on acid rain—has been a source of friction for years.

Acid rain begins when burning coal and other fuels send sulfur dioxide and similar gases into the air. These emissions, carried easily by the wind, are later deposited on the earth's surface by rain, snow, fog, and dust. Much of the acid rain in North America is generated by emissions from cars and factories in the Midwestern United States. Gases are carried eastward by the prevailing winds. When the residue falls to earth in the eastern United States and Canada, it causes billions of dollars' worth of damage by polluting lakes and killing fish, crops, and forests.

Nobody likes acid rain or what it does to the environment. Both the United States and Canada want to resolve the problem. The foreign policy issue in this case is one not of goals but of priorities. For Canadians, acid rain is a pressing problem that they want to solve as quickly as possible. For their neighbors to the south, it is only one of many environmental questions requiring attention.

Several factors have influenced these differing perceptions.

In proportion to total population, far more Canadians than Americans live in areas affected by acid rain. In addition, these are areas important to tourism, an industry that is vital to the Canadian economy. Finally, reducing harmful emissions is a bigger task for the United States than for Canada. Evidence indicates that Americans cause more of the pollution than do Canadians, who obtain a large share of their energy from nonpolluting hydroelectric sources. American factories, have, in fact, been encouraged to burn high-sulfur coal in order to lessen U.S. dependence on foreign oil.

For several years, the U.S. government has argued that more research is needed before it can set limits on emissions. But Canadians who want more immediate action have been joined by many Americans, especially in the Northeast; they argue that the technologies for fighting acid rain already exist and that the only way to demonstrate the effectiveness of such technologies is by trying them on a large-scale commercial basis.

The poet Robert Frost wrote that "good fences make good neighbors." In the dispute over the handling of the acid rain problem, we might say that good policy makes good neighbors.

(Editorial cartoon by Walt Handelsman, The Scranton Times)

In Iran, after the Shah was deposed in 1979, anti-Americanism led to the takeover of the U.S. embassy in Teheran. The poster depicts President Jimmy Carter being strangled by the Iranian people.

cision making. Each usually has its own style and cast of players.

Crisis Decision Making

A crisis situation occurs when an unexpected event arises that could affect American interests substantially—usually involving violence or the threat of violence. Such crises are a regular feature of international relations. In 1946 the Soviet blockade of West Berlin sharply increased world tension and resulted in a massive U.S. airlift of supplies to Berlin. The invasion of South Korea by North Korea in 1950 (and the subsequent Communist Chinese intervention) also required a rapid response. The Cuban missile crisis of 1962 saw a direct confrontation between the United States and the Soviet Union over whether Soviet offensive missiles would be based in Cuba. Numerous civil wars and border disputes have also created threatening situations. Our involvement in Vietnam generated many crises. In 1979 a crisis occurred when the U.S. embassy in Iran was seized by terrorists. The Middle East has been the

scene of several crises in recent years. On the average, there seems to be at least one crisis every couple of years.

Policy making during a crisis tends to have certain characteristics. Without exception, the President is in charge of decision making. The chief executive must decide whether the United States will send troops, authorize other military actions, dispatch an emergency diplomatic mission, or issue a public warning. Congress, pressure groups, large government bureaucracies, and public opinion have almost no role during a crisis. Moreover, the President rarely involves more than a few aides and advisors and maybe a few congressional leaders to help make the decisions. These key participants are usually among the President's inner circle of advisors and rarely constitute the official foreign policy advising apparatus. Finally, a concern for the national interest is the dominant (though not exclusive) theme of decision making. Such goals as personal advancement, bureaucratic expansion, economic gain, or favorable publicity tend to be less important.

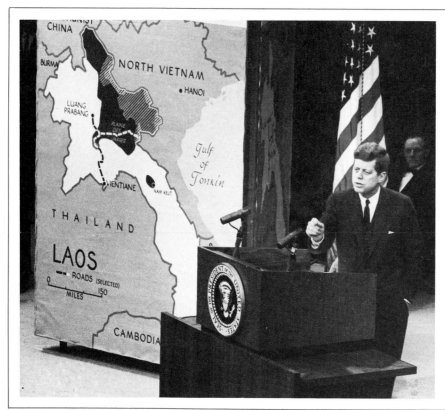

At a televised news conference in 1961, President John F. Kennedy explains the military situation in Vietnam to the American people, in an effort to generate public support for his policies.

Noncrisis Decision Making

Noncrisis decision making involves a much larger and more varied set of participants. For example, a decision on whether to sell the Soviet Union the latest computer as part of a "normalization of relations" program would involve the State Department, the Department of Defense, the Department of Commerce, the Export-Import Bank, the CIA, Congress (because there are laws covering the sale of military-related goods to foreign nations), numerous businesses and issue-oriented organizations, and the President and White House staff. Noncrisis decisions frequently involve a concern for public opinion (though not an absolute adherence to it). During our negotiations with Panama in the late 1970s over a new canal treaty, for example, there was much talk of "selling" or "educating" the public, and opinion surveys were used to pressure senators undecided on their votes. Public opinion would be less relevant if, say the President had to decide whether to use force to prevent a Communist takeover in Panama.

Because participants do not share the same perspectives on an issue, policy making is often characterized by conflict and bargaining. On an issue like the sale of computers to Russians, the Defense Department might find itself opposed by the State and Commerce departments. A division of opinion is also likely in Congress, where "get-tough-with-Russia" legislators may find themselves in conflict with lawmakers interested in greater trade and legislators from states in which computers are manufactured. Extensive bargaining might occur over the particular computers to be sold, the terms of the sale, and the political concessions to be extracted from the Russians as part of the deal. Contrary to the way decisions are reached in crisis situations, this debate could go on for months or even years. Greater disagreement over what best serves the national interest is also likely. Would the sharing of our technology help reduce U.S.—Soviet hostility, or would a technologically stronger Russia be more aggressive?

Biography: George C. Marshall

George C. Marshall was a rare combination of soldier and statesman. As an army general, he was the chief American strategist of World War II. Later, as U.S. Secretary of State, he played a crucial role in foreign policy decisions that helped shape the postwar world. For his work in promoting the program named after him— the Marshall Plan—he was awarded the 1953 Nobel Peace Prize. He was the first career soldier to be so honored.

Marshall was born in 1880 in Pennsylvania; his father was a distant relative of Chief Justice John Marshall. After attending the Virginia Military Institute, Marshall entered the Army as a second lieutenant. His dedication and obvious ability helped him rise quickly in rank and responsibility. He served in the Philippines, in France, in China, and at the Army's infantry school at Fort Benning, Georgia.

By the time World War II broke out, Marshall was in Washington with the War (now Defense) Department, and was made Army chief of staff. Under his leadership, the Army grew from a force of about 200,000 into a war machine of over 8 million, and helped win a global conflict fought on two widely separated fronts. Britain's Winston Churchill called him "the true organizer of victory."

President Harry Truman named Marshall his Secretary of State in 1947. At this time, the nations of Europe faced serious difficulties. Recovery from the rav-

ages of war was painfully slow, and many people suffered from want. In Eastern Europe, the Soviet Union was extending its Communist rule over a number of satellite nations, from Poland in the north to Albania in the south. In accordance with the policy of containment, Truman won congressional approval for military aid to prevent Communist takeovers in Greece and Turkey, but Western Europe was also in need.

In June 1947 Marshall used the occasion of a speech at the Harvard University commencement to propose his plan for European recovery. The United States would offer sizable economic aid on the condition that participating European nations agree to greater economic cooperation among themselves. Marshall's proposal did not exclude

any European nation, but the Soviet Union prevented its satellite nations from taking part.

Marshall credited others—especially State Department experts George Kennan and Dean Acheson—for their share in developing the Marshall Plan. But his diligence in lobbying for the proposal did much to win its adoption. (Even so, Congress did not act on the plan until Czechoslovakia fell under Communist rule early in 1948.) Marshall's program appealed to numerous constituencies, for its goal of limiting the spread of communism and of expanding the market for American goods. The European Recovery Program, as the plan was officially called, eventually spent some $15 billion over a four-year period. For its key role in helping Western Europe regain prosperity, the Marshall Plan was widely praised both in the United States and abroad.

Marshall was Secretary of State for only two years. (He also served one year as Secretary of Defense.) But this early period of the cold war was a critical one in American foreign policy. Marshall's immense prestige made him uniquely qualified to advance and promote a program that called for an unprecedented outlay of funds and represented a new departure for the traditionally isolationist United States. The result of his foresight and efforts was a strengthened Western alliance that bolstered America's position in an era of East–West confrontation and cooperation.

As we move from the "big" crisis decisions toward those not involving immediate threats to U.S. security, foreign and domestic decision-making processes become more alike. The authorization of funds for antipoverty programs and for foreign aid has many parallels. The President is important but does not dominate the process (and might have a limited interest in the outcome). Numerous people are involved, and the final outcome results from many compromises and the skillful advancement of particular interests. Finally, issues like foreign aid, trade agreements, and other noncrisis policies are part of an ongoing debate, with no decision likely to have immediate and dramatic consequences. Policy making is characterized by *incrementalism*—that is, adjustments are made on existing policy. (Incrementalism in domestic policy making is discussed in Chapter 14.) In contrast are such situations as the North Korean seizure of the U.S. intelligence-gathering ship *Pueblo* in international waters in 1968. The President had a day or so to decide whether U.S. military intervention (which could have triggered a war) was necessary. In the end, the President decided against direct military action, and the crew of the *Pueblo* was eventually released through negotiations with the North Koreans.

Check Your Understanding

1. What are the sources of the President's role in foreign policy making?

2. What powers does the Constitution give Congress in the area of foreign affairs?

3. In what ways can interest groups have an impact on foreign policy?

4. What role does public opinion play in the conduct of foreign affairs?

5. Describe the differences between crisis and noncrisis decision making.

WHAT ARE THE GOALS OF AMERICAN FOREIGN POLICY?

Every year government officials make hundreds of foreign policy decisions that cost billions of dollars. What overall goals motivate these decisions? What is American foreign policy supposed to accomplish? Basically, we can distinguish four broad aims: (1) maintaining national security, (2) promoting peace and international stability, (3) providing economic assistance, and (4) furthering American economic interests. Frequently these goals overlap—for example, U.S. aid to a developing nation can help American corporations that provide the assistance. Overall, the distinction provides a useful way of approaching a variety of government and private political actions.

National Security

The protection of the United States from foreign aggression has been the primary goal of American foreign policy. Candidates for public office do not question this goal; they differ only on how it can best be achieved. Without a secure territory, none of the other goals—foreign or domestic—is possible. For most of American history, security was rarely the major item on the agenda, despite its unquestioned importance. Until World War II, our geographical isolation, as well as the nature of warfare itself, allowed U.S. political leaders the benefit of not having to worry about alliances or military commitments to ensure our security. Geographical remoteness from the conflicts of Europe was sufficient.

The end of World War II, however, brought a fundamental change in U.S. national security policy. First, the advent of the atomic bomb and long-range bombers (and later, intercontinental ballistic missiles) ended the luxury of being able to take a year or two to decide whether we should enter a war and of fighting it on somebody else's territory. A Pearl Harbor-like sneak attack with atomic weapons is a terrifying thought. Second, the emergence of the Soviet Union, Communist China, and Eastern European Communist countries presented the United States with a formidable enemy committed to expansion by subversion, military invasion, or even free elections.

The Doctrine of Containing the Soviet Union

Since World War II, the central feature of American national security policy has been the containment or limitation, of Communist expansion. This goal, first clearly stated by President Truman in a 1947 speech before Congress, was for many years known as the **Truman Doctrine.** As Truman himself put it: "I believe that it must be the policy of the United States to support free peoples who are resisting attempted subjugation by armed minorities or by outside pressures." President Eisenhower called the threat of communism "global in scope, atheistic in character, ruthless in purpose, and insidious in method. Unhappily the danger it poses promises to be of indefinite duration." Al-

though recent Presidents have sought to reduce U.S.–Soviet tensions, blocking Soviet advances in Europe, Asia, Africa, and Latin America continues to be the key theme of our national security policy.

The U.S. response to Soviet expansion has taken a variety of forms. Following World War II, when the possibility of Russian military intervention in a devastated Europe seemed very real, the United States launched the **Marshall Plan** to provide economic assistance to war-ravaged European countries (the plan was named after George C. Marshall, who as Secretary of State first proposed such aid). Between 1947 and 1952, about $15 billion was given to Western European nations. In other aid programs designed to thwart Communist threats in the late 1940s, $400 million was sent to Greece and Turkey and over $2 billion to Nationalist China (the latter aid proved

A parade in Athens in 1949 marks the delivery, under the Marshall Plan, of the millionth ton of American goods shipped to Greece.

to be useless because the Communists seized control in 1949). In more recent times, economic and military assistance has been given to Thailand, Pakistan, South Korea, and many other nations to help prevent Communist takeovers.

Alliances have been a second major response to the threat of Communist expansion. The 1947 Rio Treaty, signed by the United States, Mexico, and almost all of South America, provided for mutual assistance in case of attack originating inside or outside the Western Hemisphere. NATO—the North Atlantic Treaty Organization—was created in 1949 by the United States, Canada, Western European nations, Iceland, Turkey, and Greece. SEATO—the Southeast Asia Treaty Organization, which involved the United States, Great Britain, France, Pakistan, Australia, Thailand, and the Philippines—was formed in 1954. In addition to these large-scale defensive alliances, the United States has entered into bilateral (two-nation) treaties with Japan, South Korea, Taiwan, and other nations.

With the exception of NATO, these alliances have proved of little or no national security value. Although the United States might come to the aid of treaty members, the likelihood, or instance, of a Rio Treaty member reciprocating is quite small. Moreover, military assistance supplied through treaty obligations has frequently been used for purposes other than that of containing Communism. For example, Pakistan has usually deployed its military not against possible Soviet or Chinese attack but against India. Because of the lack of political agreement among many treaty members, plus a decline in the immediacy of Communist aggression in many areas, most of these alliances—except for NATO—have become weakened or have been officially dissolved (SEATO, for example, was ended in 1977).

A third response to the perceived Communist threat was the establishment of numerous overseas military bases. Since World War II, American political and military leaders have held that the best deterrent to Soviet aggression was the threat of thermonuclear retaliation. To make the threat credible in the days before long-range missiles, the

In 1983, *following a coup, American troops land in Grenada, whose government the U.S. had opposed.*

United States surrounded the Soviet Union with large air bases from which a retaliatory attack could be launched. Military installations were established in Libya, Spain, The Azores (owned by Portugal), Turkey, Japan, Iran, and several other nations. The creation of foreign bases had far-reaching implications. Having made an expensive investment, the United States frequently felt obligated to protect it by granting the host nations trade concessions, foreign aid, or support for the local political elite. American support for the Spanish dictator Francisco Franco was justified largely by the need for keeping military bases in Spain.

The United States has engaged in numerous military operations in the name of stopping Communist expansion. The most notable, of course, were the Korean and Vietnam wars. In many other instances, U.S. intervention was more covert—that is, secret. For example, military supplies and training have been given to anti-Communist insurgents in Iran, Chile, Guatemala, Cuba, and several African nations. In 1958, when it appeared that pro-Communist forces might seize control of Lebanon, President Eisenhower ordered the Marines to that nation. President Johnson took similar action in 1965 when it appeared that the Dominican Republic might fall to Communist revolutionaries. In 1983 President Reagan ordered U.S. troops to the small Caribbean island of Grenada to prevent it from becoming a Communist base. Such intervention, even in areas far from U.S. borders and with little relevance to American economic interests, has occasionally been justified by what is called the **domino theory.** Essentially, this perspective holds that one Communist victory will lead to another, and eventually, if unchecked, the whole world will go Communist, much as one tipped domino can trigger the fall of other dominos in a row.

Promoting Peace and International Stability

A second goal of American foreign policy has been to promote world peace. Preventing war has always been an important aim, but the growing interdependence of nations and the horrible consequences of nuclear war have made the task even more crucial. Whereas a war between two small countries could once have been safely ignored, today there is always the possibility that conflict could spread and be the spark that touches off World War III.

American Support for the United Nations

Following World War II, U.S. leaders had great hope that world peace could be maintained through the United Nations. The American government was one of the moving forces in its creation and has subsequently provided the United Nations with considerable financial and material support. On numerous occasions the goal of reducing armed conflict by U.N. intervention has been realized. Between 1947 and 1949, for instance, the United Nations helped end the conflict between the Dutch and the Indonesians. United Nations troops have supervised armistices or provided a neutral buffer zone between opposing forces—for example, in Korea in 1953, in Cyprus in 1964, and in the Middle East in 1948, 1956, and 1973.

The American goal of creating an international peacekeeping force in the United Nations has not had great success, however, when world powers have been in direct conflict. Separating India and Pakistan, two long-time enemies, is considerably easier than preventing U.S.–Soviet military confrontations. When the Communist North Koreans invaded South Korea in 1950, the United Nations was powerless to stop a rapid escalation of military involvement. The United Nations was equally powerless when the Soviet Union invaded Hungary in 1956 and Czechoslovakia in 1968. Nor did the world organization fare much better in helping to end U.S. involvement in Southeast Asia. Overall, the United Nations has fulfilled American expectations in keeping peace when the issues or participants do not directly threaten U.S. or Communist bloc interests.

Direct U.S. Intervention in Conflicts

Besides working through the United Nations, the United States on numerous occasions has directly entered conflicts to promote peace. In 1973 and 1974, for example, the American Secretary of State, Henry Kissinger, dramatically intervened in the Arab-Israeli war to arrange a cease-fire and an eventual agreement on Israeli use of the Suez Canal and partial Israeli withdrawal from the Sinai desert. Perhaps the most spectacular recent American peacekeeping effort occurred in September 1978, when President Carter brought Egyptian President Anwar Sadat and Israeli Prime Minister Menachem Begin together at Camp David to resolve several long-standing Egyptian-Israeli disputes. American influence was also employed to help settle the Turkish-Greek conflict over Cyprus and several Pakistanian–Indian border disputes.

U.S.—Soviet Accords

Perhaps the most important actions taken by the United States to ensure world peace have involved attempts to create better relations with the Soviet Union. A number of programs have been established to promote greater understanding at a personal level—cultural exchanges, cooperative scientific ventures, the distribution of magazines in each other's countries, and the like. It is hoped that when Americans meet Russians with common interests, some of the mutual hostility between the nations will be lessened. Another tactic to improve U.S.–Soviet relations are occasional **summit meetings** between the President and top Soviet leaders. In this case, too, the hope is that personal contact will help each side appreciate the problems faced by the other. Summits also might help create more personal channels of communication that can prevent crises before they occur.

A third element in cooling U.S.–Soviet tension consists of treaties and agreements designed to reduce the likelihood of armed confrontation. In 1959, for example, the United States, the Soviet Union, and several other nations agreed to make Antarctica an international territory and prohibit its use for military purposes. In 1963 the United States and the Soviets established a telegraphic "hotline" to permit rapid communication in the event of an international crisis (the hotline was used during the 1967 Middle East war to prevent Soviet misunderstanding of U.S. fleet movements). The most important U.S.–Soviet accords have addressed the arms race. Beginning in 1969, a number of agreements in what is called the Strategic Arms Limitation Talks (SALT) have slowed down the development and deployment of weapons. We shall have more to say about these agreements later when we analyze the arms race.

Providing Economic Assistance

As the world's richest nation, the United States has long had a commitment to help other countries achieve higher standards of living. Of course, in many instances—for example, post–World War II help to Europe—economic assistance was motivated largely by the goal of blocking Communist expansion. Nevertheless, the United States has not been motivated solely by political self-interest. On many occasions the U.S. government has provided financial assistance or help in rebuilding after a natural disaster to nations that differed substantially with U.S. foreign policy.

In 1985 President Reagan met with Soviet Premier Mikhail Gorbachev in Geneva; earlier in the year he met with British Prime Minister Margaret Thatcher in the White House to discuss defense issues.

Foreign Aid

Much of our support for worldwide economic development has come through foreign aid appropriated annually by Congress. Between 1946 and 1984, the United States made outright grants of over $120 billion and loans of over $53 billion to other nations (and many of these loans were never repaid). Immediately following World War II, aid was given primarily to European nations, but since the mid-1950s, the emphasis has been on helping developing nations. Some of the major recipients of foreign aid in the past three decades have been Egypt, Israel, Jordan, Guatemala, Indonesia, and the Philippines. In recent years, however, there has been a trend toward using multinational agencies to channel U.S. economic aid. These include the World Bank; regional bodies, such as the African Development Fund; and United Nations agencies (in 1981 the United States gave more than $4.4 billion to such international organizations).

In addition to regular foreign aid assistance, the United States has enacted special programs to meet particular problems or the needs of specific areas. For example, President Kennedy was greatly concerned with U.S.–Latin American relations and helped create the Alliance for Progress, with an American commitment of $10 billion over a ten-year period to promote industrialization and economic growth in Latin America (subsequent Presidents have extended this commitment). For many years surplus farm products have been given to nations in need through the U.S. Food for Peace Program. On numerous occasions surplus American wheat prevented famine in India, Egypt, and several African nations. For example, in 1985 the government provided massive aid to relieve starvation in Ethiopia. In 1961, President Kennedy created the Peace Corps by executive order. Under this program, thousands of Americans have worked overseas to provide technical assistance on a person-to-person basis, frequently in remote areas.

Foreign Aid Through International Trade

One area of enormous importance for economic assistance is international trade. Many leaders of underdeveloped nations have argued that conces-

Egyptian President Anwar Sadat, President Carter, and Israeli Prime Minister Menachem Begin congratulate each other on a Middle East peace accord, 1979.

Starving children in Ethiopia wait for food at a distribution center. Many nations responded to the famine disaster in the 1980s.

sions, or agreements, in trade are far more valuable for economic progress than an occasional foreign aid handout. They maintain that if the United States really wanted to help, say, Ghana, it would import more cocoa beans from that country. This policy is frequently called "trade, not aid," and it is strongly endorsed by the United States. The United States insists, however, that trade concessions be reciprocal; that is, if we reduce the tariff on cocoa beans, Ghana should reduce its tax on American soybeans. Developing nations have largely rejected this position on the grounds that it would favor the industrialized nations, which would flood poor nations with their goods, thus preventing local economic development. To date, although the United States has occasionally helped developing nations by modifying its trade policy, it has not abandoned its policy of reciprocal trade concessions.

Furthering American Economic Interests

As we saw in Chapter 15, the federal government traditionally has been an important promoter of American industry, even to the extent of ensuring that American business can compete in overseas markets. In fact, several critics of American foreign policy have claimed that the promotion of American commercial interests throughout the world is *the* major goal of American foreign policy. These critics characterize American foreign policy as **imperialism**—that is, it tries to exploit the rest of the world for American advantage, especially that of American business interests. Whether government assistance is merely a helping hand or part of a comprehensive imperialist strategy is an important question that we shall consider once we have described how government promotes American business interests abroad.

American Overseas Investments

Anyone who has traveled overseas has observed American brand-name products—from Coca-Cola to Caterpillar bulldozers—in almost every country. The entry into foreign markets is neither accidental nor an indication of the quality of American goods. In 1984, direct investment by U.S. firms abroad totaled $223 billion, yielding an income of $23 billion. The federal government has taken steps to ensure that U.S. corporations can sell products in Europe, Asia, South America, or Africa. The U.S. tax code, for example, contains provisions that encourage American overseas expansion. The taxes that a U.S. business located abroad pays to a foreign government are credited against the company's U.S. taxes rather than being treated as ordinary business expenses. U.S. taxes on income earned by American businesses overseas are deferred, or delayed, until the earnings are actually brought back into the United States. This provision grants to companies what amount to interest-free loans. Both tax credits and deferred income provide major incentives to do business overseas. Moreover, under some conditions portions of various antitrust laws are suspended when American businesses cooperate with one another to conduct foreign trade.

The U.S. government has also acted to prevent foreign nations from placing excessive import duties on American products. For instance, the "Open Door" policy toward China advocated in the 1890s called for all commercial interests, whether British, French, or American, to be given equal treatment. The most significant modern example of this policy has been the General Agreement on Tariffs and Trade (GATT). In 1947 the United States played a major role in drafting this agreement, which includes most non-Communist nations, to regulate tariff policy on thousands of items in world trade. Members of GATT agree not to discriminate against other countries in their tariff rates, not to use internal taxes to substitute for tariffs, not to impose import quotas (except in special circumstances), and not to flood foreign markets with artificially cheap goods. Even though GATT contains several important escape clauses, overall it has acted to open up world trade.

In many instances government officials have negotiated directly on behalf of American business interests. Recently, for example, in response to large trade imbalances between the United States and Japan, American officials have tried to persuade Japan to import more American products and make it easier for American companies to sell in Japan. Perhaps the most obvious government efforts on behalf of American corporations occur in the sale of military hardware. For example,

when General Dynamics was trying to sell its F-16 fighter planes to several European air forces (in competition with the French F1 M53), the firm received full government cooperation.

The foreign aid program is yet another means of opening up the world for American business interests. In some instances the aid and technical assistance set up a future market—it is easier to sell a nation American tractors, airplanes, or computers once that country has become accustomed to using American technology. Foreign aid programs also pay for American corporations to explore overseas investment opportunities. It was under such a program, for example, that several American firms first located in Nigeria. Furthermore, the granting of U.S. aid (or the threat of withdrawal once granted) has been widely used to guarantee protection for American interests overseas. When Peru decided to withdraw a tax concession given to the international subsidiary of an American oil company, U.S. financial assistance was

A number of U.S. products are sold to third world nations. Here, women in Riyadh, Saudia Arabia, carry supplies for their infants.

stopped. In addition, the overseas investments of many American corporations are frequently protected by the Investment Guaranty Program, which is part of the Agency for International Development (AID).

Perhaps the most controversial use of foreign aid on behalf of American commercial interests occurs when aid is used to support a dictatorial government sympathetic to American businesses. For example, in 1964 the Socialist government of Brazil was overthrown by military officers trained by the United States. Foreign aid subsequently jumped by more than $100 million despite claims by some Brazilians that the new government was repressive. It is alleged that military aid (and CIA assistance)—given apparently for self-defense or as part of anti-Communist treaty obligation—has been used to maintain dictators who, in turn, helped American companies. The current governments in Taiwan and South Korea, for example, are both strongly pro-American business and have both received substantial military assistance, some of which has been used to intimidate political opponents.

Overseas Investments: The Imperialism Argument

That many American foreign policy decisions are directed toward helping private economic interests is beyond doubt. There is controversy, however, on the scope and intensity of the government commitment to private investment. On the one hand are those who see U.S. help as essentially no different from the aid given by the Japanese, French, or British governments to their corporations. Also, because American prosperity depends in part on the success of American business, it is reasonable for the government to provide assistance in overseas ventures. Moreover, such assistance contributes to overall world economic development by creating jobs and skills in developing nations. In short, some people believe that there is nothing evil about government promoting entry into overseas markets by American corporations.

Opposed to this perspective are several scholars who view current American foreign policy as a continuation, though by different methods, of a

long-standing policy of imperialism (sometimes labeled "dollar diplomacy"). In the past, imperialism meant the outright control of other nations, usually by military force, in order to exploit local resources. African and Asian colonies were forced to buy goods manufactured by the controlling nations, workers were paid as little as possible, local leaders were repressed or manipulated, and natural resources were extracted until used up. National and private economic interests were almost inseparable, and nations competed to carve up the developed portions of the world.

Following World War II, the old system of outright control was abandoned, and most nations in Asia and Africa achieved self-rule. Nevertheless, proponents of the imperialism argument claim that the same goals are still being pursued, although now the chief culprit is the American multinational corporation. That is, it is no longer necessary for the United States to own outright or directly administer a developing nation. Instead, a

"I see. Due to your corrupt mismanagement, the people of your country are starving and rebellious, and you urgently require American aid. Right. How many machine guns?"
Reproduced by special permission of PLAYBOY Magazine; © 1967 by Playboy

few multinational corporations, supported by the ever-present threat of U.S. government intervention, can make huge profits by controlling key industries. In Central America, for example, one American company has long dominated banana growing and marketing and thus has controlled several nations without actually running them. Especially in technologically dependent industries—for example, telecommunications and electronics—the American multinational corporation frequently dominates the local economy.

Proponents of the imperialism argument do not stop, however, with charges of government intervention to aid foreign business ventures. Imperialism can also result in wars, such as the ones in Vietnam and Korea. These wars, the argument goes, are fought not only to preserve the specific investments of American companies but to maintain American economic influence over much greater areas. In Vietnam, for example, the immediate goal was to hold on to extensive rubber and oil resources, but the long-range aim was to control an area of 200 million people and 1.5 million square miles of territory. In Africa, imperialism is expressed by supporting conservative or racist regimes that allow U.S. corporations access to supplies of copper, uranium, diamonds, and oil.

The Counterargument

Is the United States guilty of imperialism? On the whole, the more drastic claims by those who believe that it is have not been well documented. It certainly is not true that the U.S. government—in conjunction with the giant multinational corporations—is seeking to take over the world. Indeed, in many instances the government and multinationals have been in conflict. For instance, the federal government has cracked down on the payment of bribes by American corporations to obtain foreign business, despite corporate claims that bribery is essential to doing business in many nations (convicted companies are subject to a heavy fine). The wheelings and dealings of ITT in Chile were exposed in part by congressional investigations. The imperialism argument also fails to explain continued American support for Israel, when economic self-interest would dictate stronger support for the oil-producing Arab states. The argument that imperialism leads to war in order to protect U.S. domination is also open to serious question. Both the Korean and Vietnam wars undoubtedly cost more than these nations were worth economically (the war in Vietnam cost American taxpayers at least $118 billion). In addition, the willingness of American corporations to do business with Communist governments suggests that so-called imperialist wars might be unnecessary. After all, why go to war with China if you can sell to the Chinese jets and computers at a handsome profit without generating ill feeling?

Problems in Achieving Foreign Policy Objectives

Overall, the United States has had mixed results in achieving its foreign policy goals since 1945. The United States has maintained its national security, but it has also engaged in two long and expensive wars, in Korea and Vietnam, as well as a large number of skirmishes. Some people argue that the huge cost of this security has deprived millions of a better life. And given the ever-present possibility of nuclear war, no real security is possible despite the heavy costs. We have succeeded in helping countries like Japan and Germany recover from the devastation of World War II only to have them emerge as our economic competitors. Billions of dollars in aid to less-developed nations has had only a limited impact. To explain our shortcomings in foreign affairs, we must understand certain aspects of international relations.

Events Are Unpredictable

In making foreign policy choices, leaders face a world in which the unexpected frequently occurs. In 1950, for example, the invasion of South Korea by North Korea came as a complete surprise. The decision by the Chinese to enter the war also came as a shock. The Middle East has been a constant source of unpredicted events. Few experts anticipated the 1979 overthrow of the shah in Iran and his replacement by Moslem fundamentalists. Events in Lebanon, beginning in 1983, in which a multitude of religious groups battled for political control, would not have been predicted ten years earlier (Lebanon was long considered an island of peace and stability in an otherwise unstable region).

Such unpredictability will continue despite billions spent on gathering and interpreting intelligence data. The consequences of leadership changes in the Soviet Union and China are rarely clear in advance. The rise of new leaders in China, for example, has changed our relations with that nation dramatically. Nor can we anticipate events like the Soviet downing of a Korean commercial airliner in 1983 or attacks by terrorists and assassins. Such unexpected incidents can set off a long chain of events. The Arab-Israeli war of 1973, for example, resulted in Middle Eastern nations using their oil for political purposes, and the increased oil prices influenced nearly every aspect of our economy.

Knowledge is Limited

The problem of unpredictability is complicated further by our lack of knowledge in many areas of foreign affairs. For example, despite years of experience, billions of dollars, and numerous studies, the solution to helping developing nations build their economies has not been found. Nor have many problems of international trade been solved, despite being studied by many leading economists. In addition, we have only limited understanding of how wars begin or how they can be ended quickly (we shall consider this issue in greater depth below).

Goals Can Conflict

Perhaps the most enduring obstacle to a more successful foreign policy is that many of our goals conflict with each other. On numerous occasions leaders are pulled one way by domestic forces and in a different direction by foreign policy considerations. In recent years, for example, several American industries—autos, copper, shoes, consumer electronics, steel, among others—have sought protection from cheap imports. Protectionist requests are backed up by thousands of voters whose livelihood is in jeopardy. Yet to give in to these demands could very well damage our relations with many other countries, including our allies.

Another common conflict occurs over the overseas sale of American military goods and technology. This is consistent with a policy of domestic economic growth and help for American corporations. Such sales, however, can turn international disputes into destructive wars (on several occasions both sides fought with U.S.-supplied military hardware). Moreover, the selling of American technology ultimately can weaken American national security if the Soviets gain access to it. There is also the problem of poor nations using money for military goods rather than for economic development.

Check Your Understanding

1. What actions has the United States taken in response to the threat of Soviet expansion?

2. What are some of the different ways the United States has sought to promote peace around the world?

3. How has the United States tried to assist other nations economically?

4. How does the government promote U.S. economic interests abroad?

5. Describe the major problems in achieving U.S. foreign policy objectives.

CAN THE ARMS RACE BE ENDED?

Of all the issues in American foreign policy, perhaps the most enduring and important is the U.S.–Soviet arms race and the ever-present threat of nuclear war. This is a problem with many implications. The huge expenses of the arms race mean reduced government funds for human-needs programs—education, health care, housing, and the like. It has also been argued that the maintenance of a huge defense industry undermines the civilian economy by drawing away talent and investment while turning out products of limited value. Moreover, the arms race has spilled over to other parts of the world, especially developing nations, where money that could be spent on development is put into military hardware. Most important, it is claimed that the stockpiling of more and more destructive power increases the likelihood of a nuclear war.

Few people like the idea of ever-increasing military expenditures, and nobody wants a nuclear war. Yet attempts to halt present trends have met with limited success. To understand the arms race and the possibility of nuclear war, let us begin by describing the present situation and then examine some of the reasons for the arms race and the proposals to limit it.

Present Military Spending and Nuclear Force

The amount of money spent on national defense by the United States and the rest of the world is enormous. In fiscal 1983, for example, the U.S. Defense Department spent $205 billion. By way of comparison, in 1970, when the United States were deeply involved militarily in Vietnam, the defense budget was "only" $78.6 billion. According to current Pentagon plans, there will be no leveling off in the future—one forecast sees defense expenditures reaching nearly $450 billion by 1989.

The United States is not alone in its willingness to spend lavishly on the military. In 1983 it was estimated that total worldwide military expenditures had reached $660 billion annually. Some 25 million men and women served in regular armies. The international arms trade has become a very important industry. Some thirty nations are in this business, and in 1981, for example, the United States and the Soviet bloc provided nearly $15 billion in military hardware and assistance to developing nations.

This money can buy an incredible amount of destructive hardware. In 1983 the United States possessed 1,047 intercontinental ballistic missiles (ICBMs) equipped with 2,150 nuclear warheads. We also have 34 missile-carrying submarines, and the 568 on-board missiles have about 5,000 warheads. These missiles are supplemented by 328 manned bombers. In Western Europe alone, the United States maintains some 6,000 tactical nuclear weapons. The Soviets in 1983 had some 1,398 ICBMs armed with more than 5,000 warheads. Their submarine force consists of 62 ships with about 950 missiles, with a total of about 2,000 nuclear warheads. It is estimated that the Soviets deploy between 9,000 and 12,000 tactical nuclear weapons in Europe. Besides these massive arsenals of nuclear weapons, Great Britain and France possess 162 nuclear-tipped missiles. All told, in 1983, there were some 50,000 nuclear weapons in existence.

It is not easy to convey the power of these weapons. The atomic bomb dropped on Hiroshima, which nearly destroyed that city, had an explosive yield of 13 kilotons (or 13,000 tons) of TNT. By comparison, a U.S. Poseidon submarine carries 16 missiles, each of which has 10 warheads. Each of these warheads has a 40-kiloton explosive yield. In other words, one submarine can now hit 160 targets with thirty-two times the destructive power of the bomb that wiped out Hiroshima. Keep in mind that a single Poseidon submarine is only a tiny fraction of U.S. nuclear firepower and that substantial improvements in the destructive power of missile-delivery systems have been made since the Poseidons were introduced in the 1970s. Needless to say, both the United States and the Soviet Union have the capacity to destroy all life many times over.

Roots of the Present Situation

The emergence of expensive military machines heavily armed with nuclear weapons has many roots. It can be understood by examining the changing U.S. military objective, the doctrine of deterrence, the nature of modern warfare, and the politics surrounding the implementation of these choices.

Defining the U.S. Military Objective

At the close of World War II, the United States greatly reduced both its military aims and its armed forces. Until 1949, the United States enjoyed a monopoly in nuclear weapons, but little was done to build a stockpile of bombs, beef up delivery systems, or otherwise strengthen military capacity. Because the Soviet Union was still recovering from the destruction of World War II and consolidating its gains in Eastern Europe, this policy had widespread appeal.

In 1949 the Soviet Union exploded a nuclear device. Events in China (it fell under Communist rule), Korea, and Europe convinced many people that the Soviets had become an expansionist force. In response, the United States redefined its primary military goal as containment of the Soviet Union through the threat of **massive retaliation:** an attack on, say, Western Europe would trigger attacks by manned bombers with nuclear weapons on Soviet industrial and population centers. This could be accomplished relatively inexpensively. A few hundred B-36s or B-52s, which had a range of 10,000 miles, could withstand Soviet attack and by themselves could inflict enormous damage. It was an all-purpose strategy. These bombers could, in principle, deter Soviet aggression anywhere by holding Soviet cities hostage.

In the 1960s the emergence of the Soviet nuclear strike capacity, especially with long-range missiles, broadened the military's mission. With the Russians able to match U.S. nuclear threats, nuclear power was now a stand-off. The role of conventional, or nonnuclear, forces in the defense of Europe and Japan thus gained in importance. Also, it was argued that by improving conventional forces—infantry, armor, tactical airpower, and so forth—escalation to a nuclear conflict could be avoided. The conventional warfare mission was far more complex and costly than the 1950s-style massive-retaliation concept. Among other things, it required a capacity to support troops thousands of miles from home against an enemy that outnumbered them two or three to

one. Thousands of technologically sophisticated tanks and airplanes had to be substituted for a few B-52s.

Since the 1960s, a number of military objectives have been added. Because of the heightened importance of Middle East oil, the U.S. military now must concern itself with maintaining political stability in the region and keeping vital sea lanes open during an international crisis. Increasing Soviet influence in many developing nations has made it necessary for the United States to develop a capacity to intervene militarily, directly or indirectly, in a number of nations. If we allow for a major war fought against both the Soviet Union and China, the responsibilities of the military become enormous.

In sum, since World War II the U.S. military has added several complex goals. It must deter Soviet aggression by both nuclear and conventional forces in far-apart areas of the world. It must also be able to respond quickly and effectively to the so-called brushfire wars in Africa, the Middle East, South America, or Asia. Each of these potential conflicts has different military requirements. This is an important change from the days when a few nuclear armed bombers kept the peace around the world.

The Doctrine of Deterrence

A second factor that helps explain the existence of a large military establishment with enormous nuclear destructive power is the doctrine of **deterrence.** This theory, basically, is that an enemy can be discouraged or deterred from aggression if the consequences of such aggression would be overwhelmingly negative. In other words, if Soviet leaders know that an attack on the United States would result in the destruction of the Soviet Union, it would be senseless for them to launch an attack. Deterrence is a simple idea, but its implementation often results in complexities and what can appear to be irrational behavior.

A key element in deterrence theory is that a nation must have a credible **second-strike capacity.** If the Soviet Union launches an all-out **first strike** on the United States, we should still have sufficient power to inflict enormous damage on

The Air Force KC-135 provides aerial refueling for strategic bombing and tactical aircraft. The aim of the U.S. military is to deter a first strike by the Soviet Union.

the attacker. As long as a nation knows that a first strike cannot be totally effective, it will think long and hard about launching one. The idea of "if you seriously wound me, I'll cripple you" is generally known as **mutual assured destruction (MAD).**

Maintaining a credible second-strike capacity requires the deployment of vast destructive power. Having thousands of missiles and bombers when only a few dozen could destroy the Soviet Union is called **overkill** (the capacity to use greater force than needed to destroy a population or a facility). Thus, if the United States possesses 1,000 missiles and the Soviet first strike disables 950 of them, the 50 surviving ones must still be able to inflict massive destruction. The need by both sides to guarantee a second-strike capacity encourages never-ending increases in destructive capability. Assume that the United States deploys 100 ICBMs. The U.S.S.R. then must deploy 110 missiles to guarantee a credible second strike. Faced with 110 missiles pointing at it, the United States brings its force up to 150 to ensure a retaliatory force. There is never an end, as each side continues to add destructive capacity in order to maintain second-strike readiness.

A credible second-strike capacity also requires a degree of invulnerability—that is, the ability to survive a first-strike attack from the enemy and still be able to strike back. A small, highly vulnerable U.S. missile force might tempt a Soviet first strike. The need for invulnerability has several consequences. First, a retaliatory force must be diversified to increase the chances of survival. Since the 1950s, the U.S. deterrent has been based on the so-called **triad of weapons;** land-based missiles, manned bombers, and submarine-carried missiles are the three "legs" of our defense system. Second, survivability requires the continuous development of new techniques. The advent of spy satellites in the 1970s, for example, meant that immobile ICBMs were much more vulnerable. Technological breakthroughs—laser weapons, radar-invisible aircraft—must be anticipated and adjusted to or else a new weapons system will give the enemy an overwhelming advantage. However, the continuing quest for invulnerability could encourage a **preemptive strike** before invulnerability can be achieved. That is, if the Soviets believed that the United States, but not Russia, would be invulnerable in five years, they might decide, "Let us attack while there is some chance we still can win."

There is an important psychological side to the concept of deterrence. Deterrence requires that the enemy believe that you will strike to deter aggression or launch a second strike if attacked. One must act with a degree of toughness or else aggression might be risked. On the other hand, being too aggressive might encourage a first strike in the hope of avoiding what is perceived to be a likely first strike by a warmonger. Obviously, displaying the toughness needed to make deterrence credible adds to the tension that fuels the arms race.

In short, the doctrine of deterrence has led to a growing buildup of nuclear weapons, a continuing search for new arms, and a style of political action that indicates a willingness to use nuclear force.

The Nature of Modern Warfare

A third factor that helps to explain why the United States spends so much money on defense is the nature of the weapons used in modern warfare. The American military does not depend on millions of soldiers armed with cheap rifles supported by inexpensive tanks and airplanes. For better or worse, it has come to emphasize sophisticated weapons based on complex technology.

The decision to stress technology rather than personnel derives in part from political and population differences between the Western nations and the Soviet bloc. The Soviet bloc has fielded a very large military machine. Table 16.1 compares the forces deployed in Europe in 1983. Because the United States and other Western nations are unwilling to have standing armies of equivalent size, technology is substituted. It is hoped that a smaller number of troops backed by sophisticated hardware can more than match numerically superior Communist forces.

The reliance on technology creates a very expensive military machine. Consider, for example, the cost of a tank. In World War II the United States mass-produced tens of thousand of simple, durable tanks at about $50,000 each. In the 1970s, to counter the huge number of Soviet-bloc tanks, the United States developed the sophisticated M-1, which incorporated a laser-guided fire control system and a gas turbine engine. The cost of developing this "supertank" was enormous. The original price was supposed to be $900,000 per unit but soon exceeded $3 million when development and operating expenses were included. The pattern of cost escalation can be multiplied a hundredfold. Even leaders sympathetic to a strong military have criticized the Pentagon for allowing equipment costs to skyrocket.

Some cost escalation is inherent in the idea of a technologically sophisticated military. Huge amounts of money must often be committed to develop a totally new technology that might or might not work. For example, in 1983 and again in 1987, President Reagan called for the development of an anti-ICBM missile defense based on high-energy particle beams. Several scientists argued that this "Star Wars" approach was technologically impossible. Dead ends and cost overruns are expected under these circumstances. It is also true that unexpected changes in Soviet weaponry can render expensive weapons systems useless.

Another important consequence of the reliance on technology is a great incentive to sell U.S. arms to other nations. Developing new weapons involves a huge financial investment. If only a small number of units are sold, the cost per unit is much too high. To make the product more attractive to

Comparison of NATO and Warsaw Pact Military Forces, 1987*	NATO†	Warsaw Pact
Divisions	110	133
Main battle tanks	21,600	32,000
Antitank weapons	14,370	18,000
Artillery pieces	17,200	23,000
Armored personnel carriers	40,850	38,000
Attack helicopters	1,100	960

*The figures are for forces in place in Europe; they do not include reinforcements from non-European areas. The Warsaw Pact includes all Eastern European Communist nations except Yugoslavia and Albania, plus the Soviet Union.

†These figures include Spain and France, although these countries do not participate in the integrated NATO military structure.

Source: Center for Defense Information news release, April 28, 1987.

TABLE 16.1

U.S. military preparedness entails both high-technology training and extensive field maneuvers.

the U.S. military and to increase corporate profits, the hardware is sold vigorously overseas.

Political Factors

Underlying the military and technological drive for huge defense expenditures are several powerful domestic political forces. First, the defense budget constitutes a major source of jobs, local taxes, and other economic benefits in many parts of the country. Thus, every time the Defense Department wants to abandon a weapons system or close a base to save money, it generates strong political opposition from public officials in these areas. Strong political support also exists for potential military projects. Throughout the 1970s, for example, a number of legislators from California advocated the full deployment of the B-1 bomber, a highly expensive plane that would have been manufactured by the California-based Rockwell Corporation (in 1983 construction of one hundred B-1Bs did begin, at a total cost of $20 billion).

Second, defense contractors engage in vigorous lobbying both for their products and for a general commitment to a large defense budget. Such lobbying is understandable given the fact that most of the business of several multibillion-dollar companies, such as Gruman, General Dynamics, and McDonnell Douglas, is defense work done for the government. The lobbying takes several forms. Most defense contractors have well-financed political action committees (PACs), which disburse numerous campaign contributions, especially to legislators serving on the House and Senate Armed Services committees and the Appropriations subcommittees dealing with national defense. In addition, defense contractors almost always have their own well-staffed lobbying organizations in Washington, often supplemented by public relations consultants and law firms with special ties to government. A large number of trade organizations represent companies with defense business—the Aerospace Industries Association of America, Shipbuilders Council of America, National Electronic Manufacturers, among others. Both the company lobbies and the trade associations exert influence by supplying information, testifying at hearings, and providing public officials with such courtesies as free meals, hospitality suites at conventions, and similar benefits.

Lobbying by defense contractors is often greatly facilitated by what has been called the "revolving door" between the defense industry and government. That is, many defense company employees are former Defense Department officials (and vice versa) and can use their inside knowledge and friendships to advantage. According to the Defense Department, between 1977 and 1979, 1,623 defense employees moved to private industry, and 79 moved from private industry to government. These figures do not include the many members of Congress and aides from executive branch agencies who left government to work for defense-related companies.

Besides corporations with a direct financial stake in a large military budget, there are a number of organizations that lobby on behalf of a strong defense posture. Some, such as the Committee on the Present Danger and the Navy League of the United States, sponsor educational activities with a pro-military outlook. Veterans' groups, such as the American Legion, are also allies of defense-minded officials. In recent years several fundamentalist Christian groups, such as the Moral Majority, have added their voices to the chorus of those who believe that the best deterrent to communism is a strong military.

The Case Against the Arms Race and Nuclear Deterrence

We have explored the many forces that encourage spending ever-larger sums for ever-more-powerful weapons. Moreover, the pattern seems to be worldwide. Let us examine some of the arguments against an arms buildup. We then shall consider justifications for it and conclude with an analysis of whether anything can be done about it.

Increased Odds of a Nuclear Holocaust

Perhaps the strongest argument against the present policy is that, sooner or later, it will lead to a war that will all but destroy the planet. The odds of such a war at any one time might be small; however, given a sufficient number of rolls of the dice, so to speak, such a war can happen. No system of preventing war is foolproof so long as human beings must make decisions.

One possible source of war is accident. According to one study, over one eighteen-month period the U.S. nuclear warning system showed 147 false warnings of a Soviet missile attack.[3] It is possible that some future false warning might occur during an international crisis when a Soviet first strike might appear reasonable. The United States either could react with a genuine strike or could take other action that might convince the Soviet Union that we were attacking first. Another possibility is that a nuclear weapon will detonate accidentally

Fear of nuclear disaster has pressured the superpowers to enact some arms control treaties.

atomic weapons or have the capacity to develop them. Such nuclear arsenals are tiny compared to those of the superpowers, but under some circumstances they could trigger an all-out nuclear exchange, especially by an unstable, unpredictable government in desperate trouble.

Finally, it can be argued that continued development of new weapons systems raises the possibility of a breakthrough that will encourage a massive first strike. Currently there is what has been called a nuclear **balance of terror**—because each side can intimidate the other, a stand-off exists—but events could change quickly. For example, one side might develop an impenetrable antimissile defense system. A situation in which one side had a commanding position occurred in 1945, when only the United States had nuclear weapons, and it could happen again.

The Economic and Social Costs of the Arms Race

A second broad attack on the arms race focuses on its nonmilitary consequences. Obviously, the hundreds of billions spent on missiles and tanks could be invested in education, health care, rebuilding of cities, and so on. The money for a single Trident submarine—more than $1 bil-

in such a way as to give the impression of an attack. According to the Defense Department, between 1950 and 1980 there were thirty-two accidents involving nuclear weapons (and in one case, a U.S. submarine accidentally launched a live but nonnuclear missile).

Miscalculation by political leaders could also trigger a war nobody wants. Deterrence requires a demonstrated willingness to use nuclear force. Imagine that a Middle East war grew larger and involved the United States and the Soviet Union more and more deeply. The United States, incorrectly believing that the Soviets were going to intervene directly, believed that vital American oil supplies would be jeopardized. To prevent intervention, all U.S. forces were placed on full alert. The Soviets might mistakenly see this as the beginning of a U.S. attack and launch a first strike in the hope of minimizing the damage.

A third, and increasingly likely, source of nuclear war derives from what is called **nuclear proliferation**—the spread of nuclear weapons among smaller nations. Besides the major world powers (the United States, Great Britain, France, the Soviet Union, and China), a number of other countries—notably India, Israel, South Africa, Pakistan, and Brazil—either already possess

Crises are handled in the emergency conference room at the National Military Command Center in Washington.

lion—could probably provide comprehensive health care for thousands of poor people. In addition, ending the exportation of arms to developing countries would free an enormous amount of money for humanitarian purposes (and the arms-exporting nations would also have substantial sums of money to use in helping developing countries).

Less obvious than lost opportunities to improve the quality of life is the inflationary impact of military spending. Inflation is particularly harmful to the poor and elderly on fixed incomes. Military spending contributes to inflation in several ways. First, such spending creates spendable income but not products for that income to buy, so that more and more money "chases" a fixed supply of civilian goods. Second, the defense segment of the economy is characterized by a high rate of obsolescence, few incentives for cost reduction, and considerable inefficiency—all factors pushing prices upward. Finally, the purchase of military hardware by developing nations helps to raise the cost of their exports to developed nations. In the 1970s, for example, one of the strongest advocates of higher oil prices was Iran, which needed the money to pay for huge arms purchases.

It has been claimed that heavy investment in military production undermines overall industrial productivity and technological development. Research money and personnel that could be dealing with problems such as energy conservation instead are allocated to tasks without clear social benefits (for example, increasing the accuracy of ICBMs). Because the military is almost always willing to pay top dollar in the competition for scientific resources, most of our best scientific talent is largely wasted.

Finally, opponents of huge defense outlays assert that such expenditures foster unemployment. Although building tanks and missiles provides jobs, economic analyses suggest that fewer jobs per dollar are created by defense expenditures than by expenditures in the civilian sector. Moreover, defense jobs are often so specialized that unemployment—which is common, given the ups and downs of defense contracts—can be solved only by extensive, and very expensive, retraining.

Defending Military Spending and Nuclear Weapons

The most basic defense of the arms race and the reliance on nuclear weapons rests on the premise that the Soviet Union is committed to a policy of world domination that is pursued through a variety of techniques—subversion, propaganda, economic policies—but whose chief mechanism is military force. So long as the Soviet Union seeks this goal, the United States must continue to be strong militarily. The expenditure of hundreds of billions for defense is a necessary price to pay to preserve the independence of the United States and much of the rest of the world from communism.

It can also be argued that the emphasis on nuclear deterrence is preferable to the alternatives of large standing armies and a dependence on military alliances and foreign bases. That alternative would probably not be much cheaper, would mean a large peacetime draft, and might require regular U.S. involvement in the affairs of foreign nations to protect vital security interests. The "nuclear shield," on the other hand, requires relatively small personnel and foreign political commitments.

Defenders of U.S. defense policy also point to the absence of U.S.–Soviet military confrontation since World War II, despite repeated crises and skirmishes. In other words, the present system basically works. The fear that a small war in the Middle East or an upheaval in Eastern Europe would escalate into a nuclear war has proven groundless. Even though the Soviet Union continues to be expansionistic, it has moved relatively cautiously. It knows that the United States has both the force and the will to deter outright aggression. Often it has used its **client states,** such as Cuba or Vietnam, rather than risk engaging the United States in combat. Direct military action by the Soviets has always been close to home where Soviet interests were directly threatened (for example, Hungary in 1956, Czechoslovakia in 1968, and Afghanistan in 1979).

The economic aspects of huge military expenditures can be defended too. A defense budget of more than $300 billion might appear enormous in isolation, but in the context of the American economy it is not so large. In 1985, a year of rapid increases in defense spending, total defense outlays were only about 6.6 percent of the gross national product (GNP) and 26.5 percent of federal expenditures. Moreover, compared to the 1950s and 1960s, these proportions are low—in 1955, for example, defense spending made up 11.2 percent of the GNP and 62.4 percent of all federal outlays. Nor can it be assumed that a dollar spent on defense is a dollar less for a humanitarian goal. A reduction in defense spending might be translated into reduced taxes, not social spending. Ronald Reagan was elected President in 1980 on a platform of greater military spending *and* tax cuts, to be paid out of reduced social spending. Finally, there are civilian-related benefits from defense outlays, especially in the field of high technology. Although these benefits might be achieved more cheaply in the nondefense sector, it can be argued that without the motivation of national security, the large initial investments would not be made.

Ending the Arms Race and Reducing the Threat of Nuclear War

Even though the present worldwide confrontation between the United States and the Soviet Union has not yet resulted in a nuclear holocaust, most people agree that steps ought to be taken to reduce the likelihood of nuclear war. Just what steps are necessary and possible, however, is a matter of great dispute. Let us review and evaluate some of the proposals that have been made.

Unilateral Disarmament

This proposal views the current situation as a ticking time bomb that will eventually explode unless one side takes drastic action. Proponents suggest that the United States and its allies should disarm without promises from the Soviet side to follow suit. Advocates of unilateral disarmament believe that the Soviets would soon join the West, because the burden of national defense weighs especially heavy on them. The worst possible outcome under this proposal would be Soviet domination, but this alternative is preferable to a world destroyed by nuclear war.

Support for unilateral disarmament has ebbed and flowed since World War II and has occasionally attracted the endorsement of some notable intellectual and religious leaders. Nevertheless, its basic premises—that the Soviets will follow the West's lead and that Soviet rule is better than death—are rejected by most people and by most public officials in the United States and Western Europe. One-sided disarmament, it is asserted, will result in war, because the Soviets will believe they could defeat a militarily weakened West. Overall, regardless of its merits, unilateral disarmament is unlikely to receive serious political attention.

Nuclear Freeze

Like the advocates of unilateral disarmament, proponents of a nuclear freeze see the world as inching toward disaster unless the nuclear arms race is ended. As an important first step, the United States, the Soviets, and other nuclear powers should stop deploying ever more nuclear weapons. Such actions would not eliminate the danger of war, but they at least would stop an expensive and danger-filled escalation. This idea has drawn extensive support, especially in Western Europe but also in the United States. One 1983 public opinion poll showed that 80 percent of Americans were in favor of a freeze.[4] And unlike unilateral disarmament, it has received support from many public officials.

The proposal has also been extensively criticized. Many American conservatives believe that a freeze would only solidify what they see as a present Soviet advantage in nuclear weapons and missiles. And there is the problem of deciding just what should be frozen and at what levels. No doubt all parties would support a version of the freeze that would permit them to deploy their latest weapons while stopping the other side from doing the same. Also, as in any arms agreement, there is the troublesome issue of monitoring compliance—that is, making sure the other side doesn't "cheat." Finally, the present array of nuclear weaponry is designed largely to inflict heavy damage on civilian populations. A freeze would lock us into this weaponry and stop the trend toward more accurate but less destructive missiles.

Arms Control

The arms control approach emphasizes the use of negotiated agreements on the number of weapons, their type, deployment, and the development of new systems. Like the nuclear freeze solution, it seeks to stop escalation, but it also attempts to lessen tension by reducing existing weapons or by keeping nuclear weapons out of some areas of the world. In principle, the idea of arms control has widespread support among almost all U.S. and Soviet officials. There is even a government body—the Arms Control and Disarmament Agency—to formulate and implement agreements.

The arms control process has been going on periodically since the end of World War I. In 1925, for example, a number of nations agreed to ban the use of nerve gas and bacteriological weap-

U.S. Secretary of State George Shultz, left, meets in Moscow with his Soviet counterpart, Eduard Shevardnadze, 1987. They seek better relations between the superpowers and accord on arms control.

ons in warfare (neither the United States nor Japan ratified this treaty). Most arms agreements, however, have occurred since the 1960s (Table 16.2 lists these agreements and their major provisions). There have been some genuine accomplishments. The Limited Test Ban Treaty of 1963, for example, helped to reduce radioactive pollution from atomic testing. The Nuclear Nonproliferation Treaty that became effective in 1970 has put greater restrictions on the exportation of nuclear technology to prevent more nations from acquiring nuclear weapons. The SALT I agreement (1972) has undoubtedly stopped a very costly and perhaps pointless race to build antiballistic missiles (ABMs).

Despite these accomplishments, many doubts remain on the effectiveness of arms control. The most serious criticism is that arms control does not deal with the root cause of the arms race and the threat of a nuclear holocaust. Even a sizable reduction in offensive firepower would still leave the two superpowers locked in conflict with enough weaponry to destroy each other and the rest of the world. The goal of U.S.–Soviet negotiations ought not to be the elimination of a few obsolete bombers or an agreement to do something the two countries would do anyway, such as limit technology transfers. Rather, arms control talks should discuss the sources of tension and hostility.

Even supporters of the idea of arms control acknowledge numerous problems. The banning or limiting of one type of weapon often results in the development of an alternative not covered by the agreement. For example, the SALT I limit on ICBM launchers encouraged the development of **cruise missiles,** which can be launched from almost anything (including commercial airliners). Complex agreements pose serious difficulties in monitoring compliance. In recent years both the United States and the Soviet Union have accused each other of violating agreements, and because there are no provisions for on-site inspection, compliance can never be completely assured. Serious differences also occur in how the two sides view different weapons. For example, the United States considers its F-16 airplanes, stationed in

Arms Control Agreements and Other Treaties Dealing with Nuclear War

Year*	Name	Major Provisions
1959	Antarctica Treaty	Prohibits any military use of Antarctica, including testing of nuclear weapons or disposing of nuclear waste.
1963	Limited Test Ban Treaty	Prohibits nuclear weapons tests "or any other nuclear explosion" in the atmosphere, outer space, and under water. Below-ground explosions are permitted if radioactive debris does not go beyond the tester's borders.
1967	Outer Space Treaty	Bans the sending of nuclear weapons or other weapons of mass destruction in orbit around the earth or other celestial body. It also makes the moon and other celestial bodies off-limits to military use.
1968	Nuclear Nonproliferation Treaty	Prohibits the transfer of nuclear weapons or nuclear technology to nations without such weapons. It provides controls to ensure that peaceful nuclear activities will not be redirected to military uses.
1971	Seabed Treaty	Bans the placing of nuclear weapons or other weapons of mass destruction on seabeds beyond a 12-mile coastal zone.
1971	Reduce the Risk of Accidental Nuclear War Agreement	Pledges the U.S. and U.S.S.R. to take steps to reduce chances of nuclear war. Notification is required of accidental nuclear explosions and missile testing.
1972	Convention on Biological Weapons	Prohibits the development, production, and stockpiling of biological or toxic agents for military purposes. Existing supplies are to be destroyed
1972	Strategic Arms Limitation Treaty (SALT I)	Limits the U.S. and U.S.S.R. to two fixed antiballistic missile (ABM) sites and limits development of new ABM technology (reduced in 1974 to one ABM site).

TABLE 16.2 **(continued)**

	Year	Name	Major Provisions
Arms Control Agreements and Other Treaties Dealing with Nuclear War (continued)	1972	SALT I Interim Agreement	Freezes the number of land-based fixed ICBMs. Limits were put on modification of existing launchers and ceiling put on submarine missile systems.
	1973	Prevention of Nuclear War Agreement	Commits the U.S. and U.S.S.R. to reduce the chance of nuclear war by action and consultation.
	1974	Threshold Test Ban Treaty	Bans underground nuclear explosions exceeding 150 kilotons. Provisions include exchange of data on such tests.
	1974	Peaceful Nuclear Explosion Treaty	Limits the size of nuclear explosions for peaceful purposes and provides procedures for verification.
	1977	Environmental Modification Convention	Prohibits the modification of the environment, including ocean currents, ozone layer, climate, or ecological balance, for hostile purposes.
	1979†	SALT II	Reduces the total number of strategic nuclear weapons delivery systems, bans the construction of new land-based ICBMs, and limits the development of new weapons systems. Provisions also cover verification.
	1981	Inhumane Weapons Convention	Bans certain types of fragmentation bombs and limits weapons, such as mines and incendiary bombs, for use against military targets. U.S. has not signed this treaty.

*Dates are for U.S. agreement. In several cases the agreement came into force at a later date.

†SALT II has not been ratified by the United States, but Presidents have agreed to abide by its provisions.

TABLE 16.2

Western Europe, as a weapon deployed against an attack by conventional forces. Given its long range and capacity to carry nuclear weapons, however, the Soviets can see the F-16 as an offensive weapon. Some Soviet bombers could be considered long-range weapons if they were to be ordered on a one-way suicide mission.

Paralleling the problems of reaching an arms control agreement are the domestic difficulties of ratifying the agreement. A treaty that gave the Soviets a numerical superiority in some areas— even if the "superiority" was militarily meaningless—would encounter strong opposition. An insistence on numerical equality could lead the Soviets to reject the proposal, because equality might disadvantage them (for example, if their missiles were smaller and less accurate). Moreover, there are often attempts to link U.S.–Soviet arms accords to much larger political issues—the Soviet invasion of Afghanistan or Soviet treatment of Poland. Such "linkages" make negotiations even more difficult.

Military Solutions

The three previous approaches all focus on the quantity of weaponry. Their underlying premise is that the greater the destructive power the superpowers possess, the greater the likelihood of a devastating war. In contrast, supporters of the military approach believe that U.S.–Soviet conflicts can be made less dangerous by taking cautious military measures. A nuclear holocaust can result not from powerful weapons themselves, but from having the wrong type of weapons and inadequate decision-making procedures governing their use.

One major element in the military solution is to replace the "all or nothing" deterrence of MAD with a wider array of potential responses to Soviet aggression. We should be able to meet a Soviet attack on Western Europe, without having to rely on atomic weapons. Equally important, if the conflict becomes nuclear, targets ought to be military, not civilian. Thus, older, highly destructive but not very accurate missiles should be replaced by more accurate and less destructive systems. In addition, the existing nuclear strike force should

be made less vulnerable, to reduce the likelihood that the Soviets will be tempted to strike first. Decreased vulnerability would be accomplished through **hardened missile silos** (well-protected launch sites), deployment of mobile missiles, and a greater reliance on submarine-launched missiles.

Reinforcing these shifts in weapons would be changes in decision making. To avoid an accidental war, we should publicly renounce the "strike on warning" doctrine (that is, we will attack only after an attack has been confirmed, rather than in anticipation of it). Provisions must be made for absolute verification of an attack and for identification of the attacker (to reduce the chances of a terrorist group starting a war by setting off a single bomb). Improvements must be made in the military chain of command so that a battlefield decision made under pressure does not set off a nuclear exchange. Communication channels between U.S. and Soviet leaders can be improved, so that even in the midst of an international crisis or full-scale conventional war the chances of catastrophic misperceptions will be reduced.

The military approach has widespread support among top U.S. leaders. As we have mentioned, since the 1960s, the U.S. military has increased its capability to fight several different types of wars. In the mid-1970s the United States began shifting the emphasis from MAD to a **counterforce strategy**— nuclear strikes aimed at military, not civilian, targets. The purpose of the shift was to allow a selective and limited response to Soviet aggression that would not lead automatically to wholesale destruction. In the 1980s, much effort has been invested in making U.S. weapons less vulnerable to a Soviet first strike (one such proposal was the now-abandoned plan to build a huge field of underground, mobile MX missiles that could be fired from as many as five thousand openings).

Like all the other proposals, the military solution has been heavily criticized. Obviously, it does not lighten the heavy financial burdens of national defense, because the cost of possessing a range of military options plus a new generation of ICBMs is considerable. Critics also charge that such a solution is unstable, because technological breakthroughs cannot be anticipated and we cannot predict how leaders might behave at the onset of a limited nuclear exchange. What might occur, for instance, if U.S. leaders believed that the Soviets suddenly possessed some new "superweapon" and were about to use it?

Perhaps the most serious criticism of a military solution is that it encourages, not discourages, war. Basically, it is claimed, the likelihood of conflict is increased by providing leaders on all sides with a variety of military options short of all-out nuclear war. The development of an accurate counterforce capacity in particular can lure leaders into the mistaken belief that a nuclear war is winnable—one press of the button and the enemy's capacity to attack is destroyed. Such is not the case under the **countervalue strategy**—the destruction of Soviet cities and industries would soon be followed by the devastation of American cities and factories. Indeed, it can be argued that the only value of a counterforce system is to launch a first strike, because a retaliatory attack on empty missile silos is pointless.

Making Choices

It is obvious that there are no easy answers to these questions. The choice of solutions depends on a complex evaluation of our national goals, how leaders might behave in a crisis, how technology might change, and what unlikely events might occur. If, for example, one believes that Soviet leaders genuinely reject world domination, unilateral disarmament makes sense. At the other extreme, if one does not trust the Soviets, a military solution has the most appeal. The nuclear freeze and arms control positions fall somewhere in between. Different courses of action also flow from varying beliefs about the consequences of growing military destructive capacity: it is suicidal to support anything short of disarmament if one believes that nuclear firepower will be employed some day.

Important choices must also be made as to what costs are worth bearing. For some people the idea of living under communism is far worse than death by nuclear explosion. The hundreds of bil-

lions spent yearly on weapons can be viewed as a burden necessary for the preservation of peace; such expenditures can also be considered a major cause of world hunger, illness, and wasted human potential. Matters are made even more difficult because the tradeoffs are so hard to calculate. For example, does doubling our defense budget make us twice as secure? Does a small reduction in an enormous arsenal of weapons really decrease the likelihood of war?

In sum, whether the present situation is acceptable or fast approaching catastrophe is difficult to answer. While most people do not want an arms race and nobody wants a nuclear war, people differ sharply on what steps are to be taken. The arms race can be ended, but differences occur over whether the benefits outweigh the costs. The differences of opinion have their roots in numerous assessments, beliefs, and judgments of acceptable risks and burdens.

Check Your Understanding

1. How has U.S. military strategy changed since World War II?

2. Describe the doctrine of deterrence.

3. List major arguments against the arms race.

4. List the arguments in favor of military spending.

5. What are some of the possible ways to reduce the threat of nuclear war?

THE POLITICS OF MORALITY AND REALITY IN AMERICAN FOREIGN POLICY

Our analysis of America's foreign policy has reviewed a wide range of goals and problems. Beneath all of these specific issues is a long-standing controversy over what direction American foreign policy *ought* to take. We have not considered this question thus far, but it is fundamental. Essentially, the issue involves the role of morality in international affairs. We can distinguish two opposing perspectives in this debate: the "power-politics" or "political realism" position and what might be called the "democratic-idealism" perspective.

Advocates of the power-politics position see international affairs as a competition among nations without rules. Whereas domestic conflict is regulated by laws enforced by the police and the courts, no such provisions exist among nations except for relatively unimportant matters (for example, postal rates). Ultimately, as in the jungle, power is decisive. In a crisis, organizations like the United Nations are powerless because they cannot marshal force. Under such circumstances, the primary national goal is survival. Moreover, people cannot be trusted to behave in moral, generous ways. Given a choice, people are selfish and ruthless. A policy of helping other nations, unless such aid directly helps you, is wasteful or even dangerous. Advocating vague idealistic goals, such as human rights, will lead only to diaster. The goal of national survival should be pursued by whatever

means possible. Policy making typically involves secrecy, deception, shows of force, "dirty tricks," and whatever else is necessary. Foreign policy is the pursuit of national self-interest. As President Reagan put it: "I will be firm in my intentions to preserve the interests of the United States and, as President, I will choose the methods by which this shall best be accomplished."

In contrast is the position we have called democratic idealism. Its ultimate goal is the creation of an international order based on humanitarian principles by which disputes are settled by law, not violence. This perspective assumes that people are basically good and are capable of generosity and cooperation. The failure of previous efforts, such as the League of Nations, does not rule out future successes. After all, at one time the idea of a United States of America seemed impossible. U.S. relations with other countries should be based on how well those nations pursue peaceful, humanitarian goals, and under no condition should we support repressive, dictatorial regimes. American foreign policy ought to be made openly and be governed by the same principles as domestic policy. It should stress international cooperation, international law, human rights, and steps to abolish the arms race and war. Assassinations,

Cooperation among countries may help avert war. Here, President Carter meets with other members of the Organization of American States, representing Latin American nations.

STADOS UNIDOS   SECRETARIO GENERAL   PANAMA

blackmail, and "dirty tricks," are not acceptable at home and should not be used abroad. A humanitarian world order cannot be achieved by deceitful means.

Both perspectives have been popular among American leaders at different times. Woodrow Wilson idealistically sought to bring international peace following World War I. World War I was often justified as a "war to end all wars." U.S. support for the United Nations following World War II was rooted in this perspective. More recently, President Carter's emphasis on human rights as a cornerstone of American diplomacy was in the tradition of democratic idealism. The power-politics position has also had its advocates. Many of America's strongest allies have been repressive dictators, who have frequently used U.S. military aid to crush opponents.

Obviously, it is difficult to decide which approach the United States ought to follow. It seems apparent, however, that American foreign policy will continue to employ both. In fact, it seems that we sometimes combine the two perspectives in a strange blend. We practice power politics but call it democratic idealism. One analyst suggests that this odd blend serves a useful purpose. We can preserve our lofty ideals while surviving in an often-hostile world.[5] For example, we enter into alliances with dictatorships to protect the "free world." In Vietnam, the United States justified its massive intervention on the grounds that the Vietnamese ought to be free to decide their own fate. We sell billions of dollars' worth of arms at a considerable profit in the name of world peace. We are not suggesting that American foreign policy is an evil conspiracy justified by high-sounding phrases. Rather, both the power-politics and the democratic-idealist perspectives have strong appeals to leaders, and sometimes it is difficult to separate one from the other.

CHAPTER SUMMARY

1. How is American foreign policy made? The President, based on constitutional grants of power and on necessity, is the most important participant in the making of American foreign policy. Other officials in the executive branch, Congress, interest groups, multinational corporations, and public opinion also play a role in formulating and implementing policy. The President's role is most prominent during a crisis. In noncrisis periods, foreign policy making resembled the formulation of domestic policy.

2. What are the goals of American foreign policy? The primary aim has been national security, which since 1947 has been defined in terms of halting Soviet aggression. Other important objectives are to promote world peace, to encourage economic development, and to help American economic interests overseas. There are several problems, however, in achieving these goals. Events are unpredictable, our knowledge is limited, and goals can conflict.

3. Can the arms race be ended? The United States and the Soviet Union now spend vast sums on defense and possess enormous destructive capacity. For the United States, this situation has its roots in its changing military responsibilities, the doctrine of deterrence, the nature of modern warfare, and several political factors. The arms race has been criticized on both military and economic grounds. Various solutions, from unilateral disarmament to shifts in military preparedness, have been proposed; each has its merits and disadvantages.

IMPORTANT TERMS

Explain the following terms.

crisis decision making
domino theory
summit meeting
imperialism
deterrence
preemptive strike
nuclear proliferation
counterforce strategy
countervalue strategy

THINKING CRITICALLY

1. Modern Presidents have come to dominate U.S. foreign policy making. Would a stronger congressional role in foreign affairs reduce the likelihood of global conflict? Why or why not?

2. Do you think Congress was justified in passing the War Powers Act? Why or why not? What effect has the act had on the role of Presidents in foreign policy making?

3. How responsive to public opinion should our government officials be in making foreign policy choices? Are foreign and domestic politics different in this regard? Explain your views.

4. What obligation does the United States have to try to settle arms disputes around the world? Explain your response.

5. Sometimes presidential decisions in foreign policy must be made in secret. How can the need for secrecy be balanced against the right of Congress and the public to be informed?

6. Many nations receive millions of dollars in economic aid from the United States. Should support for U.S. foreign policy be a condition for receiving U.S. economic aid? Why or why not?

7. If the arms race ended tomorrow, do you think that the money normally spent on defense would be spent on humanitarian causes? Why or why not?

8. Some of the nations the United States supports are dictatorships. Can the United States be morally justified in supporting these dictatorships? Discuss your answer.

EXTENDING YOUR UNDERSTANDING

1. Television news has sometimes been accused of presenting an incomplete picture of other nations. Watch one week of the same national news program. Observe closely the news stories relating to events overseas, noting the references to violence and disorder, accomplishments, and the particular problems faced by citizens in each country. Based on your observations, what conclusions can you draw about this program's coverage of events outside the United States? Present your findings in a report.

2. You are the newly appointed head of the federal agency charged with formulating U.S. foreign aid policy. Your first assignment is to talk to a group of citizens who say that we should take care of our own people before helping people in other countries. Prepare a speech for this group that outlines reasons for continuing foreign aid.

3. Your local library probably has directories of national interest groups (such as *Washington Information Directory*). Select an antiwar group and write to it requesting information on its proposals for reducing or ending the arms race. Analyze these proposals in terms of their underlying assumptions and their feasibility. Present your conclusions in a report.

4. Divide the class into two groups, one representing country X and the other representing country Y. The two nations are on friendly terms. Conduct negotiations on an exchange of high school textbooks between the two nations. Prepare for the negotiations by listing the problems that might arise in the discussions and your suggested solutions to these problems.

MAKING DECISIONS

You are head of a congressional task force responsible for helping to increase Congress' role in foreign policy making. What recommendations would you make? What foreign policy-making powers should Congress have? Prepare a presentation of your recommendations for the class.

Chapter 17
The Politics of State and Local Governments

The national government is the dominant government in the United States; it is more visible and holds the ultimate power. Nevertheless, state and local governments are just as important, if not more so, in their daily impact on the lives of citizens. Such issues as the amount of money for education, construction and maintenance of roads, law enforcement, public assistance to the needy, licensing of lawyers and doctors, and zoning and land use are decided by state and local governments. Despite the popular image of an ever more powerful national government dominating state and local governments, states and municipalities have held their own. In fact, they have expanded much more rapidly than the national government. State and local governments in the United States are far from being insignificant. Our analysis examines three important questions regarding governments below the national level:

- How are state and local governments organized?
- What are the major responsibilities of state and local governments?
- Is the present system adequate for solving contemporary problems?

PREVIEW

How are state and local governments organized? States follow the national model of separate legislative, executive, and judicial branches. However, the specifics of government organization vary considerably from state to state. Within a state there are numerous types of political jurisdictions— counties, townships, cities, special districts, and even metropolitan governments. Legally the state government is supreme over these units, but in practice contemporary fiscal federalism has provided these jurisdictions a degree of independence from state authority (and areas once completely under state control have now at least partially come under federal control).

What are the major responsibilities of state and local governments? In terms of expenditures, education constitutes the most important state activity followed by public welfare, highways, and health and hospitals. Considerable variation exists, however, on how much states spend in these areas. These variations are due to such factors as the nature of the problems faced by states, differences in financial resources, and what citizens want. The other side of expenditures is raising revenue, and here too, we find sizable differences among the states. Some states stress regressive sales taxes, others more progressive income taxes.

Is the present system adequate for solving contemporary problems? Much of the present state and local government system has its roots in the eighteenth and nineteenth centuries, and it has been criticized as inadequate. Among the major criticisms are that existing geographical boundaries are no longer relevant, the multiplicity of governments leads to unnecessary complexity, government responsibilities and capacities are frequently mismatched, and state and local governments are overwhelmed by modern problems. The adequacy of the present system can, however, be defended. Many people see the system as adaptable to new demands, no worse than having all key decisions made in Washington, and the arrangement that most citizens prefer. It is important to keep in mind that much of the debate over who should be responsible for a certain policy really involves what policy is to be chosen.

HOW ARE STATE AND LOCAL GOVERNMENTS ORGANIZED?

Most citizens believe that state and local governments follow the organizational pattern of the government in Washington, D.C. There is a governor instead of a President; there is the state legislature instead of Congress; and a state court system corresponding to the federal court system. At the local level, equivalent government offices would be the mayor, city council, and municipal court. Moreover, many people also believe that the system of national-state-local government is organized like a pyramid: local governments are subordinate to the states in the same way that states are subordinate to the national government.

This image of fifty miniature national governments that, in turn, govern many smaller, similarly organized local governments is only partially correct. State and local governments might sometimes appear to be this way, but in fact these governments are varied and complex. To understand state and local politics, we must begin by examining this diversity and complexity. Our analysis will first consider the various forms government structures take at the state levels. We shall then examine the relationship of governments at different levels.

The Structure of Government in the Fifty States

State governments are generally modeled on the national system of separate executive, legislative, and judicial branches. However, the specifics, such as terms of office, which state officials are elected, and the powers of the branches of government, vary from state to state. Each state seems to have developed its own system, and these differences can frequently explain why politics is not the same in, say, California as it is in Tennessee.

The Office of Governor

Consider, for example, the office of governor in the fifty states. In three states the governor may serve for only two years. In the remaining states

Governors and lieutenant governors perform a variety of functions as leaders of their states.

there is a four-year term, but the states differ as to whether a governor may run for more than one term. As of 1986, twenty-eight states place limits (usually two consecutive terms) on how long a governor may serve. Salaries of governors vary considerably—in 1986 they ranged from $35,000 in Arkansas and Maine to $100,000 in New York (most fall between $60,000 and $75,000). A major departure from the national model occurs in twenty-one states, in which the lieutenant governor is elected separately from the governor. Because an independently elected lieutenant governor frequently has his or her own political ambitions and might be of a different political party than the governor, this can heighten political conflict.

The power of the state's chief executive varies even more. Although the President can appoint Cabinet-level administrators, in many states these top administrators are elected independently. For example, in forty-three states the important position of attorney general is elected; in thirty-eight states the state treasurer is elected; and in sixteen states the superintendent of education is elected. Many states also make it difficult for a governor to remove an appointee; they require that the governor give some concrete reason—not just a disagreement over policy—to the legislature for such removal (a President does not have to provide any explanation for removing top executive branch officials). Also, while the President maintains complete control over preparing the national budget, governors in ten states must share budgeting power with the legislature, a civil service appointee, or an independent agency.

The governor's relationship to the state legislature also differs from the national model. All states except North Carolina give the governor veto power over legislation, but wide variations exist on how large a legislative vote is necessary to override a veto. Most states specify a two-thirds vote; others, a simple majority. The President lacks one important power given to forty-three governors, the *item veto*—the power to veto a portion of a bill while leaving the rest of the legislation intact (the governor in Wisconsin can even veto a sentence or a word). Most governors can also call a special ses-

sion of the state legislature (and frequently decide the agenda of the session). Especially where state legislative service is a part-time job, the governor can use a special session as a potent weapon, because few legislators want to spend more time than necessary at the state capitol. The President may likewise call a special session of Congress, but this power has become less relevant as congressional sessions now occupy most of the year.

The State Legislature

Like Congress, the legislatures of the fifty states are responsible for creating legislation. The procedures in state legislatures also generally follow the pattern of Congress. After a bill is introduced, it goes to committee, where it is debated, changed, and then passed on for a floor vote. Of course, many states have their own special rules and customs. For example, a number of states limit the length of legislative sessions. Also like Congress, state legislatures generally have two chambers. The one exception is Nebraska, which has had a **unicameral** (one-house) legislature since 1934. The terms for state senator in all but twelve states are for four years, and the terms for lower-house legislators are for two years in all but four states. The size of the state legislature differs considerably from state to state. The lower house of the New Hampshire legislature has 400 members, compared to the lower houses of Alaska and Nevada, where there are only 40 members (state senates are much smaller—most are in the 40–60 range).

A major difference between Congress and the average state legislature is the demands made on the legislator. Serving in the U.S. Congress is a full-time job; serving as a state legislator is usually a part-time job. In the past it was customary for a state legislature to meet once every two years, and although this has changed in most states, seven states still hold only one session every two years. Even where there is an annual session, this session is likely to run for only a few months (North Dakota in 1976 responded to the press of legislative business by increasing its legislative session from sixty to eighty days). Also, because state legislators are sometimes within an automobile drive of home, the legislative week may be a short one

Biography: Nelson Rockefeller

A man of great personal wealth and enormous ambition, Nelson Rockefeller wanted very much to be President. "When you think what I had," he once said, "what else was there to aspire to?" Rockefeller competed for the Republican nomination several times but failed to win it. The forceful and ebullient New Yorker had far more success as governor of his state, a position to which he was elected four times. (Only the state's first governor, George Clinton, held the office longer.) As New York's chief executive, Rockefeller wielded much more power than he did as Vice President, a post he later held.

Rockefeller, a grandson of oil magnate John D. Rockefeller, was born in 1908. After graduating from Dartmouth College, he worked in several family enterprises, including real estate developments in New York City and oil installations in Venezuela. He then held various posts in the Roosevelt and Eisenhower administrations, among them Assistant Secretary of State for Latin American affairs and Undersecretary in the Department of Health, Education, and Welfare (now Health and Human Services).

In 1958 Rockefeller ran successfully for his first four-year term as governor of New York. Although inexperienced in state politics, he was tolerated by Republican leaders mainly because he could finance his own campaign. The new governor soon made his

mark by launching a number of ambitious projects. Under his leadership, the state university system increased from 38,000 students on 28 campuses to 246,000 students on 71 campuses. The state built 200 water-treatment plants, 90,000 housing units, and 23 new mental-health facilities. Additional construction included an impressive state office complex in the state capital of Albany—erected at a cost of $1.5 billion—and 29 other state office buildings. Programs to benefit the New York City metropolitan area included aid to public transportation.

The cost of all of this activity was high. The state budget more than quadrupled during Rockefeller's administration, from $2 billion to almost $9 billion. New

York imposed its first state sales tax. And the annual tax burden for individuals jumped from $94 to $460 for every man, woman, and child.

Ironically, Rockefeller's success in New York stood in his way when he sought the presidency in 1960, 1964, and 1968. His reputation as a big spender and as a man concerned with urban problems marked him as a liberal among Republicans at a time when leaders like Arizona Senator Barry Goldwater—the Republican presidential candidate in 1964—were turning the party in more conservative directions.

In his last five years as governor, Rockefeller himself became more conservative, probably in an effort to gain support from party regulars outside the state. He began to stress the need to hold down state spending. He proposed a residency requirement for welfare recipients—a proposal he had condemned when Goldwater advanced it in 1964. Liberal critics faulted him most for his failure to go to the scene of a 1971 prison riot at Attica, New York, which resulted in the deaths of twenty-nine inmates and ten hostages.

In 1974, after Richard Nixon's resignation as President brought Vice President Gerald Ford to the Oval Office, the latter named Rockefeller as his Vice President. Rockefeller served for two years (he died in 1979). It was the closest "the eternal governor" ever got to the presidency.

(and frequently absenses are encouraged by the fact that most legislators have other, full-time occupations).

Another difference between members of Congress and state legislators is that a state legislator receives less support than a member of Congress. This is most notable in legislative salaries. Many states still pay legislators less than $15,000 per biennial (two-year) session. New Hampshire pays the lowest, $200. On the high end of the pay scale are Illinois ($32,500 per year) and New York ($43,000 per year). In most states, however, legislative pay would not be considered a good income for a skilled worker or college graduate. Legislative staffs and other resources are also limited in most states. Support facilities of the type enjoyed by Congress (research services, organizations to make investigations, expert legal advice, and the like) are generally found in the larger, more industrialized states, such as New York and California. Given low salaries and meager legislative resources, it is not surprising that the turnover in state legislatures is fairly high. New Hampshire, with its $200 per biennial pay, had a turnover of some 40 percent in its lower house in 1984, for example.

One final important distinction between Congress and state legislatures concerns legislative *apportionment* (population per district and the shape of legislative districts). Although U.S. senators represent different numbers of people, representation within a state for both houses must closely follow population size. Before 1962, lower state houses frequently experienced severe **malapportionment**—one state representative would be elected by a few thousand voters, another by 10 or 20 times that number. State senates—like the U.S. Senate—tended to represent geographical units (for example, counties), and they too did not accurately translate population into legislative voting strength. Beginning with the *Baker v. Carr* decision in 1962, however, several key Supreme Court decisions forced state legislatures to apportion *both* houses strictly on the basis of population. The analogy between the U.S. Senate and a state senate was declared invalid in the *Reynolds v. Sims* (1964) case because political subdivisions of states, unlike the states themselves, were never

sovereign units. (Apportionment on the national level is discussed in Chapter 5.)

The State Judicial System

Like the office of governor and the bicameral state legislature, the state judicial system generally resembles the federal system. At the top of each state's court system is a court of appeals of three to nine judges (it is given a variety of names—supreme court, court of appeals, or even supreme court of errors). Below this state version of the Supreme Court, twenty-seven states have an intermediate court of appeals. The bulk of state judicial business is conducted in district courts, which cover a specific geographical area (a variety of names are used—circuit court, district court, superior court, or chancery court). Most states also maintain several specialized courts to deal with matters such as juvenile crime, the probation of wills, and family relations.

The area in which the practices of state court systems differ the most from federal court customs is in the selection of judges. All federal judges are appointed by the President and are either confirmed or rejected by the Senate. In the states, however, some judges are elected. This election can take a variety of forms. Most states elect almost all state judges in either partisan or nonpartisan elections. Several states use a combination of appointment and election. For example, the governor of Arizona, upon recommendation of a special commission, appoints judges to the state supreme, appellate, and certain district courts; judges for all other state courts are elected. Some states follow the federal model; the governor, with the consent of the state senate, appoints all judges. In a few states the legislature itself appoints judges. In other cases there ia division of labor—some judges are appointed by the governor, others by the state legislature.

Ten states use an interesting variation for selecting judges, called the **Missouri plan,** or **merit plan.** Under this plan a committee of distinguished judges, lawyers, and ordinary citizens gives a list of possible judges to the governor. The governor selects one judge from the list; after one year on the bench, the judge must be approved by

Much of the day-to-day work of the nation's judicial system is carried out in state, county, and municipal courthouses like the ones shown here.

the voters (there is no competing candidate, just "approve" or "disapprove"). The purpose of this plan is to balance expert judgment, input from the governor, and popular participation. Almost without exception, judges chosen by the Missouri plan gain popular approval and serve long terms through repeated reelection.

Do these variations in selecting state judges make much difference? Apparently not, according to several studies. One study of alternative selection plans found that they resulted in few differences in education, experience, or social background of judges (except that state legislatures were more likely to appoint their colleagues to the bench). Nor do the judges seem to decide cases differently. Elected judges, for example, are no more likely to decide in favor of defendants in criminal trials, in favor of weaker economic interests, or against corporations than appointed judges. How a judge is selected also has little impact on his or her tenure in office—elected judges are rarely defeated for reelection. Like appointed judges, they have long careers. However, unlike federal judges, most state judges face mandatory retirement ages.

Finally, although states are sometimes willing to have part-time, poorly paid, and insufficiently staffed legislatures, state courts are generally more professional. Even though only four states require judges to be lawyers, higher-level state judges are usually lawyers who work at their jobs full time. Judges are also fairly well paid, usually earning between $50,000 and $75,000 a year (sometimes more, depending on whether counties supplement state salaries). Only in municipal courts, especially **justice of the peace courts** in rural areas, is justice occasionally dispensed by part-time, poorly trained, nonlawyer judges who depend more on their wits than on expert assistance.

The Relationship of Governments Within the Fifty States

Although each of the fifty state governments conducts the business of politics in its own way, this variety is modest compared to the variation (and complexity) of governments *within* each of the fifty states. In 1982 the number of governments below the state level was 82,290, and a county or township in one state could be quite different from a county or township in a neighboring state (or even in the same state). Some of the key political units below the state level are described below.

Counties

All states except Connecticut and Rhode Island have a system of county government (in Louisiana, counties are called parishes, and in Alaska, boroughs). This form of government, which goes back to William the Conqueror of England, began in America during the colonial period. In 1982 there were some 3,041 counties; they varied enormously in size. Los Angeles County, for example, has 7 million people; Cook County, which includes Chicago, has 5.1 million citizens. But there are also hundreds of counties in the West and Southwest with 10,000 or fewer citizens. The variation in population is matched by the diversity in administrative organization. Most counties are run by committees with names such as board of supervisors, county commissioners, or just county board (very few counties have a single executive). Counties also have various elected or appointed officials with countywide responsibilities (for example, county attorney, assessor, sheriff, judge, and treasurer). In many states there are also countywide boards with authority over hospitals, public welfare, taxes, and libraries.

County government plays a vital political role, especially in rural areas. The county handles law enforcement and road construction and maintenance, administers elections, records legal information (such as deeds and mortgages), and provides help to the poor. County seats in rural areas are frequently impressive places with economic importance, because they are magnets for people. Urban county governments more closely resemble city governments; they are responsible for such things as providing recreation, flood control, sewage-treatment facilities, and countywide fire and police protection.

Township or Town Government

About one out of every five Americans lives in a town or township. This type of government is found in twenty states, especially in New England and the Midwest. Townships are subdivisions of a county and carry out many functions of county government (for example, education, highways, fire protection, and law enforcement). In 1982 there were 16,734 townships. Rural townships can cover many square miles of territory and provide important government service to villages.

The best-known town form of government is the democratic town meeting in New England states. These meetings are open to all eligible voters, who collectively make important policy decisions. The voters appoint a board, whose members are usually called selectmen, to administer these decisions. As government has become more complex, these town meetings have given greater power to the board members. Outside New England, however, rural township governments have become less important, as school boards have taken over what was once a major responsibility of township government. Nevertheless, there are still parts of the country outside of New England where township government remains important. In some suburban areas they play a key role in delivering government services.

Special District Government

County and township governments have deep roots in U.S. history. Special districts, however, are more recent innovations. They have arisen from both America's transition from rural to urban life and the desire of existing governments to shift the costs of certain services to the users of these services. Special districts are a popular new arrangement. Between 1952 and 1982, the number of special district governments (other than school districts) more than doubled, to 28,600. The most popular type of special district government is the school district, which might run schools involving several towns and thousands of students. In 1982 there were more than 15,000 school districts. Other popular responsibilities of special district governments are fire protection, soil conservation, housing, cemeteries, flood control, hospitals, and libraries.

The powers and responsibilities of these special-purpose governments vary considerably. Perhaps the most important difference among

Commentary: Forms of City Government

Government at both the national and state levels is organized into the familiar legislative-executive-judicial pattern. That is, there is a single executive, a sizable legislature, and a judiciary. At the municipal level, however, there are some important variations on this single executive, separate legislature arrangement. Cities have one of three types of governmental structure: mayor-council, council-manager, or a commission form of government.

The mayor-council system has an independently elected mayor and an independently elected city council. This is the most traditional form of government and it typically—but not always—encourages strong executive leadership. This form of government is most popular in large cities and in the East. Graphically, the mayor-council system is as shown in the top example.

The mayor-council form of government also has two variations: strong-mayor and weak-mayor systems. The distinction is

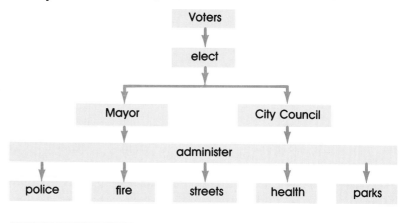

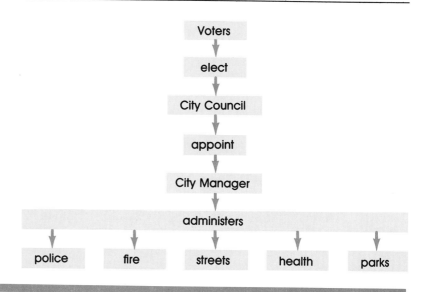

these governments concerns their independent power to raise revenue. Many special districts are limited to user charges—for example, a charge for supplying water or fire protection. But more than half can levy, or impose, property taxes or special assessments on property rather than a direct charge for services or benefits. Others have the additional power to raise revenue by issuing bonds. The rules regulating the creation of these districts and the selection of people to run them are enormously varied. Some districts are created by the state; others are created by the municipal governments.

Members of some districts are appointed; others are elected.

Cities

In contemporary society, cities are generally the most important political unit below the level of state government. In 1980 there were some 2,205 cities of more than 10,000 residents. Cities are not only where most of us live; they also contain many of our social and economic problems. Crime, air pollution, drug addiction, inadequate transporta-

not absolute, but strong-mayor systems allow mayors considerable power in administering, appointing department heads, preparing the budget, and vetoing actions of the city council. A weak mayor, however, must share administrative decision making with the city council.

The council-manager form of government has no elected chief executive. Instead, voters elect a council, and this council chooses a professionally trained city manager who runs the day-to-day business of the city (the manager can be fired by the city council). This system is intended to separate policy making (the job of the council) from administration (the job of the manager). This system is especially popular in middle-sized cities in the West; a little more than half of the cities of 25,000 or more have this system of government. The council-manager system is illustrated in the center example.

The third, and least common, form of government is the commission form, shown in the third example. This system combines executive and legislative authority into a single council of commissioners. One commissioner may be designated as mayor, but he or she has little special power. Typically, each commissioner is responsible for a specific city service. Only about 10 percent of U.S. cities have this form of government.

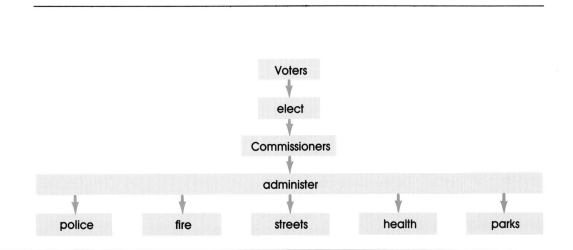

tion, and other problems are largely, though not exclusively, urban problems.

It is important to realize that a city is not merely a large number of people living near each other. "City" is a legal term. To become a city a group of people must meet the requirements of incorporation specified in state law. Typically, this involves the filing of an incorporation petition with the state, verification that petition signers are a majority of the residents, a state review of the adequacy of the proposed city (for example, population density, impact in adjacent areas), and finally, procla-

mation that the area is a city. The number of people necessary to become a city is usually fairly low—frequently less than 1,000.

Once the residents have crossed the legal dividing line to be designated a city; they can then form a local government and take actions. They can make local laws (**ordinances**), grant licenses and permits in the name of the city, and provide their own police, fire, and social services. However, despite these opportunities to exercise political power, the city is not an independent unit, sovereign within its borders. What cities can and cannot do always depends on state law. Cities can do more than what their state-granted charters spell out. Cities frequently do have significant leeway in some areas (for example, their form of government), but the states grant such discretion and can take it away by acts of the state legislatures. In some cases cities are allowed significant authority, and this is frequently called **home rule.** Home rule is found in about two-thirds of all cities with populations greater than 250,000.

Metropolitan Governments

Many problems, such as mass transportation, air and water pollution, and education, have grown beyond the borders and financial resources of individual cities. As a result, a new form of government called metropolitan government has received widespread attention. The basic idea behind metropolitan government is to preserve the identity and local functions of established cities, and at the same time to provide efficient, large-scale solutions to problems beyond the capacity of these individual governments. This solution has taken two forms: metropolitan government and metropolitan area coordination. The special district governments described earlier are a third "metropolitan" solution when they include several cities within their service jurisdiction.

Metropolitan government is currently found in only about two dozen areas, mainly in the South. These metropolitan governments have usually been created from county governments. The county government is turned into a metropolitan government with wider responsibilities and greater legal powers. In 1957, for example, voters of Dade County, Florida (in which the city of Miami is located), made their government into a metropolitan government with jurisdiction over the area's water supply, sewage, traffic, transportation, central planning, and several other services. Cities within this metropolitan system retain their powers over other services, although the Miami metropolitan government can set minimal standards. The Dade metropolitan government is run by a commission of five members elected at large, five from districts, and one commissioner elected by each city. A similar solution was adopted in Jacksonville, Florida, in 1967.

A second approach to metropolitan government is the creation of **metropolitan councils of government** (or COGs). COGs are associations of government officials in a geographical area. Their purpose is to discuss, research, and coordinate efforts to solve common problems. Even though these councils might have a budget and a professional staff, they are not true governments. They can make recommendations but they may not make laws, raise revenue, or otherwise act as gov-

Commentary: Why Arizona? Why Not Mississippi?

The enormous diversity of U.S. local government is reflected in the names of towns and cities. Although some names are used often (for example, there are nineteen Springfields), others reflect the peculiarities of the area. Here are some of the more interesting place names in the United States:

Ben Hur, Arizona
Why, Arizona
Peanut, California
Coffee Pot Rapids, Idaho
Rural, Indiana
Ordinary, Kentucky
Monkey's Eyebrow, Kentucky
Whynot, Mississippi
Double Trouble, New Jersey
Glen Campbell, Pennsylvania

Source: These and other interesting names are reported in "61 Curious Place Names in the United States," in David Wallechinsky and Irving Wallace, *The People's Almanac #2* (New York: Bantam Books, 1978). p. 1124.

To meet the needs of their residents, cities depend on a large number of public employees to provide a wide range of services, including traffic control, mass transportation, and health care facilities.

ernments. In the last two decades the national government has encouraged the creation of these councils as a means of coordinating grant proposals made by local governments (some states have also encouraged these COGs). Nevertheless, without any legal powers and because of the need for voluntary cooperation from groups with differing viewpoints, these councils have had only a limited impact.

Power of Government Units Within the States

We have seen that states can have numerous types of governments within their borders. Moreover, the jurisdictions of these governments frequently overlap. A citizen can be governed simultaneously by city, town, county, special district, and metropolitan officials (and also pay taxes and fees to all these authorities). How can all these forms of political life coexist? Is there a sort of political chain of command in which one unit dominates the one below it, which in turn dominates the one below it?

Understanding the relationship among hundreds or even thousands of governments is both an easy and a difficult task. If we take a purely legal view of the distribution of political power in a state, the relationships among different political units are simple. Without exception, state government ultimately controls political subdivisions in the state, whether these subdivisions are huge cities, sewer districts, or hamlets of five residents. The relationship among these subdivisions is also defined by state government. Local authority over taxes, the delivery of services, form of government, educational curriculum, zoning, pollution control, and taxes exist at the pleasure of the state government. Unlike a state in the federal system, a city or county in a state has no claim of ultimate authority, although in practice it may exercise considerable judgment.

The nature of contemporary federalism has made the relationship among governments within a state highly complex. In particular, the national government's willingness to provide grants-in-aid directly to political subdivisions of a state, without state control, has in practice increased local independence (although legally the state is dominant). In 1976, for example, when local governments needed money to combat unemployment, they appealed to Washington for relief, not to the state capitals. By 1983, local governments were receiving some $21 billion in federal aid. Such reliance on federal funds has fostered a new sense of political independence among city and county officials.

Equally important, it is the national legislature and court system that now make the key decisions on such local issues as school integration, regulation of health and safety, housing regulations, crime control, waste disposal, and other areas once considered largely under complete state control. Hence, a mayor might be legally subordinate to the state government, but he or she is also likely to pay great attention to national regulations on how to integrate a school or clean the water. In short, in legal theory, local governments are completely subordinate to the state government; in practice, however, financial assistance from the national government has freed local governments to a large degree.

Check Your Understanding

1. List at least three ways in which the office of governor can differ from that of President.

2. List three ways in which state legislatures differ from Congress.

3. In what important way does the selection of state judges differ from that of federal judges?

4. What is the difference between metropolitan government and metropolitan councils of government?

5. How have federal grants-in-aid changed the relationship between state and local governments?

WHAT ARE THE MAJOR RESPONSIBILITIES OF STATE AND LOCAL GOVERNMENTS?

We have seen that state and local governments have not disappeared as a result of the enormous growth of the government in Washington. In fact, in several areas (for example, number of employees) state and local governments have kept pace with or even surpassed the national government. The question that we now can ask is: What is it that all of these governments do? We shall approach this complex question by focusing on money. Rather than list all the thousands of services performed by state and local governments, we ask instead how money is allocated—how much for welfare, police protection, and so on. This way we can see where governments make their major commitments. Our analysis of state and local government responsibilities begins with spending. Then we shall examine the other side of expenditures—how all this money is raised.

Spending in States and Cities

What do state and local governments spend their money on? In fiscal 1983 the fifty states and all the governments within them spent some $567 billion. As Figure 17.1 shows, the largest expenditures were on education—$163 billion in fiscal 1983, or 35.7 percent of all state and local expenditures. No other state or local cost comes close to the cost of education. Public welfare, the second largest expenditure category, comprised only 12.9 percent of all expenditures. The importance of education is not new, though the slice of the budget going to education has gradually risen in the twentieth century. In 1902, for instance, education received 25.2 percent of all expenditures (highways were second, with 17.3 percent); in 1950 education was up to 30.1 percent (highways were again second, with 16.7 percent).

This general analysis is not true for all states and localities. Considerable variation exists in how state and local governments fulfill their obligations to their citizens. Table 17.1 shows the per capita (per person) expenditures for the five states with the largest levels of spending and the five states with the lowest levels. Note that Alaska spends four and a half times the national average for governmental services and more than 6 times as much as Arkansas. New York spends about twice as much per citizen as does Arkansas. In general, states in the South tend to spend less per person on services, such as education, public welfare, health care, and police protection.

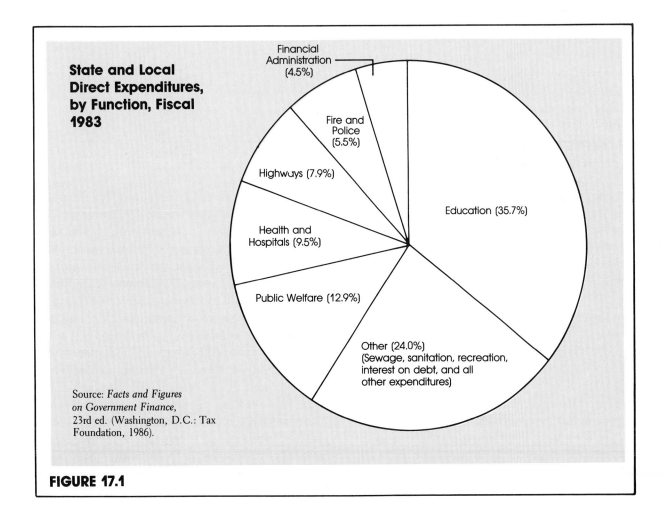

State and Local Direct Expenditures, by Function, Fiscal 1983

Financial Administration (4.5%)
Fire and Police (5.5%)
Highways (7.9%)
Health and Hospitals (9.5%)
Public Welfare (12.9%)
Education (35.7%)
Other (24.0%) (Sewage, sanitation, recreation, interest on debt, and all other expenditures)

Source: *Facts and Figures on Government Finance*, 23rd ed. (Washington, D.C.: Tax Foundation, 1986).

FIGURE 17.1

Per Capita State and Local Direct General Expenditure by Function, Five Highest and Five Lowest State Levels, Fiscal 1983

			Category			
Five states with largest per capita expenditure level	Total	Education	Highways	Public Welfare	Health and Hospitals	Police and Fire
Alaska	$8,663	$2,059	$872	$377	$294	$351
Wyoming	3,569	1,356	496	149	343	149
New York	2,790	827	162	434	290	156
Hawaii	2,411	694	151	283	181	118
Minnesota	2,404	811	241	356	207	94
Five states with lowest per capita expenditure level						
Arkansas	$1,372	$ 543	$145	$170	$144	$ 53
South Carolina	1,448	605	79	139	209	61
Missouri	1,479	545	138	164	160	90
Tennessee	1,493	518	136	156	196	76
Mississippi	1,548	552	195	169	250	58
National average	$1,988	700	157	253	189	109

Source: *Facts and Figures on Government Finance*, 23rd ed. (Washington, D.C.: Tax Foundation, 1986).

TABLE 17.1

Data on per capita expenditures in major urban areas show a greater range of governmental expenditures for services. In 1983, for the largest forty-nine cities, the average per capita expenditure for all city services was $1,083. However, New York City spends more than twice that amount per resident ($2,321); other cities spending much more than the average were Baltimore, Boston, and San Francisco. At the other end of the scale are cities like El Paso, Texas ($341 per capita); San Antonio, Texas; San Diego; Houston; and Omaha, Nebraska.

These figures include a wide discrepancy among states and localities in the spending of money. We must be cautious, however, in interpreting the meaning of this type of information. It is misleading to assert that merely because a state or city spends more money on, say, education, it therefore better serves its citizens. Several factors must be kept in mind when examining differences in how states and cities spend their money.

One factor is the cost of providing a given level of service. In sparsely populated Western states, for example, states must construct hundreds of miles of highway among towns with relatively low populations. This is expensive when calculated on a per person basis. Wyoming in fiscal 1983, for example, spent $496 per person on highways; Rhode Island, with its small size and great population density, got by with $102 per person. Citizens of both states might have equally decent highways, but decent highways cost nearly five times as much in Wyoming as they do in Rhode Island. Another good example of this difference in service costs can occur with police protection. Nevada, because of the presence of gambling and millions of visitors, spent $175 per resident in 1983 on police protection; North Dakota spent

In sparsely populated rural areas, facilities such as highways often cost more than in more densely settled regions.

$63 per citizen for law enforcement. Factors such as climate, population density, terrain, soil types, and availability of water can all affect state expenditure levels. These factors help explain why, for example, Alaska and Hawaii must spend so much more than the other forty-eight states.

A second element that helps account for the range of expenditures is the problems facing a particular government. Consider state support for higher education. Since World War II, the states have increasingly provided opportunities for higher education. In many Eastern states, numerous privately supported colleges and universities have taken much of the burden of support for higher education off state government. In many Western states, however, no extensive system of private colleges existed. Therefore, after World War II, as the demand for college education increased, states had to enter the education business. In 1983, for example, 88 percent of all students enrolled in institutions of higher learning in California were attending publicly supported colleges; in Massachusetts, because of the existence of numerous private colleges, only 44 percent of college students were in tax-supported schools. A similar pattern occurs at the local level—some cities in Arizona and other states have relatively low educational expenditures, because many residents are retired people with no school-age children.

A third factor that helps to explain why states and localities can differ so much in their financial policies is that financial resources vary considerably among state and local governments. In 1983, for example, the average per capita income in Connecticut was $11,808. In Mississippi the figure was $6,180, $5,628 less than in Connecticut. Large differences also exist in the value of real estate, the value of manufacturing facilities, and locations of business offices. These differences in wealth lead to differences in what problems are approached and how they are solved. California, because of its huge tax base, can afford to spend a good deal more per pupil than Mississippi. Wealthy towns may solve the problem of recreation by hiring a recreation staff and building tennis courts. Less affluent towns may post a sign warning motorists that children are playing in the streets.

A fourth consideration to keep in mind when viewing differences in state and local financial commitments is that state and local expenditures tell only part of the story of how much money is

From community college to graduate school, state higher education systems may enable residents to attend college regardless of the students' ability to pay.

spent. Our analysis has focused on *direct* state and local financial efforts. Recall, however, that the national government, through grants and revenue sharing, contributes significantly to state and local services. In 1983 the federal government provided some $90 billion in aid. The importance of this federal aid is that it can sometimes help reduce some of the sharper differences in expenditure patterns among the states, or at least provide minimal levels of services. Although nationally the federal government contributed $385 per capita in 1983, this figure was much higher for some states than for other states. For example, in New Mexico this figure was $619; in Ohio it was $310. Such federal expenditures do *not* necessarily equalize spending for education, health care, welfare, and the like. Rather, these federal contributions allow states and localities to offer services that are not reflected in their own direct expenditures.

The final point about how state and local governments provide services is that these services do not depend only on financial factors. In contemporary society all governments must provide certain types and levels of services. Imagine public reaction if a local government decided not to offer police protection or education because such services had become too expensive. However, beyond these minimal levels (which frequently are legally required) and the limits imposed by the availability of resources, much leeway exists. Some states, such as California, might want an extensive system of higher education, whereas others (for example, New Jersey) might decide that such a system is not needed. In the field of public welfare, Wisconsin, with its long tradition of government involvement in social problems, spent more than twice as much per capita in 1983 on social welfare as Utah, which has a tradition of greater reliance on the private sector. In New York City, garbage removal is a service provided by the government; in San Francisco it is a service provided by private companies.

How much money will be spent and on what projects is frequently decided through the political process. In the 1960s, as governor of New York, Nelson A. Rockefeller committed the state to ambitious new projects in higher education, the construction of public buildings, increased aid for the needy, and other expensive, innovative projects. Despite the increased tax burdens, Rockefeller was elected to four consecutive terms. Other candidates might try to outdo one another with promises of lower taxes and balanced budgets. Interestingly, this process does not seem to depend greatly on such factors as party affiliation of leaders, political competition in a state, or amount of citizen participation. That is, a Republican-dominated state is not automatically likely to spend more (or less) than a Democratic-dominated state.

Taxing in States and Cities

So far our analysis has focused on the expenditure side of state and local government activity. We have seen how much money states and localities spend on different services and why variations occur. Besides benefiting from education, highways, and the like, taxpayers are also the ultimate supporters of these services. And because the question "Who pays?" is certainly as relevant as "What do we get?" we must also examine the revenue side of state and local government. First we will analyze the various ways state and local revenue can be raised. We shall then consider how such revenue is actually generated as well as differences among states in the amount of money raised.

State and local governments can use a variety of methods to finance their services. Many services can be supported by charging a fee for their use. Parents of schoolchildren could pay tuition for education; highway users can pay either tolls, license fees, or a special tax on gasoline; people who had fires can be assessed fees for fire department services; and so on. A different method of raising money would be for governments to operate income-producing businesses—liquor stores, hospitals, or even state lotteries (a variation would be to collect fees for things like oil, gas, or coal taken from the state). A third method is taxation; taxes can be levied on everything from income to property to consumer purchases.

All three of these ways of raising money can be found in the United States. Even though all three are used, it would be a mistake to believe that a dollar raised one way is the same as a dollar raised another way. Each method of raising money has benefits for some people and disadvantages for others. Some techniques, such as taxes on property, taxes on food and other necessities, or fees for state licenses, are usually regressive (poor people pay a larger proportion of their income to taxes than do wealthy people). User fees (for example, school tuition) can sometimes place a heavy burden on small groups of citizens, whereas those who benefit indirectly pay nothing. From the perspective of poor citizens, government revenue derived wholly from a graduated income tax (one in which the wealthy pay a higher percentage of tax on their income than do the less wealthy) would be most desirable. They would pay little—absolutely and in percentage terms—compared to the wealthy.

What types of taxes are used most commonly by state and local governments? In fiscal 1983, the general sales tax accounted for 35.2 percent of all state and local revenue. State income (both individual and corporate) taxes in general brought in 36.7 percent of state revenue (most states have state corporation income taxes, but they are financially significant in only three states—New York, Pennsylvania, and California). The property tax is the most important source of tax revenue for local governments. The property tax contributed only slightly to state government revenue.

Predictably, considerable variation exists in states' reliance on different techniques of raising revenue. In 1983, such states as Oregon, Delaware, and Minnesota relied rather heavily on income taxes to finance state and local government. On the other hand, Nevada, Texas, and Wyoming have no state income tax. Several states—Connecticut, Florida, and Mississippi, for example—depended heavily on sales taxes.

States and localities also differ significantly in key details of taxation. Although a sales tax is

Highway tolls, a type of user fee, are one method states use to raise money.

Homeowners in many communities pay property taxes based on the assessed value of their real estate.

generally regressive, it can be made even more regressive if the rate is high and if it is applied to food (because food expenses typically make up a large proportion of expenditures for poor people). In 1983, state sales taxes varied from 3 percent to 7.5 percent. However, about half of the states allowed localities to add to the general sales tax; as a result, citizens of some areas were paying as much as 9 percent in sales taxes on their purchases. Half the states taxed food, and seven taxed prescription drugs. Income tax rates and provisions display an even greater variety among the states. Illinois, for example, has a simple system of 2.5 percent, regardless of income. Iowa has a sharply graduated system that begins at 0.5 percent for incomes under $1,000, whereas incomes over $75,000 are taxed at a 13-percent rate. Many cities, such as New York, Detroit, Philadelphia, and Kansas City, add their own city income taxes to the burden.

When considering types of taxes, the question is: How much does it cost the taxpayer? In fiscal 1983 the average per capita state and local tax burden in the United States was $1,216 (up from $308 in 1967 and $169 in 1957). Citizens of Alaska, California, Massachusetts, Wyoming, and New York have the heaviest tax burdens. Many southern states placed a much lighter burden on their citizens (Arkansas' per capita taxes amounted to only $771). However, this does not necessarily mean that citizens of high-tax states are being overwhelmed by their state taxes. States differ considerably in their taxable wealth. Thus a low tax bite in a poor state could be as much of a burden on citizens as a large bite in a wealthy state. For the most part, states with high per capita tax burdens (for example, New York and California) are also states with the greatest wealth. Therefore, the discrepancy between, say, California and Arkansas should not be interpreted to mean that Californians are being impoverished by their taxes, even though taxes are twice as high.

What can we conclude from the numerous figures on state and local expenditures and revenue collection? Although all state and local governments provide certain crucial services—education, public welfare, highways, and recreation, for example—there is no one fixed level of these services. Education might be funded lavishly in some states, whereas in others little more than the minimum is provided. Such variations depend on both nonpolitical factors (for example, difficulty of providing the service) and factors expressed through the political system (for example, a desire by elderly citizens to have taxes kept to a minimum). A second point is that a given level of services can be financed in many different ways. Regressive property and sales taxes or progressive income taxes are all capable of raising sufficient revenue, but each type of tax has its costs and benefits to different citizens. In short, providing services to citizens requires numerous choices.

Check Your Understanding

1. What are five factors that contribute to the differences in how states and cities spend money?

2. What are three main ways states can raise money?

3. Why are taxes on food and other necessities usually regressive?

4. Why does the fact that taxes are high in a state not necessarily mean that citizens in that state are overburdened by those taxes?

IS THE PRESENT SYSTEM ADEQUATE FOR SOLVING CONTEMPORARY PROBLEMS?

Our basic form of state and local government derives from decisions made more than a hundred years ago. Such "modern" innovations as the unicameral legislature, special districts, metropolitan government, and the federal grant-in-aid system are minor adjustments in a nineteenth- or even eighteenth-century system. It is not surprising, then, especially as the burdens of government continue to mount, that the present system has been challenged. Such challenges involve far more than a call for a new law or increased financial assistance to a city; they question such matters as state boundaries, the legal division between city and suburbs, and other aspects of the present system. Let us begin our analysis of the adequacy of the present system by reviewing some major criticisms of it. We shall then consider some possible defenses.

Geographical Divisions Are No Longer Relevant or Useful

The boundaries of the thirteen original states frequently derived from charters granted by English kings, early political disputes, and decisions by surveyors. Rivers, migration patterns, and military victories against foreign nations commonly defined the boundaries of subsequent states. Within states, city and county boundaries often depended on railroad routes, river junctions, and other aspects of the transportation system. Although there have been enormous population shifts in the last fifty years, the basic legal jurisdictions of state and local governments still largely reflect the decisions and circumstances of the eighteenth and nineteenth centuries.

It can be argued that these well-established boundaries are not the most efficient way of dividing political authority in contemporary society. One problem with existing boundaries is that population centers frequently cross state lines. For example, there is a Kansas City, Missouri and a Kansas City, Kansas. East St. Louis, an important industrial suburb of St. Louis, Missouri, is across the river in Illinois. In terms of its work force, transportation facilities, and economic impact, New York City is located in three states—New Jersey, Connecticut, and New York. This situation is reflected in the following humorous conversation between two couples on vacation:

First Person: I hear you are from New York.
Second Person: Yes, I am. Are you?
First Person: Oh, yes, we're from Stamford, Connecticut. What part of New York are you from?
Second Person: Why, we're practically neighbors. We're from Tenafly, New Jersey.[1]

The existence of inappropriate legal boundaries has greater significance than that of producing "New Yorkers" from Connecticut and New Jersey. The historical accidents of boundaries can provide major artificial obstacles to solving contemporary problems, such as in the area of air and water pollution. For example, several small communities in northern New Jersey are almost wall-to-wall chemical factories and oil refineries whose pollution greatly affects residents of New York City.

Cooperation between localities in providing efficient transportation systems is essential. Construction of the Brooklyn Bridge, completed in 1883, linked Manhattan with its neighbor across the East River.

Despite bearing much of the cost of such pollution (health problems, damaged property, and so on), residents of New York City have no say in this matter except, perhaps, by trying to obtain federal legislation. Because most of these New Jersey cities (and the state, to a lesser extent) enjoy substantial tax revenue from these polluting industries, the motivation to help the politically unimportant New York residents is slight.

Another policy area in which existing geographical borders can create unnecessary problems is that of transportation routes. For example, two states might design a perfectly good road system for the needs of each state, yet unless these two systems are coordinated, the overall result can be inefficient. This problem was illustrated some years ago when Connecticut and Rhode Island decided that there should be a road between New London, Connecticut, and Providence, Rhode Island. Acting according to its best economic interests, Connecticut built a northerly oriented route; Rhode Island decided that it needed a more southerly oriented route. For a few years these modern highways did not meet, and motorists traveling between New London and Providence could not take advantage of this highway system. Eventually, however, the two highways were connected.

Such problems are not limited to relationships among states. Consider, for instance, how the existence of separate cities and towns can play havoc with the racial integration of schools. It is now public policy to eliminate racial segregation of schools. But what if whites move out of a town, leaving the school system almost all black? Because the school systems of most cities (or special districts) are separate from one another, nothing can be done. This is true even if blacks live near the schools that lie outside their city or school district. In other words, the existence of legal—not physical—boundaries blocks a public goal. And because people who flee integrated schools realize this, these legal divisions can in fact help create the problem. We are not claiming that a single statewide school system would bring instant social integration; rather, eliminating artificial district lines could remove one barrier to this goal.

The Multiplicity of Governments Leads to Unnecessary Complexity

Although the first criticism of the existing system focused on the inappropriate boundaries of state and local governments, the sheer number of governing authorities is itself a problem. That is, when travel was time-consuming and population widely dispersed, it might have made sense to have lots of cities and counties. However, as the populations of towns expand toward each other and eventually merge, and modern transportation allows a "nearby" government to be thirty miles away, there is little justification for almost eighty thousand government units. This is especially true in large metropolitan areas where the only divisions between hundreds of communities are legally defined boundaries. In 1975, for example, there were some 1,214 local governments in the Chicago, Illinois, metropolitan area (and 7,815 elected officials for these governments). The New York City metropolitan area was "governed" by some 363 governments and almost three thousand elected officials.

One of the unfortunate consequences of so many governments, most with their own rule-making and taxing power, is a bewildering variety of rules and regulations. Consider, for instance, the building code situation. A building code is a locally designed and enforced set of standards that details the building practices permitted in a particular area. A building code deals with such things as what kinds of pipes can be used (plastic or copper), the materials of electrical wiring, septic systems, inspection requirements, and much more. There are presently four widely recognized "model" building codes, but only 15 percent of all governments of five thousand or more citizens use these or similar codes. As a result of pressures from local builders, modern prefabrication techniques and innovative materials are generally prohibited. The impact of this diversity of building codes and the power of local interests is that it is nearly impossible for manufacturers of housing to market inexpensive, mass-produced, preassembled parts of buildings. Because of these local requirements,

Points of View: The U.S. Map Redrawn

The problems with present state boundaries led former geography professor G. Etzel Pearcy to propose a new thirty-eight-state United States (see map below). These boundaries are drawn to reflect population densities, location of metropolitan areas, and common political, social, and economic concerns. The thirty-eight states would be approximately equal in size and would be compact in shape.

In a more radical division of the United States, which also includes Canada and the Caribbean islands, the writer Joel Garreau has separated North America into a number of large areas which he calls "nations" (see map at right). The "nine nations" he identifies are based on economic, historical, geographical, and even life style factors. Some traditional regions,

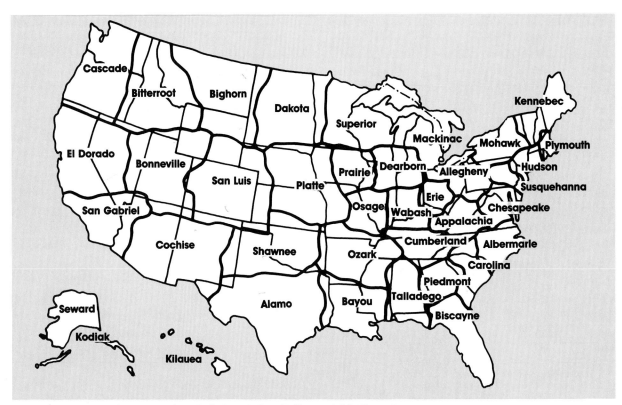

Source: G. Etzel Pearcy, A Thirty-Eight State U.S.A. (Fullerton, Calif.: Plycon Press, 1973), pp. 22–23.

each unit must be custom built, and this adds substantially to housing costs.

The existence of hundreds of independent communities, each with the power to define land use in its jurisdiction (called zoning power) can also discourage rational economic planning. Consider the problems of matching housing, commercial, and transportation needs in most multigovernment suburban areas. Community A encourages building office buildings or factories. But the workers in these offices or factories might have to travel thirty miles to work because neigh-

such as the American South—here called "Dixie"—are represented on the map. The Latino influence in the Southwest is indicated by the "Mex-America" nation; the distinctive life style of the Pacific Northwest is suggested by the label "Ecotopia," a term that combines the words "ecology" and "utopia." One possible drawback of the "nine nations" scheme is that there is no recognition of the economic, ethnic, or other significance of urban areas within and beyond the region in which they are located.

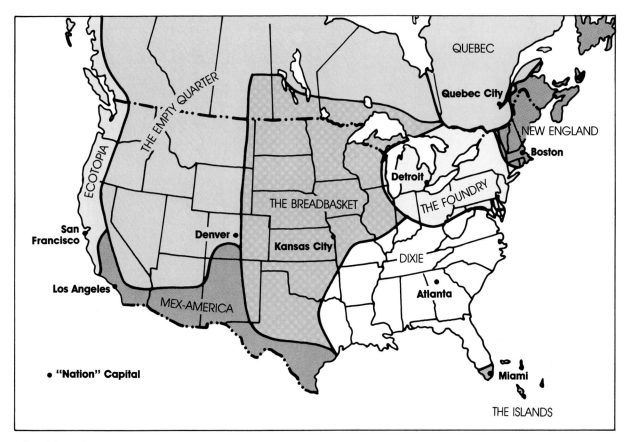

Adapted from *The Nine Nations of North America*, by Joel Garreau. Copyright © 1981 by Joel Garreau. Reprinted by permission of Houghton Mifflin Company.

boring communities, by limiting lot size, prohibiting multioccupancy dwellings, and the like, effectively keep these new workers out. Meanwhile, communities between Community A and where the workers in the new facilities live find their roads overcrowded. Getting numerous independent governments to agree on such issues as location of new industry, placement of low-income housing, road improvements, and so on, is difficult because local officials must face their own voters at election time, not the voters of the larger geographical area.

Under the Present System the Responsibilities and Capabilities of Government are Frequently Not Matched

During the 1960s, many local government officials were fond of saying that the federal government had the money, the state government had the power, and city governments had the problems. Because of greatly increased federal aid to state and local governments in the 1970s, this characterization is now less accurate. Nevertheless, if we examine the problems faced by many government units and then consider their legal and financial capacities to handle these problems, we can see that mismatches persist. Such mismatches are especially evident in the field of education, where money and power are not in the hands of the educators.

Even though the federal government has funneled huge amounts of money into state and local communities for public education, state governments retain ultimate legal control. In education, states remain the dominant unit of government. In 1984, the federal contributions to primary and secondary schools totaled about 6.2 percent of all expenditures. In all fifty states the ultimate control of education firmly rests in state hands, although the responsibility for schooling is given to local authorities. The states control such things as length of school term, minimum teacher salaries, operation of local school boards, qualifications of teachers, and general curriculum content. Some states even regulate what books can be used, acceptable methods of teaching, and approved type of penmanship. Through its overall power to regulate local finances, the state exercises a powerful influence over local school revenue raising. Local educational autonomy exists only when the state allows it to exist.

The difficulty with this state domination is that local communities with the largest educational problems are very limited in their ability to respond to these problems. For example, poor communities with many disadvantaged students must follow state, not community, standards. They must also finance a major educational effort from their limited tax base, since on average almost half of all school revenues come from local property taxes. When local residents want to use unconventional teaching techniques, have a longer school term, or develop new textbooks, they will probably be frustrated by state regulations and the limits imposed by an inadequate property tax base. The mismatch between need and capability can be seen by examining spending differences between a wealthy and a poor community in New Jersey. In 1974, Englewood Cliffs had $246,000 in assessed property value for each pupil and was able to spend $2,000 a year for each student. The much poorer city of Camden had only $18,000 of assessed property value per student and, despite a tax rate almost twice that of Englewood Cliffs, could spend only $1,000 per student. In short, it is the poor communities that must solve major education problems, yet a city like Camden lacks the political power and the financial capacity.

State and Local Governments are Overwhelmed by the Demands of Modern Society

The argument is that states and localities might have been perfectly capable of solving problems of the nineteenth and early twentieth centuries, and they still might be able to handle some contemporary problems, but the tough problems are beyond them. Especially in such areas as public welfare, economic planning, crime control, and enforcement of civil rights, state and local governments cannot be effective in meeting their responsibilities. This argument is supported by several pieces of evidence.

The office of governor is frequently very limited. Governors typically must deal with independently elected cabinet officials and powerful, independent boards and commissions. Moreover, many states limit the time a governor may serve. Terry Sanford, governor of North Carolina from 1961 to 1965, put it this way: "Almost no governor in the country has authority that even approaches his responsibility. The state constitutions fairly adequately prevent the governor from committing evil. That was perhaps the intent. They also hinder his attempt to pursue excellence."[2] Nor, for

Many of the nation's working people depend on publicly financed, low-cost housing, like this garden apartment.

that matter, are many state legislatures equipped to deal effectively with complex modern problems. As we saw, state legislatures tend to be characterized by high turnover, part-time legislators, and limited staff resources.

Another aspect of state government that tends to limit effectiveness is the existence of lengthy, detailed state constitutions. A constitution should describe basic institutions, their interrelationships, and key principles of government. It cannot provide specific rules for each situation without running the risk of creating a rigid legal straitjacket for future action (remember that one of the virtues of the U.S. Constitution is its generality). Unfortunately, many state constitutions are lengthy documents that unnecessarily hinder effective governing. Oklahoma, for example, has a 63,569-word constitution; the Texas constitution runs to 54,000 words. Lengthy constitutions such as these can spell out details of taxation policy, regulate public utilities and insurance companies, set maximums on taxes and debts, and in the case of South Carolina, define what is to be a hard-surface road in Greenville.

Finally, some people question the capacity of state and local government to raise sufficient revenue. Three points are usually made. First, the federal government can readily borrow needed money, but states and local governments typically operate under tight debt restrictions (many of these are in the state constitution itself). Second, unlike

the national government, a state must worry that increased taxes will put it at a competitive disadvantage in relation to other states. Industry an wealth will "migrate" if state and local tax become too high. Third, the sources of tax revnue readily available to states and communities— sales and property taxes in particular—are much more limited because of their regressive character. Although an income tax can exclude poor people, sales and property taxes will almost always fall on poor people, and if these taxes are too high, poor people will enter the welfare system. The possibility exists of relying more on state income taxes. Many states are moving in this direction, but the already high federal income tax rates probably preclude large state income tax rates. In sum, meeting modern needs requires a capacity to raise large sums of money, and states and cities lack a capacity comparable to that of the national government.

Defending the Adequacy of the Existing System of State and Local Government

Few people claim that the existing system is perfect. Attempts to make major changes are an enduring tradition—one delegate to the Constitutional Convention of 1787 even suggested that the thirteen original states redraw their boundaries so that each would have equal population. Nevertheless, despite all the obvious flaws, the present sys-

Problems like pollution control cannot ordinarily be solved by individual communities but require regional planning and, probably, financial aid from the federal government.

tem can be defended. Let us briefly consider three general defenses of our system of state and local government.

The System Can Adapt to Changing Circumstances

The legal and geographic roots of state and local governments go back hundreds of years, and few would argue that a nineteenth-century system could handle the problems of the 1980s. Yet if we look closely at the present arrangement, we can see that significant changes have occurred to allow an old system to meet new needs. New government authorities were created to solve problems beyond the legal and financial power of existing governments. For example, in response to the difficulties of coordinating the transportation and shipping problems of New York City, New York

State and New Jersey created the Port of New York Authority, a powerful agency with its own sources of income. To meet the problem of fragmentation of government, public officials have joined together in organizations such as the National League of Cities, the National Governors Conference, and the National Conference of State Legislatures. Also recall that since the 1960s many adjacent local governments have created councils of government to discuss and coordinate their actions.

Perhaps the most important adaptation of the old system to meet modern needs has been the federal government's financial help to state and local governments. This assistance has frequently allowed governments with limited resources to tackle expensive problems, such as pollution, vocational education, and hospital construction.

Federal assistance has been especially important in the field of helping the needy. At one time, "helping the poor" was strictly a state or local matter, but as many poor began congregating in large cities and the costs of providing assistance rose, the national government stepped in. In 1976, for example, the federal government contributed more than $90 billion for such welfare benefits as Social Security and Medicare (another $18 billion was given for various types of public assistance). To be sure, cities and counties themselves still must fund a large burden of welfare costs, but providing adequate services will now no longer exhaust local resources.

Shifting Power to Washington Is Not Necessarily a Cure

A major criticism of our present system is that with so many state and local officials each having "a piece of the action" and each jealously guarding his or her turf, the coordination necessary to solve problems is impossible. Thus, some claim, a necessary first step in resolving many contemporary problems is to centralize power in Washington. However, this line of reasoning can be challenged on the grounds that shifting power to Washington merely substitutes a new set of problems for some old problems.

First, the image of replacing dozens of state and local officials with a central, all-powerful national authority is highly misleading. When it comes to dealing with issues such as education, welfare, and transportation, there are numerous officials in Washington, each with his or her own perspective and power. Thus, instead of having to get dozens of local officials to agree to a plan, one now has to get dozens of Washington officials to agree, and this is not always easy. A regional solution to water transport proposed by the Army Corps of Engineers could easily get bogged down in disputes involving the Environmental Protection Agency, the Department of Transportation, and 535 members of Congress. Washington might be as unable to make rapid, encompassing decisions as state and local officials, despite the image of "centralized power" in the national government.

Second, even if Washington could exercise centralized power, experience has shown that solutions made in Washington are not always better than choices made in Smallville. Consider, for example, the problems with the federal urban renewal program. Created by the Housing Act of 1949, this program poured billions of dollars into cities to rebuild slums and to provide adequate housing for the poor. Despite these intentions and much federal effort, the net impact of urban renewal has been to decrease the well-being of poor central city residents. Typically, slum housing was replaced with high-income housing or commercial property, and the relocation of slum residents helped to create new slums but with higher rents. When low-income housing was built, it frequently helped to increase problems of crime, sanitation, and feelings of alienation. The disaster of this Washington-made policy has, in fact, directed people toward a new emphasis on programs involving more decentralization (for example, giving neighborhood groups a voice in planning).

The Present System Is What Most Citizens Want

Although feelings of loyalty toward one's state and community are undoubtedly not as great as they were a hundred years ago, few citizens are so filled with national spirit that they would willingly abolish existing states and localities to create more national entities. How many New Yorkers are willing to merge with, say, New Jersey, for the purpose of saving money and better coordinating state services? Even though some towns might have physically merged into one (for example, Bloomington and Normal, Illinois), legal mergers are rare. Efforts to create "consolidated" government in metropolitan areas by merging county and city governments have also had only limited success.

We must also realize that one person's disadvantages might be another person's benefits. For example, while everyone wants a "good" network of highways, nobody wants modern highways going through his or her own neighborhood. To the

Smaller communities can deal more effectively with crime if citizens work with law enforcement authorities in seeking solutions.

extent that each small town has some control over highway location, citizens can better protect themselves from a possible forced relocation (of course, the net impact of such protection is frequently inaction on new roads).

A system of numerous small governments can also have political benefits for many people. In particular, although dozens of separate governments in an area can discourage overall coordination, the smallness of such governments allows each citizen a greater role in affecting his or her political destiny. A citizen concerned about education, law enforcement, and zoning stands a better chance of being effective politically in a town of 10,000 than in a metropolitan area government of one million. This chance to make one's voice heard could well be worth the costs of some overall inefficiency. Moreover, a local political group with some degree of local influence would probably lose much of its power if local governments were consolidated. In short, to change the current system might require many citizens to lose a degree of political influence.

To return to our original question of whether or not the existing system of state and local government is adequate for solving contemporary problems, obviously, the evidence is mixed. Certainly there are many drawbacks to the present system—geographical boundaries do not always make sense; there has been a great increase in governments; governments do not always have the power to match their responsibilities; and governments below the national level can be overwhelmed by modern problems. Nevertheless, to acknowledge these problems is not to endorse drastic and large-scale changes. The present system can be defended, if only on the grounds that proposed remedies are worse or at least no better. Ultimately, "adequacy" seems to come down to the balance between weaknesses and strengths. For some people—especially those who seek change—the multiplicity of governments, limitations on state and

Every March, in communities across the state, Vermonters gather on Town Meeting Day. They may discuss issues ranging from school budgets to nuclear disarmament.

local governments, and the like are grave weaknesses that overshadow any virtues. However, for someone largely content with existing policies, the present system offers protection against rapid change and is thus a good system worthy of preservation.

Check Your Understanding

1. List three reasons why the existing geographical boundaries of states might no longer be useful.

2. Why is it often difficult for independent communities to agree on local issues?

3. List three reasons supporting the view that state and local governments are ineffective in providing essential services.

4. Why is reliance on the national government not necessarily helpful to local governments?

5. In what ways can the present system of numerous small governments be an advantage?

PERSPECTIVE ON STATE AND LOCAL GOVERNMENTS

The debate between those who would shift power toward Washington and those who would strengthen state and local government has been an enduring one. Much of this debate has focused on the capacities of the different governments. Supporters of a larger federal role usually speak of the national government's greater financial capacity, the national talent it can draw on, its ability to provide overall coordination, and other advantages that come with size. Proponents of state and local government typically stress that such governments are "closer to the people," have a better grasp of local problems, and can act faster and with less red tape. To advocates of local government, Washington means clumsy bureaucracy. To those in Washington, state and local politics is colored by small-town provincialism, amateurism, and domination by local economic interests.

This debate is more than a philosophical discussion over the merits of local rule versus a central government. The debate has practical consequences. Whether the decision is made on a federal or a local level greatly affects the outcome. People who want political decisions made in one place typically also want a certain *type* of decision. For example, advocates of tax reduction would generally favor giving greater power over tax policy to state and local officials, because these officials have traditionally resisted increased taxes. Supporters of greater government action, however, would prefer to see tax power in the hands of the national government. However, if we look behind many of the conflicts over education, taxes, welfare, and criminal justice, we find that the policy, not where the decision is made, is the true cause of the conflict.

CHAPTER SUMMARY

1. *How are state and local governments organized?* In general, states follow the federal plan of governmental organization, but each state has its own variations. Below the state level there are numerous types of political jurisdictions, and the forms and powers of these units differ considerably across states. Legally, all these jurisdictions are subordinate to state government, even though money from Washington has provided the local jurisdictions with some autonomy.

2. *What are the major responsibilities of state and local governments?* Education, followed by public welfare, highways, and health care are the major areas of state and local policy. What is important, however, is that states and communities vary considerably in how they meet their responsibilities—their response depends on many factors, including needs, resources, and people's values as they are transmitted through the political process. Wide variations also exist in how the necessary revenue is generated.

3. *Is the present system adequate for solving contemporary problems?* There are clearly some problems with the present system. A few criticisms are that geographical boundaries do not always make contemporary sense, there are probably too many local governments, and not all local governments can handle their responsibilities. However, the system can be defended on the grounds that it is adaptable; centralization is not necessarily a solution; and it is a system that most of us want.

IMPORTANT TERMS

Explain the following terms.

malapportionment
Missouri *or* merit plan
home rule
metropolitan government
metropolitan council of government

THINKING CRITICALLY

1. Many states permit the governor to serve only a limited number of terms. What are the advantages and disadvantages of such a policy?

2. A two-house national legislature (Congress) was the result of a compromise, at the Constitutional Convention, between states with large populations and those with smaller populations. Do you think that a bicameral state legislature serves the interests of a state better than a unicameral legislature? Explain your answer.

3. Should judges running for office be permitted to accept large campaign contributions? Should there be restrictions on who can contribute? Explain your answer.

4. Many large urban areas consist of hundreds of separate local governments. One approach to improving coordination is to establish metropolitan councils of government. At present, these have little or no legal power. Should these councils be given more authority? Why or why not?

5. Does the national government have an obligation to ensure that citizens receive adequate levels of essential public services, such as education and police and fire protection, even if a

state cannot afford to pay for such services? Explain your answer.

6. The sales tax is generally regressive—that is, the poor spend a larger share of their income on sales taxes than do the middle class and the wealthy. Should states reduce their reliance on this tax and instead use less regressive types of tax? Why or why not?

7. Suppose a poor central city were surrounded by wealthy suburbs. Should some of the taxes raised in these suburbs be spent in the city to equalize levels of public services? Defend your answer.

8. What would be the advantages and disadvantages if the national government gave states and communities financial aid with no strings attached?

ing special districts and school district authorities). How are the officials of these bodies selected? How are these governing bodies financed? Are all these separate bodies necessary? Explain your answer.

3. Who decides on the level of taxes in your city or town? Do the decision makers have a wide range of choices as to type and level of taxes? To what extent does your local government rely on state and national funds? Present your findings in a report.

4. Attend a meeting of your local government. What issues were discussed? Were any important decisions made? What seemed to be the major problems? Present your findings in a report.

EXTENDING YOUR UNDERSTANDING

1. Make a chart of the most important officials (governor and so on) in your state. Indicate which officials are elected and which are appointed. Show also the length of each official's term of office. Compare the responsibilities of these officials with those of similar officials on the national level.

2. Draw up a list of all the governing bodies in your county or other local government (includ-

MAKING DECISIONS

As a member of the zoning board in your community, you must make decisions about how local land can be used. A group of business people are asking the zoning board for permission to build a shopping mall and a threater in an area currently zoned for residential use. What questions would you ask the business people? What factors would you take into account in making your decision? Present your conclusions to the class.

Epilogue: Making Intelligent Political Choices

In Chapter 1 we saw that all citizens confront political choices. Even apathy represents a choice—a decision to do nothing. We also noted that the opportunity to participate does not guarantee success. Just as people can make unwise economic decisions, people can also be inept in achieving their political goals. Indeed, people often favor policies they later oppose or invest resources in hopeless causes. But given the complexity of American politics, it is not surprising that many people are unsuccessful or are too overwhelmed even to try.

There are no simple rules for making wise political choices. Nevertheless, knowledge of the material covered in the preceding seventeen chapters should help to improve the chances of success. In some instances—the flow of national legislation described in Chapter 9, for example—the relevance of the information is apparent. However, in many other situations the material's relationship to personal political choices is less than clear. Therefore, some of these implications should be made more explicit. What follows are general guidelines to political action drawn from previous chapters.

Not All Goals Are Achievable Through Government Intervention

Chapter 1 made clear that we have a "limited government." Decisions made by government can influence every aspect of our lives, but government makes no claim to exercise authority over each and every aspect of society. This is not true in totalitarian governments, such as the Soviet Union, where almost every aspect of life is subjected to government intervention. Of course, the line separating governmental and nongovernmental spheres of authority is often imprecise and can change over time.

The nature of our form of limited government has several implications. First, a particular political objective might be outside the traditional realm of the government. For example, the federal government has almost always been reluctant to interfere in the internal affairs of religious groups, because the First Amendment prohibits government from abridging the free exercise of religion. On occasion, as the examination of the secular regulation rule in Chapter 13 shows, the government has even tolerated religious-related behavior that violates the law. Thus, if you are disturbed by the doctrines and practices of certain religious cults, taking action against them through the political process is difficult. Even officials sympathetic to your goals may be hesitant to become involved in what has always been an off-limits area.

Limits are imposed on government action even when the government is within its authority. Recall from the discussion of the principles underlying the Constitution (Chapter 2) that the Founders greatly feared a government with unlimited power. Checks and balances, separation of powers, federalism, and the use of supermajorities were intended to impede government action. Moreover, public officials are limited further by constitutional guarantees of due process and numerous statutes dealing with such issues as secrecy, spending money, nondiscrimination, and the like.

The Government Often Lacks Sufficient Resources to Solve a Problem

We have seen that under our political system some policy areas and actions are off-limits to government. Even when the government can act with full authority, however, officials at all levels cannot do as they please. Indeed, a frequent complaint of public officials is that they cannot accomplish much despite the size and power of modern government. In the pursuit of an objective, a key question must be: "Can government do it?" To pressure government to do something it cannot accomplish is wasteful and can do more harm than good.

One obvious limit on government is money. Attacking such problems as pollution, poverty, illiteracy, and unemployment can be expensive. Sometimes the costs of a complete solution can be beyond the capacity of even the federal government. Consider the problem of providing adequate health care to the elderly. Programs in this field have expanded dramatically in the last two decades. But even if funds were doubled or tripled, not much more help is possible for many elderly who suffer from chronic, debilitating diseases. It might take hundreds of millions a year spent on medical research and intensive care to solve the health problems of the elderly.

Even though the federal government in principle possesses sufficient funds for such an undertaking, it might be undesirable to make such a mammoth financial commitment. Increased spending in one area always means reduced spending in others. A huge increase in spending for medical research might mean less money for education, highway safety, reducing pollution, or other worthy causes. As noted in Chapter 14, all policy choices have tradeoffs—maximum attention to one set of goals means less attention to others.

Even when government possesses sufficient financial resources, there still is no guarantee that a problem can be resolved. Public officials cannot address each and every issue. Our discussion of Congress and the President showed that these officials face enormous demands on their time. Getting the attention of a member of Congress or of the President is not easy. A legislator might show little interest in the plight of the elderly unless there were many such people in his or her district or the legislator served on a committee with jurisdiction in that area. This attitude does not reflect a lack of sympathy; rather, officials simply lack the time to be interested in every important subject. Placing a new issue on the agenda can mean pushing an old one aside.

Besides limits on money and time, government often lacks the knowledge necessary to accomplish a goal. In our discussion of economic policy (Chapter 15) we saw that policymakers have often used "hit ot miss" tactics to deal with the highly complex relationships among unemployment, inflation, government spending, the deficit, and other economic factors. Despite the existence of numerous reports, analyses, and the work of professional economists, miscalculations and mistakes do occur. We also saw in Chapter 16 the problems government faces in promoting economic development in poorer nations. The best of intentions and the commitment of ample resources means little if officials lack proper knowledge.

These considerations are not intended to discourage political action. Rather, they should be used as guides for choosing objectives that have a reasonable chance of success and benefits that will outweigh the costs.

Certain Enduring Features of Our System Have an Impact

One of the persistent themes running through the previous seventeen chapters is that the way the political system is organized has an important impact, even though activists immersed in day-to-day conflicts rarely give much thought to such matters. These factors shape political conflict and influence who wins and loses, yet they are rarely issues on the political agenda. Sophisticated citizens know that to ignore the basic character of American politics is to reduce sharply one's chances of success. On numerous occasions, small, unrepresentative interests have achieved a goal because they better understood the nature of American politics.

One important feature of our political system is that power is fragmented. This is by design— remember that the Founders believed that the concentration of power would lead to tyranny. At the national level, power is divided among three branches of government, and as we saw in Chapter 3 (Federalism), many powers are divided between the national government and the states. Fragmentation is also present within institutions. Our description of Congress (Chapter 9) emphasized the lack of centralized power. Dozens of committees, subcommittees, and party officials can influence, but not dictate, legislation. Fragmentation of authority is even present in the judicial system—the Chief Justice of the Supreme Court cannot control the eight other justices, nor can the Court itself easily impose its will on lower courts.

A related feature is that policy making is usually a cooperative activity involving numerous institutions and officials. The image that Congress enacts a law, the President enforces it, and that is the end of it is highly misleading. Consider what might happen in the implementation of pollution policy. Congress passes a law dealing with toxic waste disposal that gives the Environmental Protection Agency (EPA) authority over this matter. The EPA strictly enforces the law. Industries hurt by the policy enlist their friends in Congress who sit on the relevant oversight committees to investigate what they believe to be arbitrary and unworkable EPA standards. Meanwhile, some state pollution agencies also disagree with the EPA's policies and refuse to cooperate. Pressure is put on the President by the Commerce and Agriculture departments as well. The EPA, sensing political reality, cuts back on its enforcement efforts. This change generates a counter-reaction. Interest groups concerned with reducing pollution bring suit in federal court to force the EPA to follow the letter of the law. Additional pressures might come from state officials, local citizen's groups, and members of Congress. Advocates of tough enforcement might find allies in Congress, within the EPA, and among presidential advisors. The actual policy may therefore vary over time, and different sets of people may simultaneously be involved in its formulation and administration.

A third important feature of the U.S. political system is its fluidity. Change is natural and constant. Much of this change is built in through the electoral process. In the twenty-four years between 1960 and 1984, the United States has had six different Presidents and almost the entire membership of Congress has changed. Even though federal judges are appointed for life, death and retirement make change inevitable in the courts too. In Chapter 11 (the Bureaucracy) we saw that top appointed officials usually have limited tenure

in their positions. Of course, the population itself undergoes many changes, as a result of varying birth and death rates, as well as immigration. And people's opinions change over time and according to the circumstances of their lives.

A fourth feature is the dispersion and variety of political resources. The American political system is not a system in which one resource exists and only one interest controls it. We know not all interests are equal, but virtually everyone can have some impact.

What do these four features of American politics mean in terms of being an informed and effective participant? Overall, they suggest that any attempt to bring about far-reaching change will encounter numerous obstacles. Given the decentralization of power in our system, influence will have to be exerted in a variety of settings. If you want legislation enacted, success in the House means little unless you also succeed in the Senate. Having the President on your side does not necessarily mean that executive branch officials responsible for implementing policies will follow presidential directives. The situation becomes even more complex when state and local officials are involved.

The broad division of political resources also means that policy battles can be long and difficult. Even though most citizens and public officials might support your goal , industry opponents can, and probably will, wage a major campaign against such regulation.

In sum, quick easy victories are rare. Even when a victory is achieved, it might not be permanent. The very nature of our political system requires persistence and far-reaching involvement for success.

Simple Approaches Are Not Always Solutions

Political conflicts, almost by their very nature, oversimplify complex issues. Slogans such as "no taxation without representation" are employed to rally supporters. The virtues of one's own position and the evils of the opposition's are exaggerated.

Issues such as nuclear power, tax reform, and the rights of criminals are typically reduced to sharply contrasting views. For some people the U.S.– Soviet arms race is simply a question of whether you are for or against the continued survival of the human race.

A degree of simplification is usually necessary in political conflicts. An attempt to influence people with two-hour fact-filled speeches accompanied by 200-page handouts is not a strategy calculated to appeal to the average citizen. Moreover, for at least some people, a few simple ideas or slogans are sufficient. They might have neither the ability nor the inclination to seek more than a superficial understanding. Even the most informed citizens occasionally reduce complex issues to battles between good and evil.

The problem occurs when political activists themselves begin to oversimplify the world.'What might make for a good strategy in drumming up public support can result in ineffectiveness and frustration. And future credibility can be destroyed when simplistic solutions do not work despite prior claims of their effectiveness. Enormous investments of time, money, and energy are wasted.

Oversimplification takes several forms. Perhaps the most common in many recent political movements is the failure to think through the impact of a proposal. In Chapter 7 we mentioned that reformers within the Democratic party during the late 1960s argued that the party would be revitalized by having more primaries and recruiting more women and minorities. They automatically assumed that increased participation by voters in the party's decision-making process would lead to electoral success. This logic was, to their minds, self-evident but not based on past experience. Judging by the party's success rate since the reforms—one presidential victory in four elections, for example—the opening-up process was hardly a cure. Indeed, some critics assert that matters were made worse because internal party divisions were increased.

Another common mistake rooted in a simplistic view of politics is that good intentions produce good results. In other words, if well-meaning peo-ple, working on behalf of a good cause, persuade government to do something good, the end result will be good. Such reasoning often ignores the limitations of the proposed solution as well as what can happen in the real world.

Well-intentioned people advocating good causes also frequently underestimate the power of the opposition. These advocates may believe that other citizens and public officials will be persuaded by the sheer righteousness of the cause once they understand it.

An unrealistic belief about the power of the law is another common error. On many occasions groups become so focused on the passage of a particular bill that they ignore everything else. Our discussion of civil rights legislation in Chapter 13 demonstrated that Congress can pass a law, or even a constitutional amendment, to protect blacks, but this action can be rendered meaningless by lack of enforcement, public hostility, or defiant court interpretation. If every law worked as intended, crime would vanish. More than once a group has worked for legislation only to discover that the enacted law is not being enforced or be unenforceable (recall our analysis of the problems of enforcing laws regulating lobbying in Chapter 8). Passing a law is a means to an end, not the end in itself.

To summarize, simple ideas and slogans are essential in political conflict, but political reality is rarely simple. Great care must be given to the consequences of political actions, and good intentions are almost never enough. Nor does merely believing that a cause is just guarantee success. Finally, it is unwise to view the passage of a law as the final victory.

Success Usually Requires Persistence and Sacrifice

The history of political conflict shows that easy victories are very rare. Remember the battle to adopt the Constitution—every step of the process, from getting delegates to Philadelphia to final ratification, was a struggle. On several occasions it looked as if the effort would fail. In our analysis of the legislative process we saw that most bills fail to get through the congressional obstacle course. As we have stressed repeatedly, our entire political system is designed to check drastic and one-sided change.

One important piece of advice, particularly relevant to students, is to stick with an issue rather than going from cause to cause as if politics were like fashion. In the past few years many people have involved themselves in environmentalism, opposition to nuclear power, the nuclear freeze movement, protests against U.S. involvement in Central America, and other causes. These are all complex issues that do not lend themselves to rapid change despite impassioned pleas from concerned citizens—whether young people or adults. Moreover, if you and your allies are not willing to stick with the cause for more than a short time, the opposition may simply delay any decision until your group loses interest. Regularly changing one's cause may heighten the excitement of politics, but it usually leads to ineffectiveness.

Another related problem concerns a distaste for the dull, routine aspects of political conflict. There can be a great deal of excitement in politics, but much of the essential work can be boring. For someone who feels outraged by the government's willingness to spend lavishly on defense at the expense of human needs, sifting through hundreds of technical reports or listening to congressional testimony might not seem worthwhile. This person might prefer instead to organize a public demonstration or picket the Pentagon. But without huge investments of time in unexciting work, his or her efforts are likely to be superficial and short-lived.

Besides, having to overcome an impatience with the dull side of politics, sophisticated participants also know that they must be able to deal with individuals they may dislike. An unwillingness to suspend differences in political views, personal values, and lifestyle can be counterproductive. Success in our system requires cooperation and compromise, and this can lead to strange coalitions. The environmental movement, for example, owes much of its effectiveness to alliances with hunting and fishing groups.

Our examination of all the aspects of American government and the political process has shown both the flaws and the advantages of our system. Though change is not easy to achieve, it can be done—with a good deal of hard work and compromise. Even though the political process can frustrate the best of efforts and exhaust the energies of even the most dedicated activists, the system has demonstrated its value. It is flexible enough to respond to the pressures of many interests and yet stable enough to resist takeover by special interests. It has proved capable of maintaining a delicate balance between the rights of the individual and the concerns of the majority. It has withstood crises and gathered strength from them. Born out of compromise, our system of government continues to survive through the spirit of accommodations, providing a strong foundation for the country—in the past, in the present, and for the future.

Appendix A

THE DECLARATION OF INDEPENDENCE IN CONGRESS, JULY 4, 1776

The Unanimous Declaration of the Thirteen United States of America,

When in the Course of human events, it becomes necessary for one people to dissolve the political bands which have connected them with another, and to assume among the Powers of the earth, the separate and equal station to which the Laws of Nature and of Nature's God entitle them, a decent respect to the opinions of mankind requires that they should declare the causes which impel them to the separation.

We hold these truths to be self-evident, that all men are created equal, that they are endowed by their Creator with certain unalienable Rights, that among these are Life, Liberty and the pursuit of Happiness. That to secure these rights, Governments are instituted among Men, deriving their just powers from the consent of the governed. That whenever any Form of Government becomes destructive of these ends, it is the Right of the People to alter or to abolish it, and to institute new Government, laying its foundation on such principles and organizing its powers in such form, as to them shall seem most likely to effect their Safety and Happiness. Prudence, indeed, will dictate that Governments long established should not be changed for light and transient causes, and accordingly all experience hath shown, that mankind are more disposed to suffer, while evils are sufferable, than to right themselves by abolishing the forms to which they are accustomed. But when a long train of abuses and usurpations, pursuing invariably the same Object evinces a design to reduce them under absolute Despotism, it is their right, it is their duty, to throw off such Government, and to provide new Guards for their future security.—Such has been the patient sufferance of these Colonies; and such is now the necessity which constrains them to alter their former Systems of Government. The history of the present King of Great Britain is a history of repeated injuries and usurpations, all having in direct object the establishment of an absolute Tyranny over these States. To prove this, let Facts be submitted to a candid world.

He has refused his Assent to Laws, the most wholesome and necessary for the public good.

He has forbidden his Governors to pass Laws of immediate and pressing importance, unless suspended in their operation till his Assent should be obtained; and when so suspended, he has utterly neglected to attend to them.

He has refused to pass other Laws for the accommodation of large districts of people, unless those people would relinquish the right of Representation in the Legislature, a right inestimable to them and formidable to tyrants only.

He has called together legislative bodies at places unusual, uncomfortable, and distant from the depository of their Public Records, for the sole purpose of fatiguing them into compliance with his measures.

He has dissolved Representative Houses repeatedly, for opposing with manly firmness his invasions on the rights of the people.

He has refused for a long time, after such dissolutions, to cause others to be elected; whereby the Legislative Powers, incapable of Annihilation, have returned to the People at large for their exercise; the State remaining in the mean time exposed to all the dangers of invasion from without, and convulsions within.

He has endeavoured to prevent the population of these States; for that purpose obstructing the Laws for Naturalization of Foreigners; refusing to pass others to encourage their migrations hither, and raising the conditions of new Appropriations of Lands.

He has obstructed the Administration of Justice, by refusing his Assent to Laws for establishing Judiciary Powers.

He has made Judges dependent on his Will alone, for the tenure of their offices, and the amount and payment of their salaries.

He has erected a multitude of New Officers, and sent hither swarms of Officers to harass our people, and eat out their substance.

He has kept among us, in times of peace, Standing Armies without the Consent of our legislatures.

He has affected to render the Military independent of and superior to the Civil Power.

He has combined with others to subject us to a jurisdiction foreign to our constitution, and unacknowledged by our laws; giving his Assent to their acts of pretended Legislation:

For quartering large bodies of armed troops among us:

For protecting them, by a mock Trial, from Punishment for any Murders which they should commit on the inhabitants of these States:

For cutting off our Trade with all parts of the world:

For imposing taxes on us without our Consent:

For depriving us in many cases, of the benefits of Trial by Jury:

For transporting us beyond Seas to be tried for pretended offences:

For abolishing the free System of English Laws in a neighbouring Province, establishing therein an Arbitrary government, and enlarging its Boundaries so as to render it at once an example and fit instrument for introducing the same absolute rule into these Colonies:

For taking away our Charters, abolishing our most valuable Laws, and altering fundamentally the Forms of our Governments:

For suspending our own Legislatures, and declaring themselves invested with Power to legislate for us in all cases whatsoever.

He has abdicated Government here, by declaring us out of his Protection and waging War against us.

He has plundered our seas, ravaged our Coasts, burnt our towns, and destroyed the lives of our people.

He is at this time transporting large armies of foreign mercenaries to compleat the works of death, desolation and tyranny, already begun with circumstances of Cruelty & perfidy scarcely paralleled in the most barbarous ages, and totally unworthy the Head of a civilized nation.

He has constrained our fellow Citizens taken Captive on the high Seas to bear Arms against their Country, to become the executioners of their friends and Brethren, or to fall themselves by their Hands.

He has excited domestic insurrections amongst us, and has endeavoured to bring on the inhabitants of our frontiers, the merciless Indian Savages, whose known rule of warfare, is an undistinguished destruction of all ages, sexes and conditions.

In every stage of these Oppressions We have Petitioned for Redress in the most humble terms: Our repeated Petitions have been answered only by repeated injury. A Prince, whose character is thus marked by every act which may define a Tyrant, is unfit to be the ruler of a free people.

Nor have We been wanting in attentions to our British brethren. We have warned them from time to time of attempts by their legislature to extend an unwarrantable jurisdiction over us. We have reminded them of the circumstances of our emigration and settlement here. We have appealed to their native justice and magnanimity, and we have conjured them by the ties of our common kindred to disavow these usurpations which, would inevitably interrupt our connections and correspondence. They too have been deaf to the voice of justice and of consanguinity. We must, therefore, acquiesce in the necessity, which denounces our Separation, and hold them, as we hold the rest of mankind, Enemies in War, in Peace Friends.

We, therefore, the Representatives of the United States of America, in General Congress, Assembled, appealing to the Supreme Judge of the world for the rectitude of our intentions, do, in the Name, and by authority of the good People of these Colonies, solemnly publish and declare, That these United Colonies are, and of Right ought to be Free and Independent States; that they are Absolved from all Allegiance to the British Crown, and that all political connection between them and the State of Great Britain, is and ought to be totally dissolved; and that as Free and Independent States, they have full power to levy War, conclude Peace, contract Alliances, establish Commerce, and to do all other Acts and Things which Independent States may of right do. And for the support of this Declaration, with a firm reliance on the Protection of Divine Providence, we mutually pledge to each other our Lives, our Fortunes and our sacred Honor.

Appendix B

THE CONSTITUTION OF THE UNITED STATES OF AMERICA

Spelling, capitalization, and punctuation are as they appear in the original document. Headings and explanations have been added and are printed in color. The explanations follow the portions of the Constitution to which they refer. The parts of the Constitution that are no longer in effect are printed in *italic type.*

[PREAMBLE]

WE THE PEOPLE of the United States, in Order to form a more perfect Union, establish Justice, insure domestic Tranquility, provide for the common defence, promote the general Welfare, and secure the Blessings of Liberty to ourselves and our Posterity, do ordain and establish this Constitution for the United States of America.

The Preamble, or introduction, establishes the principle of rule by the people and lists the six basic purposes of the Constitution.

ARTICLE I   [THE LEGISLATIVE BRANCH]

Section 1   [Legislative Powers]

All legislative Powers herein granted shall be vested in a Congress of the United States, which shall consist of a Senate and House of Representatives.

Section 2   [House of Representatives]

The House of Representatives shall be composed of Members chosen every second Year by the People of the several States, and the Electors in each State shall have the Qualifications requisite for Electors of the most numerous Branch of the State Legislature.

Representatives are chosen by those "Electors" (that is, voters) in each state who are qualified to vote for members of the lower house of the state legislature.

No Person shall be a Representative who shall not have attained to the Age of twenty-five Years, and been seven Years a Citizen of the United States, and who shall not, when elected, be an Inhabitant of that State in which he shall be chosen.

Representatives and *direct Taxes* shall be apportioned among the several States which may be included within this Union, according to their respective Numbers, *which shall be determined by adding to the whole Number of free Persons, including those bound to Ser-* *vice for a Term of Years, and excluding Indians not taxed, three fifths of all other Persons.* The actual Enumeration shall be made within three Years after the first Meeting of the Congress of the United States, and within every subsequent Term of ten Years, in such manner as they shall by Law direct. The Number of Representatives shall not exceed one for every thirty Thousand, but each State shall have at Least one Representative; *and until such enumeration shall be made, the State of New Hampshire shall be entitled to chuse three, Massachusetts eight, Rhode-Island and Providence Plantations one, Connecticut five, New-York six, New Jersey four, Pennsylvania eight, Deleware one, Maryland six, Virginia ten, North Carolina five, South Carolina five, and Georgia three.*

Direct taxes—those paid directly to the federal government—are supposed to be apportioned (divided) according to a state's population. The only direct tax now in effect is the income tax. The first passage in italics has thus been superseded by the Sixteenth Amendment, which allows a tax to be levied on individual incomes rather than according to state populations.

The second passage in italics refers to indentured servants ("those bound to Service") and slaves ("all other Persons"). The "three-fifths compromise" for counting slaves was invalidated by the Thirteenth and Fourteenth amendments.

The third italic passage was a temporary provision. It was in effect only until the first census ("enumeration"), in 1790. In 1929, Congress passed the Reapportionment Act, setting the size of the House of Representatives at 435 members.

When vacancies happen in the Representation from any State, the Executive Authority thereof shall issue Writs of Election to fill such Vacancies.

When a vacancy occurs in a state's representation in the House, the governor ("Executive Authority") calls an election to fill it.

The House of Representatives shall chuse their Speaker and other Officers; and shall have the sole Power of Impeachment.

Section 3   [The Senate]

The Senate of the United States shall be composed of two Senators from each State, *chosen by the Legislature thereof,* for six Years; and each Senator shall have one Vote.

The phrase in italics was changed by the Seventeenth Amendment, which provided that senators are to be elected directly by the voters, not by state legislatures.

Immediately after they shall be assembled in Consequence of the first Election, they shall be divided as equally as may be into three Classes. The Seats of the Senators of the first Class shall be vacated at the Expiration of the second Year, of the second Class at the Expiration of the fourth Year, and of the third Class at the Expiration of the sixth Year, so that one third may be chosen every second Year: *and if Vacancies happen by Resignation, or otherwise, during the Recess of the Legislature of any State, the Executive thereof may make temporary Appointments until the next Meeting of the Legislature, which shall then fill such Vacancies.*

The "three Classes" were chosen only in the first Senate, so that a third of its members could be replaced at each successive election. The passage in italics was modified by the Seventeenth Amendment, which provides that a state's governor can name a temporary replacement, who will serve until the next election, to fill a senatorial vacancy.

No person shall be a Senator who shall not have attained to the Age of thirty Years, and been nine Years a Citizen of the United States, and who shall not, when elected, be an Inhabitant of that State for which he shall be chosen.

The Vice President of the United States shall be President of the Senate, but shall have no Vote, unless they be equally divided.

The Senate shall chuse their other Officers, and also a President pro tempore, in the Absence of the Vice President, or when he shall exercise the Office of President of the United States.

Pro tempore is Latin for "temporary." The Senate's president pro tem, as the officer is usually called, is always a leading member of the majority party.

The Senate shall have the sole Power to try all Impeachments. When sitting for that Purpose, they shall be on Oath or Affirmation. When the President of the United States is tried, the Chief Justice shall preside: And no Person shall be convicted without the Concurrence of two thirds of the Members present.

Judgment in Cases of Impeachment shall not extend further than to removal from Office, and disqualification to hold and enjoy any Office of honor, Trust or Profit under the United States: but the Party convicted shall nevertheless be liable and subject to Indictment, Trial, Judgment and Punishment, according to Law.

When someone is found guilty after being impeached, punishment by the Senate is limited to removal from office. But the person ("the Party convicted") can still be tried in a regular court for the same offense.

Section 4 [Elections and Meetings of Congress]

The Times, Places and Manner of holding Elections for Senators and Representatives, shall be prescribed in each State by the Legislature thereof; but the Congress may at any time by Law make or alter such Regulations, except as to the Places of chusing Senators.

The Congress shall assemble at least once in every Year, *and such Meeting shall be on the first Monday in December*, unless they shall by Law appoint a different Day.

The Twentieth Amendment changed this date to January 3.

Section 5 [Congressional Rules and Procedures]

Each House shall be the Judge of the Elections, Returns and Qualifications of its own Members, and a Majority of each shall constitute a Quorum to do Business; but a small Number may adjourn from day to day, and may be authorized to compel the Attendance of absent Members, in such Manner, and under the Penalties as each House may provide.

Each House may determine the Rules of its Proceedings, punish its Members for disorderly Behaviour, and, with the Concurrence of two thirds, expel a Member.

Each House shall keep a Journal of its Proceedings, and from time to time publish the same, excepting such Parts as may in their Judgment require Secrecy; and the Yeas and Nays of the Members of either House on any question shall, at the Desire of one fifth of those present, be entered on the Journal.

The *Congressional Record*, a printed journal of House and Senate proceedings, is published every day that either house of Congress is in session.

Neither House, during the Session of Congress, shall, without the Consent of the other, adjourn for more than three days, nor to any other Place than that in which the two Houses shall be sitting.

Section 6 [Pay and Privileges]

The Senators and Representatives shall receive a Compensation for their Services, to be ascertained by Law, and paid out of the Treasury of the United States. They shall in all Cases, except Treason, Felony and Breach of the Peace, be privileged from Arrest during their Attendence at the Session of their respective Houses, and in going to and returning from the same; and for any Speech or Debate in either House, they shall not be questioned in any other Place.

After stating that members of Congress are to be paid, this paragraph discusses *congressional immunity.*

With certain exceptions, members of Congress are exempt from arrest. "They shall not be questioned in any other place" means that members cannot be sued for libel or slander in court for things they write or say in the course of their legislative duties.

No Senator or Representative shall, during the Time for which he was elected, be appointed to any civil Office under the Authority of the United States, which shall have been created, or the Emoluments whereof shall have been encreased during such time; and no Person holding any Office under the United States, shall be a Member of either House during his Continuance in Office.

Section 7   [Lawmaking Procedures]

All Bills for raising Revenue shall originate in the House of Representatives; but the Senate may propose or concur with Amendments as on other Bills.

Every Bill which shall have passed the House of Representatives and the Senate, shall, before it become a Law, be presented to the President of the United States; If he approve he shall sign it, but if not he shall return it, with his Objections to that House in which it shall have originated, who shall enter the Objections at large on their Journal, and proceed to reconsider it. If after such Reconsideration two thirds of that House shall agree to pass the Bill, it shall be sent, together with the Objections, to the other House, by which it shall likewise be reconsidered, and if approved by two thirds of that House, it shall become a Law. But in all such Cases the Votes of both Houses shall be determined by yeas and Nays, and the Names of the Persons voting for and against the Bill shall be entered on the Journal of each House respectively. If any Bill shall not be returned by the President within ten Days (Sundays excepted) after it shall have been presented to him, the Same shall be a Law, in like Manner as if he had signed it, unless the Congress by their Adjournment prevent its Return, in which Case it shall not be a Law.

A bill becomes a law when the President signs it. If the President vetoes it, Congress can repass the measure by a two-thirds majority in both houses. A bill also becomes a law if the President fails to sign or return it to Congress within ten days. If Congress adjourns within that time, however, the bill is automatically vetoed; this procedure is known as the pocket veto.

Every Order, Resolution, or Vote to which the Concurrence of the Senate and House of Representatives may be necessary (except on a question of Adjournment) shall be presented to the President of the United States; and before the Same shall take Effect, shall be approved by him, or being disapproved by him, shall be repassed by two thirds of the Senate and House of Representatives, according to the Rules and Limitations prescribed in the case of a Bill.

Section 8   [The Powers of Congress]

The Congress shall have Power

To lay and collect Taxes, Duties, Imposts and Excises, to pay the Debts and provide for the common Defence and general Welfare of the United States; but all Duties, Imposts and Excises shall be uniform throughout the United States;

This list of taxes is meant to be complete rather than strictly logical, because duties, imposts, and excises are all forms of taxation. Duties and imposts are taxes on imports or exports. An excise is a tax placed on goods made or sold within a country.

To borrow Money on the Credit of the United States;

To regulate Commerce with foreign Nations, and among the several States, and with the Indian Tribes;

To establish an uniform Rule of Naturalization, and uniform Laws on the subject of Bankruptcies throughout the United States;

Naturalization is the process by which a noncitizen becomes a citizen.

To coin Money, regulate the Value thereof, and of foreign Coin, and fix the Standard of Weights and Measures;

To provide for the Punishment of counterfeiting the Securities and current Coin of the United States;

To establish Post Offices and post Roads;

To promote the Progress of Science and useful Arts, by securing for limited Times to Authors and Inventors the exclusive Right to their respective Writings and Discoveries;

To constitute Tribunals inferior to the supreme Court;

To define and punish Piracies and Felonies committed on the high Seas, and Offences against the Law of Nations;

To declare War, grant Letters of Marque and Reprisal, and make Rules concerning Captures on Land and Water;

"Letters of Marque and Reprisal" are government licenses that give merchant ships (privateers) the right to attack enemy vessels in time of war.

To raise and support Armies, but no Appropriation of Money to that Use shall be for a longer Term than two years;

To provide and maintain a Navy;

To make Rules for the Government and Regulation of the land and naval forces;

To provide for calling for the Militia to execute the Laws of the Union, suppress Insurrections and repel Invasions;

The militia refers to National Guard units, which may be called into federal service in emergencies.

To provide for organizing, arming, and disciplining, the Militia, and for governing such Part of them as may be employed in the Service of the United States, reserving to the States respectively, the Appointment of the Officers, and the Authority of training the Militia according to the discipline prescribed by Congress;

To exercise exclusive Legislation in all Cases whatsoever, over such District (not exceeding ten Miles square) as may, by Cession of particular States, and the Acceptance of Congress, become the Seat of the Government of the United States, and to exercise like Authority over all Places purchased by the Consent of the Legislature of the State in which the Same shall be, for the Erection of Forts, Magazines, Arsenals, dock-Yards, and other needful Buildings;—And

Congress has the power to govern the "Seat of the Government of the United States"—the region that eventually became the District of Columbia.

To make all Laws which shall be necessary and proper for carrying into Execution the foregoing Powers, and all other Powers vested by this Constitution in the Government of the United States, or in any Department or Officer thereof.

This is the "necessary and proper" clause (or "elastic" clause). It gives Congress the right to implied powers—those not specifically listed in the Constitution but necessary to carry out the legislature's enumerated powers.

Section 9 [Powers Denied the Federal Government]

The Migration or Importation of such Persons as any of the States now existing shall think proper to admit, shall not be prohibited by the Congress prior to the Year one thousand eight hundred and eight, but a Tax or duty may be imposed on such Importation, not exceeding ten dollars for each Person.

This temporary provision prohibited Congress from regulating the overseas trade in slaves ("such Persons") for twenty years. The provision outlawed the trade in 1808.

The privilege of the Writ of Habeas Corpus shall not be suspended, unless when in Cases of Rebellion or Invasion the public Safety may require it.

The writ of habeas corpus permits a prisoner to appear before a judge to inquire into the legality of his or her detention.

No Bill of Attainder or ex post facto Law shall be passed.

A bill of attainder is a law that declares a person guilty and specifies punishment without a trial. An ex post facto law punishes a person for an action committed before the law was passed.

No Capitation, or other direct, Tax shall be laid, unless in Proportion to the Census or Enumeration herein before directed to be taken.

This restriction on a head ("Capitation") tax or other direct tax was modified by the Sixteenth Amendment.

No Tax or Duty shall be laid on Articles exported from any State.

No Preference shall be given by any Regulation of Commerce or Revenue to the Ports of one State over those of another; nor shall Vessels bound to, or from, one State, be obliged to enter, clear, or pay Duties in another.

No Money shall be drawn from the Treasury, but in Consequence of Appropriations made by Law; and a regular Statement and Account of the Receipts and Expenditures of all public Money shall be published from time to time.

Although this clause appears in the negative, it actually gives Congress the important power of controlling the nation's funds—its "Receipts and Expenditures."

No Title of Nobility shall be granted by the United States: And no Person holding any Office of Profit or Trust under them, shall, without the Consent of the Congress, accept of any present, Emolument, Office, or Title, of any kind whatever, from any King, Prince, or foreign State.

Section 10 [Powers Denied the States]

No State shall enter into any Treaty, Alliance, or Confederation; grant Letters of Marque and Reprisal; coin Money; emit Bills of Credit; make any Thing but gold and silver Coin a Tender in Payment of Debts; pass any Bill of Attainder, ex post facto Law, or Law impairing the Obligation of Contracts, or grant any Title of Nobility.

Among other things, states are forbidden to issue paper money ("emit Bills of Credit"). They can use only gold and silver coins as legal money ("Tender") to pay debts. And they cannot interfere with "the Obligation of Contracts"—that is, weaken the commitments that people assume when they enter into legal agreements.

No State shall, without the Consent of the Congress, lay any Imposts or Duties on Imports or Exports, except what may be absolutely necessary for executing its inspection Laws: and the net Produce of all Duties and Imposts, laid by any State on Imports or Exports, shall be for the Use of the Treasury of the United States; and all such Laws shall be subject to the Revision and Controul of the Congress.

No State shall, without the Consent of Congress, lay any Duty of Tonnage, keep Troops, or Ships of War in time of Peace, enter into any Agreement or Compact with another State, or with a foreign Power, or engage in War, unless actually invaded, or in such imminent Danger as will not admit of Delay.

"Duty of Tonnage" is a tax based on a ship's cargo-carrying capacity.

ARTICLE II   [THE EXECUTIVE BRANCH]

Section 1   [President and Vice President]

The executive Power shall be vested in a President of the United States of America. He shall hold his Office during the Term of four years and, together with the Vice President, chosen for the same Term, be elected as follows.

Each State shall appoint, in such Manner as the Legislature thereof may direct, a Number of Electors, equal to the whole Number of Senators and Representatives to which the State may be entitled in the Congress; but no Senator or Representative, or Person holding an Office of Trust or Profit under the United States, shall be appointed an Elector.

The Electors shall meet in their respective States, and vote by Ballot for two Persons, of whom one at least shall not be an Inhabitant of the same State with themselves. And they shall make a List of all the Persons voted for, and of the Number of Votes for each; which List they shall sign and certify, and transmit sealed to the Seat of the Government of the United States, directed to the President of the Senate. The President of the Senate shall, in the Presence of the Senate and House of Representatives, open all the Certificates, and the Votes shall then be counted. The Person having the greatest Number of Votes shall be the President, if such Number be a Majority of the whole Number of Electors appointed; and if there be more than one who have such Majority, and have an equal Number of Votes, then the House of Representatives shall immediately chuse by Ballot one of them for President; and if no Person have a Majority, then from the five highest on the List the said House shall in like Manner chuse the President. But in chusing the President, the Votes shall be taken by States, the Representation from each State having one Vote. A quorum for this Purpose shall consist of a Member or Members from two thirds of the States, and a Majority of all the States shall be necessary to a Choice. In every Case, after the Choice of the President, the person having the greatest Number of Votes of the Electors shall be the Vice President. But if there should remain two or more who have equal Votes, the Senate shall chuse from them by Ballot the Vice President.

This procedure was replaced by the one outlined in the Twelfth Amendment.

The Congress may determine the Time of chusing the Electors, and the Day on which they shall give their Votes; which Day shall be the same throughout the United States.

No Person except a natural born Citizen, or a Citizen of the United States, at the time of the Adoption of this Constitution, shall be eligible to the Office of President; neither shall any Person be eligible to that Office who shall not have attained to the Age of thirty five Years, and been fourteen Years a Resident within the United States.

In Case of the Removal of the President from Office, or of his Death, Resignation, or Inability to discharge the Power and Duties of the said Office, the Same shall devolve on the Vice President, *and the Congress may by Law provide for the Case of Removal, Death, Resignation, or Inability, both of the President and Vice President, declaring what Officer shall then act as President, and such Officer shall act accordingly, until the Disability be removed, or a President shall be elected.*

This clause was modified by the Twenty-fifth Amendment.

The President shall, at stated Times, receive for his Services, a Compensation, which shall neither be encreased nor diminished during the Period of which he shall have been elected, and he shall not receive within that Period any other Emolument from the United States, or any of them.

Before he enter on the Execution of his Office, he shall take the following Oath or Affirmation:—"I do solemnly swear (or affirm) that I will faithfully execute the Office of President of the United States, and will to the best of my Ability, preserve, protect and defend the Constitution of the United States."

Section 2   [Powers of the President]

The President shall be Commander in Chief of the Army and Navy of the United States, and of the Militia of the several States, when called into the actual Service of the United States; he may require the Opinion, in writing, of the principal Officer in each of the executive Departments, upon any Subject relating to the Duties of their respective Offices, and he shall have Power to grant Reprieves and Pardons for Offences against the United States, except in Cases of Impeachment.

The phrase relating to "the principal Officer in each of the executive Departments" is the constitutional basis for the Cabinet.

He shall have Power, by and with the Advice and Consent of the Senate, to make Treaties, provided two thirds of the Senators present concur; and he shall nominate, and by and with the Advice and Consent of the Senate, shall appoint Ambassadors, other public Ministers and Consuls, Judges of the supreme Court, and all other Officers of the United States, whose Appointments are not herein otherwise provided for, and which shall be established by Law; but the Congress may by Law vest the Appointment of such inferior Officers, as they think proper, in the President alone, in the Courts of Law, or in the Heads of Departments.

The President shall have Power to fill up all Vacancies that may happen during the Recess of the Senate, by granting Commissions which shall expire at the End of their next Session.

Section 3 [Duties of the President]

He shall from time to time give the Congress Information of the State of the Union, and recommend to their Consideration such Measures as he shall judge necessary and expedient; he may, on extraordinary Occasions, convene both Houses, or either of them, and in Case of Disagreement between them, with Respect to the Time of Adjournment, he may adjourn them to such Time as he shall think proper; he shall receive Ambassadors and other public Ministers; he shall take Care that the Laws be faithfully executed, and shall Commission all the Officers of the United States.

The President delivers a "State of the Union" address at the opening of each new session of Congress. Woodrow Wilson was the first President since John Adams to read his message in person. Franklin D. Roosevelt and his successors followed Wilson's example.

Section 4 [Impeachment]

The President, Vice President and all civil Officers of the United States, shall be removed from Office on Impeachment for, and Conviction of, Treason, Bribery, or other high Crimes and Misdemeanors.

"Civil Officers" include executive and judicial officials but not members of Congress or officers in the armed forces.

ARTICLE III [THE JUDICIAL BRANCH]

Section 1 [Federal Courts]

The judicial Power of the United States, shall be vested in one supreme Court, and in such inferior Courts as the Congress may from time to time ordain and establish. The Judges, both of the supreme and inferior Courts, shall hold their Offices during good Behaviour, and shall, at stated Times, receive for their Services, a Compensation, which shall not be diminished during their Continuance in Office.

Judges in federal courts hold their offices "during good Behaviour"—that is, for life.

Section 2 [Jurisdiction]

The judicial Power shall extend to all Cases, in Law and Equity, arising under this Constitution, the Laws of the United States, and Treaties made, or which shall be made, under their Authority;—to all Cases affecting Ambassadors, other public Ministers and Consuls;—to all Cases of admiralty and maritime Jurisdiction;—to Controversies to which the United States

shall be a Party;—to Controversies between two or more States;—*between a State and Citizens of another State;*—between Citizens of different States;—between Citizens of the same State claiming Lands under Grants of different States, *and between a State, or the Citizens thereof, and foreign States, Citizens or Subjects.*

The Eleventh Amendment prevented a citizen from suing a state and restricted the jurisdiction of federal courts in cases involving other nations.

In all Cases affecting Ambassadors, other public Ministers and Consuls, and those in which a State shall be Party, the supreme Court shall have original Jurisdiction. In all the other Cases before mentioned, the supreme Court shall have appellate Jurisdiction, both as to Law and Fact, with such Exceptions, and under such Regulations as Congress shall make.

The Trial of all Crimes, except in Cases of Impeachment, shall be by Jury; and such Trial shall be held in the State where the said Crimes shall have been committed; but when not committed within any State, the Trial shall be at such Place or Places as the Congress may by Law have directed.

Section 3 [Treason]

Treason against the United States, shall consist only in levying War against them, or in adhering to their Enemies, giving them Aid and Comfort. No Person shall be convicted of Treason unless on the Testimony of two Witnesses to the same overt Act, or on Confession in open Court.

Treason is the only crime defined in the Constitution. The word is rigorously defined in order to prevent the government from making loose charges against those it wishes to prosecute.

The Congress shall have Power to declare the Punishment of Treason, but no Attainder of Treason shall work Corruption of Blood, or Forfeiture except during the Life of the Person attainted.

Congress can punish someone for treason, but attainder (the loss of civil rights) affects only the person convicted. It cannot "work Corruption of Blood"—that is, extend the punishment to his or her descendants.

ARTICLE IV [RELATIONS AMONG THE STATES]

Section 1 [Official Acts and Records]

Full Faith and Credit shall be given in each State to the public Acts, Records, and judicial Proceedings of every other State. And the Congress may by general Laws prescribe the Manner in which such Acts, Records and Proceedings shall be proved, and the Effect thereof.

The "full Faith and Credit" clause means that every state must accept the decisions of every other state in civil (but not necessarily criminal) cases.

Section 2   [Mutual Obligations]

The Citizens of each State shall be entitled to all Privileges and Immunities of Citizens in the several states.

A Person charged in any State with Treason, Felony or other Crime, who shall flee from Justice, and be found in another State, shall on Demand of the executive Authority of the State from which he fled, be delivered up to be removed to the State having Jurisdiction of the Crime.

A fugitive from justice must be returned to the state where the crime was committed if the governor of that state requests his or her return. The delivery of a fugitive from one authority to another is known as *extradition*.

No Person held to Service or Labour in one State, under the Laws thereof, escaping into another, shall, in Consequence of any Law or Regulation therein, be discharged from such Service or Labour, but shall be delivered up on Claim of the Party to whom such Service or Labour may be due.

The phrase "Person held to Service or Labour" refers to a slave. Thus this provision was nullified by the Thirteenth Amendment.

Section 3   [New States and Territories]

New States may be admitted by the Congress into this Union; but no new State shall be formed or erected within the Jurisdiction of any other State; nor any State be formed by the Junction of two or more States, or Parts of States, without the Consent of the Legislatures of the States concerned as well as of the Congress.

Although Congress is prohibited from creating a new state out of an existing one without the latter's consent, it did make one exception. During the Civil War, the forty counties of western Virginia (a Confederate state) remained loyal to the Union and were admitted as West Virginia.

The Congress shall have Power to dispose of and make all needful Rules and Regulations respecting the Territory or other Property belonging to the United States; and nothing in this Constitution shall be so construed as to Prejudice any Claims of the United States, or of any particular State.

Section 4   [Federal Guarantees to the States]

The United States shall guarantee to every State in this Union a Republican Form of Government, and shall protect each of them against Invasion; and on Application of Legislature, or of the Executive (when the Legislature cannot be convened) against domestic Violence.

ARTICLE V

[Amending the Constitution]

The Congress, whenever two thirds of both Houses shall deem it necessary, shall propose Amendments to this Constitution, or, on the Application of the Legislatures of two thirds of the several States, shall call a Convention for proposing Amendments, which, in either Case, shall be valid to all Intents and Purposes, as Part of this Constitution, when ratified by the legislatures of three fourths of the several States, or by Conventions in three fourths thereof, as the one or the other Mode of Ratification may be proposed by the Congress; *Provided that no Amendment which may be made prior to the Year One thousand eight hundred and eight shall in any Manner affect the first and fourth Clauses in the Ninth Section of the first Article*, and that no State, without its Consent, shall be deprived of it's equal Suffrage in the Senate.

An amendment may be proposed in either of two ways and may be ratified in either of two ways. To date, all the amendments have been proposed by Congress and all but one have been ratified by state legislatures; the Twenty-first Amendment was ratified by state conventions.

The passage in italics, a temporary provision, became irrelevant after 1808.

ARTICLE VI

[Debts, Supremacy, Oaths of Office]

All Debts contracted and Engagements entered into, before the Adoption of this Constitution, shall be as valid against the United States under this Constitution, as under the Confederation.

This Constitution, and the Laws of the United States which shall be made in Pursuance thereof; and all Treaties made, or which shall be made, under the Authority of the United States, shall be the supreme Law of the Land; and the Judges in every State shall be bound thereby, any thing in the Constitution or Laws of any State to the Contrary notwithstanding.

This "supremacy clause" means that federal laws always override state legislation in cases of conflict.

The Senators and Representatives before mentioned, and the Members of the several State Legislatures, and all executive and judicial Officers, both of the United States and of the several States, shall be bound by Oath or Affirmation, to support this Constitution; but no religious Test shall ever be required as a Qualification to any Office or public Trust under the United States.

ARTICLE VII

[Ratifying the Constitution]

The Ratification of the Conventions of nine States, shall be sufficient for the Establishment of this Constitution between the States so ratifying the Same.

The Constitution was ratified by conventions in the thirteen original states beginning on December 7, 1787, and ending on May 29, 1790. It became effective on March 4, 1789.

DONE in Convention by the Unanimous Consent of the States present the Seventeenth Day of September in the Year of our Lord one thousand seven hundred and Eighty seven and of the Independance of the United States of America the Twelfth. *In Witness* whereof We have hereunto subscribed our Names.

AMENDMENTS TO THE CONSTITUTION

The first ten amendments are known as the Bill of Rights. The date in brackets indicated for each amendment is the year in which it became law.

AMENDMENT I   [1791]

[Freedom of Religion, Speech, Press, Assembly, and Petition]

Congress shall make no law respecting an establishment of religion, or prohibiting the free exercise thereof; or abridging the freedom of speech, or of the press; or the right of the people peaceably to assemble, and to petition the Government for a redress of grievances.

AMENDMENT II   [1791]

[The Right to Keep and Bear Arms]

A well regulated Militia, being necessary to the security of a free State, the right of the people to keep and bear Arms, shall not be infringed.

Each state has a right to maintain a National Guard. Both the states and the federal government can and do regulate firearms by such means as licensing.

AMENDMENT III   [1791]

[Quartering of Soldiers]

No Soldier shall, in time of peace be quartered in any house, without the consent of the Owner, nor in time of war, but in a manner to be prescribed by law.

This provision grew out of the British practice of quartering (housing) soldiers in colonists' homes without their consent.

AMENDMENT IV   [1791]

[Search and Seizure]

The right of the people to be secure in their persons, houses, papers, and effects, against unreasonable searches and seizures, shall not be violated, and no Warrants shall issue, but upon probable cause, supported by Oath or affirmation, and particularly describing the place to be searched, and the persons or things to be seized.

AMENDMENT V   [1791]

[Rights of The Accused; Property Rights]

No person shall be held to answer for a capital, or otherwise infamous crime, unless on a presentment or indictment of a Grand Jury, except in cases arising in the land or naval forces, or in the Militia, when in actual service in time of War or in public danger; nor shall any person be subject for the same offence to be twice put in jeopardy of life or limb; nor shall be compelled in any criminal case to be a witness against himself, nor be deprived of life, liberty, or property, without due process of law; nor shall private property be taken for public use, without just compensation.

Among the safeguards listed here is the protection against being tried twice for the same offense, or *double jeopardy*. Another provision allows defendants to refuse to testify against themselves, thus avoiding *self-incrimination*. The final clause involves *eminent domain*—the right to take private property for public use; the government is forbidden to exercise this right without paying owners a fair price.

AMENDMENT VI   [1791]

[The Right of the Accused]

In all criminal prosecutions, the accused shall enjoy the right to a speedy and public trial, by an impartial jury of the State and district wherein the crime shall have been committed, which district shall have been previously ascertained by law, and to be informed of the nature and cause of the accusation; to be confronted with the witnesses against him; to have compulsory process for obtaining Witnesses in his favor, and to have the assistance of counsel for his defence.

A person accused of a crime is assured of a speedy public trial by jury. He or she must be able to see and hear witnesses for the prosecution. And the accused must also have access to a "compulsory process"—that is, the subpoena—to obtain witnesses.

AMENDMENT VII   [1791]

[Civil Suits]

In Suits at common law, where the value in controversy shall exceed twenty dollars, the right of trial by jury shall be preserved, and no fact tried by a jury, shall be otherwise reexamined in any Court of the United States, than according to the rules of the common law.

"Suits at common law" are civil, as opposed to criminal, proceedings. That is, they do not involve crimes but rather disputes between groups or individuals.

AMENDMENT VIII   [1791]

[Bails, Fines, Punishments]

Excessive bail shall not be required, nor excessive fines imposed, nor cruel and unusual punishments inflicted.

AMENTMENT IX [1791]

[Rights Not Listed]

The enumeration in the Constitution, of certain rights, shall not be construed to deny or disparage others retained by the people.

AMENDMENT X [1791]

[Powers Reserved to the States or to the People]

The powers not delegated to the United States by the Constitution, nor prohibited by it to the States, are reserved to the States respectively, or to the people.

AMENDMENT XI [1798]

[Suits Against States]

The Judicial power of the United States shall not be construed to extend to any suit in law or equity, commenced or prosecuted against one of the United States by Citizens of another State, or by Citizens or Subjects of any Foreign State.

AMENDMENT XII [1804]

[Election of President and Vice President]

The Electors shall meet in their respective states, and vote by ballot for President and Vice-President, one of whom, at least, shall not be an inhabitant of the same state with themselves; they shall name in their ballots the person voted for as President, and in distinct ballots the person voted for as Vice-President, and they shall make distinct lists of all persons voted for as President, and of all persons voted for as Vice-President, and of the number of votes for each, which lists they shall sign and certify, and transmit sealed to the seat of the government of the United States, directed to the President of the Senate;—The President of the Senate shall, in presence of the Senate and House of Representatives, open all the certificates and the votes shall then be counted;—The person having the greatest number of votes for President, shall be the President, if such number be a majority of the whole number of Electors appointed; and if no person have such majority, then from the persons having the highest numbers not exceeding three on the list of those voted for as President, the House of Representatives shall choose immediately, by ballot, the President. But in choosing the President, the votes shall be taken by states, the representation from each state having one vote; a quorum for this purpose shall consist of a member or members from two-thirds of the states, and a majority of all the states shall be necessary to a choice. And if the House of Representatives shall not choose a President whenever the right of choice shall devolve upon them, *before the fourth day of March next following*, then the Vice-President shall act as President, as in the case of the death or other constitutional disability of the President.—The person having the greatest number of votes as Vice-President, shall be the Vice-President, if such number be a majority of the whole number of Electors appointed, and if no person have a majority, then from the two highest numbers on the list, the Senate shall choose the Vice-President; a quorum for the purpose shall consist of two-thirds of the whole number of Senators, and a majority of the whole number shall be necessary to a choice. But no person constitutionally ineligible to the office of President shall be eligible to that of Vice-President of the United States.

The phrase in italics was changed by the Twentieth Amendment.

AMENDMENT XIII [1865]

[Abolition of Slavery]

Section 1

Neither slavery nor involuntary servitude, except as a punishment for crime whereof the party shall have been duly convicted, shall exist within the United States, or any place subject to their jurisdiction.

Section 2

Congress shall have power to enforce this article by appropriate legislation.

AMENDMENT XIV [1868]

[Citizenship]

Section 1

All persons born or naturalized in the United States, and subject to the jurisdiction thereof, are citizens of the United States and of the State wherein they reside. No State shall make or enforce any law which shall abridge the privileges or immunities of citizens of the United States; nor shall any State deprive any person of life, liberty, or property, without due process or law; nor deny to any person within its jurisdiction the equal protection of the laws.

This section defines citizenship. Its major purpose was to give former slaves full civil rights. It was also used to protect business interests after the Supreme Court interpreted the concept of "person" to include "corporation." The final "equal protection" clause has served as the legal foundation for many civil rights cases.

Section 2

Representatives shall be apportioned among the several States according to their respective numbers, counting the whole number of persons in each State, excluding Indians not taxed. But when the right to vote at any election for the choice of electors for President and Vice President of the United States, Representatives in Congress, the Executive and Judicial officers of a State, or the members of the Legislature thereof, is denied to any of the *male* inhabitants of such State, being *twenty-one* years of age, and citizens of the United States, or in any way abridged, except for participation in rebellion, or other crime, the basis of representation therein shall be reduced in the proportion which the number of such *male* citizens shall bear to the whole number of *male* citizens *twenty-one* years of age in such State.

This section nullifies the three-fifths formula of Article I, Section 2. It also provides penalties for states that unlawfully limit the suffrage. The words in italics were invalidated by the Nineteenth and Twenty-sixth Amendments.

Section 3

No person shall be a Senator or Representative in Congress, or elector of President and Vice President, or hold any office, civil or military, under the United States, or under any State, who, having previously taken an oath, as a member of Congress, or as an officer of the United States, or as a member of any State legislature, or as an executive or judicial officer of any State, to support the Constitution of the United States, shall have engaged in insurrection or rebellion against the same, or given aid or comfort to the enemies thereof. But Congress may by a vote of two-thirds of each House, remove such disability.

This section prevented many men of the former Confederacy from voting.

Section 4

The validity of the public debt of the United States, authorized by law, including debts incurred for payment of pensions and bounties for services in suppressing insurrection or rebellion, shall not be questioned. But neither the United States nor any State shall assume or pay any debt or obligation incurred in aid of insurrection or rebellion against the United States, or any claim for the loss or emancipation of any slave; but all such debts, obligations and claims shall be held illegal and void.

Debts incurred by the Confederacy were not to be paid by the federal government or state governments. Nor would former owners be compensated for the loss of their slaves.

Section 5

The Congress shall have power to enforce, by appropriate legislation, the provisions of this article.

AMENDMENT XV [1870]

[Suffrage for Blacks]

Section 1

The right of citizens of the United States to vote shall not be denied or abridged by the United States or by any State on account of race, color, or previous condition of servitude.

This amendment was designed to give black Americans, particularly the newly freed slaves, the right to vote. By setting up qualifications other than "race, color, or previous condition of servitude"—for example, the payment of poll taxes or literacy tests—many states circumvented this amendment and denied blacks the vote. This kind of discrimination was not abolished until the 1960s, with the enactment of laws and the Twenty-fourth Amendment.

Section 2

The Congress shall have power to enforce this article by appropriate legislation.

AMENDMENT XVI   [1913]

[Income Tax]

The Congress shall have power to lay and collect taxes on incomes, from whatever source derived, without apportionment among the several States, and without regard to any census or enumeration.

AMENDMENT XVII   [1913]

[Popular Election of Senators]

The Senate of the United States shall be composed of two Senators from each State, elected by the people thereof, for six years; and each Senator shall have one vote. The electors in each State shall have the qualifications requisite for electors of the most numerous branch of the State legislatures.

When vacancies happen in the representation of any State in the Senate, the executive authority of such State shall issue writs of election to fill such vacancies: Provided, That the legislature of any State may empower the executive thereof to make temporary appointments until the people fill the vacancies by election as the legislature may direct.

This amendment shall not be construed as to affect the election or term of any Senator chosen before it becomes valid as part of the Constitution.

AMENDMENT XVIII   [1919]

[National Prohibition of Liquor]

Section 1

After one year from the ratification of this article the manufacture, sale, or transportation of intoxicating liquors within, the importation thereof into, or the exportation thereof from the United States and all territory subject to the jurisdiction thereof for beverage purposes is hereby prohibited.

Section 2

The Congress and the several states shall have concurrent power to enforce this article by appropriate legislation.

Section 3

This article shall be inoperative unless it shall have been ratified as an amendment to the Constitution by the legislatures of the several States, as provided in the Constitution, within seven years from the date of the submission hereof to the States by the Congress.

This amendment was repealed by the Twenty-first Amendment. Note that this is the first constitutional amendment to provide for enforcement by both the national and state governments and also the first to specify how and when ratification should take place.

AMENDMENT XIX [1920]

[Women's Suffrage]

The right of citizens of the United States to vote shall not be denied or abridged by the United States or by any State on account of sex.

Congress shall have power to enforce this article by appropriate legislation.

AMENDMENT XX [1933]

[Terms, Sessions, Succession]

Section 1

The terms of the President and Vice President shall end at noon on the 20th day of January, and the terms of Senators and Representatives at noon on the 3d day of January, of the years in which such terms would have ended if this article had not been ratified; and the terms of their successors shall then begin.

Section 2

The Congress shall assemble at least once in every year, and such meeting shall begin at noon on the 3d day of January, unless they shall by law appoint a different day.

Section 3

If, at the time fixed for the beginning of the term of the President, the President elect shall have died, the Vice President elect shall become President. If a President shall not have been chosen before the time fixed for the beginning of his term, or if the President elect shall have failed to qualify, then the Vice President elect shall act as President until a President shall have qualified; and the Congress may by law provide for the case wherein neither a President elect nor a Vice President elect shall have qualified, declaring who shall then act as President, or the manner in which one who is to act shall be selected, and such person shall act accordingly until a President or Vice President shall have qualified.

Section 4

The Congress may by law provide for the case of the death of any of the persons from whom the House of Representatives may choose a President whenever the right of choice shall have devolved upon them, and for the case of the death of any of the persons from whom the Senate may choose a Vice President whenever the right of choice shall have devolved upon them.

Section 5

Sections 1 and 2 shall take effect on the 15th day of October following ratification of this article.

Section 6

This article shall be inoperative unless it shall have been ratified as an amendment to the Constitution by the legislatures of three-fourths of the several States within seven years from the date of its submission.

This is known as the "lame duck" amendment because it shortened the time between elections and the beginning of the terms for President, Vice President, and members of Congress. Officeholders who lose an election or do not run are known as "lame ducks" during their last weeks in office because their powers are weakened—like those of crippled fowl.

AMENDMENT XXI [1933]

[National Prohibition Repealed]

Section 1

The eighteenth article of amendment to the Constitution of the United States is hereby repealed.

Section 2

The transportation or importation into any State, Territory, or possession of the United States for delivery or use therein of intoxicating liquors, in violation of the laws thereof, is hereby prohibited.

Section 3

This article shall be inoperative unless it shall have been ratified as an amendment to the Constitution by conventions in the several States, as provided in the Constitution, within seven years from the date of the submission hereof to the States by the Congress.

This is the only amendment to nullify an earlier amendment. Although Section 1 abolishes national prohibition, Section 2 protects states that wish to be "dry."

AMENDMENT XXII [1951]

[Presidential Tenure]

Section 1

No person shall be elected to the office of President more than twice, and no person who has held the office of President, or acted as President, for more than two years of a term to which some other person was elected President shall be elected to the Office of the President more than once. But this Article shall not apply to any person holding the office of President when this Article was proposed by the Congress, and shall not prevent any person who may be holding the office of President, or acting as President, during the term within which this Article becomes operative from holding the office of President or acting as President during the remainder of such term.

Section 2

This Article shall be inoperative unless it shall have been ratified as an amendment to the Constitution by the legislatures of three-fourths of the several states within seven years from the date of its submission to the States by the Congress.

AMENDMENT XXIII [1961]

[Suffrage for the District of Columbia]

Section 1

The District constituting the seat of Government of the United States shall appoint in such manner as the Congress may direct:

A number of electors of President and Vice President equal to the whole number of Senators and Representatives in Congress to which the District would be entitled if it were a State, but in no event more than the least populous State; they shall be in addition to those appointed by the States, but they shall be considered, for the purposes of the election of President and Vice President, to be electors appointed by a State; and they shall meet in the District and perform such duties as provided by the twelfth article of amendment.

By providing for electors, this amendment gives residents of Washington, D.C., the right to vote for President and Vice President.

Section 2

The Congress shall have power to enforce this article by appropriate legislation.

AMENDMENT XXIV [1964]

[Abolition of Poll Taxes]

Section 1

The right of citizens of the United States to vote in any primary or other election for President or Vice President, for electors for President or Vice President, or for Senators or Representative in Congress, shall not be denied or abridged by the United States or any State by reasons of failure to pay any poll tax or other tax.

Section 2

The Congress shall have power to enforce this article by appropriate legislation.

AMENDMENT XXV [1967]

[Presidential Succession and Disability]

Section 1

In case of the removal of the President from office or his death or resignation, the Vice President shall become President.

Section 2

Whenever there is a vacancy in the office of the Vice President, the President shall nominate a Vice President who shall take office upon confirmation by a majority vote of both houses of Congress.

Section 3

Whenever the President transmits to the President pro tempore of the Senate and the Speaker of the House of Representatives his written declaration that he is unable to discharge the powers and duties of his office, and until he transmits to them a written declaration to the contrary, such powers and duties shall be discharged by the Vice President as Acting President.

Section 4

Whenever the Vice President and a majority of either the principal officers of the executive departments or of such other body as Congress may by law provide, transmit to the President pro tempore of the Senate and the Speaker of the House of Representatives their written declaration that the President is unable to discharge the powers and duties of his office, the Vice President shall immediately assume the powers and duties of the office as Acting President.

Thereafter, when the President transmits to the President pro tempore of the Senate and the Speaker of the House of Representatives his written declaration that no inability exists, he shall resume the powers and duties of his office unless the Vice President and a majority of either the principal officers of the executive department, or of such other body as Congress may by law provide, transmit within four days to the President pro tempore of the Senate and the Speaker of the House of Representatives their written declaration that the President is unable to discharge the powers and duties of his office. Thereupon Congress shall decide the issue, assembling within forty-eight hours for that purpose if not in session. If the Congress, within twenty-one days after receipt of the latter written declaration, or, if Congress is not in session, within twenty-one days after Congress is required to assemble, determines by two-thirds vote of both Houses that the President is unable to discharge the powers and duties of his office, the Vice President shall continue to discharge the same as Acting President; otherwise, the President shall resume the powers and duties of his office.

AMENDMENT XXVI [1971]

[Voting Age]

Section 1

The right of citizens of the United States, who are eighteen years of age or older, to vote shall not be denied or abridged by the United States or by any State on account of age.

Section 2

The Congress shall have the power to enforce this article by appropriate legislation.

Appendix C

THE EXECUTIVE BRANCH

Dates following names of executive bodies indicate the year of establishment.

EXECUTIVE OFFICE OF THE PRESIDENT

White House Office
Office of Management and Budget
Council of Economic Advisors
National Security Council
Office of Policy Development
Office of the United States Trade Representative
Council on Environmental Quality
Office of Science and Technology Policy
Office of Administration

EXECUTIVE DEPARTMENTS

Department of Agriculture   1889
Conducts research on animal and plant diseases; works to improve farm production; administers price support, food stamp, meat inspection, and school lunch programs.

Department of Commerce   1903
Promotes trade and economic growth; regulates weights and measures; issues patents; directs census; operates National Weather Service.

Department of Defense   1947
Formed by union of departments of War and Navy, both established in 1789. Directs operations of Army, Navy (including Marines), and Air Force; operates military bases and service academies.

Department of Education   1979
Administers federal aid to state and local agencies; offers special services for the blind and deaf.

Department of Energy   1977
Coordinates energy research and development; regulates hydroelectric power; operates hydroelectric projects.

EXECUTIVE DEPARTMENTS (Continued)

Department of Health and Human Services   1953
Originally the Department of Health, Education, and Welfare; assumed present name in 1979. Works to prevent and control spread of communicable diseases; administers Social Security, Medicare, and Medicaid; protects consumers through Food and Drug Administration.

Department of Housing and Urban Development   1965
Manages federal housing programs; encourages urban rehabilitation through grants to localities.

Department of the Interior   1849
Administers federal lands; operates Bureau of Indian Affairs and National Park Service.

Department of Justice   1870
Grew out of office of Attorney General, established in 1789. Enforces federal laws; operates federal prisons; administers Antitrust Division, Federal Bureau of Investigation, and Immigration and Naturalization Service.

Department of Labor   1913
Administers federal labor laws, including those involving the minimum wage and workers' compensation; promotes worker safety through Occupational Safety and Health Review Commission.

Department of State   1789
Maintains diplomatic relations with foreign countries through embassies and consulates; issues passports to U.S. citizens and visas to foreigners.

Department of Transportation   1966
Administers federal highway programs; supervises Coast Guard and U.S. portion of St. Lawrence Seaway; regulates air safety through Federal Aviation Administration.

Department of the Treasury   1789
Prints and coins money; borrows funds by issuing government bonds; collects federal taxes through Internal Revenue Service; supervises customs; operates Secret Service.

INDEPENDENT REGULATORY AGENCIES

Commodity Futures Trading Commission   1974
Regulates commodity exchanges and futures trading in agricultural products, metals, and other commodities.

Consumer Product Safety Commission   1972
Sets and enforces standards for a wide range of consumer products; investigates deaths, injuries, and illnesses related to consumer goods.

INDEPENDENT REGULATORY AGENCIES (Continued)

Federal Communications Commission   1934
Regulates interstate and foreign communication by radio, television, wire, satellite, and cable.

Federal Election Commission   1971
Administers and enforces federal laws regulating campaign contributions, spending, and disclosure.

Federal Energy Regulatory Commission   1977
Regulates the prices of natural gas, oil pipelines, and electricity at wholesale level; licenses hydroelectric projects.

Federal Maritime Commission   1961
Licenses and regulates waterborne commerce; establishes freight rates for domestic off-shore trade.

Federal Reserve System   1913
Supervises U.S. banks; helps establish and directs monetary policy.

Federal Trade Commission   1914
Enforces federal laws against price-fixing and illegal combinations; regulates advertising, packaging, and labeling.

Interstate Commerce Commission   1887
Regulates commercial transportation by trains, trucks, buses, and domestic water carriers.

National Labor Relations Board   1935
Safeguards employees' right to organize; conducts elections to determine union representation; investigates charges of unfair practices by employers and unions.

Nuclear Regulatory Commission   1974
Supervises civilian use of atomic energy by licensing and inspecting nuclear reactors.

Securities and Exchange Commission   1934
Regulates stock exchanges, brokerage houses, and sales of stocks and bonds.

OTHER IMPORTANT INDEPENDENT AGENCIES AND CORPORATIONS

ACTION   1971
Administers voluntary public service programs, including VISTA (Volunteers in Service to America) and Foster Grandparents program.

Central Intelligence Agency   1947
Obtains and evaluates intelligence; advises National Security Council; carries out covert operations.

OTHER IMPORTANT INDEPENDENT AGENCIES AND CORPORATIONS (Continued)

Commission on Civil Rights 1957
Collects and studies information on discrimination occurring in public accommodations, voting, and on other civil rights matters.

Environmental Protection Agency 1970
In cooperation with state and local governments, coordinates activities aimed at eliminating pollution related to air, water, solid waste, pesticides, radiation, and toxic substances.

Export-Import Bank 1934
Encourages the export of American goods and services by financing loans and issuing insurance.

Federal Deposit Insurance Corporation 1933
Insures individual deposits up to $100,000 in national banks, state banks that are members of the Federal Reserve System, and other qualifying banks.

General Services Administration 1949
Constructs and operates federal office buildings; obtains and distributes supplies; manages transport, traffic, and communications; stockpiles strategic materials.

National Aeronautics and Space Administration 1958
Explores space with vehicles carrying payloads and sometimes astronauts; researches problems of flight within and beyond earth's atmosphere.

National Archives and Records Administration 1985
Collects and stores government documents; displays Declaration of Independence and Constitution; manages presidential libraries.

National Foundation on the Arts and the Humanities 1965
Promotes the arts and the humanities by awarding grants to individuals and groups.

National Science Foundation 1950
Makes grants and offers awards in all the scientific and engineering disciplines; maintains astronomical observatories.

Panama Canal Commission 1979
Maintains and operates the Panama Canal.

Peace Corps 1961
Trains, places, and supervises volunteers who work in Latin America, Africa, the Middle East, Asia, and the Pacific.

Selective Service System 1940
Supervises registration of male citizens 18- to 26-years-old; administers military draft when necessary.

OTHER IMPORTANT INDEPENDENT AGENCIES AND CORPORATIONS (Continued)

Small Business Administration   1953
Helps small businesses through loans and obtaining of government contracts; aids victims of floods and other catastrophes.

Tennessee Valley Authority   1933
Supervises electric power distribution, flood control, conservation, and other programs in Tennessee Valley.

U.S. Arms Control and Disarmament Agency   1961
Handles negotiations with Soviet Union and other countries on arms limitation and prevention of nuclear proliferation; monitors flow of arms trade.

U.S. Information Agency   1953
Operates overseas information and cultural programs through cultural centers and libraries; administers Voice of America and Fulbright scholarships.

U.S. International Development Cooperation Agency   1979
Administers economic assistance programs designed to help developing nations.

U.S. Postal Service   1970
Began as executive department in 1872. Maintains mail service throughout the United States.

Veterans Administration   1930
Provides for housing, educational, and medical needs of veterans.

Appendix D

Getting Information

Getting accurate, up-to-date information is often critical in politics. Two sources of information are government agencies and private interest groups which specialize in collecting information and providing it to the public. Below is the latest contact information for them.

GOVERNMENTAL SOURCES

Congress

Clerk, House of Representatives, The Capitol, Washington, D.C. 20515 (202) 225-7000. General information on the House.

Secretary of the Senate S-221, The Capitol, Washington, D.C. 20510 (202) 224-2115. General information on the House.

Office of Public Information, General Accounting Office, 441 G Street NW, Rm. 7015, Washington, D.C. 20548 (202) 275-2812. An investigative arm of Congress.

Office of Intergovernmental Relations, 1111 20th Street NW, Washington, D.C. 20036 (202) 653-5540. Provides information on budgetary matters.

Superintendent of Documents, Government Printing Office, Washington, D.C. 20402 (202) 783-3238. General source of documents and reports.

The Judicial Branch

Clerk, United States Supreme Court Building, 1 First Street NE, Washington, D.C. 20543 (202) 479-3011. General information on the Court.

Director, Administrative Office of the United States Courts, Washington, D.C. 20544 (202) 633-6097. Information on the lower federal courts.

Information Specialist, Federal Judicial Center, Dolly Madison House, 1520 H Street NW, Washington, D.C. 20005 (202) 633-6011. Conducts research on the federal court system.

Executive Branch and Independent Agencies

The White House Office, 1600 Pennsylvania Avenue NW, Washington, D.C. 20500 (202) 456-1414. The President's top aides and advisors.

Office of Management and Budget, Executive Office Building, Washington, D.C. 20503 (202) 395-3000. Key agency in planning the President's legislative agenda.

Office of Governmental and Public Affairs, Department of Agriculture, Washington, D.C. 20250 (202) 447-2791. Can provide more specific direction for dealing with the Department of Agriculture.

Office of Public Affairs, Department of Commerce, Washington, D.C. 20230 (202) 377-4190. A source of materials from the Census Bureau, National Bureau of Standards, and numerous other divisions of the Commerce Department.

Staff Assistant for Public Correspondence, Office of the Assistant Secretary of Defense (Public Affairs), The Pentagon, Washington, D.C. 20301 (202) 697-5737. A starting point for dealing with the vast defense bureaucracy.

Department of Education, 400 Maryland Avenue SW, Washington, D.C. 20024 (202) 245-8564. Supplies information on the Education Department, including federal student loan programs.

Director, National Energy Information Center, James Forrestal Building, 1000 Independence Avenue SW, Washington, D.C. 20585 (202) 252-8800. Collects and disseminates energy-related information.

Public Information Center, Department of Health and Human Services, 200 Independence Avenue SW, Washington, D.C. 20201 (202) 245-6296. Provides information on the many responsibilities of the Health and Human Services Department.

Program Information Center, Department of Housing and Urban Development, 451 Seventh Street SW, Washington, D.C. 20410 (202) 755-6422. Offers literature and program information on the department's activities.

General Information Office, Department of the Interior, C Street between Eighteenth and Nineteenth Streets NW, Washington, D.C. 20240 (202) 343-1100. A good place to begin looking for information about national parks, public lands, and other Department of the Interior areas of responsibility.

The Department of Justice, Constitution Avenue and Tenth Street NW, Washington, D.C. 20530. Contains several politically important divisions including:

Antitrust Division	(202) 633-2421
Civil Division	(202) 633-3301
Civil Rights Division	(202) 633-4224
Criminal Division	(202) 633-2601
FBI	(202) 633-3444

General information can be obtained from the Office of Public Affairs, at the above address, or by telephoning (202) 633-2000.

Office of Information and Public Affairs, The Department of Labor, 200 Constitution Avenue NW, Washington, D.C. 20210 (202) 523-7316. Offers further information on the programs and activities of Labor.

Office of Public Affairs, Department of Transportation, 400 Seventh Street SW, Washington, D.C. 20590 (202) 426-4570. Provides information on the Department, which includes such well-known divisions as the Federal Aviation Administration and the Federal Highway Administration.

Office of the Assistant Secretary (Public Affairs), Office of the Secretary, Treasury Department, Fifteenth Street and Pennsylvania Avenue NW, Washington, D.C. 20220 (202) 566-5252. Makes available general information on the Treasury. Information about the Internal Revenue Service, part of Treasury, can be obtained from any district IRS office or from IRS Headquarters, Department of the Treasury, 1111 Constitution Avenue NW, Washington, D.C. 20224 (202) 566-5000.

Information Office, Commission on Civil Rights, 1121 Vermont Ave. NW, Washington, D.C. 20425 (202) 376-8312. Offers information on discrimination in many areas—education, jobs, voting, and so on.

Office of Public Communications, Federal Election Commission, 1325 K Street NW, Washington, D.C. 20463 (800) 523-4089. Offers information on federal election laws and data on campaigns.

Office of Public Affairs, Board of Governors, Federal Reserve System, Twentieth Street and Constitution Avenue NW, Washington, D.C. 20551 (202) 452-3000. Supplies information on the Federal Reserve System.

Director, Office of Public Affairs, Federal Trade Commission, Pennsylvania Avenue at Sixth Street NW, Washington, D.C. 20580 (202) 523-3830. Offers information on consumer protection, deceptive advertising, and unfair economic competition.

Office of Public Affairs, Nuclear Regulatory Commission, 1717 H Street NW, Washington, D.C. 20555 (301) 492-7715. Provides information on the use of nuclear energy and the hazards it poses.

Interest Groups

Interest groups are often an excellent source of information. In many instances group-supplied information is easier to use and more up-to-date than government-supplied data. Of course, since these are advocacy groups, a degree of caution concerning their version of events is necessary.

Civil Rights for Blacks and Other Minorities

National Association for the Advancement of Colored People (NAACP), 1025 Vermont Avenue NW, Washington, D.C. 20005 (202) 638-

2269. A long-established group interested in many black-related issues.

National Congress of American Indians, 804 D Street NE, Washington, D.C. 20002 (202) 546-9404. The advocate of American Indian tribes.

National Council of La Raza, 20 F Street NW, Washington, D.C. 20001 (202) 618-9600. A civil rights organization for Hispanics.

National Urban League, 1111 14th Street NW, Washington, D.C. 20005 (202) 898-1604. A nationwide organization concerned with eliminating discrimination against blacks in all areas of life.

Organization of Chinese Americans, Inc., 2025 Eye Street NW, Washington, D.C. 20006 (202) 223-5500. Advocates the rights of Chinese Americans and works to preserve their heritage.

Women's Rights

National Organization for Women (NOW), 1401 New York Avenue NW, Washington, D.C. 20005 (202) 347-2279. Lobbies for the rights of women in society.

National Women's Law Center, 1751 N Street NW, Washington, D.C. 20036 (202) 328-5160. A law firm working for women and women's organizations.

Natural Resources and the Environment

Chamber of Commerce of the United States, Resources and Environmental Quality Division, 1615 H Street NW, Washington, D.C. 20062 (202) 659-6172. A business lobby interested in energy and conservation.

Environmental Policy Center, 218 D Street SE, Washington, D.C. 20003 (202) 547-5330. A consumer-oriented group with wide-ranging interests.

Environmental Law Institute, 1616 P Street NW, Washington, D.C. 20036 (202) 328-5150. Conducts legal research on environmental issues.

Friends of the Earth, 530 7th Street SE, Washington, D.C. 20003 (202) 543-4312. A citizens' group working for preserving natural resources.

Resources for the Future, 1616 P Street NW, Washington, D.C. 20036 (202) 328-5000. Research-oriented group interested in conserving and developing natural resources.

Law and Justice

Alliance for Justice, 600 New Jersey Avenue NW, Washington, D.C. 20001 (202) 624-8390. Nonprofit organization dedicated to increasing the role of citizens in the judicial process.

American Bar Association, Criminal Justice, 1800 M St. NW, Washington, D.C. 20036 (202) 331-2260. Concerned with analyzing and reforming criminal law.

Civil Liberties

American Civil Liberties Union, 132 W. 43rd Street, New York, NY 10036 (212) 944-9800. Works on behalf of civil liberties, criminal justice, and minority rights.

Amnesty International USA, 332 8th Avenue, New York, NY 10001 (212) 807-8400. Works for the freedom of those imprisoned for their beliefs.

International Affairs and National Security

American Conservative Union, 38 Ivy Street SE, Washington, D.C. 20003 (202) 546-6555. Advocates the conservative viewpoint in foreign policy.

American Peace Society, 4000 Albemarle Street NW, Washington, D.C. 20016 (202) 362-6195. Works for peaceful resolution of international conflict.

Arms Control Association, 11 Dupont Circle NW, Washington, D.C. 20036 (202) 797-6450. Promotes public interest in arms control.

Carnegie Endowment for International Peace, 11 Dupont Circle NW, Washington, D.C. 20036 (202) 797-6400. Conducts research on ways to bring about world peace.

Center for Defense Information, 1500 Massachusetts Avenue NW, Washington, D.C. 20005 (202) 862-0700. Especially interested in matters relating to the military.

Committee on the Present Danger, 905 16th Street NW, Washington, D.C. 20006 (202) 628-2409. Conservative group that conducts research and sponsors educational activities.

Business and Economic Regulation

The Business Council, 888 17th Street NW, Washington, D.C. 20006 (202) 298-7650. Composed of top officers of major corporations who meet to discuss government and business.

Ethics and Public Policy Center, 1030 15th Street NW, Washington, D.C. 20005 (202) 628-1200. Concerned with business, government, and ethics.

Institute for Research on the Economics of Taxation, 1331 Pennsylvania Avenue NW, Washington, D.C. 20004 (202) 437-9570. Conducts research on the tax system.

National Association of Manufacturers, 9005 Congressional Court, Potomac, MD 20854 (301) 365-4080. Voice of manufacturing industry on public policy.

Public Citizen, Inc., Tax Reform Research Group, 215 Pennsylvania Avenue SE, Washington, D.C. 20003 (202) 546-4996. Works for tax reform on behalf of the average citizen.

Health and Safety

Action on Smoking and Health, 2013 P Street NW, Washington, D.C. 20036 (202) 659-4310. Works on behalf of nonsmokers.

American Council on Science and Health, 1995 Broadway, New York, NY 10023 (212) 362-7044. Provides information on chemicals in the environment and their impact on health.

Center for Science in the Public Interest, 1501 16th Street NW, Washington, D.C. 20036 (202) 332-9110. Conducts research on food and nutrition.

Food and Drug Law Institute, 1701 K Street NW, Washington, D.C. 20006 (202) 833-1601. Sponsors research and seminars on food and drug issues.

Public Citizen Health Research Group, 2000 P Street NW, Washington, D.C. 20036 (202) 293-9142. Citizen protection group concerned with dangerous drug practices.

Tobacco Institute, 1875 Eye Street NW, Washington, D.C. 20006 (202) 457-4800. Lobbying organization for the tobacco industry.

Education

Americans United for Separation of Church and State, 8120 Fenton Street, Silver Spring, MD 20910 (301) 589-3707. Works to prevent federal money from reaching private schools.

Council for Educational Freedom in America, 2105 Wintergreen Avenue, Forestville, MD 20747 (301) 350-0979. Works for reducing government interference in schools.

Institute for Educational Leadership, 1001 Connecticut Avenue NW, Washington, D.C. 20036 (202) 822-8405. Conducts research and organizes seminars for professional educators.

National Community Education Association, 119 N. Payne Street, Alexandria, VA 22307 (703) 683-6232. Offers information on community education.

National Education Association, 1201 16th Street NW, Washington, D.C. 20036 (202) 833-4000. Teacher-oriented group.

Science and Technology

American Association for the Advancement of Science, 1515 Massachusetts Avenue NW, Washington, D.C. 20005 (202) 467-4400. Organization of scientists.

Federation of American Scientists, 307 Massachusetts Avenue NE, Washington, D.C. 20002 (202) 546-3300. Interested in legislation dealing with science and technology.

Public Technology Inc., 1301 Pennsylvania Avenue NW, Washington, D.C. 20004 (202) 626-2400. Works to apply technology to improve public services.

Citizen Participation

League of Women Voters, 1730 M Street NW, Washington, D.C. 20036 (202) 429-1965. Promotes citizen participation and voter registration; issues publications on government.

Notes

CHAPTER 3

1. Michael D. Reagan and John G. Sanzone, *The New Federalism*, 2nd ed. (New York: Oxford University Press, 1981), pp. 136–137.
2. David L. Cingranelli, "The Effect of State Lobby Offices in Washington on the Distribution of Federal Aid to States," paper presented at the 1984 Annual Meeting of the American Political Science Association, Washington, D.C.
3. Data supplied by the Northeast-Midwest Congressional Coalition, 1984.
4. Cited in David R. Francis, "A War Between the States: Home-Grown U.S. Trade Barriers Costly," *Christian Science Monitor*, September 20, 1984, p. 23.

CHAPTER 4

1. John P. Katosh and Michael W. Taugott, "The Consequences of Validated and Self-Reported Voting Measures," *Public Opinion Quarterly* 45 (1981): 519–535.
2. Howard Schuman and Stanley Presser, *Questions and Answers in Attitude Surveys* (New York: Academic Press, 1981), p. 285.
3. Cited in Tom W. Smith, "The Polls: American Attitudes Towards the Soviet Union and Communism," *Public Opinion Quarterly* 47 (1983): 286.
4. Cited in Everett Carll Ladd, "Clearing the Air: Public Opinion and Public Policy in the Environment," *Public Opinion*, February/March 1982, p. 16.
5. Data recalculated from M. Kent Jennings and Richard G. Niemi, *Generations and Politics: A Panel Study of Young Adults and Their Parents* (Princeton, N.J.: Princeton University Press, 1981), p. 91.
6. M. Kent Jennings and Richard G. Niemi, *The Political Character of Adolescence: The Influence of Families and Schools* (Princeton, N.J.: Princeton University Press, 1974), Chapters 7 and 8.
7. Lee H. Ehrman, "An Analysis of the Relationship of Selected Educational Variables with the Political Socialization of High School Students," *American Educational Research Journal* 6 (1969): 559–580.
8. These studies are summarized in Charles K. Atkins, "Communication and Political Socialization," in Dan D. Nimmo and Keith R. Sanders, eds., *Handbook of Political Communication* (Beverly Hills, Calif: Sage, 1981), pp. 301–305.
9. See, for example, Alan M. Rubin, "Child and Adolescent Television Use and Political Socialization," *Journalism Quarterly* 55 (1978): 125–129.
10. Joseph R. Dominick, "Television and Political Socialization," *Educational Broadcasting Review* 6 (1972): 48–55.

11. James R. Lewellen, "Mass Media and Political Participation," *Social Education* 40 (1976): 457–461.
12. David Easton and Jack Dennis, *Children in the Political System: Origins of Political Legitimacy* (New York: McGraw-Hill, 1969), pp. 114–117.
13. George F. Bishop, Robert W. Oldendick, Alfred J. Tuckfarber, and Stephen E. Bennett, "Pseudo-Opinion on Public Affairs," *Public Opinion Quarterly* 44 (1980): 201.
14. Benjamin I. Page and Robert Y. Shapiro, "Effects of Public Opinion on Policy," *American Political Science Review* 77 (1983): 170–190.
15. Alan D. Monroe, "Consistency Between Public Preferences and National Policy Decisions," *American Politics Quarterly* 7 (1979): 3–19.
16. Robert Weissberg, *Public Opinion and Popular Government* (Englewood Cliffs, N.J.: Prentice-Hall, 1976), Chapters 6 and 7.
17. Robert A. Seigel, "Image of the American Presidency: Part II of an Exploration into Popular Vision of Presidential Power," *Midwest Journal of Political Science* 10 (1966): 123–137.

CHAPTER 5

1. Steven J. Brams and Peter C. Fishburn, *Approval Voting* (Boston: Birkhauser, 1983), especially Chapter 1.
2. Raymond E. Wolfinger and Steven J. Rosenstone, *Who Votes?* (New Haven: Yale University Press, 1980), pp. 71–75, 130.
3. Henry M. Bain, Jr., and Donald S. Hecock, *Ballot Position and Voter's Choice* (Westport, Conn.: Greenwood Press, 1973).
4. Charles S. Bullock III, "The Effects of Redistricting on Black Representation in Southern State Legislatures," paper presented at the annual meeting of the American Political Science Association, 1983.
5. Richard L. Engstrom and Michael D. McDonald, "The Election of Blacks to City Councils: Clarifying the Impact of Electoral Arrangements in the Seats/Population Relationship," *American Political Science Review* 75 (1980): 344–354; Margaret Latimer, "Black Political Representation in Southern Cities: Election Systems and Other Causal Variables," *Urban Affairs Quarterly* 15 (1979): 65–86; Albert K. Karnig, "Private-Regarding Policy, Civil Rights Groups, and the Mediating Impact of Municipal Reforms," *American Journal of Political Science* 19 (1975): 91–106.

CHAPTER 6

1. David Glass, Peverill Squire, and Raymond Wolfinger, "Voter Turnout: An International Comparison," *Public Opinion*, December 1983/January 1984, p. 54.

2. Herbert F. Weisberg and Bernard Grofman, "Candidate Evaluations and Turnout," *American Politics Quarterly* 9 (1981): 197–220.

3. Howard L. Rester, "Why Is Turnout Down?" *Public Opinion Quarterly* 43 (1979): 297–311.

4. D. Roderick Kiewiet, "American Voting and Nonvoting," *Society*, July/August 1984, p. 25.

5. Paul R. Abramson, John H. Aldrich, and David W. Rohde, *Change and Continuity in the 1980 Election*, rev. ed. (Washington, D.C.: CQ Press, 1983), pp. 128–129.

6. William Schneider, "An Uncertain Consensus," *National Journal*, November 10, 1984, p. 2130.

7. Center for Political Studies, University of Michigan, Ann Arbor, American National Election Study of 1980.

8. Thomas E. Patterson, *The Mass Media Elections: How Americans Choose Their Presidents* (New York: Praeger, 1980), pp. 153–159.

9. These studies are summarized in Garrett J. O'Keefe and L. Erwin Atwood, "Communication and Election Campaigns," in Dan D. Nimmo and Keith R. Sanders, eds., *Handbook of Political Communications* (Beverly Hills, Calif.: Sage, 1981), pp. 338–340.

10. O'Keefe and Atwood, "Communication and Election Campaigns," pp. 340–342.

11. Thomas E. Patterson and Robert D. McClure, *The Unseeing Eye: The Myth of Television Power in National Politics* (New York: Putnam, 1976), pp. 111–112.

12. Jack Sean McClenghan, "Effect of Endorsement in Texas Local Elections," *Journalism Quarterly* 50 (1973): 363–366.

13. John P. Robinson, "Perceived Media Bias and the 1968 Vote: Can the Media Affect Behavior After All?" *Journalism Quarterly* 49 (1972): 239–246.

14. Harold Mendelsohn, "Election-Day Broadcasts and Terminal Voting Decisions," *Public Opinion Quarterly* 30 (1966): 212–255, and Douglas A. Fuchs, "Election-Day Radio-TV and Western Voting," *Public Opinion Quarterly* 30 (1966): 226–236.

15. Evidence that the media have no impact on voter turnout is presented in Laurily K. Epstein and Gerald Strom, "Election Night Projections and West Coast Turnout," *American Politics Quarterly* 9 (1981): 479–491. Contrary data are reported in John E. Jackson, "Election Night Reporting and Voter Turnout," *American Journal of Political Science* 27 (1983): 615–635.

16. Sam Tuchman and Thomas E. Coffin, "The Influence of Election Night Television Broadcasts in a Close Election," *Public Opinion Quarterly* 35 (1971): 305–326.

17. Jackson, "Election Night Reporting and Voter Turnout," p. 631.

18. These are summarized in Sidney Kraus and Dennis Davis, eds., *The Effects of Mass Communication on Political Behavior* (University Park: Pennsylvania State University Press, 1976), pp. 140–141.

CHAPTER 7

1. Center for Political Studies, University of Michigan, Ann Arbor, American National Election Study of 1980.

2. Center for Political Studies, American National Election Study of 1984.

3. Frank B. Feigert and M. Margaret Conway, *Parties and Politics in America* (Boston: Allyn & Bacon, 1976), p. 138.

4. The 1980 data are from the Center for Political Studies, American National Election Study of 1980; 1983 data were collected by the National Opinion Research Center and reported in "Opinion Roundup," *Public Opinion*, October/November 1983, p. 27.

5. Martin Plissner and Warren Mitofsky, "Political Elites," *Public Opinion*, October/November 1981, p. 47.

6. *National Journal*, May 1982.

CHAPTER 8

1. Robert H. Salisbury, "An Exchange Theory of Interest Groups," *Midwest Journal of Political Science* 13 (1969): 1–32.

2. Jack L. Walker, "The Origins and Maintenance of Interest Groups in America," *American Political Science Review* 77 (1983): 403.

3. Jeffrey M. Berry, *Lobbying for the People: The Political Behavior of Public Interest Groups* (Princeton, N.J.: Princeton University Press, 1977), pp. 71–77.

4. W. P. Welch, "Campaign Contributions and Legislative Voting: Milk Money and Dairy Price Supports," *Western Political Quarterly* 35 (1982): 478–495.

5. Diana Evans Yiannakis, "PAC Contributions and House Voting on Conflictual and Consensual Issues: The Windfall Profits Tax and the Chrysler Loan Guarantee," paper presented at the Annual Meeting of the American Political Science Association, Chicago, 1983.

6. Henry W. Chappell, Jr., "Campaign Contributions and Congressional Voting: A Simultaneous Probit-Tobit Model," *Review of Economics and Statistics* 64 (1982): 77–83; Benjamin Ginsberg and John Green, "The Best Congress Money Can Buy," paper presented at the Annual Meeting of the American Political Science Association, Washington, D.C., 1979.

7. E. E. Schattschneider, *The Semi-Sovereign People* (New York: Holt, Rinehart and Winston, 1960), pp. 29–36.

8. Kay Lehman Schlozman, "What Accent the Heavenly Chorus? Political Equality and the American Pressure System," paper presented at the Annual Meeting of the American Political Science Association, Washington, D.C., 1984.

CHAPTER 9

1. Warren E. Miller, "Majority Rule and the Representative System of Government," in Erik Allardt and Yijo Li-

tunen, eds., *Cleavages, Ideologies and the Party Systems* (Helsinki: Academic Bookstore, 1964), pp. 343–376.

2. Roger H. Davidson, *The Role of the Congressman* (New York: Pegasus, 1969), especially Chapter 4.

3. Richard F. Fenno, Jr., *Home Style: House Members in Their Districts* (Boston: Little, Brown, 1978), Chapter 1.

4. Davidson, *The Role of the Congressman*, pp. 121–126.

CHAPTER 15

1. See James Tobin, "On Limiting the Domain of Inequality," *Journal of Law and Economics* 13 (1970): 263–277.

2. Cited in Everett Carll Ladd, Jr., and others, "The Polls: Taxing and Spending," *Public Opinion Quarterly* 43 (1979): 129.

3. Barry Susman, "Tax Overhaul: Support for a Plan Many Don't Understand," *Washington Post National Weekly Edition*, February 11, 1985, p. 37.

4. Cited in "Regulatory Growth and Reform Efforts," in *Spring 1985 Guide, Current American Government* (Washington, D.C.: Congressional Quarterly, 1985), p. 45.

CHAPTER 16

1. Roger Hilsman, *The Politics of Policy-Making in Defense and Foreign Affairs* (New York: Harper & Row, 1971), p. 18.

2. James A. Robinson, *Congress and Foreign Policy-Making*, rev. ed. (Homewood, Ill.: Dorsey Press, 1967), p. 65.

3. Ruth Leger Sivard, *World Military and Social Expenditures: 1981* (Leesburg, Va.: World Priorities, 1981), p. 15.

4. Cited in Ruth Leger Sivard, *World Military and Social Expenditures: 1983* (Washington, D.C.: World Priorities, 1983), p. 29.

5. Robert E. Osgood, *Ideals and Self-Interest in America's Foreign Relations* (Chicago: University of Chicago Press, 1953).

CHAPTER 17

1. Adapted from Ben J. Wattenberg with Richard M. Scammon, *This U.S.A.* (New York: Doubleday, 1965), p. 72.

2. Terry Sanford, *Storm Over the States* (New York: McGraw-Hill, 1967), p. 31.

Glossary

A

Absentee ballot. A ballot distributed before the election for use by people who will not be present at the polling place on election day.

Absolutist position. The view that government cannot in any way interfere with speech. All speech—even obscenity—is equally protected.

Administrative oversight. Monitoring by Congress (usually by a committee or subcommittee) of the executive branch, its agencies, and its activities.

Affirmative action program. A program in government, business, or education in which an extra effort is made to recruit members of groups that have been discriminated against in the past (minorities, women, the handicapped, and so on).

Agency clients (or clientele). Groups with especially close ties to specific government agencies. Almost all agencies have such clients.

Amicus curiae brief. Information supplied to a court by an individual or group that is not an actual participant in the case. Such a brief typically goes beyond the specific legal details of the case.

Anarchy. A society without government.

Anti-Federalists. The name given to those who opposed ratification of the Constitution.

Apportionment. The allocation of legislative seats according to a standard such as population size or area.

Approval voting. A proposed system that would allow all citizens to cast as many votes as they wish, but no more than one vote per candidate. The candidate with the most votes would win. The system is intended to reveal the one candidate who has the greatest overall support.

Aristocracy. A small group of nonelected individuals who owe their position of power to such factors as noble birth, wealth, ability, or social rank. Hereditary aristocracy, of course, is based on family line.

Articles of Confederation. The agreement among the states that created a national government. This government consisted of a one-house legislature of limited power, with each state casting a single vote.

At-large election. A system in which all elected officials are chosen by all the voters in a given political unit, rather than having voters divided into geographical districts. Typically, voters cast as many votes as there are positions to be filled, and the number of candidates chosen equals the number of vacancies (in other words, if there are ten city council seats, the top ten finishers win).

Australian ballot. A ballot printed and administered by the government rather than by a political party.

Automatic plan. A proposal to reform the **electoral college** so that (1) electors would be legally bound to follow the popular vote and (2) House members would vote individually, not as state units, if no presidential candidate received a majority in the electoral college.

B

Backdoor spending. The practice of postponing the cost of a program into the future.

Balanced budget amendment. A proposed constitutional amendment that would require federal government expenditures to match revenues except in wartime, unless three-fifths of both houses approved a deficit. It is intended to constrain government spending.

Balance of payments. The net difference between what a nation receives from foreign countries and what it spends overseas. Income derives from such things as exports, money spent by foreign tourists, and return on foreign investments; this revenue is balanced against imports, overseas military expenditures, foreign aid, overseas tourist spending, and the like.

Balance of terror. A situation in which each side possesses sufficient force to create a stand-off and therefore no violence occurs.

Balancing test. An approach used by judges to decide which rights must be abridged in a specific situation. The need to restrict a right is balanced against all other competing rights and values.

Bicameral legislature. Two-chamber (two-house) legislature, like the U.S. Congress. A one-house legislature is called unicameral.

Bill of attainder. A law directed at a specific person.

Bill of Rights. Popular name given to the first ten amendments to the Constitution. This name was applied many years after adoption of those amendments. Most of these amendments protect citizens against government interference.

Binding primary. An election for delegates to the presidential nominating convention in which delegates are legally required to support the candidate they are pledged to (this pledge, however, is usually binding only for the first vote at the convention).

Block grant. Funds given to states for a general purpose, with relatively broad guidelines for their use.

Boss. Title given to the leader of a strong party organization, or **party machine.** Today, the term has a strong negative connotation.

C

Calendar-determined election. An election whose date (month, day, and year) is fixed by law. In the United States most elections are for two- or four-year terms.

Capital case (or offense). A crime punishable by death.

Capital gains. Profits made from the buying and selling of property.

Categorical grant. Funds authorized for a specific project, to be spent according to specific regulations.

Caucus. Organization in Congress consisting of members of the same party.

Censure. A formal action of Congress in which a member is reprimanded for unbecoming conduct.

Central clearance. The procedure within the executive branch in which agencies sending bills to be introduced in Congress must submit them first to the Office of Management and Budget. This allows OMB to coordinate the President's overall legislative program.

Checks and balances. The organization of government so that each branch of government (executive, legislative, and judicial) has some power over the actions of the other. This ensures that officials of each branch depend, in part, on the cooperation of those in the other two branches. The purpose is to prevent the emergence of a dominating branch.

"Christmas tree" bill. Legislation that contains district-related benefits for a large number of legislators.

City manager. An appointed official in charge of administering the day-to-day operations of city government. He or she is hired by elected officials and usually has professional training for the position.

Civil case. A court proceeding that involves a dispute among individuals. Typical civil cases concern such matters as breach of contract, damage suits, and the like. In contrast are *criminal cases*, in which the government prosecutes a violation of criminal law. The government may also sue in civil cases.

Civil liberties. Freedoms that protect individuals from arbitrary government interference. For example, free speech is a civil liberty that prevents government from interfering with citizens' rights to express themselves.

Civil rights. Freedoms that protect citizens from discriminatory and arbitrary acts of government or other individuals, and provide remedies for such violations. For example, the 1964 Civil Rights Act bans discrimination in public accommodations and provides mechanisms for enforcement.

Civil servants. Government employees who are hired on the basis of written examinations and/or special training. They are removable only for cause and are protected from political pressure.

Civil service. A system of filling government jobs

through examinations and special training. Once gained, a government job is protected by rules that prevent firings except for cause.

Civil suit. A court case involving disputes among private individuals. Such cases usually deal with business affairs, automobile accidents, or family matters.

Class action suit. A legal action brought by one person on behalf of a group of people in similar circumstances.

Clear and present danger test. A standard by which to judge whether the government can limit speech. If the speech would lead to a dangerous, preventable situation, the speech can be banned.

Client state. A nation that is highly dependent economically and militarily on another nation, especially one of the two superpowers.

Closed primary. A **primary** limited to members of a political party. Typically, participants must declare their party affiliation in advance of the primary.

Cloture. A parliamentary device used in the Senate to end debate. Cloture can be invoked to end a **filibuster.** Presently, a motion to invoke cloture requires the signature of sixteen senators and the votes of three-fifths of the Senate to pass (sixty senators if no vacancies exist).

Cluster sampling. A procedure in which the large group from which a sample is to be drawn is divided into groups of close proximity (for example, two cities within a state). Respondents are then randomly selected from within these groups. The cities may be further broken down into blocks before random selection occurs.

Coalition. A temporary alliance of two or more groups.

Code law. A system of law in which a judge applies a rule drawn from an elaborate legal code to a particular case. Unlike **stare decisis,** there is no attempt to be consistent with past court rulings.

Committee of the Whole. A convenient device by which the House can conduct its business with a small quorum (100 instead of the regular quorum of 218). The Committee of the Whole cannot itself pass a bill.

Communism. A political system in which all major economic elements are state-owned and state-controlled. Central planning rather than the marketplace decides levels of production, allocation of resources, prices, and all other key economic issues.

Communist front. An organization secretly controlled by Communists, although members were generally not aware of the control. Typically, Communist-front organizations advocated goals such as world peace or justice.

Competitive capitalism. An economic system in which people are free to make whatever voluntary transactions they desire and are informed in their actions.

Concurrent power. An authority possessed by both the national government and the states within a specific area. For example, both the national government and the states have the power to tax.

Concurrent resolution. A measure passed by one house, with the concurrence of the other, that does not need the President's signature. Concurrent resolutions, which do not have the force of law, are used to fix the time of adjournment, express feelings on issues, and deal with certain budgetary matters.

Confederation. A government created by other governments that has no direct authority over citizens and that remains subordinate to the power that established it.

Confederation Congress. The name of the national legislature under the Articles of Confederation.

Conference committee. A committee composed of members of both houses of Congress to resolve House-Senate differences on a particular bill.

Congressional casework. The help that members of Congress and their staffs give to individual constituents and groups.

Congressional oversight. The authority of Congress, especially of a committee or subcommittee, to monitor and review the work of executive branch agencies.

Connecticut Compromise. The proposal submitted by the Connecticut delegation to solve the representation issue that combined elements of the Virginia and New Jersey plans. The lower house would be based on population, with legislators representing citizens. The upper house, however, would give each state two votes and legislators would represent states.

Consent Calendar. In the House of Representatives, the agenda of noncontroversial bills that can be dealt with quickly. Bills on the Consent Calendar were originally placed on the **Union Calendar** or **House Calendar.**

Contempt of Congress. A formal declaration of Congress stating that a person has acted contrary to its rules. The matter is then turned over to the federal judiciary for possible prosecution.

Contempt of court. An action that obstructs the work of a court. Being held in contempt of court can result in a fine and/or jail term.

Continental Congress. Group of delegates from the American colonies that first met in 1774 to protest British rule. It eventually became the first central government of the United States.

Cost-benefit analysis. The evaluation of a program in terms of whether the benefits outweigh the costs.

Counter-bureaucracy. A bureaucracy established to duplicate some of the responsibilities of an existing one. By staffing the new bureaucracy with loyal appointees, a President or other executive can attempt to overcome the resistance or incompetence of the original bureaucracy.

Counterforce strategy. The strategy of directing an attack at military rather than at civilian targets. It is the opposite of **countervalue.**

Countervalue strategy. The strategy of targeting civilian population centers and industries in an attack. It is the opposite of **counterforce.**

Covert operations. Actions taken by the government, usually overseas, that are not publicly admitted. These secret operations may be conducted by foreign nationals but with the support, financial and otherwise, of the U.S. government. Common covert operations include gathering intelligence information, supporting pro–U.S. groups, and undermining enemies through peaceful or sometimes violent methods.

Criminal conspiracy. A plan among two or more people to commit an unlawful act or to commit a lawful act by illegal means.

Cruise missile. An air-breathing, relatively inexpensive but accurate missile that can be launched in large numbers from airplanes, ships, or land bases.

Cube law. A proposition that describes the relationship between votes received and seats won in a **winner-take-all** system. In particular, if the vote is divided in the ratio of A:B, seats will be divided A^3:B^3. In practice, the cube law does not always operate.

D

Democratic socialism. A system in which government owns and administers key economic activities but individuals still possess considerable freedom in economic matters (for example, freedom to change jobs). Government-owned industries are run for the overall public good. The system is democratic because leaders are held accountable through elections.

Depreciation. The allocation for tax purposes of the cost of an item over a period of time. For example, a business that buys a $5,000 tractor may deduct or depreciate this tractor at the rate of $1,000 a year for five years. Depreciation is set by the tax code, not by "real-life" endurance. Allowing a car to be depreciated over a three-year rather than a five-year period means larger initial deductions from income. In turn, this provides an incentive to buy a new car after three years.

Deterrence. The doctrine that aggression can be prevented by the threat of a strong counterattack.

Dilatory motion. A request for a parliamentary action (for example, to read the minutes) or the offering of an amendment when the purpose is to delay the legislative process. Such a motion is banned in the House of Representatives but not in the Senate.

Diplomatic recognition. The formal acknowledgment of the legitimacy of a foreign government. When the United States grants diplomatic recognition, it intends to treat the nation like other established countries—to exchange ambassadors, engage in commercial relations, and so on.

Direct action tactics. Methods of influencing government policy that involve activities by citizens rather than or in addition to leaders. Common direct action tactics include letter-writing campaigns, petition drives, boycotts, and demonstrations.

Direct democracy. A form of government in which the people themselves decide all important political issues. Leaders merely implement the will of the people.

Direct election plan. A proposal to abolish the **electoral college.** The President would be selected by a simple majority vote with a runoff election if necessary.

Discharge petition. A petition signed by a majority of members of the House of Representatives that requires a committee to forward to the full House a bill it has considered for thirty days or more.

District plan. A proposed reform of the **electoral college** in which each state would be divided into districts of one electoral vote, and the district winner would receive that vote. Presently, except for Maine, the candidate who carries a state receives all the state's electoral votes.

Divine right. The principle that the authority of a leader was God-given and therefore only God—not the people themselves—could depose a leader. This concept was employed by some European monarchs from the fifteenth through the eighteenth centuries.

Doctrinaire party. A political party that puts commitment to an ideology ahead of electoral victory.

Domino theory. A belief that Communist success in one nation will lead to Communist victories in neighboring countries until a whole region is Communist-dominated.

Double jeopardy. A procedure under which someone is brought to trial twice for the same crime. It is prohibited by the Fifth Amendment.

Dual federalism. The doctrine that the states and the national government are coequal in sovereignty. Moreover, unless the Constitution expressly grants the national government a power, this power is retained by the states.

Due process. The principle that for the government to deprive an individual of life, liberty, or property, certain procedures must be followed. This includes informing the accused of the charges and allowing a proper defense. Experts differ on the precise requirements of due process.

Due process clause. The section of the Fourteenth Amendment guaranteeing due process to all citizens. Although "due process" has no precise definition, it is generally understood to be a guarantee that in judicial proceedings, individuals will be notified of any charges and allowed to defend themselves, the proceedings will be conducted fairly, and witnesses can be brought and questioned.

E

Electoral college. The 535 **electors** who choose the President.

Electorally safe districts. Districts in which the incumbent faces little or no competition for his or her seat.

Electors. Individuals selected by voters in a state who then vote for the President and Vice President. In practice, these electors almost always follow the popular majority. The individuals, who are selected by party organizations as an honor, meet as the **electoral college.**

Entitlement program. A program that guarantees benefits regardless of the availability of funds.

Enumerated power. A grant of power to the national government mentioned specifically by the Constitution. The power to collect taxes is an enumerated power.

Equal Rights Amendment (ERA). A proposed amendment to the Constitution sent to the states by Congress in 1972. The amendment failed to receive a positive vote in three-quarters of the state legislatures. It stated that equality under law could not be abridged, or reduced, on account of sex.

Excise tax. A tax collected on items sold. It may be a fixed amount or a percentage of an item's cost.

Exclusionary rule. The principle, established by the Supreme Court, that evidence obtained illegally cannot be used in a trial.

Exclusive power. An authority, specifically given by the Constitution to the national government, which cannot be assumed by other levels of government.

Executive agreement. A written understanding between the President and the head of a foreign nation. Unlike a treaty, it does not require Senate approval. Executive agreements usually involve filling in the details of laws and treaties, but they can represent important policy decisions in their own right.

Executive order. A document issued by the President to implement laws or treaties. It has the full force of law. Since 1946 all executive orders are published in the *Federal Register*, a daily compilation of new government regulations and announcements.

Executive power. Generally taken to mean the President's authority to act in emergencies and, when necessary, to take action not specifically provided for in the existing laws. The term is the subject of some controversy, though, in regard to how far the President can go.

Executive privilege. The principle that the President and subordinates do not have to reveal their deliberations to the other branches of government. It derives from the doctrine of separation of powers and has also been invoked by Presidents as a means of refusing to testify before congressional committees.

Exit poll. A survey of voters immediately after they have voted. Exit polls enable the media (1) to make predictions about the election's outcome before the official ballots are counted and (2) to describe which types of voters supported which candidate.

Ex post facto law. A law that makes a crime retroactive—that is, that makes an act illegal after it has been committed.

F

Faction. A group working toward a self-serving political goal.

Factional conflict. Conflict among groups, with the composition of groups changing as the issues change.

Federalism. A system in which two or more levels of government have authority over the same citizenry, with each level having at least one area in which it sets policy independently of the other.

Federalists. The name taken by those in favor of ratifying the Constitution. Originally, the term *federal government* referred to a weak central authority, so the use of *federalist* to describe pro-Constitution forces was somewhat deceptive.

Fighting words. Speech that incites people to violence. Fighting words are not constitutionally protected free speech.

Filibuster. A device used by one or more senators to speak on and on to delay the Senate's business. Such stalling, or the threat to stall, is intended to block legislation.

Filter question. A query that measures interest in or concern about an issue or is otherwise designed to weed out respondents who lack knowledge about an issue. The purpose is usually to ensure that only people with real opinions answer substantive questions. They are also used to spot people not qualified to answer a particular question—for example, "Are you eighteen?" could be used before "Did you register to vote?"

First strike. A nuclear attack made without being attacked first.

Fiscal policy. The regulation of the economy by the use of the federal budget.

Fiscal year. The twelve-month period employed by the federal government in calculating its financial activities. The fiscal year currently begins on October 1.

Flat tax. A tax on income in which all income is taxed at the same rate.

Formula grant. Financial assistance given by the government to all those who are eligible. Aid is given according to a specific formula.

Free-rider problem. The challenge, faced by interest groups, that nonmembers can gain from successful group actions without having to become members.

Frostbelt. Name given to the Northeast and upper Midwest. It is generally an area characterized by slow population growth, older industry, and cities with a declining economic base.

G

Gag order. A ruling issued by a judge to prevent newspapers and other media from describing trial-related events. Gag rules are intended to ensure a fair trial.

General revenue sharing. The transfer of money collected by the national government to states and localities, with very few restrictions.

Gerrymandering. The practice of drawing election district boundaries to give one's political interest an advantage.

Grand jury. A jury whose purpose is to determine whether the evidence is sufficient for a trial. Grand juries are intended to prevent prosecutors from using trials to harass citizens.

Grants-in-aid. The general name given to funds provided by Congress to state and local governments.

Grantsmanship. Nickname for the ability to obtain government grants. Grantsmanship usually involves skill at writing applications, and a familiarity with the bureaucratic complexities of grant administration.

Great Society. The name given to the package of programs, enacted during President Lyndon Johnson's administration, to improve the quality of life for many citizens. Programs ranged from rebuilding cities and educating the disadvantaged to beautifying the highways.

Gunboat diplomacy. The use of force and intimidation to accomplish diplomatic objectives. The phrase originates in the once-common practice of powerful nations threatening weaker ones by dispatching naval vessels to bombard coastal targets unless demands were met.

H

Hardened missile silo. A missile launch site that has been protected to make it virtually invulnerable to attack.

Hearing. A forum in which individuals testify on a proposed piece of legislation or on some other government action.

"High-wall" perspective. The belief that there should be a clear line between religion and government.

Home rule. Independence granted by the state to cities in certain policy areas (for example, the right to decide their own form of government).

House Calendar. In the House of Representatives, the agenda of general bills that do not involve financial matters.

I

Impact evaluation. The evaluation of a program according to whether it has achieved the intended results.

Impeachment. A process in which the House of Representatives formally brings charges of misconduct against the President, Vice President, or any other civil officer (members of Congress are excluded). The impeached person is tried by the Senate.

Imperialism. The policy of taking advantage of developing nations for the benefit of wealthier countries, especially their business interests.

Implementation. The period between the enactment of a policy and its completion.

Implied power. An authority of the national government that comes from a specifically mentioned power but is not itself authorized by the Constitution. For example, the power to create a national bank is implied by the enumerated power to collect taxes and pay debts.

Incorporation. The process by which the provisions in the Bill of Rights have been applied to the states through the **due process clause** of the Fourteenth Amendment.

Incrementalism. An approach to policy making that accepts existing programs as givens and makes only small changes to meet new situations.

Incumbent. The person occupying a political office.

Independent. An individual who does not identify with a political party.

Indexing. The adjustment of tax rates so that inflation-caused increases in income would not be taxed at a higher percentage. Under a system using a **progressive tax, inflation** can cause higher tax rates with no increase in real income.

Inflation. The process by which the value of the dollar drops and prices go up.

Inherent power. An authority possessed by the national government because of its rule over a sovereign nation. Such powers exist through custom rather than being stated or implied in the Constitution.

Initiative. A process that allows citizens to enact legislation directly by proposing a law, putting it on the ballot, and permitting voters to accept or reject it. Though initiatives are fairly common, states and cities frequently place many restrictions on their use.

Interest group. A collection of people acting together to influence government policy.

Interest group liberalism. A concept of society in which public policy is made by many private groups but the decisions are enforced by the government.

Interposing. The doctrine that holds that a state can place itself between its citizens and the national government to prevent the enforcement of an illegal or unconstitutional national law.

Iron triangle. A relationship—involving an executive branch agency, a committee or subcommittee of Congress, and an interest group—in which all three cooperate for mutual advantage.

Issue public. A group of people who are especially concerned about a particular public policy.

Item veto. A veto of only a portion of a bill, a right exercised by thirty-nine governors. The President lacks an item veto—a bill passed by Congress must be either completely accepted or completely rejected.

J

Jawboning. A President's use of persuasion rather than legal threats to influence economic behavior in private industry. Persuasion is often based on appeals to the public good.

Jim Crow laws. Laws, common especially in the South until about the 1950s and 1960s, that required racial segregation in such areas as education, public transportation, hotels, restaurants, and recreational facilities.

Joint committee. A committee composed of members of the House and Senate.

Joint resolution. A measure that in Congress follows the same procedure as a bill.

Judicial activism. The philosophical position that the courts ought to view the law in an overall context and take actions that address general issues, not just the particulars of a case.

Judicial restraint. The philosophical position that the proper role of the courts is to settle disputes, not to make policy.

Judicial review. The power of courts to declare laws and executive actions unconstitutional and thus null and void.

Judicial temperament. General suitability for a judgeship, as reflected in traits such as respect for and knowledge of the law, integrity, and esteem in the legal community.

Jurisdiction. The right to hear cases and settle controversies.

Justice of the peace courts. Judicial officers who try minor cases such as traffic violations or disturbances of the peace. They are most common in rural areas and are usually elected.

L

Laissez-faire. The philosophy that the government should interfere as little as possible, or not at all, in economic activities (French for "allow to act").

Laissez-faire capitalism. A system in which government economic involvement is minimal. All property is privately held, and economic decisions result from competition among individuals in the marketplace.

Land-grant college. A college established by a state on land provided by the federal government.

Latent or potential group. A collection of people sharing a common concern who are not yet organized but who might become so if their interests are threatened.

Legislative Calendar. A printed agenda of the business before the House, divided into different types of legislation or other action.

Legislative veto. A provision of a law that allows Congress to block action of executive branch officials. Congress may be given the power to veto an action, or the executive branch official may have to obtain permission before acting. Legislative vetoes, which can be exercised by either or both houses—depending on the law—were declared unconstitutional by the Supreme Court in 1983.

Libel. Defamation of character in print or by other visual means. Libel can be punished through the legal process.

Limited government. The idea that many areas of an individual's life are beyond the direct reach of government.

Literacy test. A test that required a prospective voter to demonstrate an ability to read. The ability to interpret a law was sometimes also required. Testers were given wide judgment in deciding who passed. The test served partly to improve the quality of the electorate, but has also been used to prevent poor and minority citizens from voting.

Lobbyist. An agent who deals with public officials on behalf of a political or interest group. The term originated from the fact that such agents once gathered in the lobbies of legislatures.

Logrolling. The exchange of support on legislation. One member of Congress supports a project another member wants and, in return, receives backing for his or her own project.

Loyalty oath. A signed statement affirming that one has not been, is not, or will not be engaged in any activity intended to bring about the overthrow of the existing government. Loyalty oaths were largely used to prosecute former members of Communist-affiliated organizations.

M

Malapportionment. A situation in which legislative seats are not allocated according to an appropriate standard. In contemporary politics this usually means that legislative districts have populations that differ substantially in size.

Mark-up session. A committee review and vote on each section of a legislative proposal.

Marshall Plan. A program by which the United States provided economic aid to nations of Western Europe to help them rebuild after World War II and resist Communist domination. It was named after Secretary of State George C. Marshall, who first proposed it.

Massive retaliation. The doctrine that any Soviet aggression would be met by a large-scale atomic attack on the Soviet Union.

Merit system. A personnel policy in which hiring, firing, and promotion are based on objective standards and regular evaluation according to specific standards.

Metropolitan councils of government (COGs). Associations of government officials from an area who meet to discuss and coordinate their actions. These councils have no independent power.

***Miranda* rules.** A set of rules, established by the Supreme Court, that require police to tell apprehended suspects that (1) they have the right to remain silent, (2) anything they say may be held against them, and (3) they have the right to a lawyer before and during police interrogation.

Missouri plan (or merit plan). A method of choosing judges in which a committee prepares a list of nominees, the governor chooses one, and the public, after a time period, is allowed to accept or reject this choice.

Mixed economy. A system in which there is both private enterprise and government control of economic activities. Many nations have mixed economies, and the specifics in each nation vary.

Monetary policy. Actions taken to regulate the amount of money (cash plus funds in checking accounts) and credit in the economy.

Moot case. A case that is hypothetical.

Multiple advocacy model. An approach to decision making in which several different and conflicting viewpoints are sought before the final choice is made. An alternative would be for a President to require advisors to make a single recommendation.

Multinational corporation. A firm that has substantial operations in several countries. Corporate self-interest may be separate from the particular self-interest of any host nation.

Mutual assured destruction (MAD). The doctrine that peace can be maintained if the two superpowers can destroy each other, even if one side strikes first.

N

National debt. The amount of money owed by the national government. Congress sets the permitted size of the debt.

Natural rights. Liberties that are inherent. Such rights do not require laws for their existence and are inalienable—they cannot be taken away.

Necessary and proper clause. A broad grant of power given to Congress in Article I, Section 8 of the Constitution. The provision enumerates various explicit powers of Congress and then adds that Congress can also make all laws "necessary and proper" for executing those responsibilities. It is also known as the "elastic clause" because of the flexibility it provides.

New Jersey Plan. The proposal submitted by the New Jersey delegation to the Constitutional Convention. The plan called for a strengthening of the central government under the Articles of Confederation. The principle of a one-house national legislature, with each state possessing one vote, would be retained.

"New politics." The style of campaigning that focuses on candidates rather than on political parties. Extensive advertising, professional consultants, and modern technology usually replace party workers. Generally, greater emphasis is placed on issues and personalities than on specific material rewards for votes.

"No-knock" entry. The process by which police can enter premises without announcing themselves if such an announcement would jeopardize the search.

Nonconnected PAC. A political action committee not run by a corporation or a labor union. Nonconnected PACs generally favor particular issue positions.

Nongermane amendment. In Congress, an item tacked on to a bill being considered that has nothing to do with the bill. Nongermane amendments are generally forbidden, but it is not always clear what is or is not germane.

Nonpartisan election. An election in which political parties are legally prohibited from participating, though in some instances these prohibitions are ignored. Party labels are not on the ballot. Nonpartisan elections are most common at the local level.

No prior restraint. The principle that newspapers and magazines can be punished only after, not before, they publish something.

Nuclear proliferation. The spread of nuclear weapons. Countries that now possess such weapons are sometimes called members of the "Nuclear Club."

Nullification. The nineteenth-century doctrine that held that states could declare national laws and orders null and void, or lacking in force. The doctrine is no longer accepted.

O

Open-ended question. On a poll, a question that does not offer specific alternatives as answers. Respondents are free to give any answer, using their own words. The opposite is sometimes called a close-ended question—the respondent must select from a limited set of specific alternatives.

Open primary. A **primary** that does not require participants to declare or demonstrate loyalty to a political party.

Opportunity cost. The benefits that are lost by pursuing one course of action rather than another.

Ordinances. Laws passed by a city government.

Original jurisdiction. The authority of a court to hear a case when it is first tried. It contrasts with *appellate jurisdiction*, in which a case is heard after another court has already considered it (that is, the case is *appealed* to a higher-level court).

Output theory of democracy. A concept that holds that government decisions are made in behalf of the people. The people themselves, however, do not make the decisions.

Overkill. The capacity to expend greater force than needed to destroy a population or military facility.

Oversight process. The monitoring of executive agency performance by Congress, especially congressional committees.

P

Pack journalism. The coverage of a news story by a group of journalists who share a perspective on the story. No journalist wants to differ from his or her colleagues for fear of missing the "obvious" story.

Participatory democracy. An approach, especially current in the 1960s, that emphasizes direct citizen involvement in decisions affecting people's lives. The philosophy calls for decentralized government and greater social and economic equality.

Partisan affiliation. A feeling of loyalty to and identification with a political party.

Partisan elections. Elections in which candidates are identified by political party label, and parties are allowed to campaign. In a *nonpartisan election* there is no party designation on the ballot.

Party affiliation. A psychological identity with or attachment to a political party.

Party caucus. All members of a political party in a legislative chamber.

Party identification. The feeling of loyalty or attachment to a political party.

Party machine. A very well organized party organization that controls nominations for office, can usually win the election, and possesses numerous resources such as government jobs and contracts. Machines lost much of their influence beginning in the 1950s.

Party platform. A statement of the programs and policies formulated at presidential nominating conventions that represent the future goals of the party.

Party system. The arrangement of political parties in a political system. Relevant factors include the number of parties, their strength, diversity of issue positions, and types of membership. The United States has a two-party system; several European nations have multiparty systems; the Soviet Union has a one-party system.

Patronage or "spoils" system. The use of government jobs to reward campaign supporters. The term "spoils" comes from the expression "to the victor belong the spoils."

Plebiscite. A vote in which citizens are asked to accept or reject a policy offered by government. It is the government that defines the issue and administers the selection process.

Pluralist democracy. An approach to democracy that sees society as composed of a number of groups, each having resources and each seeking to accomplish its goals through compromises. Government acts to keep conflict fair.

Plurality. A winning total that is less than a majority, that is, less than 51 percent. If candidates A and B each receive 30 percent of the vote and candidate C receives 40 percent, candidate C wins by a plurality.

Pocket veto. A veto in which legislation dies because the President does not sign a bill and Congress adjourns within ten days (excluding Sundays). If Congress remains in session and the President does not sign, the bill automatically becomes law.

Political action committee (PAC). An organization established by a group to collect and disburse campaign funds. Corporations, unions, and groups of private citizens can organize PACs. Their operation is closely regulated by the Federal Election Commission.

Political socialization. The process by which political identities and preferences develop. Political socialization can occur at any age.

Poll tax. A fee to be paid in order to vote. The poll

tax frequently replaced the more restrictive ownership-of-property requirement. In some instances, unpaid fees from previous elections had to be paid before a person was allowed to vote in the current election. Poll taxes in national elections were abolished by the Twenty-fourth Amendment, ratified in 1964.

Pork-barrel politics. The practice by members of Congress of bringing federal projects and other benefits to their districts in hopes of ensuring their reelection.

Potential group. A group that is not organized but could become so if its interests were threatened.

Poverty index. A government-devised calculation of the cost of supporting a family. It is periodically adjusted and does not include the value of government benefits.

Power elite. A supposed group of nonelected individuals whose vast economic influence allows them to control government.

Preferred position doctrine. A view that holds that some rights—for example, free speech—are more important than others and thus may be limited only under extreme circumstances.

Precinct. The most basic unit in a political party organization. A precinct frequently has less than a thousand voters. It is headed by a *precinct leader* (sometimes called *precinct captain*).

Preemptive strike. A nuclear strike launched in anticipation of an enemy attack.

Presidential electors. Individuals, selected in accordance with rules set by state legislatures, who choose the President. Originally these presidential electors were chosen by state legislatures. Today they are chosen directly by the voters.

Prestige press. Newspapers and magazines read by influential people in government and business.

Primary constituency. Those voters in a district who supported a legislator in the primary.

Primary election. An election held by a political party to determine who will run under the party label in the general election.

Private bill. Proposed legislation dealing with particular individuals or groups. Private bills often grant exceptions for individuals in the areas of immigration, claims against the government,

land titles, and so on. Such bills are usually accepted unanimously.

Private Calendar. The House agenda of all bills dealing with matters affecting the affairs of private individuals.

Privilege. A legal or moral claim to some benefit that is given to some citizens and can be more easily taken away or limited than a **right**.

Process evaluation. The evaluation of a program in terms of its stated guidelines. The emphasis is on carrying out the program according to strict administrative standards.

Progressive tax. A tax whose rate increases as the taxpayer's income increases.

Project grant. Financial assistance given by the government for a specific project. This aid must be applied for by a government agency or unit; it is not given automatically to all those who may be eligible for assistance.

Proportional plan. A proposal to reform the **electoral college** by dividing a state's electoral vote according to the proportion of votes each candidate received.

Proportional representation (PR). A system of allocating legislative seats to political parties based on the number of votes received. Citizens vote for party lists of candidates. The system is popular in many European democracies. There are many important variations in PR systems.

Public-interest group. An **interest group** that defines its mission as working for the overall public good rather than for the narrow concerns of one sector of society.

Pure speech. The peaceful expression of ideas before a willing audience.

Q

Quota sampling. A method in which the entire group from which a sample is to be drawn is divided into different groups—for example, men, women, union, nonunion. Respondents are then selected so that the final sample has the same proportion of each group as does the population as a whole. Where final selection is random, the quota technique closely resembles **stratified sampling.**

R

Racehorse journalism. An approach to campaign coverage that emphasizes who is ahead at any given moment and which tactics the candidates are using. Little or no emphasis is placed on long-term issues, the consequences of proposals, or other more abstract aspects of the campaign.

Radicalism. A political perspective favoring large-scale, rapid change in public policy. There are many different versions of radicalism—some accepting violence to accomplish change—with much disagreement on what change is supposed to accomplish.

Random sample. A selection of people from a group, in which each person has an equal chance of being chosen. The sample is the subgroup; randomness is the method of selection. Not all samples are random. The entire group from which the sample is drawn is usually called the population.

Ranking member. Member of a committee who has the most seniority after the chairperson if the party is in the majority. The ranking minority member is the member of the minority party with the most committee seniority.

Realigning election(s). An election (or series of elections) that has a major impact on the policy direction of government and on long-term voting patterns; also sometimes called *critical election*.

Recall. A procedure by which citizens can request an official to run again for election before the end of his or her term. Though legally permissible in several states and many cities, recall is infrequently used.

Reconciliation. The process by which the budget committees in the House and Senate bring in line the total expenditures called for by the two committees and the totals proposed by other appropriations committees.

Rediscount rate. The interest rate changed by the Federal Reserve on money loaned to member banks. This rate affects the amount of money that banks can lend out.

Red tape. An expression for what appears to be unnecessarily complex regulation. The term comes from the British practice of tying legal records together with red ribbon.

Reelection constituency. All those people in a district who voted for a legislator in the general election.

Referendum. A mechanism by which the legislature places an issue before the public in an election for its approval or rejection. In many states a change in the state constitution or permissible level of indebtedness must be approved by referendum.

Registration. A requirement that prospective voters become enrolled before the election. This allows records to be verified and limits the possibility of fraud. Most states use permanent registration. Voters remain registered unless they move or fail to vote in a series of elections.

Regressive tax. A tax whose rate decreases as income increases. A tax with a fixed rate, such as a sales tax, can be regressive in its actual operations. A 5-percent sales tax can place a heavier burden on poor people if poor people spend a larger proportion of their incomes in taxable items.

Reindustrialization. A proposed policy in which a major government effort would be made to revitalize declining U.S. industry.

Representative democracy. A form of government in which citizens, through regular and fair elections, choose leaders, and the right to influence government is protected. It is an attempt to balance citizen influence against the existence of a large, complex modern society.

Resolution. A vote by Congress that lacks the force of law and does not require a President's signature. Resolutions can be enacted by either house (*simple resolution*) or by both houses together (**concurrent resolution**). Resolutions are used to express sentiments on issues, establish chamber parliamentary rules, set the time for adjournment, and propose constitutional amendments to be ratified. A *joint resolution*, if signed by the President, has the force of law but is usually reserved for relatively minor matters. One important joint resolution is a *continuing resolution*—a legislative authorization for an executive branch agency to continue to spend funds without a specific budgetary appropriation.

Retrospective voting. The practice of casting a vote on the basis of an incumbent's past performance rather than on an expectation of future performance.

Reverse discrimination. The practice of giving special favor or opportunities to members of groups once discriminated against.

Rider. An amendment attached to a bill that may or may not be relevant to the subject matter of the bill (if irrelevant, the rider is a **nongermane amendment**). Often riders are used to enact legislation unlikely to pass if it stood on its own.

Right. A legal or moral claim to some benefit. A right can be taken away or limited only under special circumstances and for good cause.

Roll call vote. A vote in which the preference of each legislator is formally recorded.

Run-off election. A contest between the two candidates with the largest vote totals from a previous election in which no candidate received a majority. The purpose is to guarantee the election of a candidate with a majority of votes.

S

Sales tax. A tax collected on items or services sold. It is almost always a percentage of the item's cost.

Secession. The doctrine that individual states could withdraw from the United States, because the original union was not intended to be eternal. The Civil War settled the issue.

Second-strike capacity. The ability to launch a devastating attack after absorbing an attack.

Secular regulation rule. The principle, established by the courts, that the right to religious beliefs is absolute but that religious behavior may be restricted by appropriate laws or rules.

Select and special committees. Committees that deal with less important issues (for example, legislative printing services) or a temporary matter such as an investigation into corruption charges against a government official. These committees are generally not permitted to report bills to the full chamber.

Self-incrimination. A statement by an individual that serves to implicate that person in a crime. The Fifth Amendment protects individuals against self-incrimination.

Senatorial courtesy. The custom by which the President consults with the senior senator from his or her party before making a federal judicial appointment in the senator's state.

Senior Executive Service (SES). A group of top bureaucrats who may be transferred from agency to agency without loss of rank. The SES was created by the 1978 Civil Service Reform Act.

Seniority. The continuous length of service in a legislative house while belonging to the same party. There is both seniority in general (continuous service in a chamber) and committee seniority (continuous service on a committee).

Sense of political efficacy. A belief that one can make a difference politically and that one's views count.

Separation of powers. The principle by which authority is dispersed among three branches of government. No single branch of government exercises legislative, executive, and judicial power.

Shays' Rebellion. An armed insurrection in western Massachusetts from 1786 to 1789. Led by Daniel Shays, it was an attempt to protect debtors from foreclosures. The uprising was defeated but it alarmed many wealthy citizens.

Sherman Antitrust Act. A law enacted in 1890 that forbids contracts, monopolies, or conspiracies or trade that interfere with commerce.

Shield laws. Laws that permit newspaper reporters the right not to reveal their sources in criminal proceedings. Such laws exist in some states, but not at the federal level.

Single-issue group. An organization that is concerned only with one particular topic—for example, abortion or pornography—rather than with a broad range of subjects.

Slander. Oral defamation of character. Slander can be punished through the legal process.

Social movement groups. Loose collections of organizations and individuals working toward a common political goal, especially at the citizen level. Definitions of membership, of lines of authority, and of organizational structure are minimal.

Special district governments. Local or regional units created to administer a particular function such as education or sanitation.

Speech plus. A means of expression that involves behavior—for example, picketing.

Split ticket voting. The practice of casting a vote for candidates of both parties in a single election. Choosing a Democrat for President and a Republican for the Senate candidate is an example of split ticket voting.

Staggered elections. The arrangement of election schedules so that terms of office overlap. In the Senate, for example, one-third of that chamber is up for reelection every two years.

Standing committee. A more or less permanent committee that deals with a general and important topic—defense, agriculture, commerce, for example.

Standing to sue. The right to take a legal action.

Standing vote. A vote taken by having supporters and opponents of a measure stand and be counted.

Stare decisis. Latin for "let the decision stand." This is the principle, widely applied in the U.S. legal system, by which judges rely on similar, appropriate past decisions when they rule on cases.

Statute. A law passed by a legislature.

"Stop-and-frisk" laws. Laws that permit the police to search people if there is a reasonable suspicion of wrongdoing, even though no arrest occurs.

Straight party ticket. A vote cast only for candidates of one party. The selection of candidates of different parties is called a **split ticket vote.**

Stratified sampling. A procedure in which the entire group from which the sample is to be drawn is subdivided into groups (for instance, according to race or sex) and random selection occurs within groups. As opposed to **cluster sampling,** the group members may not be in close proximity.

Straw poll. An opinion poll in which people themselves decide to participate; they are not selected by those conducting the survey. People can vote more than once and little attempt is made to ensure that participants resemble a cross section of the population.

Subpoena. A legal order compelling a person to be present at a legislative or judicial proceeding.

Subsidy. Government assistance to encourage some economic behavior. Subsidies may be direct payments or a reduction in a financial obligation.

Substantive due process. The principle that the Supreme Court could decide what economic activities the government could and could not regulate. If government regulation of a business was deemed unacceptable, the Court would conclude that such regulation was a violation of due process.

Suffrage. The right to vote.

Summit meeting. A diplomatic meeting between the President and top Soviet leaders.

Supermajority. A majority larger than 50 percent plus 1 (which is called a *simple majority*). Common supermajorities are two-thirds and three-quarters.

Sunbelt. Name given to the South and Southwest, a region experiencing population growth and economic expansion.

Supremacy clause. Article VI, paragraph 2, of the Constitution, which states that the Constitution and the laws made under it are the supreme laws of the United States.

Suspect classification. A doctrine employed by the courts that says that if a law deals with racial or nationality differences, the law must be very closely examined. To be valid, such a law must advance a compelling state interest and the distinction must be necessary to accomplish its purpose.

Symbolic speech. The manipulation of symbols—for example, the flag or a black armband—to express an idea.

Syndicalism. A philosophy calling for worker ownership of all industry, to be brought about by violent means if necessary. The concept was once closely associated with Communism.

T

Tariff. A tax on imports. Tariffs can be used to raise revenue or protect domestic industry from foreign competition, or both.

Tax expenditure. A reduction in tax liability for a group or interest. It is the equivalent of a payment and is thus an "expenditure."

Tax shelter. An investment whose primary objective is to reduce taxes rather than to generate income.

Teller vote. In Congress, a vote taken by having supporters and opponents file past recorders ("tellers") who tally the results. It is used only in the House. Usually no record is kept of how each member voted.

Theocracy. A government based on religious law, in which power is held by church officials.

Ticket. A group of candidates for office who run under a common party label; also sometimes called a *slate*.

Totalitarian government. A government that claims the authority to regulate all aspects of society and the lives of its citizens.

Totalitarian state. A government that claims the authority to control all aspects of citizens' lives.

Trade deficit. A negative dollar difference between the value of exports and imports. If the value of exports exceeds the value of imports, a *trade surplus* exists.

Triad of weapons. The U.S. policy of relying on three types of weapons for defense. Presently, the United States employs manned bombers, land-based missiles, and submarine-based missiles (the three systems make it a triad; two would be a dyad).

Truman Doctrine. U.S. policy opposing Communist expansion into any nation.

Two-step flow of communication. The passing on of information from a small group that receives it directly to a larger group that has no direct contact with the message. When teachers read articles and then tell their students about the material, a two-step flow of communication takes place.

U

Unanimity rule. The rule that for a jury to convict an individual, the jury's verdict must be unanimous.

Unanimous consent agreement. An agreement among Senate leaders on the order and terms of debate on a bill. It is similar to the agreements reached by the House Rules Committee.

Unicameral. A one-house legislature. A two-house legislature like the U.S. Congress is called a bicameral legislature.

Union Calendar. In the House of Representatives, the agenda of all bills that directly or indirectly appropriate or raise revenue. Bills are listed in the order in which they are reported from committee.

Unitary government. A system in which all power ultimately resides in the central government, though for convenience some responsibilities may be delegated to local or regional officials.

Unit vote system. In a presidential election, the practice by which a state casts all its **electoral college** votes for the candidate with the largest number of popular votes. In the nineteenth century several states divided their electoral college votes proportionately among candidates.

V

Value-added tax (VAT). A sales tax charged at each stage of an item's production rather than at the final point of sale.

Veto. Latin for "I forbid." It is the act of a President to prevent a bill passed by Congress from becoming law. A presidential veto can be overridden by a two-thirds vote of both houses of Congress.

Virginia Plan. The proposal submitted by the Virginia delegation at the Constitutional Convention that called for (1) a strong, two-house national legislature apportioned according to population; (2) a separate national executive; and (3) a separate national judiciary.

Voice vote. A legislative vote in which members say "aye" or "nay" on a bill or motion and the presiding officer decides the outcome. No record is kept of how individual legislators voted.

W

Welfare state. A collection of government programs to provide comprehensive care for citizens of all ages. In the United States the term has a somewhat negative meaning.

Wide-open, or **blanket, primary.** A **primary** in which voters can select nominees of both parties at the same time.

Winner take all. A procedure in which only the top votegetter wins election. The opposite occurs when seats are distributed in proportion to votes received.

Writ of certiorari. A court order requesting records from a lower court. In practice, *writ of certiorari* is the expression used by the Supreme Court to grant a review of an appeal.

Write of habeas corpus. A court order directing an official holding an individual in custody to show cause for the person's detention. The purpose of the writ is to prevent imprisonment without reason.

Writ of mandamus. A court order requiring some action to be taken (Latin for "we command").

Index

Photo Credits